Fundamentals of
Labor Economics

Fundamentals of Labor Economics

SECOND EDITION

Thomas Hyclak

Lehigh University

Geraint Johnes

Lancaster University Management School

Robert Thornton

Lehigh University

SOUTH-WESTERN
CENGAGE Learning·

Australia · Brazil · Japan · Korea · Mexico · Singapore · Spain · United Kingdom · United States

SOUTH-WESTERN
CENGAGE Learning·

**Fundamentals of Labor Economics,
Second Edition**
Thomas Hyclak, Geraint Johnes,
Robert Thornton

Senior Vice President, LRS/Acquisitions &
Solutions Planning: Jack W. Calhoun

Editorial Director, Business & Economics:
Erin Joyner

Editor-in-Chief: Joe Sabatino

Acquisitions Editor: Michael Worls

Developmental Editor: Ted Knight

Editorial Assistant: Elizabeth Beiting-Lipps

Art and Cover Direction, Production
Management, and Composition:
PreMediaGlobal

Media Editor: Anita Verma

Brand Manager: Robin Lefevre

Market Development Manager: John Carey

Manufacturing Planner: Kevin Kluck

Marketing Communications Manager:
Sarah Greber

Cover Image: © donatas/shutterstock

Rights Acquisitions Specialist: John Hill

For product information and technology assistance, contact us at
Cengage Learning Customer & Sales Support, 1-800-354-9706

For permission to use material from this text or product,
submit all requests online at **www.cengage.com/permissions**
Further permissions questions can be emailed to
permissionrequest@cengage.com

Library of Congress Control Number: 2012947817

ISBN-13: 978-1-133-56158-3

ISBN-10: 1-133-56158-6

South-Western
5191 Natorp Boulevard
Mason, OH 45040
USA

Cengage Learning is a leading provider of customized learning solutions
with office locations around the globe, including Singapore, the United
Kingdom, Australia, Mexico, Brazil, and Japan. Locate your local office at:
www.cengage.com/global

Cengage Learning products are represented in Canada by
Nelson Education, Ltd.

For your course and learning solutions, visit **www.cengage.com**

Purchase any of our products at your local college store or at our preferred
online store **www.cengagebrain.com**.

Printed in the United States of America
1 2 3 4 5 6 7 16 15 14 13 12

Contents

CHAPTER 5

The Supply of Labor: Hours of Work   89

CHAPTER 6

Human Capital Analysis   114

CHAPTER 7

Labor Market Equilibrium   153

CHAPTER 8

Information and Job Search   185

CHAPTER 12

Unions and Collective Bargaining   301

CHAPTER 13

Labor Market Discrimination   355

Preface

Fundamentals of Labor Economics, 2nd ed., is intended to serve as a core text for the one-semester introductory labor economics course offered at the undergraduate level. Its purpose is to help students understand the fundamental forces underlying the complex operation of modern labor markets. In writing this book, we have assumed that students have taken a prior course in Principles of Economics but not necessarily any other economics courses. While some familiarity with regression analysis might also be useful, we understand that many students may not have taken a course in statistics; and we have thus provided a very readable yet thorough review of regression analysis in the appendix to Chapter 1. Although in a few cases our analysis and examples also make use of elementary calculus, students whose mathematics background is limited to algebra will have no difficulty understanding the theory and empirical evidence explored in this text.

Text Overview

This book provides a comprehensive treatment of the theory of labor market behavior, supported by a wealth of empirical evidence. One of the novel features of this textbook is its international focus. Reflecting the diverse international experience and background of the authors, the book draws examples not just from the United States but also from Canada, Europe, Australia, the Pacific Rim, and other countries. Labor economists have come to rely on international comparative studies to examine the impact of institutional and legal influences on the labor market as these influences vary most widely across country borders. We have used labor data from a number of countries in this manner to provide student-accessible "tests" of various hypotheses.

The first seven chapters focus on what might be called the neoclassical supply and demand analysis of the determination of wages and employment in labor markets. These chapters establish the foundation for the economic analysis of labor issues. Chapters 8 through 13 examine wage and employment determinants that go beyond traditional supply and demand forces. These include market imperfections, imperfect and asymmetric sources of information, legal restrictions, collective bargaining, employer use of incentive compensation schemes, and race and gender discrimination. The final chapters provide extensive treatments of unemployment and wage and income inequality.

Fundamentals of Labor Economics addresses several topics that we believe have not been given adequate attention in other labor economics textbooks. Most notable is our emphasis on labor market monopsony, which (together with the topic of minimum wages) comprises an entire chapter (Chapter 9). Labor market information and job search have also been given a chapter of their own (Chapter 8) as has the emerging subfield of personnel economics, including incentive pay systems and career compensation (Chapter 11). Finally, in this second edition we have added a section on occupational licensing, an institution that now directly affects nearly 30% of workers in the United States.

Pedagogical Features

The applied focus of this book is apparent with a glance at any chapter. Each chapter begins with focus questions that set the stage for the material to be covered. Key terms introduced in the chapter are listed at the end of the chapter, along with a set of problems that ask students to apply what they have learned. Within each chapter, three types of boxes reveal and clarify the economics of the world of work. In *The Way We Work* boxes, specific issues relating to life at work are explored. *Putting Theory to Work* boxes showcase current research on work habits, performance, and compensation. *Around the World* boxes summarize interesting research on employment practices and policies in countries outside the United States. All of these features provide additional real-life evidence of the complexity of modern labor markets.

Acknowledgments

We would like to thank our colleagues and students for their input and encouragement along this road. We are especially grateful to Simon Medcalfe of Augusta State University and Ed Timmons of St. Francis University for writing the sections dealing with discrimination in professional sports and occupational licensing, respectively. In addition, we are grateful to the reviewers who have provided useful critical comments on each manuscript draft of both the first and second editions. In particular, we thank John T. Addison, University of South Carolina; Thomas Creahan, Morehead State University; Abdollah Ferdowsi, Ferris State University; James W. Henderson, Baylor University; Robert M. LaJeunesse, Colorado State University; Meghan Millea, Mississippi State University; Daniel L. Millimet, Southern Methodist University; and David Zimmerman, Williams College. We also thank our editors at Cengage and previously at Houghton Mifflin, in particular Michael Worls, Ted Knight, Ann West, Julie Hassel, and Jennifer DiDomenico, for their support and encouragement, and the many others who helped to see this book through to completion. Rene Hollinger and Diane Oechsle labored diligently over numerous drafts and redrafts, and we thank them for their efforts.

Thomas Hyclak
Geraint Johnes
Robert Thornton

What is labor economics all about?

Why do we study theory and institutions and policy?

How do we test our ideas with real world data?

The Study of Labor Economics

The Study and Scope of Labor Economics

One of the first lessons we learn in economics is that we all have to make choices about how best to use the scarce resources we possess. For our personal standard of living, this problem of scarcity usually boils down to having a limited amount of money to spend in comparison with the cost of buying all the things we would like to have. And for the vast majority of us, the money we earn in the labor market determines our spending power.

We know that different people earn different amounts of money from their work. For example, in 2011 a reporter in Oregon earned $26,000, an advertising account executive in Massachusetts earned $76,000, a social media manager in Iowa earned $42,000, and a computer programmer in Kansas earned $45,000.[1] What determines the amount of money a person can earn in the labor market? Why does this amount differ so much from person to person and place to place?

Perhaps you could earn more money if you had the time to undertake more paid work, or if you had more marketable skills. Your current situation is the result of choices you have made about how much time to spend at work, how much time to spend at leisure, and how much time to invest in acquiring skills.

While you are making these choices, employers are also making decisions about how best to produce their firms' output. How many workers should they employ? What wage

---

[1] Every year *Parade* magazine publishes a special report on what people earn. These earnings amounts and many others were in *Parade*'s "What People Earn" report of 2011.

will they need to pay to attract enough qualified workers to the firm? It is these choices, made by individuals, firms, and public organizations, that are the subject of this book.

Labor economics can be defined as the study of the factors that underpin choices made concerning employment, wages, and other terms and conditions of employment for an individual or group of workers. Examining these factors may seem at first glance to be a fairly straightforward task. However, when you begin to consider more closely the determinants of employment and wages, the scope of topics considered as part of labor economics widens rapidly. Because buyers and sellers are engaged in transactions over the use of people's time and because wages earned through employment are the main source of income for most people, labor market transactions are complex. The complexity increases when we consider the impact of laws and regulations, customs and traditions, and trade union and corporate policies on the outcome of labor market transactions. The purpose of this book is to help you understand the fundamental forces underlying the complex operation of modern labor markets.

Three concepts dominate our discussions of the labor market. As in any market, demand and supply are two important considerations. They have much to do with the way in which wages are determined and the way in which employment levels are set. The third concept is institutions, which we understand broadly to include government, unions, and other organizations. But institutions also include the customs and norms "imported" into the economic sphere from the society in which the economy operates. Institutions are particularly important in the labor market.

The Method of Labor Economics

Mainstream economists generally employ a common method of analysis that involves three activities: (a) the collection and analysis of data to identify problems and issues; (b) the application to problems and proposed policies of economic theory (often the **neoclassical theory**, which is based on the behavior of profit maximizing firms and utility maximizing individuals); and (c) a return to the collection and analysis of data to test the predictions derived from theory and to evaluate policies.

However, labor economists differ slightly from most other economic specialists in two ways. First, data collection and analysis is a relatively more important part of the method of labor economics than of other branches of the discipline. In many fields, theorists working solely on extensions and applications of economic theory without using data analysis dominate the list of influential economists. In labor economics, however, it is difficult to think of a prominent practitioner who has not made important contributions through empirical analysis. Second, labor economics is more heavily influenced by institutional considerations than are most other economic specialties.

Labor Market Theory

Wages and employment are determined in labor markets, where buyers and sellers interact. Thus, when performing **labor market analysis**, it is natural for economists to extend the theory of demand, supply, and market coordination to the study of labor issues. Chapters 2 through 5 develop the essential elements of the theory of labor demand and labor supply. The demand for labor is derived from two things: (a) the demand for the good or service produced by workers and (b) the production function linking workers, machinery, and other inputs to the output of a profit maximizing firm. A key consideration in labor demand is the degree to which labor and other inputs are interchangeable in production. The theory of labor supply is seen as derived from a model that maximizes the utility resulting from the individual's choice between the consumption of leisure and the consumption of goods and services. A key consideration is the individual's need to work to obtain the income required to buy things.

The application of demand and supply analysis to labor markets may seem very familiar on the surface, but we must think seriously about the meaning of the term *market* when it is applied to labor. Markets for different goods, services, or inputs differ in many ways; a key consideration is the length of time needed for markets to reach equilibrium. In some markets, such as those for financial assets and commodities, buyers and sellers have good information and meet on organized exchanges. In these markets, supply and demand changes are quickly reflected in market prices. Thus prices move the market to equilibrium quickly after a shift in demand or supply.

Labor markets, like housing markets, are on the other end of the "speed of adjustment" continuum. In labor markets the market transaction usually establishes a relationship that is expected to last for some period of time—otherwise known as a "job"—so there is an advantage to establishing a good match between worker and employer. Not all workers are equally suited for a given job, and not every job is suitable for a given worker. But employers have only partial information about workers, and workers don't have full information about job characteristics. As a result, much of the activity in the labor market (interviews and site visits, for example) involves information gathering and processing, which means that many transactions take a long time to complete. Although demand and supply forces operate in labor markets, these markets are unlikely to move quickly to a new equilibrium when there is a shift in demand or supply. As a result, labor economists pay close attention to the differences between the short- and long-run aspects of markets and consider how markets behave in disequilibrium.

A key result in labor and housing markets is that each transaction is a unique match. In financial or commodity markets, the **law of one price** can be expected to hold—if a share of XYZ Corporation stock is selling for $1, everyone can buy or sell it at that price. (Of course, what John Doe pays in commissions and so forth to make a trade might be different from what Jane Doe pays, but that's a different issue.) In labor and housing markets we can talk about market forces determining the *average* price for a certified public accountant (CPA) or a two-bedroom bungalow, but the law of one price is unlikely to hold. There will be a distribution of wages paid to newly hired CPAs that depends on worker and job characteristics. Workers differ from one another (as do jobs), and labor economists must consider this. As a result, empirical studies of labor market outcomes very often focus on data for individual workers instead of using the one price generated by market equilibrium.

Labor Market Institutions

When economists speak of **institutions**, they generally mean social organizations other than markets that have an effect on economic outcomes. There are three main types of institutions encountered in the study of labor economics: political institutions, economic institutions, and social beliefs and customs.

When governments impose direct legal restrictions on market outcomes, such as anti-discrimination legislation, the police power of the state is used to determine or influence wages and employment. Employer associations, trade unions, and other lobbyists try to influence political institutions in ways favorable to the interests of the groups they represent. However, the political process may not take much notice of the market in wielding the police power of the state.

Economic institutions such as business firms can be thought of as social organizations that substitute authority, rules, and procedures for market forces in determining economic outcomes. Internal firm decisions about pay raises, promotions, work organization, pensions, and other fringe benefits (human resource management) affect wages and employment in ways that might be influenced only partly by labor market conditions. Trade unions are organizations that act as the agents of workers in trying to affect their wages and other conditions of work and bind employer decisions with contracts. Union or agent bargaining power may be more important than supply and demand in determining wages for a given group of workers.

The third type of institution consists of the social beliefs and customs in that society. The existence of racial discrimination in labor markets or the description of certain occupations as "women's work" flows from the social customs defining the status and opportunities available to different groups in society. If customs and beliefs are strong enough, some people may forgo the opportunity to achieve more profitable outcomes (e.g., by hiring lower-paid women) in order to comply with them. This means that labor market conditions are only partially reflected in the observed wages and employment opportunities available to different groups.

The relative importance of institutional factors in labor markets is at the heart of all the main challenges to neoclassical theory in the history of economic thought. The German historical school, which evolved in the mid-1800s, proposed an inductive approach to uncovering economic relationships from the detailed analysis of historical data. The objective was to promote sound policies of national economic development, and it rejected the attempt to identify general economic "laws" through deductive reasoning. Marxian analysis is based on property rights, class conflict, and exploitation of labor, and it rejects the concept of harmonization of interests through the operation of markets. Institutional economists emphasize the evolution and impact of institutions and the interrelationship between economic, belief, power, and legal systems. Institutional labor economists have typically viewed government as the principal social process affecting the evolution of institutions.[2]

Although modern labor economics is grounded in economic theory, and mainly neoclassical theory at that, these alternative ideas about the relative importance of institutions in the method of analysis have had a very considerable influence on this field of study. New extensions of economic theory have attempted to explain the origin and evolution of certain labor institutions based on the concepts of profit and utility maximizing behavior.[3] An examination of institutions is therefore a necessary complement to economic theory in the study of labor economics.

---

[2] Francesca Schinzinger, "German Historical School," John E. Roemer, "Marxian Value Analysis," and Warren J. Samuels, "Institutional Economics," in *The New Palgrave: A Dictionary of Economics*, eds. John Eatwell, Murray Milgate, and Peter Newman (London: Macmillan, 1987).

[3] See Oliver E. Williamson, *The Economic Institutions of Capitalism* (New York: Free Press, 1985), and Edward P. Lazear, *Personnel Economics* (Cambridge: MIT Press, 1995).

Empirical Analysis

The collection and analysis of data to describe problems and issues, to test hypotheses derived from theory, and to evaluate policy actions are a very important part of the method of labor economics. Actually, most labor economists leave the collection of data to others, preferring to use databases developed largely by government agencies or independent research organizations. Faced with the need to evaluate calls for labor regulation and to respond to social critics of the economic system, most governments have been engaged in the collection and dissemination of data on wages, employment, and other labor market variables since the early 1800s.

Types of Data

Labor economists commonly analyze three types of data. **Time series data** include observations over time and are usually aggregated across firms or individuals—data may be for the entire national economy, regional labor markets, industries, or occupations. So, for instance, we may investigate how the national unemployment rate varies over a period of five years. **Cross-sectional data** encompass information about many individual respondents or firms, all collected at a single point in time. Cross-sectional data may be aggregated across individual units (e.g., a study using data on unemployment rates for each of the 50 U.S. states drawn from the 2010 Census), or the data may contain information on individuals, in which case we have information about individual people, and we know whether each individual has a job or not. Much labor economics research uses *microdata*— cross-sectional information on large numbers of individual workers at a moment in time. A cross-sectional database allows us to investigate, for example, whether people from a given social class are more likely to be unemployed than other people—at a single point in time. (The fact that we're investigating this at a single point in time is a good thing. It means that the state of the economy and other time-dependent factors are automatically held constant for all observations, giving us a comparison that is based on a level-playing field.) Finally, **panel data**, often referred to as **longitudinal data**, combine information across subjects with time series data for each subject. These data sets are much harder to come by, but they have a number of advantages. Using a panel data set, we could, for example, analyze the impact on wages of a part-time training course undertaken by workers; because everything about each worker except the training course stays the same, any change in the wage must be attributable to the training. Economists rarely have an opportunity to conduct laboratory experiments, but panel data often let them come pretty close.

Techniques

The analysis of data from any database can be done with quite simple techniques; sometimes a visual examination of data presented in charts or tables is sufficient to establish support for the existence of an empirical relationship between variables. More typically, however, labor economics researchers employ some variant of **multiple regression analysis** to test hypotheses about the relationship between two or more variables.

We use multiple regression analysis because of the *ceteris paribus* (or "other things being equal") condition that applies to all economic hypotheses. For example, in a principles of economics course, we are quick to point out that the law of demand predicts that a rise in the price of a product will lower the quantity demanded of that product—but only on the condition that all of the other variables that also affect the quantity demanded remain unchanged. Multiple regression analysis allows us to use statistics to hold constant other variables while we examine the relationship between two variables such as price and quantity demanded.

As we go through our treatment of the fundamentals of labor economics, we will often have occasion to refer to the estimated coefficients from multiple regression analyses as evidence for empirical relationships between variables. These regression estimates are important pieces of our knowledge about labor economics. To be sure you understand how labor economists come up with these estimates, review the appendix to this chapter, which provides a quick refresher course.

Policy Analysis

Labor economists use theory, institutional analysis, and empirical analysis for two purposes. The first is to understand how wages and employment are determined for a given set of workers in a given economy at a given point in time. This activity is described as **positive economics**. The second activity, often referred to as **normative economics**, is to evaluate the way labor problems might be alleviated by public policy. Policy analysis is an important part of the study of labor economics because governments have taken many steps over the years to achieve political and social objectives by regulating labor markets.

Policy analysis may involve examining a labor problem with an eye toward proposing a policy that would reduce or eliminate the problem. It also involves evaluating existing public policy to determine the extent to which policy itself is the cause of labor problems and how policy might be improved. For example, most European countries experienced sharp increases in unemployment during the 1980s and saw unemployment stubbornly remain at very high levels during the 1990s. Labor economists have exerted considerable effort trying to understand why this happened and what policy steps might be taken to reverse this situation. Much of the analysis has led to the conclusion that policies that limit labor market flexibility—such as high minimum wages, restrictions on hours, part-time work and dismissals, and generous unemployment compensation—have contributed to the unemployment problem. The results of policy analysis in this case are to recommend reforms that enhance flexibility.[4]

Policy analysis, both in terms of suggesting new policies to address problems and in evaluating the effectiveness and side effects of existing policies, is an important part of our study of labor economics.

International Comparisons

In recent years labor economists have begun to pay closer attention to international comparisons.[5] Because different countries have different legal environments and different

---

[4]Many articles develop this theme. See, for example, Stephen Nickell, "Unemployment and Labor Market Rigidities: Europe Versus North America," *Journal of Economic Perspectives* 11 (1997): 55–74, and "Chronic Unemployment in the Euro Area: Causes and Cures," *IMF World Economic Outlook*, June 1999.

[5]For example, Richard B. Freeman, ed., *Working under Different Rules* (New York: Russell Sage Foundation, 1994).

institutional structures, cross-country comparisons may be extremely helpful in isolating the relative impact of these factors on changes in the structure of wages and employment. Countries may also differ in the extent to which broad economic changes, such as the growing globalization of trade and finance, have affected labor market outcomes.

A good way to examine these changes is through explicit international comparisons, and we have incorporated international comparisons in this text wherever they are appropriate. In addition, we emphasize the application of economic theory, institutional analysis, and empirical analysis in an international comparative fashion, where possible, in our examination of positive and normative labor economic issues.

The Plan of This Book

This book starts with the basic theory of labor markets. Chapters 2 and 3 develop the theory of labor demand for profit maximizing producers facing a technical relationship between the amount of a good or service produced and inputs of labor and other inputs. The basic theory of labor supply—the decision to work or not work and how much time to devote to working—is developed in Chapters 4 and 5. Here the choice framework examines the allocation of time to different activities by a utility maximizing individual.

Labor supply also involves investment choices relating to the acquisition of education, training, and other human assets required for entry into particular labor markets. This aspect of labor supply is examined in Chapter 6, which presents the basics of **human capital** theory.

Chapter 7 concludes the treatment of basic labor market theory with a discussion of the way supply and demand decisions interact in both the short run and the long run. An important long-run feature is the way in which different labor markets—in different regions or with different occupations—are connected by the movement of workers and employers toward the market offering the greatest advantage. Here we look at regional convergence, compensating differentials, and the manner in which international trade links labor markets in different countries.

We then turn to a discussion of some important extensions of the basic theory of labor markets. Basic labor market analysis assumes that buyers and sellers have good information about wages, job conditions, and the opportunity cost of decisions. However, in the real world much of the activity in labor markets involves information gathering and processing as individuals and employers try to find a good match between people and jobs. Chapter 8 develops the theory of job search behavior and the way job search activities by individuals and employers affect labor market outcomes.

Basic labor market analysis also assumes there are large numbers of potential buyers and sellers. In Chapter 9 we consider the way the market works when there is only one buyer of labor, or a very small number of firms, on the demand side of the market. Policy analysis is emphasized throughout the text because many labor issues have been the focus of policy proposals. In Chapter 9 we provide a comprehensive review of one such policy— legislation to establish minimum wages. Minimum wage laws were among the earliest labor policies adopted by industrial countries, and, partly because strong conclusions about minimum wages can be derived from rudimentary supply and demand analysis, these laws have been the subject of much debate. Interestingly, many careful empirical labor market studies have reached conclusions at odds with the rudimentary supply and demand analysis. The heated debate and mixed evidence make minimum wage policy a subject for comprehensive examination.

The first nine chapters of this book focus on an explication of neoclassical labor market theory. At the same time, we review data and the results of empirical studies for evidence of the ability of the theory to explain reality. Beginning in Chapter 10, however, we extend our coverage to include the study of labor market institutions.

Chapter 10 considers the rationale for and impact of internal labor markets, recognizing that the pricing and allocation of labor within organizations is often only weakly linked to the market outcomes external to the firm. The main explanation for internal labor markets is the importance of long-run relationships between employers and workers for productivity and profitability. The main consequence of internal labor markets is the creation of market segments and wage rigidity that affect wage inequality and unemployment.

Chapter 11 examines the internal labor market in greater detail, focusing on the way organizational structure and compensation methods influence worker productivity. This subject has become known as *personnel economics* because it provides an economic explanation (based on profit and utility maximizing behavior) for many organizational practices included in personnel administration or human resource management.

Trade unions may be the most widely studied labor market institutions around the world. This in part reflects the high drama associated with conflicts between labor and management over the past century or so. Chapter 12 examines the economics of trade unions—the factors that cause workers to join; the objectives and constraints to union negotiations; and the consequences of trade union activity for union members, other workers, firms, and the economy.

Labor market discrimination on the basis of race, gender, religion, ethnic origin, sexual orientation, or disability is also treated as a labor market institution. Such discrimination is one way in which social customs and beliefs may have pervasive effects on wages and employment opportunities in many economies around the world. Chapter 13 examines discrimination—where it comes from, how it works, and what its consequences are—and the policies designed to address discrimination and its consequences.

The final two chapters discuss macro–labor economics topics. The focus is on national or regional levels of unemployment (Chapter 14) and the distribution of wages across all workers in a nation or region (Chapter 15). These two issues have been the focal point of much academic and policy research in the past quarter-century due to developments in Europe and the United States since the 1980s. In Europe, most countries experienced a steady rise in overall unemployment rates and a very sharp increase in youth joblessness. In the United States, wage and income inequality have been increasing steadily. Rising European unemployment and U.S income inequality have been seen by some authors[6] as related responses to the impact of technological change and increased globalization on labor markets in industrialized countries. These trends worsened considerably as the world economy suffered through the global economic crisis of 2008–09, known widely as the "great recession," and then recovered very slowly in the following years. Considerable attention once again was focused on the problems of high unemployment rates for many, long durations of unemployment for some, and rising wage and wealth inequality.

---

[6] See Stephen Nickell, "Unemployment and Labor Market Rigidities: Europe Versus North America," *Journal of Economic Perspectives* 11 (1997): 55–74.

Summary

Labor economics covers a range of topics that should prove very interesting to you. We are considering the world of work, where nearly all of us spend most of our adult life. Learning about the fundamental forces that affect our own wages and employment opportunities seems well worth the effort. In addition, the scope of labor economics includes topics that are often in the news. Unemployment, falling wages for unskilled workers, union strikes, government consideration of minimum wage increases, and concerns about the shortage of certain workers are just a sampling of the subjects we consider. Knowledge of labor economics will make you a more informed voter and a better business manager.

Labor economics draws heavily on economic theory, extrapolating from it to consider the unique characteristics of information gathering and job search behavior in labor markets. But labor economics also considers the role of labor institutions as determinants of labor market outcomes, including procedures and practices of firms, actions and objectives of trade unions, and government interventions. Because these outcomes depend on both market and institutional forces, labor economics is essentially an empirical subject where information drawn from studies of real world data has considerable influence on the field and where international comparisons of data and empirical studies play an increasingly important role. In this book, we illustrate labor market theory with many examples of present-day labor institutions and policy and the results of empirical studies from the United States and many other countries.

KEY TERMS

neoclassical theory

labor market analysis

law of one price

labor market institutions

time series data

cross-sectional data

panel or longitudinal data

multiple regression analysis

human capital

positive economics

normative economics

PROBLEMS

1. Identify a current news article related to labor economics. (Sources could be newspapers, magazines, or Web pages. A good Web site for economic news and data is www.dismal. com.) Briefly discuss the positive and normative elements in the story you have identified.

2. List three ways in which the movement of workers from Germany to other countries would be good or bad for Germany, other countries, and the workers who decide to move.

3. Think of your summer or part-time job. How were your wages affected by the labor market (was there a shortage or surplus of potential workers, for example), by institutions, and by public policy?

4. Empirical studies show that the wages earned by U.S. high school dropouts fell by more than 20% over the last decade or so. Is this fact sufficient reason for the government to consider labor market policies that would help these workers earn higher wages?

APPENDIX

Regression Analysis

Regression analysis is a statistical tool widely used in labor economics, and familiarity with it is essential for students and researchers alike. This review is intended to serve either as a refresher for those of you who have studied regression analysis but may be a little rusty or as a very brief introduction for those who have had no prior exposure to regression. In this review we will cover these topics:

- What a regression equation is, how to compute it, and how to interpret it.
- The major goodness of fit measures in regression (the standard error of estimate and the coefficient of determination).
- How to conduct hypothesis tests of regression coefficients.

An Example

Suppose we would like to investigate the degree to which earnings are related to various worker characteristics such as years of education, work experience, and gender for a sample of 300 individuals. Table 1.A.1 provides some representative data for our sample. (The gender variable has been specified as a dichotomous or "dummy" variable, taking on a value of 1 for males and 0 for females.) A close inspection of the values in the table indicates that earnings tend to be higher for those in the sample with more years of education, but the relationship between earnings and the other two variables is less clear.

How can we tell how much earnings on average tend to change as years of education and the other variables change? Let's fit a linear regression equation to the data in Table 1.A.1. The criterion that we use to determine the "best-fitting equation" in regression analysis is known as the *least squares criterion*.[7] When we use earnings as the *dependent variable* (y) and education, experience, and gender as the *independent variables* (x_1, x_2, and x_3, respectively), the equation has the form:

$$\hat{y} = b_o + b_1 x_1 + b_2 x_2 + b_3 x_3 \qquad \text{(1A-1)}$$

---

[7]According to this criterion, the equation that best fits the data is the one for which the sum of the squared deviations of the actual values of y from the predicted values of y (indicated by $\hat{y}$) is less than for any other equation. For this reason, regression analysis is more precisely called "least squares" regression analysis.

TABLE 1.A.1   Earnings, Education, Work Experience, and Gender for a (Hypothetical)
Sample of 300 Individuals

Individual	Annual Earnings ($000)	Years of Education	Work Experience (years)	Sex (M = 1) (F = 0)
1	55	16	15	1
2	60	17	20	0
3	45	13	13	0
4	52	15	18	1
5	30	14	8	0
6	34	13	10	0
7	45	14	12	1
8	26	12	2	1
9	48	15	10	1
10	75	18	25	0
11	80	17	25	0
12	85	19	27	0
13	60	15	15	1
14	25	8	20	1
...	...	...	...	...
...	...	...	...	...
...	...	...	...	...
300	35	12	20	0

In the equation b_0 is known as the *y-intercept term* (the predicted value of earnings if the values of all the independent variables are zero), and b_1, b_2, and b_3 are the regression slopes or *coefficients*.[8] Because regression analysis usually requires laborious computations, statistical software programs (e.g., EXCEL) are generally used to compute the numerical values of the intercept and coefficient terms. We have in fact used EXCEL to estimate the regression equation for the data in our example, and the EXCEL output is depicted in Table 1.A.2. Reading the column labeled *Coefficients*, we can see that our regression equation turns out to be:

$$\hat{y} = -43.368 + 4.976x_1 + 1.208x_2 + 4.377x_3 \qquad (1A\text{-}2)$$

How do we interpret the equation? The intercept term (−43.368) tells us that if an individual has no education, has no work experience, and is a female, then we would expect her earnings to be *negative* $43,368. (Remember that our earnings data are in $000.) Clearly this prediction is nonsensical, the major reason being that it lies far outside the range of the information in Table 1.A.1. The coefficients of the three independent variables are more interesting. The b_1 value of 4.976 tells us that each additional year of education

---

[8] The equation that we fit here is called a *multiple regression equation* because we have several independent variables. *Simple regression* refers to the case where there is only one independent variable.

TABLE 1.A.2   EXCEL Regression Output

SUMMARY OUTPUT

Regression Statistics

Multiple R	0.9675998
R Square	0.936249372
Adjusted R Square	0.918862837
Standard Error	5.443747122
Observations	300

ANOVA

	df	SS	MS	F	Significance F
Regression	3	4787.355123	1595.785041	53.84911	7.29772E−07
Residual	296	325.97821	29.63438273		
Total	299	5113.333333			

	Coefficients	Standard Error	t-statistic	p-value
Intercept	−43.36844042	8.820975286	−4.916513086	0.000459
Education	4.976623174	0.604156047	8.237314185	4.94E−06
Experience	1.208262655	0.243830224	4.955344076	0.000432
Gender	4.377102449	3.11872801	1.403489639	0.188065

© Cengage Learning

is associated with (on average) $4,976 higher annual earnings when each of the other variables is held constant. Similarly, every additional year of experience is associated with annual earnings that are $1,208 higher, again holding the other variables constant. Furthermore, being a male brings with it earnings that are on average higher by $4,377, once more holding the other variables constant.

How well does our regression equation actually explain the earnings of the individuals in Table 1.A.1? Remember that even though it is the best-fitting equation according to our least squares criterion, the equation just described still might not be able to explain much of the variation in earnings. For the purpose of describing the *goodness of fit* of the regression equation, two important measures are used:

1. The standard error of estimate
2. The coefficient of determination.

The standard error of estimate is roughly a measure of average prediction error. Its value (here given as 5.443, or $5,443, in the fourth row of the Regression Statistics section of Table 1.A.2) indicates how far away on average the actual earnings values for our 300 individuals are from the earnings values predicted by the regression equation.

The coefficient of determination is our second measure of the goodness of fit of the regression equation. Written as R^2 (or R Square in the Regression Statistics section of Table 1.A.2), the coefficient of determination tells us what proportion of the variation in the dependent variable is explained by the independent variables. The closer the R^2 value is to 1 (or 100%), the better the fit of the regression equation. For our earnings equation, the R^2 value of .936 indicates that the three independent variables—education, experience, and gender—in the regression equation explain nearly 94% of the variation in earnings.[9]

Statistical Inference in Regression

In regression analysis the researcher is usually interested in generalizing the results beyond the sample that was used. For example, we might wish to infer how much of an effect differences in education, experience, or gender on average have on the earnings of *all* individuals of the type considered here. For the purpose of making such generalizations, it is helpful to think of our regression equation as a sample estimate of a corresponding "theoretical" or "population" relationship between earnings and the independent variables we have used to explain earnings. We can depict this population regression relationship in the following way:

$$Y_0 = \beta_0 + \beta_1 X_1 + \beta_2 X_2 + \beta_3 X_3 + \varepsilon \tag{1A-3}$$

The population intercept (β_0) and coefficients (the other βs) can be interpreted in the same manner we have interpreted our sample regression intercept and coefficients. However, the population regression equation is a theoretical relationship only, so we will never be able to determine the "true" values of the coefficients. In addition, the last term in the population regression equation (ε), the *error term*, indicates that our regression equation does not describe an exact relationship between the dependent and independent variables. A good way of thinking about the error term is that it embodies all the other factors influencing the dependent variable over and above those that have been included as independent variables.

As mentioned, in regression analysis the researcher is usually interested in generalizing the results to see what the sample might tell us about the "true" relationships between the dependent variable and the independent variables. One question is particularly important in this regard: Is it possible that for the population there is *no* relationship between the dependent variable and all of the independent variables? In other words, could the values of the coefficients (βs) of the population regression equation be zero? In such a case, the sample regression coefficients may have taken on nonzero values only by chance—or, as statisticians say, because of sampling error.[10] To judge whether this may be the case, we can undertake the following hypothesis test for the regression coefficients:

$$H_0: \beta_1 = \beta_2 = \beta_3 = 0$$
$$H_1: \text{Not all the } \beta s = 0 \tag{1A-4}$$

H_0 above is referred to as the null hypothesis, and H_1 is called the alternate hypothesis.

---

[9]The *Adjusted R Square* value, given just below the *R* Square value in Table 1.A.2, is simply the *R* Square value adjusted for degrees of freedom. Its value will ordinarily be slightly less than the unadjusted *R* Square.

[10]Just as when we flip a perfectly fair coin a number of times we may get unequal numbers of heads and tails, so also may we observe a nonzero relationship between earnings and the number of years of education, for example, even when for the population as a whole there might be no relationship between the two.

To test the null hypothesis that all of the population regression coefficients are equal to zero, we undertake an analysis of variance test (an F test). The results of this test are given in the middle section of our EXCEL output, the ANOVA table. The F-value in the table (53.84) is accompanied by a level of significance of 7.29772E−07, or .000000729. This value, also sometimes called a *p-value*, tells us that we could expect to get an F-value of as high as 53.84 only about 7 in 10 million times if the null hypothesis were true. Because this is not a very high probability, we reject the null hypothesis and conclude that at least one of the population regression coefficients is not equal to zero.

Since the F test has led us to reject the null hypothesis that all the regression coefficients are equal to zero, we are then justified in proceeding to test the individual regression coefficients. In other words, we will undertake the following hypothesis test for *each of* the regression coefficients:

$$H_0 : \beta_i = 0$$
$$H_1 : \beta_i \neq 0$$
(1A-5)

As a rule of thumb for large samples, if a sample regression coefficient (b_i) is at least *twice* the value of its standard error (s_{bi}), the null hypothesis (H_0) of no relationship between the dependent and the respective independent variable (i.e., $\beta_i = 0$) will be rejected. Another way of putting it is that the t-statistic for that coefficient must be at least 2.0.[11] In such a case, there is said to be a *statistically significant* relationship between the dependent variable and the corresponding independent variable. The underlying rationale is that, if the population regression coefficient β_i were really zero, there would be less than a 5% chance that a sample regression coefficient would have a magnitude as large as two standard deviations above zero.

How does each of the coefficients of our sample regression equation stack up against their respective null hypotheses? Turning to the bottom section of the EXCEL summary output in Table 1.A.2, the t-statistics of each of the regression coefficients are presented in column 4. The value of the t-statistic for the coefficient of the education variable is 8.237, signifying that a statistically significant relationship exists between earnings and education, just as we might have expected. Similarly, with a t-statistic of 4.955 the coefficient of the experience variable also is statistically significant. However, the coefficient of our third independent variable (gender) produces a t-statistic of only 1.403. This indicates that, at least for our sample, gender does not have a significant effect on earnings.

As an alternative to using the t-statistics, the p-values in the column next to the t-statistic column may also be used to test the null hypotheses that each of the β_i values is equal to zero. Like the interpretation that we gave to the F-statistic in the ANOVA section, each of the p-values indicates the probability of getting a sample regression coefficient as high as the one that we have calculated if the respective population regression coefficient were equal to zero. As can be seen from the p-value column, the p-values for both the education and the experience coefficients are very small. But the p-value of the gender coefficient (.188) is high

---

[11] The t-statistic is defined as $(b_i - \beta_i)/s_{bi}$.

enough to lead us to conclude that the population regression coefficient for the gender variable might be equal to zero.[12]

Causality and Regression Analysis

The mainstream positivist approach to economic investigation is based on the idea of "if …, then …" relationships. Economic theory is based on the idea that *if* a certain set of assumptions holds, *then* a certain set of consequences will arise. Likewise, empirical economics is typically based on the estimation of statistical relationships that tell us that *if* there is a change in the value of an explanatory variable *then* there will be a change in the value of the dependent variable. This means that economists are very concerned about the *direction of causality* between variables.

On its own, regression analysis tells us nothing about causality. If the data show a statistical relationship between two variables we cannot, from a simple regression line, tell which variable influences which. It may even be the case that each variable influences the other in a complex simultaneous relationship—we often call this a chicken-and-egg relationship because of the familiar conundrum: which came first, the chicken or the egg? An example of such a chicken-and-egg relationship in economics is the relationship between education and occupational choice: do people choose to get educated to a certain level because of the job they want to do, or is the job they do conditioned on the education they have received? If we want to use regression analysis to inform policy, it is vitally important that we know what the effect of changing a policy variable will be, so we have to have a way of sorting out this direction of causality puzzle.

This conundrum has led to the development of a variety of statistical tricks that help to establish exactly what is going on in such complex relationships between economically relevant variables. Without going into too much detail here, we will outline two such methods that have come to be commonly used by economists studying labor markets.

Natural Experiments

Unlike physical scientists, economists rarely have the opportunity to conduct controlled experiments in laboratories. But sometimes situations arise that offer data from a "natural experiment," and thus allow economists to separate out cause and effect. We consider several examples of such experiments in Chapter 6 when we look at the impact of education on individuals' earnings. One of these examples concerns how changes in legislation on the minimum school leaving age meant that some workers *had* to have more education than otherwise identical individuals (regardless of their intended career), simply because of the random fact that they were born in later years. If this extra education led them to earn more, then we know that education had an effect on earnings. The change in legislation acts as a natural experiment and we sometimes refer to it as an *instrument*.

---

[12] Generally a *p*-value that is less than 5% indicates that there is a statistically significant relationship present, whereas a *p*-value that is greater than 5% indicates that there is not.

Difference-in-Differences Studies

A related technique involves situations in which we can analyze changes in outcomes across time and across different groups, where one of the groups has been subject to a change in treatment while the other has not. A classic example in labor economics is the study, discussed in Chapter 9, in which the impact is assessed of different minimum wage policy adjustments in Pennsylvania and New Jersey. In this type of study, the focus is on how outcomes vary across time and across groups of individuals (e.g., a "treated" and an "untreated" group); we study the change (or difference) in outcome across both time and groups—hence the term "difference in differences."

A neat way of evaluating the magnitude of the effects of policy change on an outcome variable is to run a regression of the form

$$\hat{y} = b_0 + b_1 t + b_2 z + b_3 tz \tag{1A-6}$$

where t is a time dummy that takes the value 1 for the period after the policy change and 0 for the period before the change, z is a state dummy that takes the value 1 for the state in which the policy changed and 0 for the state where the policy did not change; hence tz is the interaction of policy change and state. In this regression, b_1 captures changes in the outcome over time, while b_2 captures differences across states. The key coefficient is b_3, which shows how the outcome variable responded to the policy change (in the one state where the policy did indeed change). Since differences across time periods (due to, say, the macroeconomic environment) and across states (due to, say, different institutional environments) have been accounted for by b_1 and b_2 respectively, the impact captured by b_3 must be a pure measure of the effect of the policy.

The availability of such a pure measure has made difference-in-differences estimation very popular among applied labor economists in recent years. But it should be borne in mind that it is not always possible to conduct analyses of this kind—it is fairly unusual for policy changes to be staggered across different groups of subjects. Where they are (perhaps where new policy proposals are being piloted on some groups but not others), it is worth taking the econometric evidence seriously.

2

The Demand for Labor

If schoolteachers in Gotham City receive a 10% pay increase, will the number of teachers employed change as a result?

If the federal minimum wage were raised, what would happen to the quantity demanded of low-paid workers such as teenagers and others with low levels of skill and experience?

If a university raises tuition to $75,000 per year, what will happen to the demand for professors?

The market for labor, like other markets, comprises both a demand side (employers who want to hire labor) and a supply side (workers who want to be employed). Adjustment to a demand and supply equilibrium may be complicated by institutional factors, but we would nevertheless expect demand and supply to be major influences on labor market outcomes. Indeed, how well the market adjusts to the forces of demand and supply is an indication of the degree of competitiveness within the labor market. It is appropriate, then, to begin by studying in some detail the character of the demand and supply of labor. In this chapter we focus on the demand side of the market.

The basic purpose of analyzing the demand for labor is to see how much labor—how many workers or how many labor units—employers will want to hire at various pay levels. Clearly, labor is needed in the production process; firms can produce things only if labor is there to do the producing. This applies to services such as education or health care just as much as it does to manufacturing. So we begin with an analysis of the part played by labor in a firm's production function. Then we examine how labor is demanded alongside other factors of production, such as capital. We distinguish between the demand for labor in the short run (when the amount of capital employed cannot be adjusted) and labor demand in the long run (when all inputs are variable). We also distinguish between the demand for workers and the demand for hours of labor. In doing all of this, we'll see how the productivity of labor—the contribution that labor makes to the production process—is key to determining labor demand. Next we study the influences on the shape of the demand for labor schedule. In particular, we'll look at the determinants of the elasticity of labor demand. Finally, we address some caveats that must be attached to the notion that productivity is what drives the demand for labor.

Labor Demand

Over the years the National Education Association (NEA), the largest teachers' union in the United States, frequently issued reports called *Teacher Demand and Supply*. Usually in the reports the NEA argued that teacher demand was something on the order of 50% to 100% more than the supply of teachers, which would signify a very sizeable shortage of teachers. But what the NEA meant by "demand" was something very much different from what economists mean by that term. The NEA began with what it referred to as a "desirable" teacher–pupil ratio (about 20 students per teacher in all classrooms) and then projected how many teachers would be required to achieve this ratio. Rather than demand, the NEA referred to what might better be called a perceived need, a goal, or maybe just wishful thinking. To economists, the demand for teachers is a need backed up by the ability and the willingness to actually hire the number of teachers in question. Ironically, in many years that the NEA claimed (by its accounting) that teacher demand exceeded teacher supply, there was actually a *surplus* of teachers, with more teachers looking for teaching jobs than there were openings.

The Production Function

The very first thing to understand about the demand for labor is that it is a derived demand. Nobody, and no firm, wants labor for its own sake. So the demand for labor is unlike the demand for hamburgers, for example. Firms want to hire labor only because there is a demand for the goods and services that labor can help to produce. If the demand for the goods and services didn't exist, then there wouldn't be a demand for labor either.

The demand for labor is derived from the demand for what labor can produce, so a natural starting point in the discussion of labor demand is the **production function**. The production function maps the amounts of labor (and also the amounts of other inputs, such as capital[1] used in the production process) employed by a firm onto the output of the firm. This can be expressed mathematically by an equation of the form

$$Q = f(K,L) \tag{2-1}$$

where Q represents output, K represents capital, and L represents labor input. (The "f" in this equation stands for "is a function of"; so, the equation simply says that output is a function of capital and labor.) But at this stage it is probably easier to represent the production function diagrammatically.

A simple production function is illustrated in Figure 2.1. As inputs of labor and capital (Input 1 and Input 2) increase, so also does the output of the firm. The production function shown in this diagram is concave—it has the appearance of a dome. This shows

---

[1] By *capital*, we mean the plant, the office, the machines, and so forth.

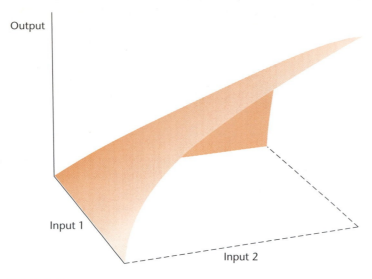

Output

Input 1

Input 2

FIGURE 2.1 A Production Function

that although extra inputs result in the production of extra output, the rate at which inputs can be converted to output deteriorates as the firm becomes bigger.

The production function shown in Figure 2.1 is three-dimensional; it looks just like a piece of a mountain. This image shows two inputs (labor and capital) and one output. It is possible to deal with more complex production functions, but such functions cannot be represented in this way because they have too many dimensions for us to picture. Even a three-dimensional graph has its problems, not least of which is the fact that the paper on which it is drawn is only two dimensional. Fortunately, there are ways around these problems. Geographers and cartographers depict the lay of the land on a map by using contour lines. We shall do something similar here.

Figure 2.2 shows some of the contour lines that could be drawn to depict the three-dimensional production function shown in Figure 2.1 in two dimensions. You will see that the axes of Figure 2.2 have been labeled L (for labor) and K (for capital). These correspond to east and north on a map. What has happened to output (which we labeled Q)? Just as altitude is represented by the contour on a map, the level of output is represented by an **isoquant** on our diagram, a convex curve that slopes downward from left to right. The diagram shows three isoquants, labeled Q_1, Q_2, and Q_3. The term *isoquant* is derived from the Greek word *iso*, meaning the same, and the English word "quantity." So everywhere along any one of these isoquants, the firm is producing the same quantity of goods or services. On isoquant Q_1, the firm is producing Q_1 units of output; on isoquant Q_2, it is producing Q_2 units of output, and so on. We know that Q_2 must be greater than Q_1 (and Q_3 greater than Q_2) because, for a given amount of capital, more labor is needed to produce Q_2 than Q_1 (and more is needed to produce Q_3 than Q_2).

Why is each isoquant downward sloping? If the firm employs less capital, it can keep output constant only by employing more labor. The downward slope, therefore, implies that capital and labor are, to some extent, substitutes for one another in production. Is this true? To answer that question, we invite you to consider the following examples.

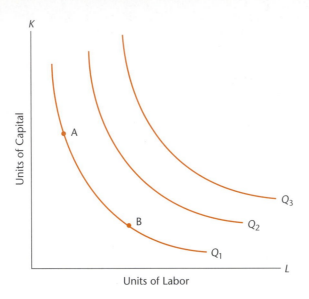

FIGURE 2.2 Isoquant Curves

If your university used advanced sound and video relay equipment, you could be taught in a lecture class of 8,000 students rather than the much smaller class you are in right now. The recent history of the automobile industry in which robotics has largely replaced human labor in the production process indicates that there are many ways to produce a car. And Budweiser employs a mix of capital and labor that is very different from that used by Stoudt's, a small brewery in eastern Pennsylvania. (Of course, Budweiser brews many more bottles of beer each year than Stoudt's, which would put the pint for Budweiser [sorry, the *point* for Budweiser] on a much higher isoquant, as well.) But as the proverb says, there is more than one way to skin a cat.

Why is each isoquant convex? This is because capital and labor are not *perfect* substitutes for one another. Capital can be used to increase class sizes, but a professor is needed to teach the class, and someone must grade your work. Although robots can be used to build cars, humans are still needed to design them. And even though machinery is used intensively in the production of beer, the whole process is overseen by humans. Just as these processes cannot be executed by capital alone, they cannot be performed by humans alone either. You need books, pens, and paper for your education; you need tools to manufacture an automobile; and you need at least a bucket to make beer.

An isoquant is really nothing more than a contour line of the production function, and its shape is determined by the shape of the production function. Capital and labor map onto output in a way that reflects the imperfect substitutability of the two inputs.

Now let's compare two points along the same isoquant. In Figure 2.2, we've labeled two points on isoquant Q_1. Point A is high up on the isoquant, and tells us that we could produce Q_1 units of output using only a little labor as long as a lot of capital is used. In other words, this represents a capital-intensive process of production. Meanwhile, point B is relatively low down on the isoquant, indicating that Q_1 can also be produced using only a little capital as long as a lot of labor is used. This is a labor-intensive process of production.

Notice that at point A the isoquant is a lot steeper than it is at point B. The slope of the isoquant is known as the **marginal rate of technical substitution (MRTS)**. If a firm producing at point A wants to keep output constant but employ one unit less of labor, it would need to employ a lot more capital. This is because, at point A, production is already capital intensive; at this point, it is not easy to further substitute capital for labor. The same is not true of a firm that operates at point B. Here, the firm could keep output at Q_1 while reducing labor input by one unit, and it could do so without having to employ very much more capital. This is because it is relatively easy to substitute capital for labor when the firm is labor intensive.

To make this point clear, think of two automobile firms: one makes extensive use of robots on the production line, whereas the other relies on human labor. Which firm will find it easier to raise its capital intensity? If you said the second one, that's correct. All that firm needs to do is to go some way toward emulating the first firm. This explanation is based on the fact that the slope of the isoquant (the MRTS) is much greater at point A than at point B. As we move to the right, the MRTS declines; this is known as the diminishing marginal rate of substitution.

So far, we have considered only the case of a smooth isoquant. Now let's consider an extreme case in which inputs are perfect complements—that is, no substitution between inputs is possible (see Figure 2.3). This arises from what is known as a "fixed coefficients" production function, and here the only sensible point at which production would take place is point A. Anywhere else on the isoquant the firm would be employing inputs that are not needed to produce the given level of output; and because it would presumably be paying to employ these superfluous inputs, the firm would not be maximizing its profits.

Figure 2.4 illustrates one more feature of a production function, a region of uneconomic production. If we were to keep adding more and more labor, at some point the slope of the isoquant would become positive. The isoquant would "bend back on itself."

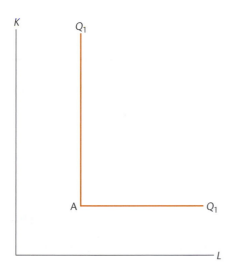

FIGURE 2.3 A Production Function with No Capital–Labor Substitution Possibilities

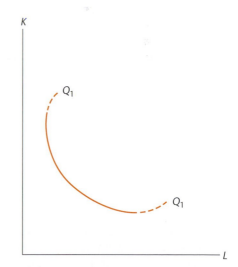

FIGURE 2.4 A Production Isoquant Showing the "Uneconomic" Region of Production

At this point not only could we not afford to give up any more capital, but we would actually have to *increase* the amount of capital with which labor is working to keep output the same. Such a course of action—increasing both capital and labor but with no increase in output—would make no sense because input costs rise with input usage, but the firm has no more product to sell. And in fact the region of Q_1 indicated by the dotted lines is sometimes referred to as the uneconomic region of production.

We've seen that the demand for labor is a derived demand, and that it originates from the ability of labor to combine with other inputs to produce output. How well labor combines with the other inputs determines labor's productivity, and how productive labor is determines its attractiveness to a firm. In the next section we examine how the productivity of labor is related to a firm's demand for labor.

The Marginal Product of Labor

What set of conditions would lead the manager of a business firm to hire an additional worker? Clearly, if the firm is in business to make money for its owners, it would not hire an extra worker if the cost of doing so was greater than the extra revenue generated by the labor of that worker. To make a hiring decision, then, the manager needs to know the additional cost to the firm in paying wages and fringe benefits to the employee (plus any costs due to taxation and other overhead) and the extra revenue generated by selling the extra output produced by that employee. The extra output produced by adding one more worker to the staff of a business is called the **marginal product of labor**. If worker compensation is set by labor market conditions, and the price at which the extra output can be sold is known to the firm, the marginal product of labor becomes the key determinant of labor demand. This is a very important idea—indeed it's the cornerstone of our analysis of the demand side of the labor market. Let's examine it in more detail.

The Short-Run Demand for Labor

In the period of time economists refer to as the short run, at least one factor of production is considered to be fixed. In analyzing labor demand, we usually think of capital as the fixed factor of production and labor as the variable factor. In other words, we assume that the employer may vary the hours worked or, through layoffs or hires, may vary the number of workers employed, but that capital is fixed.

The Short-Run Demand for Labor: An Example

How do we evaluate the demand for labor in the short run? To answer this question, let's set up a simple numerical example. Suppose you are running a small resumé preparation service called Acme. The workers in your business combine their labor with some capital—most notably the computing equipment needed to prepare the documents. To some extent, it might be possible to substitute capital for labor in this environment—for example, by using a word processor with an advanced spell checker or by buying dedicated software that provides a template for the resumés. Either of these might save some labor time and increase productivity. So the production function of your business gives

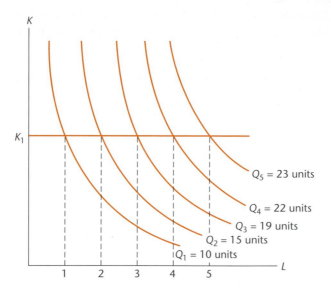

FIGURE 2.5 Diminishing Returns to Labor

rise to isoquants of the kind that we've already met. But it is not possible to exploit the substitutability that these isoquants imply because capital is fixed. So how can you decide, in the short run, how many workers to employ?

The isoquant map for Acme Resumé Preparation Services is illustrated in Figure 2.5. The isoquants slope downward from left to right and are convex to the origin. Each isoquant shows how many resumés can be prepared by the firm over a given time period, such as a day. The horizontal line labeled K_1 indicates the amount of capital the firm already has at its disposal. This is what is fixed in the short run. Regardless of how many workers you choose to employ, these workers must work with the fixed amount of capital already at their disposal (so no new word processors). Because the firm cannot, in the short run, depart from this line, all the interesting points in this diagram lie along the line K_1.

Your decision about how many workers to employ clearly must depend on how many resumés you want to process. If you don't want to process any resumés at all, you do not need to employ any labor. If you want to process up to 10 resumés per day, then you need to employ one worker. If you want to process 11 resumés each day, however, you need to hire a second worker, but then neither worker will be fully employed. The isoquant map tells us that it is simply not possible for a single worker to process 11 resumés, but two workers can process up to 15 resumés per day. Note that the second worker is not as productive as the first; the *marginal product* of the second worker is lower than that of the first. This does not mean that the second worker is lazy or less able than the first—rather, it results from the fact that both workers are using the same fixed stock of capital. A single worker has exclusive use of the word processor and other equipment, but two workers must share this equipment. If both workers want to use the same equipment at the same time, one worker must wait, leading to some downtime and loss of productivity. We can see the same effect happening as labor input is increased to three workers—the third worker adds only four resumés to the potential daily output of the firm. In general, as the amount of labor employed increases, each change in labor produces a smaller change in output. This phenomenon is known as the **law of diminishing returns**—if additional amounts of one factor of production are combined with a fixed factor, at some point the *increase* or *increment* to total output (not total output itself) begins to decline. And, as you probably remember from your principles of economics class, the law of eventually diminishing returns is universally true. Otherwise we could produce all the world's food needs in a flowerpot, and the subject of economics (which is all about meeting unlimited wants with scarce resources) would not exist.

Next, we can formalize this diminishing returns relationship by means of the marginal product function. The marginal product is the change in output that results from the addition of one more unit of labor input. Mathematically:

$$MP = \Delta Q / \Delta L \qquad (2\text{-}2)$$

We use delta notation here—the Δ denotes the change in the variable that follows. Hence the right hand side of the equation denotes the change in output divided by the change in the amount of labor employed. Figure 2.6 depicts the marginal product function, which declines as more labor is added due to diminishing returns. The region where the MP function falls below the horizontal axis corresponds to the uneconomic region of production we noted on the isoquant map—a region that could also be labeled one of negative returns.

Another important functional relationship is the average product of labor (AP). The average product is defined simply as:

$$AP = Q / L \qquad (2\text{-}3)$$

As labor input increases, so does output. At low levels of labor input, output might be expected to rise quite sharply, and AP will follow a rising path as labor increases. But

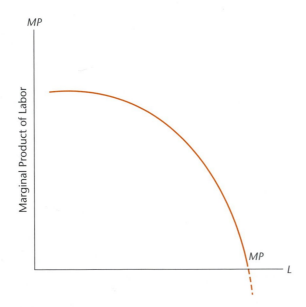

FIGURE 2.6 The Marginal Product of Labor

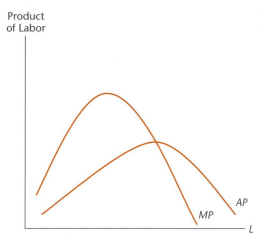

FIGURE 2.7 The Relationship between Marginal and Average Product of Labor

eventually, because capital is fixed, the amount of output added by additional workers must fall. Consequently, *AP* will peak and turn downward (see Figure 2.7).[2]

The marginal product of labor is an extremely important concept because it is a key determinant of the employer's demand for labor. Indeed, if we think of the worker's wages as being paid in units of the good that the worker is producing, then the marginal product function constitutes the demand schedule for labor for a competitive, profit-maximizing employer. In other words, given any wage that the employer would have to pay, he or she would choose to hire the amount of labor corresponding to that point where the wage intersects the *MP* schedule. To understand why this is so, look at Figure 2.8. If the wage happens to be *w*, the employer would not stop at hiring only L_1 workers because the marginal product of the last worker hired exceeds the cost of hiring that worker. The employer would increase the level of profit by hiring more workers. Similarly, the employer would not hire L_3 workers, because the marginal product of the last worker is less than the wage the employer would have to pay that worker. Only at L_2 is the worth of the last worker (the marginal product) exactly equal to what the employer would have to pay (in units of the good being produced) to hire that worker. Using similar reasoning, you can see that whatever the wage is, it always "pays" the employer to hire only up to the point where $w = MP$. That's why we call the *MP* function the demand schedule for labor.

---

[2] *AP* will intersect *MP* at the former's maximum point, as shown in Figure 2.7. The reasoning that underlies this observation is quite simple, and will be demonstrated here by way of an example. Suppose you put a number of economics professors in a sack, weigh the sack, and calculate the average weight of the professors. Now put into the sack one extra (i.e., a marginal) professor. If the marginal professor weighs more than the average, he will push the average up. (This is why the *AP* rises to the left of the point where *AP* and *MP* cross.) But if the marginal professor weighs less than the average he or she will pull the average down (so, to the right of the intersection of *AP* and *MP*, *AP* falls).

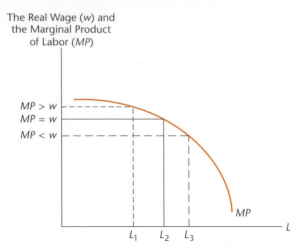

The Real Wage (*w*) and
the Marginal Product
of Labor (*MP*)

FIGURE 2.8 The Real Wage and Marginal Product of Labor

So far our analysis has been in "real" terms; that is, the marginal product has been measured in physical units (numbers of resumés produced). The same is true for the wage. In most situations involving employment and pay, however, the transaction is conducted in money or "nominal" terms. In short, we have to put a "price tag" on our demand for labor. For a firm operating in a competitive product market, this is easy: simply multiply the marginal product by the price of the product or service. The result ($MP \times P$) is the **value of the marginal product (VMP)**. So, if Acme charges $30 for each resumé prepared, the *VMP* is the marginal product times $30. Simply put, the value of the marginal product tells us what the *value* of the additional output will be if the employer hires one more worker. And here's the important point: the *VMP* represents the employer's demand schedule for labor in nominal terms. Under certain conditions, the employer will hire labor only up to the point where the *VMP* is equal to the wage he or she has to pay. To hire beyond this point would have the effect of reducing profits. To hire short of this point would be to forgo the opportunity to increase profits.

Before proceeding further, we should note one other thing. All that the marginal product theory boils down to is the following truism: A profit maximizing employer will hire someone only if the person is worth hiring. Marginal product theory really is this basic. So far in this chapter we've conjured up a number of concepts—production functions, isoquants, diminishing returns, and the marginal rate of substitution—and to what end? To argue that employers will normally hire a person only if that person is "worth" hiring— worth it in the sense that the value of what that person produces is just equal to what it would cost to hire him or her.

Table 2.1 puts into systematic form some of the facts we have learned about Acme Resumé Preparation Services. (We are assuming here that the firm can hire workers only in discrete units—e.g., one, two, three.) The first column indicates the number of employees the firm might conceivably hire. The second column is derived from the isoquant map in Figure 2.5. Recall that this tells us how high an isoquant the firm can reach given that it employs the number of workers in the corresponding row of column 1. The third column shows the marginal product of labor. For example, as the firm increases employment from

TABLE 2.1   Acme Resumé Preparation Services

(1) Employees (L)	(2) Resumés (Q)	(3) Marginal Product ($\Delta Q/\Delta L$)	(4) Average Product (Q/L)	(5) $ Price (P)	(6) $ Value of Marginal Product (VMP)
0	0			30	
1	10	10	10	30	300
2	15	5	7.5	30	150
3	19	4	6.33	30	120
4	22	3	5.5	30	90
5	23	1	4.6	30	30

three to four, output rises by three resumés. The increase in output doesn't happen when three workers are employed or when four workers are employed, but rather as employment is *increased* from three to four.

In column 4, we report the average product of labor, and price is reported in column 5. The final column tabulates the value of the marginal product and is obtained by multiplying the marginal products in column 3 by the (constant) price of $30. It is this value of the marginal product that determines the short-run demand for labor in money terms.

Now for the big question. How many workers would you desire to hire if the wage that you would have to pay is $90 per day? The answer is four. Why? If you employed fewer than four workers, you would not be maximizing your profits because adding extra workers would increase your revenues (measured here by the *VMP*) more than it increases your costs. When you employ the fourth worker, you are adding just as much to your revenue as you are adding to your costs. It would not be worth hiring a fifth worker because this worker would be paid $90 but would bring in only $30 (the worker's *VMP*) more to the firm. Therefore, only with the fourth worker is the worth of the worker exactly equal to the cost of employing the worker, and it is when four workers are employed that you are maximizing your profit.

Conditions for the MP to Represent Labor Demand

Although the analysis seems straightforward so far, we've pretty much avoided mentioning the specific conditions—let's call them assumptions—for the marginal product schedule (and the value of the marginal product) to serve as the demand schedule for labor. Some are obvious, but others are not. In any case, here are the assumptions in no particular order:

1. *The employer is trying to maximize profits.* That the employer is a profit maximizer is implied by the fact that he or she seeks to hire *up to but not beyond* the point where the wage (the marginal cost of labor) is equal to the value of the marginal product (the marginal return from one more unit of labor). Do most employers seek to maximize profits? Aside from the government and the not-for-profit sector (e.g., most hospitals and colleges), it is safe to assume that the quest for profits drives most employers.

If a for-profit firm is not a profit maximizer, its managers are likely to be removed by the shareholders who are seeking the best return on their investment in the company. The shareholders would then put in place new management that would pursue the goal of profit maximization.[3]

2. *The period is the short run.* The marginal product schedule is a short-run schedule. Capital, in other words, is fixed. Later we'll turn to the matter of the demand for labor in the long run when all factors of production are variable.

3. *The wage is the only cost of labor to the employer.* Does this mean that we are assuming the workers get no fringe benefits such as employer pension contributions, health insurance, and the like? For the moment, yes; but this is an easy assumption to dispose of, and you will learn the implications of doing so a little later on.

4. *All workers are of the same quality.* The assumption of worker homogeneity can fairly represent some types of workers (e.g., assembly-line workers) but clearly not others.

5. *The labor market is competitive.* This assumption means essentially that the labor market comprises a large number of employer firms, none of which hires a sufficiently large number of workers to be able to exercise control over the market wage. In our resumé preparation firm example, it meant that we could effectively hire all the workers we wanted at a wage of $90.

6. *The product market is also competitive.* This, of course, means that the firms that make up the product (or service) market are also numerous, with no one firm able to exercise control over the price of the product or service. In our resumé preparation example, we implicitly assumed that the price at which we could sell our resumés remained at $30, no matter how many or how few of them we sold.

7. *The marginal product is the demand for labor only over a certain range.* The usual range is bounded by the peak of the average product function (see Figure 2.7) and the horizontal axis (where the wage is zero). No firm would pay more than the average product for its labor because this would entail incurring a loss, and no firm would pay less than zero as a wage because it could not attract workers if it did so.

What we are saying, essentially, is that for the marginal product function to serve as the demand for labor, these seven conditions must characterize market and employer behavior. But aren't these assumptions rather restrictive? The answer is yes, they are somewhat restrictive, but perhaps not as much as you might be thinking. With just a few modifications we can make our marginal product analysis much more general and useful.

The Demand for Labor in Noncompetitive Product Markets

For the VMP to serve as the employer's demand schedule for labor (see assumption 6), the product or service market in which the employer is operating must be *competitive*—that is, a market composed of a large number of sellers, none of whom exercise control over the price of the product. But what if this condition does not characterize the market in

---

[3] Empirical evidence for this comes from Vojislav Maksimovic and Gordon Phillips, "The Market for Corporate Assets: Who Engages in Mergers and Asset Sales and Are There Efficiency Gains?" *Journal of Finance*, 56 (2001): 2019–2065.

TABLE 2.2 Acme Resumé Preparation Services (noncompetitive product market)

(1)	(2)	(3)	(4)	(5)	(6)	(7)
		Marginal		Value of Marginal	Total Revenue	Marginal Revenue
Employees (L)	Resumés (Q)	Product ($\Delta Q/\Delta L$)	Price (P)	Product (VMP)	Product (TRP)	Product ($\Delta TRP/\Delta L$)
0	0		50		0	
1	10	10	30	300	300	300
2	15	5	28	140	420	120
3	19	4	26	104	494	74
4	22	3	24	72	528	34
5	23	1	22	22	506	−22

question? What if there are only a few sellers, or maybe even just one? This is called a noncompetitive or monopolistic market—not monopolistic in the strongest sense of the term (literally, one seller) but in the sense that some firms possess some monopoly power, such as control over price.

To see how the demand for labor would change if the product market is noncompetitive, let's return to the example of our resumé preparation service. Table 2.2 depicts the same worker productivity information as Table 2.1, except that we now assume that the market for resumés is not competitive. In other words, Acme Resumé Preparation Services has some market power. If the company wants to sell more resumés, it must reduce the price at which it sells them. Another way of saying this, of course, is that the company now faces a less-than-perfectly-elastic demand schedule for its product. (In the previous scenario, the company could produce and sell all the resumés it desired without having to lower the price it charged—now it cannot.)

Notice first of all that the numbers in the value of the marginal product (*VMP*) column (column 5) of Table 2.2 are falling faster (after the first worker) than they did in Table 2.1. This is the result of the fall in price that is necessary if the firm is to sell more resumés. It's a good example of how things going on in one market (in this case, the product market) can spill over into what goes on in another (such as the labor market). But how many workers will you hire now if the wage is, as before, $90? Your first impulse might be to hire only three workers because the *VMP* of the fourth worker ($72) is now less than the wage that the fourth worker would have to be paid. However, in this case you should not hire even the third worker. Why not? Because in a noncompetitive product market situation like this one, the value of the marginal product no longer measures the worth of the worker to the employer. The reason is simple. Because of the noncompetitive nature of the product market, beyond some point the employer has to lower the price of the product to sell more. But the price will be lowered not just for the output of the last (or marginal) worker but for the output of the first two workers as well—that is, unless the producer can discriminate in the price charged to different customers. Put simply, hiring the third worker will result in revenue effects resulting from the price being lower for *all* of the firm's output.

But if the *VMP* no longer measures the true "worth" of the marginal worker, what does? The answer can be seen in columns 6 and 7 of Table 2.2. Column 6, first of all, shows the *total revenue product* (*TRP*) of the workers. The *TRP* is the result of multiplying output (*Q*) times the price (*P*) at which that output could be sold. It represents the revenue that the firm would receive if it hired *L* workers. For example, employing three workers would result in $494 in revenue (*TRP*) for the firm. What would happen to revenue if a fourth worker were hired? The table shows that *TRP* would increase to $528. In other words, the *change* in *TRP* resulting from hiring a fourth worker would be $34. So what would the worth of the fourth worker be? That's right, $34. The change in the total revenue product resulting from hiring one more worker is the **marginal revenue product (MRP).** If the wage you must pay is $90, how many workers will you hire? The answer is two. Only with two workers does the wage (the cost of labor) not exceed the *MRP*. If you hired a third worker, the cost of the third worker would be greater than the revenue that worker brings into the firm.

In light of this discussion, can we generalize any further about the demand schedule for labor? We have already seen that in a competitive product or service market it is the *value of the marginal product* (*VMP*) that serves as the employer's demand schedule for labor. And in a less-than-competitive market it is the *marginal revenue product* (*MRP*) that serves as the employer's demand schedule. The *VMP* is the marginal product of labor multiplied by the price of the product, or $MP \times P$. Although we won't formally demonstrate it here, the *MRP* can be shown to be equal to the marginal product of labor multiplied by the marginal revenue in the product market, with marginal revenue being the change in total revenue resulting from the sale of one more unit of the product. In other words, $MRP = MP \times MR$. In a perfectly competitive product market, price and marginal revenue are equal, so the *MRP* and *VMP* schedules are the same. Therefore, we can consider the *MRP* to be the demand for labor whether the product market is competitive or not. This is the more general, all-inclusive concept.

What Determines the Position of the Short-Run Demand for Labor?

Because the short-run demand for labor is determined by a mix of product market considerations (*MR*) and productivity (*MP*), the position of the demand for labor schedule depends on things that are going on in both the product and labor markets. Anything that affects the marginal revenue a firm receives for its output will affect labor demand. This means that demand and supply forces in the product market will affect the demand for labor because both demand and supply affect the product market price. Hence the demand for labor will shift outward if product market demand rises owing to increases in income, a rise in the population, a favorable change in the prices of substitutes and complements of the good being produced, or a change in tastes in favor of the good being produced. All of these things affect product market demand, so they will also affect the demand for labor.

Product market supply depends on the number of firms in the industry, input prices, choice of technology used in production, and any taxes or subsidies that might be in place. All of these things can affect the level of supply in the product market; through this effect, they influence marginal revenue in the product market and so also the marginal revenue product of labor.

Changes in labor productivity that emanate from outside the firm can also result in shifts of the labor demand curve. In the short run, the most obvious source of such a productivity change can be found in the agricultural sector, where surprise changes in climate can lead to labor becoming more or less productive. When uncharacteristically bad weather results in a poor harvest, the demand for labor tends to fall because the productivity of labor has fallen. More generally, surprise shocks in productivity, arising from whatever source, can affect the position of the short-run demand for labor.[4]

A Note on Exploitation

Because an employer will not ordinarily pay a wage greater than the worker's marginal revenue product, the interesting concept of **exploitation** arises. Exploitation has a long history of usage in economics, and beginning with Karl Marx the term has often evoked a very emotional response. According to Marxian thinking, only labor creates value in the production process.[5] Therefore, any monetary payment or return to a non-labor factor of production (such as entrepreneurs, landowners, or money lenders) is by definition "exploitative" of labor because labor would then not be getting paid what it is worth for its contribution to the production process. This Marxian definition of exploitation is somewhat different from the definition used by most mainstream economists.

What then do we mean when we say that labor is "exploited" with respect to the wage that it receives? Very simply, if labor receives a wage lower than their marginal revenue product, then wage exploitation is present.[6] Labor's marginal revenue product represents what labor is worth, and any wage below the *MRP* means that workers are being paid less than what they are worth to the employer. We should stress that when using this economic definition of exploitation, it is possible for a worker (e.g., one with no skills or experience) to receive a very low wage yet not necessarily to be exploited. Conversely, a worker receiving a very high wage (e.g., a professional athlete) might still be exploited in the sense that we are using the term here.

The Demand for Labor in the Long Run

So far we have restricted ourselves to the short run, the period of time during which at least one factor of production (here, capital) is considered to be fixed. But what does the employer's demand schedule for labor look like in the long run when *all* factors are

---

[4] In the long run, of course, productivity can also be influenced by the amount and quality of capital employed by the firm. In the short run, capital is fixed, however, so this is not a consideration we need to deal with here.

[5] These issues are studied in Marx's classic work, *Capital*, volume 1, chapter 9. This was originally published in 1867.

[6] This is a tricky concept. In defining exploitation as a situation where workers are paid wages lower than their marginal revenue product, we must remember that we are referring to the marginal revenue product *of the last worker hired*. To see this, refer back to Table 2.2. If the wage rate happened to be $74, then 3 workers would be hired because the *MRP* of the third worker is also $74. But, you might be thinking, why shouldn't the first person hired receive a wage of $300 (the *MRP* associated with $L = 1$) and the second person hired receive a wage of $120 (the *MRP* for $L = 2$), while the third worker gets a wage of $74? There are several reasons. First, remember that all workers are assumed to be of the same quality and can thus be considered interchangeable when it comes to the hiring order. (Put another way, if the third worker would have been the first hired and the first person would have been the third, the *MRP*s shown in Table 2.2 would be the same.) A second reason is that if each worker received a wage equal to that individual worker's *own MRP*, then all the revenues emanating from production (the Total Revenue Product, *TRP*) would be going to workers, with nothing left over for the other factors of production (capital, entrepreneurship, land). In the example from Table 2.2, the *TRP* is 494 and so would be the sum of total wages (which we call the total wage bill.)

variable? If changes in wage rates occur, employers will be both willing and able to make adjustments in the amounts of labor and other factors that they use. For example:

- Facing high union wage demands, some employers have chosen to move their operations to a new location (from the northern to the southern United States, from Western to Eastern Europe, from developed to developing countries) where wages are lower or where unionism is less widespread.
- Given rising wage costs, some employers switch to more capital-intensive methods of production, trying to substitute relatively cheaper capital for relatively more expensive labor.
- Some labor employment practices in various parts of the world that appear to be inefficient may be perfectly sound when the relative costs of labor and capital are considered. For example, streetcars in Beijing have two crew members, a car operator and a fare collector; delivery trucks may have both a driver and one or two delivery boys. Where labor is relatively cheap, it makes sense to produce with a high ratio of labor to capital.

To analyze the demand for labor in the long run, let's return to our production function in terms of capital and labor (see Figure 2.9). And here a new concept is important, the **budget constraint**. The budget constraint determines how much labor (L) and how much capital (K) a firm can purchase with its current budget. Letting B refer to the budget level, and w and r refer to the per-period price of labor and capital, respectively, the budget constraint may be written as follows:

$$B = w \cdot L + r \cdot K. \tag{2-4}$$

(We are here using the dot symbol ($\cdot$) to denote multiplication and will do so in all subsequent equations.) Notice in Figure 2.9 that if the firm were to spend all of its budget

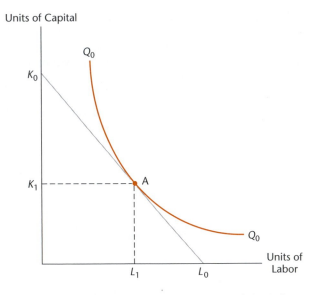

FIGURE 2.9 The Cost Minimizing Amount of Capital and Labor for a Given Output

dollars on capital and none on labor (not very likely), then the firm could employ $K_0 = B/r$ units of capital. Conversely, if the firm chose to employ only labor but no capital (again, not very likely), then it could hire $L_0 = B/w$ units of labor. Since K_0/L_0 refers to the slope of the budget constraint, an alternative way of expressing the slope would be $(B/r)/(B/w)$ or, canceling terms, w/r. This is important because it enables us to express the slope of the budget constraint as the ratio of the prices of labor and capital.

Assume that at the moment the employer is at point A in Figure 2.9, employing L_1 units of labor and K_1 units of capital. Since A is a point of tangency between the isoquant and the lowest attainable budget constraint, the employer is producing the given level of output at the lowest possible cost. So at this point the employer is employing an optimal amount of labor, with the MRP just equal to labor's wage. Similarly, the employer is employing just the right amount of capital. Although we have not specifically analyzed the employer's decisions regarding the employment of capital, it is easy to see that the desire to maximize profits would lead the employer to employ capital up to the point where its marginal product (let's call it MRP_K) is just equal to the price of capital (r). The expressions that the marginal revenue products of each of the two factors are equal to their respective prices, $MRP = w$ and $MRP_K = r$, can easily be divided by one another and the terms rearranged to show that for the profit maximizing employer of labor and capital:

$$\frac{MRP}{w} = \frac{MRP_K}{r} = 1 \qquad (2\text{-}5)$$

What equation 2-5 signifies is that the optimal combination of labor and capital is reached when the ratios of the marginal product of each factor to its own price are equal to unity. This is an important relationship, and we will return to it shortly.

Now what would happen to the firm's demand schedule for labor in the long run if the price of labor were to fall? First, notice that if the price of labor falls, the slope of the budget constraint, w/r, becomes flatter. In fact, the budget constraint rotates counter-clockwise about point K_0, as is shown in Figure 2.10, rotating[7] from K_0L_0 to K_0L_0''. This rotation of the budget constraint allows the firm to hire more labor than it did before the wage decline. But how much more labor? The answer depends on several "effects" emanating from the wage change; these are called substitution and scale effects.

The **substitution effect** is the effect of a fall in the price of labor on the quantity of labor demanded *if output (Q) were to remain unchanged*. In Figure 2.10 the magnitude of the substitution effect is shown by first constructing another budget constraint line ($K_0'L_0'$) parallel to the rotated budget constraint line and making this budget line just tangent to the *original* production isoquant (Q_0Q_0). Notice that the point of tangency occurs at point B. The distance AB (or $L_2 - L_1$) indicates the magnitude of the substitution effect. Because of the shape of our production isoquant, a fall in the price of labor will always result in the substitution effect leading to more labor being employed. This result

---

[7]To understand why the budget constraint rotates in this way, consider the following: if the firm were to employ only capital and no labor, a fall in the wage would not affect the amount of capital that it can employ (it would remain unchanged at K_0); but if the firm were to employ only labor and no capital, then the fall in the wage would allow it to increase labor employment from L_0 to L_0''.

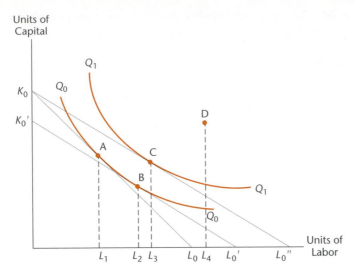

FIGURE 2.10 The Price and Scale Effects of a Lower Price of Labor

is intuitively obvious. With labor now being relatively less expensive than capital in the production process, in the long run the employer will be inclined to substitute now-cheaper labor for the relatively more expensive capital factor.

But as we've already said, scale effects will also be present if the price of labor falls. Scale effects result from a change in the price of labor that changes the scale of operations. The first of these scale effects is the **output effect**. As shown in Figure 2.10, the decline in the wage, signified by the rotation of the budget constraint line, also enables the employer to attain a higher level of output (point C on isoquant Q_1Q_1) with the same budget expenditure level. The magnitude of the output effect on the quantity of labor employed is signified by the horizontal component of distance BC, or $L_3 - L_2$.

What's the intuition underlying the output effect? The decline in the price of labor has not only allowed the employer to substitute now-cheaper labor for more expensive capital (the substitution effect), but it has also increased the real value of the employer's budget. The same dollar value now enables the employer to hire more labor and more capital as well. (Notice that the amount of capital associated with point C is greater than that associated with point B.) The result of more labor and more capital being used is that output will increase, hence the term "output effect." The logic underlying the output effect depicted in Figure 2.10 can further be seen by the fact that the magnitude of the effect (BC) results from a *parallel shift* of the budget constraint from $K_0'L_0'$ to K_0L_0''. The parallel shift of the line signifies an increase in the real value of the budget but with the prices of labor and capital held constant. In short, then, the substitution effect tells us how much of the total change in the amount of labor utilized (AC) is due to the pure price effect (with output held constant). The output effect tells us how much of the change is due to the greater scale of operations (with prices held constant).

At point C the firm is minimizing costs for a given output, but this does not necessarily mean that it is maximizing profits. The diagram contains only input and output information. It includes no data about product prices, so we cannot tell from it where the profit maximizing output level is. Put more formally, the output effect is not the only scale effect that will occur. Although both the substitution and output effects will increase the amount of labor used by the employer, point C in Figure 2.10 merely represents the optimal amounts of the labor and capital inputs *for the given budget constraint*. Rather, the profit maximizing level of output—and the corresponding amounts of the labor and capital inputs required to attain that output level—would lie on yet a *higher* output isoquant attainable only with a *higher* budget constraint. The change in the amount of labor (and capital) associated with the movement from C to this higher level of output (which is depicted as point D in Figure 2.10) is known as the *maximizing effect*. The profit-maximizing amount of labor associated with point D is L_4, as shown in Figure 2.10.

An explanation of why point C does not give us the profit maximizing amounts of output, labor, and capital can be seen through equation 2-5. This equation showed that the employer will maximize profits if labor and capital are each hired up to the points where their marginal product/wage ratios are equal to one. Point C is not such a point. Although at point C the two marginal product/price ratios will be equal to one another, their ratios will each exceed one. That means that to maximize profits the employer will need to employ still more labor and capital, even though a higher budget will be required to do so. The reason we cannot analyze the maximizing effect any further than we have done in Figure 2.10 is that it requires information on product demand and corresponding revenues, while our analysis so far has been restricted to analyzing product and factor costs.[8]

To summarize and to see how each of the effects works to give us the long-run demand schedule for labor, let's now turn to Figure 2.11. Suppose that the employer's initial demand schedule for labor was MRP_1 and that the initial wage rate was w_1. The employer would therefore have hired L_1 units of labor at point A. But when the price of labor fell to w_2, the substitution effect caused the employer to substitute labor for capital. The substitution effect would thus cause the original *MRP* schedule to shift to the *left*. This may seem counterintuitive, but remember that the position of the *MRP* schedule is a function of how much capital the labor factor is working with. If the substitution effect causes the employer to use less capital, the *MRP* schedule will fall. Labor will be less productive because it has less capital to help it do the work. Notice, though, that with the drop in the wage to w_2, the employer will still be using more labor than before. In other words, point B is to the right of point A.[9] What about the scale effects? Because the scale

[8] The analysis above assumes that there is perfect competition in the product market. That is, the increase in this particular firm's output will not lower the market price of the product (or service) being produced. But if there is not perfect competition in the product market (or if the decline in the wage were to be experienced by *all* firms), then the price of the product would decline and yet another scale effect—the *revenue effect*—would result. This effect would result in the equilibrium point in Figure 2.10 (call it point E—we're really running through the alphabet here) being somewhat lower and to the left of point D. The best explanation of all four effects is contained in C. E. Ferguson, *Microeconomic Theory*. Homewood, Illinois, Irwin (1969), chs. 13–14.

[9] The fall in the price of labor cannot cause the capital–labor ratio to decline enough to reduce the short-run demand for labor below its starting level. To see why this is so, think about what the implications would be of B being to the left of A. If this were to happen, it would imply that the firm could maximize its profits by employing less labor and less capital than it does at point A. But since the firm was already maximizing profits at point A, this is impossible.

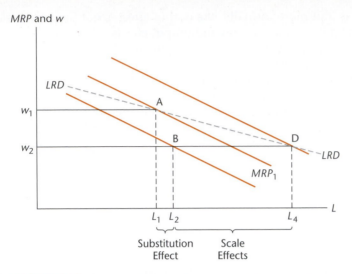

FIGURE 2.11 Marginal Revenue Product and the Long-Run
Labor Demand Curve

effects result in the employer using *more* capital, the *MRP* schedule will consequently shift to the right, as the movement from B to D in Figure 2.11 shows. The net result is that the effects will cause the *MRP* to shift to the right.[10]

What about the long-run demand schedule of labor? Since point D reflects the net result of both the substitution and scale effects of a change in the wage, point D represents one point on the long-run demand for labor. Other points could be constructed in a similar fashion. If we assume that the long-run demand schedule is linear, then we can extend a line through initial point A and point D and represent the long-run demand schedule accordingly as *LRD*, as we have done in Figure 2.11. The slope of the long-run demand schedule is flatter than that of the short-run schedule, which means roughly that the long-run demand schedule of labor is more elastic than the short-run demand schedule. Intuitively, since capital can be substituted for labor in the long run, the demand for labor becomes more price sensitive.

Summary

Let's briefly review what we've learned in this chapter. First, we've learned why the study of labor demand is important. Principally, labor demand analysis enables us to see how many workers employers will want to hire at various pay levels. We analyzed labor demand in the short run, developing and applying the marginal productivity theory.

---

[10]This is so unless the factor is what we call an "inferior" factor. If this is the case, then the long-run demand for labor would be steeper than the short-run demand for labor.

According to the marginal productivity theory, the employer's demand schedule for labor is (under a certain set of conditions) equivalent to the marginal revenue product. Turning to the long run, we found that the employer's long-run demand for labor was more elastic than short-run demand because other factors of production can be substituted for labor if the wage rate changes.

In Chapter 3 we continue our treatment of labor demand, focusing on the elasticity of labor demand. We begin by analyzing several important measures of labor demand elasticity and then explain how we can deduce and estimate the magnitudes of these elasticities.

KEY TERMS

production function

isoquant

marginal rate of technical substitution (MRTS)

marginal product of labor

law of diminishing returns

value of the marginal product

marginal revenue product

exploitation

budget constraint

substitution effect

scale effects

output effect

maximizing effect

PROBLEMS

1. Use the following table showing Joe's Barber Shop's short-run production function to answer the questions that follow

Number of Barbers	Haircuts per day	AP	MP	VMP	MRP
1	20				
2	32				
3	42				
4	50				
5	56				
6	59				

a. Assume that both the labor market for barbers and the product market for haircuts are competitive. Assume the current barber wage is $100 per day and that Joe's can charge customers $15 per haircut. Fill in the missing values in the table above.

b. Making the same assumptions as you did in part a, how many barbers should Joe's hire?

c. Assume that the labor market for barbers is competitive, but now assume that the product market for haircut is not competitive. (To get more customers to come to his shop for haircuts, Joe has to lower the price.) The current wage is still $100 per day. Fill in the missing values in the table that follows.

Number of Barbers	Haircuts per day	Price of a haircut	AP	MP	VMP	MRP
1	20	15				
2	32	12				
3	42	10				
4	50	9				
5	56	8				
6	59	7				

   d. Making the same assumptions as you did in part c, how many barbers should Joe hire?

2. Figures 2.10 and 2.11 explained the effects of a decrease in the wage rate on the long-run demand for labor. Use similar diagrams to show the substitution and scale effects of a wage *increase* on the long-run demand for labor.

3. What would be the effects of each of the following changes on an employer's long-run demand curve for labor? Start with a diagram like Figure 2.10 and show the substitution and scale effects.
   a. An increase in the cost of capital.
   b. A decrease in the cost of capital.
   c. An increase in the wage rate and an increase in the cost of capital.

4. Can you think of three examples that you have experienced where relatively high-priced labor has led to the substitution of capital for labor? We will give you three hints:
   a. Go to the supermarket and purchase some groceries.
   b. What have some apartment and office buildings done to deter crime and increase safety?
   c. Have you ever had to wait for long stretches of time at a tollbooth on an interstate highway?

5. The table shows the short-run weekly production function for the Ace Swimming Pool Company, which installs above-ground pools.

Pools Installed Per Week	Number of Workers Employed
2	1
3	4
4	9
5	16
6	25

   a. Calculate the marginal product and average product of labor.
   b. Suppose the going price of a pool is $2,500. Calculate the value of the marginal product of labor.
   c. If Ace hires nine workers, what is the weekly cost of labor to Ace?

6. Suppose that a firm has the following production function:

$$Q = K^{\frac{1}{2}} \cdot L^{\frac{1}{2}} = \sqrt{KL} \tag{2-6}$$

a. Using calculus, the marginal product of labor for this production function may be calculated as:

$$\partial Q / \partial L = \frac{1}{2} \left(\frac{K}{L} \right)^{\frac{1}{2}} = \frac{1}{2} \sqrt{\frac{K}{L}} \qquad (2\text{-}7)$$

Use this formula for the marginal product of labor to figure out how much labor will be hired if $K = 100$ and the real wage of workers is 2.5 (measured in units of output).

b. How much labor will be hired if the real wage drops to 2?

c. Calculate three different combinations of K and L that would allow this firm to produce 100 units.

d. Show that the marginal rate of technical substitution ($\Delta K / \Delta L$) decreases as the firm's capital-to-labor ratio (K/L) decreases. (This is what happens if you would move from, say, point A to point B on the isoquant in Figure 2.2.)

APPENDIX

Technological Change and Labor Demand

Throughout our analysis of labor demand, we have implicitly assumed that the technology an employer utilizes is fixed. We must be careful here about how we think of technology. If an employer decides to alter the "mix" of labor and capital used, it does not necessarily mean that he or she is using a different technology. Economists define a given technology as the *set* of options or choices that an employer has regarding labor and capital input combinations. If you think of technology in this way, you will see that in Figure 2.A.1 a given technology is depicted by all the possible capital–labor input combinations represented by a given set of production isoquants.

But what if technology changes? What will happen to the employer's demand schedule for labor? First of all, a change in technology for the better will result in a *leftward* shift of

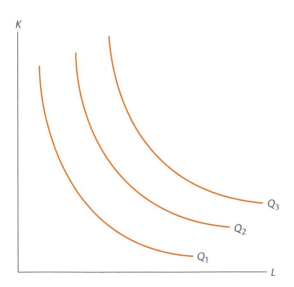

FIGURE 2.A.1 The Production Function with Two Variable Inputs

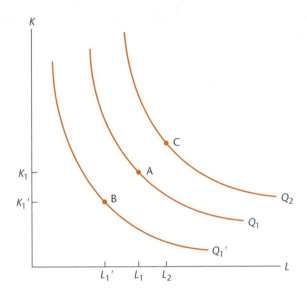

FIGURE 2.A.2 Technological Change and the Production Function

the production isoquants. This means that the same level of output can now be produced with less labor and/or less capital than before. In Figure 2.A.2, the change in technology can be depicted by the shift of Q_1 to Q_1'. As the figure shows, the amounts of both labor and capital needed by the employer to produce the same level of output has, at least initially, fallen. If the proportionate fall in the amount of labor utilized is greater than the proportionate fall in capital, the technological change is said to be "labor saving." If the fall in capital is proportionately greater, the change is said to be "capital saving."

What kind of an effect does technological change have on jobs? Your first impulse is probably to answer that it must destroy jobs. After all, isn't that what Figure 2.A.2 shows? The answer is not as simple as this, however, for point B (and employment level L_1') in Figure 2.A.2 does not represent the final outcome. Although the technological change has indeed shifted the production isoquant to the left, there is no reason to suppose that the employer will desire to produce the same output level (Q_1) as before. The technological change has meant that the cost of producing output Q_1 has fallen. This will in turn be likely to result in a reduction of the price of producing the product and an increase in the quantity demanded by consumers. If this all sounds familiar, it certainly should! We're referring again to the *scale effects* discussed earlier in this chapter. Whether the scale effects will be strong enough to actually increase the level of employment for this firm beyond where it was initially (say to L_2) is uncertain, however. Still, even if the level of employment is lower for the firm (and perhaps for the industry), it does not mean that employment in the entire economy will be lower. Because the technological change has resulted in lower prices, the real incomes of consumers generally have increased. And with higher real incomes and greater purchasing power, the level of spending on goods and services elsewhere will rise, and with it new jobs will be created.

We can see this scale or output effect in data for the aggregate private non-farm business sector in the United States.[11] From 1949 to 1998, firms in this sector substituted capital for labor. Capital per hour of labor input rose by 2.6% per year, on average. There was also technological change. Multifactor productivity rose by 1.2% per year, on average, from 1948 to 1998. But because of strong output growth (an average annual rate of growth of 3.7%), labor input rose by 1.8% per year on average over these 50 years.

Here are some of the more significant examples of technological change that we have all experienced in recent decades:

- *Automatic teller machines (ATMs).* Although ATMs may have reduced employment of tellers and bank clerks, they have certainly increased employment for individuals needed to build and service the machines.
- *Office software.* Has the widespread use of office software reduced the employment of secretaries? Maybe or maybe not. But it certainly has increased employment for those who manufacture, sell, and service personal computers and related equipment (printers, ink cartridges, paper, etc.).

The bottom line, then, is that in the long-run technological change does *not necessarily* reduce the overall number of jobs at the level of the firm, the industry, or the economy. It may indeed reduce the number of *certain* jobs, but not the number of jobs overall.

---

[11] U.S. Department of Labor, "Multifactor Productivity Trends, 1998," *News,* September 21, 2000.

CHAPTER

3

Topics in Labor Demand

If the wage increases by 10%, does the quantity of labor demanded change by a lot or a little?

If the salaries of finance professors increase significantly, will the quantity demanded of economics professors go up, go down, or stay the same?

Do workers get paid their marginal product?

In Chapter 2 we derived a long-run labor demand schedule; now we are ready to more completely analyze the **elasticity of labor demand**. In general, the elasticity of demand tells us what the percentage change in the quantity demanded of something will be, given a certain percentage change in the price of that something. Knowledge of the elasticity of demand for certain types of labor can be very useful. For example, it could tell us what might happen to the number of workers employed if the federal minimum wage were raised to $12 per hour or if a union demanded a 20% increase in its negotiated wage level. In fact, understanding the adverse employment effects stemming from a wage demand of this magnitude can serve as a brake on union wage demands generally.

In this chapter, we first look at three important labor demand elasticities: the wage elasticity of labor demand, the cross-elasticity of labor demand, and the elasticity of substitution. We then turn to some useful extensions and embellishments of marginal productivity theory, such as efficiency wage theory. We conclude this chapter by posing a simple but important question: On average, are workers paid about what they are worth to their employers? To put it another way, do their wages tend to equal their marginal product?

Elasticities

The Wage Elasticity of Labor Demand

The wage elasticity of the demand for labor is the percentage change in the quantity of labor demanded divided by the percentage change in the wage. The symbol η is often used for this elasticity, and we can express η as follows:

$$\eta = \Delta\%L/\Delta\%w \tag{3-1}$$

Equivalently, for those of you familiar with calculus, η can also be expressed as $\partial(\ln L)/\partial(\ln w)$.[1]

The wage elasticity of labor demand can range from 0, in which case a given change in the wage would have no effect on the quantity of labor demanded (the demand schedule would be vertical), to $-\infty$ (minus infinity), in which case the demand schedule would be horizontal. The wage elasticity of labor demand is sometimes also referred to as the *own-wage* elasticity of labor demand. This is to distinguish it from the cross-elasticity of labor demand which we discuss below.

The Cross-Elasticity of Labor Demand

Because firms may employ several categories of workers and factors of production, the demand for workers in one category may be affected by what has happened to the price of workers in another category or even to the price of a completely different type of input, such as capital. For example, how will the demand for skilled workers change if the wages of unskilled workers rise? What will happen to the demand for labor if the price of capital falls? In such cases we are interested in the **cross-elasticity of labor demand**. Letting i refer to one factor (e.g., skilled labor) and j to another (e.g., unskilled labor), we can denote the cross-elasticity of demand this way:

$$\eta_{ij} = \%\Delta L_i / \%\Delta w_j \tag{3-2}$$

Note that the wage elasticity of demand is really just a special case of this cross-elasticity, with $i = j$. (That's why the former is sometimes referred to as the *own-wage* elasticity.) But unlike the own-wage elasticity of demand, whose sign is generally expected to be negative, the sign of the cross-elasticity of demand may be either positive or negative. If $\eta_{ij} > 0$, then the factors are **gross substitutes**. In other words, if the price of factor j (unskilled labor) should rise and if the employer consequently uses more of factor i (skilled labor), then clearly skilled and unskilled labor are substitutes for one another, and $\eta_{ij} > 0$ reflects this fact. On the other hand, if $\eta_{ij} < 0$ and the price of factor j rises, the employer would use less of factor i. In this case, factors j and i are **gross complements**.

The reasoning here is a little tricky, and factors that are considered to be gross substitutes or gross complements should not be confused with factors that are substitutes or complements in the production process. For example, in Figure 3.1 unskilled labor and skilled labor are *substitutes* in the production process. A change in the relative prices of these factors would (if output Q were constant) lead the employer to substitute one factor for the other (as shown by distance AB). Equivalently, the marginal rate of substitution of skilled labor for unskilled labor is not zero. Contrast the situation in Figure 3.1 with that of Figure 3.2, which depicts two factors that are *complements* rather than substitutes in the production process. The marginal rate of substitution of the two factors is zero,

---

[1] A small absolute change in a variable when expressed in natural logarithm values is approximately the same as the *percentage change* in the values of the variable. For example, suppose that the wage changes from $100 to $103. This is clearly a 3% (.03) change in the wage. But if we take the natural logarithm of $103 (4.6347) and subtract from it the natural logarithm of $100 (4.6052), we also get (approximately) .03. Expressing values in natural logarithms is a common practice in labor economics.

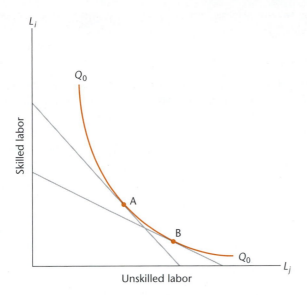

FIGURE 3.1 Inputs that are Substitutes in Production

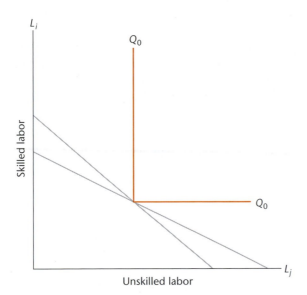

FIGURE 3.2 Inputs that are Complements in Production

and a change in the relative prices of the factors will have no effect on the quantities of the factors utilized by the employer.

   In deciding whether factors are substitutes or complements in the production process, we look only at the substitution effect. But when we consider the question of whether

THE WAY WE WORK

The Changing Occupational Mix

When we study the demand for labor, we are implicitly studying employers' demands for workers in many different types of occupations and jobs. And it is not surprising that there have been pronounced changes in the occupational structure of most developed countries in the last century. For example, in the U.S. in 1910 only about 25% of workers had jobs in the professional, managerial, clerical, sales, and service (except household) worker categories. In that year over 30% of all employment was in the category of farmer and farm worker. But by the year 2000 about 75% of workers had jobs in the first set of categories (professional et al.), while the farm and farm worker categories had now shrunk to include fewer than 1% of all workers. Other occupational categories that have shrunk over this time period include operatives (a category that includes operatives of motor vehicles and machinery (from about 16% to 10%) and laborers (not including farm laborers, from about 10% to 4%). Of course over this period of time, many new occupations never even dreamed about in 1910 (except perhaps in science fiction) have emerged, mainly due to advances in science and technology. Many of these occupations have become so well-known and commonplace today (think of computer specialists, aeronautical engineers, medical technicians, and dental hygienists, for example) that we don't really think of them as "new." But the point we are making here is that the occupational mix of most developed countries is constantly changing, with new types of jobs emerging all the time. In a recent survey by the U.S. Department of Labor, an extensive list of what have been dubbed as "new and emerging" (N&E) occupations was compiled. Interestingly most of these N&E occupations were in small firms (fewer than 100 employees) and were fairly broadly distributed across industries. The N&E list includes such occupations as technology coordinator, sanitation technician, urine sample collector (yuk), pharmacokineticist, cheer worker, polysomnographic technician, and bar-proof checker. Have you heard of any of them? You probably soon will.

Sources: Ian D. Wyatt and Daniel E. Hecker, "Occupational Changes during the 20th Century," *Monthly Labor Review*, March 2006, pp. 35–57. Jerome Pikulinski, "New and Emerging Occupations," *Monthly Labor Review*, December 2004, pp. 39–42.

factors are gross substitutes or gross complements, we also look at scale effects. In other words, we move off the isoquant and consider demand effects as well.

As an illustration, let's consider the case of store managers and sales assistants. A sales assistant provides certain retail services under the supervision of a manager. Certainly, assistants and managers are substitutes in production. That is to say, assistants can perform certain functions (sales, stock-checking) that a manager might otherwise perform. A fall in the price of sales assistants could create a substitution effect with stores substituting to some degree the services of assistants for those of managers. But are they gross substitutes or gross complements? How could we tell? If the price of sales assistants falls, the cost (and price) of retail services would be lower and, via the scale effect, could increase the demand for the products sold in stores generally and with it the demand for store managers. If the strength of this scale effect is sufficiently great to outweigh the substitution effect, the cross-elasticity of demand (η_{ij}) would be negative. Managers and sales assistants would thus be *gross complements*. But if the substitution effect were stronger than the scale effect, $\eta_{ij} > 0$, then the two factors would be *gross substitutes*, and a fall in the price of sales assistants would lead to a reduction in the demand for managers.

In general, if two factors are substitutes in production, they may be either gross substitutes or gross complements. However, if they are perfect complements in production (as they would be if their production isoquant resembled that in Figure 3.2), they will always be gross complements because there is no substitution effect.

The Elasticity of Substitution

Still another important labor-related measure of elasticity is the **elasticity of substitution**. Often symbolized by σ, the elasticity of substitution indicates the effect that a change in relative factor prices will have on the relative amounts of the two factors utilized if output is held constant. Suppose that our two factors of production are again labor (L) and capital (K) with prices w and r, respectively. The elasticity of substitution is defined as follows:

$$\sigma = \%\Delta(K/L)/\%\Delta(w/r)$$

or as
$$\sigma = \Delta\ln(K/L)/\Delta\ln(w/r) \tag{3-3}$$

To illustrate, suppose first that the wage rises by 1% relative to the price of capital. If $\sigma = 0$, then there would be no change in the *relative* amounts of capital and labor (the capital–labor ratio) used. The production isoquant in this case would look like that depicted in Figure 3.2. But suppose, instead, that σ was relatively high at 3. In this case a 1% rise in the relative price of labor would lead to a 3% rise in the capital–labor ratio, a situation that might look like that in Figure 3.1. The elasticity of substitution can be thought of in yet another way. It measures the relative magnitude of the substitution effect.

How Elastic Is the Demand for Labor?

We can pull together some of these concepts by looking at an important alternative way of expressing the (own-wage) elasticity[2] of the demand for labor, η:

$$\eta = -(1 - s)\sigma + s\eta_p \tag{3-4}$$

Although seemingly more complex than the basic expression for demand elasticity that we worked with in equation 3-1, this formula summarizes and highlights some of the issues discussed earlier. The terms η and σ are the wage elasticity of demand and the elasticity

---

[2]Some extra assumptions are used here: there is perfect competition (i.e., firms earn zero profits and pay factors of production the value of their marginal product), returns to scale are constant, and capital is elastically supplied. See John Hicks, *The Theory of Wages* (New York: St. Martin's Press, 1966), pp. 241–244.

THE WAY WE WORK

The Case of the Vanishing Bank Teller

After many decades of growth, employment in the banking industry began to fall about 1989. The employment of bank tellers has been especially hard hit since then. Why the decline? A drop in the demand for banking services has not taken place, but numerous substitutes for banking labor have appeared. The most important one, of course, is the growth of automatic teller machines (ATMs). In 1975, fewer than 10 million ATM transactions were made in the United States, involving a total of $1 billion. Currently, it has been estimated that some 14 billion ATM transactions take place in the United States each year and that ATMs dispense more than $1 trillion dollars to consumers. ATMs are not the only technological change that has altered the way banking services are provided. For example, electronic scanners now quickly record check entries, a process previously done by hand. Thus the decline in banking employment can largely be explained by a substitution of cheaper and more productive capital equipment for labor. Because employment in banking has declined, we can deduce that the substitution effect (resulting in more capital and less labor used) has outweighed the scale effects (which would increase the usage of *both* capital and labor). We can also deduce that banking labor and capital are gross substitutes.

What has happened to those workers who lost their jobs in banking? According to the Bureau of Labor Statistics, between 1988 and 1996 an average of 20 to 25% of people employed in banking moved out of the industry annually. But only a relatively small proportion (about a sixth) of those represented in the gross flows wound up unemployed. Rather, most found work in a variety of other industries where labor remains relatively highly valued. What about bank tellers? After many years of decline, the employment of bank tellers in the U.S. is projected to grow once again, but at a relatively slow rate. To attract customers, banks have been opening more branches, and have also been staying open for longer hours and on weekends.

Sources: Ben Craig, "Where Have All the Tellers Gone?" *Economic Commentary*, Federal Reserve Bank of Cleveland, April 15, 1997. Electronic Funds Transfer Association, "ATM Fraud: Frequently Asked Questions," http://www .efta.org/archives/ATMFAQs.pdf (no date); United States Department of Labor, *Occupational Outlook Handbook*, "Tellers," 2010–2011.

---

of substitution, respectively. The term η_p refers to the price elasticity of demand for the final product.[3] The only new term in the equation is s, which stands for labor's share of the total costs of production. (If s is close to zero, then labor costs account for a very small proportion of total costs. If s is close to 1, labor costs account for the lion's share of production costs.)

---

[3] Remember that the price elasticity of demand for the final product (η_p) is usually negative according to the law of demand.

The second term on the right-hand side of equation 3-4 refers to the impact on labor demand of *scale effects* (see Figure 2.11); that is, it concerns the impact on labor demand of the increase in product market demand that results from the feed-through of lower wages into lower product prices. This is the **scale elasticity** of demand for labor. The first term on the right-hand side of equation 3-4 is the **constant-output elasticity**[4] of demand for labor.

We can make some inferences about the likely magnitude of the own-wage elasticity of labor demand by looking closely at equation 3-4. The demand for labor will tend to be less elastic under the following conditions:

- When the price elasticity of demand for the product or service produced by that labor (i.e., the absolute value of η_p) is low
- When it is difficult to substitute other factors of production for labor (i.e., when the elasticity of substitution, σ, is low)
- When the proportion of total costs that are accounted for by labor costs, s, is low (assuming $\sigma < \eta_p$)
- When the supply of substitutes for labor is inelastic (i.e., the firm cannot easily switch from the employment of labor to the employment of labor substitutes).

These conditions,[5] sometimes referred to as the Marshall-Hicks determinants of labor demand elasticity, can only give us (at best) a rough idea of how elastic or inelastic the demand for a particular type of labor might be. Fortunately in recent years a rather large number of econometric studies have presented empirical estimates of the elasticity of demand for labor for various time periods, industries, occupations, and countries. These estimates are called *empirical* because they are based on actual numerical observations on how the demand for labor changes as wages change.

In his book *Labor Demand*, Daniel Hamermesh[6] summarized and refined the estimates of more than 200 studies of labor demand elasticities. This is what he found:

- The value of the constant-output elasticity of demand for homogeneous labor, which is $-(1-s)\sigma$, tends to fall between the range of -0.15 and -0.75 for the typical firm, with -0.30 being a best single-value estimate. In other words, the substitution effect elasticity is not particularly large.
- There have not been that many good studies of scale elasticities, but Hamermesh's best estimates put this value at about -0.70.[7]
- As a result of what we know about the magnitudes of the substitution and scale elasticities, this would mean that -1.0 would be a good estimate of the *total* elasticity of demand in the long run. One word of caution though: these values are averages

---

[4] This is also known as a "substitution elasticity."

[5] They are referred to as the Marshall-Hicks determinants of labor demand in honor of the economists who first identified them. See Alfred Marshall, *Principles of Economics*, 8th ed. (London: Macmillan, 1930), pp. 385–386; and John Hicks, *The Theory of Wages* (New York: St. Martin's Press, 1966), pp. 241–242. Notice again that condition 3 above only holds if $\sigma < \eta_p$. If $\sigma > \eta_p$, then the demand for labor is less elastic if the proportion of total costs that are labor costs is *high*. The reasoning is tricky, but Saul Hoffman provides a clear explanation: "Revisiting Marshall's Third Law: Why Does Labor's Share Interact with the Elasticity of Substitution to Decrease the Elasticity of Demand?" *Journal of Economic Education* 40 (2009): 437–445.

[6] Daniel Hamermesh, *Labor Demand* (Princeton, NJ: Princeton University Press, 1993).

[7] Daniel Hamermesh and Albert Rees, *The Economics of Work and Pay*, 5th ed. (New York: HarperCollins, 1993), p. 153.

based on a large number of studies, and there is considerable variation with respect to firms and industries studied, time periods, countries, and so forth.

- The elasticity of substitution (σ) between capital and homogeneous labor appears to be approximately 1.0.
- Capital and *skilled* labor are apparently complements, but capital and *unskilled* labor seem to be substitutes.[8]

Of course, not all labor is homogeneous. Different types of labor exist, not least because people have different skills. Some empirical studies have estimated the own-wage elasticities associated with a variety of occupational or industry groups. One study shows that the elasticity of demand for production labor in U.S. manufacturing has become increasingly elastic over time, with the constant-output elasticity varying from around −0.6 in the 1960s to −1 in the 1990s. Meanwhile the corresponding elasticity for nonproduction labor has changed from around −0.7 to about −0.6 over the same period.

PUTTING THEORY TO WORK

DO IMPORTS FROM LOW WAGE COUNTRIES REDUCE THE DOMESTIC DEMAND FOR LABOR?

Many observers strongly believe that imports of goods and services from developing countries, where workers earn very low wages, reduce the demand for labor in developed nations. Evidence from Australia, however, raises doubts about this notion.

Christis Tombazos examined the factors affecting the aggregate demand for labor in Australia from 1967 to 1992.* He estimated that a 10% *decrease* in the price of imported goods from Southeast Asia relative to Australian wages would result in a 9.7% *increase* in the demand for labor in Australia during this period, holding aggregate output and the prices of other inputs constant. This evidence of a *complementary* relationship between imports from low-wage countries and Australian labor demand reflects the fact that a high proportion of these imports are in the form of raw materials and intermediate goods that require further processing before being sold to end users.

Tombazos also found that a 10% drop in the relative price of imports from the United States and Canada would decrease labor demand by 9% in Australia, and a similar drop in the relative price of imports from the United Kingdom would lower labor demand by a whopping 20%. Imports from high-wage countries are more likely to *substitute* for domestic labor because most of these products are finished goods sold directly to end users.

Of course, this empirical study looks only at the relationship between imports and labor demand in the aggregate. We examine the impact of trade on employment opportunities and wages for different groups of workers in more detail in later chapters.

*Christis G. Tombazos, "The Impact of Imports on the Demand for Labor in Australia," *Economics Letters*, 62 (1999): 351–356.

---

[8] Some further recent evidence that capital and skilled labor are complementary as inputs is provided by John Duffy, Chris Papageorgiou, and Fidel Perez-Sebastian, "Capital-Skill Complementarity? Evidence from a Panel of Countries," *Review of Economics and Statistics* 86 (2004): 327–344. The study analyzed a panel of 73 developed and less-than-developed countries over a period of 25 years.

These changes may be related to the increase in international trade over this time frame; hikes in the pay of production workers have led to increased imports and reduced domestic employment, but it has not been easy to import the output of nonproduction or service workers.[9] More recently, however, U.S. firms have begun to shift more of their service activities abroad, to both affiliated and unaffiliated firms. The process has become known as "offshoring" and includes such jobs as telephone operators, telemarketers, proofreaders and copy markers, and correspondence clerks.[10]

Extensions and Embellishments of Marginal Productivity Theory

Despite being the foundation of labor demand theory, marginal productivity theory has not been without its critics. Some of the criticisms have merit; others do not. One of the most often heard complaints about the theory is that employers in the real world don't actually use terms like "marginal revenue product" when they make decisions about pay and hiring. Because the relations and concepts that compose marginal productivity theory are not explicitly used, the implication is that they must therefore be useless. Those who express such criticisms are at best only half correct. It is true that employers don't directly utilize many of the labor concepts developed in this chapter. But this doesn't mean that employers don't act in a way that is consistent with labor demand theory or that the theory has no relevance or predictive power.

Imagine that you are driving along a two-lane highway and are thinking about passing that slow-moving truck you've been behind for the last 10 miles. Before deciding whether to pass or not, a physicist would tell you that you should take into account the speed of the truck, the speed of any cars coming toward you in the other lane, and the speed at which you intend to pass. The physicist could even tell you the appropriate formulae to use, with time, speed, acceleration, and distance variables all included. Now no one—not even a physicist (we think)—*explicitly* makes driving decisions this way. Instead, we simply decide to pass the truck based on whether we think we can make it safely. But isn't it true that we *implicitly* consider all of these factors (speeds, distances, acceleration, times) anytime we pass, without ever thinking about—indeed without necessarily even knowing anything about—the physicist's variables or equations? Likewise, employers may not explicitly calculate the marginal revenue products of workers, but in deciding to hire a worker an employer has implicitly estimated that the worker is "worth" the wage to be paid. In other words, the employer has acted in accordance with marginal product principles—just as if the employer were comparing the marginal revenue product with the wage. In short, the fact that employers may not be familiar with the concepts of marginal productivity theory does not constitute a valid criticism of the theory. The crucial question is whether employers act in a manner consistent with the theory.

---

[9] Matthew J. Slaughter, "International Trade and Labor-Demand Elasticities," *Journal of International Economics* 54 (2001): 27–56.

[10] Roger J. Moncarz, Michael G. Wolf, and Benjamin Wright, "Service-providing Occupations, Offshoring, and the Labor Market," *Monthly Labor Review* 131 (December 2008): 71–86.

Other more potentially serious problems and concerns with marginal productivity theory are examined in the following sections. Some of these concerns deal with the assumptions underlying the basic model that we analyzed earlier. Others deal with the time frame over which employers make wage and employment decisions. As you will see, most of these concerns and problems can be dealt with nicely by extending the basic model.

The Independence of Wages and Productivity

Throughout our discussion of labor demand so far, we have assumed that the marginal product function—that is, the short-run labor demand curve—and the wage rate are *independent* of one another. That is, if the wage rate rises or falls, the demand schedule itself does not change, and employers respond to wage changes by either increasing or reducing employment along the constant demand curve. Is this always reasonable, or are there situations in which a change in the wage rate might be expected to cause a change in the entire demand schedule? Economists argue that there are two types of situations in which a wage change can shift the demand schedule itself: (a) efficiency wages and (b) shock effects. Let's look briefly at each of these situations.

Efficiency Wages

Economists have long recognized that higher wages can sometimes improve worker productivity. This could happen in a very poor underdeveloped country where incomes are so low that many workers are undernourished and in poor health. Higher wages might have the effect of enabling workers to eat better and to become healthier, more productive employees. In Figure 3.3, the effects of such a phenomenon are depicted. At the initial

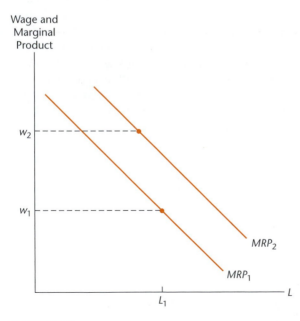

FIGURE 3.3 Marginal Revenue Product When Higher Wages Lead to Higher Productivity

wage w_1, the employer's demand schedule is MRP_1, and L_1 workers will be hired. But if the wage rate were higher, say at w_2, the employer's marginal revenue product schedule shifts upwards to MRP_2. The marginal product of workers at each level of employment depicted is actually higher than it was before. As a result, higher wages need not necessarily lead to lower levels of employment.

Efficiency wages is the term generally used to describe a situation where higher wages lead to higher worker productivity and, as a result, "pay for themselves." But is there evidence that efficiency wages do, in fact, exist? The answer to that question seems to be "yes." A very long time ago Henry Ford discovered that by paying his Ford Motor Company workers the highest pay in the industry (in 1914 that was $5 per day) he was able to raise worker productivity and reduce worker turnover. In more recent times, some professional athletes, unhappy with their pay, have refused to play up to their potential performance levels.

The Shock Effect

A second situation where higher wages might lead to higher worker productivity is called the **shock effect**.[11] The shock effect is very much like the efficiency wage effect except that here the higher productivity emanates not from workers but rather from management. Sometimes areas or pockets of inefficiency, slack, and waste exist in a firm. If wages rise (and with them labor costs), management might be "shocked" into eliminating these inefficiencies, which might have otherwise gone unnoticed or been ignored.

Shock theory has sometimes been called on to justify minimum wage hikes. Minimum wages can sometimes lead to lower levels of employment, which is the reason many economists oppose them. But as others have argued, if an increase in the minimum wage "shocks" employers into looking for other ways to reduce labor costs, the adverse employment effects might not be as severe or might not occur at all. Shock effects have the same effect on the labor demand as we have shown for efficiency wages in Figure 3.3—namely, they raise the MRP schedule. And in terms of the production isoquant (see Figure 2.2), shock effects result in an inward shift of the isoquant, a movement toward the origin. In other words, the same amount of output (Q) can be produced with less labor and less of the other factors of production.

However, it should be noted that the idea of a shock effect calls into question the notion that firms are maximizing their profits. We argued earlier that there are strong reasons to accept profit maximization as a working hypothesis. So we would not expect shock effects of this kind to be particularly large, and we would not expect them to be observed often.

Fixed Costs of Employment

Despite the logical simplicity of the marginal productivity theory, you may be thinking that in the real world questions involving labor demand are far more complex than the theory seems to allow for. For example, we have so far treated the wage as if it

---

[11] Sumner H. Slichter, James J. Healy, and E. Robert Livernash, *The Impact of Collective Bargaining on Management* (Washington, DC: Brookings, 1960).

were the *only* cost of employing labor. But anyone who has ever been involved in hiring workers knows that there are **fixed costs of employment** that are unrelated to the wage. These costs generally fall into four categories: hiring costs, training costs, taxation, and fringe benefits.

Hiring Costs

Hiring costs include advertising job openings and screening and interviewing job applicants. Many firms have become increasingly sophisticated in their hiring strategies in recent years. They know it is important to get as good a match as possible between the skills a worker has and the skills needed to do a job well. As a result, aptitude tests, psychometric tests, evaluations of applicants' abilities to work in teams, and other similar recruitment tools have increasingly come into use. But such sophistication is bought at a price. The time involved in running these tests imposes relatively high costs on the firm, and the firm must balance the benefits of sophisticated recruitment against these costs.

Training Costs

Training costs are just what they imply: teaching new employees the skills associated with the job. These costs represent an important type of nonwage cost that our marginal productivity theory has so far ignored. For some types of jobs, they can be quite substantial. Where this is the case, we would expect employers to do all they can to ensure that workers stay with the firm for a long time once they have been recruited.

Taxation

In some countries, firms must pay taxes that can take the form of a fixed cost on employment. An example is the employer contribution to national insurance in the United Kingdom, which until recently required employers to pay 10% of each employee's earnings as a tax, up to a maximum contribution of £58.50 per employee per week. For employers whose workers were highly paid, this entailed payment of a fixed tax of £58.50 on each person employed.[12] Clearly, taxes of this type are not a good idea if the government wishes to encourage firms to hire a lot of labor.

Fringe Benefits

Nonwage benefits—or "fringes" as they are sometimes called—make up yet another type of nonwage cost associated with employment. Fringe benefits include such items as employer-paid health insurance, pension schemes, company cars, and paid vacations. Of all the types of nonwage labor costs, fringe benefits usually loom as the most sizeable to the employer, comprising about 30% of compensation costs in private sector firms

---

[12] This was the rate for the tax year 2002–2003. No payment had to be made for employees earning £89 or less per week, and this consequently encouraged many firms in the United Kingdom to make jobs available on a part-time basis.

TABLE 3.1   Fringe Benefit Costs as a Percent of Total Compensation, 1986–2011

Year	Private Sector Workers	State and Local Government Workers
1986	27.0	--
1990	27.6	--
1995	28.4	30.4
2000	27.0	29.2
2005	29.0	31.7
2011	29.3	34.5

Source: Bureau of Labor Statistics, U.S. Department of Labor, "Employer Costs for Employee Compensation," various years (March), 1987–2011. The Department of Labor has collected this data annually since 1986.

(see Table 3.1) and slightly more in the state and local government sector. (Why do you think this is so?)

We have ignored such nonwage costs so far, even though they are obviously important. Many costs, such as the cost of a health care plan or of a company car, are fixed whether a worker works full time or part time. Furthermore, some of these costs are "one-time costs," such as the costs of recruiting a new worker, whereas others are "recurring costs," such as paid vacations. Wages, by way of contrast, are usually considered to be variable costs because (except for salaried employees) they vary with the hours workers put in. Walter Oi has called these nonwage costs "quasi-fixed costs"[13] because some of them are not completely fixed even though they do not vary with hours of work.

Two questions arise at this point: (a) why does it matter whether some of these costs are fixed or quasi-fixed, and (b) what are the consequences for marginal productivity theory? Addressing the first question, the distinction between fixed and variable labor costs has implications for how a firm might respond to an increase in product demand. Will it perhaps choose to hire new workers, or will it instead stretch out its existing work force by offering or requiring overtime hours? Notice in Figure 3.4 that the increase in labor demand will (by definition) result in more labor services ($L_2 - L_1$) being utilized by the employer. But up to this point we have not said whether the increase will take the form of more workers or more hours, or even some combination of the two. Does it matter to the employer?[14]

Suppose that the increase in product demand, and therefore in the demand for labor, is expected to be only temporary. In such a case the employer would most likely not undertake a search for new workers and incur the associated search and hiring costs, not to mention the training costs and extra fringe benefit costs. Instead, meeting the increase in product demand through overtime hours might be the more sensible course of action, and it is a more easily reversible solution.

---

[13] Walter Oi, "Labor as a Quasi-Fixed Factor," *Journal of Political Economy* 70 (1962): 538–555. "Quasi" is a Latin word meaning "as if" or "having some resemblance to."

[14] See Daniel Hamermesh, *Workdays, Workhours, and Work Schedules: Evidence for the United States and Germany* (Kalamazoo, MI: W.E. Upjohn Institute for Employment Research, 1996).

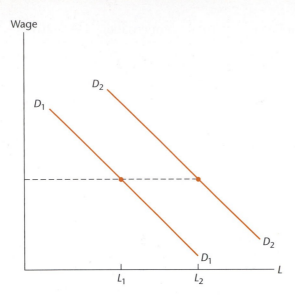

Wage

FIGURE 3.4 An Increase in Labor Demand with
Fixed Labor Costs

But overtime hours can be costly too. The U.S. Fair Labor Standards Act requires employers to pay time-and-one-half pay to hourly workers for weekly hours in excess of 40. Legal requirements for premium pay for hours worked in excess of some weekly maximum are a common feature in many other countries as well. In Canada, for example, time-and-one-half pay is required for hours worked beyond 40 to 48 per week, depending on occupation and industry. One province, British Columbia, requires that all hours worked in excess of 12 in a day must be compensated at twice the normal rate. In other countries, such as the United Kingdom, overtime requirements are set by collective bargaining. But even so, premium pay for overtime hours might still be less costly to the employer than the additional nonwage costs associated with hiring new workers.

What about the opposite situation—that of a decline in product demand and the demand for labor? The analysis here is similar to that just presented. In the case of a decline in labor demand, the employer is faced with the decision of laying off some workers, cutting worker hours, or perhaps doing neither—allowing instead a certain amount of idle, "standing around doing nothing" time. If the employer decides to lay off some workers, it may later turn out that the decline in demand was only temporary. The employer might then have to incur the fixed costs of searching for, hiring, and training new workers once demand returns to its former level. Because of this uncertainty, many employers prefer to meet declines in demand by reducing hours or by doing nothing, at least if the demand decline is expected to be short term.

How can the employer decide on the most appropriate course of action in case of an increase or a decline in the demand for labor? Should the employer hire more workers or simply stretch out the existing workforce by having them work more hours? The employer can utilize the very same reasoning as was used to decide on the appropriate "mix" of factors of production. As equation 2-5 pointed out, the profit maximizing employer should hire all factors up to the point where the ratios of their marginal products to their marginal costs are equal to 1. In other words, in deciding whether more workers or more hours should be used, the employer should compare the following ratios:

$$\frac{MRP_{\text{new workers}}}{MLC_{\text{new workers}}} \; \substack{\leq \\ = \\ >} \; \frac{MRP_{\text{additional hours}}}{MLC_{\text{additional hours}}} \tag{3-5}$$

The marginal cost (MLC) of hiring new workers includes all of the wage and fixed costs we have discussed; the marginal cost of additional hours includes principally the time-and-one-half pay premium the employer might have to pay to workers. Because the fixed costs associated with hiring additional workers can be quite high, it is not surprising that so many employers "stretch out" their existing workforce when demand increases. Moreover, it is also not surprising that over the years pro-worker groups in many countries have tried to reduce the maximum weekly hours of work and to increase the overtime pay penalty. By raising the costs of overtime, it is argued, such a change would encourage employers to hire more workers (by lowering the right-hand term in equation 3-5).[15]

Another important implication of the presence of fixed costs to employers relates to the different layoff experiences of skilled workers versus unskilled workers during recessions in economic activity. During such downturns, employees with lower levels of education and training are much more likely to experience layoffs than are employees with higher levels of education and skills. When economic recovery eventually sets in, it is easier and less expensive for employers to hire new unskilled workers, or to rehire those who were laid off, than it is to do the same for skilled workers. Not only are the search and hiring costs likely to be much greater for skilled workers, but so are the training costs. Some economists have referred to the greater reluctance of employers to let go of skilled workers during recessions as "labor hoarding."

Now let's turn to the second question: What are the consequences of fixed costs of employment for the marginal productivity theory of labor demand? Can we modify the theory to take into account such costs, or should the theory be unceremoniously dumped? Before we considered fixed costs, our model implied that employers always equated current MRP with the current wage (which was equal to the marginal labor cost, MLC) in their employment decisions. In other words, $w = MLC = MRP$. But if there are hiring (H) and training (T) costs associated with the employment of a new worker, then our earlier analysis would imply that the marginal cost of employing a worker will necessarily exceed the worker's marginal revenue product, at least some of the time. How can we reconcile this fact with marginal productivity theory?

To do so, let's move one step closer to reality and assume that a firm expects to employ the worker for some definite period of time into the future, say for t periods (years). Wages must, of course, be paid in each period, but the hiring and training costs

---

[15] At first sight it seems curious that overtime payments have been legislated in the United States, but there is a historical reason for this. Many people don't realize that the overtime pay provisions of the Fair Labor Standards Act of 1938 were designed to help pull the nation out of the Depression by encouraging employers to hire new workers when demand rose rather than providing more hours of work to those already employed. In 1938, nonwage costs of employment (especially fringe benefits) were much lower than they are today.

that we have discussed are incurred only once. We can therefore express the present value (*PV*) of the costs of this worker to the firm over the *t* periods as follows:

$$PV_{costs} = H + T + w_0 + w_1/(1+r) + w_2/(1+r)^2 + \ldots + w_t/(1+r)^t \qquad (3\text{-}6)$$

with *r* as the interest (or discount) rate. Likewise, the present value of the worker's expected marginal revenue products to the firm over the *t* future employment periods can be expressed as:

$$PV_{MRP} = MRP_0 + MRP_1/(1+r)^1 + MRP_2/(1+r)^2 + \ldots + MRP_t/(1+r)^t \qquad (3\text{-}7)$$

Instead of suggesting that the employer will hire a worker only if that worker's marginal revenue product is expected to equal the wage in *each* future period, our marginal productivity theory can be modified to say that employers will seek to ensure that the *present value* of the costs associated with hiring a worker will be no greater than the *present value* of the worker's expected marginal products over future periods. This modification, of course, makes the marginal productivity theory much more realistic in explaining employer behavior. But it also now means that it is no longer necessarily true that the wage will be equal to the worker's MRP in each (or even in any) future period. In passing, it is worth noting that the employer's means of coping with the one-shot costs of employment is to turn employment into a long-term relationship; this relationship is an institution, and we call it a *job*.

Are Workers Paid Their Marginal Product?

Putting aside for the moment the notion of hiring and training costs (which over the life cycle of the worker are likely to be relatively small anyway), do workers on average tend to be paid about what they are "worth" to their employers—that is, their marginal revenue product? If we should find out that workers are in fact paid about what they are worth, it would tend to validate marginal productivity theory. If the evidence suggests otherwise, it could be due to any of several reasons. It could mean that labor on average may be "exploited" in either of the senses that we defined exploitation earlier, which could reflect the fact that labor markets are for various reasons not competitive. Evidence that some workers are paid less than their marginal revenue products could also be a reflection of other factors such as labor market discrimination. Finally, some workers may be paid wages that are *greater* than their marginal product, for example, where unions may have succeeded in negotiating wage and employment levels above what the employer would have otherwise paid.

What does the evidence say? Surprisingly, there are few studies of how wages compare with marginal products for individual occupations. In a study of major league baseball players, Gerald Scully found evidence that before free agency came into being in the 1970s, star players received only 10 to 20% of their worth to the teams they played for. Now that players have won the (still somewhat restricted) right to negotiate with and move to other teams, star ballplayers' salaries are more closely in line with their marginal products.[16]

---

[16] Gerald Scully, *The Business of Major League Baseball* (Chicago: University of Chicago Press, 1989), p. 156.

In a study of professors, real estate agents, and car salesmen, Robert Frank found that the most productive workers in a given organization tended to be paid *less* than their marginal product, and the least productive workers were paid *more* than their marginal product. As an explanation for this somewhat surprising finding, Frank suggests that highly paid workers are also high-status workers. The price these workers are willing to pay for remaining in their high-status jobs is a level of pay below what they are actually worth.[17] If Frank's surmise is correct, then an institution, in this case status, is distorting the operation of market forces.

Summary

The demand for labor is a derived demand; it is derived from the demand for the products that labor produces. This means that to analyze labor demand we must first analyze the role labor plays in the firm's production process. The firm's demand for labor in the short run is given by the marginal revenue product of labor (under certain assumptions), and in the long run it is more elastic than is the case in the short run because other factors can be substituted for labor in the long run.

The elasticity of demand is related to the product market price elasticity of demand for the good that labor produces, the elasticity of substitution between labor and capital, the share of labor in the firm's costs, and the elasticity of supply of substitutes for labor. Typical estimates of the constant-output own-price elasticity of labor demand lie in the range from -0.15 to -0.75, and estimates of the total wage elasticity of demand for labor are about -1.0.

Efficiency wages and shock effects present us with two reasons higher wages might lead to higher productivity. In addition, changes to the simple theory of marginal productivity are needed when a significant proportion of remuneration is in the form of fringe benefits. Changes may also be needed when institutions play a significant role in the behavior of firms.

What comes next? As you surely are aware by now, economists never talk about demand without also bringing up the subject of supply. So it's on to the study of the supply of labor in Chapter 4.

KEY TERMS

elasticity of labor demand

cross-elasticity of labor demand

gross substitutes

gross complements

elasticity of substitution

scale elasticity

constant-output elasticity

efficiency wages

shock effects

fixed costs of employment

---

[17] Robert H. Frank, "Are Workers Paid Their Marginal Products?" *American Economic Review* 74(4) (1984): 549–571. Similar results have also been obtained by Stephen Machin, Alan Manning, and Stephen Woodland, "Are Workers Paid Their Marginal Products: Evidence from a Low Wage Labor Market," CLE Discussion Paper 158, London School of Economics, 1993.

1. We know that the growing volume of international trade has for some time now been characterized by the loss of some manufacturing jobs in the U.S. and in other developed countries to lower-cost firms in developing countries. But the "offshoring" of service jobs is a relatively new phenomenon.
   a. In addition to those examples of offshoring mentioned earlier in this chapter (telephone operators, telemarketers, and proofreaders), can you compile a list of six additional service jobs in the U.S. that have been subject to offshoring?
   b. Do those service jobs that have been most subject to offshoring have any common characteristics that would distinguish them from jobs not likely to be offshored? (For example, the job of automobile mechanic is not likely to be offshored.) Think of at least four such common characteristics.

2. a. As you might have suspected, employee nonwage (fringe) benefits make up a much larger percentage of labor costs in the United States today than they did a few generations ago. For example, according to the U.S. Chamber of Commerce, on average fringe benefits in larger firms comprised 39% of payroll in the year 2001 compared to only about 24% in 1959. Do you think the growing fringe-benefit share of labor costs has made the level of employment more responsive or less responsive to changes in labor demand over the business cycle? Explain.
   b. What about the average number of hours worked per week by employed workers? Do you think that this growing fringe-benefit share of labor costs has made the average number of hours worked more or less responsive to changes in labor demand over the business cycle? Explain.

3. H. Hogan runs a small convenience store in Hollywood. Currently he keeps the store open from 9 a.m. to 5 p.m. Monday through Saturday (these are not very convenient hours for a convenience store are they?), and he runs the store completely by himself. He has been informed that he could probably see his weekly revenues rise by 30% if he keeps his convenience store open until 10 p.m. every day.
   a. Make a list of all the factors he should take into account in his decision to possibly extend his store hours.
   b. What are the conditions that would lead Mr. Hogan to decide to hire another worker instead of increasing even further his own working hours?

4. The numbers in the first table below represent values of Q (output), K (capital), L (labor), w (the wage rate), and r (the price of capital) for a business firm for two periods.

Period	K	L	w	r	Q
1	30	50	200	100	500
2	40	55	180	100	510

   a. Use this information to calculate the own-wage elasticity of labor demand.
   b. Use the information in the next table below to calculate the cross-elasticity of labor demand (relative to a change in the price of capital) for the next two periods.

Period	K	L	w	r	Q
3	40	55	180	100	510
4	45	60	180	80	550

c. From what you have calculated in part b, are labor and capital gross substitutes or gross complements?

5. In Table 3.1, you saw that state and local government workers (such as teachers, firefighters, and police) on average have a higher percentage of their compensation in the form of fringe benefits than do workers in the private sector.

a. What are some possible reasons for the difference?

b. At the time of this writing (2012), several states (e.g., Wisconsin) have passed legislation restricting or eliminating collective bargaining by state and local government workers. The reason given has been that public sector workers and their unions are too powerful. Why is the existence of the public sector/private sector differences in Table 3.1 *not necessarily* supportive of this contention?

APPENDIX

A Test of the Marginal Productivity Theory: A Cobb-Douglas Exercise

In addition to the (not all that many) attempts to see if workers in various occupations tend to be paid wages equal to their marginal product, there have been a number of attempts to examine the question at the macroeconomic level as well. For this purpose a specific type of production function—the Cobb-Douglas production function—has been used. We look first at what this production function is and then see how it relates to the question of whether workers tend to be paid wages equal to their marginal products.

More than 80 years ago, Paul H. Douglas (an economist at the University of Chicago) and mathematician Charles Cobb formulated the following production function:

$$Q = AL^{\alpha}K^{\beta} \tag{3A-1}$$

where Q refers (as before) to output, L to the labor input, and K to the capital input. The term A is simply a multiplicative factor (not that important to our analysis), while α and β are, respectively, output elasticities for labor and capital. In other words, α tells us what the percentage change in output (Q) would be, given a 1% change in the labor input (L). That is:[18]

$$\alpha = \frac{\partial Q/Q}{\partial L/L} \tag{3A-2}$$

The Cobb-Douglas production function is commonly used in economic analysis because it is relatively simple and possesses some features and properties that correspond fairly well with what we know (or suspect) about production and demand in the real world. For example, it can be shown that the slope of the marginal product ($\frac{\partial Q}{\partial L}$) of a Cobb-Douglas production function is negative, just as we suggested that a demand schedule for labor should be. It can also be shown that the elasticity of substitution (σ) of the Cobb-Douglas production function is always unity, a value that matches the empirical estimates of Daniel Hamermesh.[19]

---

[18] To show that the output elasticity with respect to the labor input equals α, simply take the first partial derivative $\partial Q/\partial L$ of $AL^{\alpha}K^{\beta}$ and multiply the result by L/Q. The result will equal α.

[19] As Hamermesh states on p. 392 of *Labor Demand*, "A reasonable estimate of the elasticity of substitution between labor and homogeneous labor is one. A Cobb-Douglas function is [thus] a good approximation to the structure of two-factor production."

How can the Cobb-Douglas production function be used to judge whether workers as a whole tend to be paid wages equal to their marginal product? The first thing we need to do is to derive the marginal product function from the Cobb-Douglas equation. It can be shown that:[20]

$$\frac{\partial Q}{\partial L} = \frac{\alpha Q}{L} \qquad (3A\text{-}3)$$

Now, if labor is paid a wage on average equal to its marginal product (we're keeping all units in *real* terms), then:

$$w = \frac{\alpha Q}{L} \qquad (3A\text{-}4)$$

Let's now think of what labor's share of total output would be if, again, labor is paid a wage equal to its marginal product. Multiplying the average wage (w) times L and dividing by Q gives us labor's share of output:

$$\frac{wL}{Q} = \frac{\frac{\alpha QL}{L}}{Q} = \alpha \qquad (3A\text{-}5)$$

Canceling terms, the right-hand side of equation 3A-5 will collapse to α. In other words, what we have found is that *if* the Cobb-Douglas function correctly describes production in the aggregate and *if* workers are paid wages equal to their marginal products, then labor's share of national output will equal the output elasticity with respect to labor. By comparing what we know about labor's share of national output with independent estimates of output elasticity, we can tell whether workers tend to be paid wages equal to their marginal products.

What is labor's share of national output, and how closely does it compare with estimates of α? Very early research by Cobb and Douglas and later studies by Douglas[21] along with several other colleagues found α and labor's share of output to be remarkably close (about 2/3), not only for the United States but for a number of other countries as well (Australia, Canada, New Zealand, the United Kingdom, and South Africa). Later estimates by R. Craine[22] for the United States (1942–1967) also show a close correspondence between the two values. However, a study by L. Thurow[23] for the period 1929–1965 does not show a close correspondence between the marginal product of labor and average compensation. So, at the present time, we have to say that the

---

[20] To show this, again take the first partial derivative $\partial Q/\partial L$ of $AL^{\alpha}K^{\beta}$ and this time multiply the result by L/L. (Hint: $AL^{\alpha-1}K^{\beta}L = Q$)

[21] C. W. Cobb and Paul Douglas, "A Theory of Production," *American Economic Review* 19 (1928): 139–165; P. H. Douglas, "The Cobb-Douglas Production Function Once Again," *Journal of Political Economy* 84 (1976): 903–915.

[22] Roger Craine, "On the Service Flow from Labor," *Review of Economic Studies* 40 (1973): 43.

[23] Lester Thurow, "Disequilibrium and the Marginal Productivity of Capital and Labor," *Review of Economics and Statistics* 50 (1968): 25.

evidence as to whether labor in the aggregate tends to be paid its marginal product is rather mixed. More recently, though, Alan Krueger has noted that the calculation of labor's share of national income is plagued by serious measurement problems. Furthermore, it is increasingly difficult to divide labor and capital income neatly into mutually exclusive categories, as the rise of employee stock ownership and pension funds demonstrates.[24]

---

[24] Alan Krueger, "Measuring Labor's Share," *American Economic Review* 89 (1999): 45–51.

4

The Supply of Labor: Labor Force Participation

If the real wage increases, will some students leave school to find a job?

If a person wins the lottery, will he or she be less likely to be in the labor force?

How do social security benefits affect the labor supply decisions of senior citizens?

In Chapters 2 and 3 we discussed labor demand and labor demand elasticities. The other side of the market is labor supply. When we analyze labor supply, we are asking about the amount of work that an individual, a family, a labor market, an area, or even the whole economy is willing to offer at various possible wage levels. Why is it important to study labor supply and to know how the amount of work offered responds to wages?

From a macro perspective, the amount of labor supplied is an indication of the work effort and the commitment to productive activity of a country's population. All other things equal, countries with a stronger commitment to work should enjoy higher material living standards. Also, knowing the relationship between wage changes and the amount of work offered is useful for evaluating certain types of policies such as antipoverty policies. The U.S. poverty threshold[1] for a single person in the year 2011 was $11,702. If the United States provided a monetary payment just sufficient to put any person above the poverty level whose income fell below the poverty threshold, what effect would that have on that person's incentive to work?

If our vantage point is that of the economy as a whole, the total amount of labor supplied depends on the following factors:

1. The size of the population
2. The proportion of the population that chooses to be in the work force

---

[1] To determine who is in poverty and to estimate poverty rates, the U.S. Census Bureau uses a set of money income thresholds that vary by family size. If a family's total income is less than that poverty threshold, then that family and every individual in it are considered to be in poverty. The official poverty thresholds are updated each year for inflation using the Consumer Price Index. (http://www.census/gov/hhes/www/poverty/about/overview/measure.html)

3. The number of hours that those in the labor force work
4. The quality of work and the effort put in by those choosing to work.

Each of these four aspects of labor supply—even the size of the population[2]—is influenced to some degree by the wage rate. We will not be looking at the economics of population growth, but in this chapter and Chapter 5 we focus on the supply of labor as measured by the labor force participation rate (the second factor in our list) and by hours of work (the third factor). In Chapter 6 we analyze the labor supply from a quality focal point.

Labor Force Participation

Ask someone how he or she would define the labor force, and you're very likely to get an answer like this: "It's the number of people who have jobs." In fact, though, the **labor force** includes not only those who are working for pay or for profit but also those who are unemployed. Now this definition may sound rather silly to some because, of course, at any moment everybody in the population is either working or not working. So what's the difference between the labor force and the population? There are several important differences:

- The labor force includes only persons of "working age,"—that is, 16 years or older.[3]
- The labor force excludes persons who are "institutionalized" (e.g., those in prisons).
- The term *unemployed* has a technical definition, and it does not have the same meaning as "not employed." People are counted as unemployed only if they are looking for a job in the labor market, waiting to be recalled to a job from which they were laid off, or waiting to report to a new job. In other words, just because a person is without work does not mean that the person is unemployed. An unemployed person may usefully be thought of as being a full-time job searcher.

Almost paradoxically, this definition of the labor force means that some people who are working are not counted as being in the labor force, whereas some others who are not working are counted as being in the labor force. People who do housework full time within the family surely work, but they are not part of the labor force; people who are unemployed but looking for work are part of the labor force. Notice also that to be counted as in the labor force and working a person needs to work as little as one hour per week. Although the precise definition of unemployment varies across countries (here we have used the U.S. definition), broadly similar definitions are used by the governments of many countries and by international organizations such as the Organization for Economic Cooperation and Development (OECD).

---

[2] How can the size of the population be influenced by wage rates? The decisions of people to marry and to raise families are at least to some degree affected by their incomes. See, for instance, T. Paul Schultz, "Marital Status and Fertility in the United States: Welfare and Labor Market Effects," *Journal of Human Resources* 29 (1994): 637–669.

[3] In many countries where there is a statutory retirement age, an upper limit is imposed as well.

TABLE 4.1 An International Comparison of Labor Force Trends, 1979–2010

Country	Year	Civilian Working Age Population	Labor Force	Employment	Unemployment
		(Data are in Thousands)			
Australia	1979	10,575	6,519	6,111	408
	1999	14,698	9,414	8,762	652
	Change (1979–99)	39.0%	44.4%	43.4%	59.8%
	2010	17,854	11,868	11,247	621
Canada	1979	17,663	11,392	10,561	831
	1999	23,385	15,398	14,326	1,072
	Change (1979–99)	32.4%	35.2%	35.7%	29.0%
	2010	27,250	18,263	16,969	1,294
France	1979	39,371	22,604	21,392	1,212
	1999	45,769	25,915	23,285	2,630
	Change (1979–99)	16.3%	14.6%	8.8%	117.0%
	2010	49,656	28,067	25,423	2,644
Japan	1979	88,000	55,210	54,040	1,170
	1999	107,590	66,730	63,920	2,810
	Change (1979–99)	22.3%	20.9%	18.3%	140.2%
	2010	110,260	65,100	62,000	3,100
United Kingdom	1979	42,228	26,463	25,031	1,432
	1999	45,828	28,786	27,058	1,728
	Change (1979–99)	8.5%	8.8%	8.1%	20.7%
	2010	49,756	31,421	28,944	2,477
United States	1979	164,863	104,962	98,824	6,137
	1999	207,753	139,368	133,488	5,880
	Change (1979–99)	26.0%	32.7%	35.1%	−4.18%
	2010	237,860	153,889	139,064	14,825

Sources: U.S. Department of Labor, Bureau of Labor Statistics, Office of Productivity and Technology, "Comparative Civilian Labor Force Statistics, Ten Countries, 1959–1999," December 20, 2000; U.S. Department of Labor, Bureau of Labor Statistics, Division of International Labor Comparisons, "International Comparisons of Annual Labor Force Statistics," March 20, 2011.

Table 4.1 presents information on trends in the working age population, the labor force, and employment and unemployment in six large countries, comparing data for selected years from 1979 to 2010. For the period 1979–99, first of all, we can see that the countries with the fastest population growth (Australia, Canada, and the United States) also experienced increases in their labor force and employment levels that exceeded the rate of population growth. In these three countries, the fraction of the working age population in the labor force and employed was higher in 1999 than it was 20 years earlier. In France and Japan, however, labor force and employment growth lagged behind population growth with the result that more people were out of the labor force in 1999 than in 1979. Also, in France and Japan (and the United Kingdom, too), employment growth not only lagged behind population growth but was slower than labor force growth. As a result, many more French and Japanese were unemployed in 1999 than in 1979. For the period 1979–99, the U.S. experience is unique among the countries in Table 4.1. In the U.S. employment grew much more rapidly than the labor force, resulting in far fewer unemployed people in 1999 than in 1979. Clearly, variation across countries in population, labor force, and employment growth has a lot to do with differences in unemployment. Do the relationships among population growth and changes in labor force, employment, and unemployment continue to hold from 1999–2010? We have left this as an exercise in problem 6 at the end of this chapter. (Don't be too surprised at the results. During this period we have experienced the Great Recession!)

It is the **labor force participation rate**, however, that is our labor supply measure of interest. What is the labor force participation rate? It is the percentage of the working-age population that is in the labor force at any moment of time. An equivalent way to express the labor force participation rate (LFPR) algebraically is as follows:

$$\text{LFPR} = (E + U)/(E + U + N) \tag{4-1}$$

where E represents the number of employed persons, U represents the number of unemployed, and N stands for those in the working-age population who are not in the labor force.

In Table 4.2 we report data on labor force participation rates for men and women in three separate age groups in these same six countries for 1990, 1999, and 2009. A careful look reveals several interesting patterns:

- Labor force participation rates are generally lower for younger and older male and female workers in comparison with workers in the prime working ages from 25 to 54.
- Participation rates are generally lower for women than for men for all age groups and in all six countries, with the lone exception of young workers in Japan. Among prime-age (aged 25–54) women, the labor force participation rates vary quite a bit across the countries shown here, while more than 90% of prime-age men were in the labor force in all countries for all years. Interestingly, the labor force participation rate for prime-age women in Sweden in 1999 was 86.7%, while in Mexico it was 44.8%. (Neither is shown in Table 4.2.) This tells quite a vivid story about social customs toward work in different countries.
- Participation rates for prime-age men tended to fall over the period shown here, but participation rates for older men (aged 55–64) have risen since 1999, after having fallen during the 1990s.
- Except for Japan, there has been a tendency toward falling labor force participation rates for young men and women over the period analyzed.
- In contrast to the trend for prime-age men, participation of women in the 25–54 and 55–64 age groups rose in all six countries over the 20-year time frame.

In addition to the differences in levels and trends in labor force participation rates by age and sex detailed in Table 4.2, participation rates also rise steadily with education level.

TABLE 4.2   An International Comparison of Labor Force Participation Rates % by Age and Sex

		Men			Women		
	Year	*15–24* (%)	*25–54* (%)	*55–64* (%)	*15–24* (%)	*25–54* (%)	*55–64* (%)
Australia	1990	73.0	93.1	63.2	67.7	66.6	24.9
	1999	72.6	90.4	61.0	68.6	69.5	32.6
	2009	70.2	90.3	69.3	67.6	75.6	52.9
Canada	1990	72.2	93.1	64.3	67.3	75.4	34.9
	1999	65.3	91.1	60.7	61.7	78.2	39.4
	2009	65.4	90.7	67.7	65.1	82.2	56.3
France	1990	39.6	95.4	45.8	33.1	72.9	31.1
	1999	32.1	94.1	42.6	24.6	78.4	32.5
	2009	43.5	94.4	44.3	37.1	83.5	38.9
Japan	1990	43.4	97.5	83.3	44.8	64.2	47.2
	1999	47.7	97.1	85.2	46.7	66.4	49.8
	2009	43.0	96.1	84.4	44.8	71.1	53.5
United Kingdom	1990	83.5	94.8	68.1	72.4	72.9	38.7
	1999	73.3	91.6	63.5	65.1	75.8	41.1
	2009	67.4	91.5	70.3	60.9	78.5	50.8
United States	1990	71.8	93.4	67.8	62.9	74.0	45.2
	1999	68.0	91.7	67.9	62.9	76.8	51.5
	2009	58.5	89.7	70.3	55.2	75.6	60.0

Source: Organization for Economic Cooperation and Development Employment Outlook. Paris: OECD, June 2000, Labour Force Statistics, 1989–2009. Paris: OECD, 2010. The first age category is 16–24 (rather than 15–24) for the United Kingdom and the United States.

For example, in the United States the 2009 labor force participation rate was 46.5% for those who were not high school graduates, 62.1% for high school graduates, and 77.5% for college graduates.[4]

These are interesting statistics that show both remarkable changes over time and substantial differences between age and gender groups. How do we explain these changes and differences? Let's look at the theory of labor supply to see how it can help explain the decisions of workers to enter the labor force.

The Theory of Labor Force Participation for an Individual

Economists explain the decision of an individual to participate (or not) in the labor force as a decision of how best to allocate time between work (i.e., labor market activity) and nonwork (including such activities as school, housework, and enjoying leisure pursuits).

---

[4]U.S. Census Bureau, *Statistical Abstract of the United States*, 2011, Table 592.

More specifically, let's assume that time can be broken down into three major components: work time, leisure time, and subsistence time (the time needed for such activities as eating, sleeping, and personal necessities). Although we will ignore subsistence time as not much influenced by economic variables (it's exogenous), we can express our complete time breakdown as follows: the total amount of time (T) available is made up of time spent in work (L), at leisure (l), or engaged in subsistence activity (s). Hence

$$T = L + l + s \tag{4-2}$$

Next, let us assume that individuals get satisfaction (or **utility**) from leisure time (l) and from income per period (which we'll designate as Y).[5] We can express this by saying that a person possesses a utility function, with the level of utility (U) a function of Y and l, or:

$$U = f(Y, l) \tag{4-3}$$

Notice how similar this utility function is to the production function that we encountered in equation 2-1 and Figure 2.1. Utility depends on the consumption of two goods, income and leisure. As the consumption of each of these goods increases, so does utility. If consumption of income goes down, then utility can remain the same only if the amount of leisure taken goes up, and vice versa. So the utility function gives rise to a set of contour lines very similar to the production isoquants described previously. In this case the contour lines are called **indifference curves** because they indicate combinations of income and leisure between which the worker is indifferent.

The utility function is graphically depicted by the indifference map of contour lines shown in Figure 4.1, with income on the vertical axis and hours of leisure on the horizontal axis. The graph shows a number of indifference curves and supposes that the individual regards both income and leisure as "goods." Higher levels of utility are signified by moving in the northeast direction of the graph (to levels U_1, U_2, and so on); as the worker moves in this direction, he or she receives both more income and more leisure. Notice that if we consider hours spent on subsistence as fixed and outside the scope of our analysis, then any additional hour devoted to leisure is one less hour devoted to work (and vice versa). Therefore, we can read the number of leisure hours by moving from left to right along the horizontal axis and the number of work hours by moving from right to left.

For any given level of utility (e.g., U_1), various combinations of income (Y) and leisure (l) will provide the same level of satisfaction. However, the rate at which an individual is willing to give up income for more leisure varies along the utility curve. At point A, for example, an individual is working many hours and has very little leisure. To be induced to give up an hour of scarce leisure time would most likely require a very large additional amount of income (unless the person is a workaholic—but such a person would not have the type of indifference curves we're dealing with here). The slope of the utility curve at point A tells us just how much more income a person would require in return for giving up an additional hour of leisure if the level of utility is to remain the same. As we saw in Chapter 2, we call this slope the *marginal rate of substitution* of income for leisure (MRS),

---

[5] We could equivalently think of Y as all the goods and services that income can buy.

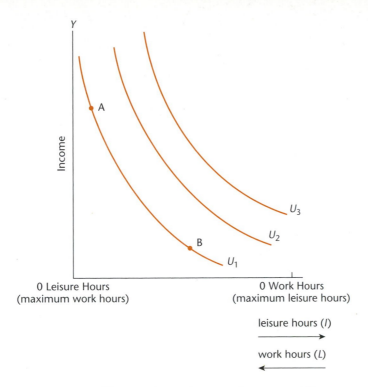

FIGURE 4.1 Indifference Curves between Income and Hours
of Work or Leisure

and it is clear that at point A the MRS is very large. At point B, however, the situation is just the reverse. Here the individual has very little income but a lot of leisure. How much value would this individual place on yet another hour of leisure as measured by the amount of income he or she would be willing to give up? Not very much, as the small slope of the U_1 curve (the MRS) signifies to us.

Let's turn next to income and wage rates and see what role they play in the decision of an individual to work or not work. Income, of course, can come not just from market work but also from other sources, such as winning the lottery, bank interest, or capital gains from dealing in equities. Therefore, we can express Y as the sum of earnings from work—the wage rate (w) times hours of work (L)—plus income from all other sources (Z). Algebraically:

$$Y = (w \times L) + Z \tag{4-4}$$

Figure 4.2 depicts two different income lines. In line ABC, nonlabor income, or income not due to market work, is represented by the vertical distance Z_1 (or AB). In other words, the person whose income line is depicted by ABC would receive an income of Z_1 even if he or she doesn't work a single hour. Earnings from different possible amounts of market work are shown by the line segment BC. The slope of BC represents the *hourly wage rate,* showing how much more income will result from giving up an additional hour

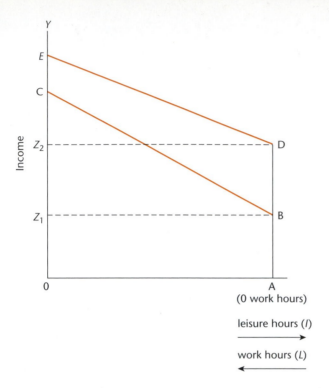

FIGURE 4.2 Budget Constraints

of leisure and working that additional hour instead. In general, then, the wage rate can be expressed as

$$w = -(\Delta Y / \Delta l) \tag{4-5}$$

Line ADE, by way of contrast, represents the income line of a person with a higher level of nonlabor income (Z_2) but with a lower market wage.

Now how can we use the utility function and the income line together to explain the decision of a person to enter or not to enter the labor force? In Figure 4.3 our hypothetical person has an income line of ABC, with nonlabor income of AB and a market wage represented by the slope of line BC. Will this person choose to enter the labor force? The answer is "no." The highest level of utility that can be attained with income line ABC is U_2, and at utility level U_2 this person will choose the maximum amount of leisure possible (A)—that is, no work.

Take a closer look at Figure 4.3 to see why our hypothetical person won't enter the labor force. The marginal rate of substitution (MRS) of income for leisure at point B (which depicts zero work) is greater than the market wage that he or she can command. In other words, the subjective value the individual places on leisure time at that point is greater than the wage employers are willing to pay for that time. The marginal rate of substitution at the zero work point is called the **reservation wage**; this is the lowest wage that will induce a person to enter the labor force.

so, we should take into account the following aspects of labor market performance in industrialized countries during the past several decades:

1. Family incomes have risen in real terms (although not evenly over time), and the share of personal income from nonlabor sources has also changed. For example, in the United States real median family income increased by 12.2% from 1980 to 1998, although from 1998 to 2009 it has shown almost no growth. In addition, the share of personal income derived from interest and dividend payments rose from 14.7% in 1980 to 16.6% in 1998, but has since fallen to 15.8% as of 2009. And the share of personal income from government social benefits (such as social security and welfare benefits) has increased from 11.8% in 1980 to 12.5% in 1998 to 17.2% in 2009.[10] These data give some indication of the magnitude of changes in the Z term in our labor supply model.

2. There has been a rise in the wages of females relative to those of males in most developed economies. The gender wage gap (defined as the difference between male and female median full-time earnings as a percentage of male earnings) fell from 18.8% to 14.4% in Australia, from 35.3% to 20.0% in the United Kingdom, and from 36.6% to 21.6% in the U.S. over the period 1980–2004. Declines were also seen in France (from 19.7% in 1980 to 11.7% in 2003—although the gap in France has been inching up again) and in Japan (from 41.7% in 1980 to 33.9% in 2000).[11] This continues a trend evident since at least 1960 in these countries,[12] which has increased the opportunity cost for women of remaining out of the labor force.

Now let's look at four specific groups to investigate how the labor supply has changed in recent years.

Young Workers

As Table 4.2 shows, the LFPRs of young men and women (aged 15–24 years) are significantly below those registered for prime-age workers (25–54). Furthermore, the participation rates for these groups fell in most countries during the 1990s and the 2000s. Can our model of labor supply with its emphasis on substitution and income effects explain some of these differences and changes?

Of course the main reason for low LFPRs for younger as compared to older workers is that many younger men and women are full-time students. This is clearly the case for those younger than age 18 and increasingly the case for those in their early 20s. The decrease in participation rates over time largely reflects the fact that people in this age range are more likely to remain in education longer than was true of previous generations. For example, in 1970 only 10.7% of the U.S. population aged 25 years and over had completed four or more years of college, compared to 29.5% in 2009. And in 1970 only about 52% of the U.S. population aged 25 years or more had completed high school, whereas the

---

[10] These data are from tables in the *Economic Report of the President*, February 2000 and February 2011.

[11] Data from *Society at a Glance*, OECD Social Indicators, 2006, Table EQ3.3, p. 73.

[12] Jacob Mincer, "Intercountry Comparisons of Labor Force Trends and of Related Developments: An Overview," *Journal of Labor Economics* 3 (1985): S1–S32.

corresponding percentage as of 2009 was 86.7%.[13] In a real sense, young people today are far more likely to substitute school (leisure) for work than were their counterparts of several generations ago.[14]

In terms of the theory of labor supply, this reflects two factors. For youth, nonlabor income can be defined as the income earned by the household head and other wage earners in the family. Over time, as family income has risen, families have decided to allocate resources to support the further education of their children. For the labor supply decision of young people, this has the effect of raising Z, which reduces the likelihood of labor force participation by this group. In addition to a higher level of Z, we can also factor in what amounts to a decrease in the value of w for less well-educated youths as the wage return to higher education has increased. In our models we have looked only at the wage as the price of leisure and ignored any opportunity cost of working. If we expand the choice set to include work, leisure, and remaining in school, we have to recognize that the wage return to further education is a big part of the opportunity cost of entering the labor force after high school. Without making the theoretical analysis more complicated, as the wage premium associated with having a college degree increases, the opportunity cost of working instead of going to school increases. This in turn reduces the likelihood that individuals of high school or college age would choose to enter the workforce rather than continue their education. The real wage return to working, which is w minus the present value of future wage enhancements associated with higher education, falls while nonlabor income Z rises; and both factors work to reduce labor force participation among school-age people.

You may be wondering why the level of labor force participation is not even lower and why the decline in participation rates of young people has not even been more dramatic than Table 4.2 indicates. After all, in some countries the decline has been rather modest (or an increase has occurred—e.g., France) while the proportion of young men and women going on to higher education has risen greatly. The fact is that many individuals are both in the labor force *and* going to school full time. Remember that persons working part time are still counted as in the labor force if they work at least one hour per week for pay or are actively searching for a full- or part-time job. As to why so many are working while attending school, just look at the cost of automobile insurance or your college tuition bill! Both have increased in real terms over recent years.

The fact that many young people choose to study rather than to supply their labor is interesting in that it serves to emphasize the extent to which dynamic considerations enter the process of decision making. You may be studying now in order to increase your chances of getting a good job in the future, but your decision to study now is also determined in part by decisions that you have made in the past. Each of us could choose many different pathways through our careers—we all make choices about the type of work we do and about whether to work, or to be educated, or to do neither at

---

[13] U.S. Department of Commerce, *Statistical Abstract of the United States, 2011*, Table 225.

[14] Some of you may be aghast at our characterization of schooling as "leisure." Of course, our definition of leisure is intentionally broad and includes all sorts of activities outside the labor market. But you might be interested to know that the origin of the word *school* is from the classical Greek word σχωλη, which really does mean leisure.

each point in our lives. We are, therefore, instinctively making complicated calculations in order to choose which of these pathways will suit us best. Economists have successfully drilled down into this complex decision-making process in order to derive insights into the career decisions made by young people, and by doing so have been able to make predictions about how the occupational structure of the economy will unfold in years to come.[15]

Older Male Workers

In most countries the labor force participation rates of older men are lower than those of prime-age men. And this is certainly true for the six countries shown in Table 4.2, with participation rates for 55- to 64-year-old men averaging about 20 to 30 percentage points lower than the corresponding rates for 25- to 54-year-old men. Although the table does not depict rates for men aged 65 and older, those levels are much lower still. For example, in 2009 the participation rate for men aged 65 and over in the U.S. was 21.9%.

In fact, labor force participation rates for men aged 55–64 fell steadily for the greater part of the twentieth century. This was true not just for the United States but for most other OECD countries as well. However, in the last two decades a reversal has taken place, with LFPRs of older men leveling off and beginning to rise in many countries. This can be seen clearly in Table 4.2, where participation rates in five of the six countries depicted rose over the period 1999–2009, in some cases quite sharply.

Can our model of labor force participation explain what has happened to LFPRs of older men—first the secular decline and, more recently, the leveling off and upturn? The secular decline is easy to explain with our model. Old age brings with it various infirmities and disabilities, which would encourage many to leave the labor force. (Using the terminology of our model, these would cause the reservation wages of older people to rise.) But although this explains why participation rates of the elderly male population are below those of younger groups, it does not readily explain why elderly male participation rates have fallen over most of the twentieth century. A more plausible explanation is the more widespread availability of retirement pensions (including social security) for the elderly population. It has only been since the end of World War II that private pensions have become widespread in the United States, and social security dates back only to 1935. By providing people with income that does not stem from work, pension income acts as a type of pure income effect (Z), which reduces the incentive to work just as equation 4-7 predicts.

There are three factors to consider in analyzing the impact of social security and other pensions on work incentives. These are the earliest age at which workers can begin receiving benefits, the replacement rate (i.e., how high the benefits are as a proportion of labor income), and the implicit tax rate for continued work. Information on these three aspects of the social security systems in 11 countries is presented in Table 4.3. In most countries workers can retire at age 60. Italy allows workers who are 55 to retire and begin receiving benefits, whereas the early retirement age in the United States is 62. So workers begin

---

[15] See, for example, Michael Keane and Kenneth Wolpin, "The Career Decisions of Young Men," *Journal of Political Economy* 105 (1997): 473–522.

TABLE 4.3   Characteristics of Social Security in Various Countries

Country	Early Retirement Age	Replacement Rate	Implicit Tax Rate
Belgium	60	77%	82%
Canada	60	20%	8%
France	60	91%	80%
Germany	60	62%	35%
Italy	55	75%	81%
Japan	60	54%	47%
Netherlands	60	91%	141%
Spain	60	63%	−23%
Sweden	60	54%	28%
United Kingdom	60	48%	75%
United States	62	41%	−1%

Source: Jonathan Gruber and David Wise, "An International Perspective on Policies for an Aging Society," NBER Working Paper 8103, January 2001. Available online at www.nber.org/papers/w8103. Also in Stuart Altman and David Schactman, eds., *Policies for an Aging Society* (Baltimore and London: Johns Hopkins University Press, 2002), pp. 34–59.

facing the retirement decision at a fairly young age in these countries. In addition to these social security programs, workers in many countries may be able to "retire" even earlier if they are eligible for disability benefits or preretirement benefits for the long-term unemployed.

The replacement rate is calculated as the ratio of retirement benefits to preretirement earnings for the median social security recipient. This measure of the generosity of social security benefits varies widely among the countries listed in Table 4.3. In Canada, social security benefits "replace" just 20% of the preretirement earnings of those leaving the work force at age 60. In the United States the replacement rate is 41%. However, social security benefits are much more generous in Europe, with early retirees in France and the Netherlands receiving benefits that are only slightly less than the wages a worker could get on the job. The theory of labor supply predicts that the availability of retirement benefits reduces labor force participation by adding to nonlabor income (Z). As Figure 4.6 illustrates, there is a negative relationship between the labor force participation rate of older male workers and the social security replacement rate in this small sample of countries.

The final characteristic of social security systems detailed in Table 4.3 is the implicit tax on the wages of those who decide to continue to work beyond the early retirement years. This tax is "implicit" in that it represents the opportunity cost of not taking early retirement rather than an actual tax that must be paid by the individual. The opportunity cost stems from lost pension benefits. In many countries, the monthly social security benefit is not increased for workers retiring later even though they are likely to collect benefits for a shorter time period. Because of this "actuarially unfair" treatment, workers who postpone retirement lose part of their lifetime social security wealth for every year that they delay retirement.

The last column of Table 4.3 shows estimates of this implicit tax on work as a fraction of earnings for a worker at the early retirement age. The lost pension wealth is a very high fraction of after-tax wages in many countries, reaching 141% in the Netherlands. Only in

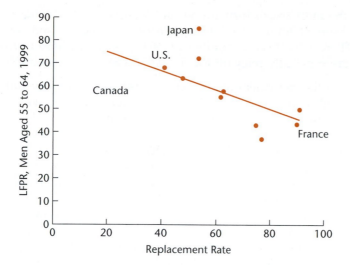

FIGURE 4.6 Social Security Benefits and Participation

Sources: OECD Employment Outlook. Paris: Organization for Economic
Cooperation and Development, June 2000; and Jonathan Gruber and
David Wise, "An International Perspective on Policies for an Aging
Society," NBER Working Paper 8103, January 2001. Available online
at www.nber.org/papers/w8103.

the United States, which increases social security benefits for each year worked until the
age of 70, is the social security system approximately neutral with regard to the incentive
to work. Spain is unusual in this small sample of countries by offering workers a substantial subsidy (an implicit tax rate of −23%) for delaying retirement. In the countries with a
positive implicit tax rate, the social security program has the effect of reducing the real
wage earned by those who continue to work. This subtraction from wage earnings, like
the added nonwage retirement benefit, would lead many workers to withdraw from the
labor force according to our model of labor supply.[16]

Considerable empirical evidence links international differences in the low level of and
decrease over time in the labor force participation rates of older workers to the characteristics of the social security system.[17] These results are consistent with the predictions of
the model of labor supply developed in this chapter. Making it easier to retire early with
generous benefits adds to nonwage income and therefore reduces participation. Putting
an implicit tax on the wages of those not choosing early retirement flattens the income
line and also reduces participation. Many European countries indeed may have structured
early retirement incentives to reduce LFPRs for older workers in the belief that this would
open job opportunities for younger workers in high unemployment economies.

---

[16] Private and occupational pensions operate differently from the social security systems in many countries.
The former typically pay out an amount that is positively related to years of contribution, thereby providing a
disincentive to retirement. But the coverage of such schemes is patchy, especially for lower income workers.

[17] Jonathan Gruber and David Wise, "Social Security and Retirement: An International Comparison," *American
Economic Review* 88 (1998): 158–163; Axel Borsch-Supan, "Incentive Effects of Social Security on Labor Force
Participation: Evidence in Germany and across Europe," *Journal of Public Economics* 78 (2000): 25–49.

But what can explain the most recent turnaround and increase in the LFPRs of older workers that have been observed for most of the countries in Table 4.2 and for many other countries as well? There have been a number of factors at work here in the past 20 years or so, some that are especially relevant for the United States. For example:

- The gradual increase in the retirement age at which workers can receive full social security benefits. The full retirement age in the United States was formerly age 65, but is being gradually raised to 67. In addition, every year that workers delay retirement beyond their full retirement age produces an 8% increase in their level of social security benefits, thereby creating an additional incentive for many to continue working. (In the United Kingdom, the "state pension age" for women is being raised gradually from 60 so that those born after April 1978 will have a state pension age of 68.)
- The fact that levels of social security benefits have been growing at a slower rate than in the past and that they are now subject (up to 85% of social security income) to federal income taxes.
- The elimination of the social security "earnings limit" after the full retirement age is reached. This earnings limit (also called the "earnings test") formerly restricted the amount of earnings from work that social security recipients could make without losing some of their social security income. The earnings limit effectively acted as a tax on additional earnings from work, and the elimination of the limit effectively meant an increase in the wage rate for seniors receiving social security income who chose to also continue to work.
- The fact that average life expectancy has grown. Since 1970 the average life expectancy in the United States for males has increased by about four years and by about three years for females. (Of course, female life expectancy is still longer than that for males by about five years.) What this means is that many people must work more years to cover their retirement income needs.
- The abolition of mandatory retirement policies for most workers. It is now illegal for most employers to compel their employees to retire at a certain age.
- The fact that private sector employers are now less likely to provide or pay for health care benefits for workers who have retired.
- The fall in the number of defined benefit retirement plans. Defined benefit plans, just as their name implies, provide workers with a fixed amount of income at retirement, an amount that does not rise should workers decide to delay retirement. Instead, these plans have been largely replaced by defined contribution plans, with the dollar amounts depending on how much workers and employers have invested into the retirement plans.

What most of the factors listed above have done is to either increase the effective wage rate from working or to reduce the level of Z, nonlabor income, for workers who are nearing retirement age. In other words, either the substitution effect or the income effect is working in most of the above cases to encourage some workers to continue to work rather than to retire. (Can you identify which effect is working for each of the above factors?)

Finally there is one additional factor that may also help explain the recent rise in the LFPRs of older men—not just in the United States but in many other countries as well. It is the recent increase in participation rates of older women. Remarkably, for each of the six countries described in Table 4.2, the LFPRs of women 55–64 years of age have risen, in some cases quite dramatically, over the period of time shown. But how can this rise in older female participation rates possibly explain the *rise* in older men's rates? After all, since many of these women are married, by working they raise the income of their families. Therefore don't they create an income effect (a higher level of *Z*) that would *discourage* some men from remaining in the labor force? The surprising answer to this question is that such an increase in nonlabor (spousal) income need not necessarily lead to lower participation rates for the other spouse. It is possible that some married couples may have a preference for *shared* leisure time. According to this reasoning, husbands might not enjoy their leisure time as much when their wives are working, and in such instances may actually increase their labor force participation rates. In this case the leisure (and work) of the spouses would be considered to be complements. In researching this question, Tammy Schirle has estimated that a substantial portion of the recent increases in the LFPRs of older men can be explained in just this way—by the increase in participation rates of their wives—with wives' leisure time thereby being complementary to that of their husbands. She estimates that about one-third of the recent increase in older males' participation rates in both the United States and the United Kingdom (and about one-half of the increase in Canada) can be explained as responses to the increased participation of their wives.[18] We will take up this matter at greater length in Chapter 5 when we analyze family models of labor supply.

Women

As we have seen in our analysis of participation rates of young workers and older men, differences across countries and over time can, to a large degree, be explained with the help of our elementary model of labor supply using income and substitution effects. The analysis of labor supply becomes more challenging when we turn to the case of female participation, a subject that has attracted much research attention in recent decades.

One of the most noteworthy labor market trends over the second half of the twentieth century was the rapid rise in female labor force participation rates, which largely reflected sharp increases in the fraction of married women working outside the home. The rise in LFPRs, especially for prime-age women, can easily be seen in Table 4.2, although the increase began long before 1990. (For example, in the United States the LFPR for prime-wage women in 1972 was 51% while in 1950 it was only 37%.) As we have done for the case of males, let's see to what extent our model of labor supply can explain the changing patterns of female labor force participation rates. With married women in particular, we must recognize that the utility maximizing choice is not just between leisure and work but also between work in the production of goods and services in the home versus work in the labor market.

A number of factors are important in explaining the general trend toward increasing labor force participation of married women in particular. Over long periods of time, changes in the occupational structure of the economy have interacted with changes in the education, wealth, fertility, and preferences of women to make work in the labor market more attractive and available to women than work in the home. Of course, labor-saving technology and home-care products that have been introduced over the past several generations (such as automatic washers and dryers, dishwashers, microwave ovens, and

[18] Tammy Schirle, "Why Have the Labor Force Participation Rates of Older Men Increased Since the Mid-1990s?" *Journal of Labor Economics* 26 (4) (2008): 549–594.

slow-cookers) have reduced the amount of time that many women have had to spend on household tasks. And medical advances (such as birth control) have provided women with more choices in marriage and pregnancy decisions, thereby giving them more opportunity to work outside the home. These changes have also eroded cultural distinctions between "women's work" and "men's work," which in turn have spurred further increases in female participation. In all countries, increasing labor force participation rates for women are associated with smaller family sizes and higher divorce rates.[19]

An important factor explaining rising female participation is the elasticity of the participation rate with respect to the real wage earned by women and the real wage earned by men. A detailed analysis[20] of studies in a dozen major countries in the mid-1980s showed that, on average, the elasticity of female participation rates with respect to the real wage earned by women was equal to +1.0. This indicates that, other things unchanged, a 1% increase in the real wage paid to women would lead to a 1% increase in the participation rate. At the same time, the elasticity with respect to the real wage earned by men was, on average, −0.4. Therefore, a 1% increase in the male wage would lower the female participation rate by four-tenths of 1%. As our model suggests, other things being equal, a rise in w (the real wage earned by women) leads to an increase in the LFPR of women, whereas a rise in married women's unearned income Z (due to a rise in the real wage earned by men) leads to a reduction in the LFPR of women.

Because the elasticity with regard to w is greater than the elasticity with regard to Z in these estimates,[21] an increase in the female real wage relative to the male real wage would result in an increased female LFPR. This can be seen in Figure 4.7, which shows the relationship between the female–male wage ratio in the mid-to-late 1990s and the female participation rate in 1999 across several countries. Notice that there is a slight positive relationship between the variables as suggested by the theory of labor supply and the evidence on elasticities discussed previously.

Just as we saw earlier in the case of the rising LFPRs of older males, there have occurred some recent unexpected changes in the participation rates of women in the United States. Specifically, the first decade of the new century has seen a *decline* in the LFPR of women in many categories—especially among single women, women without children, and highly educated women with children. This decline can clearly be seen in Table 4.2 for women in the 15–24 and 25–54 age categories. It is not clear at this point just why the declines have occurred. Some observers have referred to it as the "opt out" revolution, while some have claimed that it is due to discrimination rather than choice, while still others argue that the decline is a cyclical phenomenon fueled by recessions. Whatever the reasons, as one observer puts it: "The received wisdom regarding women's labor force participation has been turned on its head in the last decade or so."[22]

---

[19] Dora L. Costa, "From Mill Town to Board Room: The Rise of Women's Paid Labor," *Journal of Economic Perspectives* 14 (2000): 101–122.

[20] Jacob Mincer, "Intercountry Comparisons of Labor Force Trends and of Related Developments: An Overview," *Journal of Labor Economics* 3 (1985): S1–S32.

[21] There is evidence that both elasticities have fallen slightly since the mid-1980s but that their relative size has remained the same. See Costa (2000) op. cit.

[22] Diane Macunovich, "Reversals in the Patterns of Women's Labor Supply in the United States, 1977–2009," *Monthly Labor* Review, November 2010, p. 31.

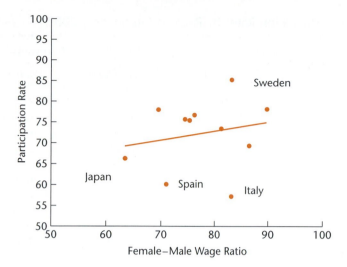

FIGURE 4.7 Gender Wage Ratio and Female Participation Rate

Sources: Authors' calculations using data from Francine Blau and Lawrence Kahn, "Gender Differences in Pay," *Journal of Economic Perspectives* 14(4) (2000): 75–99, and the Bureau of Labor Statistics Web site.

Race and Residence

Data for the United States show that LFPRs for white males tend to be several percentage points higher than for black males, whereas the reverse is true for females. In 2008, for example, the participation rates were 73.7% for white males, 66.7% for black males, 59.2% for white females, and 61.3% for black females. Black–white wage differences may account for the lower participation rate of black men relative to whites (black men employed full-time earn about 75% of what white men earn); but this factor cannot explain racial differences for women. In fact, the average earnings of full-time employed black females are only slightly less than that of white females. Therefore, the substitution effect cannot explain the higher black female participation rate. What factors can? One reason for the difference lies in the fact that black families are much more likely than white families to have a female head of household. The absence of a male income earner in many black families means that, for black females considering entering the labor force, the level of family income without their earnings (Z) is low. For such females, therefore, the income effect is working to increase the likelihood of their participating in the work force.

Black labor force participation rates are also affected greatly by the fact that blacks make up a disproportionate share of the residents of inner city neighborhoods in most large cities. Table 4.4 illustrates the importance of residential location on the labor force participation rates of blacks and whites living in 11 major metropolitan areas in 2007, a year of relatively low unemployment in the United States. In 2007, 63.7% of blacks and 66.4% of whites were in the national labor force. The LFPRs of both white and black central city residents were well below national levels and levels for metropolitan area

TABLE 4.4   U.S. Labor Force Participation Rates by Race and Residence, 2007

| | Central City Residents | | Metropolitan Area Residents | |
Metropolitan Area	Black (%)	White (%)	Black (%)	White (%)
Baltimore	58.7%	60.5%	65.8%	66.6%
Chicago	66.2%	68.8%	59.6%	68.9%
Cleveland	48.1%	57.9%	60.2%	68.4%
Dallas	64.0%	68.8%	68.4%	71.2%
Detroit	56.4%	46.2%	58.5%	62.8%
Houston	59.2%	62.6%	62.9%	65.6%
Los Angeles	54.1%	70.3%	60.1%	67.3%
Milwaukee	67.5%	67.1%	69.2%	69.4%
New York	58.2%	59.3%	60.8%	63.6%
Philadelphia	54.4%	53.1%	60.2%	66.0%
St. Louis	61.2%	62.0%	72.2%	69.8%

Source: U.S. Department of Labor, Bureau of Labor Statistics. *Geographic Profile of Employment and Unemployment, 2007.* Bulletin 2736, June 2011.

residents in most cases. Participation rate disparities are even more pronounced when we look at data for neighborhoods within the central city.

William Julius Wilson has explained the disappearance of work from high poverty urban neighborhoods in part as a result of decreased wages in the inner city following industrial change and the suburbanization of businesses.[23] He also points to opportunities to earn income in illegal activity, the underground economy, or from government programs as other important deterrents to inner city labor force participation. This explanation is consistent with the hypothesized effects of w and Z on LFPR drawn from our labor supply model.

Summary

In this chapter we looked closely at the theory of labor supply from one focal point, that of labor force participation. We examined the theory of the labor force participation decision for individuals as well as the determinants of labor force participation rates for various groups, such as young people, older workers, and women.

Two variables—the real wage rate available to a person who works and the nonlabor income available to a person—are key determinants of the decision to enter the labor force. Changes in real wages and nonlabor income provide plausible explanations for observed changes in labor force participation rates for different age and sex groups in many countries. As our discussion of labor force participation by older men indicates,

---

[23] William Julius Wilson, *When Work Disappears: The World of the New Urban Poor* (New York: Alfred A. Knopf, 1996).

public policy programs, such as social security retirement pensions, may have significant work disincentives built into them.

By itself, however, the labor force participation rate is a limited measure of labor supply. It can only indicate whether an individual is in the labor force or what percentage of people in a certain group choose to offer their services in the labor market. It does not tell us how much work an individual or a group is willing to offer. In this respect, therefore, the number of hours of work—per day, per week, or per year—is a superior measure of labor supply. And it is to this subject that we turn in Chapter 5.

KEY TERMS

labor force
labor force participation rate
utility
indifference curves
reservation wage

income effect
substitution effect
added worker effect
discouraged worker effect

PROBLEMS

1. News reports have indicated that the steep drops in U.S. stock prices from 2000 to 2003 and from 2008 to 2009 have caused many people to delay their retirement and to remain in the labor force instead. Use the labor force participation model to explain the relationship between the stock market and retirement decisions.

2. Use the data in the following table to calculate the labor force participation rate for each of the seven countries.

Thousands of People in 2010

	Civilian Working Age Population	Employment	Unemployment
Australia	17,854	11,247	621
Canada	27,250	16,969	1,294
France	49,656	25,423	2,644
Germany	70,856	38,209	2,980
Sweden	7,641	4,534	409
United Kingdom	49,756	28,944	2,477
United States	237,830	139,064	14,825

3. Which of the countries in problem 2 above has the highest and the lowest unemployment rates? Is there any association between unemployment rates and labor force participation for all seven countries?

4. What does the term *workaholic* really mean—one who simply works very hard (like the authors of this book), or one who gets more pleasure from working than from leisure

(not like the authors of this book)? First try mapping out the shape of such a person's utility isoquants. Then use the income-labor-leisure model to depict and explain the labor supply preferences of a workaholic and how he or she would react to changes in wages.

5. Applications to MBA programs in the United States dropped significantly in 2000 when the unemployment rate fell to 4% (the lowest rate in decades). Then in 2008 and 2009 with the unemployment rate rising, MBA applications also rose rapidly. Does the theory of labor force participation help explain this inverse relationship between the strength of the economy and the volume of MBA applications?

6. We saw in Table 4.1 that from 1979 to 1999, the countries with the fastest rate of growth in population also generally experienced increases in their labor force and employment levels that exceeded that of population growth. Do the same general relationships among population growth on the one hand and labor force and employment growth on the other hand continue to be the case from 1999–2010?

The Supply of Labor: Hours of Work

When might a higher wage result in a reduced quantity supplied of labor?

Why do Americans work more hours per year than people in other countries?

What characteristics of welfare programs have disincentives for work?

Let's turn now from our discussion of labor force participation rates and focus on an alternative measure of labor supply—hours of work. Remember that to be counted as being in the labor force a person needs to put in only one hour per week of paid employment. So labor force participation rates only measure whether that person is in the labor force, not how strongly committed to work that person is. There have been some interesting developments with respect to hours of work in recent years, and we discuss these trends in this chapter.

First we examine the trend in hours of work over time. Most of us know that the workweek, for example, is much shorter today than it was 75 or 100 years ago. But what about most recently? And what about the average workday or work life? Then we discuss the principal determinants of working hours. Why have working hours declined over the long term? Next we explore the theory of the supply of working hours, which will help us determine the shape (positive or negative) and the elasticity of the labor supply schedule. Finally, we use this theory to turn our sights to some interesting and important policy issues.

The History of Working Hours

Few people today have an appreciation of just how long hours of work used to be. In the *Encyclopedia of the Social Sciences* in 1932, Wladimir Woytinsky stated that no reliable statistics are available for the period around 1800, but it was pretty well known that a "working day of 14 hours was customary, one of 16 hours attracted little attention, and only a working day of 17 or 18 hours was considered an abuse." Furthermore, Woytinsky goes on to say, "such excessively long hours were worked not only by men but also by women and children, whose labor was used on a particularly large scale in the textile factories." Moreover, the workweek at that time was not five days but six. Even as late as 1840, the workweek averaged about 69 hours in England, about 78 hours in the United States, and 83 hours in Germany.[1]

To imagine what the quality of life must have been like at that time for some workers, let's do a little quick arithmetic. Most people need to sleep 8 hours per night. Preparing and eating meals may take up another 2 hours per day. Travel time to and from work may be 1 hour or so, and perhaps another hour is spent on personal necessities. If we add these 12 hours to a 13-hour workday, we are already into the next day. Not much free time for recreation and pleasure is left, is there? With workdays like these characterizing the lives of many workers of the time, it's not hard to understand the concerns of reformers such as Karl Marx, who deemed inevitable the overthrow of the capitalist system.

THE WAY WE WORK

The Good Old Days?

Working life has come a long way in the past 120 years. Consider these 1872 regulations for a New Jersey carriage manufacturing firm:

- Employees will daily sweep floors, dust the furniture and shelves.
- Each day, fill lamps, clean chimneys, and trim wicks. Wash windows once a week.
- Each worker will bring in a bucket of water and a scuttle of coal for the day's business.
- Make your pens carefully. You may whittle your nibs to your individual tastes.
- The building will open at 7:00 a.m. and close at 8:00 p.m. daily, except on the Sabbath on which day it remains closed. Each employee is expected to spend the Sabbath by attending church and contributing liberally to the cause of the Lord.
- Men employees will be given an evening off each week for courting purposes, or two evenings a week if they go regularly to church.
- After an employee has spent his hours of labor, he should spend time reading the Bible and other good books.
- Any employee who smokes cigars, uses liquor in any form, gets shaved in a barber shop, or frequents pool and public halls will give good reason to suspect his worth, intentions, integrity, and honesty.
- The employee who has performed his labors faithfully and without fault for a period of five years and who has been thrifty and attentive to his religious duties will be given an increase of five cents per day, provided a just return in profit from the business permits it.

Source: During the nineteenth century the above set of office rules was apparently quite common. Variants of these work rules can be found on many Internet sites such as http://bsdfortunes.tumblr.com/post/2682530243.

---

[1] Hours of Labor, *Encyclopedia of the Social Sciences*, 1932, p. 480.

Interestingly, most employers and even the general public saw little wrong with such excessively long hours at that time. Why? Well, it was the norm, for one thing. But there was also the prevailing religious conviction about the virtue of hard work: "Satan finds mischief for idle hands" was a popular sentiment. During a strike in 1825, for example, Boston carpenters' demands for a 10-hour workday (but still on a six-day work-week) were characterized by their employers as "fraught with pernicious evils," and if it should happen to spread to other communities, it could "open a wide door for idleness and vice."[2] As one historian notes, in an era when the sun-up to sun-down system "was normal for the vast majority of the population, the carpenters could not find much sympathy; they lost the strike."[3]

Hours of work today are nothing like those of these early times. Figure 5.1 shows the trend in weekly hours worked in the U.S. economy over roughly 110 years. The average weekly hours worked by manufacturing production workers declined rapidly over the first several decades of the 1900s. Since the 1940s, though, the average workweek for these workers has remained stable at a little over 40 hours. Figure 5.1 also shows the average weekly hours worked by all private sector workers in the U.S. economy over the past 50 years. Weekly hours worked declined from 1959 to 1989, leveled off at about 34.5 hours per week during the 1990s, and have declined again to just under 34 hours during the first decade of the new century.

FIGURE 5.1 Average Weekly Hours Worked in the U.S. 1899–2009

Source: Historical Statistics of the United States and Economic Report of the President, February 2012.

---

[2] Quoted in Allan Cartter and F. Ray Marshall, *Labor Economics,* 2nd ed. (Homewood, IL: Irwin, 1972), p. 430.

[3] Joseph Rayback, *A History of American Labor* (New York: The Free Press, 1966), p. 60.

TABLE 5.1   International Comparisons of Average Annual Hours Worked per Person in Employment

	1979	1999	2010	Percentage change, 1979–2010
Australia	1,833	1,860	1,686	−8.0%
Canada	1,841	1,806	1,702	−7.6%
France	1,868	1,596	1,562	−16.4%
Western Germany	1,770	1,456	1,409	−20.4%
Ireland	1,902*	1,692	1,664	−12.5%
Japan	2,126	1,810	1,733	−18.5%
Norway	1,580	1,398	1,414	−10.5%
Spain	1,930	1,816	1,663	−13.8%
United Kingdom	1,813	1,719	1,647	−9.2%
United States	1,829	1,847	1,778	−2.8%

*For the year 1983

Source: OECD Employment Outlook, June 2003 and 2011.

Table 5.1 gives a different picture of working hour trends, comparing developments in annual hours worked across 10 countries over the last 30 years. Vacations and holidays differ and many work at part-time jobs or hold more than one job, so these data cover average hours worked per year by all workers in the economy.[4] The United States clearly stands out from most other countries on this list in two ways: the work year is somewhat longer, and the rate of decline has been lower than in most other countries.[5] On average, U.S. workers spend 92 more hours at work per year than workers in Australia and 364 more hours per year than the average Norwegian. In addition, the length of the work year fell by more than 15% in France, Western Germany, and Japan over this period, whereas the average U.S. work year fell by less than 3%. In fact, over part of this period (1979–1999), the average number of hours per year worked by the typical American worker actually rose slightly—from 1,829 to 1,847 hours.

Why have hours of work generally declined over time? What factors were at work to bring about the drop in the workweek in the United States and most other countries during the first half of the twentieth century? Why has the trend toward fewer hours at work slowed in the United States in the past two generations? Many reasons have been offered, among them technology and productivity growth, restrictive hours legislation, trade union demands, and the wishes of employers; but labor economists tend to emphasize the importance of changes in workers' preferences for fewer hours of work per period as the driving force behind these trends.

---

[4] The data in Figure 5.1 refer only to hours worked in the main job held. Work hours in manufacturing tend to be lower than in other sectors, partly as a result of union pressure. In Table 5.1, by way of contrast, the data refer to hours worked in all sectors of the economy and allow for the incidence of double job-holding.

[5] The average annual work year actually increased by 6.8% in Sweden over this same period. The relatively high figure for the work year in the United States is largely due to shorter vacations in this country than elsewhere.

Worker Preferences and Hours Worked

The shorter workweek that we enjoy today has to a large degree been the result of changing worker preferences—a desire on the part of workers to consume more "leisure" time. Other factors that have been emphasized by some observers, especially unions and legislators, have served as the *channels* through which worker preferences have been expressed. Productivity growth has been the *means* through which workers have been able to put in fewer hours at work without experiencing a fall in income. But worker preferences appear to be the driving force behind the secular fall in hours.

Now what would you say to the following objection to the argument that we have just laid out: "Excuse me, haven't you overlooked one very important additional reason for the decline in the workweek—the fact that the population has grown? Because of the growing population, hours of work simply *had* to fall. If they hadn't, there wouldn't be enough work to go around for everybody." This type of reasoning is fallacious. A person using such an argument is assuming that the potential number of jobs in the economy is constant and that, if the population grows, then either hours of work must fall or the unemployment rate must rise. In fact, the potential number of jobs in the economy is a function of the level of potential aggregate demand. As the population grows, so also does the level of potential aggregate demand and with it the potential number of jobs.

Economists sometimes call this reasoning the "**lump of labor**" fallacy.[6] It amounts to assuming that at any moment of time there is only so much work to go around. Unfortunately, a lot of people fall victim to this type of faulty reasoning, supporting proposals to cut the workweek in times of recession to "spread the work around" or opposing immigration because immigrants "take away jobs from our own people."[7]

Now back to our main point. Worker preferences have been a very important reason for the secular decline in the workweek. Some of you still might not be convinced, wondering just how much leeway or freedom workers actually have in determining the number of hours per week that they work. The simple fact is that workers have a surprising amount of freedom in determining how many hours to work. We're not saying that a worker can just go up to his or her boss and say something like this: "Mr. Dithers, I think I'd like to put in only 32 hours next week." But remember the following:

- The labor force also includes people who are self-employed, and if you are self-employed you can choose your own hours (generally long hours).
- Although a 35–40 hour workweek might be, in some sense, typical for full-time workers, there are a large number of workers who have longer or shorter working weeks than this. In 2011 about 25% of workers in U.S. nonagricultural industries typically worked more than 40 hours per week, and a similar percentage typically worked fewer than 35 hours per week. In 2010, 38% of working men in the United Kingdom worked fewer than 40 hours per week, while in Japan for the same year the percentage was only 22%. South Koreans seem to work more hours per

---

[6] Paul Krugman, "Lumps of Labor," *New York Times*, October 7, 2003.

[7] This is a particularly objectionable phrase. But the point we're trying to make is not that this sentiment is morally offensive, although it is to us, but rather that the logic behind the reasoning is faulty.

week than workers in many other developed countries, with nearly 60% working 45 hours per week or more as of the year 2007. What all these numbers indicate is that if you have a preference for a nonstandard workweek, there are jobs out there to suit your preference.[8]

- Many people in the labor force have more than one job; that is, they "moonlight."
- Many workers work overtime when the opportunity arises. Granted, not all over-time work is voluntary, but a goodly portion of it is.[9]

In other words, workers do have a considerable number of options and a surprising amount of flexibility in arranging or seeking out work schedules that fit their preferences.

The Theory of Hours of Work for an Individual

Let's now turn to the subject of how economists theorize about the labor supply decisions of individuals. Given that worker preferences play an important role in the determination of work hours, how do we model these preferences?

We laid the foundation for our analysis of the supply of hours decision in the discussion of the theory of labor force participation in Chapter 4. As Figure 5.2 shows, a worker who is faced with a market wage offer of BC will choose to be in the labor force because his utility will be maximized at point D, which depicts a nonzero number (L_1) of hours of work. Remember that the horizontal axis depicts hours of leisure, if we read from left to right, and hours of work, if we read from right to left. At point D the wage line BC is just tangent to the utility isoquant U_3, which means that the wage rate and the marginal rate of substitution of income for leisure are equal.

What would happen to our typical worker if he or she experienced an increase in non-labor income? Figure 5.3 (which is virtually identical to Figure 4.5) shows that he or she would probably prefer to work fewer hours and enjoy more leisure. In other words, L_2 is to the right of L_1. This again is the pure income effect; and just as an increase in nonlabor income was earlier seen to have the effect of lowering the labor force participation rate for a group of individuals, here we see that such an increase would be expected to reduce the number of hours of work offered by an average individual. It is of course possible for G to lie to the left of D, but this would imply that leisure is an inferior good. So long as leisure is a normal good, G must be to the right of D, and an increase in nonlabor income necessarily implies a reduction in preferred working hours.

But what effect would an increase in the wage rate be expected to have on workers' hours preferences? This question gets right to the core of the labor supply question because the labor supply schedule is defined as the relation between wage rates and the

[8] U.S. Department of Labor, Bureau of Labor Statistics, "Labor Force Statistics from the Current Population Survey," Table 19, Annual Averages: Persons at Work in Agriculture and Nonagricultural Industries by Hours of Work, 2011; OECD Labour Force Statistics, 2011, Chart LMF2.1.A, "Distribution of the Working Population by Usual Working Hours per Week, by Gender, 2010"; Susan Fleck, "International Comparisons of Hours Worked: An Assessment of the Statistics," *Monthly Labor Review*, May 2009, pp. 3–30.

[9] The Institute for Workplace Studies, *Overtime and the American Worker* (Ithaca, NY: New York State School of Industrial and Labor Relations, 1999), reports that some 60% of workers work overtime, and of these about 33% are compelled to do so by their employers. So most overtime is voluntary.

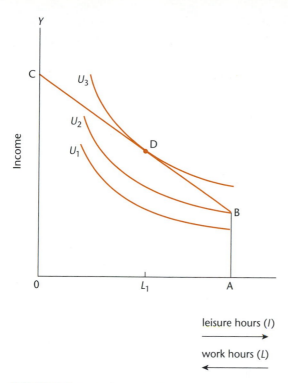

FIGURE 5.2 An Individual Worker's Optimal Number of Work Hours

number of work hours offered. In our analysis of labor force participation rates, we were able to state unequivocally that a rise in wages would cause the labor force participation rate (LFPR) of a group to increase. The higher wage would make leisure more expensive and, according to the substitution effect, lead some persons in the group to substitute work for leisure. However, in the case of hours of work, the effect of an increase in wages on the supply of hours offered is uncertain.

To see why this is so, refer to Figure 5.4. Line BC represents the original wage, and at this wage our utility-maximizing worker would prefer to be at point D on utility isoquant U_1 while offering L_1 hours of work. Now suppose the wage offer rises to line BE. At this higher wage, our worker would now maximize utility at point H on utility isoquant U_2. Notice that point H is associated in this case with L_3 hours of work offered, which represents *fewer* hours of work (and more hours of leisure) than before, not what you might have expected. The increase in the wage from BC to BE carries with it two effects—an income effect and a substitution effect—and these two effects work in the opposite direction to each other in influencing the supply of work hours offered.

Clearly the wage increase has put our worker on a higher utility isoquant (U_2) as he or she moves from initial point D to final point H. But how much of this is due to the change in income per se (the income effect), and how much is due to the fact that leisure has now become relatively more expensive than it was before (the substitution effect)? To examine this, let's consider the worker's position after the wage change. How much

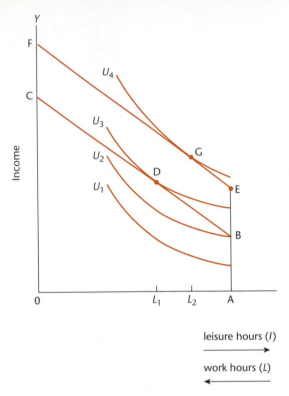

FIGURE 5.3 A Change in Nonlabor Income

income could we take away so that the worker is no worse off than before the wage change? Let's start at point H, along wage line BE, and shift the BE line down toward the origin, parallel to itself, until it is just tangent to indifference curve U_1. Doing this gives us the dotted wage line GF, which is tangent to U_1 at point I. The distance EF (or, equivalently, BG) shows us how much income the wage change has been "worth" to the worker. The horizontal distance between I and H (or, equivalently, the distance between L_2 and L_3) shows how much more leisure the worker now demands owing to this higher level of income. This is what is meant by the income effect. The income effect is positive because leisure is a normal good. As the worker's income effectively rises from GF to BE, the worker demands more leisure and tends to supply fewer labor hours.

So the **income effect** is the horizontal distance between I and H. But what about the substitution effect? The substitution effect can be defined as the effect of a change in the wage rate on work hours, but this time holding the level of income constant.[10] In Figure 5.4, the **substitution effect** is the horizontal distance between I and D (or, equivalently, the distance between L_1 and L_2). At point D, the wage rate is the initial wage (given by the slope of BC), whereas at point I the wage rate is the new higher wage (given by the slope of GF, which is parallel to BE), but at both points D and I the utility

---

[10] Holding the level of income constant here is considered tantamount to keeping utility the same.

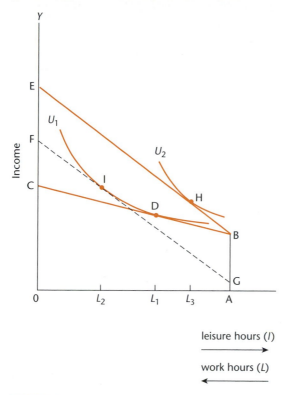

FIGURE 5.4 Situation Where the Income Effect is Larger than the Substitution Effect

level is constant at U_1. So the distance between I and D represents the effect of an increase in the *relative* wage rate (the relative price of leisure) alone on the number of hours preferred. It is clear from the diagram that point I must lie to the left of D; the substitution effect alone therefore implies that more labor will tend to be supplied (and less leisure demanded) as the wage rate increases.

To recap, an increase in the wage rate has two separate effects on a worker's preferred hours of work. The income effect tends to reduce the number of work hours offered (because leisure is a normal good) whereas the substitution effect tends to increase work hours. In Figure 5.4 the income effect (IH) is much larger than the substitution effect (ID), and as a result the net effect of a wage increase on work hours is negative. However, there is no reason to suspect a priori that the income effect will in fact be the larger of the two effects. It is just as plausible that the substitution effect of a wage increase could be larger than the income effect, and that the number of work hours preferred would therefore rise. This is precisely what Figure 5.5 depicts with the income effect (IH) being dwarfed by the substitution effect (ID).

Notice, finally, what our analysis implies about the slope of the supply of labor schedule. If the income effect dominates the substitution effect, the labor supply schedule will be **backward-sloping**, as shown in Figure 5.6b. That is, wage increases will elicit a decrease in hours of work. But if the substitution effect tends to dominate the income effect, the labor supply schedule will be forward-sloping as in Figure 5.6a, and wage increases will lead to an increase in hours of work offered.

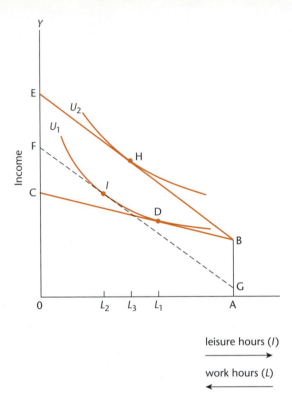

FIGURE 5.5 Situation Where the Income Effect Is
Smaller than the Substitution Effect

When we analyzed the effect of a wage change on the labor force participation decision, we did not separate the effect of the wage change into an income effect and a substitution effect as we have just done in this analysis of the hours decision. There the wage change only brought about a substitution effect. The reason? Remember that the labor force participation decision is a dichotomous decision. By this we mean that a person is either in or not in the labor force. Because of this, a wage increase could not produce an income effect that would result in a person's dropping out of the labor force.

In a somewhat similar situation, that of an increase in the overtime pay premium, a wage change could not produce an income effect that would reduce the hours of work. Workers often receive a premium over their base hourly pay rate for hours worked in excess of 40 hours per week. In the United States this premium is 50% (sometimes called time-and-a-half pay). Suppose a worker is currently working exactly 40 hours per week, and the law (or maybe a union contract) is changed to require two times the base pay rate for overtime (double-time, as some call it). If we were to analyze this worker's possible supply response, we would probably be inclined to say that it would depend on whether the income effect or the substitution effect of the increase in the overtime rate were stronger. If the stronger effect were the substitution effect, the worker would increase his or her hours of work; if the income effect were dominant, the worker would reduce his or her hours. But wait, you may be thinking. If the income effect were stronger than the substitution effect, it would mean that our worker, who had been working 40 hours,

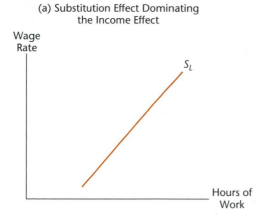

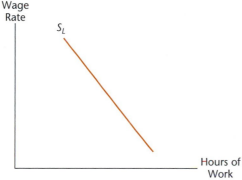

FIGURE 5.6 Labor Supply Schedules

would now reduce his or her hours to less than 40. But at less than 40 hours, the overtime pay provisions do not come into effect. In this situation, therefore, it would be impossible for the income effect of a wage increase to dominate the substitution effect.

Applications of the Theory

Let's return to the data on trends in hours worked. How does the theory of labor supply explain the decrease in work hours over long periods of time? Our explanation should sound very familiar because it echoes our discussion in Chapter 4 of differences in labor force participation rates across demographic groups and countries. Over time there has been a steady rise in both nonlabor income from accumulated wealth and government transfer payments and a rise in real wage rates. The income effect of the rise in the importance of nonlabor income for family budgets is expected to increase the demand for leisure and lower the preferred hours of work. If the income effect of higher real wages dominates the substitution effect, then higher real wages would also lead to a rise in the demand for leisure and a decrease in the preferred hours of work. Labor supply theory suggests that rising real wages and nonlabor income are major determinants of changing work hours preferences.

What about the unusual behavior of working time in the United States over the span of two decades from 1979 to 1999? Although annual hours worked continued to fall in most other developed countries, there was an increase in the average U.S. work year from 1979 to 1999, as Table 5.1 pointed out. Perhaps a good part of the explanation is the fact that the United States was the only major economy to experience falling real wages during that 20-year period. The average hourly wage of manufacturing production workers, adjusted for inflation, fell by 9.4% from 1979 to 1999. In comparison, the same real wage measure rose by 8.3% in Canada, 25.8% in Australia, 28.8% in the United Kingdom, 36.1% in France, and 39.5% in Japan over the same time span.[11] If the income effect of a wage change dominated the substitution effect, this could help explain the rising work year in the United States and the falling work year elsewhere. Of course a number of other factors would need to be taken into account in addition to these wage trends for a complete explanation of recent hours trends in the U.S. economy.

A closer look at a study of labor supply illustrates how economists empirically test the hypotheses derived from theories as well as some empirical information on the supply curve in a given occupational labor market. Let's look at the results reported by Victoria Phillips in her study of the hours of labor supplied by nurses in Great Britain, using data on 403 female nurses.[12] The theory suggests that hours supplied per week (H) would be affected by nonlabor income (Z), the wage rate (w), and factors affecting the individual's utility for work versus leisure, broadly defined to include work in the home (U). For a woman, these utility factors might include the number and age of children in her care as well as personal characteristics, such as age and education.

The hypotheses could be expressed as the following linear equation:

$$H = a + b(Z) + c(w) + d(U) + e \qquad (5\text{-}1)$$

where H, Z, w, and U are the variables defined above; a, b, c, and d are parameters to be estimated by regression techniques; and e is a random error term. This method can be used to test hypotheses by examining the statistical significance of the estimates of the parameters a, b, c, and so on. If an estimated coefficient is statistically significant, this information leads us to reject the null hypothesis of no relationship between H and that variable. Phillips reported the following parameter estimates, with starred (*) coefficients indicating that they are statistically different from zero:

$$H = 39.7^* - 0.076\,(Z)^* + 7.53\,(lnw)^* - 0.15\,(Age)^* - 13.77\,(Wales)^* - 7.45\,(Adv.$$
$$Training)^* - 1.08\,(No.\ of\ children) - 1.50\,(Had\ Mortgage) - 2.04\,(Experience)$$

---

[11] These rates are calculated from data on hourly compensation costs in national currency for manufacturing production workers contained in U.S. Department of Labor, Bureau of Labor Statistics, "International Comparisons of Hourly Compensation Costs for Production Workers in Manufacturing, 1975–2001," Supplementary Tables for BLS News Release USDL 02-549, September 27, 2002.

[12] Victoria L. Phillips, "Nurses' Labor Supply: Participation, Hours of Work, and Discontinuities in the Supply Function," *Journal of Health Economics* 14 (1995): 567–582.

This says that the labor supply of nurses in Britain was negatively related to Z and positively correlated with the natural log of w, which is consistent with the theory of labor supply developed previously. Also older nurses with advanced training living in Wales supplied significantly fewer weekly hours of work than younger nurses without advanced training living in other parts of Great Britain. The remaining variables in Phillips's regression were not statistically significant determinants of the hours of work supplied by these people. The estimate of the coefficient on the wage suggests that the labor supply curve in the market for nurses in Britain in 1980 had a positive slope.[13]

Variations on the Wage Line

So far in our analysis of worker hours preferences, we have implicitly assumed that the hours opportunities open to the worker are unconstrained. That is, by depicting the wage line as linear and continuous, we have in effect said that the worker has the option of choosing as many or as few hours of work per week as he or she wishes. Of course, we know that often this will not be the case. Let's look briefly at a couple of such situations to see how this affects our analysis of labor supply.

First, consider a situation where a worker cannot choose more than a certain number of hours of work because at the moment only part-time employment (e.g., 20 hours per week) is available. In such a case, the wage line would look as depicted in Figure 5.7a with a kink at 20 hours of work. Here the worker would, depending on the shape of the utility isoquant, be able to maximize utility only at 20 or perhaps fewer hours of work. Similarly, if only full-time (40 hours per week) employment were available with the possibility of overtime, the relevant wage line would be like that depicted in Figure 5.7b, with the kink at 40. Although the worker's options are again somewhat constrained, he or she might choose to work at the full-time job, work more than 40 hours per week (by working overtime), or perhaps instead choose not to enter the labor force. This would be the case if, in Figure 5.7b, the highest utility attainable is at zero work hours.

Finally, consider a situation in which we took into account the fact that certain monetary costs are associated with working, such as commuting costs, work clothing, child care costs, and the like. To see what would happen, first ignore all the lines and curves on Figure 5.8 except for utility isoquant U_3 and wage line DE. The situation depicted is that of an individual who has nonlabor income of DA and faces a rather low wage of DE. Because the highest level of utility that this person can attain is U_3, but this occurs only at the zero hours of work point (D), this worker will choose not to be in the labor force. A wage just a little bit higher than that depicted by wage line DE would encourage this person to enter the labor force, however. Remember that we refer to the wage that is just high enough to induce a person to enter the labor force as the reservation wage.

Now suppose that the fixed costs associated with working, such as commuting and child care costs, are equal to DB. Then the wage line for an individual entering the labor force would begin not at point D but rather at point B. Wage line BF has been

---

[13] For reasonable values of the wage and unearned income variables, the substitution effect exceeds the income effect.

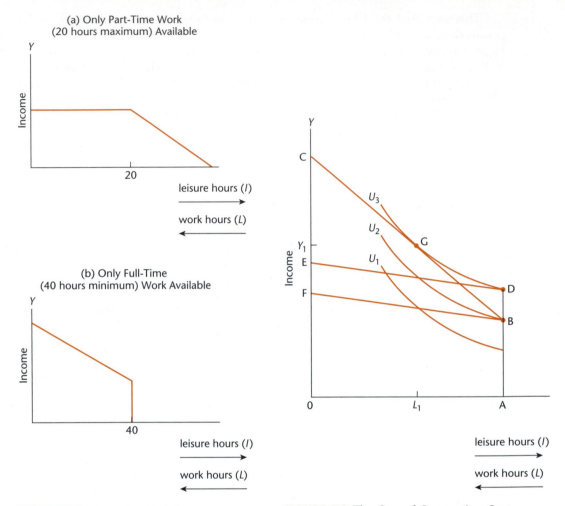

FIGURE 5.7 Wage Line Variations

FIGURE 5.8 The Case of Commuting Costs

drawn parallel to wage line DE to depict this situation. Intuition tells us that if this individual chose not to enter the labor force when there were no fixed costs of working, then he or she would be even less inclined to enter the labor force if there were such costs. And Figure 5.8 certainly confirms our intuition because the highest level of utility now available to this worker would only be U_2. But what wage would induce this person to join the labor force? Begin at point B (the level of nonlabor income net of the fixed costs of working) and rotate wage line BF clockwise about point B until the resulting line is just tangent to utility isoquant U_3. We can see that the resulting wage line BC will be tangent to isoquant U_3 at point G. The slope of wage line BC can therefore be said to be the reservation wage if the fixed costs of working are DB because BC represents the wage that is just high enough to encourage our individual to jump into the labor force. The level of utility if the individual chooses to work L_1 hours and receive an income of Y_1 (point G) is just the same as if the individual decides not to work at all and receives nonlabor income of DA.

THE WAY WE WORK

The Great Hours Debate

Back in the 1990s, an ongoing academic debate spilled over into the popular press about whether Americans were on average working longer hours than they had been a few decades ago. In her book *The Overworked American*,* Juliet Schor claims that there has been a pronounced increase in the effective number of working hours people are putting in. She says that the increase has not shown up in the government statistics on scheduled work hours. But instead Schor cites such arguments as more married women and teenagers at work, employers demanding more time at work, shrinking vacations, the time squeeze at home (bigger houses to keep clean, taking kids to soccer practice, and so forth), and rampant consumerism (the "shop till you drop" syndrome). Schor also claims that capitalism has a built-in tendency toward longer hours at the workplace (remember the quasi-fixed cost reasoning in Chapter 3) and that unions (who in the past had pushed for shorter hours) have declined in strength.

In a later study, *Time for Life*,† John Robinson and Geoffrey Godbey present evidence that is strongly at odds with Schor's thesis. Using information from time diaries, Robinson and Godbey have estimated that Americans by the end of the century had on average five more hours of free time per week than those who lived in the 1960s. The authors claim that Americans seriously overestimate the time they spend at work, both on the job and at home. Where does this extra free time go? Robinson and Godbey argue that virtually all the added leisure time that we have added over the last several decades is being spent in front of the TV. Television viewing now occupies about 40% of our free time, according to Robinson and Godbey. Is it true, then, that America really has become a nation of couch potatoes?

Notes: *Juliet Schor, *The Overworked American* (New York: Basic Books, 1991).
†John Robinson and Geoffrey Godbey, *Time for Life* (University Park, PA: Penn State University Press, 1997).

Welfare Programs and Labor Supply

Now let's apply some of the fundamental concepts we have learned to a hypothetical policy proposal similar to one put forth by the U.S. Congress a number of years ago. To help alleviate the problem of poverty, suppose that a policy is designed that would give every adult person a $4,000 grant. To help pay for the costs of this program, Congress proposes to raise the average rate of taxation from a level of 15% to a level of 20%. For simplicity, let's assume that the tax rate is a "flat" one; that is, the tax rate is constant rather than progressive across all income levels. What effects would this proposal have on labor force participation rates and hours of work? The question is important because we would not want this program to have such adverse effects on people's work efforts that the benefits of poverty alleviation are offset. After all, it's only as a result of people working that income is generated that can be redistributed to the poor!

Suppose that an average individual faces an after-tax market wage rate of AB, as depicted in Figure 5.9. In other words, the slope of line AB is equal to 85% of the market

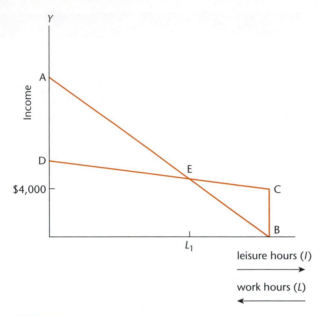

FIGURE 5.9 The Incentive Effects of a Simple Grant Program

wage, the other 15% representing the tax payment. If the grant proposal were passed, however, the worker would receive nonlabor income of $4,000 (BC in Figure 5.9). Also, the worker's after-tax wage would now be only 80% of his or her market wage, as line CD depicts (because the tax rate has risen to fund the $3,000 grant). What kind of effect on the individual's work incentives would result? The answer depends on whether the individual is currently in the labor force and, if so, how many hours of work he or she is putting in.

To explain further, suppose that before enactment of the grant program our hypothetical individual was not in the labor force: that is, the highest level of utility the individual could attain was at point B. Because the grant program will result in nonlabor income rising, the income effect would tend to serve to further discourage labor force participation for groups of people like this. Furthermore, since the post-tax wage rate is lower as a result of the program, the substitution effect will also act as a disincentive to participate in the labor force. In other words, people who were not in the labor force before will have even less incentive to work if the program is enacted. The same reasoning would apply to people who are already working any number of hours less than L_1. (Remember that hours of work, L, are read from right to left here.) For them both the income effect (higher income) and the substitution effect (lower net wage) would encourage people to offer fewer hours of work. Notice that this is true despite the fact that people will be enjoying higher levels of utility, for all points on line segment CE are associated with higher utility levels than all points on line segment BE.

Now this reasoning is correct only up to point E, which we sometimes call the **break-even point**. Any individual at point E will be just as well off—no better and no worse—under the new program as under the old. What levels of earnings and hours of work are represented by point E? The answer can be easily found by solving for Y (earnings income) in the following equation:

$$.85Y_{before} = .80Y_{after} + 4,000 \qquad (5\text{-}2)$$

The result is that the break-even level of income is $80,000. People whose Y and L combinations lay to the right of point E would be subject to work disincentives as we've already seen, but what about people with prior Y and L combinations to the left of point E? First of all, these people would find themselves worse off under the grant program than they were before. Utility levels attainable with line segment DE are clearly lower than U-levels attainable with line segment AE. Furthermore, because the after-tax income of such people is lower, the income effect would encourage them to work more. (Remember, with lower income the demand for leisure falls.) However, just as before, the substitution effect would encourage them to work less (the cost of leisure is lower at lower wage rates). The net effect, with the income and substitution effects of the program working in opposite directions, is unclear. It depends on which effect is stronger, income or substitution.

Some Extensions of the Individual Model

Family Models

We've looked very closely at the theory of individual choice regarding the optimum number of hours of work. Now let's extend the model somewhat to make it more realistic and powerful as an explainer of what's been happening on the hours of work front.

First of all, with most families today having more than one wage earner, it is not always reasonable to assume that an individual's labor supply decision is made independently of others. For example, the decision of a married woman to enter the labor force and the question of how many hours of work to put in will almost certainly depend on the income and hours of work of her husband (and, of course, vice versa). As a result, much recent research on labor supply has focused on the family and on the **household labor supply**, rather than on the individual as the decision-making unit.

One very simple model of the labor supply decision from the focal point of the family has been called the "male chauvinist model." In this model, the husband and the wife each possess a utility function where utility is a function of income and leisure, just as was the case for the individual worker. In her labor supply decision, the wife views her husband's income as a kind of nonlabor income, just as we depicted earlier in Figure 4.5 and Figure 5.3. The husband, meanwhile, regards the wife's earnings as "pin money," which does not enter his utility function at all. In this model, as the husband's earnings rise, the wife will likely choose to offer fewer hours of work to the labor market. And what about the earnings of the wife? What effect would it be likely to have on the labor supply of the husband? Well, none. (Why do you think that this model has been called the male chauvinist model?)

Gary Becker has refined this model by emphasizing the fact that market goods and time are both determinants of the utility we get from activities we undertake.[14] So, for

---

[14] Gary Becker, "A Theory of the Allocation of Time," *Economic Journal* 75 (1965): 493–517.

example, to have a meal we must acquire the ingredients and we must spend time preparing and eating the food. Acquiring the ingredients could mean buying them from a store, but equally it could mean growing them in a garden. The balance between buying the ingredients from a store (using money earned in the labor market) and producing the ingredients within the household is one important decision that the household must make. Another decision concerns the degree to which the food has been prepared. Should the household combine the ingredients itself, or should it buy TV dinners? And finally— here's the key point—the household needs to make a decision about how to allocate the time of the various members of the family, because that allocation of time has implications for the household's consumption possibilities. So household members who are *relatively* efficient at working in the labor market will tend to do more labor market work (and less household production) than others. If you are hopeless at both gardening and cooking, but your partner is good at both, and if you are good at labor market work, but your partner is not, then it is likely that you will spend a lot of time working in the labor market while your partner spends a lot of time engaged in household production. If you and your partner are hopeless at both cooking and gardening, perhaps you will eat out more, especially if your partner is good at labor market activities. Note that this theory implies that a change in the wage paid in the labor market to any member of the household will have an impact on the extent to which *all* members of the household engage in the labor market. This is so because it is the *relative* efficiencies that matter.[15]

Becker's insight led to the development of another model focusing on the family as the labor supply unit. This is the so-called family utility/family budget constraint model.[16] Here the utility to be maximized is *total family utility*, with family utility a function of total family income and total family leisure. This is a very popular method of analyzing labor supply, but it becomes much more complex than the individual labor supply model. For one thing, in the case of a wage change on the part of a family member, there occur *two* substitution effects:

1. an own-wage substitution effect, which can be written as

$$\Delta L_i / \Delta w_i \qquad (5\text{-}3)$$

where i refers to the family member in question (say, the husband)

2. a cross-substitution effect, which can be written as

$$\Delta L_i / \Delta w_j \qquad (5\text{-}4)$$

where j refers to another family member (the wife).

---

[15] No pun is intended. A parallel may usefully be drawn between the allocation of labor market production and household production between members of the family, on the one hand, and the theory of comparative advantage in international trade on the other.

[16] This approach was developed by Marvin Kosters, "Effects of an Income Tax on Labor Supply," in *The Taxation of Income from Capital*, eds., Arnold Harberger and Martin Bailey (Washington, DC: Brookings, 1969). Jane Leuthold, "An Empirical Study of Formula Income Transfers and the Work Decisions of the Poor," *Journal of Human Resources* 3 (1968): 312–323, has extended this model to the case in which the husband and wife have separate utility functions but retain a common budget constraint. A good reference on these models is Mark Killingsworth, "Must a Negative Income Tax Reduce Labor Supply? A Study of the Family's Allocation of Time," *Journal of Human Resources* 11 (1976): 354–365.

Although the sign of the own-wage substitution effect should be positive as expected, the sign of the cross-substitution effect (CSE) could be either positive or negative. How so? Consider the case of a family in which the wife receives a huge promotion with a pay increase so substantial that the husband decides to leave his lesser-paying job to stay home and take care of the kids. In this case the CSE is negative, and the market work of the husband and wife would be considered *substitutes*.

On the other hand, it is also possible to imagine a situation where a wage increase for the wife would encourage not only more work hours on her part (as we would expect) but more work hours on the part of her husband as well. Rather than leave work and go home to an empty house, the husband might simply prefer to stay longer at the office. Here the CSE would be positive, and the labor of the husband and wife would be considered *complements*.

It is important to note that labor supply theory cannot predict whether the CSE will be positive or negative. In other words, it is, as economists like to say, an "empirical question." However, the evidence suggests that the labor supply of prime-age males is on average largely independent of the wage of their spouses. In other words, their CSE tends to be about zero. However, evidence also suggests that the CSE for married women tends to be negative, the result being that an increase in the husband's wage will on average induce the wife to work less.[17] Even so, recent research suggests that married women's labor supply is becoming less responsive to the wages of their husbands than in the past.[18]

At any rate, household or family models often provide a more realistic theory of labor supply than individual models, and that is a clear advantage of using this approach. However, as we have seen, these models are more complex, and that is a clear disadvantage. In some contexts the household models may become too unwieldy to be useful, so it is important for us to study both individual and household decision-making models.

Life-Cycle Model

A second interesting extension of the individual labor supply model is the class of models known as **life-cycle models**. These models extend the analysis over many periods of time in an individual's life. Many people's labor–leisure decisions vary depending on their ages, or the stages of their lives. Figure 5.10a describes a typical inverted U-shaped age–hours profile for males, with weekly hours rising over the early stages of their work lives and then falling later in life.[19]

Life-cycle models of labor supply generally begin with a multiperiod utility function, with lifetime utility (U) a function of consumption of goods and services (C) and leisure (l)

---

[17] See, for example, Dean R. Hyslop, "Rising U.S. Earnings Inequality and Family Labor Supply: The Covariance Structure of Intrafamily Earnings," *American Economic Review* 91 (2001): 755–777.

[18] Francine Blau and Lawrence Kahn, "Changes in the Labor Supply Behavior of Married Women: 1980–2000," *Journal of Labor Economics* 25 (3) (2007): 393–438.

[19] See Mary Coleman and John Pencavel, "Changes in Work Hours of Male Employees, 1940–1988," *Industrial and Labor Relations Review* 46 (1993): 262–283. Coleman and Pencavel examine the relationship between weekly hours and years of work experience rather than age, but the two are very closely correlated for males. Interestingly, they also find that the inverted U-shape has become more pronounced (p. 270).

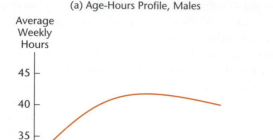

(a) Age-Hours Profile, Males

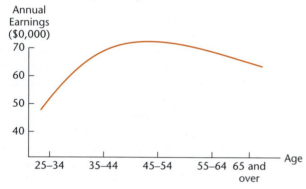

(b) Age-Earnings Profile, Males, 2009

FIGURE 5.10 Age–Hours and Age–Earnings Profiles for Men (Year-Round, Full-Time Workers)

Source: (b) U.S. Department of Commerce, *Statistical Abstract of the United States, 2012*, Table 703, p. 459.

at every period t (e.g., a year) of a person's expected life (N periods). Such a utility function could be written as:

$$U_{\text{lifetime}} = \sum_{t=0}^{N} [U_t(C_t, l_t)/(1 + R)^t] \tag{5-5}$$

This equation simply says that in each period individuals get utility (U) from consumption (C) and from leisure (l). The R term represents the rate of time preference or the rate at which an individual prefers present consumption over future consumption. It can also be called an individual's implicit rate of interest. If R is large, an individual strongly prefers present consumption or leisure over that in the future and vice versa. To go along with the multiperiod utility function, an individual could also be considered to possess a multiperiod budget constraint, which might be formulated as follows:

$$\sum_{t=0}^{N} [(w_t L_t - C_t)/(1 + r)^t] = 0 \tag{5-6}$$

Although the budget constraint formula seems complicated, the intuition is simple. In each period an individual can choose to work and earn income of wL (wage times hours of work), and out of this he or she can then choose to spend (consume) a certain amount C. What is not spent in any period will be carried over (saved) for a future period.[20] Earlier in our single-period model, we assumed that an individual desired the combination of income and leisure that would maximize utility subject to his or her budget constraint. In this multiperiod model, we are assuming the same thing: that is, an individual seeks to maximize *lifetime utility* subject to a *lifetime* budget constraint. But unlike in the single period model, we can see that lifetime utility maximization might result in different combinations of work and leisure at different stages of people's lives, just as Figure 5.10a shows.

Why might people choose to supply different amounts of labor at different stages of their lives? There are many individual reasons, of course, among them health; the presence of children; or the desire to buy a home, a new car, and so on. But to help explain the regularly observed inverted U-shaped age–hours profile, let's look at Figure 5.10b, which depicts the age-earnings profile. As the figure shows, there is a not surprising tendency for earnings to rise with age, reach a peak, and then perhaps decline as a person nears retirement age, much like the age–hours profile. What does the age–earnings profile tell us about how labor supply varies with age?

As an individual moves up the age–earnings profile, accumulating experience, raises, and promotions, according to the *substitution effect* we would expect that the person would tend to supply more hours of work. Leisure, again, is more expensive if a person's wages are higher. There's nothing new here. But what about the *income effect*, which, as we saw earlier, would tend to cause a reduction in that individual's hours of work if his or her wages were to rise? Here is where the life-cycle model's predictions differ from those of the single-period model.

To explain, we must introduce the concept of **permanent income**, or the expected *lifetime* income or wealth of the individual. Most people expect that their incomes will rise over time. They certainly expect it, for example, when buying a house whose monthly payments might be a little expensive for them at the moment but that will become progressively easier later on. In other words, people often gear their consumption and labor supply decisions not to what their incomes happen to be *at the moment* but rather to what they expect the course of their incomes to be *over time*. But if this is the case, then increases in wages over time would not carry with them an income effect. That is, the person's permanent income has not gone up because it was already "expected" or anticipated. From a life-cycle point of view, this means that the supply of labor should be forward sloping rather than backward bending because of the dominance of the substitution effect. The only type of situation where a wage increase would produce an income effect that might reduce the number of hours of work is if the wage increase is *unanticipated*.

---

[20] In the multiperiod budget constraint, future income is discounted by the market interest rate r, just as in the multiperiod utility function we discounted future utility by the individual's implicit rate of time preference R.

We have seen that labor supply models can vary in several ways, by focusing on the individual or on the family or by analyzing a single period or the life cycle. However, although these models can tell us much about what we would *expect* the shapes and elasticities of labor supply schedules to be, only empirical evidence can tell us for sure. And it is to such evidence that we now turn.

Empirical Evidence on Labor Supply Elasticities

What evidence do we have on the shape of labor supply schedules in the long run for groups of individuals? We've seen how weekly hours of work have fallen substantially over the last 100 to 150 years, a period that has also witnessed tremendous growth in the real wages of workers. Because only limited credit for this reduction in hours can be given to unions and government legislation, does this inverse correlation between hours of work and wages argue for a backward-bending, long-run aggregate labor supply schedule? The answer is … maybe. The reason the negative long-term association between work hours and wages is not indisputable proof of a backward-bending supply schedule is that this ignores other factors, such as the growth in nonlabor income (pensions, income of working spouses, and so forth). It also ignores demand considerations, although we have seen that the presence of fixed costs of employment would be expected generally to cause employers to prefer longer work schedules.

Recent decades have also seen an impressive body of empirical evidence put forth by labor economists dealing with labor supply elasticities. For example, Dora Costa has estimated that the wage elasticity of hours worked for all male workers in the 1890s was about −0.12, in 1973 about −0.08, and in 1991 about 0.04. Clearly the elasticity of supply has been very low—highly inelastic—over this 100-year period.[21] Table 5.2 summarizes the results of about two dozen such studies as reported by Mark Killingsworth in his survey of the labor supply literature.[22] As can be seen from the table, the estimated own-wage elasticities of labor supply differ for men and women. For men, the elasticity seems to be negative but very small, indicative of a backward-sloping schedule with the income effect exceeding (but only barely so) the substitution effect. For women, however, the average own-wage elasticity is positive and somewhat greater than unity, hinting at a forward-sloping labor supply schedule. It should be stressed that the figures in the table are averages, however, and that there is considerable variation in the results across the different studies as the rather large standard deviations (especially for women) show.

A more recent summary of several dozen studies by Blundell and MacCurdy indicates that the average wage elasticity of supply estimate for men was slightly positive but at 0.08 still extremely small, while for married women the average elasticity estimate was

---

[21] Dora Costa, "The Wage and the Length of the Work Day: From the 1890s to 1991," *Journal of Labor Economics* 18 (1) (2000): 156–181.

[22] Mark Killingsworth, *Labor Supply* (Cambridge: Cambridge University Press, 1983).

TABLE 5.2   Estimates of Labor Supply Wage Elasticity

	Men		
	Own-Wage Elasticity	*Substitution Effect*	*Income Effect*
Mean	−.10	.26	−.36
Median	−.07	.19	−.28
Standard Deviation	.15	.30	.29
	Women		
Mean	1.30	1.42	−.13
Median	.47	.56	−.11
Standard Deviation	2.80	2.80	.16

Source: Mark Killingsworth, *Labor Supply* (Cambridge: Cambridge University Press, 1983), Table 4.3. Results for men are averages from 11 different studies summarized by Killingsworth; the results for women are averages from 21 studies.

much larger at 0.69.[23] And still more recent evidence by Blau and Kahn have tended to confirm the finding that married women's labor supply tends to be much more responsive to changes in their wages than does men's labor supply.[24]

Why should it be that the slopes and the elasticities of the supply schedules for men and women differ? One very plausible explanation attributed to Jacob Mincer and Glen Cain[25] argues that women have traditionally had more choices in how to allocate their time than have men. For women the choices involve how much time to devote to market work, home work (child care, housework, and so forth), and leisure. For men, however, the traditional choice set has included only market work and leisure. Even today with more and more married women participating in labor force activity, men tend to devote only about 10–12 hours per week to household services compared to women's 30–40 hours.[26] Why should this make a difference in the shapes of the labor supply schedules? Well, in general the strength of the substitution effect should depend on the number of substitutes there are for one's time. Because women on average have more substitutes than men,

---

[23] "Labor Supply: A Review of Alternative Approaches," in *Handbook of Labor Economics*, vol. 3A, eds., Orley Ashenfelter and David Card (Amsterdam: Elsevier, 1999). The average estimates are calculated from Tables 1 and 2, pp. 1646–51.

[24] Francine Blau and Lawrence Kahn, "Changes in the Labor Supply Behavior of Married Women: 1980–2000," *Journal of Labor Economics* 25 (3) (2007): 393–438. For two recent studies of labor supply elasticities for particular occupational groups, see also Colin Camerer, "Labor Supply of New York City Cabdrivers: One Day at a Time," *Quarterly Journal of Economics* (May 1997): 407–441; and Gerald Oettinger, "An Empirical Analysis of the Daily Labor Supply of Stadium Vendors," *Journal of Political Economy* 107 (2) (April 1999): 360–392.

[25] Jacob Mincer, "Labor Force Participation of Married Women," in *Aspects of Labor Economics*, ed. National Bureau of Economic Research (Princeton, NJ: Princeton University Press, 1962); Glen Cain, *Married Women in the Labor Force* (Chicago: University of Chicago Press, 1966).

[26] See John Douglass, Genevieve Kenney, and Ted Miller, "Which Measures of Household Production Are Best?" *Journal of Forensic Economics* 4 (1990): 25–45.

it is not surprising that the substitution effect of a wage increase should be stronger for women. Column 3 of Table 5.2 shows just how large the substitution effect tends to be for women; it is sufficient to offset the relatively small income effect and produce a positively sloped supply schedule.

Summary

In Chapters 4 and 5 we have examined both the theory and the evidence relating to labor supply from the focal points of labor force participation and hours of work. In particular, we have investigated the determinants of individuals' labor market participation decisions and looked at the influences on the labor market participation rate for various groups, including youths (who face a trade-off between participation and education), older workers (who face a trade-off between participation and retirement), and women (many of whom face a trade-off between participation and household production). Hours of work have declined steadily in most countries over the last century, but the decline has been less pronounced in the United States.

Our exploration of the determinants of individuals' choices of hours of work noted the possibility that, in the long run, the aggregate supply of hours to the labor market can be backward bending. This might well explain the decline in hours worked as remuneration has increased in many countries. However, in the short run, the aggregate supply of hours must rise as the wage increases (recall the empirical evidence on nurses).

Our analysis is affected if people cannot choose their working hours; but at the same time we have observed numerous ways in which people can control the length of their working week (by taking on overtime or second jobs or by choosing to work part time). We also adjusted our theory to take into account what happens when labor supply decisions are made in the context of families. Empirical estimates of labor supply elasticities are generally consistent with the predictions of our basic theory of labor supply.

As yet, however, we have not considered the quality dimension of labor supply. Nor have we discussed how labor supply is related to training and education. Both of these questions are closely connected to what economists call investment in human capital, the subject of Chapter 6.

KEY TERMS

demand for leisure

"lump of labor" fallacy

income effect

substitution effect

backward-sloping supply of labor

break-even point

household labor supply

labor supply elasticity

life-cycle models

permanent income

PROBLEMS

1. Do you think it is possible in the short run for the total quantity of labor supplied to a labor market to fall as market wages rise? Explain.

2. Suppose that the government is considering imposing one of two types of taxes: (a) a per capita tax of a certain dollar amount, which reduces nonlabor income, or (b) a proportional (fixed rate) tax (t) on earnings, where the tax paid equals ($t \cdot w$). The government is worried, however, that people may work less in response to the tax that is imposed. Which of the two taxes—per capita or proportional—is more likely to lead a person in the labor force to supply less time to the labor market—that is, to work less? Explain carefully and depict graphically.

3. Suppose that a person has the following (multiplicative) utility function: $u = y \cdot l$. As in this chapter, y is income and l is leisure. Find the utility maximizing number of hours worked per day (L) in each of the following situations:
   a. The hourly wage (w) = 1
   b. The hourly wage (w) = 2
   c. The hourly wage (w) = 3
   Assume that all hours are spent either working or at leisure (that is, $l + L = 24$).

4. In her article "The Wage and the Length of the Work Day: From the 1890s to 1991" (*Journal of Labor Economics*, 2000), Dora Costa discovered a remarkable change over the past 100 years in the relationship between the wage and the length of the work day for highly-paid groups vs. those of low-paid groups. In the 1890s the most highly paid workers worked fewer hours than the lowest-paid workers. But 100 years later, the reverse was true—highly paid workers now work longer hours than the lowest paid workers.
   a. What does this imply about the elasticity of labor supply back in the 1890s vs. 100 years later?
   b. One of the complaints of the protest movements that took place in New York (Occupy Wall Street) and in many other cities in the years 2011 and 2012 was that income inequality in the United States was much too large. How could you use Dora Costa's finding about the length of the workday to shed light on the question of just how large the degree of income inequality actually is?

5. Can the two different conclusions in the U.S. "great hours debate" be reconciled? In other words, do you think people have more or less leisure time today? (You might wish to ask your parents and grandparents for their perspective.) Could Americans have more leisure time while working more hours per year than Norwegians?

Human Capital Analysis

Why do economists look at the decision to spend a year in school as equivalent to a capital investment?

What are the private and social returns to investment in education?

What is the difference between general and specific human capital?

In our discussion of labor supply so far, most of our attention has been focused on the effect of current wages on worker labor supply decisions. But many times such decisions involve a substantial initial "investment" on the part of the worker before the stream of earnings begins. This investment might involve the time and money costs of going to college, undergoing a period of training, or learning a trade. For these types of labor supply decisions, both *current* wages and expected *future* wages are important factors. These considerations give our analysis of labor supply a long-run focal point, and to the extent that education and training also improve the productivity of labor, we have added a quality dimension as well.

What is human capital? **Human capital** is the stock of knowledge, skills, aptitudes, education, and training that an individual or a group of individuals possess. Just as with physical capital, acquiring human capital is costly. (Think how much it is costing you to attend college in terms of tuition and time—including the loss of earnings that you would have made had you used that time differently.) Just as with physical capital, investment in human capital can generate returns in the form of higher future earnings. Unlike the case with physical capital, however, ownership of human capital cannot generally be transferred.

Some Background

Before we launch into a formal analysis, let's take a quick look at how the modern analysis of human capital began and just how important human capital is to an individual and to a nation. In the 1950s and 1960s Simon Kuznets and a number of other economists began to study the determinants of the growth of gross national product (GNP). They observed that there were great differences in GNP growth rates across nations, and they wondered why some economies grew more quickly than others. Was the abundance of natural resources the most important factor? Was investment in physical capital the key to rapid growth? Perhaps it was the quality of a nation's labor force, or was it something else?

To help answer these questions, many of these "growth accountant" economists began with a simple model of the macro economy such as the **Cobb-Douglas aggregate production function** (see the appendix in Chapter 3), which assumes that output (Q), which is GNP in this case, is related to the amount of capital (K) and labor (L) inputs according to the following functional relationship:

$$Q = AL^{\alpha}K^{\beta} \tag{6-1}$$

The term A is a multiplicative factor, and α and β are output elasticities for labor and capital, respectively. In other words, α represents the percentage change in GNP given a 1% change in the nation's labor force (L). By converting each of the terms in the Cobb-Douglas function to natural logarithms, equation 6-1 can be rewritten as follows:

$$\ln Q = \ln A + \alpha \ln L + \beta \ln K \tag{6-2}$$

What's the advantage of such a transformation? Remember from Chapter 3 that a change in a natural logarithm of a value is approximately equal to a percentage change in that value. Therefore, equation 6-2 could be equivalently expressed as:

$$\Delta Q/Q = \Delta A/A + \alpha \Delta L/L + \beta \Delta K/K \tag{6-3}$$

In other words, with information on the growth rates of GNP, the labor force, and the capital stock, along with independent estimates of the values of the output elasticities α and β (thought to be about 0.75 and 0.25, respectively), we ought to be able to measure the relative contributions of labor and capital to GNP growth. However, only about half of the growth in the GNP of the United States can be explained in this way. The unexplained residual, represented by changes over time in the A term, was thought to reflect the influences of technological change as well as changes in the quality (called "vintages") of labor and capital. Robert Solow, Edward Denison, John Kendrick, and other growth economists then tried to estimate the separate contributions of these other influences, and Solow later won the Nobel Prize for his efforts. But what is important for our purposes is simply this. Anyone, not just economists and students of economics, would guess that the attainment of higher levels of GNP and higher living standards is influenced not just by quantities of labor and capital but also by their quality. Otherwise, the relative contribution to GNP of a busker (a street corner musician), a trash collector, a car plant operative, a nuclear scientist, a professional economist, and the president of the United States all would be the same! (Notice we have not said whose contribution really is more important. We'll leave that to you.[1]) Before the research of these growth economists, few recognized the overwhelming importance of the quality of a nation's human capital stock to GNP. For example, Denison has estimated that education was the source of 30% of the growth of output per person in the United States from 1929 to 1982.[2] Another way of putting this

---

[1] See David Colander, *Why Aren't Economists as Important as Garbagemen?* (Armonk, NY: M. E. Sharpe, Inc., 1991).

[2] Edward Denison, *Trends in American Economic Growth, 1929–1982* (Washington, DC: Brookings, 1985), p. 15.

is that if individuals in the 1980s had on an average the same amount of education as their grandparents, their standard of living would have been about 30% lower.

To make the point in yet another way, the World Bank devised a new system for valuing the wealth of nations, including the value of natural resources, physical capital, and human capital.[3] In its listing of the wealth of 92 countries, the United States came in at first place, with a per capita wealth of $401,000. How much of this wealth is comprised of natural and physical capital? Only 23% is; the remaining 77% represents human capital. The same pattern holds for many other countries. For instance, in both Canada and Australia human capital accounts for 66% of all wealth, and in the United Kingdom it accounts for a massive 79%. The same is not true, however, of many of the world's poorest countries. The country with the lowest wealth level in the study is Rwanda, where wealth amounts to just $5,000 per capita. Of this, only 39% is attributable to human capital. It is no exaggeration to suggest that education represents a major source of the difference in incomes and wealth across countries. Most of the world's wealth is "locked up," so to speak, in human beings.

These surprising numbers indicate how enormously important human capital is as a component of the wealth of an individual or of a nation. It also explains why some countries have been able to recover so quickly after a major war even though a huge amount of their physical capital was destroyed. The recovery experiences of Japan and Germany after World War II are both good examples.

As you can see, our analysis of labor supply, which so far has consisted of looking at the decision to participate or not participate in the work force and how many hours of work to offer, has not gone far enough. It has ignored the activity of individuals who, like many readers of this book, are not at work and not quite at leisure either. Rather, you are investing time and money to secure an education. One reason for your investment of time and money is so that you will be able to supply future work activity that will be of higher quality and that will enable you to generate higher earnings than you otherwise would.

In this chapter we first look at how earnings vary over the life cycle, both for educated workers and for those with less education. Then we examine the ways of measuring the net payoffs to training using the net present value (NPV) approach and the internal rate of return (IRR) approach. We also examine a further approach known as the earnings function approach to evaluating investments in training. Next we examine what the evidence on net present values and rates of return for different levels of education looks like. In other words, does it "pay" to attend college, and if so, how much? Also, who should pay for different types of human capital acquisition? Should it be firms, individuals, or the government? Finally, we discuss the accuracy of the estimates we have of the impact of education on earnings. There may be some sources of bias in our estimates. In particular, it's important to recognize that, while human capital analysis has helped us understand a lot of issues in labor market analysis, it is not the only game in town—there are other explanations for many of the phenomena that we shall be exploring in the pages that follow. We'll finish the chapter by exploring these alternative explanations, and by investigating how serious the resultant biases can be.

---

[3] Arundhati Kunte, Kirk Hamilton, John Dixon, and Michael Clemens, *Estimating National Wealth: Methodology and Results* (Washington, DC: World Bank, 1998). See also Peter Passel, "The Wealth of Nations: A 'Greener' Approach Turns List Upside Down," *New York Times*, September 19, 1995, Section C, p. 1.

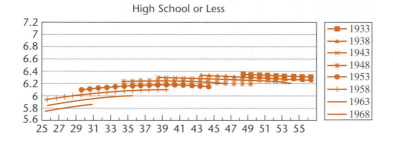

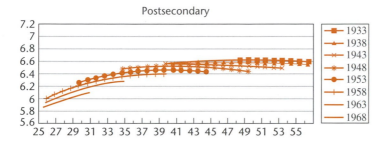

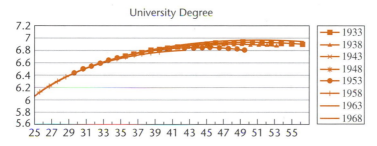

FIGURE 6.1 Dynamic Age-Earnings Profiles, Males, USA

Source: James E. McDonald and Christopher Worswick, "Earnings and Employment Probabilities of Men by Education and Birth Cohort, 1982–96: Evidence for the United States, Canada and Australia," mimeo, Carleton University, 2000.

Education and Age-Earnings Profiles

To get an idea of the relationship between age, years of education, and earnings, let's begin by looking at some dynamic **age-earnings profiles**,[4] which show how earnings vary over the life cycle for workers who have different levels of educational attainment. We have provided data for three countries: the United States (Figure 6.1), Canada (Figure 6.2), and Australia (Figure 6.3).

It is important to understand just how these graphs have been put together. One way of drawing an age-earnings profile is to look at a cross section of individuals of different

---

[4] James E. McDonald and Christopher Worswick, "Earnings and Employment Probabilities of Men by Education and Birth Cohort, 1982–96: Evidence for the United States, Canada and Australia," mimeo, Carleton University, 2000.

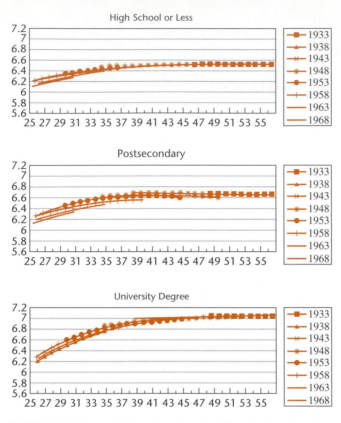

FIGURE 6.2 Dynamic Age-Earnings Profiles, Males, Canada

Source: James E. McDonald and Christopher Worswick, "Earnings and Employment Probabilities of Men by Education and Birth Cohort, 1982–96: Evidence for the United States, Canada and Australia," mimeo, Carleton University, 2000.

ages at a single point in time. This allows us to see how earnings vary with age, but it is also potentially misleading. Any differences in remuneration earned by people of different ages could be due to either of two things: a genuine age effect or an effect (a "cohort effect") attributable to unobserved differences over time (for instance, in the quality of their education).

To overcome this problem, the dynamic age-earnings profiles in these figures plot the age-earnings relationship separately for different cohorts of workers, showing the way in which earnings vary with age separately for men who were born in the early 1930s, the late 1930s, the early 1940s, and so on through the late 1960s. Using three graphs for each country, we can separate workers who entered the labor market straight from high school from those with some postsecondary education and from those with a university degree.

Several features stand out. Let's look at the United States first (see Figure 6.1). For workers without a university degree, earnings of a typical worker peak around age 40 and then decline a little. This is the characteristic inverted-U shape of the age-earnings profile. For workers with a university degree, earnings rise steeply up to age 40 and then flatten out. So for all workers, earnings initially rise but later stagnate or decline.

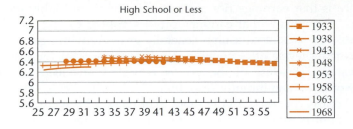

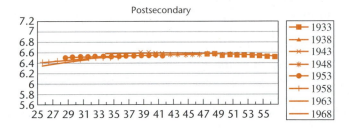

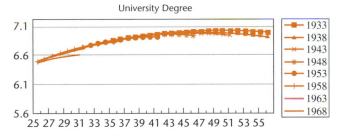

FIGURE 6.3 Dynamic Age-Earnings Profiles, Males, Australia

Source: James E. McDonald and Christopher Worswick, "Earnings and Employment Probabilities of Men by Education and Birth Cohort, 1982–96: Evidence for the United States, Canada and Australia," mimeo, Carleton University, 2000.

Why does the age-earnings profile reach a peak and then decline? In other words, why do younger cohorts of workers eventually overtake older workers with respect to earnings? There are several reasons for this phenomenon. First, working time tends to fall as workers become older. On average, older workers work fewer hours per week and fewer weeks of the year. Workers' skills also depreciate in value as workers age. Why don't workers continue to invest in training to keep their skills from depreciating in value and perhaps even becoming obsolete? The answer to that is that it doesn't pay to continue to invest in training because there is a shorter remaining work life to amortize the investment costs.[5] Finally, as people age, their health tends to become poorer. Some work less, and others drop out of the labor force entirely.

[5] Yoram Ben-Porath, "The Production of Human Capital and the Life Cycle of Earnings," *Journal of Political Economy* 75 (1967): 352–365.

The next thing to notice is that earnings rise more steeply for more highly educated individuals than for others. This means that earnings profiles appear to "fan out," with the distance between successive levels of education generally growing with age.

Finally, look at the changing levels of remuneration across cohorts for those workers with relatively little education. The fate of the poorly educated unskilled worker in developed countries has worsened significantly over time. In the late 1950s, 25-year-old workers who were highly educated earned a little more than those who were not. Today a substantial earnings premium is attached to education, not only later in the life cycle but as soon as one leaves college. This is most easily seen in the left-hand side of the top panel where the lines fan out with the most recent cohorts appearing at the bottom.

Two theories have been put forward to explain the worsening labor market conditions faced by the unskilled: globalization and skill-biased technical change. The globalization hypothesis suggests that increased international trade has resulted in greater competition for the producers of tradeable goods; thus the fact that clothing can be produced in emerging economies where wages are low puts downward pressure on the wages of workers in the clothing industry in developed economies. Skill-biased technical change implies that recent changes in technology (especially computing) have increased the productivity (and remuneration) of relatively well-paid skilled workers more than these changes have increased the productivity of workers with lower skill levels.

The graphs for Canada look fairly similar to those for the United States (see Figure 6.2), but the picture is very different in Australia where the age-earnings profiles for less educated workers are almost perfectly flat (see Figure 6.3). This reflects the relatively equal distribution of income in Australia. Yet even in Australia the earnings profile for university graduates rises sharply with age, so here, too, the profiles fan out across education categories.

These data refer only to men; women's age-earnings profiles are much flatter. Why the gender difference? One reason, of course, is that women are more likely than men to leave the work force, especially for the purpose of having children. Thus the average woman tends to have less experience and less seniority than the average man, and both of these factors are associated with higher earnings. Moreover, if women expect to leave the work force more often than men, it can shape their preferences for certain types of work. Jobs that allow relatively easy entry to and exit from the labor force without serious depreciation of skills and jobs where hours of work fit in well with family commitments (such as elementary school teaching) may be more attractive to many women. Finally, labor market discrimination may also explain differences in the gender age-earnings profiles, and we have much more to say about this in Chapter 13.

Clearly there is a relationship between age and earnings. Why might this be so? One person should not be expected to be more productive than another simply by virtue of being older, but it is reasonable to suggest that experience makes workers more productive. As a result of working on a particular set of tasks over a long period, workers discover for themselves the tricks of the trade. In some fields, it may take many years for workers to achieve their full potential. For instance, an economic researcher learns many skills while at university. But it is practice that makes perfect, and it may be decades after graduation before a researcher produces his or her best work.

The empirical estimation of an earnings-experience relationship is not straightforward, however, and data for labor market experience are not always easily obtained. To analyze data sets in which information on actual labor market experience is not available, two

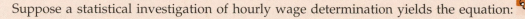

PUTTING THEORY TO WORK

THE AGE-EARNINGS CURVE AGAIN

Suppose a statistical investigation of hourly wage determination yields the equation:

$$\ln \text{wage} = -0.214 + 0.059 \times \text{age} - 0.00067 \times \text{age}^2 + 0.098 \times \text{years of schooling}$$

How can we plot this on a graph? First, suppose that years of schooling equals 10. For various ages, we can calculate the expected value of the log wage as $0.766 + 0.059 \times \text{age} - 0.00067 \times \text{age}^2$. The antilog of this will tell us what the wage is expected to be. So for a 25-year-old, the expected wage is \$6.19. For a 40-year-old, the expected wage is \$7.80, and the corresponding figure for a 60-year-old is \$6.65.

We can plot these figures on a graph and join them with a curve. If we increase schooling to 15 years, the whole curve shifts up vertically parallel to itself.

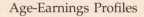

Age-Earnings Profiles

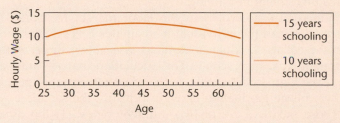

How can we calculate the age at which the curve peaks? One way to do this is by inspecting the curve; in the current diagram earnings peak somewhere in the mid-40s. We can pinpoint this with greater accuracy using a little calculus. If we differentiate the wage equation with respect to age and set the result equal to zero (so that we are looking for the point where the slope of the curve is zero) we get

$$\partial(\ln \text{wage})/\partial(\text{age}) = 0.059 - 0.00134 \times \text{age} = 0$$

This implies that $0.00134 \times \text{age} = 0.059$, and so the age at which the earnings function is flat is 44.03.

This age-earnings relationship is very similar to those in Figure 6.1 through Figure 6.3. The inverted U-shape of the function results from the inclusion on the right-hand side of the regression equation of linear and quadratic terms in age. Kevin Murphy and Finis Welch have argued that cubic and quartic terms should be included too. Most studies find that the quadratic specification approximates the data well enough.

Source: Kevin M. Murphy and Finis Welch, "Empirical Age-Earnings Profiles," *Journal of Labor Economics* 8 (1990): 202–229.

approaches have been used. The first approach involves the calculation of *potential* experience. This is done by subtracting from the respondent's age the age at which the respondent left full-time education. This approach is somewhat crude, especially in the case of women who may have experienced time out of the labor market to raise children. The second approach calculates *imputed* experience; for women this involves making a further deduction from the estimate of labor market experience based on the number of children the respondent has borne.[6]

In the next section, we discuss how the returns to education can be estimated using real world data. As you will see, the relationship between earnings and both schooling and experience is fundamental to the evaluation of the benefits of education.

Calculating the Returns to Education

Let's begin by considering the various ways of measuring the value of human capital investments in education. Suppose an 18-year-old is considering starting four years of college but wonders whether this will most likely pay off for him or her. (We could just as easily use as examples a person thinking about "investing" in an MBA degree program, an apprenticeship training program, or any other type of training investment.) The individual sees a stream of potential earnings ahead (see Figure 6.4), along with costs should he or she choose to undertake this investment in training.

Figure 6.4 shows that an individual who works in the labor market from age 18 onward starts to earn four years earlier than the individual who attends college.[7] But soon after entering the labor market, the college graduate's earnings rise above those of the individual who entered work straight from high school. The calculation that we must all do, implicitly at least, when we leave high school is this: Is the gross return we expect to make from enhanced salaries after college graduation enough to justify the sacrifices we must make to go to college?[8] Those sacrifices are of two different types: (1) the direct costs of tuition and purchase of books and other materials and (2) foregone earnings (opportunity costs). Weighing the costs of prolonged education against the benefits is not easy because the costs and benefits occur at different times. It is therefore necessary to find a way of comparing sums of money that are enjoyed in the future with costs that are incurred now. Much of the rest of this chapter is about just that.

There are two nearly equivalent approaches to calculating the return or the worth of such an investment: the net present value approach and the internal rate of return approach. We will look briefly at each one. Then we discuss the earnings function approach.

The Net Present Value Approach

First, let's examine the **net present value** approach. To compute the present or discounted value of the earnings stream associated with a college education, we take the earnings expected at each year of an individual's working life, adjust it by an appropriate discount

---

[6] Antonio Zabalza and Jose Luis Arrufat, "The Extent of Sex Discrimination in Great Britain," in *Women and Equal Pay: The Effects of Legislation on Female Employment and Wages in Britain*, eds., Antonio Zabalza and Zafiris Tzannatos (Cambridge: Cambridge University Press, 1983).

[7] We realize that many college students have part-time jobs. But let's keep things simple.

[8] We say "sacrifices," but actually student life is quite pleasant!

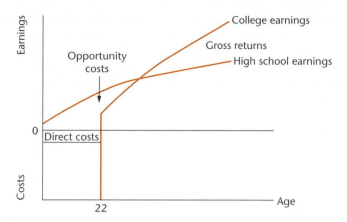

FIGURE 6.4 Paths of Costs and Returns to General Training and Education

factor, and then sum all of the resulting discounted earnings. The associated formula, familiar to anyone who has calculated a present value, can be written as follows:

$$PV = \sum_{t=18}^{n} \frac{Y_t}{(1+r)^{t-18}}$$ (6-4)

Here PV stands for the present value of the earnings stream, t is the individual's age, n is the expected age at retirement, Y is the earnings expected at each year t, and r is the rate of interest or discount rate.[9] What is the appropriate value of r to use? The discount rate r should represent the rate of interest or the opportunity cost of capital. If you happen to have the funds to pay for college, r would be the interest rate you could have earned on these funds if they were invested in an opportunity of equivalent risk.

A natural question to ask at this stage is how can we estimate the earnings expected at each year into the future? This is not an easy question to answer. It involves making best guesses. The most commonly used method is to look at what people of different ages and with different levels of education currently earn, and then to average (or "smooth") those data. So it is assumed that the life-cycle earnings of an individual who entered the labor market directly from high school will look much the same over the life cycle as the average experience of other workers (of various ages) who likewise ended their education at high school. Of course, this is only a guess; it is entirely possible that the demand for high school graduates will rise or fall in the future, and this would lead to an increase or decrease in the rate of return. But the point is that the best that anyone can do when making decisions about whether to invest in their own human capital is to make a realistic guess at what the future will hold. That being so, it seems reasonable to use smoothed experience-earnings profiles for each education level as a guide.

---

[9] For those unfamiliar with discounting, the discounted or present value of a future amount is merely the worth today of some amount payable in the future. For example, if the interest rate were 6%, then the present value of $100 payable one year from now would be equal to $100/(1.06) or $94.34. This is the amount that, if invested at 6% interest, would just equal $100 in one year. Similarly, the present value of $100 payable two years from now would be $100/(1.06)^2 or $89.00.

What about the direct costs of attending college, such as tuition and fees? These can be entered into equation 6-4 as negative income through the college years. (Don't include the indirect costs of college such as the earnings you would have made had you gone to work after high school rather than gone on to college. You'll see why in a minute.)

Putting it all together, we can calculate the present value of the expected lifetime earnings of a college graduate using equation 6-4. Is a college education a worthwhile investment? If the present value of the discounted earnings stream of a college graduate exceeds the present value of the earnings stream of a high school graduate, then the college education investment is indeed a good one. A perfectly equivalent way of putting this is if the difference between the two present values (the net present value) is positive, as equation 6-5 states,[10]

$$\text{Net } PV = \sum_{t=18}^{n} \frac{(Y_t^c - Y_t^{hs})}{(1+r)^{t-18}} \tag{6-5}$$

where Y_t^c and Y_t^{hs} denote the income expected in time t for an individual educated to college level and to high school level, respectively.

The Internal Rate of Return Approach

The second method, the **internal rate of return** approach, is used much more frequently by economists than the net present value approach in estimating the worth of investments in training. Using the same symbols as those in equations 6-4 and 6-5, let us first consider the total costs (C) of attending college, including both direct costs (tuition, fees, and so forth) and indirect or opportunity costs (earnings forgone). We can express the present value of these costs over one's working life as:

$$PV_{\text{costs}} = \sum_{t=18}^{n} \frac{C_t}{(1+r)^{t-18}} \tag{6-6}$$

Similarly, let's tally the present value of returns associated with going to college—that is, the expected earnings of a college graduate—via equation 6-7:

$$PV_{\text{returns}} = \sum_{t=18}^{n} \frac{Y_t^c}{(1+r)^{t-18}} \tag{6-7}$$

Now let us calculate the discount rate r that will make the present value of the *returns* to college exactly equal to the present value of the *costs* associated with college or, equivalently, the r that will make the net present value (the difference between the two present value streams) equal to zero. This value of r is called the internal rate of return (IRR) and is formally expressed in equation 6-8:

$$\sum_{t=18}^{n} \frac{(Y_t^c - C_t)}{(1+r)^{t-18}} = 0 \tag{6-8}$$

---

[10] Because we compute the difference between the two expected earnings streams, we do not include the earnings "opportunity costs" in the college graduate's earnings stream. To do so would be double-counting.

Basically, the IRR indicates the "payoff" to an investment and can be used to judge whether an investment is worthwhile. If the IRR exceeds the interest rate you could earn on alternative investments (the opportunity cost of capital) or the interest rate you would have to pay to finance a college education, then the investment is worthwhile and should be undertaken.

The net present value approach and the internal rate of return approach are virtually equivalent ways of calculating the worth of an investment.[11] The IRR approach has been preferred by most economists seeking to calculate the magnitude of the payoff. However, IRR calculations can be extremely laborious. Moreover, the data requirements of both methods can be demanding. For example, we might not have good information on the expected level of earnings for each year. For these reasons, economists often utilize different estimation techniques, as we explain in the next section.

The Earnings Function Approach

For the purpose of calculating actual rates of return to educational investments, economists often make use of **earnings functions**. Earnings functions are one of the most widely used sets of models in labor economics, and their popularity is largely attributable to the work of Jacob Mincer.[12] This approach makes a number of restrictive assumptions, but it has the advantages of simplicity and of being relatively undemanding in its data needs.

The earnings function approach begins by estimating a statistical model, which explains remuneration by reference to workers' schooling, labor market experience, and any other relevant variables. This is done using the method of least squares regression in which the dependent variable is the natural logarithm of the wage. Years of schooling, experience, and experience squared appear as right-hand variables.[13] Data for all these variables are collected for a group of individuals, each individual constituting a single observation. Formally, the regression equation may be written as

$$\ln w = \alpha + \beta S + \gamma X + \delta X^2 + \text{other explanatory variables} \tag{6-9}$$

where w denotes the individual's wage, S is the number of years of schooling received, and X is the work experience of the individual; the Greek letters represent the constant coefficients, which are estimated by the regression program. Other things being equal, it is expected that an increase in the years of schooling of an individual will lead to an increase in his or her earnings. Hence the coefficient on this variable, β, is expected to be positive. If, for example, the coefficient is 0.1, then one extra year of schooling is expected to raise the log wage by 0.1; this is equivalent to an increase in the level of the wage of about 10%.[14]

---

[11] We say "virtually equivalent" because sometimes there may be more than one IRR for any given stream of costs and returns. This can happen if the stream of future returns turns negative in some periods.

[12] Jacob Mincer, *Schooling, Experience and Earnings* (New York: Columbia University Press, 1974).

[13] Experience squared is included to capture the phenomenon that the age-earnings profile typically rises as workers reach prime age, but then levels off or falls prior to retirement from the labor force. We saw this in Figures 6.1 to 6.3, but we'll investigate the nonlinear nature of the wage-experience relationship in greater detail later.

[14] Strictly speaking, 10.52%. This is calculated as $100(e^\beta - 1)\%$. An adequate and often used approximation is simply 100β.

THE WAY WE WORK

What Good Does a Degree Do?

An analysis of the lifetime earnings of students who left the University of Alabama in 1995 shows that those leaving with a bachelor's degree receive earnings, on average, that are $400,684 higher than the earnings of college dropouts. A master's degree raises lifetime earnings by a further $125,706.*

Studies from other countries confirm this pattern. In Scotland, lifetime earnings for men amount to £301,000 for those with a degree, compared with just £203,000 for those who fail to complete secondary education.[†] The corresponding figures for women are lower, at £231,000 and £113,000, respectively. In Australia, women without children have discounted lifetime earnings of A$468,887 if they have a degree, but only A$226,378 if they have not completed high school.[‡]

The message that education pays should not surprise you. If you are taking a course in labor economics, you are probably sacrificing, for a while, the opportunity to be employed full time. You are also likely to have paid tuition and to have bought this book—at least we hope you didn't steal it! So you must think that education is, in some sense, worthwhile. But you might be surprised by the size of the earnings difference, which suggests that even an expensive higher education is likely to prove to be a good investment.

Notes: *Samuel Addy and Ahmad Ijaz, "Economic Impacts of the University of Alabama: An Update," 1999. Available online at http://cber.cba.ua.edu/pdf/uaimpact.pdf. This study assumes a 3% discount rate.
[†]David Bell, "Higher Education in Scotland: A Report for the Cubie Committee," 1999. Available online at http://www.stir.ac.uk/Departments/Management/Economics/staff/dnfb1/scotland/Investment%20in%20Human%20Capital.pdf. The Scottish figures are based on data for 1997–98 and assume a 5% discount rate.
[‡]Bruce Chapman, Yvonne Dunlop, Matthew Gray, Amy Liu, and Deborah Mitchell, "The Foregone Earnings from Child Rearing Revisited," 1999. Available online at http://cepr.anu.edu.au/pdf/DP407.pdf. The Australian data are measured at 1996 prices using a 5% discount rate.

If the only cost to the individual of this additional year of schooling is foregone earnings, then by sacrificing 100% of the wage throughout the present year, an additional 10% can be earned in all subsequent years. So long as the individual is fairly young (so that the remaining working life can, without too much loss of accuracy, be assumed infinite), it is easy to show that this implies that the rate of return on the investment in education is also 10%.[15]

In showing how β can be interpreted as a rate of return, we assumed that loss of earnings represents the only cost of education. This might have made you balk. Of course, many university students make substantial contributions to the cost of their tuition.

---

[15]Let costs (foregone earnings, w) equal benefits (the present value of returns) so that $w = \beta w (\delta + \delta^2 + \delta^3 + ...)$, where $\delta = 1/(1 + i)$ and i is the rate of return. Dividing both sides by βw, denoting for conciseness the term in parentheses by k, and noting that $(1 + k)/k = 1/\delta \Rightarrow k = \delta/(1 - \delta)$, straightforward substitution reveals that $\beta = i$.

This fact means that the earnings function approach to estimating the rate of return to education is only appropriate for levels of education where tuition is paid by the government. This holds true for most primary and secondary education. It also holds true for university education in some countries; but increasingly university education has come to be funded through "cost-sharing" mechanisms where students are required to pay tuition fees. This is certainly the case in the large English-speaking countries of Australia, Canada, New Zealand, the United Kingdom, and the United States.

Let's pause for a moment to think a little more about the meaning of the rate of return that might be estimated using the statistical method. Suppose we estimate a rate of return for higher education in Finland, a country where students themselves do not pay tuition fees. The rate of return thus calculated gives us a good idea of how the individual regards his or her investment in a university education. It informs us about the trade-off between the earnings opportunity given up to enter full-time schooling and the earnings enhancement received as a result of this extra education. But the rate of return does not tell us anything about how society should regard this investment. Because the full cost of the investment (which includes the cost of tuition as well as the cost of foregone earnings) does not enter the calculation, the government cannot use the Mincerian rate of return as a guide to determine how much it should invest in its people's education. For this reason, the rate of return that is estimated by the statistical method should be regarded as a **private rate of return**; it tells us the return that the individual gains from his or her own private investment in schooling. This will generally differ from the **social rate of return**, which tells us the return that society gains from an investment in schooling, because in calculating the social rate of return all the costs of education (including tuition) must be taken into account.

Think about it a little and you will realize that there are some further differences between the private rate of return and the social rate of return. First, the private rate of return should be calculated using after-tax earnings (because the individual does not directly benefit from taxes paid), but the social rate of return should be calculated using pretax earnings (because society benefits from the government expenditures that are made possible by the individual's tax payment). Second, the social rate of return should include an allowance for the positive externalities that arise from education. These are very difficult to measure, but they are known to include enhanced productivity of co-workers, improved health, more democratic systems of government, less crime, and an improved environment.[16]

The earnings function approach assumes that there is no interaction between age and the effect schooling can have on earnings. The premium on earnings is assumed to be constant across all ages, but you can probably think of many reasons this might not be so in practice. For example, basic schooling may teach people at an early age how to learn; individuals with a strong background of formal education may therefore be more responsive than others to vocational training received later in life so that the earnings premium increases over the life cycle. We investigate this in more detail later in the chapter. In the meantime, the earnings function approach, for all its strong assumptions, does offer us a relatively easy way to estimate a rate of return for education.

---

[16]Walter McMahon, *Education and Development: Measuring the Social Benefits* (Oxford: Oxford University Press, 2000).

TABLE 6.1   Social and Private Rates of Return to Education, by Level of Education, Various Countries

Country	Social		Private	
	Secondary	*Higher*	*Secondary*	*Higher*
Australia		16.3	8.1	21.1
Denmark		7.8		
France			14.8	20.0
Germany			6.5	10.5
Italy			17.3	18.3
New Zealand	12.4	9.5	13.8	11.9
Spain	8.5	13.5		
United Kingdom	7.5	7.5		
United States	10.0	12.0		

Source: George Psacharopoulos and Harry Anthony Patrinos, "Returns to Investment in Education: A Further Update," *Education Economics* 12 (2004): 111–124.

The Evidence

The subject of human capital and rates of return to investment in education first became popular in the 1960s. Since then literally thousands of studies have been undertaken that attempt to calculate the payoff to various years of education. We can only discuss a few of these here. To begin with, let's consider some estimates of the private rate of return to education in developed economies.

Table 6.1 shows the social and private rates of return to both secondary and higher education in a variety of developed economies. The first thing to notice about these figures is that they are, in general, quite high. Compare them with the return you would get from putting your money in the bank, and you'll see that investing in education offers a pretty good deal to the average student.[17] A second thing to notice is that the private rate of return is much higher than the social rate of return, especially in the case of higher education because higher education is often heavily subsidized; recall that in many countries students do not pay for their tuition at all. This is true of the non-English-speaking countries in the table, and at the time to which these estimates refer it was true also of Australia, Great Britain, and New Zealand. In countries with such high private rates of return to education, an excess demand for university education was sure to emerge. This has been managed by restricting access to higher education so that only the most able benefit from schooling at this level. In effect, there are two prices: a dollar price and an ability price.

---

[17] The bit about the *average* student is quite important. The marginal student, the one with the least to gain from education, likely earns a rate of return that is not so favorable. Indeed, if education is subsidized, the social rate of return to the marginal student may fall below commercially available rates of interest. This is the case of over-education. See John Ashworth, "A Waste of Resources? Social Rates of Return to Higher Education in the 1990s," *Education Economics* 6 (1998): 27–44.

TABLE 6.2 Estimates of the Private Rate of Return to an Additional Year of Schooling, USA

Study	Schooling Coefficient
Ashenfelter and Krueger (1994)	0.084
Behrman et al. (1994)	0.094
Miller et al. (1995)	0.064
Ashenfelter and Rouse (1998)	0.102
Rouse (1999)	0.105
Behrman and Rosenzweig (1999)	0.118

Source: Omar Arias and Walter W. McMahon, "Dynamic Rates of Return to Education in the US," *Economics of Education Review* 20 (2001): 121–138.

Let's look now at just one country in a little more detail. Table 6.2 summarizes the findings of several recent studies, all of which establish the rate of return for higher education in the United States. On average, the private rate of return to a college education appears to be about 10%, with the estimates falling in the 7 to 12% range.

Does an investment in education pay off? Well, the rates of return associated with most other investments of similar risk would appear to be less than this. And certainly the interest rates that most students and their parents pay on loans to finance a college education are much lower as well. In short, then, a college education seems on average to be a good investment.

This question has been asked also in England, where tuition fees for undergraduates have risen very rapidly since their introduction in 1998. Initially fixed at £1000 per year, these fees were raised to £3000 in 2006. Evidence suggests that, in 2010, the rate of return to an undergraduate education amounted to 15% for men and 14% for women.[18] In view of these high rates of return, universities have, since 2012, been allowed to raise their tuition fees up to £9000, but there is now substantial variation across universities in the level of fee charged.

A number of studies have calculated rates of return for graduate levels of education: master's and PhD degrees. In general, these studies have found rates of return substantially lower than those for bachelor's degrees. The internal rates of return are usually in the single digits and sometimes are even negative.[19]

So much for developed countries. What about other parts of the world, where even a basic education is not available to everybody? Table 6.3 summarizes the results of a large number of studies that have been conducted around the world. A number of features stand out from this table.

[18] Gavan Conlon and Pietro Patrignani, "The Returns to Higher Education Qualifications," Department for Business, Innovation and Skills Research Paper 45, 2011. Available online at http://www.bis.gov.uk/assets/biscore/higher-education/docs/r/11-973-returns-to-higher-education-qualifications.pdf. It is worth noting that this report is coy about the rates of return that are to be expected once tuition fees rise to £9000; in this scenario the authors "at no point in the report...estimate either the net graduate premium, net Exchequer benefit or associated rates of return" (p. 107).

[19] See, for example, Walter W. McMahon and Alan P. Wagner, "Expected Returns to Investment in Higher Education," *Journal of Human Resources* 16 (1981): 274–285. The Conlon and Patrignani paper cited in footnote 18 also provides evidence on the returns to masters and doctoral education.

TABLE 6.3 Social and Private Rates of Return to Investment in Education by Level of Education; Cross-Country Averages Grouped by Per Capita National Income

Country type	Social			Private		
	Primary	Secondary	Tertiary	Primary	Secondary	Tertiary
Low	21.3	15.7	11.2	25.8	19.9	26.0
Middle	18.8	12.9	11.3	27.4	18.0	19.3
High	13.4	10.3	9.5	25.6	12.2	12.4
World	18.9	13.1	10.8	26.6	17.0	19.0

Notes: The boundaries between low, middle and high income groups are defined by the per capita income figures (US dollars per annum) of 775 and 9265. The figures are obtained by averaging all countries for which data are available.

Source: George Psacharopoulos and Harry Anthony Patrinos, "Human Capital and Rates of Return," in *International Handbook on the Economics of Education*, eds. Geraint Johnes and Jill Johnes (Cheltenham: Elgar, 2004), pp. 1–57, Table 1.2.

First, the tendency that we observed earlier—for social returns to education to be lower than private returns—is confirmed in this table. This follows from our earlier discussion and indicates that in all countries studied there is an element of public subsidy of education.[20] We say something more about externalities due to education later in this chapter, but for the moment it's enough to note that governments everywhere appear to be persuaded of the justification of educational subsidies.

Second, a pattern common to many countries is that the rates of return to primary education exceed those to secondary education (high school), and the latter in turn exceed those to tertiary education (college). This pattern is particularly pronounced in less developed countries. In some respects it is very curious because an implication of rate of return analysis is that it is good policy to ensure that the rate of return available on every investment is the same. At the margin, investments should be made in those sectors where the rate of return is highest. As investment in those sectors increases, diminishing returns set in and the rate of return falls into line with that available elsewhere. An optimum is reached where rates of return in all sectors are equal.[21] So the observation that rates of return are, in developing economies, highest for primary education provides a rationale for the efforts of international agencies such as the World Bank to persuade governments in these countries to divert resources, at the margin, toward the primary sector of education.

Third, a tendency has been observed for less developed countries to have very high social rates of return to education.[22] This is indicative of undereducation in those

---

[20] Some studies do not use after-tax measures of remuneration, and this biases upward the estimate of private returns by excluding contributions made to the direct cost of education through the tax system. Nevertheless the subsidization of higher education is ubiquitous. In general, measures of social rates of return adopt the standard neoclassical assumption about the relationship between productivity and the wage.

[21] It is worth pausing here to clarify a point that often causes confusion. The rule given in the text does *not* mean that substantial (nonmarginal) investments in education should necessarily go in their entirety into the one sector that (before the investment is made) exhibits the highest rate of return: it is a rule that applies *only* at the margin.

[22] This is not so pronounced in countries with a highly regulated labor market and an egalitarian political orientation.

TABLE 6.4   Change in the Social and Private Rates of Return
to Education over an Average 15-Year Period

Educational level	Social	Private
Primary	−8.3	−2.0
Secondary	−5.7	−1.9
Tertiary	−1.7	1.7

Note: The figures are obtained by averaging all countries for which data are available.

Source: George Psacharopoulos and Harry Anthony Patrinos, "Human Capital and Rates of Return," in *International Handbook on the Economics of Education*, eds., Geraint Johnes and Jill Johnes (Cheltenham: Elgar, 2004), pp. 1–57, Table 1.A.8.

countries. Although the private sector is active in many countries in plugging gaps left by the state system of education, financial institutions are unwilling to offer unsecured loans for the purpose of education. Surprising though it may seem, this is so for two reasons, one good and one bad: slavery is illegal (that's good) and death is inevitable (that's the bad news). Were it not for these two facts, banks could make slaves of their immortal debtors, and so their loans could be secured.

Fourth, movements of the rate of return over time can be instructive. This can be seen in Table 6.4. From a global perspective, the fall documented in this table has been most rapid in the primary education sector and least rapid in the tertiary sector of education. This suggests that the fall reflects the move in many developing countries toward the provision of primary education for all. Indeed, the World Bank has set a goal of universal primary education by the year 2015. The private rate of return to *higher* education seems to be bucking the trend, however, and has been rising over time. This is an interesting finding that might well be related to skill-biased technical change: the notion that the gains in productivity and earnings over recent years have been concentrated among the most highly educated workers because computers and other high-tech tools need educated people to work them.

The time path of rates of return has been particularly well documented for the United States; increased demand for qualified labor (especially engineers) in the post-Sputnik era led to rapidly rising rates of return to college education, and this in turn led to rapidly rising enrollments. During the mid-1970s the rate of return fell sharply, leading some economists to suggest that overeducation had become a problem.[23] The rate of return to college education has since risen somewhat. Figure 6.5 shows the time path of earnings for workers in their mid-20s to mid-30s over the period since 1970. The gap between those with a university degree and those without has risen inexorably over this period.

We've covered important ground in this section, and some of the major points are worth reiterating:

- The rate of return to education is high in relation to other investments of equivalent risk. The average graduate gets a good deal from his or her education; it's a sound investment. Whether or not that is true for the marginal graduate remains unclear.

---

[23] Richard Freeman, *The Overeducated American* (New York: Academic Press, 1976).

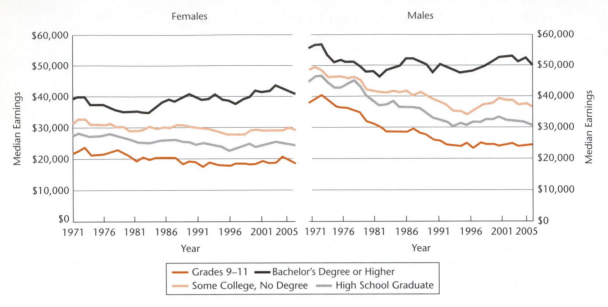

FIGURE 6.5 Median Earnings of Full-Time Workers Aged 25–34 in the United States, 1971–2005, Constant 2005 $

Source: Sandy Baum, Jennifer Ma, and Kathleen Payea, *Education pays 2010: The Benefits of Higher Education for Individuals and Society* (Washington: College Board, 2010). Available online at http://trends.collegeboard.org/downloads/Education_Pays_2010.pdf

- In developing countries, the rate of return to education is particularly high. There is too little investment in education in these countries. By increasing their stock of human capital, these countries could raise productivity and improve their level of economic development. Indeed, investments in human capital are likely to be much more profitable than investments in physical capital (such as plant and machinery) in these economies.

- In some countries, not all children receive even a primary education, but the rate of return to primary education is extremely high. This has led major international aid agencies to call for universal primary education by the year 2015. While some progress has been made toward meeting this goal, it seems unlikely to be fulfilled.

- The rate of return to education, at primary and secondary levels, has tended to decline over time as more is being invested in education. Undereducation is now less of a problem than it was in the past. At the tertiary (college) level, the picture is less clear. It looks as though there has been a recent increase in the return to education at this level, possibly owing to skill-biased technical change.

Bias in Rate of Return Estimates

Although it seems clear that education is a worthwhile investment both to individuals on average and to society, some controversies exist regarding what the evidence is really telling us. Most of these controversies concern whether the published rate of return evidence indicates the actual payoffs to education or whether the rates reflect other forces at work and are consequently "biased." Two possible sources of bias are ability bias and selection bias.

Ability Bias

When a profit maximizing firm is on its demand curve for labor, the wage equals the marginal revenue product. The relationship that this implies between productivity and wages is crucial in the interpretation of social rates of return. It suggests that we can measure the social value of increased production due to education simply by looking at the increase in wages. But what if wages don't reflect productivity in the way that theory says they should? What if education, rather than influencing productivity, merely serves as a signal to employers of the likely innate ability of the individual? **Ability bias** influences employers to pay educated workers more than uneducated ones not because their education has *made* them productive but because they are likely to be of higher ability and, for this reason, more productive than other workers. Alternatively, employers might use evidence of workers' education as a means of screening or sorting workers likely to be of high ability into more demanding jobs; again, the education does not increase productivity but merely flags workers likely to be especially productive because of their innate abilities. These ideas form what has become known as the signaling/screening critique.[24] It is also sometimes known as *credentialism* because the theory of signaling and screening assumes that it is credentials (certificates) rather than human capital that influence earnings.

An obvious question is this: If firms base their remuneration policies on workers' education levels, why don't all workers invest in a high level of education? The answer is that the cost of acquiring a high level of education is higher for less able individuals than it is for others. Completing a bachelor's degree in four years is cheaper, both in terms of direct costs and forgone earnings, than completing a degree in five or six years.

A simple example might help to make this point. Suppose there are two types of worker: high productivity, denoted by π_H, and low productivity, denoted by π_L. Suppose further that each worker can choose between a high level of education and a low level of education. The low level comes free, but workers wishing to invest in a high level of education must incur a cost. For high-productivity individuals, let's assume that the cost is $2,000. For their less able counterparts, the cost is $6,000. Suppose further that the marginal product of high-productivity individuals is $10,000, and that of low-productivity individuals is $5,000.

Now suppose the employer sets a remuneration level for all workers of $7,500. In this case, all workers are paid the same regardless of their education level so there is no reason for any workers to invest in their own education. This is known as a **pooling equilibrium** because it has the effect of pooling all productivity types into one group.

Suppose instead that the firm decides to pay a salary of $10,000 to those who have been educated to a high level, and just $5,000 to other workers. What happens now is very interesting. The more able workers will choose to invest in education because $10,000 minus the $2,000 that they spend on tuition (that is, the net remuneration of $8,000) is greater than what they would receive if they did not invest in education ($5,000). Meanwhile, the less able workers will choose not to invest in education because the pay that they receive when their education level is low ($5,000) exceeds their net

---

[24] Early proponents of this view include two Nobel Prize winners: Kenneth Arrow, "Higher Education as a Filter," *Journal of Public Economics* 2 (1973): 193–216; Michael Spence, "Job Market Signaling," *Quarterly Journal of Economics* 87 (1973): 355–379.

remuneration when they have a high education level ($10,000 − $6,000 = $4,000). By implementing a pay policy based on the educational levels of its workers, the firm arrives at what is known as a **separating equilibrium**, which ensures that the low-ability and high-ability workers have the incentive to separate themselves out into two distinct groups: the more able workers undertake more education, and the less able workers undertake less.

In general, therefore, only students who are more intellectually able tend to go on to receive a college or university education. Less able individuals find it too challenging, time consuming, and costly to extend their education. Inevitably, therefore, there is some potential for the certificates that people have acquired to come to be seen as a measure of their innate ability. This is true not only in the United States, where about 70% of school leavers go on to pursue degree-level higher education, but even more so in many other countries where admission to higher education is much more selective. The corresponding proportion is 51% in Ireland and Germany and only 17% in China.[25] All of this being the case, the question arises of whether the average rate of return found to be associated with a college education might reflect partly (or even mostly) the natural abilities of those who attend college rather than what is learned in college.

It sounds like a plausible story. You have, after all, come to university hoping that a degree will help you get a good job. So perhaps credentialism has something to it. But wait a minute. How do you get that degree? You study hard, learn things, and augment your stock of human capital! Therefore, your behavior is unaffected by whether credentialism or human capital explains wage determination. After all, students aren't interested in *why* education increases their job prospects, they are only interested in the fact that it does.[26] Unfortunately this means that we can't infer anything about signaling, screening, and human capital by looking at the choices made by students because those choices would be the same under either model. To throw light on whether the world works according to the human capital model, on one hand, or the credentialist model, on the other, we need to be a bit more imaginative.

First, some statistical studies have included a direct measure of ability as an additional explanatory variable in the wage regression. In other words, log wages are modeled as a function of schooling, experience, ability, and other controls. Not many data sets collect information on direct measures of ability, but some do, and these have given analysts an important opportunity to disentangle the effects of education and ability on earnings. Often the ability measure is based on performance in IQ tests, but sometimes performance on tests taken early on in the respondent's education is used instead. Most studies using this approach have found that the change in the coefficient of schooling that results from adding an ability term to the earnings function is rather small.[27]

A second method that has been used to separate out the effects of ability and earnings relies on the study of identical (monozygotic) twins. They are of special interest in this context because they are genetically identical and so have identical innate ability. If we study differences in earnings and schooling between each member of a pair of twins, we

---

[25] OECD Education at a Glance, available at http://www.oecd.org/document/2/0,3746,en_2649_39263238_48634114_1_1_1_1,00.html.

[26] Unless, of course, they—like you—are studying this subject.

[27] Zvi Griliches, "Estimating the Returns to Schooling: Some Econometric Problems," *Econometrica* 45 (1977): 1–22.

can establish to what extent a difference in schooling has influenced a difference in earnings. This measure of the effect of schooling on earnings is a pure measure, uncontaminated by ability bias, because we know that each member of a twin pair has identical ability to the other member. Some studies have collected information about many pairs of monozygotic twins, and statistical analyses of these data suggest that education really does affect earnings and that ability bias is small. The estimates of the private rate of return to schooling provided in Table 6.2 have all been derived using this "twins" method.

You might be tempted to ask how economists collected enough data about twins to conduct this kind of analysis. There is a town in Ohio called Twinsburg, and each summer it hosts a festival of twins. The Twinsburg festival is the largest gathering of twins in the world, attracting several thousand twins, triplets, and quadruplets. In 1991, the number of tourists visiting Twinsburg was augmented by a pair of economists (who are not twins), Orley Ashenfelter and Alan Krueger.[28] They were in Ohio to interview pairs of monozygotic twins and to collect information about their education and labor market experience. On the basis of their interviews, Ashenfelter and Krueger found that omitted ability variables did *not* result in downward bias in their rate of return estimates. In fact, their rate of return estimates averaged 12 to 16%, higher than those found in many other studies.[29] Other countries (albeit countries that do not have the luxury of towns called Twinsburg) also have data on twins that have allowed similar analyses to be conducted, with broadly similar results.[30]

A third method that has been used to try to correct for ability bias relies on some statistical trickery. The trick is to find something that influences the education people receive but does not affect anything else (and in particular is completely unrelated to ability). If we can find such a "something," we can measure the pure effect of education on earnings, cleaned up of any contamination by ability bias. The "something" is known, in technical language, as an *instrument* for education. This approach to removing ability bias therefore amounts to finding a clever instrument.

Several possible instruments have been suggested in the literature, but we focus on just a few. The first is the Vietnam draft lottery.[31] At the time of the Vietnam War, young men were drafted into the military on a random basis. Eligibility for the draft was based on the individual's birthday. Dates were drawn at random, and if an individual's birthday matched one of the dates drawn, that person could be drafted. However, it was possible during some years to postpone (or even to avoid altogether) entry into the military on the ground that an individual was engaged in education. Many young people chose to prolong their studies at this time for a reason that was unrelated to their ability, prior schooling, or expected future labor market performance. What's more, those youngsters that did prolong their schooling were a subset of those *randomly* chosen

---

[28] Orley Ashenfelter and Alan Krueger, "Estimates of the Economic Return to Schooling from a New Sample of Twins," *American Economic Review* 84 (1994): 1157–1173.

[29] In addition to correcting for ability bias, Ashenfelter and Krueger made allowance for measurement error.

[30] See, for example, Dorothe Bonjour, Lynn Cherkas, Jonathan Haskel, Denise Hawkes, and Tim Spector, "Returns to Education: Evidence from UK Twins," *American Economic Review* 93 (2003): 1799–1812.

[31] Joshua Angrist and Alan Krueger, "Estimating the Payoff to Schooling Using the Vietnam Draft Lottery," *NBER Working Paper 4067*, 1992.

to be eligible for the draft. Eligibility for the draft can serve as an instrument for schooling among this cohort of youths. Once this is done, the coefficient on the schooling variable in the earnings function can be estimated and is cleansed of ability bias. With instrumentation, the estimated private rate of return amounts to 6.6%. This compares with an estimate of 5.9% using the same data but without correcting for bias. Any bias is therefore small and leads, if anything, to an underestimate of the rate of return to education.

A second instrument to consider is raising the statutory minimum school leaving age.[32] In the United Kingdom the school leaving age was raised from 14 to 15 in 1947, and in 1973 it was raised further to age 16. Therefore, in the late 1970s and early 1980s, some older people were in the labor force who left school at age 14 along with some younger workers who were unable to leave school until they were 16 years old. Using data from this period, the change in legislation can be used as an instrument. When the earnings function is estimated using this instrument, the coefficient on schooling is estimated to be 0.1525 (implying a private rate of return of 16.5%). This compares with a private rate of return of just 6.3% when the earnings function is estimated without instrumentation. This again suggests that the rates of return reported earlier in this chapter, estimated as they are using the simpler method, are if anything underestimates of the true rate of return.[33]

A third instrument that has been used is the quarter in which an individual student was born.[34] Students that are old compared with others in their cohort (that is, those born in the quarter immediately after the start of the academic year) might, owing to the nature of state school attendance laws, be able to drop out of school at an earlier stage of their education than other students. Hence quarter of birth influences educational attainment but is uncorrelated with ability, thereby making it a suitable instrument. Instrumenting for education in this way confirms the findings of the studies referred to above—that calculations of the rate of return to education that do not correct for ability bias are not overestimates.

A fourth instrument is the distance to the nearest higher education institution.[35] Those who reside relatively close to a university might be more likely to extend their education beyond the secondary level. Studies that use this instrument, once again, typically show an absence of downward bias in OLS estimates of the rate of return to education.

Not all instrumental variable models are so supportive of the human capital model. A recent study based on interstate variation in the pass standard of the General Educational

---

[32] Colm Harmon and Ian Walker, "Estimates of the Return to Schooling in the United Kingdom," *American Economic Review* 85 (1995): 1278–1286.

[33] In this case, the underestimate is quite substantial. The explanation usually given by the authors of these studies is that there are errors in the measurement of years of schooling in the surveys they have used. This might be so, but an equally plausible explanation is that the instruments chosen (in this case, the raising of the school leaving age) are imperfect.

[34] Joshua D. Angrist and Alan B. Krueger, "Does Compulsory School Attendance Affect Schooling and Earnings?" *Quarterly Journal of Economics* 106 (1991): 979–1014.

[35] Thomas J. Kane and Cecilia E. Rouse, "Labor Market Returns to Two- and Four-Year Colleges," *American Economic Review* 85 (1995): 600–614.

Development (GED) credential provides some evidence to support signaling and screening in the United States.[36]

A fourth method that has been used to assess the validity of the signaling/screening critique divides data on workers' pay, education, and age into two or more groups. The criterion for this division is the type of occupation in which the worker is employed. On a priori grounds, we might expect to find signaling or screening to be more prevalent among some groups of workers than others. For example, there is no reason to suppose that signaling should be an important factor in the determination of the earnings of self-employed workers. Such workers should be aware of their own abilities without feeling the need to signal those abilities to themselves by acquiring unproductive education. Most studies of this type find no evidence of ability bias in estimates of rates of return due to signaling or screening.[37]

A fifth attempt to distinguish between the contribution of education to productivity and the role of education as a signaling or screening device involves the analysis of the education-wage profile at different points in the life cycle. It is likely that the screening function of education is important only for the first few years an individual spends in the labor market. Beyond that employers should be able to assess the worker's productivity using more direct measures. Any fall in the measured rate of return to education observed as the worker ages may therefore be due to the withering away of ability bias as signaling and screening factors become less important with greater work experience. Studies using this approach have shown that workers with degrees maintain their earnings premium as they age.[38] Indeed, the fanning out that we observed in the age-earnings profiles shown in Figure 6.2 through Figure 6.4 confirms this. As highly educated workers age, their earnings tend to rise faster than those of other workers. This lends further support to the theory of human capital.

Finally, some further evidence on the credentialism versus human capital debate comes from the literature on macroeconomics. Despite the popularity of rate of return analyses, the economic benefit of education to society is perhaps better measured using macroeconomic methods. Recent research into the determinants of economic growth has stimulated a number of macroeconomic studies, most of which involve cross country analysis. Education appears to exert a strong positive influence on economic growth,[39] and it appears that this influence is comparable in magnitude to the effect one would expect from microeconomic studies. Because growth arises from increased productivity, it seems

---

[36] John H. Tyler, Richard J. Murnane, and John B. Willett, "Estimating the Labor Market Signaling Value of the GED," *Quarterly Journal of Economics* 115 (2000): 431–468.

[37] Kenneth I. Wolpin, "Education and Screening," *American Economic Review* 67 (1977): 949–958; Elchanan Cohn, Billy F. Kiker, and M. Mendes de Oliveira, "Further Evidence on the Screening Hypothesis," *Economics Letters* 25 (1987): 289–294; Geraint Johnes, "Human Capital versus Sorting: New Data and a New Test," *Applied Economics Letters* 5 (1998): 665–667. An exception, which does find some evidence of screening, is John Riley, "Testing the Educational Screening Hypothesis," *Journal of Political Economy* 87 (1979): S227–S252.

[38] W. Norton Grubb, "Further Tests of Screening on Education and Observed Ability," *Economics of Education Review* 12 (1993): 125–136; Elchanan Cohn, Billy F. Kiker, and M. Mendes de Oliveira, "Further Evidence on the Screening Hypothesis," *Economics Letters* 25 (1987): 289–294; Geraint Johnes, "Human Capital Versus Sorting: New Data and a New Test," *Applied Economics Letters* 5 (1998): 665–667.

[39] Ross Levine and David Renelt, "A Sensitivity Analysis of Cross Country Growth Regressions," *American Economic Review* 82 (1992): 942–963.

that education really is a productivity enhancer.[40] In looking at the relationship between education and growth in this way, we have come full circle and are right back where we started this chapter.

So, despite the attractiveness of the signaling and screening critique, most of the evidence from the tests described previously suggests that the human capital model more faithfully describes the relationship between education and earnings. It does seem as though education really is a productivity enhancer. That said, signaling and screening are inherently plausible, and the evidence is not all one-sided, so it is likely that the debate will continue.

Selection Bias

A second important potential source of bias in estimating the rate of return to education concerns sample selection. For social reasons, this is likely to be a particularly serious problem when analyzing the rates of return faced by women. Let's see why.

Suppose you collect data on the earnings of a sample of workers, chosen at random, in order to conduct a rate of return analysis. You would want to know how much respondents are earning in their current jobs, how much experience they have (or, at least, how old they are), and the highest level of schooling that they attained. You might go on to analyze these data and produce some estimates of the rate of return to education. But there would be a problem: The sample you have collected is a random sample of workers, but it is not a random sample of the population. Some people choose not to enter the labor force, perhaps because the earnings they could receive are low because the education they have acquired yields a low rate of return. The fact that you have left these people out of your sample means that you will have overestimated the rate of return to education.

This problem is particularly acute in the case of women, especially those who interrupt their careers for family reasons. Their decision about when to return to work depends in part on their earnings potential. Women for whom the rate of return to education is unusually high are more likely than others to return to work early. After all, for them the opportunity cost associated with *not* working is high. So, by analyzing workers only, a bias is introduced into the estimation of the rate of return.

This problem has come to be known as **sample selection bias**. Some clever statistical techniques have been developed to correct for this type of bias, and these methods are used routinely in the statistical estimation of earnings functions.[41] Let's see how they work.

Let's consider the labor market experience of women in two steps. The first step involves the decision of whether or not to participate in the labor market. It is possible to model this decision using a standard statistical framework. The decision may depend on factors such as age, marital status, the number and age of any children, and education.

---

[40]Some care is needed here, however. The fact that education is shown to be a productivity enhancer in these studies does not mean that education is always, everywhere, and at all levels productive. The studies are based on average experience over many countries. In developed countries, there is some evidence of overeducation. See, for example, Alison Wolf, *Does Education Matter?* (London and New York: Penguin, 2002).

[41]James J. Heckman, "Sample Selection Bias as a Specification Error," *Econometrica* 47 (1979): 153–161.

Once this model of participation has been estimated statistically, information from the model can be used to estimate an equation that tells us how earnings are determined. To be specific, the variables that determine participation are used to estimate the probability with which each individual participates. A measure of this probability,[42] denoted by λ, is then inserted as an extra variable in the estimated wage equation. This is the second step. This corrects the wage equation for the sample selection bias. The coefficients of the wage equation estimated in this way apply to the whole population, not just to the selected sample of those who work.

From the abstract discussion that we've had so far, it's difficult to gauge how seriously we should take sample selection bias. To be sure, a simple statistical estimate of an earnings function may be based on a nonrandom sample of women (those that work), and so it *may* be biased. But whether it actually is biased depends on whether the women left out of the sample would (if they worked) have wages that were determined differently from those in the sample. That is an empirical issue.

So we must turn now to the question: Is sample selection bias important? To assess this, we'll look at one recent study, chosen to be representative of the many that have been conducted. In Table 6.5, we reproduce the results of a statistical analysis of Brazilian women of working age. The data on which these results are based come from the Brazilian National Household Survey (the Pesquisa Nacional por Amostra de Domocílios, or PNAD) for 1999.

In this table the log of the wage is expressed as a function of age, age squared, years of schooling, and a group of variables that describe the respondent's ethnicity, area of residence, workplace, and union status.[43] To interpret the coefficients, note that if the value of any variable increases by 1, the wage is expected to rise by a percentage of about 100 times the corresponding coefficient. For example, we should expect that, other things being equal, a woman living in the South earns wages that are about 25% higher than a woman living in the Central region (which is the reference region). The numbers in parentheses are t-statistics. These give an indication of how precisely the coefficients have been estimated, bearing in mind that the statistical analysis is based on a random sample, not on the whole population.[44]

Consider the first column of the table. The coefficients in this column have been estimated using ordinary least squares regression and do not correct for sample selection bias. The results look very much as you would expect them to look. There is a nonlinear relationship between age and wage, and this follows the inverted-U pattern we observed earlier in this chapter. The results suggest that earnings peak when women reach the age of 56 years. The results also suggest that living in an urban area adds 11% to women's

---

[42] Known as the Inverse Mills' Ratio in honor of the work of John P. Mills, "Table of the Ratio: Area to Bounding Ordinate for Any Portion of Normal Curve," *Biometrika* 18 (1926): 395–400.

[43] The model of participation that is used to derive the sample selection term, λ, has the same set of education, age, ethnicity, and residence variables, but excludes workplace information and union status. It also includes family composition variables. These analyses are taken from Rodolfo Hoffman and Ana Lúcia Kassouf, "Deriving Conditional and Unconditional Marginal Effects in Log Earnings Equations Estimated by Heckman's Procedure," *Applied Economics* 37 (2005): 1303–1311.

[44] So long as the standard error is at most half as big as the corresponding coefficient, the coefficient is estimated with sufficient precision for us to be about 95% sure about its sign.

TABLE 6.5   The Effects of Sample Selection Bias on Female Wage Equations

Variables	Without correction	With correction
Constant	−2.1199	−2.5397
	(37.6)	(34.0)
Education (years)	0.1106	0.1165
	(124.1)	(103.3)
Age	0.0487	0.0626
	(16.9)	(18.9)
Age squared	−0.000437	−0.000612
	(11.9)	(14.5)
Yellow	0.3328	0.3259
	(5.84)	(5.67)
Black	−0.1879	−0.1678
	(11.1)	(9.77)
Mulatto	−0.1454	−0.1409
	(16.0)	(15.4)
Urban	0.1111	0.1005
	(8.37)	(7.5)
North	0.2198	0.2206
	(11.7)	(11.7)
South	0.2528	0.2586
	(19.5)	(19.8)
Southeast	0.4087	0.3961
	(39.9)	(38.1)
Midwest	0.2728	0.2686
	(17.2)	(16.8)
Industry	0.2762	0.2783
	(12.7)	(12.8)
Service	0.3010	0.3037
	(15.7)	(15.8)
Union	0.2424	0.2412
	(22.4)	(22.3)
λ		0.1742
		(8.63)

Note: t statistics are in parentheses.

Source: Rodolfo Hoffman and Ana Lúcia Kassouf, "Deriving Conditional and Unconditional Marginal Effects in Log Earnings Equations Estimated by Heckman's Procedure," *Applied Economics* 37 (2005): 1303–1311.

earnings. This, too, is a common finding in studies of this kind. Two explanations have been proposed for this.[45] First, in urban areas a wide diversity of services are readily available, and this increases the productivity of firms located in such areas. For example, if the photocopier breaks down, firms in urban areas can get it repaired right away

---

[45] Antonio Ciccone and Robert E. Hall, "Productivity and the Density of Economic Activity," *American Economic Review* 86 (1996): 54–70.

whereas firms in rural areas may have to wait several days for a service company to come and repair it. This reduces the productivity, and so also the wages, of workers in rural areas, albeit through no fault of their own. Second, external economies of scale are associated with production in cities. For instance, technological improvements may spread more rapidly in a densely populated area than elsewhere.

But the most interesting coefficient in column 1 of the table for our purposes is that relating to education. It suggests that the private rate of return to education is between 11 and 12 percent, which is very much in line with results reported earlier in the chapter from other studies.

What happens to these figures if the equation is re-estimated correcting for sample selection bias? We can find out by looking at column 2. The coefficient on education rises slightly, so the bias is in the direction that we expected. But the rise is not particularly dramatic, only about 5 percent; so the coefficient still suggests that the rate of return is between 11 and 12 percent.[46]

An important caveat must be mentioned concerning the two-step technique described here. For this method to be statistically valid, variables should be included in the model of labor market participation that do not affect wages. If they are not, the model is said to be unidentified, and it is not valid. Some economists contend that there are no such variables because anything that affects participation must also affect the level of remuneration. After all, changes in labor supply might reasonably be expected to affect the wage, and labor supply is the summation of individuals' participation decisions. If we accept that the two-step model is unidentified, then we have to accept also that we can do nothing to correct for the problem of sample selection bias. That being the case, it is just as well that the evidence suggests that sample selection bias is typically quite slight.

General versus Specific Human Capital

So far we have discussed human capital as if all human capital is similar in type. This is an oversimplification, however, and some results quite important in the context of public policy may be obtained by introducing a bit more realism into our models.

Most education provides workers with skills that may be applied when working for any of a large number of employers. For instance, the human capital that students accumulate during an economics course can be used by many different types of firms: businesses value analytical minds with the ability to see to the heart of the matter, to set up and solve problems, and to weigh (sometimes conflicting) evidence to come up with a conclusion; they also value workers who are numerate and who can communicate succinctly and persuasively both orally and in writing. These skills constitute **general human capital**.

Other skills may be useful to the worker only when working for his or her current employer. Such skills may be acquired through education or, perhaps more often, through training, and we call these skills the worker's **specific human capital**. Human capital

---

[46] Bo Honoré, Francis Vella, and Marno Verbeek, "Attrition, Selection Bias and Censored Regressions," in *The Econometrics of Panel Data*, 3rd ed. eds., L. Mátyás and P. Sevestre (Berlin: Springer, 2008), pp. 385–418 shows that, in some other contexts, sample selection bias can be more important.

of this kind includes local knowledge of the workings of the firm and the worker's information stock about products produced within that firm that are not produced elsewhere. For example, soldiers in the army are taught skills (use of weaponry, for example) that are of limited usefulness outside the context of the army. If someone leaves the army and goes to work in a bakery, he or she still has these skills, but they are not much use to the baker and will not generate higher wages for the worker. (Although pointing a gun at the boss to try to get a wage increase might work in the short term, people tend to be put in jail for that kind of bargaining.)

The typical worker's stock of human capital includes both general and specific components. Just think of your own situation. You have some skills that can be thought of as general human capital; for example, you can read and write in English, you are numerate, and you know something about the way the world works. But you also have some much more specific skills. You are, for instance, familiar with the buildings of your university, you have been taught by the faculty who work there, and you know something about the facilities offered by the surrounding area. You may even have developed some sort of loyalty to the institution. This mix of skills makes you an ideal tour guide for those considering coming to your university to study, but they are not skills that would recommend you as a good tour guide for another higher education institution.

Because general human capital may be useful to the worker in gaining employment in any of a large number of firms, a worker's current employer will be reluctant to invest in the worker's stock of general human capital because it would always be possible for the worker to quit and move to a different employer. The worker would be equally productive, and could earn as much, anywhere. If this were to happen, the firm's investment in its employee would be lost. The theory therefore suggests that investments in general human capital should be made by the worker rather than by the firm. It is for this reason that the acquisition of skills easily transportable across firms is most commonly observed in the education system where literacy, numeracy (mathematical skills), basic craft skills, and so on are taught. When general human capital accumulation is observed within firms, this typically is the result of special arrangements such as apprenticeships in which workers (by receiving a relatively low wage) effectively pay for the training themselves. So long as this model holds, it should not be possible to observe "poaching" of one firm's trained employees by another firm.

Specific human capital is different. If an investment in a worker's stock of specific human capital is made, the return to this investment will only be realized if the worker remains with his or her current employer. The employer can make such an investment with some measure of confidence because the employer will benefit from the increased productivity in the future. In addition, once a worker has acquired some specific human capital, the firm need not pay the worker the full amount of his or her marginal revenue product because the worker is now worth more to the present firm than he or she would be worth elsewhere. Thus, the worker is not inclined to quit, and the firm makes a surplus as a result of the specific training. The employer will nonetheless wish to pay the worker some return on the investment in specific human capital to deter the worker from moving to another employer. In this case the costs of human capital acquisition are normally shared between the worker and the firm.

Although general and specific human capital may be viewed as two extremes, most situations in the real world are a mixture of these two types. Therefore, it is worthwhile

PUTTING THEORY TO WORK

FORENSIC ECONOMISTS AND VALUING A LIFE

Here's an unpleasant thought. Suppose that one afternoon one of the authors of this textbook meets an untimely death in an automobile accident where the other party is at fault. The author's family may well sue the responsible driver of the other vehicle for damages suffered by the family members (called a "wrongful death" action) as well as for damages on behalf of the deceased (in legal terminology this is called a "survival" action). How would such damages be calculated? Most likely an economist (often called a "forensic economist") would be called in to calculate the economic losses experienced by the surviving family members in the wrongful death action, and estimates would be made of how much money the deceased would have continued to provide for the support of his wife and children over his remaining life expectancy. In the survival action, however, where the basis of the suit is the losses experienced by the decedent, the economist might be asked to put a dollar value on how much the life of the decedent was worth.*

Now in one sense, of course, a human life is "priceless." There is no market for human lives. Furthermore, moral and ethical values along with religious beliefs cause some people to recoil at the thought that we might even begin to think of the value of a life. On the other hand, we can think of how much a human being might have earned over his or her remaining years in the work force and use this to estimate the *economic* value of a human life. This would simply require the calculation of the present value of expected future earnings given the person's age, educational level, current job, and so on, much as we have discussed in the previous sections involving the returns to an investment in human capital. This "discounted future earnings approach" is used in most states as the basis for damages in cases such as this. However, in some jurisdictions a broader (and somewhat controversial) approach called the "hedonic" approach has been used to place a value on a human life. This approach uses the amounts that people are willing to pay to reduce the probability of death (for example, by buying a smoke detector) or the additional amounts earned by workers in dangerous occupations (such as coal mining or law enforcement) to compensate them for added risk at work to infer the value that people on average place on their lives.

What range of estimates have economists come up with for the value of human lives? If you use the discounted future earnings approach and pick out earnings data from age-earnings profiles such as those we looked at earlier, you can see that a recent college graduate might have a lifetime earnings stream whose present value (at 6% interest, for example) could be in excess of a million dollars. However, the value of an average life according to some of the hedonic studies has been estimated to be as much as $15 million.†

What's the point of all of this? First, this example indicates that human capital analysis and techniques are widely used in the courts. Second, considering the stratospheric values that have resulted, it might be a good idea to check the liability limits of your automobile insurance policy.

Notes: *See Robert Thornton and John Ward, "The Economist in Tort Litigation," *Journal of Economic Perspectives* 13 (2) (1999): 101–112.
†See Ted Miller, "The Plausible Range for the Value of Life—Red Herrings among the Mackerel," *Journal of Forensic Economics* 3 (3) (1990): 17–39.

to distinguish a third category of human capital. **Transferable human capital**[47] consists of skills that may be transferred across a limited number of employers. In the context of transferable human capital, each employer has some degree of market power over its employees. This market power has two implications. First, as in the case of specific human capital, the firm will find it worthwhile to invest in its workers' skills. Second, the employer does not need to pay its workers as much as their marginal revenue product. So, in effect, the workers pay for some of their human capital acquisition because they receive wages that are lower than their value to the firm. If these employees were to quit to work for another firm, they would most likely choose to go to a firm where their transferable human capital enhances their productivity. But as there are only a few such firms, and these firms also have a degree of market power, the workers would be exploited there too. The upshot of all this is that firms will pay for some proportion of investment in transferable human capital (which is not entirely specific) but that poaching of employees may occur nonetheless.

Externalities, Equity, and Subsidies

We saw earlier on that difficulties can arise when the social and private rates of return to education are not the same. If the private rate of return is higher than the social rate of return, then there is an incentive for individuals to undertake education, even though this might not be in the best interests of society as a whole. This is the phenomenon of overeducation, which often arises from the fact that education is subsidized.

This raises the question: If inefficiency results from having a private rate of return to education in excess of the social rate of return, how can educational subsidies be justified? There are several answers. First, some individuals may not have access to sufficient funds to invest as much as they would like in education.[48] This reflects an imperfection in capital markets. At the higher education level, programs such as the Stafford loan have done a lot to reduce these imperfections in the United States. In other countries, other mechanisms are in place. For instance, in Britain and in Australia students have guaranteed access to loans through the Student Loans Company and through the Higher Education Contribution Scheme, respectively. So long as these mechanisms are in place, subsidies should not be necessary to correct for capital market imperfections. But in France and Germany and some other countries there are no such mechanisms, and in these cases subsidies provide important protection.

Second, a variety of externalities to education might exist that can justify the use of subsidies. For instance, education might make it easier for people to change occupations at a time when changes in the pattern of demand make such flexibility important.[49]

---

[47] Margaret Stevens, "Transferable Skills and Poaching Externalities," in *Acquiring Skills: Market Failures, Their Symptoms and Policy Responses*, eds., Alison Booth and Dennis Snower (Cambridge, New York and Melbourne: Cambridge University Press, 1996).

[48] David A. Kodde and Joseph M. M. Ritzen, "The Demand for Education under Capital Market Imperfections," *European Economic Review* 28 (1985): 347–362.

[49] Johan Moonwon Kang, "Optimum Subsidies for Education in Two-Sector Economies," *Economics Letters* 35 (1991): 373–377.

Or education might serve to make people more geographically mobile, thus enabling people to move more easily to find work. The education of one group may have a beneficial effect on other groups of workers, especially if workers work in teams. If the least productive member of a team has his or her productivity enhanced by education, the productivity of all team members can increase because they are no longer being held back.[50] Furthermore, if a high proportion of workers are educated, the remaining uneducated workers might benefit, perversely, because they have scarcity value.[51] Numerous other externalities to education have been identified. Some studies show that education reduces crime, improves the environment, is good for the health, and fosters democratic systems of government.[52] All of these things might render the true social rate of return to education much higher than has been estimated and suggest that some subsidy of education is justified.[53]

Third, it has recently been argued that the financing of education partly through the tax system is a means of enforcing gambling contracts that parents willingly enter. Parents do not know in advance what their children's demand for education will be, so they regard the partial funding of education by the public purse as a type of insurance policy. Some parents gain from this, but some lose out. To enforce payment by those who lose out, the state must be involved.[54]

Finally, equity considerations might justify government involvement in education in the form of subsidies. Governments everywhere often face a trade-off between the goals of efficiency and equity. People in different countries attach varying degrees of importance to each of these goals, and this is often reflected in the preferences they express through the political system. If voters opt for a government that emphasizes equity, even at the expense of efficiency, then the tax and spending policies of government are likely to be redistributive. In the context of education, this likely means a system that is free at the point of delivery and is paid for out of progressive taxes. This is not efficient, but it is not a bad thing; people have, after all, shown through the democratic process that they value equity.

Human Capital and Mobility

The concept of human capital has come to be applied very widely in labor economics because it helps to explain individuals' earnings. A nice example of this is the role human capital plays in workers' mobility decisions.

In a very simple neoclassical model, workers migrate to the region in which they can be paid the highest wage. This typically is the region in which the ratio of capital to labor

---

[50] George E. Johnson, "Subsidies for Higher Education," *Journal of Labor Economics* 2 (1984): 303–318.

[51] Geraint Johnes and Jill Johnes, "Policy Reforms and the Theory of Education Finance," *Journal of Economic Studies* 21 (1) (1994): 3–15.

[52] Walter W. McMahon, *Education and Development: Measuring the Social Benefits* (Oxford: Oxford University Press, 1999).

[53] An attempt to catalog the main externalities to education is made by Robert H. Haveman and Barbara L. Wolfe, "Schooling and Economic Well-Being: The Role of Nonmarket Effects," *Journal of Human Resources* 19 (1984): 377–407.

[54] Rod Garratt and John M. Marshall, "Public Finance of Private Goods: The Case of College Education," *Journal of Political Economy* 102 (1994): 566–582.

is highest because that is what makes labor productive.[55] This migration shifts the regional supply of labor, and in turn this affects the wage paid in each region. As labor migrates out of a region, for instance, the labor supply in that region declines and the wage increases. Meanwhile, in regions to which labor is migrating, the supply of labor is rising and the wages fall. These market forces serve to equalize wages across regions. When wages are equal in all regions, the migration will cease.

This model, appealing though it is in its simplicity, does not capture much of what we know about migration. Most important, we know that migration is not all one way. People tend to move both to and from regions where wages are relatively low. In a nutshell, net migration between regions is very small in comparison to gross migration flows.

The human capital model can help explain this. Migration is an investment. The act of moving is costly, and people will only undertake a move when they expect to reap returns in the future as a result of the move, and when the discounted value of these returns exceeds the cost of moving. So younger people are more likely to migrate than are older people because they have a longer working life left in which to recoup the cost of migration.

Moreover, each individual (or household) has different characteristics, and each is able to evaluate their expected earnings in each region. The human capital model does not suppose that all individuals in a labor market receive the same wage! Hence, some people might deem it a good investment to move from region X to region Y whereas others find it worthwhile to move in the opposite direction. By explaining the difference between gross and net migration, the human capital model offers considerable insight into spatial movements of labor. Migrations have been happening for a very long time indeed. Our species is believed to have evolved around 200,000 years ago in Africa. About 70,000 years ago, we started to migrate to other parts of the world—initially to southern and western parts of Asia, and, possibly as recently as 30,000–45,000 years ago, into Europe.[56] Not much is known about the reasons why these early people moved—or indeed the reasons why they did not move earlier—but one theory is that they moved in search of food. In other words, this was a migration caused by economic factors.

Present day migrations are significant in terms of the numbers of people involved. Figure 6.6 is a map of the world showing the annual migration of people at the start of this century. Most migration takes place between countries within regions of the world. This is hard to evaluate on a level playing field because some regions contain a few large countries (like North America) while others contain many small countries (like Europe or Africa)—migration across countries is, for obvious reasons, higher in the latter regions than in the former. But it is clear from the map that a lot of short range migration within regions does take place. There is also a lot of longer range migration going on: from Asia into Europe and North America; from Latin America and the Caribbean into North

---

[55] Coincident with labor migration, capital will move from areas that are capital abundant to areas where capital is more scarce and so earns a higher return. Typically, therefore, labor and capital migrate in opposite directions.

[56] For genetic and fossil evidence, see Christopher Stringer and Peter Andrews, "Genetic and Fossil Evidence for the Origin of Modern Humans," *Science* 239 (1988): 1263–1268. For linguistic evidence see Patrick Manning, "Homo Sapiens Populates the Earth: A Provisional Synthesis, Privileging Linguistic Evidence," *Journal of World History* 17 (2006): 115–158. In addition to homo sapiens, there once existed other closely related species, some of which were producing stone tools more than 2,500,000 years ago. Some of these had already settled in Europe and Asia by the time our species evolved—they too are believed to have migrated into these regions from Africa.

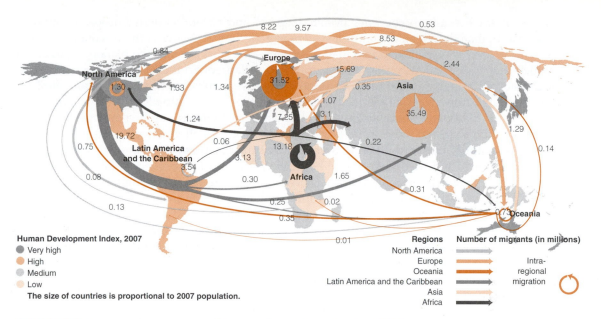

FIGURE 6.6 Origin and Destination of International Migrants, circa 2000

Source: Human Development Report (2009), http://hdr.undp.org/en/media/HDR_2009_EN_Complete.pdf

America; from Africa into Europe; and from Europe into North America and (surprisingly, perhaps) Asia. These flows are determined partly by proximity – hence people move from Africa to Europe and from Latin America to North America. But they are also clearly determined also by economic considerations. The major migrations involve movements of people from relatively poor countries to relatively rich countries.

Where large scale migration takes place, it has the potential to cause disruption in both the sending and receiving economies. Labor supply rises in the receiving economies, and this can put downward pressure on wages. Meanwhile the workers that leave the sending economies are frequently (compared with the population that stays) young, energetic and able, and there may therefore be a concern that the economies that they are leaving may suffer a "brain drain." Migration can also present non-economic challenges such as cultural assimilation. It can therefore be a somewhat emotive issue.

The United States is a country with a tradition of welcoming migrants from other countries, but concern has nonetheless accompanied the relatively recent growth in numbers of migrants—and especially of less well qualified illegal migrants—from central American countries such as Mexico. Numbers of illegal migrants from Mexico more than doubled during the 1990s, to a total of around 5 million.[57] These are very unevenly distributed around the country, and there is the possibility that uncontrolled migration has a marked impact, at least in some locations.

In Europe, meanwhile, migration has become an important issue following the expansion of the European Union in 2004. Some 10 countries joined the union at that time. These

---

[57] Gordon H. Hanson, "Illegal Migration from Mexico to the United States," *Journal of Economic Literature* 44 (2006): 869–924.

included small southern countries (Malta, Cyprus) and several eastern European countries that had operated under a communist system of government. Many of these economies faced serious problems of transition to a market system—not least because the planned markets in which they had previously sold their output had collapsed. So the eastern expansion of the EU involved bringing into the union countries that were substantially poorer than countries in western Europe such as Germany, France, or the United Kingdom. This is important because the EU operates as a single market in labor, and workers in the new member countries gained the right to move from these countries to other—often richer—parts of Europe.

It was straightforward enough to predict that the enlargement of the EU would generate labor flows, and that these would be from east to west. It proved to be much harder, however, to predict the magnitude of these flows. Forecasters had little experience on which to draw—they knew about past migration trends, for sure, but policy switches of the kind being considered here are rare and the circumstances were unique. One famous study predicted that the UK would receive at most 13,000 net immigrants per year from the accession countries—as things turned out, in the years immediately following the expansion of the EU, immigration from the new member states turned out to be more than that figure *per month*.[58] While the numbers migrating helped ease skills shortages in the period before the Great Recession, there is no doubt that the experience of the middle part of the last decade raised some serious questions about the adequacy of data on this issue. It also, therefore, raised questions about the preparedness of the authorities— particularly in some localities that were especially affected by immigration—to provide the necessary infrastructure for a rapidly expanding population.

In many countries where there have been large influxes of migrants, concern has been raised that the additional labor supply might damage the interests of workers who are already in the receiving country. In a simple model, as labor supply rises, the wage tends to fall. If wages are inflexible, the increased supply of labor may result in involuntary unemployment. So it is easy to see why concerns have arisen. Since the extent to which the nonmigrant workers in an economy might be harmed by immigration depends critically on the elasticities of labor supply and demand, and on the degree to which wages are inflexible, these concerns are essentially an empirical issue—we need to establish the statistical facts.

Several studies have been undertaken to try and establish the impact of immigration on workers in the receiving economy.[59] These studies adopt a variety of approaches.

---

[58] Christian Dustmann, Maria Casanova, Michael Fertig, Ian Preston, and Christoph M Schmidt, *The Impact of EU Enlargement on Migration Flows* (London: Home Office, 2003). Available at http://eprints.ucl.ac.uk/14332/1/14332.pdf. This study made the assumption that, in making their migration decisions, workers in the new member states would behave exactly as workers from other sending countries had historically done. The authors noted that this was a strong assumption and urged caution in interpreting their results. Such caveats are not often emphasised by the media!

[59] See, for example: David G. Blanchflower and Chris Shadforth, "Fear, Unemployment and Migration," *Economic Journal* 119 (2009): F136–F182; George J. Borjas, Jeffrey Grogger, and Gordon H. Hanson, "Immigration and the Economic Status of African-American Men," *Economica* 77 (2010): 255–282; David Card, "Is the New Immigration Really So Bad?" *Economic Journal* 115 (2005): F300–F323; Christian Dustmann, Francesca Fabbri, and Ian Preston, "The Impact of Immigration on the British Labour Market," *Economic Journal* 115 (2005): F324–F341; Christian Dustmann, Albrecht Glitz, and Tommaso Frattini, "The Labour Market Impact of Immigration," *Oxford Review of Economic Policy* 24 (2008): 477–494; Martin Kahanec, Anzelika Zaiceva, and Klaus F. Zimmermann, "Lessons from Migration after EU Enlargement," in *EU Labor Markets after Post-Enlargement Migration*, eds., M. Kahanec and K. Zimmermann (Berlin: Springer, 2009).

For example, David Card looks at the relationship between the wage differential between skilled and unskilled native workers in a sample of US cities, on the one hand, and, on the other hand, the proportion of the local labor market accounted for by unskilled immigrant workers. If there were a positive relationship, this would be evidence of immigration having an adverse effect on unskilled native workers. But Card finds no relationship at all. Likewise, Dustmann, Fabbri and Preston, in a time series investigation of data from the UK from 1983-2000, find that an increase in the ratio of immigrant to native population serves, if anything, to increase wages—though this relationship is not statistically significant in most specifications of their model.

By way of contrast, Borjas, Grogger and Hanson have drilled down a little further into the data. They have looked at the impact of immigration on the labor market performance of a very specific group, namely African-American men in the United States over the period 1960–2000. Their findings suggest that immigration causes a decline in the average wage of such men and an increase in their propensity to be unemployed. To be specific, a 10 per cent increase in the labor supply caused by immigration leads to a 2.5 per cent cut in the wages of African-American men and a 5.9 percentage point decline in their employment rate. Blanchflower and Shadforth also note that immigration into the UK imposed downward pressure on wage inflation among those most susceptible to competition from immigrant workers. They interpret this as a beneficial effect of migration in that it improves the nature of the trade-off between inflation and unemployment—in effect, the increase in the supply of labor serves to reduce the natural rate of unemployment.

What about the impact that migration has on the sending economies? In the European migration of recent years, some small countries have experienced significant changes in the structure of their population as predominantly young migrants move out. For instance, there has been substantial migration of young workers out of Latvia in recent years.[60] The loss of young—and especially relatively highly skilled young—workers poses a variety of threats for the sending economy. It reduces the number of people of working age available to pay taxes that support children and the elderly. It reduces the capacity of the economy to produce, and hence lowers gross domestic product. It reduces the scope for entrepreneurship and innovation.

Yet there may also be advantages to the sending region. Many migrants return home after a period away. Many others send money (so-called remittances) back to their families in the sending economy. If, by moving, workers can earn higher wages, it may even be the case that they can contribute more to the sending economy than they would by staying there! The World Bank estimates that remittances amounted to $325 billion worldwide in 2010.[61] In addition to remittances, migrants may benefit the sending economy through their influence on decisions of companies in the receiving economies: in particular, companies might be more prepared to engage in foreign direct investment in countries where they know (from their experience of migrants) that workers offer a high quality resource. Moreover, migrants might help in the diffusion of technological know-how to the sending countries—either by setting up businesses themselves or simply by talking

---

[60] *The Economist*, 1 October 2010.

[61] http://siteresources.worldbank.org/TOPICS/Resources/214970-1288877981391/Annual_Meetings_Report_DEC_IB_MigrationAndRemittances_Update24Sep10.pdf

about technological advances with people back home.[62] Various economists have studied the impact on sending economies of the "brain drain"—some, such as Jagdish Bhagwati, have suggested imposing a "tax on brains", that is, an exit tax on the human capital embodied in migrants leaving a country.[63] But given the arguments presented above, it is clear that the need for such a tax is an empirical issue—while there are good reasons to suspect that a case for the tax can be made, there are also some strong mitigating factors. Research on flows of Indian workers to the United States suggests that the impact on tax revenues in India is actually quite small—equivalent to around 0.14 per cent of the gross domestic product.[64] So perhaps the downside of migration for the sending regions is not so great after all.

Summary

In this chapter we introduced the important concept of human capital. Empirical studies have identified the education, training, and experience of the work force as key determinants of a country's total wealth and economic growth. Education can be studied as an investment decision, with the student, the parents, and the government paying the direct and indirect costs of acquiring a useful asset. Estimates of the rate of return to this asset all suggest that this expenditure has a monetary payoff that exceeds most alternative investment options.

An important question is whether the labor market values education because of what a student learns while in school or because a student's success in school is a signal of his or her innate ability. It is very difficult to distinguish between these two concepts by analyzing available data on individual decisions or wage returns to years of schooling. Labor economists have been quite creative in trying to make such a distinction, however, and we have some confidence in saying that the returns to schooling are in addition to the wage gains for native ability.

Another important distinction is between general and specific human capital. Specific human capital is mainly of use in a particular work setting whereas general human capital is portable between different employers and jobs. It seems clear that an employer has an incentive to invest in the specific human capital of the firm's workers because the employer can reap the benefits of that investment through the enhanced performance of these workers on the job.

Most important, we have relaxed the assumption that all labor is the same. The new material in this chapter enables us to think of workers of different abilities and with differ-

---

[62] Yingqi Wei and V. N. Balasubramanyam, "Diaspora and Development," *World Economy* 29 (2006): 1599–1609.

[63] Jagdish Bhagwati, "The United States in the Nixon Era: The End of Innocence," *Daedalus* 101 (1972): 25–47. Here Bhagwati puts his proposal in a nutshell: "The simplest device would be for the Internal Revenue Service to collect on behalf of the poor home country a tax, possibly 15 per cent of taxable income, that would be automatically transferred to that country" from which the migrant has come.

[64] Mihir A. Desai, Devesh Kapur, and John McHale, "Sharing The Spoils: Taxing International Human Capital Flows," *International Tax and Public Finance* 11 (2004): 1–31 estimate the total loss of tax revenue to India of emigration to the United States to be around $700 million per year; since India's GDP amounted to around $500 billion, this is tantamount to a tax loss of 0.14 per cent of GDP.

ent levels of education and experience. The notion that some human capital is specific to a particular employer further enriches the insight that workers are a heterogeneous bunch of people. This heterogeneity is extremely important in that it gives rise to many institutions that exist in labor markets such as employment contracts (firms want to protect their investments in specific human capital), unions (union workers have monopoly power only inasmuch as they are different from other workers), and promotion structures (if firms bought labor on a spot market, there would be no need for internal promotions). So we now are dealing with a much richer model of the labor market than we had earlier. It is also a more realistic model because we all know that human beings are different from one another.

KEY TERMS

human capital

age-earnings profiles

net present value

internal rate of return

earnings functions

private rate of return

social rate of return

ability bias

pooling equilibrium

sample selection bias

general human capital

specific human capital

transferable human capital

PROBLEMS

1. Think of six things that have been invented since your grandparents were children. How have they improved the quality of life? How do they improve productivity and the wealth of nations? What type of expertise was needed to invent them, and then to put them into production? What contribution does education make to that expertise?

2. Consider an 18-year-old who is about to embark on a three-year course of study. The total costs of the course are $18,000, payable in advance. The returns take the form of an annual $5,000 earnings premium (paid at year end) that the individual receives from age 21 through age 60. Calculate the net present value of this investment assuming a discount rate of 5%.

3. Given the costs and returns in question 2, calculate the internal rate of return to the investment in education.

4. Congratulations! You have just been given a new job as the senior government adviser on education. The president has asked you to privatize the entire education system so that there will be no public expenditure at all on education. What arguments would you make in favor of such a policy, and what arguments would you make against it?

5. In addition to the examples noted in the chapter, what other benefits (externalities) do you think that education can produce for society at large as opposed to just the individual?

6. Suppose that (contrary to what we learned in the chapter) screening is in fact the primary reason for the higher incomes that college graduates enjoy relative to those of

high school graduates. Explain why this would make for a high private rate of return to college but a low social rate of return.

7. Imagine a job that required a six-month period of specific (not general) on-the-job training. Why would an employer be hesitant to hire a person who would be likely to leave the job after working for just two years?

8. As we have noted in the boxed item "Forensic Economists and Valuing a Life," human capital analysis is sometimes used in court cases involving personal injury and wrongful death. Suppose that Marvin Jones is a 50-year-old construction laborer who earns $30 per hour. While on the job he is severely injured by an underground electric cable that the local power company failed to mark at the construction site. Marvin is so severely injured that his doctor has said he will never work as a construction worker again. He has retained an attorney to sue the power company for damages. Suppose you are a consulting economist to Marvin's attorney. What would you need to know to calculate the present value of this lost earnings?

9. Suppose you have the information in the following table for a sample of 15 individuals: annual income (in $1,000's), years of education, years of work experience, and gender (a dummy variable). Use Excel or another program of your choice to estimate the average rate of return per year of college using a Mincer-type earnings function.

Individual	Income ($000)	Years of Education	Work Experience (Years)	Gender (M = 1) (F = 0)
1	45	16	15	1
2	50	16	20	0
3	35	13	13	0
4	42	16	18	1
5	20	12	8	0
6	24	12	10	0
7	35	14	12	1
8	16	12	2	1
9	38	15	10	1
10	65	16	25	0
11	70	16	25	0
12	75	16	27	0
13	50	15	15	1
14	15	12	20	1
15	25	12	20	0

a. In other words, estimate the following regression equation:

$$\ln \hat{y} = b_0 + b_1(\text{ED}) + b_2(\text{EXP}) + b_3(\text{GEN}).$$

b. Interpret the meaning of the coefficient (slope) of the education variable.

c. The rate of return you estimated for years of education is only approximate because $\ln(1 + r)$ is only approximately equal to r. To get the exact rate of return, use this "conversion" formula: $r = e^b - 1$. What is your exact rate of return per year of education now?

7

Labor Market Equilibrium

How do short-run fluctuations in labor demand and supply affect wage rates and employment?

If people can move into high-wage markets over time, why would long-run wage differentials continue to exist?

How does trade with less developed countries affect the wage of unskilled workers in developed countries?

Now that you have learned about labor demand and labor supply in isolation, let's examine how demand and supply interact in the labor market to determine wages and employment. By applying the supply and demand model to labor markets, we can understand how shifts in demand and supply in a market for a particular group of workers affect employment and wage levels in the short and long run. This helps to explain why the average earnings of U.S. college graduates have increased so dramatically from the late 1970s to the present. Empirical evidence on labor market adjustments also helps us to understand how long the long run is in calendar time.

We also examine how migration of workers and employers between markets determines the structure of wages across occupations, industries, and regions. Why do professional athletes who have graduated from college earn average wages considerably above those earned by "normal" college graduates? The important concept of rents and compensating differentials as the long-run determinants of the wage structure are the focal point of this analysis.

Equilibrium in a Single Labor Market

It is common in economics to look at a single market in isolation from others; this is known as partial equilibrium analysis. Before we can begin to examine the interaction of supply and demand in a single market, we need to think a bit about the factors that might define the boundaries of a labor market. By a particular labor market, we usually mean a market for a specific occupation within a geographic area. Clark Kerr[1] provides this definition:

> The labor market is the area, defined occupationally, industrially, and geographically, within which workers are willing to move and do move comparatively freely from one job to another. Movement within the area is fairly easy and customary; and migration into it or out of it is less frequent and more difficult.

If we are considering the labor market for janitors, the geographic limits of the market might be commuting distance around a city. The market for CEOs, however, might be national or even international in its geographic limits because a potential supplier in this market is willing to migrate in response to a job opportunity.

Supply-Demand Models

Figure 7.1 shows the most typical version of the labor market supply and demand curves. Along the vertical axis are values of the real wage (w/p), which is the nominal compensation paid by employers and received by workers for a unit of labor (w) deflated by an appropriate price index (p). Along the horizontal axis is the number of labor units (which could be hours, weeks, or persons) offered by people and demanded by employers at each real wage. As the real wage rises, people increase their willingness to enter the labor force and may increase their work hours supplied, so we have drawn a positively sloped labor supply curve for the entire market. At the same time, higher real wages will reduce the quantity demanded of labor, so the market demand curve is negatively sloped.

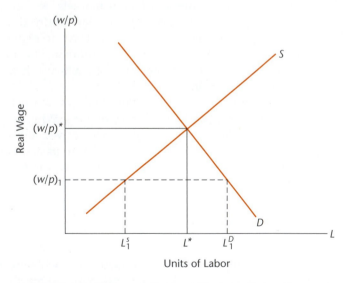

FIGURE 7.1 Real Wage Adjusts to Eliminate Excess Demand

---

[1] Clark Kerr, "Labor Markets: Their Character and Consequences," in *Labor Markets and Wage Determination: The Balkanization of Labor Markets and Other Essays,* ed., Clark Kerr (Berkeley: University of California Press, 1977), pp. 38–39.

The market supply and demand curves represent the sum of all the potential suppliers and demanders of a particular type of labor. Normally, this means that the demand and supply curves are aggregated horizontally—summing, at each value of the real wage, the demand for labor across all firms and the supply of labor across all workers. The supply of labor is limited by the number of people who have the skills and experience required for the type of job under consideration. The demand for labor adds up the demand of firms in all industries that use a particular type of worker. For example, manufacturing firms and schools are both potential buyers in the labor market for janitors, maintenance electricians, or accountants.

The equilibrium real wage is the level of w/p at which the quantity demanded of labor equals the quantity supplied. In Figure 7.1, the equilibrium values are denoted as $(w/p)^*$ and L^*. Suppose the current real wage is at $(w/p)_1$. At this real wage, the quantity demanded exceeds the quantity supplied ($L_1^D > L_1^S$), and individual firms will have an incentive to bid up the nominal wage w (thus raising the real wage w/p) to attract the amount of labor they need. As the real wage rises, the quantity of labor supplied increases and the quantity of labor demanded decreases until these quantities are in balance and there is no further impetus to push up w.

If the quantity supplied exceeds the quantity demanded at a given real wage, individual workers will have the incentive to bid down the money wage w to secure employment. This will move the real wage lower, which in turn will bring the quantity supplied and demanded in the market into equilibrium. This description of how equilibrium is arrived at is perfectly analogous to the demand and supply models that we use to describe the determination of prices and quantities in other markets. An important empirical question is whether we can observe real-world labor markets moving toward equilibrium as predicted by the model.

Two things need to be considered with regard to the concept of labor market equilibrium as applied to real-world markets. First, it is best to think of the equilibrium wage in the model as the average wage given by data on the market with a distribution of actual wages about that mean. Because of worker and job heterogeneity (not all applicants for janitorial jobs are identical nor are all janitorial positions the same in terms of working conditions, and so forth), it is very difficult to delineate a market narrowly enough so that we can have confidence that the law of one price, which is implied by supply and demand models, will prevail.

Second, even though the quantity demanded equals the quantity supplied of labor units if the market is in equilibrium, this does not mean that all jobs are filled and that all workers are employed at any given moment of time. Because of normal turnover (quits, dismissals, retirements, deaths, new entrants, and reentrants), it is far more likely that a survey taken today will find some jobs vacant and some workers unemployed even in a labor market that is in equilibrium. If we define the quantity of labor demanded as the level of employment plus unfilled positions (that the employer would like to fill) at each real wage, and the quantity of labor supplied as the number employed plus the number of job seekers at each real wage, the real-world market equilibrium occurs when vacancies are equal to the number of seekers at the current real wage. Such a market is balanced in the sense that demand equals supply—but there remains the problem that the vacancies and the unemployed workers have not "found" each other. We will return to this issue in Chapter 8.

The position of the labor supply curve in Figure 7.1 is determined by the number of potential workers; the nonwage income, including pensions and transfer payments, available to them; their preferences for leisure and consumption; and by the effect of taxes on

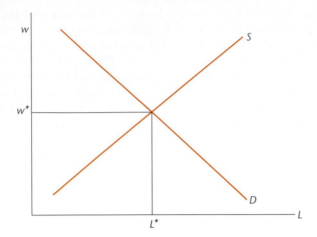

FIGURE 7.2 The Equilibrium Nominal Wage

their take-home pay. The position of the labor demand curve in Figure 7.1 is determined by the price of other inputs, by the technical possibilities of substitution among inputs in the production of the various goods and services produced with the use of this type of labor, and by the aggregate output of the firms hiring these workers. Shifts in labor demand or supply would result from changes in any of these underlying factors and would, in turn, move the labor market to a different equilibrium position.

Figure 7.2 presents a slightly different way of drawing the labor supply and demand model. Here the nominal wage (w) is measured on the vertical axis instead of the real wage (w/p). We might prefer to use this depiction of the labor market model for a couple of reasons. First, although workers and employers may be motivated by the purchasing power of the wages they receive and pay out, respectively, actual labor markets invariably express the transaction between labor suppliers and demanders in nominal terms. Only in the case of countries experiencing hyperinflation with fully indexed wages[2] can we say that the labor market determines the *real* wage. In "normal" circumstances, labor markets determine nominal wage levels.

Second, by using this framework, we can more easily take into account the different real wages motivating buyer and seller behavior. Workers make labor supply decisions by comparing the nominal wage offered with the cost of living, perhaps measured by a consumer or retail price index. Employers make labor demand decisions by comparing the nominal wage with the selling price of their products. It is possible that changes in the retail price index might differ from changes in the producer price index for the products made with the help of a given group of workers, resulting in different effects on supply and demand decisions. It is also possible that the short-run response of sellers and buyers to an equal price increase might be different.

---

[2] Hyperinflation refers to a situation where the average price level increases at an extremely rapid rate, causing the purchasing power of the country's currency to fall significantly each day. In such cases, nominal wages are often indexed; that is, they are automatically adjusted with rising prices to keep their purchasing power more or less the same over time.

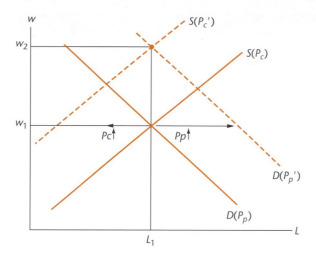

FIGURE 7.3 A Rise in Prices Results in a Higher Nominal Wage

Figure 7.3 examines how changes in the price level would affect labor market equilibrium. A rise in consumer prices (p_c) causes the labor supply curve to shift to the left at all nominal wage levels. This change in consumer prices reduces the purchasing power of each wage level, rotating the income line in toward the origin and causing some people to drop out of the workforce or to reduce their hours supplied (see Chapters 4 and 5). A rise in producer prices (p_p) causes the labor demand curve to shift to the right because the value of the marginal product of workers has risen. These changes in labor supply and demand would cause a rise in the nominal wage. If the percentage change in p_c equaled the percentage change in p_p and buyers and sellers responded to these changes in the same way, there would be no change in the equilibrium level of L. This is shown in Figure 7.3.

It is conceivable, however, that the changes in p_c and p_p would differ. For example, p_p might be determined nationally or even internationally for firms that export, whereas p_c might be heavily influenced by local factors. It is also conceivable that workers or employers might respond differently to a given change in p_c or p_p. For example, it might take some time for workers to fully realize how the cost of living has changed as a result of a rise in p_c. In these cases, both w and L might change as a result of a simultaneous change in p_c and p_p, at least in the short run.

Recall that we have held everything else constant in drawing the demand and supply curves in Figure 7.2 and in considering how they might change as the price level changes in Figure 7.3. Supply and demand shifts can occur for other reasons. An increase in income taxes would be expected to shift labor supply to the left, whereas an increase in industry output or a technological change favoring this particular type of worker would be expected to shift labor demand to the right.

Empirical Evidence

The supply and demand model of individual labor markets generates very clear hypotheses about the effect of changes in labor demand and labor supply on equilibrium wage

THE WAY WE WORK

A Strong Market for Economics PhDs in the United States

In the spring of 2001, despite a slowing U.S. economy, graduate students entering the job market for new holders of PhDs in economics were pleasantly surprised by the strength of the demand for their services. The *Wall Street Journal*[*] reported that salary offers of $70,000 to $80,000, already up 15% since 1999, were being supplemented with offers of lighter teaching loads, early sabbaticals, and generous financial support for research and summer pay. Students from top PhD-granting departments and those with expertise in financial economics received multiple job offers.

The strength of the market was traced to supply and demand shifts. Rising demand stemmed from two factors. First, there was increased recruiting of PhD economists by consulting and financial services firms, which added considerably to university and government job openings. Second, rapidly rising enrollment in undergraduate economics courses has led to increased demand for new economics faculty at the same time that large numbers of faculty are approaching retirement. At top universities without undergraduate business majors such as Harvard, economics is the most popular major on campus, with the number of majors up by more than 30% in the last five years.

At the same time, the supply of new PhDs had fallen in prior years to levels not seen since the 1950s. The attraction of MBAs and law degrees, with shorter training periods and bigger financial returns to the investment, has siphoned off many students who would be expected to pursue a PhD in economics. In addition, the very tight labor markets of the preceding few years had increased the opportunity cost of leaving the job market for five years of graduate study.

As all those new economists will say again and again during their careers, "It's all supply and demand!"

Note: *[*]Jon E. Hilsenrath, "In Hot Pursuit of Economics Ph.D.s," *Wall Street Journal*, February 20, 2001.

rate and employment levels. A large number of empirical studies of labor market adjustment have been carried out over the years. These studies help us see how well real-world markets correspond to the predictions of our model of the labor market. Empirical studies can also help us see how the process of labor market adjustment works out over time. The theory we have studied doesn't tell us much about the dynamics of adjustment, and the evidence on this topic shows us again how important it is to consider the role of institutions as well as markets in wage and employment determination.

Randall Eberts and Joe Stone completed a significant study of the wage and employment responses to demand and supply changes in local labor markets in the United States.[3] They used panel data for 21 metropolitan areas over the period from 1973 to 1987

---

[3] Randall W. Eberts and Joe A. Stone, *Wage and Employment Adjustment in Local Labor Markets* (Kalamazoo: W. E. Upjohn Institute, 1992).

to estimate labor demand and supply curves for a "representative" local labor market. These estimates were then used to simulate the response of the market to changes in demand and supply.

Eberts and Stone determined the wage elasticity of labor demand to be −1.04 and the wage elasticity of labor supply to be +4.9. This supply elasticity seems quite large; however, in a local labor market, an increase in wages may induce workers from other localities to migrate to or commute to jobs in the high-wage area. In addition, it gives residents the incentive to increase their labor force participation or their hours of work. A local wage increase can generate a substantial supply response.

The wage and employment effects of shifts in labor demand and supply implied by the model estimated by Eberts and Stone are presented in Figures 7.4 and 7.5. Figure 7.4 traces the effect over time of a 1% increase in the local demand for labor relative to labor demand in the United States as a whole. The level of both wages and employment rise in response to this increase, as we would predict from the basic labor supply-demand model. However, given their estimate of a fairly flat labor supply curve, most of the increase in labor demand results in rising employment rather than in increased wages. In the new equilibrium, which takes about a decade to reach, about 80% of the increase in labor demand is in the form of increased employment and about 20% is absorbed in a higher wage.

Figure 7.5 shows Eberts and Stone's estimate of the wage and employment effects resulting from a shift in labor supply. As expected from the basic model, an increase in supply moves the market toward lower wages and greater employment. In this case, the ultimate wage and employment changes are roughly proportional, which reflects their finding of a wage elasticity of demand about equal to −1. The effects of both supply and demand changes play out over long periods of time, suggesting that shocks to a local labor market may be felt in the community for more than a decade before the self-adjusting mechanism of the market brings wages and employment levels to a new

FIGURE 7.4 Wage and Employment Response to an Increase in Local Labor Demand

Source: Randall W. Eberts and Joe A. Stone, *Wage and Employment Adjustment in Local Labor Markets* (Kalamazoo: W. E. Upjohn Institute, 1992).

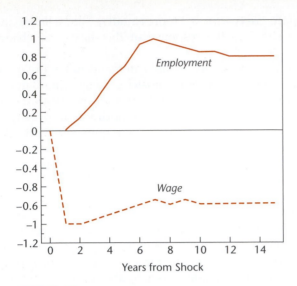

FIGURE 7.5 Wage and Employment Response to an Increase in Local Labor Supply

Source: Randall W. Eberts and Joe A. Stone, *Wage and Employment Adjustment in Local Labor Markets* (Kalamazoo: W. E. Upjohn Institute, 1992).

equilibrium. The conclusions that local labor demand shifts affect employment more than wages and that markets take a long time to return to equilibrium are also seen in other studies.[4]

Empirical studies of market responses to changes in labor demand have received considerable attention as economists try to understand how the labor market behaves during business cycle downturns. For example, Harry Holzer and Edward Montgomery examined the effects of positive and negative labor demand shifts on wage and employment adjustment in labor markets.[5] More specifically, they examined the labor demand impact of increases and decreases in product sales growth for a sample of U.S. firms in 1980 and 1982. Like Eberts and Stone, they found that short-run wage adjustments to changes in labor demand were significantly smaller than employment adjustments. They also found evidence of an asymmetric wage response: that is, wages rose when increased sales growth boosted labor demand, but wages did not drop much, if at all, when decreased sales growth led to reduced labor demand.

This asymmetric response of wages to a labor demand shock with downwardly rigid real wages is a common feature of empirical studies of the cyclical behavior of real wages

---

[4]See Timothy J. Bartik, *Who Benefits from State and Local Economic Development Policies?* (Kalamazoo: W. E. Upjohn Institute, 1991); and Olivier Jean Blanchard and Lawrence F. Katz, "Regional Evolutions," *Brookings Papers on Economic Activity* 1 (1992): 1–75.

[5]Harry J. Holzer and Edward B. Montgomery, "Asymmetries and Rigidities in Wage Adjustments by Firms," *Review of Economics and Statistics* 75 (1993): 397–408.

in the United States and other countries.[6] For example, Alun Thomas found that real wages were relatively inflexible in response to changes in labor demand in regional labor markets in Britain and the United States and in national labor markets in Europe.[7] And Mariano Bella and Beniamino Quintieri found that labor demand shifts in Italy mainly affected industrial employment and had only minor effects on wages.[8] This evidence of wage rigidity, especially in response to a decrease in labor demand, has been one of the factors leading to the study of how institutions and public policy affect wage-setting behavior.

The Phillips Curve

As we have seen, labor market studies find that labor demand shifts primarily affect employment in the very short run and that these employment changes have delayed effects on wages that take a substantial period of time to be completed. This has led to many empirical studies of the response of wages to changes in the unemployment rate, where unemployment is used as an indicator of changes in labor demand relative to labor supply. The **Phillips curve** estimates the relationship between the percentage change in nominal wages and the unemployment rate, controlling for the anticipated rate of price inflation in time series data.[9] Although the Phillips curve model has often been criticized for lacking a microeconomic theoretical foundation, the wage-unemployment relationship can be seen as essentially derived from the basic supply-demand model of the labor market explaining the nominal wage.

When the labor market is in equilibrium and demand equals supply, there will be measurable unemployment resulting from turnover and the time required for job seekers to be matched with job vacancies. The unemployment rate at labor market equilibrium has been called the **full-employment unemployment rate**. It is also called the natural or nonaccelerating rate of inflation unemployment rate. At this rate of unemployment, with balance between labor demand and supply, the real wage will not change. If the economy is experiencing price inflation, nominal wages will have to increase just enough to keep the real wage fixed. To see this, we can refer to the following equation:

$$\%\Delta(w/p) \cong \%\Delta w - \%\Delta p \tag{7-1}$$

The real wage will grow only if nominal wages increase at a faster pace than the rate of price inflation. For a given rate of inflation (such as $\%\Delta p = 5$), the real wage would remain unchanged as long as $\%\Delta w = \%\Delta p$. This would be the case with the labor market at equilibrium.

---

[6] Thomas J. Kniesner and Arthur H. Goldsmith, "A Survey of Alternative Models of the Aggregate U.S. Labor Market," *Journal of Economic Literature* 25 (1987): 1241–1280.

[7] Alun H. Thomas, "The Response of Wages and Labor Supply Movements to Employment Shocks across Europe and the United States," *IMF Working Papers*, 1994.

[8] Mariano Bella and Beniamino Quintieri, "The Effect of Trade on Employment and Wages in Italian Industry," *Labour* 14 (2000): 291–309.

[9] The Phillips curve gets its name from A. William Phillips, "The Relationship between Unemployment and the Rate of Change of Money Wage Rates in the United Kingdom, 1861–1957," *Economica* 25 (1958): 283–299.

However, an increase in labor demand would cause the unemployment rate to decline because an increased number of job opportunities relative to the number of job seekers makes it easier to match seekers with jobs. This increase in labor demand and drop in unemployment is associated with a rising real wage, meaning that the nominal wage is increasing at a faster pace than inflation. Thus, the Phillips curve views nominal wage inflation as inversely related to the unemployment rate. A tighter labor market with lower unemployment is predicted to have faster nominal wage growth for a given rate of price inflation, which will cause the real wage level to increase.

A very simple form of the Phillips curve for annual data can be written as:

$$\%\Delta w_t = \alpha + \beta_1 U_t + \beta_2 \%\Delta p_{t-1} + \varepsilon_t \tag{7-2}$$

where w is the nominal wage, U is the unemployment rate, and p is an index of average prices. Our brief theoretical discussion predicts that $\beta_1 < 0$ and that $\beta_2 > 0$. Table 7.1 presents estimates of the parameters of equation 7-2 from time series data for the home areas of the authors: Chicago, Cleveland, and Wales. These estimates are based on a particular application of multiple regression analysis that adjusts for the possibility of a simultaneous relationship between wage inflation and unemployment. The Phillips curve estimates for these three regions are consistent with predictions: during the sample periods, higher unemployment was correlated with slower wage growth, and more rapid price inflation was associated with faster nominal wage growth. The estimates of the Phillips curve parameters have been used to judge how flexible or rigid wages are in response to a change in unemployment.

The Wage Curve

The **wage curve** is a more recent empirical approach to the study of wage determination, and it also relies on the unemployment rate as a summary measure of the state of labor supply and demand.[10] In fact, David Blanchflower and Andrew Oswald, developers of

TABLE 7.1 Phillips Curve Estimates $\%\Delta w_t = \alpha + \beta_1 U_t + \beta_2 \%\Delta p_{t-1} + \varepsilon_t$

	α	β_1	β_2	R^2
Chicago 1964–86	3.27 (4.74)	−.26 (−2.17)	.82 (6.83)	.67
Cleveland 1964–86	4.38 (3.84)	−.58 (−2.76)	1.02 (5.10)	.62
Wales 1971–85	10.60 (2.60)	−.52 (−1.90)	.69 (2.90)	.60

Source: Thomas Hyclak and Geraint Johnes, "Regional Wage Inflation and Unemployment Dynamics in Great Britain," *Scottish Journal of Political Economy* 39 (1992): 188–200; and Thomas Hyclak and Geraint Johnes, *Wage Flexibility and Unemployment Dynamics in Regional Labor Markets* (Kalamazoo: W. E. Upjohn Institute, 1992).

---

[10] David G. Blanchflower and Andrew J. Oswald, *The Wage Curve* (Cambridge, MA: MIT Press, 1994).

the wage curve concept, argue that the wage curve supplants the Phillips curve in analyzing the effect of local unemployment rates on wages. The wage curve differs from the Phillips curve in two ways: (1) the level of the real wage rather than nominal wage growth is the dependent variable, and (2) estimates are typically based on individual or group data rather than on aggregate economic or regional data.

The wage curve is usually written as:

$$\log(w/p)_{irt} = \alpha\log(U)_{rt} + \beta X_{irt} + d_r + f_t + \varepsilon_{irt} \tag{7-3}$$

where the subscript i designates an individual or group, r denotes a given region or locality, and t denotes a given year. Here X stands for several individual wage determinants, such as education and experience, drawn from human capital theory; d is a separate intercept for each regional labor market, and f is an intercept for each time period. Because the real wage and unemployment rates are both measured in logarithms, the estimate of the parameter α is also an estimate of the elasticity of the real wage with respect to the regional unemployment rate.

Table 7.2 presents some estimates of the elasticity of the real wage with respect to regional unemployment rates in four countries. The estimates are all negative and statistically significant, and they show that areas with higher unemployment rates have lower real wage levels, other things being equal. The elasticity estimates are generally in the range between 0 and -0.3; most estimates are close to -0.10, which is a consistent finding in wage curve analyses and indicates that a 10% decrease in the unemployment rate within a given region would raise the real wage by 1%. Again, we see evidence of rather small wage effects from shifts in labor demand or supply. Only the results for Australia, which are in the neighborhood of -0.20, and perhaps the results for women in the United Kingdom and the United States deviate significantly from the -0.10 standard.[11]

The empirical results from the wage curve studies could be interpreted as evidence that local labor markets with a relatively high demand for labor have lower unemployment rates and higher real wages than areas with relatively weak labor demand. Blanchflower and Oswald also offer several institutional explanations for the existence of wage curves. If we stick with the idea that the wage curve is related to labor market

TABLE 7.2   Estimated Wage Curve Elasticities

Country and Period	All Workers	Men	Women
United States, 1963–87	−.098	−.119	−.064
United Kingdom, 1973–90	−.082	−.094	−.074
Australia, 1986	−.195	−.210	−.200
Canada, 1972–87	−.095		

Source: David Card, "The Wage Curve: A Review," *Journal of Economic Literature* 33 (1995): 785–799.

---

[11] A recent attempt to use meta-analysis of the results reported in a large number of studies indicates the wage curve elasticity is equal to -0.7. We discuss this result in greater depth in Chapter 14. See Peter Nijkamp and Jacques Poot, "The Last Word on the Wage Curve?" *Journal of Economic Surveys* 19 (2005): 421–449.

equilibrium, we encounter a problem similar to that seen with the Phillips curve. The wage curve allows us to predict the real wage that would result from different unemployment rates, but it does not tell us whether the labor market is in equilibrium at that real wage or how real wage levels lead the labor market to equilibrium. It is not a complete model of the labor market.

This brief review of empirical studies following different methods gives us three key insights. First, it does appear that real-world wage and employment levels respond to shifts in labor demand and supply in a manner consistent with the predictions of the basic labor market model. An understanding of the evolution of supply and demand in a given market is important to understanding why wages in that market are what they are. Second, although real-world wages respond in the hypothesized way to an increase in labor demand, there is consistent evidence that this response is small in magnitude even in the long run. Third, it appears that labor markets may require a long time to return to equilibrium after a demand or supply shift. A number of attempts to amend the basic model or to incorporate institutional features into the model of the labor market have been motivated by an interest in explaining this evidence of relative stability of wages in the face of demand shocks and the long adjustment period.

Equilibrium Across Different Labor Markets

Comparing the wages received by different workers, or groups of workers, is a widely pursued pastime by many people who are not labor economists. For example, *Parade* magazine periodically publishes a list of people in various occupations from around the United States in an explicit comparison of what different workers earn. If a teacher in Boise, Idaho makes $30,000 a year while a computer engineer in Boston makes $120,000, an important question to ask is what is behind that wage difference (our answer thus far would be supply and demand) and whether that wage difference is permanent. It is the permanence of wage differentials between labor markets that we turn to now.

The teacher in Boise could learn computer engineering and move to Boston to earn a higher wage. If a lot of people did the same thing, the increased supply of computer engineers chasing jobs in Boston should push down that wage, and the disappearance of qualified teachers from Boise should raise that wage. In analyzing whether wage differentials will persist in the long run, we need to consider the gains and costs of moving between markets to find a better deal.

Figure 7.6 illustrates the way demand and supply differences between labor markets could result in a wage differential between two groups of workers. Initially, the real wage in market A exceeds the real wage in market B, and this differential reflects labor market equilibrium in the two markets. However, the wage differential itself creates a motive for the migration of workers or employers between labor markets. Such migration would be expected to reduce or even eliminate the wage differential in the long run.

Supply Adjustments

If A and B are different local labor markets for workers in a given occupation, we might expect workers earning a lower real wage in Market B to have an incentive to migrate to Market A in search of jobs paying higher wages. If A and B represent markets for workers

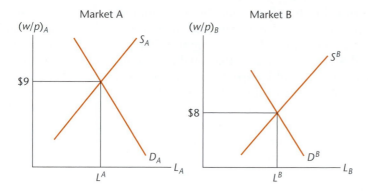

FIGURE 7.6 A Short-Run Wage Differential

with different occupations, skills, or education, those in the lower-wage jobs would have an incentive to acquire the skills needed to search for positions in the higher-wage labor market. These types of long-run responses would increase the supply of labor in Market A and lower it in Market B as people either shifted their residence or acquired the skills or education needed to switch occupations. Such a shift in supply would lower the equilibrium real wage in market A and raise the wage in market B, as indicated in Figure 7.7.

Will this adjustment in wages continue until they are the same in both markets? This is highly unlikely. An individual incurs costs of switching between labor markets. These **migration costs** may be dollar costs (to move between geographic areas or to acquire skills or education needed to enter the high-wage market), opportunity costs of the time required to find out about wage differentials and to take action to move toward the high-wage market, and psychic or disutility costs from leaving familiar surroundings to pursue a higher wage. Wage differentials between markets must be big enough to offset these costs if a supply adjustment such as that shown in Figure 7.7 is going to happen. In addition, if a shift in supply starts to reduce the wage differential between these markets, this will also reduce the incentive for individuals to incur the costs necessary to switch labor markets. Although we expect supply adjustments like those in Figure 7.7 to occur, the long-run equilibrium will still involve wage differentials that are just big enough to compensate workers for the cost of migrating.

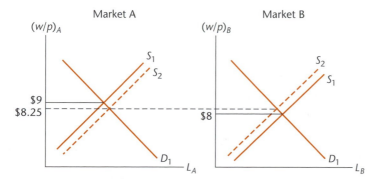

FIGURE 7.7 Migration of Workers Reduces Wage Differentials in the Long Run

In some cases, long-run supply adjustments between markets may not occur even if there is a very large wage differential between related markets. What professional athletes, corporate CEOs, and entertainers have in common is a scarce and innate skill that is limited in supply in the population and that enables them to earn average salaries substantially above what they could expect to earn in their next best alternative employment. Unlike the decision to go to college in order to qualify for a higher paying job, it is not possible for an individual to *decide* to become seven feet tall with great shooting, rebounding, and shot-blocking skills so as to qualify for a very high-paying job in the NBA. In these labor markets, only a very limited supply response is possible even in the long run. This big wage differential is described as an **economic rent**, which is the return to a skill in scarce supply (not the amount you must pay your landlord each month).

Demand Adjustments

The existence of wage differentials between labor markets also provides an incentive to employers to switch their labor demand from the high-wage market to the low-wage market. The existence of lower wages in the South motivated large numbers of U.S. textile and apparel manufacturers to move their operations out of the Northeast region of the country after World War II. The existence of even lower wages in Southeast Asia and Latin America has stimulated an additional shift in the location of this industry in recent decades. In addition, skilled workers command a substantial wage premium over unskilled workers; therefore, employers have an incentive to discover ways to substitute low-wage workers for higher-wage workers, perhaps by changing the work process.

A long-run shift in labor demand between markets toward low-wage workers acts to reduce wage disparity in the manner shown in Figure 7.8. As the demand for low-wage workers increases, their wage is bid higher. As the demand for labor shifts away from high-wage workers, their wages fall.

Long-run adjustment on the demand side of the market depends on the ability of firms to substitute low-wage labor for high-wage labor in production. In many cases, this is not possible. For example, it is unlikely that a hospital could successfully substitute radiologists for surgeons even if the wage differentials between these groups favored such a switch. Also, the firm's ability to substitute low-wage for high-wage workers

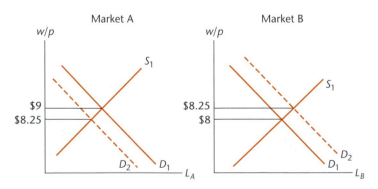

FIGURE 7.8 Demand Shifts Reduce Wage Differentials in the Long Run

might be limited by the requirement to invest in new capital equipment or new technology or to incur other costs, such as training or supervision costs, to make effective use of the low-wage workers in production. Still, in practice we would expect both supply and demand adjustments to occur over time in response to a large wage differential between different groups of workers.

In certain cases, however, long-run adjustment to eliminate or reduce wage differentials between workers can occur only on the demand side. This is certainly the case with gender or racial wage differentials. An important question that we examine in detail in Chapter 13 is why employers have been slow to respond to the opportunity of hiring women or minority workers for lower wages than they pay white males.

Compensating Differentials

Our analysis thus far has suggested that supply and demand shifts in the long run will act to reduce wage differentials between labor markets but that such differentials will not be completely eliminated. In long-run equilibrium, wage differences will remain between groups that are just high enough to compensate for other differences between the jobs held by these groups. These are known as **compensating differentials**. Workers will have to be paid a higher wage to accept employment in "bad" or "hard" jobs or to induce them to undergo the education and training necessary to fill certain positions.

A perfectly satisfactory discussion of compensating differentials can be found in *The Wealth of Nations*, written by Adam Smith in 1776.[12] He identified a number of ways in which wage inequalities might arise because of employment conditions:

- Jobs that are hard, dirty, and dangerous will pay more, other things being equal, than easier, cleaner, and safer jobs. A wage premium may be required to induce workers to fill them.
- Wages will be higher in jobs requiring more costly training. We discussed this in Chapter 6 when we examined the incentives for individuals to invest in human capital. The private return on investment in education or skill is the wage differential a worker can expect to earn over his or her work life.
- Wages will be higher in jobs that are highly seasonal, that are affected by the weather, or that involve periods of unemployment between projects. The wage premium here is needed to get workers to enter the market and maintain their skills when they often are unable to work for a complete year.
- Wages will be higher in jobs that require a higher degree of trust or responsibility. One sometimes hears people long for a job "they don't have to take home with them." A worker responsible for planning and executing operations needs to be compensated for the extra hours of worry and concentration that go into this type of activity.
- Wages will be lower in occupations that have a small chance of a large gain. This explanation for wage inequality requires a bit of thought. Consider the occupation of rock musician, in which a very small percentage of musicians have the chance of becoming stars and earning the high salaries associated with that status. As a result of the

---

[12] Adam Smith, *An Inquiry into the Nature and Causes of the Wealth of Nations* (New York: The Modern Library Edition, 1937).

numbers drawn to this occupation by the chance of great success, the average salary of all rock musicians, which is heavily weighted by those playing small clubs and dances or on the street corner, is fairly low in comparisons to most jobs. The extremely high wages of very successful musicians, actors, athletes, or lawyers obscure the fact that a large number of people in these occupations earn mediocre salaries.

- Real wages will be lower, all things being equal, in localities with attractive amenities, such as nice weather or interesting recreational activities. Because these places are more attractive to live in, workers should be willing to accept lower wages for the opportunity to live there.

For all of these nonwage job or area characteristics, we might expect to see wage differentials between related labor markets continuing to exist even in the long run when people have had the opportunity to migrate toward markets with higher wages and firms have had the opportunity to substitute, where possible, low-wage workers for high-wage workers.

Empirical Studies of Wage Differentials

Our theoretical analysis suggests two hypotheses about the wage levels in related labor markets. First, where wage differences are in excess of the cost of moving between markets for some workers or firms, supply will shift toward the high-wage market and demand toward the low-wage market. The end result is a move toward convergence of wage levels in the two markets. Second, in the long run, wage differentials between similar workers will be just high enough to compensate for differences in the nonwage characteristics of jobs or areas.

Let's consider the empirical evidence on these two hypotheses. First, we look at studies of interregional migration and wage convergence to determine if regional labor markets operate in a way that leads to reduced wage differentials over time. Then we examine the evidence on whether wage differentials serve to compensate workers for differences in job-related risks of injury or death. As you will see, this empirical evidence supports the hypotheses drawn from our supply and demand analysis of wage differentials.

Interregional Migration and Wage Convergence

Wage differentials across different regions and localities within a country have long been a matter of interest and discussion. Of particular interest to us are the many research projects investigating why people migrate between places. Labor market theory suggests that we should observe out-migration from regions with relatively low real-wage levels and in-migration to regions with relatively high real-wage levels.

In the United States, low relative wages spurred a century-long out-migration from the southern states from the late 1860s to the mid-1960s,[13] and the continued stream of illegal immigrants crossing the border from Mexico into Texas, Arizona, and California has been a public policy issue for decades. In Europe, large-scale migration from the low-income countries of southern Europe and northern Africa to the high-wage economies of western and northern Europe has been an important feature of post–World War II

---

[13] Gavin Wright, *Old South, New South* (New York: Basic Books, 1986).

THE WAY WE WORK

Family-Friendly Policies

In many firms, wages represent only a part of the reward package received by employees. Workers might benefit from travelling allowances—discounted season tickets for public transport, perhaps. In some occupations, workers might receive some of their reward in the form of accommodation that comes with the job. In cases like these, workers typically receive a wage that is lower than it otherwise would be, because the nonpecuniary benefit generates a compensating differential.

The same is true of a firm that implements family-friendly policies—these might take the form of job sharing arrangements, parental leave, flexible working hours, or offering workers the facility to take time off for family reasons and making this time up later. One might, other things being equal, expect workers to be more willing to supply their labor to a firm offering such family-friendly policies; at the same time, one would expect such policies to be costly to the firm. By raising labor supply and reducing demand, we would therefore expect firms offering these policies to pay a lower wage than other firms.

A recent study suggests that the wage differential between firms that offer family-friendly policies and those that do not is of the order of 20%. In other words, family-friendly policies are costly to provide, and firms shift (at least a substantial part of) the cost of providing these facilities onto their workers by paying wages that are quite substantially below those offered by otherwise similar firms.

Note: *John Heywood, Stanley Siebert, and Xiangdong Wei, "The Implicit Wage Costs of Family Friendly Work Practices," *Oxford Economic Papers* 59 (2007): 275–300.

developments and a source of ethnic tension in recent years. Anecdotes and news stories about major migration waves such as these seem to confirm the idea that workers will move to local and regional labor markets in response to better wage and employment opportunities. This is also the conclusion we would reach from a survey of econometric studies of the determinants of less dramatic movements of people among local labor markets.

The dependent variable in such studies is the **net in-migration rate**, which is the number of in-migrants minus the number of out-migrants to an area over a period of time divided by the population. A common finding of econometric studies is that net in-migration is positively correlated with the relative wage in a region. That is, high relative wages are associated with high positive net in-migration rates, and low relative wage levels are associated with low positive or negative net in-migration rates. Additionally, net in-migration is negatively correlated with the relative supply of local labor as measured by regional unemployment rates. Finally, the cost of moving between regions, which is usually measured by the distance between sending and receiving areas, has been found to have a negative effect on net in-migration.[14] All of these empirical relationships are consistent with the predictions of our model of wage differentials.

[14] Michael J. Greenwood, "Research on Internal Migration in the United States: A Survey," *Journal of Economic Literature* 13 (1975): 397–433.

More recent migration studies have examined the interaction between labor and housing markets.[15] If rising local labor demand, falling unemployment, and rising real-wage levels lead to tight housing markets with rising house prices and rentals, the desirability of moving to that community might be diminished. Conversely, if depressed local labor markets result in low housing demand and low house prices in regional housing markets, it may be difficult for workers to sell their homes and leave such an area. The interaction of labor and housing markets might mean that some workers will commute over long distances to jobs in areas with high wages instead of moving their residence to an area with high house prices in addition to high wages.

Table 7.3 shows the relationship between wages, unemployment, and house prices and in-commuting and in-migration among the regions of the United Kingdom. Higher and more rapidly rising full-time wages were associated with higher in-commuting and in-migration rates for these regions, holding other determinants of these rates constant. Higher and more rapidly rising unemployment rates reduced the percentage of workers commuting into an area and the percentage of population associated with net in-migration. Higher house prices in a region reduced the rate of in-migration to that region and increased the fraction of the regional workforce made up of commuters. These results are in accord with the predictions of our model of wage differentials.

Empirical evidence seems to show that workers move or commute from one geographic area to another in response to higher wages or better job opportunities. Has this movement, along with the possibility of demand shifts toward low-wage regions, also served to reduce geographic wage differentials as our theory suggests? The answer can be found in the literature on regional convergence.

Economists have looked for two kinds of evidence that regional income or wages have come closer together over time. So-called **beta convergence** is present when data indicate

TABLE 7.3   The Effect of Unemployment, Wages, and House Prices on Net Commuting and Net Migration to British Regions

Regional Characteristics	Net In-Commuting	Net In-Migration
$\Delta\ln$ (Full-Time Wage)	.265 (13.2)	.050 (11.4)
$\ln$ (Full-Time Wage)$_{t-1}$	.184 (11.5)	.024 (7.74)
$\ln$ (House Price)$_{t-1}$	.051 (5.7)	−.015 (−2.3)
Δ Unemployment Rate	−1.30 (−25.0)	
Unemployment Rate$_{t-1}$	−.24 (−5.7)	−.023 (−3.06)

Note: t statistics are in parentheses. Other independent variables were included in these regressions.

Source: Gavin Cameron and John Muellbauer, "The Housing Market and Regional Commuting and Migration Choices," *Center for Economic Policy Research Discussion Paper 1945,* 1998.

---

[15]Stuart A. Gabriel, Janice Shack-Marquez, and William L. Wascher, "Regional House Price Dispersion and Interregional Migration," *Journal of Housing Economics* 2 (1992): 235–256; Richard Jackman and Savva Savouri, "Regional Migration in Britain: An Analysis of Gross Flows Using NHS Central Register Data," *Economic Journal* 102 (1991): 1433–1450; Geraint Johnes and Thomas Hyclak, "Housing Prices, Migration and Regional Labor Markets," *Journal of Housing Economics* 3 (1994): 312–329.

that high-wage areas at the beginning of a time period had slower wage growth over that period than low-wage areas. This indicates that forces are at work to erode wage differences across areas over time. **Sigma convergence** occurs if over time the dispersion of wages across areas, as measured by the standard deviation or variance, diminishes. This indicates that wages across regions are moving toward the national average. Studies have found evidence of beta convergence across regions in many countries, but sigma convergence seems to occur much less frequently.

Most studies of regional convergence have used data on per capita income or gross domestic product rather than wage levels. Robert Barro and Xavier Sala-i-Martin found evidence for beta convergence in U.S. state per capita income over the period from 1880 to 1988 and in European regional per capita gross domestic product (GDP) from 1950 to 1985. And Serge Coulombe and Frank C. Lee found evidence for beta convergence in Canadian provincial per capita income from 1961 to 1991.[16] However, studies of regional income convergence within the small countries of Austria and Greece did not find much evidence of beta convergence.[17] With respect to wage differences, there is evidence of beta convergence for average wages across U.S. metropolitan areas from 1969 to 1995 and for Canadian provinces from 1964 to 1990.[18]

Figure 7.9 provides some information on beta convergence for the relative wage of clerical workers (the local wage as a percentage of the U.S. average wage) across 37 large U.S. metropolitan areas from 1971/72 to 1990. There is a slight tendency in these data for areas with high initial relative wages to show slower relative wage growth than those areas with lower initial wage levels. However, as is evident from the scatter diagram, this is not a particularly close relationship. The correlation coefficient between these two series is only –0.16. Still, we might take this as enough evidence for beta convergence across these areas to warrant a more complete analysis of the data. There is no evidence in these data for sigma convergence. The standard deviation of the relative wage across areas in 1971/72 was 7.50, and in 1990 it was 8.54. So, the dispersion of wages across areas increased rather than decreased over this time span.

Within Europe, too, convergence of wages has been a feature of labor markets. Paul Ramskolger has studied a panel of data over the period 1992–2005 and concluded that wage growth in western European economies exhibited strong interdependence over this period.[19] Peter Egger has studied convergence in the Czech Republic, Hungary, and Poland—three of the countries that joined the European Union in 2004, though his

[16] Robert J. Barro and Xavier Sala-i-Martin, "Convergence across States and Regions," *Brookings Papers on Economic Activity* 1 (1991): 223–251; and S. Coulombe and F. C. Lee, "Convergence across Canadian Provinces, 1961 to 1991," *Canadian Journal of Economics* 28 (1995): 886–898.

[17] Helmut Hofer and Andreas Woergoetter, "Regional Per Capita Income Convergence in Austria," *Regional Studies* 31 (1997): 1–12; and Costas Siriopoulos and Dimitrios Asteriou, "Testing for Convergence across the Greek Regions," *Regional Studies* 32 (1998): 537–546.

[18] Matthew P. Drennan and José Lobo, "A Simple Test for Convergence of Metropolitan Income in the United States," *Journal of Urban Economics* 46 (1999): 350–359; and Bakhtiar Moazzami, "Regional Wage Convergence in Canada: An Error-Correction Approach," *Canadian Journal of Regional Science* (1997): 341–350.

[19] Paul Ramskogler, "The State of Wage Convergence in the European Monetary Union," *Vienna University of Economics Working Paper 130*, 2010. http://bit.ly/mSUMeJ. Ramskogler focuses on members of the European Monetary Union, a club of countries that, prior to the introduction of the euro, ensured that the exchange rates between their currencies remained broadly stable.

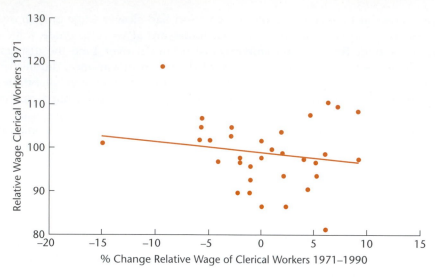

FIGURE 7.9 Wage Convergence, U.S. Metro Areas, 1971 to 1990

Source: Authors' calculations from data in "Area Wage Surveys: Metropolitan Areas, United States and Regional Summaries, 1971–72," *Bureau of Labor Statistics Bulletin* 1725–96, and "Area Wage Surveys: Selected Metropolitan Areas, 1990," *Bureau of Labor Statistics Bulletin* 3055–61.

analysis relies upon data from the period leading up to their accession.[20] He finds that sigma convergence of wages in these countries has accelerated as a consequence of the increase in intermediate goods trade resulting from greater outsourcing.

This brief survey of empirical studies of interregional migration and wage differentials gives us some measure of confidence in the predictions of our model of equilibrium in related labor markets. Workers move toward local labor markets with better wages and job opportunities, and wage differences favoring certain localities are eroded over time by market forces.

Compensating Differentials for Job Safety

Our second hypothesis about wage differentials is that in the long run wage differentials between groups will be just high enough to compensate workers for nonwage characteristics of the job. In Chapter 6, we saw how wage differences between college and high school graduates determine the return to the money and opportunity costs of acquiring a college degree. If the wage differential isn't high enough, the number of students enrolling in college will decline, the supply of college graduates will fall, and the relative wages of college graduates will begin to rise. In equilibrium, the wage difference between high school and college graduates will be just high enough to ensure that the labor supply of college graduates matches the labor demand.

---

[20] Peter Egger, "Intermediate Goods Trade and International Wage Convergence in Central Europe," *Empirica* 33 (2006): 181–192.

Another factor differentiating jobs is the risk of injury or death facing workers. The data in Table 7.4 illustrate the wide variation across countries in death rates from occupational injuries. In the United Kingdom, fewer than one worker out of every 100,000 died as a result of an accident at work, whereas in the United States, the occupational fatality rate was 3.9 workers out of every 100,000 employed. In part, the differences are due to industrial structure, with many developing economies focusing economic production in more hazardous activities such as agriculture and extraction (mining). It may also be the case that the economic incentives for firms to ensure the safety of their workforce are weaker in contexts where the value of a life (as measured by the positive hedonic wage functions that we discussed earlier—*not*, we emphasize, as measured in a normative sense) is lower.

The risk of injury and death also varies considerably across industries, occupations, regions, and individual employers within a country. This is illustrated in Table 7.5, which shows 2010 rates of fatal and nonfatal injuries by major industry group in the United States. Agriculture has the highest risk of fatal injury, and jobs in transportation and warehousing carry the highest risk of nonfatal injury. Not surprisingly, jobs in office-based occupations tend to be relatively safe.

If Adam Smith was right, similar workers in jobs with a greater risk of injury or death should receive a compensating wage differential in comparison with those in less risky positions. Testing this compensating differential hypothesis has been the focus of the quality-adjusted wage function literature (or so-called **hedonic wage functions**). A large number of empirical studies have established the conclusion that workers are indeed compensated for a higher risk of fatal and nonfatal injuries on the job.[21]

TABLE 7.4   International Comparison of Occupational Fatality Rates, 2006–07

Country	Fatality Rate
Australia	1.8
Canada	6.3
Hungary	3.0
Japan	2.1
France	2.4
Germany	2.1
Poland	3.1
Spain	2.8
Sweden	1.7
United Kingdom	0.7
United States	3.9

Source: Authors' calculations from data in the Yearbook of Labor Statistics, International Labor Office. The data refer to 2006 for the United Kingdom and 2007 for all other countries. Fatality rate is the reported number of fatal occupational accidents per 100,000 workers. http://www.ilo.org/public/ENGLISH/protection/safework/accidis/globesti.pdf

---

[21] W. Kip Viscusi, "The Value of Risks to Life and Health," *Journal of Economic Literature* 31 (1993): 1912–1946.

TABLE 7.5 Fatal and Nonfatal Injury Rates by Industry in the United States, 2010

	Fatalities per 100,000 Workers	Nonfatal Injuries per 100 Workers
Agriculture	26.8	4.8
Mining	19.8	2.3
Transportation	13.1	5.2
Construction	9.5	4.0
Wholesale	4.8	3.4
Other Services	3.0	2.7
Utilities	2.5	3.1
Professional and Business Services	2.5	1.7
Manufacturing	2.2	4.4
Retail	2.2	4.1
Leisure and Hospitality	2.2	3.9
Information	1.5	1.8
Financial Activities	1.2	1.3
Education and Health Care	0.9	4.8

Source: "National Census of Fatal Occupational Injuries in 2010 (Preliminary Results)," U.S. Department of Labor, Bureau of Labor Statistics News Release USDL-11-1246, August 25, 2011 and "Workplace Injuries and Illnesses – 2010," U.S. Department of Labor, Bureau of Labor Statistics News Release USDL 11-1502, October 20, 2011.

The method of testing for the existence of risk-related compensating differentials generally involves the estimation of a wage regression like the following:

$$w_i = \alpha + \sum \beta_j X_{ji} + \theta p_i + \varepsilon_i \tag{7-4}$$

where w is the wage or logarithm of the wage of each of the i workers in the sample, X stands for one of the j characteristics of each of the i workers and their jobs, which is used to control for wage determinants with the exception of injury rates. Finally, p is the perceived probability of fatal or nonfatal injury in the occupation or industry of employment of each of the i workers in the sample under study. An estimate of θ that is positive and statistically significant would lend support to the idea that workers are compensated for their risk of injury.

For example, a recent study analyzed the effect of the risks of both fatal injury and nonfatal injury on the wages of workers in the United Kingdom from 1991 to 2003.[22] The estimates of the responsiveness of log wages to both fatal and nonfatal injury rates in this study are close to 0.01 and the t statistics associated with these estimates are highly

---

[22] Beat Hintermann, Anna Alberini, and Anil Markandya, "Estimating the Value of Safety with Labour Market Data: Are the Results Trustworthy?" *Applied Economics* 42 (2010): 1085–1100.

PUTTING THEORY TO WORK
RISING LABOR COSTS IN CHINA

China has become a manufacturing power house on the basis of low unit labor costs. Until recently, increased labor supply from rural to urban migration has offset the increased demand for production workers from new Chinese firms and international companies who shifted the location of their operations to China. But there are indications that low wages may be a thing of the past in China.

The Economist magazine reports that wages and benefits for blue-collar workers have been rising by double digit rates for most of the past decade and that recent trends in wages and transportation costs could erase the cost differential between manufacturers in China and the United States in the near future.* Apparently, rising demand for labor is fast outstripping the ability of China's large population to fuel growth in labor supply.

*Note: *"The End of Cheap China," *The Economist*, March 10, 2012.

significant when the wage equation is estimated using ordinary least squares.[23] This would suggest that hourly wages of otherwise similar workers would rise by about 1% for every one person per 10,000 increase in the fatality or injury rate in their industry of employment. A 1% compensating differential for industry fatality risk has also been found for U.S. and Japanese workers.[24]

Estimates of θ indicate how much an individual worker's hourly wage needs to increase to induce that worker to accept a riskier job. These estimates have also been used to calculate the "value" of a worker's life. This would be the total annual expenditure necessary to induce a group of workers to accept an increase of one more death in the expected number of deaths. The estimates of the value of life for samples of workers in more highly developed economies are generally much higher than those elsewhere, reflecting the higher real wages in the former set of countries.

Such estimates of the value of life could be useful in a cost-benefit study of a proposed worker safety requirement. Suppose that some regulation concerning safety could reduce the occupational death rate by one worker per 1,000 at a cost of $1 million. If we knew that workers were collectively willing to "pay" more than $1 million for this reduction in risk by accepting lower wages for safer jobs, this would suggest that the benefits of the proposed regulation exceeded the costs. Of course, measuring the benefits of a safety regulation in this way would be bound to raise a protest from those who would argue that wages and work alone are not the full measure of a person's value. The results reported above would add another concern because they imply that a cost-benefit analysis might find that safety regulations pass this test in a high-wage economy and fail in a low-wage economy.

---

[23] It should be noted, however, that these results are not robust with respect to estimation method; when Hintermann et al. use panel data estimation techniques, the compensating differential associated with risk disappears. It is not clear, however, that the application of panel data methods in this context is appropriate, since risk associated with working in a given industry likely varies little over time.

[24] Thomas J. Kniesner and John D. Leeth, "Compensating Wage Differentials for Fatal Injury Risk in Australia, Japan and the United States," *Journal of Risk and Uncertainty* 4 (1991): 75–90. They found a 2.5% higher compensating differential in their sample of Australian workers.

Our theoretical analysis of the operation of labor markets in the long run concludes that wage differences between otherwise similar workers in different labor markets should reflect compensating differentials. We have seen that higher wages are needed to provide a return to workers who invest in more schooling. We have also seen that occupations that have a higher risk of injury or death "compensate" workers who accept this higher risk by paying them a wage premium. The evidence on compensating differentials for these and other nonwage aspects of employment suggest that Adam Smith was correct in his analysis of the reasons for differences in the wage advantages of different occupations.

International Trade and Relative Wages

Our final topic in this chapter concerns the impact of increased international trade and immigration on the wages of skilled workers relative to the wages of unskilled workers. This topic, which used to be confined to a small section in courses on international trade, has become a very important issue in recent analyses of labor market trends in the United States and Europe. This has happened because of the coincidence of two dramatic developments over the last quarter of a century.

First, there has been a rapid increase in world trade, particularly in trade between developed and less developed economies. For example, World Trade Organization data indicate that the ratio of world exports of goods and commercial services to world GDP increased by around 86% over the period from 1985 to 2008. This rise in world trade has been the result of reduced transportation, information, and communication costs, international commitments by the major economies to eliminating trade barriers, and greater pursuit of free trade as part of the development strategies of less developed economies.

At the same time, there has been a marked increase in wage inequality in the United States and other countries that is associated with rising skill differentials. For example, Claudia Goldin and Lawrence Katz have shown that the wage gap between college graduates in the United States and high school graduates widened from 40% in 1980 to 60% in 2005.[25] Economists furthermore predict that this increase in wage inequality is likely to persist.[26] The fact that inequality increased most rapidly in the United States during the 1980s, when the U.S. trade deficit also increased in dramatic fashion, has led many observers to look at international trade as the main cause of rising inequality.

Let's examine the reasoning that suggests a possible link between increased trade with developing countries and increased relative wages by skill in countries like the United States as well as the empirical evidence on the contribution of increased trade to the rise in the U.S. skilled wage premium.

The Relative Supply-Demand Model

The **relative supply-demand model** is a fairly simple extension of the basic supply and demand model shown in Figure 7.10. On the vertical axis is the ratio of the wage paid to

---

[25] Claudia Goldin and Lawrence F. Katz, *The Race between Education and Technology*, Chapter 8 (Harvard University Press: Cambridge, 2008).

[26] See, for example, Joseph Altonji, Prachant Bharadwaj, and Fabian Lange, "Changes in the Characteristics of American Youth: Implications for Adult Outcomes," *NBER Working Paper 13883*, 2008; and Geraint Johnes, "Changes in the Characteristics and Skills of British Youth," *Economics Bulletin* 29 (1) (2009): 368–374.

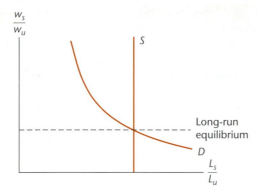

FIGURE 7.10 Labor Market Equilibrium and Relative Wages

skilled workers (w_s) to the wage earned by unskilled workers (w_u); along the horizontal axis, we measure the number of skilled workers employed divided by the number of unskilled workers hired. The short-run supply curve (S) is assumed fixed by the past investments in education and training undertaken by skilled workers. The demand curve (D) traces out a negative relationship between the relative employment of skilled workers and their relative wage. As the wage of skilled workers rises relative to that of unskilled workers, firms will attempt to substitute unskilled for skilled workers to the extent possible.

The demand curve in Figure 7.10 assumes a constant elasticity of substitution between skilled and unskilled workers and can be represented by the following equation:

$$L_s/L_u = T(w_s/w_u)^{-\sigma} \text{ or } \ln(L_s/L_u) = \log(T) - \sigma \ln(w_s/w_u) \tag{7-5}$$

In equation 7-5, the term T stands for the net effect of variables other than the relative wage on the relative demand for skilled workers, and σ is the elasticity of substitution between the skilled and unskilled.

As usual, equilibrium in the labor market occurs when the demand and supply of skilled relative to unskilled workers are equal at the going relative wage. The long-run equilibrium value for w_s/w_u is that which just compensates workers for the cost of investing in the education and training required to acquire the skill. A short-run increase in demand would cause the relative wage to rise above this value, which in turn would increase the financial reward to skilled workers. This is depicted as the movement from point A to point B in Figure 7.11. A rise in the relative wage increases the returns on investment in this skill and so would induce more people to spend the money, time, and energy necessary to acquire this skill. Eventually, the supply would increase as a result of this investment in human capital, and the relative wage would return to the long-run equilibrium level as in the movement from point B to point C in Figure 7.11. Of course, the return to the long-run equilibrium relative wage could take a considerable length of calendar time to accomplish.

Theories of Trade and Wages

The theoretical analysis of the impact of increased trade on relative wages is based on the **Hecksher-Ohlin model**. This model leads to the conclusion that countries sharing the same technology in an environment of open trade will produce and export those products that require more of the factors of production available in relative abundance and import products produced with relatively scarce factors of production. Less developed countries will produce goods that use unskilled labor intensively, and these goods will be imported by developed economies. In turn, developed economies will produce goods that use skilled labor intensively and export these products to less developed countries.

This theory leads to two predictions about wages. The **factor equalization theorem** states that an environment of completely free trade would lead to wage equalization across borders for similarly skilled workers even if workers were not able to migrate from low-wage countries to high-wage countries. However, transportation costs and consumer preferences for domestically produced goods and services may limit free trade effects. In the absence of completely free trade, the **Stolper-Samuelson theorem** predicts that an increase in trade will increase the wage of the relatively abundant factor of production used heavily to produce export goods and lower the wage of the relatively less abundant factor used by other countries to produce import goods.[27]

In terms of the relative supply and demand model, the effect of increased trade between more and less developed economies would lead to a shift to the right in the relative demand curve for skilled workers in the developed country and a shift to the left in the demand curve for skilled workers in the less developed trade partner. This would increase the relative wage of skilled workers in the developed country in the short run and widen wage inequality as a result. In effect, an increase in trade could lead to a shift like that from point A to point B in Figure 7.11 in the developed economy.

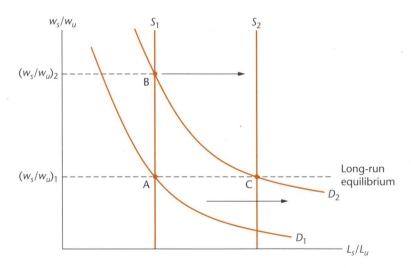

FIGURE 7.11 Short- and Long-Run Adjustments to an Increase in the Demand for Skilled Workers

[27] See Gary Burtless, "International Trade and the Rise in Earnings Inequality," *Journal of Economic Literature* 33 (1995): 800–816; and Wolfgang Stolper and Paul A. Samuelson, "Protection and Real Wages," *Review of Economic Studies* 9 (1941): 58–73.

Some economists believe that the key assumptions of the Hecksher-Ohlin theory—that trade partners have the same technology and produce the same products—are unrealistic. Adrian Wood has developed an alternative theory of trade that rejects the possibility of factor price equalization. However, his analysis still leads to the prediction that an increase in trade between less developed countries and developed economies will put downward pressure on the real wages of less skilled workers in the developed country and raise the relative wage of skilled workers.[28] Again, increased trade with less developed countries is one of the factors that could shift the demand curve to the right in Figure 7.11.

Evidence on Trade and U.S. Wages

A number of trade and labor economists have attempted to estimate the effect of increased trade on the U.S. skilled wage premium. This effort has been complicated by the fact that both the demand and supply for skilled workers has been shifting to the right over time for reasons unrelated to trade. In the United States and other countries, increased educational attainment has resulted in a steady rightward shift in the supply of skilled labor over time. Marvin Kosters has estimated that the upgrading of schooling levels in the U.S. workforce increased the ratio of skilled to unskilled workers from 0.15 in 1960 to 0.67 in 1997, for an average annual rate of growth of 4%.[29] In addition, technological change and growth in the demand for services such as medical care have led to a steady rightward shift in the demand for skilled workers relative to unskilled workers over time. George Johnson's analysis indicates that demand growth for all reasons has generally outstripped supply growth in the United States except during the decade of the 1970s.[30]

If we could observe the supply and demand curves of our relative wage model for any two years, we would expect to see the shifts shown in Figure 7.12 for the past two decades in the United States. The empirical trick is to determine how much, if any, of the shift in the demand curve and the rise in relative wages can be attributed to increased trade with developing countries.

The range of estimates of the contribution of trade to rising skill differentials in the United States runs from close to zero[31] to almost 100%.[32] However, several studies by both trade and labor economists have found that about one-fourth to one-fifth of the rise

[28] Adrian Wood, *North-South Trade, Employment and Inequality: Changing Fortunes in a Skill-Driven World* (Oxford: Clarendon Press, 1994).

[29] Marvin H. Kosters, "Government Policy and Wage Inequality: Regulation, Incentives, and Opportunities," in *The Causes and Consequences of Increasing Inequality*, ed., Finis Welch (Chicago: University of Chicago Press, 2001), pp. 201–240.

[30] George E. Johnson, "Changes in Earnings Inequality: The Role of Demand Shifts," *Journal of Economic Perspectives* 11 (1997): 41–54.

[31] Lawrence F. Katz and Kevin M. Murphy, "Changes in Relative Wages, 1963–1987: Supply and Demand Factors," *Quarterly Journal of Economics* 106 (1992): 35–78.

[32] Wood, op. cit.

PUTTING THEORY TO WORK

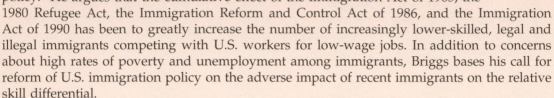

U.S. IMMIGRATION POLICY

Vernon Briggs has been one of the more outspoken critics of U.S. immigration policy.* He argues that the cumulative effect of the Immigration Act of 1965, the 1980 Refugee Act, the Immigration Reform and Control Act of 1986, and the Immigration Act of 1990 has been to greatly increase the number of increasingly lower-skilled, legal and illegal immigrants competing with U.S. workers for low-wage jobs. In addition to concerns about high rates of poverty and unemployment among immigrants, Briggs bases his call for reform of U.S. immigration policy on the adverse impact of recent immigrants on the relative skill differential.

The first part of this analysis rests on the evidence that immigrants, on average, have lower levels of educational attainment than native-born Americans. In a 1997 study, Marvin Kosters[†] finds that 34.7% of the foreign born were high school dropouts, down from 75.4% in 1960, whereas 15.6% of the native born were in this category, down from 57.4% in 1960. At the same time, the percentage of foreign born with a college degree was 24.5% as opposed to 23.8% of the native born. He estimates that the cumulative effect of increased immigration since 1980 made the ratio of skilled to unskilled workers in the United States about one-quarter of a percentage point lower in 1997.

In terms of our relative supply and demand model, this would mean that immigration policy shifted the supply curve slightly to the left of where it would otherwise have been and contributed to the rise in the skilled wage premium. But if the impact of immigration on the relative supply of skilled labor is small, we might expect the impact on relative wages also to be small. Michael Greenwood, Gary Hunt, and Ulrich Kohli simulate the effect of a 20% increase in the number of unskilled foreign-born workers in the United States. Such an increase would lower the real wages of low-skilled natives by two-tenths of 1% and the wages of unskilled foreign-born workers by two-thirds of 1%.[‡]

The debate about U.S. immigration policy will continue, but it is difficult to argue that immigration has played a big role in raising wage inequality.

Notes: *Vernon M. Briggs Jr., *Mass Immigration and the National Interest*, 2nd ed. (Armonk, NY: M. E. Sharpe, 1996).

[†]Marvin H. Kosters, "Government Policy and Wage Inequality: Regulation, Incentives, and Opportunities," in *The Causes and Consequences of Increasing Inequality*, ed. Finis Welch (Chicago: University of Chicago Press, 2001).

[‡]Michael J. Greenwood, Gary L. Hunt, and Ulrich Kohli, "The Factor Market Consequences of Unskilled Immigration to the United States," *Labour Economics* 4 (1997): 1–28.

---

in relative wages can be attributed to increased international trade.[33] Although much of the debate has centered on whether trade effects are "big" or "small" relative to other factors, for our purposes, it is sufficient to note that empirical studies are generally in line with the hypothesis that increased trade can be harmful to the lowest-paid workers and beneficial for higher-paid workers in advanced industrial economies.

---

[33]William R. Cline, *Trade and Income Distribution* (Washington, DC: Institute for International Economics, 1997).

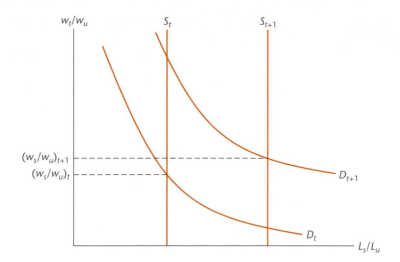

FIGURE 7.12 Shifts in the Market for Skilled Relative to Unskilled Labor

Summary

This chapter has considered the insights into the determination of wages that we can realize from a simple supply and demand treatment of the labor market. In fact, the supply and demand framework, whether in the study of wages in one labor market or in the study of relative wages in related labor markets, is a powerful device for organizing our analysis and interpreting empirical results. In particular, we have seen that the labor market adjusts to changes in demand and supply, but these adjustments are often rather slow, with the market taking up to 10 years to settle down to a new equilibrium after a shock. When the market adjusts to an increase in labor demand, most of the adjustment takes place through an increase in employment; there is also an increase in wages, but in the United States, at least this is usually relatively modest. When the market adjusts to an increase in labor supply, wages fall while employment rises.

Equilibrium across different labor markets occurs through the process of migration of labor (in the direction of higher wages) and capital (in the direction of lower wages). Consequently, we would expect wage convergence to occur across regions. Empirical evidence suggests that convergence is quite slow. Workers in unpleasant jobs, in jobs that require a substantial investment in education and training, or workers living in unpleasant or high-cost regions are typically paid higher wages than other workers. These higher wages reflect compensating wage differentials.

An increase in international trade may worsen the relative position of low-skilled workers in developed economies. A new long-run equilibrium pattern of employment for developed economies will have a higher proportion of workers attracted to skilled work than previously. But it will take some time to arrive at that new equilibrium.

Supply and demand analysis can teach us quite a lot about the things that we observe in the labor market. However, we have to remember the difference between labor markets and markets for commodities. Although labor market analysis can shed light on the determinants of the average wage in the market for college graduates or the average wage of these workers relative to the average wage of high school graduates, there is still a considerable amount of wage variation about these averages for individual workers. An understanding of supply and demand and their interaction is just the starting point for labor economics.

KEY TERMS

Phillips curve	beta convergence
full-employment unemployment rate	sigma convergence
wage curve	hedonic wage functions
migration costs	relative supply-demand model
economic rent	Hecksher-Ohlin model
compensating differentials	factor equalization theorem
net in-migration rate	Stolper-Samuelson theorem

PROBLEMS

1. Use the supply and demand model (see Figure 7.1) to analyze the effect of each of the following events on real wages and employment in the relevant labor market.
   a. The growth of e-commerce and the market for computer programmers.
   b. The demise of the Xtreme Football League and the market for free-agent offensive linemen. (The XFL was set up in 2000 but lasted for only one season.)
   c. Increased government subsidies for college education and the market for college graduates.
   d. More people opting to skip graduate school and go to work and the market for MBAs.

2. The following equations identify labor supply and demand in a market.
   Demand: $L = 150 - 2 \cdot w + 2\,p_p$
   Supply: $L = 50 + 1 \cdot w + 1/2\,p_c$

   a. If $p_p = p_c = 1.0$, determine the equilibrium quantity of labor hired and the nominal wage level.
   b. Suppose p_p rises to 1.10 while p_c remains at 1.0. Determine the equilibrium values of L, w, w/p_p, and w/p_c.
   c. Suppose the intercept of the supply curve increased from 50 to 75 while $p_p = p_c = 1.0$. Determine the equilibrium values of L, w, w/p_p, and w/p_c.
   d. What factors would result in a change like that specified in question 2c?

3. Identify three occupations for which the labor market is confined to local areas and three occupations with national labor markets.

4. Suppose a labor market is in equilibrium and the government imposes a tax equal to 10% of the wage to pay for unemployment insurance. Use supply and demand curves to determine the effect of this tax on total employment, the cost of a unit of labor to the firm, and the wage received by workers. Discuss the burden of this tax on firms and workers.

5. Studies of labor market adjustment in Europe and North America find that an increase in labor demand has a big effect on employment and a small effect on wages in the short run. If labor supply curves are positively sloped, how can a firm increase labor input without offering a higher wage?

6. Why might there be an asymmetric wage response to increases v. decreases in labor demand? What would the labor supply curve look like in this case?

7. If your wage rises from $10 an hour to $10.50 an hour and consumer price inflation is 5%, what happens to your real wage?

8. Suppose the Phillips curve is:

$$\%\Delta w = 6 - 2U + 1\%\Delta p$$

a. What rate of unemployment would result in no change in the real wage?
b. If the unemployment rate drops below this level, what happens to the real wage?

9. Compare and contrast the Phillips curve and the wage curve.

10. Are supply shifts or demand shifts or both more likely to be the mechanism that changes the following wage advantages or disadvantages? Carefully explain your reasoning.
   a. High wages for U.S. computer engineers.
   b. Low wages for Indian computer engineers.
   c. Low wages for Catholics in Northern Ireland.
   d. High wages of white males everywhere.
   e. High wages of professional athletes.
   f. High wages of accounting and finance professors.

11. Use supply and demand diagrams to explain why wages will be higher in the long run in occupations involving disagreeable or dangerous working conditions.

12. The data in this table show wages relative to the national wage for eight local labor markets in 1950 and 2012. Is there evidence of beta and sigma convergence?

Area	1950	2012
A	110	115
B	109	114
C	108	113
D	107	112
E	98	103
F	96	111
G	94	99
H	92	97

13. A labor economist is gathering data to estimate the parameters of the following equation. What does labor market theory hypothesize about the signs of b, c, and d? Explain.

$$\text{Net In-Migration} = a + b\left(\frac{\text{Local Wage}}{\text{National Wage}}\right) + c(\text{House Prices})$$
$$+ d(\text{Average Winter Temperature}) + e$$

14. Why might we expect little evidence of regional wage convergence in a small country like Greece or Austria with a major capital city?

15. Suppose in a local economy there are just two types of jobs for young men who are high school dropouts: legal jobs in the service economy and jobs in the illegal drug business. Which will offer a higher wage? Why? Is this higher wage a compensating differential?

16. Use the relative supply-demand model to explain the short- and long-run effects of the following developments:
    a. Consumer demand rises for the products of skilled workers.
    b. More firms move to this economy because of the low wage of unskilled workers.
    c. The brain drain causes highly educated workers to leave this economy for jobs in the United States.
    d. The government initiates a policy to double the number of college graduates.

17. Use the relative supply-demand model to discuss the short-run effect of increased trade between developing and highly developed countries on the relative wage of skilled workers. Assume that the relative supply of skilled workers is twice as high in the developed countries.

18. What would be the long-run effects of the changes you described in question 17?

19. Should developed countries worried about rising inequality consider restrictions on trade with less developed countries? Are there alternative policies for them to consider?

CHAPTER

8

Information and Job Search

How does the cost of acquiring information affect the search behavior of workers?

Why would more generous unemployment benefits increase the duration of unemployment?

Why does the number of new matches of workers to jobs increase when more workers are unemployed?

Our discussion of labor market equilibrium so far has sidestepped the question of how individual workers find jobs and how individual employers find suitable employees. We briefly discussed job vacancies and job seekers in labor market equilibrium in Chapter 7, but in these models economic agents possessed full information about the nature of the labor market, wages, and employment opportunities. This is at odds with what we know to be the case from casual observation: It is clear from our own job search experience that the search process is largely one of information gathering in an uncertain environment. The notion of finding a "good" job or a "good" worker is largely irrelevant in theoretical models that assume that buyers and sellers possess complete information, because under such an assumption agents will only consider trading with partners that they already know to be "good." More recent models of the labor market have added some realism by including some accommodation for imperfect information and uncertainty.

The roots of information economics, as they pertain to the analysis of the labor market, are found in the work of statisticians dating from the 1930s. The so-called secretary problem analyzed the behavior of a manager hiring a secretary and showed that the manager will continue to interview candidates for the post only until he finds a candidate who meets his criteria (on some productivity measure) satisfactorily. But when should the manager optimally stop interviewing? Since the early 1960s, routine statistical problems of optimal stopping have come to be applied to the analysis of labor markets. Some of these applications refer to the search for workers by firms, others to the search for jobs by workers, and still others consider the case where employers and workers are simultaneously searching. The earliest models, developed by George Stigler, appear in two variants.[1]

---

[1] George J. Stigler, "The Economics of Information," *Journal of Political Economy* 69 (1961): 213–225.

185

Both variants consider the case of workers that are searching for employment, and they make the basic assumption that the pattern of wages across employers follows a fixed distribution. Workers are assumed to know the characteristics of this distribution, but the position of each firm within the distribution is a matter of uncertainty. The two basic approaches adopted by Stigler are (a) to assume that workers search for jobs across a fixed size sample of firms and (b) to suppose that workers search each firm in turn, or sequentially. In both cases, the aim of the worker is to maximize expected returns.

In this chapter, we first examine the simple fixed sample search model and then move on to a variety of models of sequential job search. Variants of these models, which relax some of the assumptions of the basic model and give a rich variety of insights into the labor market, are discussed. We also consider the new generation of search models known as matching models in which the labor market search is bilateral: that is, while workers are searching for jobs, firms are simultaneously searching for workers. Finally, we analyze the properties of the wage offer distribution in greater detail to understand why firms in a labor market characterized by search offer different wages. In other words, why does the wage offer distribution exist in the first place?

The Fixed Sample Search Model

The starting point for theories of search is the problem of incomplete information. Information has value, and acquiring more information enables you to make better decisions. However, information is not free; you must devote time, energy, and money to its acquisition. In the simplest model of job search, we address this information problem by asking this question: What is the optimal number of interviews required to make a good decision about accepting a job offer?

In this model, an unemployed worker searches for a job by balancing the expected benefits to search against the expected costs of search. As in any simple utility maximizing problem, the optimal solution is found where the expected marginal benefit equates with the expected marginal cost. We use the adjective "expected" in this marginal benefit–marginal cost comparison because the outcomes of search are uncertain, and we must characterize them in terms of expected rather than known values. The **expected value** is equal to the sum of the values of each possible outcome multiplied by the probability of that outcome occurring. For example, if I win a dollar if heads comes up in a coin toss and lose a dollar if tails comes up, the expected value of tossing a fair coin is:

$$\frac{1}{2}(\$1) + \frac{1}{2}(-\$1) = 0.$$

In the case of a fixed sample search model, the relationship between costs and the number of firms searched is certain. We assume that the cost of each search is constant and is denoted by c. This means that as the number of firms searched (n) increases, the total cost of search (cn) rises linearly.

The expected benefit of search behaves in a rather different fashion. If no firms are searched, the total benefits of search activity are zero because no job will be obtained by the worker. Assume that every time a worker searches a firm, the worker receives a job offer. (This is not as restrictive an assumption as it might at first appear—offers may

TABLE 8.1   The Benefits of Continued Job Search

Firms Searched	Probability of highest offer being $20,000	Probability of highest offer being $30,000	Expected Wage	Marginal Expected Benefit
1	1/2	1/2	$25,000	
2	1/4	3/4	$27,500	$2,500
3	1/8	7/8	$28,750	$1,250
4	1/16	15/16	$29,375	$625

be of a zero wage.) If only one firm is searched, the expected total benefit will be the mean of the wage offers distribution because this is the expected value of the wage that will be obtained. If two firms are searched, we would expect the higher of the two wage offers obtained to be above the mean of the wage offers distribution.

Table 8.1 illustrates the relationship between the number of searches and the expected benefit from search. Suppose the labor market consists of two types of firms, half of which pay a starting salary of $20,000 and half of which pay a starting salary of $30,000. By searching more firms, a worker increases the chance of getting an offer from a high-wage firm. But, as Table 8.1 illustrates, the marginal expected benefit from search decreases as the number of searches increases. With one interview and half the firms paying the higher wage, the job seeker has a fifty-fifty chance of securing a high-wage offer, and the expected value of this one interview is the mean of the distribution, or $25,000.

If the job seeker has two interviews, the chances of finding a higher wage offer increase. Interviewing two firms, Acme and Ajax, yields four possible outcomes: both are low-wage firms; both are high-wage firms, Acme is high wage and Ajax is low wage; or Ajax is high wage and Acme is low wage. In only one of these four outcomes will the seeker find only the low-wage offer; in the other three at least one high-wage offer will be found. So the expected value of a two-firm search is $27,500, and the expected marginal benefit from expanding the search from one to two firms is $2,500. Looking down the rows of Table 8.1 makes the point that increasing the scope of the search increases the expected value of the search outcome. However, the marginal expected benefit from extending search activity falls as the number of searches increases. With positive search costs, this means that the optimal number of searches is less than the number that would give you the best outcome with certainty.

It should be stressed that these are statistical expectations that represent the best guesses of central location that can be made in advance of any search by a representative worker. The result for any one individual engaging in a search may differ, sometimes quite substantially, from these expectations.

Stigler gives us a formula to determine the marginal expected value of search in the more general case in which the wage offers in a labor market are normally distributed.[2]

---

[2] George J. Stigler, "Information in the Labor Market," *Journal of Political Economy* 70 (1962): 94–104.

In this case, the expected maximum wage offer a job seeker could get from n searches (where n varies from 3 to 20) is:

$$w_{\max} = 0.65n^{0.37}\sigma + w_{\mathrm{mean}} \qquad (8\text{-}1)$$

where σ is the standard deviation of the distribution of wage offers about w_{mean}.

If we take the derivative of this equation with respect to n, the number of searches, we get the following expression for the marginal expected benefit of one additional search:

$$\Delta w_{\max}/\Delta n = 0.24\sigma/n^{0.63} \qquad (8\text{-}2)$$

Again this indicates that the marginal expected benefit from one more interview declines as the number of interviews increases.

Figure 8.1 shows the marginal cost and marginal expected benefit from an additional search. The task faced by a worker engaged in a fixed sample search is to maximize the expected surplus—the expected gap between the total costs and benefits of the search activity—by searching up to the point where the marginal cost equals the marginal expected benefit. Hence, at sample size n^* we have the solution to the number of firms the worker should search. Once the worker has searched n^* firms, the job seeker stops searching and chooses to work for the firm offering the highest wage.

A fixed sample search provides us with a simple model of job search that is appropriate for analysis in a variety of rather specialized circumstances. University students approaching the end of their studies typically engage in job searches of this type. For them, entry into a new job will not be immediate but rather will take place after a few months. This gives them the opportunity to interview with more than one firm before accepting an offer. However, students do not generally search for work across hundreds or thousands of potential employers because the costs of search—filling out application forms, attending interviews, getting haircuts and cleaning suits, and so on—are sufficient to deter students from searching more than a finite (and, in practice, rather low) number of firms. They must trade off the extra cost of searching across a larger number of firms against the expected benefits in terms of the wage offer they might receive.

For many other workers, however, a fixed sample search is not efficient. In the fixed sample context, workers continue to collect offers until they have reached the optimal

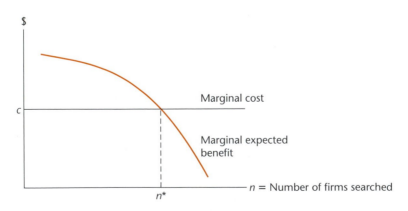

FIGURE 8.1 The Optimal Number of Searches

number of firms in the sample. If an early search yields a particularly good offer, the worker will nonetheless continue searching until n^* firms have been visited. In most contexts, it is not efficient to behave in this way, especially if the wage offers are not extended for an indefinite period—in other words, if they eventually "vanish." Rather, it can be shown that optimal search behavior is sequential. Put simply, this means that a searcher examines each job offer in turn and will quit searching once a satisfactory offer has been made. In the next part of this chapter we consider a variety of sequential search models.

The Sequential Search Model

An Example

Let's begin with a simple example of the sequential search model. Assume you are a college student on summer vacation (a short enough period to let us ignore the effects of time discounting). You decide to spend your 10 weeks of vacation at a seaside resort and begin to look for a job to pay for your accommodations and contribute to your savings or expenses upon returning to college. Suppose you know that four kinds of jobs are available in terms of their pay (other things such as working hours and nonwage conditions are identical). These four jobs pay $100, $120, $130, or $140 per week *plus the cost of your room and board*. (Perhaps the jobs you are looking for are in the hotel industry, and the hotels accommodate and feed their own workers in addition to paying a wage.). You expect that finding each of these jobs is equally likely, so there is a 0.25 probability of getting a $100 wage offer and an equal 0.25 probability of getting each of a $120, $130, or $140 offer. Assume that you are risk neutral; that is, you are neither attracted by riskier situations nor would you pay to reduce the risk you face. Finally, to make the analysis easier, let's assume you get one wage offer a week, and if you turn down an offer, you must wait a week to get another wage offer.

The first offer you get is for a job paying $100 a week. This would give you $1,000 for your summer's work *above* your costs of room and board. Should you accept this job? A rational person trying to maximize income from summer employment would compare the certain outcome of $1,000 with the *expected* outcome from waiting one week for another job offer. The expected value of an uncertain outcome is the sum of the probability times the outcome for each possibility. Table 8.2 shows the expected outcome of waiting one more week for another offer.

If you wait a week, then you have just 9 weeks to work this summer. Even so, the expected value of waiting one week exceeds the certain value of accepting a $100 a week

TABLE 8.2   Expected Value from Continuing the Job Search for a Second Week

Outcome A: $100 × 9 weeks = $900 × 0.25 = $225.00
Outcome B: $120 × 9 weeks = $1,080 × 0.25 = $270.00
Outcome C: $130 × 9 weeks = $1,170 × 0.25 = $292.50
Outcome D: $140 × 9 weeks = $1,260 × 0.25 = $315.00
Expected Value $1,102.50

offer today by $102.50, so it would be rational to wait a week. Another way of looking at this decision is that by waiting you have one chance in four of getting a worse outcome (9 weeks at $100 versus 10 weeks at $100) and three chances in four of getting a better outcome (earning more than $1,000 for the summer). In a statistical sense, this boils down to saying that four birds in the bush with an equal chance of getting one of them is worth more than one bird in the hand, but remember that we are assuming that you are risk neutral.

In this example, the $1,102.50 figure determines your reservation wage. If the current wage offer gave you a higher income than this amount, you would accept the job. So if your wage offer were $120 instead of $100 per week for 10 weeks, it would be better to accept the job than to continue searching. The reservation wage in this mathematical sense is defined as the wage that makes you indifferent between accepting an offer and continuing to search. The reservation wage is a critical variable in the theoretical analysis of sequential job search, and its value will be affected by several factors.

First, consider any explicit costs of going a week without working. If the cost of room and board were $100 a week and this had to be paid out of pocket while you remain unemployed, then we would deduct $100 from the expected value of continuing the job search. This would lower the reservation wage: $1,102.50 − $100 = $1,002.50. The higher the costs of continuing to search for a job, the lower the reservation wage.

Second, suppose that you receive some nonlabor income to cover your expenses while unemployed. Perhaps your parents are willing to pay for your room and board and give you $20 spending money each week until you find a job. This would add $20 to the expected net value of continuing to search and increase the reservation wage because $1,102.50 + $20 = $1,122.50. The receipt of "unemployment benefits" that offset some or all of the costs of remaining unemployed raises the reservation wage.

Third, the reservation wage will increase along with your estimate of the highest wage that might be offered for this job. Suppose the highest net wage available was $150 instead of $140. This would change the entry in the fourth row of the table to $150 × 9 weeks = $1,350 × 0.25 = $337.50. This in turn would raise the return to continued search by $22.50.

Fourth, the reservation wage will be affected by your estimate of the probability of getting a given wage offer. Suppose that instead of an equal probability for each wage outcome, you had the following distribution in mind: a 0.50 chance of a $100 offer, a 0.25 chance of a $120 offer, a 0.15 chance of a $130 offer, and a 0.10 chance of a $140 offer. This would make the expected value of a job offer received after waiting a week equal to $1,021.50. (Make sure you can do this calculation.)

Fifth, where (as in our example) the time horizon is finite, the reservation wage will decrease the longer you are unemployed. Suppose that you follow the reservation wage approach and pass up the offer of $100 a week during your first week of search and continue to look for a job. Suppose further that at the end of the second week of job search you get yet another offer to work at $100 a week. You turned down this wage during your first week of search, but does this mean you will also reject this wage offer if you receive it during the second week of search? Let's check the reservation wage calculation in Table 8.3.

Because continuing the job search for a third week shrinks your "work life" from 9 to 8 weeks, it lowers the expected payoff. The shorter the expected work life, the lower the reservation wage. So do you accept a job paying $100 a week for 9 weeks or continue to look for a higher paying job? With the returns to continued search being $980, it would

TABLE 8.3   Expected Value from Continuing the Job Search for a Third Week

Outcome A: $100 × 8 weeks = $800 × 0.25 = $200.00
Outcome B: $120 × 8 weeks = $960 × 0.25 = $240.00
Outcome C: $130 × 8 weeks = $1,040 × 0.25 = $260.00
Outcome D: $140 × 8 weeks = $1,120 × 0.25 = $280.00
Expected Value $980.00

make sense to turn down the job. Of course, if your parents refused to pay your bills for a second week at the beach, your returns to continued search would only be $880, and you'd now accept the job.

In this example the work life is only 10 weeks, so we don't have to worry about discounting future income to present values. If we were considering the search behavior of graduates looking for a starting position, the work life would be very long, and the incomes earned just before retirement would have little weight in determining the value of a wage offer. In such a case, remaining unemployed for another week or month is unlikely to have as big an impact on the reservation wage as in the example we have just discussed. However, as workers remain unemployed, it is possible that they may revise their estimate of the distribution of wage offers in a way that lowers the reservation wage.

A More Formal Model

In more formal sequential job search models, we again suppose that we are concerned with a searcher who is initially unemployed. To keep things simple, suppose that the worker receives no unemployment benefits or other welfare payments. The searcher is assumed to be looking for a job for life. Once the searcher accepts a job offer, all search activity ceases. We assume that, in each period, one firm is searched at a cost to the worker denoted by c. The searcher could in principle continue to search for an infinite number of periods (so long as we define the periods to be sufficiently short), although in practice this would result in infinite costs and no returns. The task for the searcher is to balance the marginal cost of search against the expected marginal benefit. To do this, we set a reservation wage, w_r, below which all job offers are rejected and above which any job offer is accepted. (Indeed, any model in which offers above the reservation wage are accepted and those below it are rejected is said to be a model with the reservation wage property.)

Although this model is dynamic—it involves different job offers being made at different points in time—the searcher's utility is maximized when he or she searches in a short-sighted fashion, making the decision of whether to accept a job offer or to continue searching one period at a time. Another way of putting this is to say that the searcher behaves myopically. The searcher does not need to plan out a search strategy over his or her whole lifetime because the searcher faces an identical problem in each time period. So long as the searcher remains unemployed, the same wage offer distribution and the same cost of an extra period of search apply.[3]

---

[3] Note that this would no longer be the case if the searcher's time horizon were less than infinite.

Calculating the reservation wage is quite straightforward. The marginal cost of a search equals c, and the marginal expected benefit is the difference between the wage offer and the reservation wage, weighted by the probability that a wage offer in excess of the reservation wage is made. We can be precise about the marginal expected benefit only if we know exactly what the distribution of wage offers looks like.[4] For example, if wage offers are uniformly distributed between \$0 and \$1, then some straightforward analysis of probability reveals that the marginal expected benefit equals $(1 - w_r)^2/2$. In this case, the optimal reservation wage chosen by the searcher will be

$$w_r = 1 - \sqrt{2c} \qquad (8\text{-}3)$$

It is easy to see from this example that as search costs (c) rise the reservation wage (w_r) will fall.

In Figure 8.2 the marginal costs and benefits of search are plotted with the reservation wage on the horizontal axis. The marginal cost is the fixed amount c. The marginal expected benefit of search clearly decreases as the reservation wage increases. This is so for two reasons: the searcher is less likely to receive an acceptable job offer when he or she sets a high reservation wage; and when w_r is high, the difference between whatever acceptable wage is offered and w_r is likely to be low. The optimal level of the reservation wage is then determined by the intersection of the two curves.[5]

As with our original example, Figure 8.2 allows us to consider the effect of changing conditions on the searcher's optimal reservation wage. An increase in the costs of search will lead to a reduction of the reservation wage as the marginal cost curve shifts up from MC_1 to MC_2 in Figure 8.3. With higher search costs, a worker can ill afford to prolong the period of unemployment and will try to price his or her way into a job. The effect of an increase in unemployment benefits, or other sources of income available to the searcher

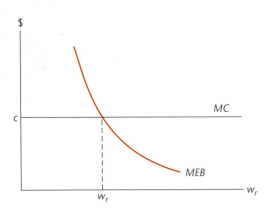

FIGURE 8.2 Determination of the Reservation Wage

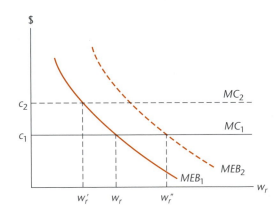

FIGURE 8.3 Changes in the Reservation Wage

---

[4] In the general case, where the probability density function of the wage offers the searcher can expect to receive is given by $\phi(w)$, marginal benefits equal marginal expected costs when $c = \int_{w_r}^{\infty} (w - w_r)\phi(w)dw$.

[5] This corresponds with the reservation wage that ensures that the equation in footnote 5 is satisfied.

PUTTING THEORY TO WORK

SEARCH IN THE LABORATORY

Tests of the theoretical predictions of labor economics models are almost always done by statistical analysis of data drawn from samples of workers or of aggregate data for regions and nations. In some cases, however, it is possible to use human subjects in laboratory experiments in these tests.

James Cox and Ronald Oaxaca report on the results of such an experimental test of search behavior, using students as human subjects.* They argue that experimental results are particularly well suited to testing search hypotheses because the experimenter can control the length of the search horizon, information about the wage offer distribution, the discount rate, and the cost or subsidy to search. It would be almost impossible to control adequately for all of these factors using the information available in most data sets, even with the most complex statistical analysis.

Cox and Oaxaca admit that they were surprised to discover that student search decisions were very close to the optimal decisions implied by theory. Over several different treatments, students exhibited the "correct" reservation wage behavior from 68% to 87% of all cases under the assumption of risk-neutral behavior. Allowing risk-averse or risk-neutral behavior pushed the success rate above 95% in almost every trial. Statistical tests for differences between actual and predicted outcomes in search duration and search income showed close correspondence in most trials.

Cox and Oaxaca conclude: "The picture that emerges from our experiments is one of reasonably close agreement between the predictions of the risk-neutral search model and observed subject behavior. However, we do find significant evidence of risk-averse behavior" (p. 322).

*Note: *James C. Cox and Ronald L. Oaxaca, "Laboratory Experiments with a Finite-Horizon Job-Search Model," *Journal of Risk and Uncertainty* 2 (1989): 301–330.

could be treated as a decrease in the costs of search. A second implication is that a wider distribution of job wage offers will, other things being equal, result in the worker setting a higher reservation wage. The increased probability of getting a very high wage offer raises the marginal expected benefit of continued search by changing the wage offer distribution. An increase in the marginal expected benefits of continued search would shift the marginal expected benefits curve from MEB_1 to MEB_2 in Figure 8.3, raising the reservation wage.

This search model has major implications for the way in which we view unemployment. In a model of this type, a worker who rejects a wage offer is essentially choosing to remain unemployed in the hope and expectation that a higher wage offer will come in the future. This is an instance of voluntary unemployment. Moreover, the choice is made as a form of investment in the worker's future earnings prospects. The investment takes the form of one period of lost income plus a marginal search cost, and the expected benefit takes the form of a wage offer earned in perpetuity higher than the wage offer rejected by the worker. Assuming that the job rejected by a worker and the one that the worker ultimately accepts both pay wages equal to the worker's marginal product, it is clear that by prolonging search the worker increases the marginal product ultimately achieved.

Job search, or unemployment, is therefore a means whereby better, more productive worker–firm matches can be secured than otherwise would be possible. In simple search models of this type, unemployment is efficient and may indeed be regarded as a good thing. That said, increasing the quality of information would lead to good matches being made more quickly, and so that would be even better.

Refinements to the Model

Length of the Search Period and the Reservation Wage

In the model just described, it has been assumed that the searcher has an infinite time horizon. This doesn't affect the calculations much for very young workers, but for the majority of the workforce this will not be the case. Most workers have a time horizon imposed either by the finite length of one's (working) life or—in a world in which capital markets are imperfect and unsecured loans to finance job search are not available—by the exhaustible nature of one's stock of savings.

Once the assumption of an infinite time horizon is relaxed, some of the key results of the simple sequential search model are altered. In particular, the property of that model that allowed the searcher to behave myopically is no longer present. A clock is now ticking that places the searcher in a different position in each period. One effect of turning down a job offer in the current period is that fewer periods now remain in which search can take place, and fewer periods remain in which the cost of investing in search can be recouped through higher per period earnings.[6] As we saw in the numerical example earlier, search with a finite time horizon implies a reservation wage that falls as the period of search lengthens.

Once we relax the assumptions of the simple model, it becomes clear that there are other reasons that might explain a decline in the reservation wage over time. Stephen Salop has suggested that workers may not be completely ignorant about which firms occupy what part of the wage offer distribution.[7] If workers do indeed possess knowledge of this kind, and if that knowledge is imperfect, they may engage in a process of systematic search in which they hunt for jobs first at the firms they believe offer good wages, and only later search at the firms they believe offer lower wages. If searchers adopt this kind of search strategy and are initially unsuccessful at finding work, they may reduce their reservation wage as their period of search lengthens to bring it into line with the wages they believe are on offer at the second-tier firms they are now searching.

Another possibility is that workers do not have certain knowledge of the shape of the wage offer distribution. Workers who are unsuccessful in attracting acceptable wage offers early in their search may attribute this to an unrealistically optimistic view of the location of the wage offer distribution. Put simply, perhaps they began their search by believing that, in general, firms pay higher wages than they actually do. An optimal response to this perception would be for the searcher to revise downward his or her idea of the shape of the wage distribution. As far as the searcher's perception is concerned, the

---

[6] Reuben Gronau, "Information and Frictional Unemployment," *American Economic Review* 61 (1971): 290–301.

[7] Stephen Salop, "Systematic Job Search and Unemployment," *Review of Economic Studies* 40 (1973): 191–201.

whole distribution shifts to the left. And in terms of the analysis shown in Figure 8.2 and Figure 8.3, the marginal benefit of the search curve shifts to the left.

The field of Bayesian statistics has been developed specifically to enable us to model this type of revision. Once the worker's perception of the wage offer distribution has shifted to the left, a new reservation wage must be calculated, and this will generally be lower than the reservation wage obtained previously. Because workers who are searching for jobs are unemployed, it is reasonable to suppose that a decline in the reservation wage over the period of unemployment might be due to a fall in the marginal utility of leisure. A short period of unemployment may be viewed as a vacation, but a lengthy period can become very tedious, causing workers to reduce their reservation wage in an attempt to price their way back into work.

A final explanation for the decline in the reservation wage over the unemployment period is that the marketable human capital stock of the worker declines as a consequence of unemployment. This may be due to a lack of practice of the workers' skills, even at the basic level of attendance, timekeeping, and responsiveness to authority. Alternatively it may result from technological change in the workplace. Either way, the tendency for workers to lose their attractiveness to potential employers as their spell of unemployment lengthens means that unemployment can have a scarring effect, such that an individual's history of unemployment reduces his or her future employability.

Relaxing the Assumption of No On-the-Job Search

In simple job search models of the type we have been discussing, it is assumed that searchers are unemployed. This is clearly at variance with the facts. For example, in 2003, some 20% of all employed U.S. workers with access to the Internet engaged in active job searches.[8] If we suppose more realistically that search may be conducted either by unemployed workers or by employed workers, the model needs to be refined. In particular, we assume that on-the-job search is more costly than searching while unemployed. This is reasonable because unemployed workers have much more free time in which to search and may find it easier to attend interviews.

Begin by considering an unemployed worker. The new context in which we are now placing our model of job search implies that the worker faces two reservation wages. The lower of these may be denoted by w_r^1. Therefore, in any given period if the unemployed worker receives a wage offer lower than w_r^1, he or she will reject it and continue to search full time in the next period. The increase in search costs the worker faces is more than offset by the benefit that the worker expects to gain by receiving a higher wage offer later. The higher of the two reservation wages is denoted by w_r^2. If the worker receives a wage offer greater than w_r^2, the worker will accept the job and quit searching. This latter reservation wage is so high that any further search while on the job would impose a marginal cost in excess of the expected marginal benefit of an extra period of search. Finally, if the worker receives a wage offer between the two reservation wages, the worker will accept it but will continue to search for a better wage while on the job. This model was constructed by Ken Burdett[9] in the context of an infinite time horizon model.

---

[8] Betsey Stevenson "The Internet and Job Search," *NBER Working Paper 13886*, 2008.

[9] Ken Burdett, "A Theory of Employee Job Search and Quit Rates," *American Economic Review* 68 (1978): 212–220.

Nonetheless, it makes predictions about individual behavior that many will deem to be reasonable and realistic. It is a fine example of the power of modern search theory.

Bilateral Search Models

In the search models we have considered so far, search is conducted on one side of the market only, namely the supply side. It may be more realistic to suppose that while workers are actively searching for jobs, firms are simultaneously trawling the labor market in search of prospective employees. Firms also operate in a world of uncertainty and spend resources on advertising, interviewing, and other aspects of recruitment. This insight has led to the development of bilateral search models.

Acknowledging the presence in the market of firms that are searching for workers might seem innocuous, although it adds some complications to the model, but the existence of bilateral search can have some rather profound implications. In particular, the fact that firms are searching for workers may result in unemployed workers searching too little[10] because such workers free-ride on the search activity of firms. Because workers recognize that firms are actively looking for workers, workers devote less energy and fewer resources to their own search activity than they would were company searches absent. For instance, the fact that some firms advertise their vacancies in the media might lead unemployed workers to search among only those firms that advertise; they then do not apply for work by visiting factory gates, even though some firms may recruit workers who do so. Meanwhile, the level of search activity by firms may also be suboptimal because firms free-ride on the search activity of workers. In this case, some firms may choose not to advertise their vacancies because they can fill them simply by waiting for workers to turn up at the factory gates asking for work. In effect, the existence of firms' search for workers imposes an externality on workers who are also searching, and vice versa.

The outcome is that, throughout the market, some economic agents are free-riders and are searching too little. As a result, job vacancies remain unfilled and workers remain unemployed for longer than would be efficient; longer, that is, than would be the case in a market where the market failures due to the externalities discussed here are absent. In the context of traditional models of the labor market, this means that the natural rate of unemployment is too high and can no longer be viewed as the level of unemployment that maximizes social welfare. This result contrasts sharply with the finding from the simple search model.

Screening and Signaling

A particularly interesting search problem involves the existence of asymmetric information. Suppose workers are either low- or high-productivity, with high-productivity workers earning a wage premium. Furthermore, workers know which type they are but employers do not. Employers can only find out which type a particular job applicant is through interaction. (This may be revealed during the interview process, but it may not be clear until the employee has completed a period of time on the job.) In this case, low-productivity

---

[10] Christopher Pissarides, "Search Intensity, Job Advertising and Efficiency," *Journal of Labor Economics* 2 (1984): 128–143.

workers have the incentive to apply for high-productivity jobs because there is some chance they will be hired and be able to earn a high-productivity wage for some time even though they were inefficiently matched to the job. Even if the hiring process weeded out all low-productivity workers, the firm would have to incur the extra costs of weighing the applications of unqualified applicants.

The **screening model of firm search** suggests that in this case it might pay the firm to employ a screening device to automatically exclude low-productivity workers.[11] As we saw in Chapter 6, the usual candidate for such a device is education. If high-productivity workers find it less costly in terms of effort to achieve a college diploma than do low-productivity workers, the employer can use a college diploma as a screening device. By requiring all applicants to possess a degree, the employer can limit applications to high-productivity workers. This implies that a degree may be required to apply for a job even if the knowledge associated with a degree is not required to do the job. As you can see, screening may not fully repair the inefficiency associated with asymmetric information.

In this framework, workers who can invest in education relatively cheaply would have an incentive to acquire educational credentials for their value as a signal to potential employers of their high-productivity status. Thus a "separating equilibrium" can emerge in which it is optimal for high-productivity workers to invest in the signal and for low productivity workers not to invest. Despite theoretical issues raised by the complexity of firm–applicant interaction in such an environment and despite difficulties of empirically disentangling screening effects from human capital effects, screening models provide some interesting insights into aspects of the joint search problem.[12]

Matching Models

A good illustration of the usefulness of job search models is the application of the theory to empirical data on flows into and out of unemployment. At the microeconomic level of the individual worker, we would expect search to be most successful when there are many vacancies but few other unemployed workers. For the individual firm searching for workers, search is likely to be most successful when there is high unemployment but a low level of vacancies in other firms.

At the macroeconomic level, the number of new matches (M) made in a given period between firms and workers (i.e., the number of new hires) will vary positively with both the number of vacancies (V) and the number of unemployed workers (U). The relationship can be expressed formally in the **matching function**:

$$M = M(V, U) \tag{8-4}$$

If there are constant returns to scale, then each of M, V, and U can be expressed as rates rather than levels by dividing each by the size of the labor force. Let the corresponding

---

[11] Michael A. Spence, "Job Market Signalling," *Quarterly Journal of Economics* 87 (1973): 355–379.

[12] For a detailed literature review see John G. Riley, "Silver Signals: Twenty-Five Years of Screening and Signalling," *Journal of Economic Literature* 39 (2001): 432–478.

rates be denoted by m, v, and u, respectively. In the constant returns scenario, the matching function may be written

$$m = m(v,u) \tag{8-5}$$

It is often more convenient to work in rates rather than levels, so the issue of whether the matching function really is characterized by constant returns to scale is empirically important. Unfortunately, the empirical evidence is rather ambiguous, depending in part on how the general matching function is specified.

The specifications that appear in equations 8-4 and 8-5 are general. They are vague about the precise nature of the relationship between the stock of vacancies, the stock of unemployment, and the flow of new hires per period. Equations 8-4 and 8-5 tell us that new hires depend on vacancies and unemployment, but they do not tell us exactly what the relationship is. To be a little more informative, we could impose some structure on the relationship. For example, we could assume that

$$M = V^{\alpha}U^{1-\alpha} \tag{8-6}$$

where α is a number somewhere between 0 and 1. This is another application of the Cobb-Douglas function (see the appendix to Chapter 3). It has several appealing properties. First, equation 8-6 implies that the number of matches or new hires (M) rises as the number of vacancies (V) increases; when more vacancies exist, it becomes easier for a given unemployed worker to find a job. Likewise, M rises as the number of unemployed workers (U) rises because firms are more likely to find suitable workers to fill their vacancies when there is a large pool of unemployed labor from which to choose. Clearly, if there were no unemployed workers or no vacancies, there could be no matches; therefore, the hiring rate must rise as U and V increase.

But equation 8-6 goes a little further than this. It suggests that as U rises (holding V constant for the moment) M will rise at a *decreasing* rate; likewise, as V rises (now holding U constant), M increases at a *slower* rate. This is a nice feature of the specification in equation 8-6 because it suggests that there is a limit in the extent to which a rise in vacancies alone (i.e., without a rise in unemployment) can increase the number of new hires.

It is easy to demonstrate that the function in equation 8-6 implies constant returns to scale; that is, if U and V are both multiplied by a constant, k, then the new value of M will be kM. This constant-returns property of equation 8-6 results from the simplicity of the functional form in which the exponents on V and U sum to one.[13]

A final attractive feature of equation 8-6 is that the parameters of the model can be estimated using regression methods.[14] If we are prepared to make the assumption that the matching function follows a constant returns to scale Cobb-Douglas form, we can establish exactly what the relationship is between new hires, vacancies, and unemployment.

---

[13] If $M = V^{\alpha}U^{1-\alpha}$, then multiplying each of V and U by k would give a right-hand side of $(kV)^{\alpha}(kU)^{1-\alpha}$, which is equal to $kV^{\alpha}U^{1-\alpha}$, which in turn equals kM.

[14] After a little manipulation, the equation may be rewritten as $\ln M = \alpha_1 \ln U + \alpha_2 \ln V$. This is a linear equation, and the parameters of the model, α_1 and α_2, can easily be estimated by applying ordinary least squares regression to time series data on M, U, and V. The hypothesis that $\alpha_1 + \alpha_2 = 1$ can then be tested statistically.

Most studies that have used this method to evaluate the matching function estimate α to be between 0.5 and 0.7.[15]

Not all of the empirical evidence suggests that the assumption of a constant-returns Cobb-Douglas form for the matching function is valid, however. For instance, Ronald Warren[16] has used a more sophisticated specification to estimate the matching function with monthly data from the U.S. manufacturing sector. His results suggest that there are increasing returns to scale in the matching technology and that the specification of equation 8-6 represents an oversimplification.

Whether returns to scale in the matching function are constant or increasing has some rather profound implications beyond those alluded to previously. Peter Diamond has constructed a model in which the trading frictions that appear in a search model can lead to a multiplicity of output and unemployment equilibria.[17] To keep things simple, suppose that all workers produce output on their own initiative and that they must sell all the output they produce to other workers. Output costs may vary (both over time and across workers); each worker knows the overall distribution of costs but does not know how to find the lowest cost opportunities.[18] So the typical worker will produce output when a low-cost opportunity arises but will prefer to remain unemployed otherwise. In effect, there is a reservation cost above which the worker will choose not to produce. Once the worker has decided to produce output in a given period, the worker must find trading partners who will buy the output.

Suppose further that there are increasing returns to scale in the matching function between buyers and sellers of output; that is, trade becomes easier as the number of traders increases simply because there are more people to trade with. (This is formally equivalent to the notion of increasing returns to scale in the matching function between firms and workers; the buyer can be thought of as an employer and the seller as a worker.) This assumption leads to an intriguing possibility: there may be more than one reservation cost, more than one equilibrium level of output, and more than one equilibrium level of unemployment. Let's see why this is the case. To any one worker, the benefit of production depends on the level of production of all other workers. If other workers produce only a little, there will be little opportunity to take advantage of the trading benefits of increasing returns to scale, so the reservation cost will likely be quite low. If all workers produced high levels of output, however, trade will be easier, and it becomes more worthwhile for each worker to set a high reservation cost and to produce a relatively high level of output.

Note that this only works if there are increasing returns to scale in the matching function, which, as we have seen, there might be, at least in some economies. Diamond's

---

[15] A key reference is Barbara Petrongolo and Christopher A. Pissarides, "Looking into the Black Box: A Survey of The Matching Function," *Journal of Economic Literature* 39 (2000): 390–431. These authors go further than estimating the values of α_1 and α_2; they also test the validity of the assumption that the matching function is a constant-returns-to-scale Cobb-Douglas equation. On their data, they find that the assumption is supported.

[16] Ronald Warren, "Returns to Scale in a Matching Model of the Labor Market," *Economics Letters* 50 (1996): 135–142.

[17] He provides a nice illustration of his model involving natives on an island jumping up to gather coconuts that, rather curiously, grow on palm trees! Peter Diamond, "Aggregate Demand Management in Search Equilibrium," *Journal of Political Economy* 90 (1982): 881–894.

[18] This is analogous to the assumption in the simple job search models that workers know the distribution of wages but do not know which firm offers which wage.

argument is consistent with the Keynesian idea that an economy can get stuck in an equilibrium that has undesirable properties—one where unemployment is high and output is low. In this scenario, a demand shock could conceivably cause all firms simultaneously to increase their employment levels and shift the economy to a more desirable high-employment, high-output equilibrium. Put bluntly, if returns to scale in the matching function are increasing, there may not be a unique natural rate of unemployment, and there may be scope for demand management policies to be effective in combating joblessness.

The conflicting results obtained in studies conducted so far suggest that more research is warranted into the returns to scale that obtain in the matching function. Far from being an esoteric topic, it is one with profound policy importance. If returns to scale are constant, then the view that a unique natural rate of unemployment exists may be correct and demand management policies cannot permanently affect the rate of unemployment. If returns to scale are increasing, however, multiple natural rates of unemployment may exist. If this is so, there may be scope for demand management policies to affect the rate of unemployment by effecting a jump from one equilibrium to another.

Equilibrium Search Models

All of the job search models discussed so far have in common the assumption that a job searcher expects to receive job offers that vary in terms of the offered wage. However, the law of one price suggests that any wage offer distribution should collapse around a single point. Indeed, if all workers were to behave identically, the failure of firms offering low wages to hire new workers would force up their wage offers; this would in turn produce a rise in the reservation wage; once again the lowest paying firms would be forced to raise their wage offers, and this process would continue until all firms offered the same wage. Some features of the job search model challenge the very existence of a wage offer distribution, and it is this distribution that underpins the model itself.

Not surprisingly, this observation has concerned labor economists. As early as 1984, James Albrecht and Bo Axel sought to bypass these difficulties by assuming heterogeneous workers.[19] It is possible, and indeed reasonable, to suppose that different workers with different preferences and skills will have different reservation wages. The existence of such worker differences would be sufficient to result in a distribution of wage offers in what might be called a search equilibrium.

In addition to worker heterogeneity, a wage offer distribution would result from differences across firms and from job search by employed individuals.[20] Suppose a variety of types of firms exist; some operate in low-productivity sectors of the economy and are able to offer only low wages whereas others are characterized by higher productivity and higher wages. If workers were identical, the process of job search would result in the former being competed out of business. Suppose, however, that we adopt a model in

---

[19] James Albrecht and Bo Axel, "An Equilibrium Model of Search Unemployment," *Journal of Political Economy* 92 (1984): 824–840.

[20] Ken Burdett and Dale Mortensen, "Wage Differentials, Employer Size and Unemployment," *International Economic Review* 39 (1998): 257–273.

which on-the-job search can take place. This means that unemployed workers may find it in their interest to accept jobs at low-paying firms while they continue their search to find work with better paying employers. If the production function is approximately linear, then firms in the low-output, low-wage sector can operate as profitably as other firms in the high-output, high-wage sector. Hence a pure search equilibrium may be obtained in which different firms optimally select different levels of productivity and offer different wages.[21]

The Duration of Unemployment and the Hazard Function

The theory of job search helps us understand two important features of unemployment. The first is the duration of unemployment, which refers to the length of time an individual could expect to remain unemployed after losing a job or moving into the labor force. The second is the probability with which an individual who became unemployed at the beginning of a year could be expected to move out of unemployment and into a job at any given point during that year. The way in which this probability of escape from unemployment changes as the duration of unemployment lengthens is referred to as the **hazard function**.

One key insight from search theory is that both the duration of and probability of escape from unemployment will be affected by the reservation wage. As we have seen, a higher reservation wage reduces the probability that a person will find an acceptable job offer in any given search period. Thus we would expect the reservation wage to be positively correlated with the duration of unemployment and negatively related to the probability of escaping from unemployment. (See the Around the World box for an example of the latter relationship in a sample of jobless Polish workers in the mid-1990s.)

Efforts to estimate hazard functions empirically have used two approaches.[22] The **parametric approach** follows the lead of insurance actuaries by assuming a particular distributional form—most frequently the Weibull or log-logistic function—in advance of estimating the parameters of the hazard function. The second or **nonparametric approach** estimates an equation relating individuals' unemployment status to a set of worker characteristics (determinants of the reservation wage and wage offer rate) plus a full set of dummy variables, one for each time period following a person's entry into unemployment. In view of the extra flexibility the second approach affords—the hazard can rise or fall in each period rather than being constrained to follow an assumed pattern—it is not surprising that it typically yields closer fits to the data and has become the primary method used in contemporary studies of unemployment duration.

It is interesting to examine the results of some of these studies. Larry Katz and Bruce Meyer have investigated the probability of escape from unemployment using data from the American Panel Study of Income Dynamics.[23] They find that the hazard rate falls as workers get older. Abstracting from these effects, a strong pattern of duration dependence

[21] Pierre Konig, Gerard J. van den Berg, and Geert Ridder, "Semi-Nonparametric Estimation of an Equilibrium Search Model," *Oxford Bulletin of Economics and Statistics* 62 (2000): 327–356.

[22] Nicholas Kiefer, "Economic Duration Data and Hazard Functions," *Journal of Economic Literature* 26 (1988): 646–679.

[23] Larry Katz and Bruce Meyer, "The Impact of the Potential Duration of Unemployment Benefits on the Duration of Unemployment," *Journal of Public Economics* 41 (1990): 45–72.

AROUND THE WORLD

The Reservation Wage of Polish Job Seekers

Under central planning, Poland and other central and eastern European economies experienced very little unemployment. However, during the transition to a market economy during the 1990s, unemployment rose rapidly to levels similar to those in western Europe. A recent study has examined the job search of unemployed Polish workers in the mid-1990s transition, looking specifically at the determinants of reservation wages, reemployment probabilities, and acceptance wages in a sample of 23,179 individuals.*

Unemployed workers were asked about their reservation wage. These stated wage levels were closely related to human capital characteristics of individual workers. Controlling for other determinants, reservation wages were lower the longer the person had been unemployed and higher for those receiving unemployment insurance benefits. These relationships are consistent with the predictions of search theory. Unemployed individuals whose previous job had been in a state-owned enterprise had lower reservation wages than those previously employed in the private sector.

The reservation wage was negatively associated with the probability of moving out of unemployment, although this relationship was not highly significant. As we might expect from our theory, those with lower reservation wages, other things being equal, would be more likely to find an acceptable offer in a given time period from the wage offer distribution. Controlling for the reservation wage and other factors, workers previously employed in the state sector were less likely to move off the unemployment rolls. It may be that previous employment in the less-efficient state sector was seen as a negative signal of individual worker productivity and, thus, as a useful screening device.

Among workers who found jobs, their reservation wage was a very important determinant of the wage offer they accepted. As our theory suggests, a higher reservation wage led to a higher wage. Wage offers were higher from private sector employers, and workers who moved from a state enterprise to a private firm, or vice versa, suffered a wage penalty.

These results lend support to the notion that unemployed Poles in the mid-1990s behaved in a way consistent with search theory. They also indicate that the shift from an economy dominated by businesses owned and managed by the government to one in which privately owned businesses are the rule had an important effect on search behavior and outcomes.

Note: *Vera Adamchik and Thomas Hyclak, "Reservation Wages, Re-Employment Probabilities and Acceptance Wages: Unemployed Polish Workers in the Transition to a Market Economy," Presented at the 17th Annual Conference of the European Association of Labour Economists, Lisbon (2004).

suggests it is more difficult to escape unemployment the longer one is unemployed. The hazard falls sharply as the duration of unemployment lengthens, although there are a few notable spikes (see Figure 8.4). The hazard rises sharply but temporarily 26 weeks and 39 weeks after workers enter the unemployment register. These spikes coincided with the maximum duration of unemployment compensation programs in the United States at the time of the study and are consistent with the idea that the resulting increase

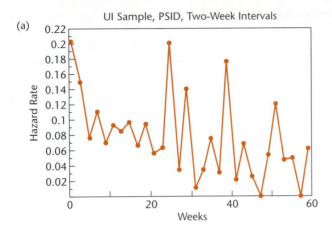

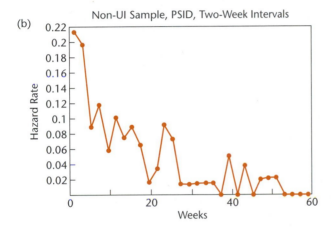

FIGURE 8.4 Total Hazard

Source: Reprinted from the *Journal of Public Economics*, Vol 41, Larry Katz
and Bruce Meyer, "The Impact of the Potential Duration of Unemployment
Benefits on the Duration of Unemployment", pp. 45–72. Copyright 1990,
used with permission from Elsevier.

in the cost of unemployment caused people to lower their reservation wage when they lost benefits.

An analysis of the hazard rate in the United Kingdom was conducted by Elena Stancanelli.[24] Like Katz and Mayer, she finds that older workers are less likely than others to escape unemployment in a given period. A relatively high rate of local unemployment also reduces the probability of escape, and workers in unskilled occupations are likely to have longer unemployment durations than others. Being married raises the hazard rate, but the presence of children reduces it. Home ownership and the level of earnings in the last job are also important determinants of the probability of escape from unemployment;

---

[24] Elena Stancanelli, "Unemployment Duration and the Duration of Entitlement to Unemployment Benefits: An Empirical Study for Britain," *Applied Economics* 31 (1999): 1043–1051.

both are associated with relatively short unemployment durations. Once these measures of worker heterogeneity have been allowed for, the hazard is found to decline very slightly as the duration of unemployment lengthens. As in the U.S. analysis, there are spikes close to the points at which welfare payments expire although in the United Kingdom these spikes do not appear to be very large.

Using Swedish data, Rheinhold Bergström and Per-Anders Edin[25] compared the results observed using parametric methods with a variety of distributional assumptions with those using nonparametric methods. Their nonparametric analysis suggests that the hazard rises during the early part of an unemployment period, and starts to decline after three or four months. The initial rise in the hazard has been found in some other studies too, and it has often been attributed to workers taking what are in effect vacations during the first few weeks of their unemployment. Once these "vacations" are over, workers start to search in earnest, and the hazard rate increases for the next three to four months.

Differences across countries in the results obtained in studies of the hazard function should not be too surprising. In most countries, the incentives for the unemployed to return to work vary with the duration of unemployment. For instance, if welfare payments are stopped in country X after a year of unemployment, this is a rather strong incentive for the unemployed to find work within a year, and we should not be surprised to find a positive duration dependence leading up to that cut-off time. Welfare systems and active labor market policies differ substantially from country to country, and the shape of the hazard must do so too.

Labor Mobility

Early models of job search came under some criticism because they failed to explain why anyone should ever quit a job. They assumed that jobs, once acquired, were held for life. Since the work of Burdett, however, the reasons workers might quit have been well understood.[26] As well as providing an explanation of unemployment, search theories offer a rationale for labor mobility.

Burdett's model of on-the-job search suggests that we should expect search activity to generate a wage profile for the individual that is increasing over time. This does not necessarily mean that the worker is mobile across jobs. It is possible that a worker who receives a wage offer in excess of his current wage can use this to secure a wage increase from his or her current employer. Essentially therefore, the relationship between on-the-job search and labor mobility is an empirical one.

It has long been appreciated that the early years of working life are typically characterized by considerable job mobility and high wage growth.[27] Implicit in this view is the assumption that workers quit jobs to accept better employment opportunities, where

---

[25] Rheinhold Bergström and Per-Anders Edin, "Time Aggregation and the Distributional Shape of Unemployment Duration," *Journal of Applied Econometrics* 7 (1992): 5–30.

[26] Ken Burdett, "A Theory of Employee Job Search and Quit Rates," *American Economic Review* 68 (1978): 212–220.

[27] William Johnson, "A Theory of Job Shopping," *Quarterly Journal of Economics* 92 (1978): 261–277; Robert Topel and Michael Ward, "Job Mobility and the Careers of Young Men," *Quarterly Journal of Economics* 107 (1992): 439–479.

the match between worker and firm is more productive and where the worker is better remunerated. Younger workers have low wages initially, so they are sure to search intensively while on the job because the potential returns to search are high.

Because workers do change employers, it is reasonable to suppose that, for these workers at least, there is a positive return to job mobility. Measuring that return empirically is rather difficult, however, because we cannot measure how much the mobile worker would have earned had he or she not moved. The standard approach used to bypass this problem is to estimate two earnings equations—one for movers and one for stayers—and the difference between the predicted wages obtained from these equations at mean values of the explanatory variables is an estimate of the average returns to job mobility. In estimating these earnings equations, however, it is necessary to correct for sample selection bias. One way this could be done is to use the approach developed by James Heckman.[28] This ensures that the coefficients of the estimated wage equations for movers and stayers are not biased by unobserved heterogeneity between movers and stayers.

Kristen Keith and Abigail McWilliams have developed a simpler method of eliminating sample selection bias.[29] These authors compare directly the mean earnings of movers and stayers but restrict their sample of stayers to those who (despite not moving jobs in the current period) move in the next period. This has the advantage of restricting the sample of stayers to those who presumably possess the same (unobserved) characteristics as movers, but it does so at the cost of throwing away a lot of data. Using data from the U.S. National Longitudinal Survey of Youth, 1979—1985, they estimate separately for women and men the returns to job mobility for those who were searching for new jobs prior to separating from their previous employer, and for those who were not.[30] For male searchers, they find that the returns to job mobility are from 11% to 12%, whereas for female searchers the returns are from 11% to 18%. For nonsearchers the estimated returns are also positive, from 2% to 4% for men and from 3% to 5% for women.

Job Search Methods and Results

The final topic in our discussion of job search concerns the various methods of job search employed by workers and the results obtained from different job search methods. An individual can pursue employment through the services of public or private employment agencies, by scanning newspaper advertisements, or by contacting employers directly. Alternatively, a job seeker could ask friends and relatives about job openings at their places of employment and ask them to "put in a good word with the boss" about an application. Finally, in recent years the Internet has provided an alternative source for finding out about openings and for circulating an applicant's resumé. Does it matter which method is used?

---

[28] James Heckman, "Sample Selection Bias as a Specification Error," *Econometrica* 47 (1979): 153–161.

[29] Kristen Keith and Abigail McWilliams, "The Returns to Mobility and Job Search by Gender," *Industrial and Labor Relations Review* 52 (1999): 460–477.

[30] The latter group comprised many layoffs but also included workers who quit to take on another job without actively searching. The returns to mobility estimated for laid-off nonsearchers are close to zero for women and negative for men.

TABLE 8.4   Job-Finding Success by Search Method

Method	Percentage of searchers using this method	Percentage of jobs obtained using this method
Job centre/public employment agency	35.9	19.8
Response to advertisements (e.g., in newspapers)	35.1	22.9
Direct contact with employer	8.2	11.0
Through contacts, friends, relatives, social networks	9.8	27.4
Private employment agency/other	9.2	18.9

Source: Paul Frijters, Michael A. Shields, and Stephen Wheatley Price, "Job Search Methods and Their Success: a Comparison of Immigrants and Natives in the UK," *Economic Journal*, 115 (2005): F359–F376.

The data in Table 8.4 come from a study of job search methods used in the United Kingdom. They show, in the first column, the percentage of unemployed workers using each of a variety of different search methods. The figures sum to less than 100 because not all unemployed workers are actively searching. In principle they could sum to more than 100 because searchers might use more than one method. It is easily observed that the most popular search methods involve job centres (public employment agencies) and responding to job advertisements.

The second column of the table shows the methods by which jobs were found by workers who were successful in their job search. The pattern of percentages across the different search methods in this column contrasts sharply with the pattern observed in the first column. A high proportion of jobs are found through informal channels—including direct inquiry at "factory gates" and through networks of personal contacts. While these findings refer to the United Kingdom, other studies have reported very similar results for many other countries, including the United States and Canada.[31]

Studies of job search by young workers also indicate that the public employment service may not be the best vehicle for a successful search. A study of the youth cohort in the 1981 panel of the National Longitudinal Survey shows that reliance on friends and relatives and direct application led to job offer and acceptance rates in the United States that were two to three times higher than the rates for using a public agency or responding to want ads.[32] In a study of Australian teenagers, 33% of those with jobs used friends and relatives, 28% used direct application, 18% answered want ads, and just 10% used the public employment agency to find work. Interestingly, unemployed

[31] Paul Frijters, Michael A. Shields, and Stephen Wheatley Price, "Job Search Methods and Their Success: A Comparison of Immigrants and Natives in the UK," *Economic Journal*, 115 (2005): F359–F376. See also Steven M. Bortnick and Michelle Harrison Ports, "Job Search Methods and Results: Tracking the Unemployed, 1991," *Monthly Labor Review* (1992): 29–35; and Lars Osberg, "Fishing in Different Pools: Job Search Strategies and Job-Finding Success in Canada in the Early 1980s," *Journal of Labor Economics* 11 (1993): 348–386.

[32] Harry Holzer, "Search Method Use by Unemployed Youth," *Journal of Labor Economics* 6 (1988): 1–20.

teens were more likely to be using ads and the employment agency as their main search method.[33]

Why do searchers choose to use the public employment agency, and why does this method have less success? Those receiving unemployment insurance benefits were significantly more likely to use the public employment agency, perhaps because of registration and monitoring requirements to receive benefits. Recall the evidence that the receipt of unemployment benefits tends to lengthen the duration of unemployment for individuals because it allows them to choose a higher reservation wage. If people using the public employment agency are more likely to be benefit recipients than those using other methods, this duration–reservation wage connection might be sufficient to explain the lower job finding rates for those relying on this method. There is also some evidence that workers with lower amounts of human capital, which might adversely affect the job offer distribution, are more likely to use the public employment service.

Our analysis of employer search and screening also helps explain why the public employment agency method is relatively unsuccessful and why references by friends and relatives are more successful in getting job offers.[34] Employers may regard the public employment agency as an inefficient way of screening applicants because all unemployed individuals have access to the service, and the agency may be judged more on the number of referrals than on the number of placements. References from current employees, however, are a potentially valuable screening device. It is likely that the applicants will be similar to current employees and that they will have good information about the vacant job, making it easier to determine if it is a good match for their skills and interests.[35]

Increasing attention is being paid to the use of the Internet as an additional job search method. The Internet has the potential of providing considerably more information about jobs and candidates at the initial stages of the search process than is available with other search methods. Three distinct types of Internet search have been identified: web sites such as Monster.com, with searchable databases of job openings or resumés; corporate web sites that provide information and solicit online applications; and employer-initiated searches to identify promising candidates.[36] Tools such as LinkedIn allow passive search by workers by allowing them to post resumés on the web, to collect recommendations, and hence to attract the attention of prospective employers who are searching for workers. In the early years of the Internet, using the web as a job search tool does not appear to have been very effective, but more recent data indicate that it is now a highly effective search tool—indeed there is evidence to suggest that unemployment durations are typically around 25% shorter where the workers have used the web in job seeking.[37]

---

[33] Alexandra Heath, "Job-Search Methods, Neighborhood Effects and the Youth Labor Market," Research Discussion Paper 1999-07 Economic Research Department, Reserve Bank of Australia, 1999.

[34] For more evidence on the success of personal references see Stephen R. G. Jones, "Job Search Methods, Intensity and Effects," *Oxford Bulletin of Economics and Statistics* 51 (1989): 277–296.

[35] James D. Montgomery, "Social Networks and Labor Market Outcomes: Toward an Economic Analysis," *American Economic Review* 81 (1991): 1408–1418.

[36] David H. Autor, "Wiring the Labor Market," *Journal of Economic Perspectives* 51 (2001): 25–40.

[37] Peter Kuhn and Hani Mansour "Is Internet Job Search Still Ineffective," *IZA Discussion Paper 5955*, available at http://ftp.iza.org/dp5955.pdf (2011).

THE WAY WE WORK

Unemployment Benefits and Wage Offers

Search theory hypothesizes that the receipt of unemployment benefits would, other things being equal, lower the cost of continued search and raise the reservation wage for an out-of-work job seeker. Two implications of this have been the subject of empirical research.

First, a higher reservation wage is associated with a longer duration of unemployment because it reduces the chance of receiving an acceptable offer within any given period of time. This implication has been examined extensively and was summarized earlier in this chapter. The finding that unemployment insurance lengthens the duration of unemployment and thus increases the measured unemployment rate has often been described as a negative side effect of a public policy designed to provide income support to the unemployed.

Second, the receipt of unemployment benefits should also allow a job seeker to search more extensively for a vacancy that best matches his or her skills and preferences. If the receipt of benefits while unemployed were positively correlated with the wage received by a person when a job offer was accepted, this would be evidence that a positive side effect of this policy was its impact on the quality of job matches.

There have been fewer studies regarding the second implication—the effect of unemployment benefits on post-unemployment wages. A review of the literature and new research results provided by John Addison and McKinley Blackburn find some evidence that people receiving benefits eventually obtained higher wage offers, about 2% higher, than out-of-work individuals who did not qualify for unemployment compensation.* This suggests that unemployment insurance indeed allows people to search longer and to find better jobs.

Note: *John T. Addison and McKinley Blackburn, "The Effects of Unemployment Insurance on Post-Unemployment Earnings," *Labor Economics* 7 (2000): 21–53.

Internet recruiting can also be considerably cheaper for firms than traditional means. Glenn Pearce and Tracy Tuten estimate that a Sunday newspaper ad for a job opening costs $1,000 and that headhunters charge 30% of the first year's compensation package whereas most web sites charge from $100 to $300 a month.[38] Their survey of recruiters at 15 large U.S. banks found that the banks used the Internet mainly to develop an inventory of active job seekers. One problem noted by bank recruiters was that the Internet generated a high volume of inquiries and applications but at the cost of a large number of low-quality applicants relative to job requirements. Employers thus need to introduce measures whereby they can filter applications effectively. Owing to the lower application costs, Internet sites reduce the incentive for job seekers to self-select only for jobs that are a good match and thus increase screening costs for employers. If the Internet results in a flood of applicants for open positions, added signaling costs are imposed on those job seekers who are well qualified for the position. In any case, Internet search has boomed

---

[38] C. Glenn Pearce and Tracy L. Tuten, "Internet Recruiting in the Banking Industry," *Business Communications Quarterly* 64 (2001): 9–18.

in recent years and now accounts for a global advertising spend by companies amounting to over $2 billion per year.[39]

Summary

In the theoretical world of neoclassical economics, workers are identical, all decision makers have perfect information, and long-run equilibrium ensures that differences in working conditions and job characteristics are reflected in compensating wage differentials. The real world differs considerably. Workers differ in their preferences and have limited information about firms and jobs, so the process of matching supply and demand for labor involves search. This chapter has reviewed some of the principal ways in which search has been incorporated in labor economic analysis.

One of the key conclusions is that search, or information gathering, is a costly activity. Individuals will have an incentive to do no more than the optimal amount of information gathering. This search reduces the uncertainty facing a decision maker, but some degree of uncertainty will remain, and decisions will have to be based on expected outcomes. In these circumstances, a sequential job seeker will base decisions on a reservation wage, which embodies the expected outcome and costs of continued search. The concept of the reservation wage is a critical component of job search models, the empirical analysis of unemployment duration, and the empirical study of the rate at which unemployed workers are matched with vacancies.

KEY TERMS

expected value
screening model of firm search
matching function

hazard function
parametric approach
nonparametric approach

PROBLEMS

1. Suppose that the currency used by citizens of Transylvania is the transo, and that the exchange rate is such that each transo is worth $1,000. Suppose further that wage offers received by typical job searchers in Transylvania are uniformly distributed between 0 and 1 transo per week. Finally, suppose job search costs amount to 0.05 transos per search and that the searcher can access one job offer per week. What reservation wage will a typical searcher set? (You may assume that the searcher has an infinite time horizon.)

2. Equation 8-2 states that the marginal expected benefit of one more search is higher if the standard deviation of the wage offer distribution is higher. Why would this be the case?

---

[39] John Janedis regularly publishes estimates of spending on online recruitment at agencies such as Monster Worldwide (MWW) and Dice Holdings Inc (DHX) in a series of press reports from UBS Securities.

3. Think about the jobs held by you and your friends last summer. Use this information to describe the wage offer distribution for summer jobs in your area last year. What will your reservation wages be this summer if the situation is the same as last year? Explain.

4. Use Figure 8.2 to analyze the effects of the following on the reservation wage:
   a. Increased nonlabor income
   b. Increased search costs and a decrease in the chances of finding a very high-wage job

5. Would you expect the reservation wage of an unemployed college graduate to be higher or lower than that of an unemployed high school dropout? Use the equation in footnote 4 and Figure 8.2 to discuss why the marginal cost and marginal benefits might differ for these two types of workers.

6. Discuss three reasons a worker's reservation wage would decrease the longer he or she remained unemployed.

7. Suppose you were employed at a job paying $10 an hour and were searching for a better job. Would $10 be your reservation wage?

8. Why would the cost of search be higher for an employed person than for an unemployed person? Why might the use of the Internet lower the cost of on-the-job search?

9. Increasing returns to scale in the matching function implies that doubling U and V more than doubles M, the number of unemployed finding a job. Why might this be the case?

10. During recessions, it is common to observe V falling and U rising. Suppose a 10% drop in V is associated with a 15% increase in U. Suppose further that $\alpha = 0.7$ in equation 8-6. What happens to the outflow rate for unemployment under these circumstances? Explain.

9

Monopsony and Minimum Wages

What is monopsony and why does it matter?

How does worker interest in a long-term employment situation convey monopsony power on employers?

Do minimum wages reduce employment opportunities for low-wage workers?

In a competitive labor market, each employer employs a small percentage of the total number of workers in that market. Individual employers are too small to have any effect on the wage rate, and every employer can hire as much labor as he or she desires without having to pay a higher wage. The supply of labor facing each employer in such a labor market is horizontal, or perfectly elastic.

Certainly this description does not characterize *all* labor markets. In some labor markets, one employer employs a relatively large proportion of that market's total labor force, or maybe the labor market is dominated by more than one employer, but still a small number. In such cases employers may have some control over the wage they must pay to attract workers, in effect facing an upward-sloping supply of labor function, which is unlike that faced by competitive employers. These are **monopsony** employers, and they operate in monopsonistic labor markets.[1] Although in a literal sense "monopoly" and "monopsony" refer to markets in which there is only *one* seller or buyer, we use the term *monopsony* in a somewhat looser sense. When we refer to a monopsonistic labor market, we are talking about a market with sufficiently few employers so that each of them has some control over the market wage and does not, therefore, face a perfectly elastic labor supply schedule.

In this chapter we first look at the theory of wage and employment determination in monopsonistic situations. Next we identify where monopsony labor markets exist. Are

---

[1] Just as the word *monopoly* means "a single seller" (from the Greek words *mono* [meaning "one"] and *polein* [to sell]), the word *monopsony* was formed to mean "a single buyer." However, in classical Greek the word "opsonein" means to buy fish or meat. So a monopsonist (taken at its literal meaning) refers to a single buyer of fish or meat products. See Robert J. Thornton, "How Joan Robinson and B.L. Hallward Named Monopsony," *Journal of Economic Perspectives* 8 (2) (2004): 257–261.

they common or rare? Do they arise in certain types of markets, and if so, where? We study in detail two markets where monopsony is often thought to be common: the markets for teachers and for professional athletes. Economists have expressed a renewed interest in monopsonistic labor markets in recent years, and we examine why this is the case. Modern theories of monopsony draw heavily on the theory of job search (see Chapter 8) and are able to explain some findings on the labor market that can seem really bizarre to people brought up on the theory of competitive labor markets. In particular, some recent findings on the economic effects of the minimum wage are comprehensible only when it is realized that labor markets can be monopsonistic. Therefore, in the latter portion of the chapter we discuss the implications of monopsony in the labor market for minimum wage policy.

Wage and Employment Determination under Conditions of Monopsony

The classic examples of labor market monopsony are the so-called company towns of the late nineteenth century, such as Pullman, Illinois, which was located just south of Chicago. Workers in Pullman produced railroad coaches known as "Pullman sleepers." In this town the sleeping-car workers all worked for the same company (the Pullman Palace Car Company), all lived in houses owned by the company, and all bought at the company store. So complete was the control of the company over the town that even the sewage from the workers' houses was pumped out and used as fertilizer on nearby farms owned by the company. Similar company towns flourished in the coal mining towns of Pennsylvania and in some textile manufacturing towns in the southern United States. Elsewhere, examples are provided by the textile towns of nineteenth century northwest England and mining towns in northeastern Australia.

The analysis of wage and employment determination in the case of monopsony can easily be built on the foundations of our analysis of wages and employment under competitive labor market conditions. Suppose an employer is literally the sole employer of labor in the relevant labor market. This employer possesses a marginal revenue product (MRP) function, which is depicted in Figure 9.1. The MRP function indicates to the employer the addition to total revenue that would result from the hiring of each new worker. As the only employer in this labor market, the monopsonist does not face a horizontal (or perfectly elastic) supply of labor schedule as was the case with our competitive labor market employers in Chapter 7. In this situation the employer's labor supply schedule is upward sloping, which means that at some point the monopsonistic employer would have to pay a higher wage to hire additional workers. In fact, because the monopsonist is the *only* employer in this labor market, the monopsonist's labor supply curve is also the market labor supply curve.

The supply of labor schedule shown in Figure 9.1 can also be called an average labor cost (ALC) schedule. That is, by showing what wage level the employer must pay to attract a certain number of workers, the schedule indicates to the employer the average labor cost associated with each level of employment. To see what the *change* in total labor cost would be if the employer decides to increase the level of employment, we have to refer to the marginal labor cost (MLC) schedule that rises above the supply or ALC schedule in Figure 9.1. Why does the marginal labor cost schedule rise faster than the

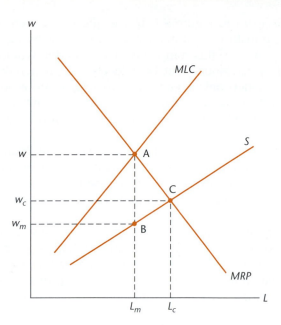

FIGURE 9.1 Wage and Employment
Determination under Monopsony

labor supply schedule? If the monopsonist wants to hire new workers, the positively sloped labor supply schedule indicates that he or she must raise the wage level to attract new workers. Unless the employer is going to pay the higher wages only to the newly hired workers, however (a situation very likely to breed bitterness among the existing workers), the wages of all workers—new and old—will increase, thus causing the marginal labor cost to rise more quickly than the average labor cost. This is called "nondiscriminating monopsony." In the converse situation, where some workers are paid more than other workers despite the fact that they are otherwise identical, the employer is referred to as a **discriminating monopsonist**.

How many workers will the nondiscriminating monopsonist employer hire in this case, and what wage will he or she pay? Following the goal of profit maximization, the employer will hire workers up to the point where their MRP is just equal to their MLC. In Figure 9.1 this occurs at point A at employment level L_m. Note, however, that the wage associated with point A (that is, w) is higher than the wage the monopsonistic employer must pay to secure L_m workers. The wage necessary to secure L_m workers is read off the labor supply curve, namely w_m.

There are several important points to note about the wage and employment levels that characterize our monopsonistic labor market situation. First, workers are receiving a wage lower than their marginal revenue product; therefore they are being exploited in the sense that they are not being paid what they are "worth" to the firm in terms of their productivity. The peculiar features of a monopsony labor market will result in a tendency for profit-maximizing employers to pay their workers a wage that is less than their MRP.

A second point to note is that there is a tendency for both the level of wages and the level of employment to be lower than they would be in competitive labor markets. This can be seen clearly by referring once again to Figure 9.1. If a magic wand were waved over this monopsonistic labor market, transforming it into a competitive one by increasing the number of employers, the level of wages in this competitive labor market would be w_c and the level of employment would be L_c. Notice that both levels are greater than the wage and employment levels of the monopsonistic employer. In fact, some economists refer to the difference between w_c and w_m as an alternative measure of the degree of monopsonistic exploitation rather than the difference between the marginal revenue product and w_m.

Third, the demand for labor is given by the wage–employment pairing at B; and since B is below the MRP, it is clear that we cannot interpret MRP as being a demand curve for labor. Indeed, in much the same way as a product market monopolist doesn't have a supply curve, we can say that the monopsonistic employer doesn't have a labor demand curve.

We can deduce a couple of other interesting features from our monopsony model. Suppose a minimum wage is imposed on the monopsony employer that is intended to eliminate wage exploitation. Such a wage minimum could be imposed by law, or it could result from a union and its collective bargaining efforts. As Figure 9.2 indicates, this minimum wage may not only reduce or eliminate the degree of monopsonistic exploitation but may *increase* the level of employment. Such a result is certainly counterintuitive because we ordinarily think of employers as desiring to employ *fewer* workers, not more, as wages rise. How could this happen? Suppose the minimum wage that the monopsonistic employer now faces in Figure 9.2 is at w_u, which is higher than it was formerly at w_m. Because the employer would be able to hire additional workers at the same wage w_u (at least up to the point where w_u meets the supply of labor schedule at point D), w_u now

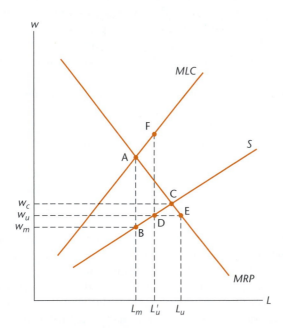

FIGURE 9.2 Minimum Wage Effects under Monopsony

serves as the (constant) marginal labor cost schedule, replacing the former upward-sloping MLC schedule.[2] The profit-maximizing employer in this case would desire to hire L_u workers, where the wage w_u intersects the MRP schedule at point E. Of course, at wage w_u only L'_u workers would be willing to work for the employer because the labor supply schedule indicates to the employer that hiring more workers than L'_u would require an increase in the wage to a level above w_u. In any case, the higher wage w_u has still caused the employer to increase employment to a higher level than before.

Several additional observations are in order concerning this paradoxical positive association between wages and employment in the case of monopsony. First, notice that the tendency for the monopsony employer to hire more rather than fewer workers as the wage rises holds true only over a limited range. If the minimum wage the monopsonist must pay were to rise above w_c, the wage that would exist if this were a competitive labor market, then the usual negative association between wage and level of employment would reappear. Wages above w_c would effectively mean that the monopsony employer would be "riding up" the MRP schedule.

There is still another curious feature about the monopsony model. As we have explained, a minimum wage of w_u would result in the monopsony employer wishing to hire L_u workers at point E. However, the constraint imposed by the labor supply schedule has meant that the employer will only be able to hire L'_u workers at this wage. At w_u the quantity of labor demanded exceeds the quantity of labor supplied; a labor shortage or excess demand situation exists. In the usual case of competitive labor markets, wages would tend to rise until the excess demand for labor is eliminated. Employers unable to fill their vacancies would bid up the wages offered until the labor shortage disappeared. But in the labor market monopsony case, no such tendency exists. Even though there seems to be an excess demand for labor in the amount of DE (or $L_u - L'_u$), point D represents the profit maximizing wage level. Any attempt to pay a wage higher than w_u would mean a marginal labor cost of F or higher to the monopsonist, a level of marginal labor cost far exceeding the MRP. Thus point D represents an equilibrium wage level while it (again paradoxically) also portrays a situation of excess demand. As you can see, funny things happen under conditions of monopsony.

Our example of bringing in a union or imposing a minimum wage requiring the monopsonistic employer to pay a higher wage might imply that one of these two courses of action is the logical solution to eliminating or paring down the degree of wage exploitation. Such a conclusion is not necessarily warranted, however. A monopsonist employer paying a wage below the MRP of his or her workers is not necessarily reaping above-normal profits. On the contrary, the employer might be producing in a product or service market that is highly competitive. For example, consider the small coal mining operators of northeastern Pennsylvania or southern Illinois of a few generations ago. As the only source of jobs in the small towns where they operated, many of these employers

---

[2] Notice that the higher wage w_u serves as the new marginal labor cost schedule only up to point D in Figure 9.2, where w_u intersects the labor supply schedule. If the employer increased employment beyond point D, he or she would have to pay a higher wage. As a nondiscriminating monopsonist—one paying the same wage to all workers of a given type—this would require the payment of a higher wage not only to the new hires beyond point D but to the existing workers as well. As a result, the marginal labor cost beyond point D would be represented by the former MLC schedule, beginning at point F. Notice that there is thus a "gap"—a discontinuity, as measured by the vertical distance DF—in the marginal labor cost schedule at point D.

possessed varying degrees of monopsony power and probably paid wages below the MRP of their workers.[3] Yet, with many such small and large producers of coal, the product market in which they sold their coal was highly competitive. As a result, locally higher wages might not necessarily have had the effect of expanding the level of employment but could actually have driven some employers out of business. This represents an important caveat to our analysis. In short, an employer might be paying a wage below workers' marginal revenue product, but it does not follow that the employer is necessarily enjoying monopsony or monopoly profits. Therefore, imposition of a minimum wage or the entrance of a union might not always have the intended effect.

Where Does Monopsony Exist?

How widespread is the phenomenon of labor market monopsony, and where does it tend to exist? How much lower are the wages of workers who work for monopsonistic employers? These questions naturally follow from our discussion of the theory of labor market monopsony.

Geographic Monopsony

Monopsony labor markets can arise as a result of geographic location. Labor history is filled with examples of employer monopsony: the textile towns of New England and Lancashire; the coal mining towns of northeastern Pennsylvania and southern Illinois; steel towns such as Pittsburgh, or Sheffield in England; railroad manufacturing towns like Pullman in Illinois, or Crewe in England. In some of these areas, one employer may have exercised such a dominant influence over the local economy that the name "company town" became appropriate. Books, movies, and popular accounts have often portrayed wages and living conditions in these towns in less than glowing terms, and bitter struggles sometimes occurred between workers and their unions on one side and employers on the other side.

Local monopsony is a much rarer phenomenon today than it was a hundred years ago. The reason is simple: workers today are far more mobile when it comes to commuting to work than they were three or four generations ago. Without a car or public transportation, a worker in a company town might have been unable to travel more than a couple of miles each day to the textile mill or coal mine. Today, however, many workers commute long distances to work. This greater degree of worker mobility has made a larger number of potential employers available to the average worker and, equivalently, a larger potential labor force available to the typical employer. In other words, monopsonistic labor markets have become—are you ready for this?—more "polypsonistic."

Labor mobility plays a key role in determining the extent of employer monopsony power and, hence, monopsony wage exploitation. Figure 9.3(a) depicts a situation in which the supply schedule of labor is extremely inelastic with respect to the wage: in other words,

---

[3] William March Boal, "Testing for Employer Monopsony in Turn of the Century Coal Mining," *Rand Journal of Economics* 26 (3) (1995): 519–536.

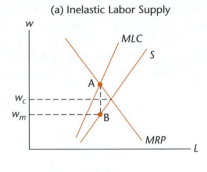

(a) Inelastic Labor Supply

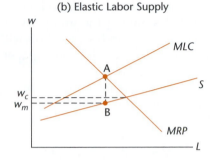

(b) Elastic Labor Supply

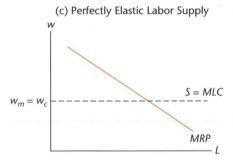

(c) Perfectly Elastic Labor Supply

FIGURE 9.3 Monopsony and the Elasticity of Labor Supply

labor is not very mobile. As a result, the difference between the competitive wage (w_c) and the wage paid by the monopsonist (w_m) is substantial, and a high degree of wage exploitation is present. In Figure 9.3(b) the labor supply schedule is highly elastic; as a result, there is not much difference between the wage paid in a competitive labor market (w_c) and the wage paid by the monopsonist. Figure 9.3(c) depicts an employer who faces a perfectly elastic supply of labor schedule; in this case there is no difference between the wages paid by monopsonistic and competitive employers.

But how can we gauge the extent to which labor markets are monopsonistic? And how can we measure the degree to which workers may be exploited as a result? In fact, discerning the degree of labor market monopsony caused by geographic factors is quite difficult (except in the most extreme cases) because we do not directly observe labor supply schedules or their elasticities. One notable attempt to do so was made by Robert Bunting several decades ago.[4] Bunting looked at 1,774 "local labor markets" (they were in fact counties) and calculated the percentage of the total labor force in each county area that was employed by the largest firm, the 4 largest firms, and the 10 largest firms. The resulting **concentration ratios**, according to Bunting, should give some indication of the extent of potential monopsony existing in these markets, with higher 1-, 4-, or 10-firm concentration ratios signifying greater degrees of monopsony. Bunting actually found a surprisingly low degree of employer concentration. In fact, the largest firm employed more than 50% of the total labor force in fewer than 1% of the areas studied. The four largest firms together employed more than 50% of all workers in only about 4% of the areas, and the 10 largest firms employed 50% of all workers in about 10% of the 1,774 areas. Not surprisingly, the most highly concentrated markets tended to be those smallest in size; there were no New Yorks, Chicagos, or L.A.s among the group. Were the most concentrated areas characterized by any particular types of industries? You will probably not be surprised to learn that the mining, textile manufacturing, and paper products industries were heavily represented in the most concentrated areas.

Bunting's findings seem to indicate that the degree of geographic concentration of employers, and the degree of local monopsony power that they wield, is not very high. But now there is a question: Was Bunting necessarily measuring monopsony when he examined concentration ratios? Notice that a high degree of employer concentration in a particular county area may not necessarily signify considerable monopsony power. Monopsony power depends rather on the geographic *extent* of the labor market area. If the extent of the labor market area is much greater than that of the county, then despite the fact that the Hi-De-Ho Manufacturing Company employs 75% of the workers in Dustball County, Hi-De-Ho possesses little or no monopsony power. Precisely this situation describes many so-called college towns, such as Urbana, Illinois, and State College, Pennsylvania, where the dominant local employer (the state university) employs a very high proportion of the area's labor force and nearly 100% of all professors in the area. But do these universities therefore possess monopsony power when it comes to hiring professors? Because the labor market for professors is far greater in extent (it is, in fact, worldwide in scope), neither the University of Illinois nor Penn State University has significant power to act as geographical monopsonists, at least when it comes to setting pay for beginning professors. On the other hand, both universities may well have monopsony power when it comes to hiring other types of workers (such as secretaries and maintenance workers), the labor market for whom might be very limited in geographic extent.

In short, it is important to realize that the existence and degree of employer monopsony power depend critically on the particular type of workers and the geographic extent of the labor market in question.[5]

---

[4] Robert Bunting, *Employer Concentration in Local Labor Markets* (Chapel Hill: University of North Carolina Press, 1962).

[5] In fact, then, any county can actually be thought of as comprising in whole or in part a large number of labor markets, depending on the occupational group in question. Interestingly, Bunting tried to see to what extent his employer concentration ratios were correlated with the average level of wages across the county areas. Although we would expect a negative correlation between wages and employer concentration, Bunting actually detected a positive correlation.

Government as a Monopsonistic Employer

Government monopsony can arise from government acting as an employer, especially at the local government level. In thousands of towns and cities across the country, the local government may be the only employer (or at least the dominant employer) of a particular type of labor, such as police personnel, firefighters, schoolteachers, trash collectors, and other occupational groups. As a monopsonistic employer, it has been argued that government may be able to exercise its monopsony power to pay wages below workers' marginal revenue products or below wages that might be paid for similar work or to workers with similar amounts of training in competitive labor markets in the private sector.

What is the evidence for the presence of monopsony pay differentials in public employment? Many research studies have tried to detect and measure the magnitude of monopsony pay differentials in the public sector. Most of these studies have focused on wage or salary differences for workers in a particular occupation (such as teachers or nurses) in different labor markets for a particular year. They have usually formulated an earnings function such as the following:

$$\ln w = b_0 + b_1 M + b_i O_i \tag{9-1}$$

where $\ln w$ refers to the natural logarithm of wages in the occupation, M is a measure of the degree of monopsony in the labor market, and O_i refers to other variables (such as the general level of wages and salaries in the area or the cost of living) that might be expected to have an effect on wage levels. The coefficient b_1 then gives a measure of the impact of monopsony on wages.

Measuring the precise degree of monopsony power can be very difficult, however. First it is necessary to specify the extent of the relevant labor market. Many studies have simply assumed that the metropolitan area or the county comprises the labor market, in effect arguing that the extent of the labor market is determined by the commuting distances of workers. Although such an assumption might be appropriate for some occupations (local transit workers perhaps), it is clearly not appropriate for others, as we have pointed out.

To measure the extent of monopsony present in the relevant labor market (that is, to specify values for M in equation 9-1), some studies have simply counted the number of employers in the local labor market, implying that there will be a small number of employers in monopsonistic markets but a large number in competitive markets. Such a simple employer "head count" might be a very unsatisfactory measure of monopsony, however. Why? Let's use the case of school districts as employers of schoolteachers as an example. A county with 100 districts, one of which hires 95% of the teachers in the county, may be far more monopsonistic than a county with only 5 districts, each hiring about 20% of the county's teachers. The first case is representative of some big city school systems surrounded by dozens of smaller suburban districts. This implies that measuring monopsony correctly is more a matter of considering the *percentage* of the market's work force that is hired by one or a few employers, not simply the *number* of employers in the area.

One measure that at first thought seems ideally suited to this purpose is the concentration ratio, the percentage of employees hired by the largest employers in the market. Concentration ratios have indeed been used in many monopsony studies, such as that of Bunting. Although concentration ratios consider both the number of employers and the degree of inequality in their sizes, one difficulty with them is that in a given market there are as many possible concentration ratios as there are employers (the 4-firm concentration ratio, the 8-firm concentration ratio, the 231-firm concentration ratio, and so on). Not only is the choice of which concentration ratio to use arbitrary, but in ranking markets according to the degree of monopsony power, it is possible to draw different conclusions depending on which ratio is selected.

But let's move on from the technical difficulties. What have analyses of the effects of governmental monopsony power found? Most of the studies have been for public school-teachers, and many found significant correlations between teachers' salaries and some measure of **school district monopsony** (concentration ratios, number of school districts in the area, etc.). However, in most cases the effects of monopsony were quite small, and some found no *significant* relationship between various monopsony measures and teacher salaries. Similar studies done for other groups of public employees (such as nurses) have also had mixed results.[6]

One study by Ransom and Sims is worth noting because it uses a somewhat different methodology than the others. (We discuss this approach at greater length later in the chapter in the section on "Dynamic Monopsony.") These authors begin by regressing district level data on the quit rate against the log of average salaries. Dividing the estimated coefficient by the average quit rate yields an estimate of the wage elasticity of the quit rate. They further note that, in equilibrium, the wage elasticity of labor supply is equal to twice the absolute value of the wage elasticity of the quit rate.[7] So this method can be used to estimate the elasticity of labor supply to the firm. In a perfectly competitive model, this elasticity should be infinite. In practice, Ransom and Sims find it to be low. Their estimates range from 1.50 to 3.75, those with the richest specifications of the model being at the upper end of this range. So their evidence confirms that the labor supply curve has a positive slope, consistent with the notion that employers have a significant degree of monopsony power.

Another noteworthy study is based on the fact that a competitive labor market presents firms with a perfectly elastic labor supply curve, while the corresponding curve under monopsony is upward sloping. This study—one that concerns the pay of nurses, not teachers—is by Douglas Staiger, Joanne Spetz, and Ciaran Phibbs.[8] They focused on Veterans Affairs (VA) hospitals in the United States. Prior to 1991, the pay of nurses in VA hospitals was determined nationally. In 1991, however, new mechanisms were put in place, and wages paid to these nurses are now based on the results of local wage surveys, which means that VA nurses' pay is responsive to local market conditions. If

---

[6] See for example, John Landon and Robert Baird, "Monopsony in the Market for Public School Teachers," *American Economic Review* 61 (5) (1971): 966–971; David Lipsky and John E. Drotning, "The Influence of Collective Bargaining on Teachers' Salaries in New York State," *Industrial and Labor Relations Review* 29 (3) (1976): 352–362; James Luizer and Robert Thornton, "Concentration in the Labor Market for Public School Teachers," *Industrial and Labor Relations Review* 39 (4) (1986): 573–584; Lori L. Taylor, "Competition and Teacher Pay," *Economic Inquiry* 48 (3): 603–620; Simon Medcalfe and Robert J. Thornton, "Monopsony and Teachers' Salaries in Georgia," *Journal of Labor Research* 27 (4) (2010): 537–554.

[7] Employment equals last period employment times (1–s), where s is the separation (or quit) rate, plus new recruitment. Noting that employment, separations and new recruitment are all dependent on the firm's wage offer, this relationship can be expressed in terms of elasticities as $\varepsilon_{Nw} = \varepsilon_{Rw} - \varepsilon_{sw}$ where the terms denote the wage elasticities of employment, new recruitment and the separation rate respectively. In equilibrium the recruitment elasticity is the negative of the separation rate elasticity, so $\varepsilon_{Nw} = -2\varepsilon_{sw}$.

[8] Douglas Staiger, Joanne Spetz, and Ciaran Phibbs, "Is There Monopsony in the Labor Market? Evidence from a Natural Experiment," *NBER Working Paper 7258*, 1999.

this switch in the wage determination mechanism results in a decrease in the relative pay of nurses in some areas, we would expect that many nurses would quit working in VA hospitals and seek jobs elsewhere. That is, after all, what an elastic supply curve is all about, and there are plenty of other hospitals around that can provide a source of employment. But this did not happen. Indeed the short-run supply curve of labor to the VA hospitals was found to be remarkably inelastic (only about 0.1). The obvious implication of this is that the VA hospitals do, in the short run at least, possess a considerable degree of labor market monopsony power.

Taking the studies of monopsony labor markets as a whole, however, the evidence seems to suggest that monopsony pay differentials probably exist, but are rather modest in scale. This presents something of a puzzle—why does the evidence provided on the elasticity of the labor supply curve seem so compelling while the evidence on the extent of pay differentials is weaker? As we saw earlier in Figure 9.3, the magnitude of the monopsony–competitive pay differential is directly related to the elasticity of labor supply: the higher the supply elasticity, the smaller should be the pay difference. But the magnitude of the monopsony–competitive pay differential is related to the elasticity of the labor *demand* schedule as well. Only in this case the *lower* the elasticity of demand (the MRP schedule), the smaller will be the pay difference. Figure 9.4 indicates how the difference in pay offered by employers in these two different types of markets shrinks (*ceteris paribus*) as the demand schedule becomes vertical. The explanation behind the graphs is that workers with inelastic demand schedules are considered to be so important to their employers that wages don't play much of a role in determining how many workers will be hired. Equivalently, the bargaining power of workers whose demand schedules are inelastic is sufficient to keep them from being exploited.

What relevance does this have for the question of monopsony pay differences in public employment? The elasticity of demand for many types of public employees tends to be quite low. Police and firefighters, for example, provide essential services without close substitutes, and both of these features would lead us to expect that these workers face inelastic demand schedules. We might also include prison guards, teachers, and perhaps even sanitation workers in this category.[9] The evidence for monopsony pay differentials in public employment may be weak precisely because the low demand elasticity for some public employees prevents them from being exploited.

The Market for Professional Athletes

There is another potential type of monopsony present in the labor market. This type of monopsony occurs as a result of outright collusion on the part of employers who agree not to offer employment to workers currently working for another employer. The most notable example of this type of monopsony can be seen in the professional sports industry, most notably, in the United States, in baseball, basketball, and football.

Let's examine the labor market for professional baseball players and see how our monopsony model applies. The baseball players' labor market is one of the oldest

---

[9] Not all public employees provide services that we would label as essential and without close substitutes, however. Tennis instructors in public parks and washroom attendants at city hall are two examples that come to mind.

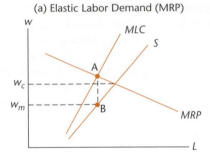

(a) Elastic Labor Demand (MRP)

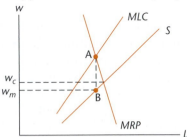

(b) Inelastic Labor Demand (MRP)

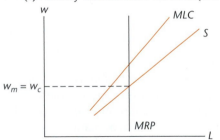

(c) Perfectly Inelastic Labor Demand (MRP)

FIGURE 9.4 Monopsony and the Elasticity
of Labor Demand

continuing examples of monopsony in the United States. It dates at least as far back as 1879 when the owners of National League teams became upset over the high salaries they had to pay to keep their players from jumping to other teams. The owners secretly agreed to exclude or "protect" five players on each team from competitive bidding. Gradually this secret agreement became both open and extended to include all players; this is the so-called reserve clause in the contracts signed by major league ballplayers. According to the reserve clause system (which was not modified until 1977), a ballplayer could play for no other team than the one he was currently signed to play for unless he was traded. Players could therefore not choose to quit and seek to offer their services to another ball club simply because they were unhappy about their pay, their playing time, or the fans in the stands. In effect, each professional baseball team permanently "owned" the services of the ballplayers in their employ. The player reserve system thus constituted a monopsony whereby there was only one buyer of labor for each player. However, the baseball monopsony is probably better characterized as a discriminating monopsony—remember the distinction we made earlier—because, of course, not all players are paid the same salary. To a very large degree salaries reflect the relative "productivity" of individual ballplayers, but they can also reflect their reservation wages.

In 1975 the baseball reserve system was struck down by an arbitrator's ruling on a grievance brought by the Major League Baseball Players Association (MLBPA), the players' union. Under the terms of a collective bargaining agreement reached by the MLBPA and the owners in 1977, baseball players are now no longer tied permanently (unless traded) to one team. Instead, after six years in the league players can become "free agents" and are free to negotiate with other teams. In effect, the monopsony structure of professional baseball still exists in a modified format and only for players with fewer than six years in the league.[10]

Before we look at how much of an impact the monopsony structure of major league baseball had on players' salaries, though, there's an interesting side issue to discuss. The owners and other defenders of the reserve clause had long insisted on the necessity of continuing the arrangement, even arguing that major league baseball's very future depended on it. Their reasoning was this: unlike an ordinary business that would not be troubled if it could weaken or eliminate its competitors, baseball would be in serious jeopardy if its financially weaker teams should fail. What does this have to do with the reserve clause? The owners argued (and quite successfully for a very long time) that the reserve clause helped to equalize team strengths. By preventing star players with financially weaker clubs from moving to richer clubs able to pay them higher salaries, they argued that the reserve clause kept the talent distribution from becoming too uneven, games from becoming too one-sided, and the financially weaker clubs from folding. Hence the reserve clause was "good for baseball," or so the owners contended.

A closer examination of this reasoning, however, reveals that it is fallacious. If we can safely assume that owners are profit maximizers, it becomes clear that it would not ordinarily be in the best interests of any ball club, however wealthy, to load up its team with all the scarce top talent that it could fill its roster with. Why not? After some point, the possible addition of yet another superstar slugger or pitcher will result in a lower net addition to the team's total revenue than the acquisition of the previously added superstars. What this means, of course, is that diminishing returns sets in, causing the marginal revenue product of baseball players to decline. This decline in the MRP can happen in either of two ways. Adding a tenth all-star slugger is not going to cause the team's run production to increase as much as the addition of the ninth all-star slugger. After all, a team can only put nine players in the lineup at any one time. The same is true for

---

[10] The 1977 agreement between the players and the owners also introduced another interesting and rather unique feature to the salary determination process: final offer salary arbitration. Players with at least three years of major league experience may request arbitration in the case of impasses in salary negotiations with owners: that is, a third party may be called in to resolve the impasse and make a determination that is binding on both parties. But whereas in usual interest arbitration cases an arbitrator is free to make whatever salary determination he or she deems appropriate, baseball's final offer arbitration system requires the arbitrator to select the best final offer of either the ballplayer or the owner. The claimed advantage of final offer salary arbitration is that it encourages both parties to be more reasonable in their demands and offers.

pitchers. The acquisition of a seventh potential 20-game winner will have a smaller effect on a team's performance than the acquisition of the previous potential 20-game winners.

These examples show that the marginal *physical* product of star baseball player labor declines as L increases. But remember that MRP ($MRP = MP \times MR$) has both a physical component (the MP) and a *value* component (MR). A team with as much talent as our hypothetical examples have would in all likelihood win so many games and by such great margins of victory that fan interest ultimately would decline. But let's return to our point: that the baseball owners' argument that the reserve clause helps to equalize team strengths is faulty. Suppose that Team A is considering making an offer to buy the contract of a star player who the team estimates has a marginal revenue product of $15 million. However, Team B, who currently owns the contract of the player, will accept nothing less than $20 million in a trade. In such a situation Team A will not offer to buy the contract of the player because the cost of adding the player to the team is higher than the player's worth to the team. Now, suppose instead that Team A happens to own the contract of the player in question, and it is Team B that makes the offer to trade for the player. Team B is located in a much larger metropolitan area, with a larger pool of fans to draw from and larger advertising revenues to reap. As a result, Team B estimates that the MRP of the star player is $20 million and offers to buy the player from Team A. Any offer from Team B greater than $15 million (Team A's estimate of the worth of the star player to itself) will result in Team A trading the star player. The point of all of this is that the reserve clause should have had no effect whatever on whether the star player was traded or kept by the team that currently owned his contract. The desire to maximize profits alone will determine whether the player will be kept, traded away, or traded for; and this decision depends only on the relation between the player's worth (his MRP) to the team that owns his contract and his worth to other teams who might trade for him. The reserve clause merely allows whatever team happens to own the player's contract at the time to pay him less than his marginal revenue product: to exploit him, in other words.

Notice that we have not said that a free market, in which players are completely free to switch teams, will necessarily make the distribution of baseball player talent any more equal than the monopsonistic reserve clause system. Theoretically, the distribution of talent would be the same under either system. To the extent that larger markets are potentially wealthier markets (there are more fans to pay to attend ball games and more potential advertisers willing to spend big dollars for prime time ad spots), a superstar is likely to be more valuable to teams playing in such markets. As a result, there is an incentive for baseball teams in such areas to trade for or to retain more, but not all (remember diminishing returns), superstar players.

Probably the most convincing evidence against the argument that the player reserve system equalized team strengths is the experience of the New York Yankees. During the heyday of the reserve system, the Yankees dominated major league baseball, winning 20 World Series, more than any other team.

We've noted all along in this chapter that monopsonistic labor markets are likely to result in worker exploitation, with pay tending to fall below the worth of workers as measured by their marginal revenue products. How much less than their MRPs were major league baseball players paid under the reserve system? In an article published in 1974[11]

---

[11] Gerald Scully, "Pay and Performance in Major League Baseball," *American Economic Review* 64 (6) (1974): 915–930.

Gerald Scully found that before free agency came about, the average ballplayer was paid only about 20% of the net revenues (MRP) he produced for his team. Superstar ballplayers were paid on average only about 15% of what they were worth. Interestingly, mediocre ballplayers were paid *more* than their marginal revenue products. This was a result of baseball's minimum salary, which was about $12,000 per year when Scully did his study. To put this minimum salary in context, beginning salaries for university professors were at about this level at that time.

Since elimination of the reserve clause in 1976–77 and the emergence of a competitive labor market, salaries have—well, how do we best put this—"fulminated." If you don't have a dictionary handy, a glance at Figure 9.5 will give you a pretty good idea of what this word means. It is a pretty safe bet that free agency has eliminated much of the salary exploitation in professional baseball.

A form of reserve clause also still operates in the European soccer leagues. Players are contracted to play for a particular team, but players can be traded by teams for substantial transfer fees. There have been signs in recent years that this monopsony is crumbling, much as the reserve clause crumbled in baseball. The Bosman ruling of the European Court of Justice in 1995 ensured that players could freely move from one team to another once their contract expired without the former club being compensated.[12] Some top players have taken advantage of this to increase their wages. If their new team does not

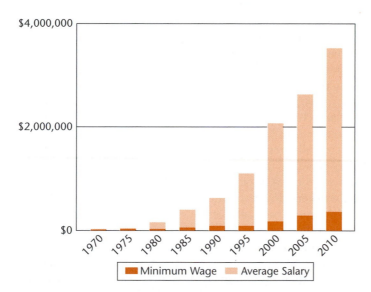

FIGURE 9.5 Average Baseball Player Salaries

Source: Baseball Almanac, http://www.baseball-almanac.com/charts/salary/
FC2StackedColumn2.swf?IsLocal=1&dataURL=salaries.xml

---

[12] Until then, the team with which a player had been contracted could demand a transfer fee even after the contract had expired. Jean-Marc Bosman wished to transfer from FC Liege to Dunkirk in 1990 but was prevented from doing so because Liege set a transfer fee that Dunkirk was unwilling to meet. Furthermore, Liege imposed a wage cut on Bosman. He took his case to the courts with consequences that continue to resonate in the world of European soccer.

have to pay a transfer fee, the team can pay an equivalent sum directly to the players in the form of a higher salary. Certainly footballers' salaries in Europe have increased dramatically in the years since the Bosman ruling, but it is hard to say how much of this is due to the new flexibility in the transfer market. Other factors have been at work too, including the escalation of fees for television rights and the increased interest of sports clubs in commercial development.

Dynamic Monopsony

The examples of monopsony labor markets discussed so far might have led you to think, "Interesting, but is monopsony really important?" The answer to this question is "yes." Monopsony has much wider relevance than these admittedly rather esoteric examples. To understand why this is the case, we need to introduce a little refinement into our analysis.

The classical model of labor market behavior—where demand meets supply and that determines the wage and employment levels—is appealing, but it supposes that workers arrive at the market at the start of a day and that the price for which their time will be sold is settled upon quickly. On this assumption, if workers are left unhired at the end of the day, the price falls until someone comes along to hire them. Each new day brings about a new deal. Of course, in real life, workers are not strawberries, and their time is not sold on a market that adjusts in this way.

Put another way, the market for labor is not a spot market. Rather, a worker, once hired, builds a relationship with his or her employer that is expected to last some time: maybe a month, maybe three months, maybe three years, maybe a lifetime. In addition, the deal struck when a worker is hired is not subject to renegotiation each and every day.

Workers form long-term relationships with firms for a variety of reasons, one being that it would be very costly for workers to behave as if their labor were traded on a spot market. They would have to search for work every day. That would entail looking through the job ads in the newspaper, writing letters and filling out application forms, contacting references, getting haircuts, traveling to and attending interviews, and even buying the occasional new suit! In other words, workers would have to incur all the costs of search (see Chapter 8) even if they were already employed, and they would have to incur them often. To avoid these costs, workers do the obvious thing—they search for jobs, but only occasionally. The rest of the time, they act just like loyal employees of their current employer.

But here is the catch. If the current employer knows that its workers are not constantly on the lookout for jobs elsewhere, it knows also that it is the *only* firm in the market for those workers during the current time period. In other words, the fact that workers cannot constantly search for alternative employment means that *all* firms are monopsonists in the labor market. This is known as **dynamic monopsony**—*dynamic* because a firm's monopsony power relies on the commitment of workers to the firm in a relationship that is expected to last over many time periods.[13] The development of a theory of dynamic

---

[13] Alan Manning, *Monopsony in Motion: Imperfect Competition in Labor Markets* (Princeton: Princeton University Press, 2003); Venkataraman Bhaskar, Alan Manning, and Ted To, "Oligopsony and Monopsonistic Competition in Labor Markets," *Journal of Economic Perspectives* 16 (2002): 155–174; Orley C. Ashenfelter, Henry Farber and Michael R. Ransom, "Labor Market Monopsony," *Journal of Labor Economics* 28 (2010): 203–210.

monopsony is extremely important because it explains how monopsony can be the norm for the labor market. (It also explains why the competitive case of a firm facing a perfectly elastic supply curve of labor can be viewed as a deviation from this norm.)

The degree to which firms can exploit this monopsony power is limited. If a firm were to reduce wages far below the competitive level, its workers would soon start to search for jobs elsewhere with greater intensity. But the costs attached to this search mean that there must still be some scope for firms to pay workers less than their MRP on a permanent basis.

All of this has a number of implications: among them is the idea that firms are not wage-takers. Different firms can pay different wages for similar work. This opens up all kinds of possibilities. For example, monopsony power makes it possible for some firms to discriminate against some workers on the basis of gender, ethnicity, or religion. (In a competitive model such **discrimination** is hard to rationalise because it would be competed away.)[14]

Another example concerns the tendency for larger firms to pay higher wages than those paid by smaller firms.[15] The key to understanding why this might happen is to note that the wage-employment solution under conditions of monopsony lies to the left of the labor demand curve. The level of employment that obtains at the monopsonistic equilibrium is constrained by labor supply; at the low, indeed exploitative, wage that the firm is offering, relatively little labor is willing to work. If more people could be persuaded to work at this low wage, the firm would increase its profits. Monopsonistic firms, in effect, face a menu of choices. A firm could either employ few people at low wages or more people at a higher wage; the number of people employed is essentially determined by the labor supply. And what's more, two firms could be making exactly the same amount of profit while behaving differently from one another: one firm might employ just a few people at a low wage, and another could employ many people at a relatively high wage. Economists call this the **firm size wage effect**. Large firms tend to pay better wages than do smaller firms. (Bear that in mind when you're looking for jobs.) This is one of the stylized facts about the labor market that has been widely observed in a lot of different countries, yet it's a fact that was little understood until the idea of dynamic monopsony came along.

Dynamic monopsony is quite an exciting new development. It turns on its head the view that we can, with a few exceptions, model labor markets as if they were competitive markets. The norm is for firms to have some degree of monopsony power and, therefore, to have some real discretion over what wages they pay their workers.

The next question is an obvious one. How important are dynamic monopsony effects in practice? Do they dampen wages by 50%, 5%, 0.5%, or less? In other words, does monopsony matter? The short answer is "yes." Evidence from the south coast of England

[14] A model of discrimination based on monopsony is provided by Erling Barth and Harald Dale-Olsen, "Monopsonistic Discrimination and the Gender Wage Gap," *NBER Working Paper 7197*, 1999.

[15] Ken Burdett and Dale Mortensen, "Wage Differentials, Employer Size, and Unemployment," *International Economic Review* 39 (1998): 257–273. Some compelling empirical evidence on this issue is provided by Francis Green, Stephen Machin, and Alan Manning, "The Employer Size-Wage Effect: Can Dynamic Monopsony Provide an Explanation?" *Oxford Economic Papers* 48 (1996): 433–455.

PUTTING THEORY TO WORK

THE WAGE PENALTY

In a monopsonistic labor market, firms have considerable power in wage setting. Such a labor market is a mirror image of a unionized market wherein unions put upward pressure on wages. It should not be surprising, therefore, to find that (compared to a competitive market) workers under monopsony are typically underpaid.

Using a statistical technique known as stochastic frontier analysis, Duncan Watson* has estimated the extent of the wage penalty due to dynamic monopsony in the United Kingdom. He finds that, on average, male workers who are not members of a trade union are paid some 18% less than they would be in the absence of monopsony effects. The corresponding figure for females is 19%.

The wage penalty suffered by young men is greater than that suffered by prime-age men, to the tune of about 1.5 percentage points. This may be because young men are willing to engage in job shopping activity, taking on temporary work at relatively low pay, before they choose a career.

Better-educated workers are less prone to monopsonistic exploitation than are other workers. Workers with a degree suffer a wage penalty three-quarters of a percentage point less than workers with no qualifications. Highly educated workers are less likely than others to suffer prolonged spells of unemployment, and they are better able to finance effective job search, thereby forestalling monopsonistic exploitation.

Note: *Duncan Watson, "UK Wage Underpayment: Implications for the Minimum Wage," *Applied Economics* 32 (2000): 429–440.

PUTTING THEORY TO WORK

IS BIGGER BETTER?

Consider two firms that are identical in all respects apart from the number of employees. One firm is smaller than average, and the other is larger than average. To be more precise, the first firm employs one standard deviation fewer workers than the average, and the second employs one standard deviation more.

Now consider a worker at the first firm, and compare her with an identical worker (in an identical job) at the second firm. According to estimates provided by Charles Brown and James Medoff,* the worker at the larger firm will earn wages that are between 8 and 12% higher than are earned by her counterpart at the smaller firm. The effect of firm size on wages can therefore be quite substantial—comparable with the effect that unions have!

Note: *Charles Brown and James Medoff, "The Employer Size-Wage Effect," *Journal of Political Economy* 97 (1989): 1027–1059.

suggests that the effect of monopsony power on workers' pay is not insubstantial. Alan Manning[16] used data from a survey of nurses in this region to conclude that monopsony depresses wages by about 10%. Further evidence on this issue is provided in the Putting Theory to Work feature.

Where does this leave us? Should the competitive model of the labor market be thrown out the window as a useless relic of a (possibly fictional) bygone age? We think not. Economic models are not, after all, designed with realism in mind; that would make them far too complicated to be useful. Rather, models are designed to provide us with a helpful guide in understanding the way the real world works. And, for many purposes, the competitive model of the labor market does just that. Nonetheless, you need to be aware that some things that happen in the real world cannot be explained using the competitive model. For instance, it doesn't explain why discrimination takes place. When we encounter topics such as this, we do what any good craftsperson would do: we pick the right tool for the job. Often, the competitive model works rather well, but at other times the monopsonistic model of the labor market will suit our needs better.

Minimum Wages

In the previous section, we gave two examples of economic phenomena that can be explained by the theory of dynamic monopsony—discrimination and the firm size wage effect. In this section, we consider in some detail a third example, namely, the effect on employment of **minimum wage** legislation. Earlier in the chapter (see Figure 9.2) we saw that introducing or raising a minimum wage can have positive effects on employment in a monopsony setting. This was a startling finding because it contrasts so sharply with the prediction of the competitive model that minimum wages must lower employment. At the very least, the new theory of dynamic monopsony makes clear the fact that the employment effect of the minimum wage is an empirical issue. Therefore, we devote some time here to analyzing the results in a number of recent studies of the minimum wage.

In a 1998 report, the Organization for Economic Cooperation and Development (OECD) identified 17 member nations with comprehensive minimum wage requirements based on national legislation.[17] Other countries have adopted minimum wage laws since then, and still others allow collective bargaining to establish minimum wages for workers, including workers who are not covered directly by a labor contract. Comprehensive minimum wage laws cover most workers, although disabled people, apprentices and trainees, public sector employees, and managerial employees are exempted from coverage to a varying degree across countries. In most cases the minimum wage requirement is national in scope, although U.S. states and Canadian provinces can enact local minimum wages in excess of the national level. In Japan and Mexico, however, only provincial governments set the minimum wage.

---

[16] Alan Manning, "Labor Markets with Company Wage Policies," *Centre for Economic Performance Discussion Paper 214*, London School of Economics, 1994.

[17] "Making the Most of the Minimum: Statutory Minimum Wages, Employment and Poverty," *OECD Employment Outlook*, June 1998, pp. 31–80.

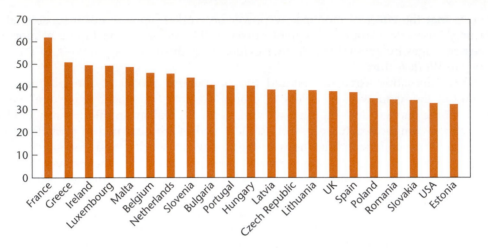

FIGURE 9.6 Minimum Wages as a Percentage of the Average Wage in 2004,
Various Countries

Source: Thorsten Kalina and Claudia Weinkopf "Ein gesetzlicher Mindestlohn auch in Deutschland?,"
Institut Arbeit und Technik – Report (2006) 2006–06, available at http://www.econbiz.de/archiv1/2008/
51694_mindestlohn_deutschland_modellrechnung.pdf.

Figure 9.6 presents some information on differences in the minimum wage across
countries. In this comparison, France has the most generous minimum wage at 62% of
the mean wage, and the United States and Estonia are at the less generous end of the distribution, each at around 32 or 33%.

A consequence of the relatively high minimum wage in countries such as France is
that, in these economies, a high proportion of workers qualify for the minimum wage.
Around 16% of workers in France qualify, while the corresponding figure in the United
States is just a little over 1%. Table 9.1 presents more detailed information on the characteristics of U.S. workers earning wages at or near the minimum wage level. In comparison
with the overall work force, a much higher fraction of low-wage earners are teenagers,
part-time workers, and workers who have not completed high school.

TABLE 9.1   Characteristics of Minimum Wage Workers ($7.25 per hour) in the United States: 2011

Percentage of all hourly-paid workers with wages at or below the federal minimum wage	5%
Percentage of hourly-paid teenagers with wages at or below the federal minimum wage	23%
Percentage of all full-time workers with wages at or below the federal minimum wage	2%
Percentage of all part-time workers with wages at or below the federal minimum wage	13%
Percentage of hourly-paid men with wages at or below the federal minimum wage	4%
Percentage of hourly-paid women with wages at or below the federal minimum wage	6%
Percentage of hourly-paid workers without a high-school diploma with wages at or below the federal minimum age	11%
Percentage of hourly-paid workers with a high-school diploma (but with no college) with wages at or below the federal minimum wage	5%

Source: U.S. Department of Labor, Bureau of Labor Statistics, "Characteristics of Minimum Wage Workers: 2011," March 2, 2012.

In addition to work force coverage, another factor that potentially limits the impact of the minimum wage is the extent to which the legislated wage keeps up with the rate of inflation. In the United States, legislation establishes a federal nominal minimum wage that is changed only occasionally. There are, however, several states that set their own minimum wages above the federal level, and in some of these the overall minimum wage is linked to price indices so that cost-of-living adjustments are automatically made. In many other countries, the minimum wage is not automatically adjusted for inflation, though it is periodically reviewed. Clearly, over the period in between such reviews, the inflation-adjusted value of the nominal minimum wage declines steadily. The OECD survey identified only Belgium and Luxembourg as countries that indexed the minimum wage to a consumer price index.

Empirical Evidence on the Employment Effect of Minimum Wages

Much of the recent attention given to the minimum wage issue resulted from an interesting study of a so-called natural experiment, and we begin with a detailed summary of this evidence. The employment effect of the minimum wage has also been extensively studied using traditional econometric methods, and we examine some of that evidence later in this section.

The Card-Krueger "Natural Experiment" Study

The humble quarter-pound hamburger has come to play a crucial role in the minimum wage debate. Burger chains employ many workers at very low wages, and the availability of shift work makes such work appealing as part-time employment for students, ensuring that fast-food restaurants enjoy a plentiful supply of labor. But it is also one reason the wage is low—a high supply of labor meets a limited demand. It is not the only reason for low wages in this sector, of course. Much of the work suits youths who left the education system relatively early and began work with low stocks of human capital.

In April 1992, the state of New Jersey raised its minimum wage from the federal minimum of $4.25 to $5.05. At the same time, in neighboring Pennsylvania the minimum wage remained at the lower level of $4.25. Two economists who, at that time, lived near the border between the two states realized that this legislative change presented a great opportunity to investigate the employment effects of the minimum wage. Because the minimum was being increased in one state but not the other, David Card and Alan Krueger[18] realized that they had the chance to conduct a **natural experiment**, something that rarely presents itself in economics. The two states share a border, local economic conditions are similar in the border region of the two states, and national legislation affects both states equally. The *only* thing that differed between the two states was the fact that the minimum wage changed in April 1992 in New Jersey but not in Pennsylvania. Examining the data on wages and employment on both sides of the state line both before and after the change

---

[18] Their work is reported in David Card and Alan B. Krueger, "Minimum Wages and Employment: A Case Study of the Fast Food Industry in New Jersey and Pennsylvania," *American Economic Review* 84 (1994): 772–793.

is rather like performing an experiment under laboratory conditions in one of the physical sciences. The results of the analysis allow the "pure" effect of minimum wages on employment to be evaluated.

Fortunately for Card and Krueger, the hike in the New Jersey minimum wage was announced several months in advance, so they were able to collect data on a "before and after" basis. They first approached fast-food restaurants on both sides of the state line in February and March of 1992 (before the change), and they collected a second set of data in November and December of the same year. In all, they obtained information from about 400 fast-food outlets; about 80% of these were based in New Jersey, the remainder being drawn from eastern Pennsylvania. With this data set, they investigated the change in employment in the New Jersey restaurants due to the change in the minimum wage.

At the beginning of 1992, about one-third of all restaurants in both Pennsylvania and New Jersey paid their workers starting wages of $4.25 per hour, the minimum wage (see Figure 9.7). The remaining two-thirds paid more, but very few workers received more than $5.05 per hour. By late 1992, starting wages in Pennsylvania were distributed fairly evenly across the range between $4.25 and $5.05. In New Jersey, meanwhile, almost everybody on starting wages received exactly $5.05 per hour by the end of 1992.

So the increase in the minimum wage certainly led to an increase in wages paid, but what about the effect on employment? In Pennsylvania, average employment per restaurant[19] fell slightly during 1992, from 23.33 to 21.17. This is not altogether surprising; the economy as a whole was not doing very well at the time. In New Jersey, however, average employment per restaurant rose, from 20.44 to 21.03, over the study period. This is not a huge increase; but when put alongside the fall that occurred in neighboring Pennsylvania, it is enough to suggest that the minimum wage hike did not harm employment.

To say that Card and Krueger's results caused a stir would be putting it mildly. Their work seemed to challenge the very foundations on which most economists' views of the world were constructed. This was in an area of keen interest to policymakers because their decisions could make a real difference to the lives of many people living in relative poverty. Moreover, the impact of the Pennsylvania and New Jersey natural experiment was felt over a much wider geographical area. In the United Kingdom, for example, the Conservative government had stubbornly resisted adoption of a national minimum wage as part of the European Union's Maastricht Treaty. Yet here was evidence that seemed to undermine the economic underpinnings of the government's case.

The results of the New Jersey and Pennsylvania experiment shocked many economists into looking afresh at the issue of minimum wages. The data used by Card and Krueger have come under particularly close scrutiny.[20] David Neumark and William Wascher

---

[19] This was measured as full-time equivalent workers. Many workers in fast food restaurants are part-time; to make the comparisons fair, it was important that Card and Krueger measured employment in this way. The count of full-time equivalent workers is based on the number of hours that each worker puts in. So two workers who work half-time would be counted as one full-time equivalent.

[20] The exchange between Card and Krueger and two other economists, David Neumark and William Wascher, is a great example of economic fisticuffs with gloves off. See David Neumark and William Wascher, "Minimum Wages and Employment: A Case Study of the Fast Food Industry in New Jersey and Pennsylvania: Comment," *American Economic Review* 90 (2000): 1362–1396; David Card and Alan B. Krueger, "Minimum Wages and Employment: A Case Study of the Fast Food Industry in New Jersey and Pennsylvania: Reply," *American Economic Review* 90 (2000): 1397–1420.

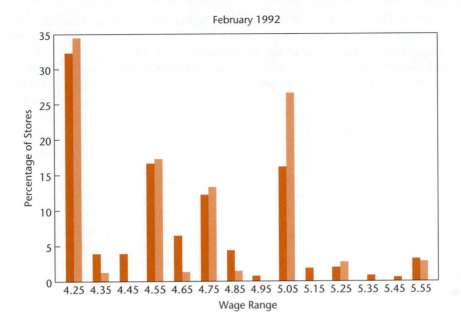

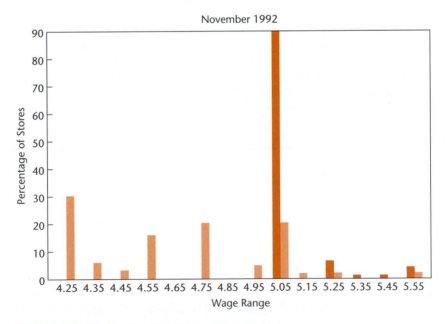

FIGURE 9.7 Distribution of Starting Wage Rates

Source: David Card and Alan B. Krueger, "Minimum Wages and Employment: A Case Study of the Fast Food Industry in New Jersey and Pennsylvania," *American Economic Review* 84 (1994): 772–793.

suggested that the data used were of poor quality. Using data from an alternative source,[21] these authors found that average employment levels in New Jersey *fell*, and by more than in Pennsylvania, in the wake of the minimum wage hike.

Card and Krueger responded by using Bureau of Labor Statistics data[22] to repeat their analysis. This new analysis once again showed that there was, if anything, a small rise in New Jersey employment relative to the Pennsylvania experience during 1992 in the wake of the minimum wage increase. The new analysis also casts some doubt on how representative the sample of restaurants chosen by Neumark and Wascher was. In particular, the results are extremely sensitive to the inclusion or otherwise of one particular restaurant operator in Pennsylvania.

You might be tempted to ask at this stage, "Is the minimum wage all about hamburgers?" This is an important question because the market for fast food is not necessarily the same as the market for many other things. One way restaurant operators in New Jersey could get around the problems posed by a higher minimum wage is to raise the prices of their burgers. They could do this in the knowledge that a modest rise in the product price would not have much of an effect on demand. Consumers would not drive all the way to Pennsylvania, incurring time and travel costs, just to buy a burger that was perhaps 10 cents cheaper. The burger would be cold by the time they got home! Burgers are not goods that are typically traded across state lines.

Consider, however, the case of a furniture manufacturer that pays the minimum wage to its workers. It is not so easy for such a firm to raise the price of its product in response to an increase in the minimum wage because furniture is a traded good. People in Ohio buy furniture made in Montana, or in Sweden. Furniture makers operate in a reasonably competitive product market, and it is not easy for them to change the price in response to a local increase in the minimum wage. If they did so, they would risk pricing themselves out of the market. Although the experience of the fast food industry is interesting, it is not necessarily all that instructive. Different industries might have very different responses to changes in the minimum wage.

Nevertheless the initial work done on the New Jersey and Pennsylvania natural experiment clearly stirred up a hornets' nest. After more detailed consideration of the problem, the best that one can say about the evidence is that it is mixed. Now let's look at some other pieces of evidence on the employment effects of the minimum wage.

Other Minimum Wage Studies

Some evidence from the U.S. Current Population Survey[23] suggests that a rise in the minimum wage increases the number of young people in full-time employment. To be more specific, the elasticity (with respect to the minimum wage) of the probability

---

[21] The Employment Policies Institute (EPI) collected some of the data, and Neumark and Wascher collected the remainder themselves. Their data on employment and wages are based on personnel records rather than on answers to a telephone interview; they argue, plausibly enough, that this should make the data more reliable.

[22] These data are derived from unemployment insurance payroll tax records.

[23] David Neumark and William Wascher, "Minimum Wage Effects on School and Work Transitions of Teenagers," *American Economic Association Papers and Proceedings* 85 (1995): 244–249.

with which a teenager is not in education but is in employment is 0.57. If the minimum wage rises by 10%, the probability of an individual being employed and not in education rises by 5.7%. This seems to support the central finding of the New Jersey and Pennsylvania natural experiment. But a word of caution is needed here: the elasticity of the probability of being in education and not in employment is −0.1. In other words, an increase in the minimum wage diverts young people out of education and into the labor market. If youths are being encouraged to leave school prematurely, the positive employment effects of the minimum wage might not be an unambiguously good thing.

There is interesting evidence from other countries too. Much of this was collected in response to the commitment in the Maastricht Treaty of 1992, which requires member countries of the European Union to have national minimum wages.

In the United Kingdom, for example, there was no national minimum wage until 1999.[24] In earlier years, various industries had been subject to an industry-specific wage minimum, but these were allowed to erode (and were eventually abolished) during the 1980s as the Conservative government led by Margaret Thatcher encouraged the development of a flexible labor market. The employment effects of the erosion of industry-specific minimum wages appear to have been small, and moreover they seem to contradict the predictions of the competitive model.[25] Indeed, as the toughness of the minimum wage policy was eroded, employment seemed to fall—the reverse of the rise predicted by the theory of competitive markets. The British experience suggests that employment is maximized when the minimum wage is set at 56% of the average industry wage. An increase in the minimum wage from this level can lead to substantial declines in employment. But a decline in the minimum wage can also lead to a cut in employment levels. The employment level when the minimum wage is 56% of the industry average wage is 0.1% higher than it would be in the absence of a minimum wage. This is a very small employment gain, to be sure, but it certainly suggests that over some range minimum wages are not harmful to full employment.

In France,[26] regions that experienced lower initial wage levels (and so were most affected by changes to the minimum wage) tended to experience relatively high employment gains from the 1960s through 1980s, a period during which the minimum wage rose rapidly. In the Netherlands during the early 1980s, the youth minimum wage was reduced to a lower proportion of the adult minimum wage, but this had virtually no impact on the share of employment accounted for by youths in any of the traditional low-wage sectors. In Spain, an increase in the toughness of minimum wage legislation from 1978 to 1992 appears to have been associated with an increase in employment growth.

---

[24] The United Kingdom had negotiated an opt-out from the social chapter of the Maastricht Treaty. The new Labor government, elected in 1997, adopted the social chapter, and it is this that paved the way to the introduction of the minimum wage.

[25] Stephen Machin and Alan Manning, "The Effects of Minimum Wages on Wage Dispersion and Employment," *Industrial and Labor Relations Review* 47 (1994): 319–329.

[26] Stephen Machin and Alan Manning, "Minimum Wages and Economic Outcomes in Europe," *European Economic Review* 41 (1997): 733–742.

Econometric Studies

Several studies of the minimum wage employment effect have involved time series or panel estimation of a regression equation such as:

$$E = \alpha + \beta w_m + \delta X + \varepsilon \qquad (9\text{-}2)$$

where E is the level of employment for a particular group in time period t, usually measured as a fraction of the group's population; w_m measures the minimum wage, usually as a fraction of the median or mean wage in the economy; X is a vector of variables used to control for the business cycle and other determinants of group employment; α, β, and δ are parameters estimated by the regression method; and ε is a random error term. The parameter of interest is β, which is hypothesized to be significantly less than zero. If the employment and minimum wage variables are measured in logarithms, then β is an estimate of the elasticity of employment with respect to the minimum wage.

A review of the empirical literature on U.S. workers found that the estimated elasticity of employment with respect to the minimum wage for teenagers (ages 16 to 19) ranged from −0.01 to −0.03; estimates for young adults were negative but smaller than these amounts.[27] A more recent study using data from 1975 to 1996 for Belgium, Canada, France, Greece, Japan, the Netherlands, Portugal, Spain, and the United States also found a very inelastic employment response to the minimum wage. For teenagers aged 15 to 19, the elasticity estimates were in the range of −0.2 to −0.4; for youths aged 20 to 24 and adults over 25 the elasticity estimates were not generally significantly different from zero.[28] This study found that changes in teenage employment over time were much more responsive to other determinants than to the minimum wage.

If you are feeling confused, it's likely that you've understood everything perfectly! A few years ago, economists thought they had a clear grasp of the employment effects of the minimum wage. Recent evidence shows that the matter really isn't that straightforward and that we can't be sure what the employment effects of a moderate minimum wage are likely to be. At modest levels, at least, a minimum wage probably does not raise unemployment and might even reduce it. But at modest levels, the benefits of the minimum wage to those who remain in employment are modest too.

Other Effects of the Minimum Wage

We have focused on the employment effects of the minimum wage so far. However, even if minimum wages are harmful to employment, that doesn't mean they are a bad thing. The gain in income to those that benefit from the minimum wage might offset the disutility felt by people who are displaced out of the labor market. A checklist of the effects of the minimum wage would include these points:

---

[27] Charles Brown, Curtis Gilroy, and Andrew Kohen, "The Effect of the Minimum Wage on Employment and Unemployment," *Journal of Economic Literature* 20 (1982): 487–528.

[28] "Making the Most of the Minimum: Statutory Minimum Wages, Employment and Poverty," *OECD Employment Outlook*, 1998, pp. 31–80.

PUTTING THEORY TO WORK

A LIVING WAGE?

Since the pioneering effort of the City of Baltimore in 1994, more than 80 U.S. cities, counties, and school districts have adopted living wage laws.* These local government ordinances require companies doing business with the local government or receiving grants or other forms of assistance from the government to pay wages that are significantly above the federal minimum wage.

These wage floors are called "living" because they are set at a level designed to allow a full-time worker to live above the U.S. government's poverty level of income. In 2012, a full-time worker with a family of four needed to earn more than $23,050 to be above the official poverty level. Working 2,000 hours a year at the federal minimum wage, however, would bring in just $14,500.

Cities faced with grassroots campaigns to adopt living wage ordinances are also faced with the kind of debate surrounding changes in the minimum wage. Those in favor emphasize the positive gain in wages earned by low-income workers and the reduction in poverty that results. Critics emphasize the negative effect of higher wage costs on the number of low-income workers hired and on business investment within the city's boundaries.

Like many studies of the minimum wage, there seems to be little evidence of large negative effects of living wage laws. These laws affect relatively few workers, and these workers are employed largely by firms paid under contracts with the local government that sets the living wage.[†] In addition, lax enforcement and loopholes in the language of some laws allow employers to escape the provisions of the laws.[‡]

A major study of the effects of living wage laws sponsored by the Public Policy Institute of California found that a living wage 50% above the federal minimum wage would lower the local poverty rate by 1.8 percentage points. This positive effect was seen as outweighing the employment displacement associated with such laws.[**]

Notes: *Robert A. Jordan, "Living Wage Movement Grows Despite Critics," *Boston Globe*, April 11, 2002; [†]Jeff Madrick, "Living Wages Are Practical and Don't Let Theory Get in the Way," *New York Times*, July 5, 2001; [‡]Alison Grant, "Cleveland's Living-Wage Law Weak, Report Finds," *Plain Dealer*, March 20, 2002; [**]Justin Pritchard, "National Study Concludes That 'Living Wage' Reduces Poverty," *Associated Press State and Local Wire*, March 14, 2002, and Gene Koretz, "The Case for Living Wage Laws," *Business Week*, April 22, 2002.

- The effect on any people who are displaced out of employment
- The effect on income of those who remain in work
- The effect on the income distribution

If unemployment rises as the result of the minimum wage, then the first of these effects is clearly negative. The second effect, meanwhile, is clearly positive. The third effect is more ambiguous: An increase in unemployment tends to widen the income distribution, whereas the enhanced earnings of those who stay employed tends to narrow it.

If **social welfare** is thought of as, among other things, a weighted average of all three effects, it is clear that the welfare effect of the minimum wage could be positive or negative. The precise effect will depend on the extent to which the minimum wage affects income and employment, but it will also depend on the extent to which these things figure into the social welfare function.

Most evidence that we have[29] suggests that employment has considerable weight in the social welfare function. Certainly we know that unemployment makes people very unhappy. Some estimates suggest that the act of transiting from employment to unemployment has as much impact on an individual's happiness as does a pay cut of $30,000 per year—and that is in addition to the loss of earnings implied by the job loss. This being the case, it is understandable that most of our focus has been on the employment effects of the minimum wage.

A cynic might take the view that the minimum wage represents an attempt by governments to pass the buck. Rather than pay for social policies through the system of taxation and government expenditure, imposing a minimum wage passes the cost of reducing poverty onto firms. The temptation for governments to do this is entirely natural —after all, we all like to vote for political parties that can find ways of reducing the need for high taxes. But if the aim of the minimum wage is to reduce poverty, it really isn't all that clear that this is a policy well suited to the objective. After all, the minimum wage helps those who are employed, but it doesn't do much to help those who are not. In addition, the minimum wage targets individuals who have low rates of pay, but it is the income of households, not of individuals, that matters when we come to consider who lives in poverty. Many of those who benefit from the minimum wage are young people living with their parents, and they would not be in poverty in the absence of the minimum wage. Welfare benefits are more costly to the public purse, but there is little doubt that they represent a more precise weapon than the minimum wage in the struggle against poverty.

Table 9.1 provides some U.S. evidence on this, but it is fair to say that the evidence is not all that clear cut. There is a concentration of part-time workers and youths in the group of workers who receive earnings at or close to the minimum wage. These workers are typically not protected by membership in trade unions. Yet more than half of minimum wage workers are adults, and about 30% are working full time. On the other hand, when an analysis was done of the potential consequences of an increase in the minimum wage from $5.15 an hour to $7.25 in 2007, it was estimated that only about 15% of the additional wages would go to workers who lived in poor families.[30] What does all this tell us about whether the minimum wage is hitting its target group? We think the evidence is ambiguous, at best.

To shed more light on this issue, Figure 9.8 presents some comparative international data on the household income of workers who earn low wages. In most countries the majority of low-wage earners do not live in poor households but rather in households with moderate to high levels of income. Even in the United States, only about 20% of workers who are paid wages at or below the minimum wage are in families whose incomes are at or below the poverty threshold.[31] What this suggests is that a considerable

---

[29] See, for example, Andrew Clark and Andrew Oswald, "A Simple Statistical Method for Measuring How Life Events Affect Happiness," *International Journal of Epidemiology* 31 (2002): 1139–1144.

[30] United States Congress, Congressional Budget Office, "Response to a Request by Senator Grassley About the Effects of Increasing the Federal Minimum Wage Versus Expanding the Earned Income Tax Credit," January 9, 2007.

[31] Ralph Smith and Bruce Vavrichek, "The Minimum Wage and Family Incomes: An Update," United States Congress, Congressional Budget Office, November 16, 1993.

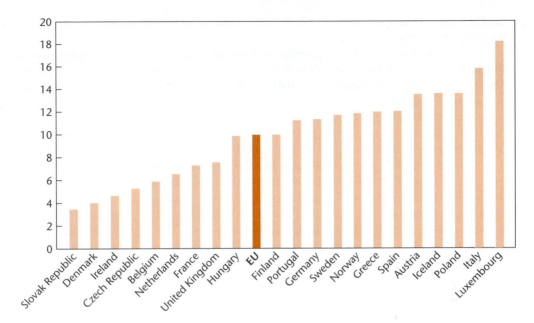

FIGURE 9.8 OECD (2009), OECD Employment Outlook 2009: Tackling the Jobs Crisis, OECD Publishing. http://dx.doi.org/10.1787/empl_outlook-2009-en

amount of the potential benefits of the minimum wage accrue to individuals who are not in poverty.

What can we conclude about the minimum wage? We think it is probably doing some good, but were we to grade the minimum wage like we would a term paper, we would write "Could do better." At modest levels, the minimum wage may not raise unemployment, as was once thought, but neither is it as effective a tool against poverty as some observers might have us believe.

Summary

In this chapter we have explained wage and employment determination in markets that do not fit the "large number of buyers" assumption of the competitive labor market model. We have seen that, other things being equal, in such monopsonistic labor markets both wages and employment levels tend to be below what they would otherwise be if the market were competitive.

Existing research indicates that pure monopsony may not be all that widespread a phenomenon and that in any case the negative effects on wages appear to be small (except for pre-1977 baseball players, and even back then "exploited" ballplayers did not receive a lot of sympathy from fans).

But the more refined concept of dynamic monopsony has opened up a whole new can of worms. The available evidence suggests that this phenomenon exists and that its effects are nontrivial. Moreover, a variety of economic phenomena—such as labor market discrimination and the firm size wage effect—can plausibly be explained by dynamic monopsony.

Arguably the most startling result to have emerged from recent empirical analysis of the labor market is that the minimum wage is not necessarily harmful to employment. The most plausible explanation for this result is that monopsony effects are at work.

As we come to the end of this chapter, it is worth thinking about the source of dynamic monopsony a little more deeply. Remember that dynamic monopsony arises because workers are not perpetually searching for alternative employment; they typically have a long-term relationship with their employer. Either explicitly or virtually, employers and workers have contracts with one another that bind them to each other over lengthy periods of time. This contractual relationship makes the market for labor very different from other markets studied by economists. It is not a market that can be expected to clear on a day-to-day basis. Instead, it is a market where the future and the past matter as well as the present. Workers choose which employer to work for on the basis of expected future wages, not just on the basis of the current wage. The next two chapters highlight some of the profound implications this has for our analysis of the labor market.

KEY TERMS

monopsony

local monopsony

discriminating monopsony

concentration ratio

government monopsony

school district monopsony

dynamic monopsony

discrimination

firm size wage effect

minimum wage

natural experiment

social welfare

PROBLEMS

1. Eureka, Nevada, is a small town with only one restaurant, DJ's Diner. For the purposes of this exercise, you may consider DJ to be a geographical monopsonist. Assume further that DJ sells only one type of product (burgers) at $2 each. His production function is given by the data on labor input and output in the following table. The labor supply curve is given by the data on labor input and the hourly wage.

Labor input	Output (burgers per hour)	Wage (per hour)
1	10	10
2	18	11
3	24	12
4	28	13
5	30	14

Use the information in the table to calculate the following at each level of labor input:
a. Marginal product
b. Marginal revenue product

    c. Total labor cost

    d. Marginal labor cost.

2. Use your calculations in question 1 to determine the level of employment at DJ's Diner. How would your answer change if this restaurant operated in a competitive labor market?

3. (Greater degree of difficulty) Suppose a monopsonist has a production function given by

$$Y = \sqrt{L}$$

and faces a labor supply schedule given by

$$w = 10 + L/2$$

where Y represents output, L is labor input, and w is the hourly wage. For various levels of labor input, calculate the following:

    a. Marginal product

    b. Marginal revenue product (assuming that product price [p] $= 50$)

    c. Total labor cost

    d. Marginal labor cost and, hence, establish the level of labor input this monopsonist will choose.

4. In the dynamic monopsony model, employers gain market power from the inability of workers to be constantly seeking alternative employment. What, then, would be the effect on the extent of monopsony power of:

    a. An increase in the real cost of travel

    b. An increase in annual leave entitlement

    c. Creation of an Internet site that advertises job vacancies in a specific field

    d. Introduction of human resource management methods that make the recruitment process more time consuming for applicants.

5. If small firms pay lower wages than larger firms, how can smaller firms attract workers?

6. How have geographical monopsonies been affected by improved transportation? Are such monopsonies more likely to be observed nowadays in North America (where the population is small in relation to the land area) than in Europe (where the reverse is true)? Explain.

7. Suppose that a monopsonist is able to distinguish between the labor supply schedules for men and women and that the wage elasticity of labor supply is greater for men than for women. What does this imply for the wages paid to men and women?

8. Outline the alternative courses of action open to the manager of a fast-food restaurant faced with an increase in the minimum wage. How might the higher wage affect her ability to attract new job applicants? Would it affect her pricing decisions?

9. A study found that the wages paid by national fast food chain restaurants located within a medium-sized U.S. city varied, ranging from the (then) legal minimum wage of $5.15 an hour to $6.75 an hour.

    a. Explain how this would be evidence of monopsony.

    b. How would this affect your analysis of the local employment effects of an increase in the minimum wage?

10. The following table gives estimates of the elasticity of labor demand relative to the minimum wage obtained from regression analysis. Do the estimates for the different groups make sense? Explain.

Worker Group	Elasticity Estimate
Men ages 16 to 19	−0.30
Women ages 20 to 25	−0.15
Men ages 26 to 30	0.0

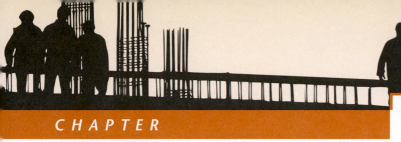

10

Internal Labor Markets

Why do employers invest so heavily in identifying the best candidate for a vacant job?

Why are many senior positions filled by promotions from within the company?

What distinguishes "good jobs" from "dead-end jobs"?

As we have seen in the first half of this book, the competitive model of the labor market is an extremely useful tool for studying certain aspects of labor economics. Competition among workers for jobs and among firms for workers determines a unique equilibrium wage for a given labor market and a unique structure of wages across labor markets. As Adam Smith noted long ago, the equilibrium wage structure reflects the impact of compensating differentials.[1] These differentials may compensate for the cost of investment in skill acquisition, for workers' willingness to work in disagreeable or unsafe jobs, for the level of responsibility, or for wage fluctuations associated with a given occupation. All of these factors can be neatly explained by the supply and demand model you have already mastered.

However, the competitive labor demand and supply model is, like all models, an abstraction from the real world, and it is designed to concentrate on certain features of real-world labor markets at the expense of others. The competitive labor demand and supply model depends on key assumptions that allow us to ignore some features of the real world while focusing on those that are most useful for an understanding of the important determinants of long-run wage differentials. This is a common practice when we develop a theory. For example, we probably would not worry about the people crammed in their seats, the flight attendants pushing carts up and down the aisles, or whether there was an

---

[1] Adam Smith (*The Wealth of Nations.* Modern Library Edition, 1937, p. 100) wrote: "The wages of labour vary with the ease or hardship, the cleanliness or dirtiness, the honourableness or dishonourableness of the employment. Thus in most places, take the year round, a journeyman tailor earns less than a journeyman weaver. His work is much easier. A journeyman weaver earns less than a journeyman smith. His work is not always easier, but it is much cleanlier. A journeyman blacksmith, though an artificer, seldom earns so much in twelve hours as a collier, who is only a labourer, does in eight. His work is not quite so dirty, is less dangerous, and is carried on in daylight, and above ground."

in-flight movie if we were making a model to test the stability of a new airliner design using a wind tunnel or a computer simulation. However, these might be major issues of concern if our problem were, instead, to figure out how to get the most revenue from the limited space inside the airliner's cabin.

This chapter, and also Chapter 11 on personnel economics, examines what happens when we relax two of the key assumptions built into the competitive labor demand and supply model. The first of these assumptions is that, at the equilibrium wage, workers don't care which employer they work for, and firms don't care which workers they get to fill their jobs. Workers along the supply curve and jobs along the demand curve are assumed to be homogeneous in the competitive model, and we challenge that assumption in this chapter. The second assumption that we challenge is that the firm can obtain the maximum output from different combinations of labor and other inputs in a way that is independent of the wage and of the specific workers hired. That is, we confront the assumption that productivity is determined by technological factors alone.

Competitive labor market analysis treats labor as though it is traded on a spot market (like flowers or peaches), but we know from casual observation that matches between workers and firms are not really like that. When you buy a peach, you pay for it and eat it. The next time you buy a peach, it may or may not be from the same store. When a firm buys a unit of labor—for example, an hour of a worker's time—it makes a match with that worker. But the match does not end after an hour. The relationship between a firm and its workers is typically much longer lasting than that.[2] In addition, a firm's hiring decisions have implications for the future, so the firm will care greatly about the characteristics of the workers it hires. Firms also appreciate that their relationship with their workforce can be nurtured so that decisions about wages and working conditions made today can affect workers' productivity in the future.

This chapter explores the nature of the long-term relationship between workers and firms. The analysis of internal labor markets (ILMs) considers the effect of such long-term employment relationships in organizations and the productivity incentives of compensation packages on wage setting and employment opportunity.[3] As you will see, the study of ILMs opens up a whole new world in which labor markets do not always clear—where demand and supply do not determine wages in a straightforward manner, where unemployment and discrimination can and do exist and persist. It is an uncomfortable world, but it gives us great insight into the world in which we live.

First we look at the characteristics of internal labor markets and examine how internal markets connect with the external labor market (ELM). Next, we examine the evidence concerning the historical evolution of ILMs and the related question of whether ILMs serve a useful purpose in the modern economy. Some have argued that the recent wave of corporate downsizing, the upward trend in the use of contingent workers, and the reorganization of many manufacturing workplaces signals a significant shift away from ILM-type work organizations. The third part of this chapter considers the efficiency aspects of ILM organizations, and finally we explore the implications of ILMs for the structure of the labor market.

---

[2] There are good reasons for this longevity of employment relations. Searching for new matches is costly, as we saw in Chapter 8.

[3] Peter Doeringer and Michael Piore, *Internal Labor Markets and Manpower Analysis* (Lexington: Heath, 1971).

Insights from our ILM analysis will prove helpful in chapters to come. For example, when workers are represented by trade unions, this can be seen as an ILM with an explicit contract binding workers, their union representatives, and employers. In addition, to the extent that wages within ILMs only partially adjust to demand and supply shifts, this theory can help form the basis for an understanding of how wage rigidity contributes to unemployment. Finally, our study of labor market discrimination will be enhanced by understanding how entry into ILMs may be blocked for specific groups. ILM analysis is also helpful in explaining short-run changes in wage inequality.

The Characteristics of ILMs

The Importance of Long-Term Employment Relations

The first characteristic of ILMs is that they are found in places where both employees and employers anticipate that the employment relationship will last for a long period, if not for the worker's entire working life. In the competitive labor market, workers can quit their job without imposing costs on the firm because workers can easily be replaced by perfectly adequate substitutes. The ILM develops in situations where a quit does impose costs on the firm. These costs derive from investments in establishing the work relationship and in enhancing the specific skills[4] of the worker. Once these investments are made, the firm has the incentive to find ways of reducing quits and stabilizing employment to maximize its return on these investments.

To illustrate this, we can compare two jobs with vastly different fixed costs of employment. Suppose you were the owner of a neighborhood diner with an opening for a part-time dishwasher. Your recruitment costs might be limited to posting a sign or might include the cost of running a classified ad in the local newspaper. Word-of-mouth advertising among your other workers and customers would likely be sufficient to ensure an adequate supply of applicants. The application process would probably be rather informal. There would be no need to continue the process once someone convinced you they were reliable and capable of doing the job. And the training period, even in the operation of an expensive dishwashing machine, would be fairly short. With a bit of luck, you could fill the job with a fully productive worker in a day's time.

Hiring and training a new dishwasher costs time and energy, which has an opportunity cost, and money for ads and for the wages paid to the worker while he or she is learning the job. You might not be very happy if the worker quit as soon as the first paycheck was handed out, making you go through the hiring process all over again, but at least the costs of that process are not high. On the other hand, it would not take very long to determine whether your new hire is up to the job. Because the costs of dismissing the worker and searching anew are not high, you could fairly easily make the decision to replace this worker. This type of employment relationship is consistent with the treatment of turnover

---

[4] Recall from our discussion of human capital that specific skills are those fully useful only while working in a specific job for a specific employer, whereas general skills can be used in any employment situation. An employer has the incentive to invest in specific skills because the firm can obtain the return on that investment. An employer would be reluctant to invest in general skills because the worker could capture the return.

in the competitive market model: Worker turnover is not a big deal because little is invested in establishing the employment relationship or in training new hires.

Now consider the case where you are the chair of a university department of economics with an opening for an assistant professor to teach labor economics (among other courses). Here the costs of establishing the employment relationship are quite high; the typical department will establish a recruitment committee; place ads in national or international publications such as *Job Openings for Economists*, *The Chronicle of Higher Education*, or the *Times Higher Educational Supplement*; have the committee review the applications to identify a subset to interview; send the committee to the national, and possibly regional, conferences to interview those candidates; have the committee reduce the list to the three or four top candidates, invite those candidates to campus to interview with the entire department and the administration, and, finally, select a top candidate and offer him or her the job. And if the candidate declines, the whole process might start over again!

When we total up the time, energy, and money spent in this recruitment process, we quickly reach a large sum. Because it is very important for us to find someone who is a good match with the particular teaching needs, research expectations, and "culture" of the department, and because it is very difficult to ascertain how a new PhD recipient will fit in, the recruitment process is likely to be much more complex and expensive than is the case when a restaurant hires a dishwasher. And the costs do not stop there. Monitoring the performance of an academic is more difficult and more costly than monitoring the performance of a dishwasher. The need to observe whether the new recruit's teaching is adequate, whether research programs pan out, and whether the recruit develops into a good colleague who participates in the team management of the department all add to the cost of hiring. Because the recruitment process is itself costly, the department has an incentive to take steps to lower the chance that the new faculty member will quit shortly after being hired. All the ingredients are in place to make sure that the relationship between the worker and the university will be a long-term one.

This type of work situation fits very snugly into the ILM model of long-run employment relationships. The university promises the job applicant that if she is hired and meets the department's expectations, she will successfully pass through the probationary period and subsequently enter a long-term employment relationship. In other jobs where it is important and difficult to find the right person to match a job vacancy and where a period of specific training follows the hiring decision, employers will likewise have the incentive to find ways of reducing turnover to maximize the return on their investment.[5]

Employees in certain situations also make specific investments in their jobs that increase their interest in a stable long-run relationship. Even the dishwasher in the diner has friends at work and a comfortable work routine that result in a small, but not unimportant, cost of changing jobs. A university professor who develops her courses to meet the particular needs of the student mix at her school, who adapts her research activity to the particular research "infrastructure" at her school, who finally learns enough about the catalog and arcane course requirements to be an effective adviser at her school, and who gets to know

---

[5] In some cases, employers require a bonding arrangement whereby workers receiving skill enhancing investments commit themselves to a subsequent minimum period of employment with the organization making the investment. Examples include medical and other professional education and training opportunities provided by the armed services and arrangements for junior faculty at universities in emerging economies to spend a several years in developed countries studying at major centers of learning.

enough about the people and practices of her school to effectively participate in its administration faces even higher costs of changing jobs. In employment situations where both the employer and the employee make specific investments in establishing and preparing for the employment situation, there are incentives for long-run employment relationships.

Are the costs of establishing the employment relationship high? The results from various surveys reported by Daniel Hamermesh[6] suggest that **hiring costs** in 2010 dollars ranged from around $1,200 for secretaries to more than $7,500 for professional and managerial employees. In addition, managers typically spend 42.5 hours recruiting and training the typical new hire during the first month on the job, and training and career development costs run from 1.0 times annual earnings for car salespeople to as much as 2.5 times annual earnings for pharmaceutical employees. A 2009 Survey of UK firms by the Chartered Institute of Personnel and Development (CIPD) found that the average number of weeks required to fill a vacancy was 5.9 for manual/craft jobs, 12.5 for managers and professionals, and 17.1 for senior managers.[7] They also found that the median cost of recruitment for all types of workers was £4,000 (about $6,200). Clearly, business firms are willing to invest a considerable amount of time and money in identifying the best applicant for a given job opening.

Do workers typically enjoy long-term employment relationships? The data on **job tenure** for several countries presented in Table 10.1 indicate that long-term relationships are quite common for wage earners in the prime of their working years from age 45 to 49. A very high percentage of these men and women had been employed with the same firm for 10 or more years both at the beginning and end of the last decade. In 2009 this percentage ranged from a third of Australian men and a quarter of women in that country to more than 6 out of 10 French men and women, with the incidence of long-term employment particularly high in continental Europe. The data in Table 10.1 also suggest

TABLE 10.1   Employee Job Tenure

Percent of Wage Earners Age 45-49 Working 10 or More Years for the Same Employer

Country	Men		Women	
	2000/01	*2009/10*	*2000/01*	*2009/10*
Australia	43.9	34.8	33.0	26.6
Canada	55.3	48.3	46.9	42.8
France	70.3	64.8	63.7	62.1
Germany	60.7	62.0	47.8	52.6
Spain	64.5	57.9	58.7	47.6
UK	52.8	45.2	41.7	38.0
US	49.0	43.7	41.4	38.0

Sources: US data for 2000 and 2010 are from "Employee Tenure in 2010" BLS News Release, Sep. 14, 2010 and available at: http://www.bls.gov/news.release/pdf/tenure.pdf.

Data for other countries are for 2000 and 2009 (except 2001 and 2009 for Australia) and are available at: http://stats.oecd.org/Index.aspx.

---

[6] Daniel S. Hamermesh, *Labor Demand* (Princeton: Princeton University Press, 1993).

[7] CIPD, "Recruitment, Retention and Turnover," *Annual Survey Report*, 2009. Available at: ww.cipd.co.uk.

THE WAY WE WORK

Number of Jobs and Job Tenure during a Worker's Life

A sample of U.S. men and women were surveyed annually from 1979 to 1994 and biennially from 1994 to 2008 about various aspects of their labor market experiences. From these longitudinal data, we can get a picture of the number of jobs and length of job tenure for the same group of 7,757 individuals over their work life.

The average male in this sample held jobs with 11.4 different employers from age 18 to age 44, with almost 8 of these during the first decade of work. The average woman held 10.7 different jobs from age 18 to 44. For men, those with less education had more jobs and more during their younger years. Among women, those with more education held a greater number of jobs than those with less schooling.

The table below summarizes the duration of employment in jobs started at different ages for the workers in this sample. In general, older workers had longer job tenures than younger workers, but even among those starting a job in the 39 to 44 age range, about a third left that job within a year. A small percentage of workers stayed with the same employer for their entire work life until age 44.

Duration of Employment Relationships in Jobs Started from Age 18 to 44

Age at Start of a Job	% of jobs lasting less than one year	% of jobs lasting 5 or more years	% of Jobs lasting until 2008
18 to 22	71.8	6.2	1.2
23 to 27	59.0	11.5	3.3
28 to 32	51.4	15.7	5.7
33 to 38	41.3	21.2	11.1
39 to 44	33.5	32.4	28.5

Note: Bureau of Labor Statistics, "Number of Jobs Held, Labor Market Activity, and Earnings Growth among the Youngest Baby Boomers: Results from a Longitudinal Survey," *News Release* USDL-10-1243, September 10, 2010. Available at: http://www.bls.gov/news.release/pdf/nlsoy.pdf.

that in all countries but Germany the fraction of middle aged workers with long-term employment relationships declined a bit over the decade from 2000 to 2009. We'll return to a discussion of changes in the relative importance of ILMs later in this chapter.

Job Hierarchy and Internal Wage Structures

The second key characteristic assigned to ILMs concerns the organization of jobs and compensation within the organization.[8] Generally, well-defined entry level jobs are connected to a hierarchy of employment opportunities, sometimes described as a career

[8] Paul Osterman, "Employment Structures within Firms," *British Journal of Industrial Relations* 20 (1982): 349–361; Paul Osterman, "Choice of Employment Systems in Internal Labor Markets," *Industrial Relations* 26 (1987): 46–67.

ladder. Using the college professor example, the entry level academic job in the U.S. is at the assistant professor level, and the career job ladder involves the possibility of promotion to associate professor and professor. With the exception of instructors, who may or may not be eligible for promotion to higher ranks, these three ranks encompass the **job hierarchy** for academic employees of U.S. colleges and universities. Institutions of higher learning in other countries have similar job hierarchies with different job titles. For example, titles in the UK academic hierarchy run from lecturer to senior lecturer to professor.

In an ILM, most employees are hired into the organization at the entry level and are promoted from within to higher ranks. Thus, the entry level job, sometimes referred to as the **port of entry**, is the main point of contact between the ILM and the external job market. This concept of a job hierarchy suggests that most of the hiring of people into the organization will occur at the entry level. This seems to be the case with academic job markets. Among the 256 job openings for U.S. full-time, tenure track faculty listed in the October 2010 issue of *Job Openings for Economists*, 55% were at the assistant professor level, and the majority of the remaining ads were for positions that would be filled at either the assistant professor or associate professor level. Although people are hired in colleges and universities at all ranks, the typical hire occurs at the entry level; there is a relatively limited demand on the external market for senior level professors.[9]

Along with a hierarchy of jobs within the firm, another characteristic of ILMs is the existence of an internal wage structure with two key characteristics. First, relative wages within the firm are closely tied to the job hierarchy in a way that is fairly rigid. Thus, an important determinant of increases in an individual worker's pay level is promotion to higher job levels within the department or career job ladder. Workers with more responsibility need to be paid more than those with less, so as a worker ascends the job hierarchy, he or she receives increases in pay. This is partly a compensating differential phenomenon—more responsibility calls for more compensation—but it also results from the need to ensure that supervisors have more status than the workers they supervise. The second characteristic is that the compensation system is "back-loaded" with significant increases in pay and the value of fringe benefits for more senior employees. As you will see in more detail later in this chapter, these characteristics of an ILM—the hierarchy of jobs filled mainly by promotions from within and a pay structure that particularly rewards promotions and longevity with the firm—can be viewed as mechanisms to provide incentives for the long-term employment relationships that ensure an adequate return on the firm's investments in hiring and training.

Figure 10.1, which we like to refer to as the "wind-blown hair" diagram, provides a detailed depiction of the wage structure within the ILM for managerial workers in a single firm.[10] What is particularly informative is that it allows us to see what happened over time to the wages of new hires entering the managerial work force of this firm each year (the dark solid line) and what happened to the real earnings of each cohort of managerial

---

[9] In some other countries, such as Australia and the United Kingdom, this is less clearly so. There, job ads for senior professors are not so uncommon. But both of these countries have higher education systems that are more closely integrated than is the case in the United States, with reasonably homogeneous institutions financed largely from the public purse. So the conditions favoring the development of an ILM within each university are not so strong. The whole higher education system in these countries might, however, be regarded as an ILM.

[10] George Baker, Michael Gibbs, and Bengt Holmstrom, "The Wage Policy of a Firm," *Quarterly Journal of Economics* 109 (4) (1994): 921–955.

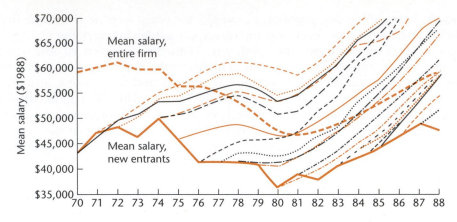

Size of entering cohort   222 222 170 286 388 712 251 420 509 510 550 795 706 690 606 782 925 1002 987

FIGURE 10.1 Salary Paths for Employee Cohorts in a Firm

Source: George Baker, Michael Gibbs, and Bengt Holmstrom, "The Wage Policy of a Firm," *Quarterly Journal of Economics* 109 (4) (1994): 921–955.

workers over their work life (the light lines that give this chart its nickname). Thus we can see that the 222 workers hired in 1970 earned around $44,000 in real pay during their first year on the job, whereas the pay in constant dollars for the 222 workers starting in 1971 was around $47,000. Workers who started in 1970 and stayed with the firm until 1984 saw their average real pay rise to around $70,000.

Two features in Figure 10.1 are relevant for our discussion of internal labor markets. The first is the clear cohort wage effect; wages within the ILM progress fairly steadily with tenure, and the wages of adjacent cohorts often move in parallel over time. This is entirely consistent with the description of the ILM wage structure presented previously: workers hired in a given group can anticipate a rising real wage over their career with the firm, with the rate of increase determined by annual increases, promotion increases, and the increased benefits related to seniority.

The second important feature of Figure 10.1 is that from year to year the average wage of a given cohort of workers is much less volatile than the average wage of new hires, or even the average wage of all workers taken together. This is due to the fact that wages of workers at entry ports to the ILM are determined by external market forces, whereas those of workers elsewhere in the ILM are to some extent insulated from the vicissitudes of demand and supply. The mean real salary of new entrants is responsive to external labor market conditions, falling during the recessions of 1974–75, 1979–80, and 1981–82 and rising steadily during the long business cycle expansion of the mid- to late 1980s. A similar, although much smoother, pattern can be seen in the line depicting the movement of the overall average wage over time.

In contrast, the average real wage of each cohort seems less responsive to the business cycle. The groups hired in the early 1970s saw their average wage rise during the 1974–75 downturn, and the groups hired in the late 1970s experienced only slight slowdowns in their average earnings during the recessions of the early 1980s. This early 1980s period did cause a downturn in the path of real wages for cohorts hired in the early 1970s. But even in these cases, the fluctuations in starting salary generally appear more pronounced than the fluctuations in cohort salary. One characteristic of ILMs is that they shelter workers from the full effect of external labor market developments. This is supported by the data in Figure 10.1 and can be seen in the fact that cohort salaries had a positive trend throughout the period from 1972 to 1981, when the average firm salary was falling, and rose at a much faster pace than the average firm salary from 1981 to 1988.

Evidence for the importance of job level and promotions as a determinant of a worker's compensation level and for the insulation of internal wages from external market developments can be found in recent econometric case studies of workers at a university; blue- and white-collar workers at a German manufacturing plant; all workers at a US company; and three groups of workers at a large Taiwan auto dealer.[11] Further evidence supporting the conclusion that the wages of workers in ILMs are partially sheltered from current labor market developments is provided by recent studies of large samples of individual workers in Denmark, Sweden, and the United States.[12] So the key wage propositions of ILM analysis seem to prevail in labor markets around the globe.

Types of ILMs in the U.S. Economy

John Dunlop, arguably one of the most important institutionally oriented labor economists, has attempted to classify working situations in the U.S. economy according to the degree of ILM influence on the structure of jobs and wages.[13] In his classification, which excludes managerial, supervisory, or executive workers, Dunlop defines eight categories of work situations that can be clustered in three main groups that each included about a third of the US workforce:

- *Little ILM Influence.* This area includes workers in small enterprises where human resource management is more personal and where the employment situation is inherently less stable due to highly competitive product markets; workers in temporary, part-time, or substitute worker pools where wages and work rules are determined by the subcontractor rather than the firm where the work is located; and owner-operators. In 1990, with wages and employment heavily influenced by the external labor market, this group numbered around 40 million workers in the United States.
- *Heavy ILM Influence.* This cluster includes two large groups of workers: (1) public sector, civil service employees who work in an environment where human resource

---

[11] Catherine Haeck and Frank Verboven, "The Internal Economics of a University—Evidence from Personnel Data," *CEPR Discussion Papers 7843*, 2010; Christian Pfeifer, "An Empirical Note on Wages in an Internal Labour Market," *Economics Letters* 99 (2008): 570–573; Michael Gibbs and Wallace Hendricks, "Do Formal Salary Systems Really Matter?" *Industrial and Labor Relations Review* 58 (2004): 71–93; Ming-Jen Lin, "Opening the Black Box: The Internal Labor Markets of Company X," *Industrial Relations* 44 (2005): 659–706.

[12] Tor Eriksson and Axel Werwatz, "The Prevalence of Internal Labour Markets—New Evidence from Panel Data," *International Journal of Economics Research* 2 (2005): 105–124; Edward Lazear and Paul Oyer, "Internal and External Labor Markets: A Personnel Economics Approach," *Labour Economics* 11 (2004): 527–554; and Darren Grant, "The Effect of Implicit Contracts on the Movement of Wages over the Business Cycle: Evidence from the National Longitudinal Surveys," *Industrial and Labor Relations Review* 56 (2003): 393–408.

[13] John T. Dunlop, "Organizations and Human Resources: Internal and External Markets," in *Labor Economics and Industrial Relations: Markets and Institutions*, eds., Clark Kerr and Paul D. Staudohar (Cambridge: Harvard University Press, 1994).

policies are largely prescribed by law, and (2) those employed in large establishments in manufacturing, utilities, and some services. This is the group on which many of the observations and studies of ILMs have been made. The capital intensity and use of specialized capital in these firms leads to multiple tiers of job classifications, and the market power of firms leads to management or collective bargaining determination of ports of entry and assignment of workers to job levels. Dunlop estimates that this cluster, where the impact of the external labor market is indirect and restricted, included 33 million U.S. workers, or 30% of total employment, in 1990.

- *Moderate ILM Influence.* Between the extremes are three groups of workers in situations with lots of points of entry to the firm and very short job hierarchies. First are retail and service sector jobs, with only a few layers in the entire hierarchy of the establishment and a heavy external market influence on entry level jobs. Second are clerical-oriented organizations, such as banks or insurance operations. The third group includes technical-professional organizations, such as universities, research organizations, and consultancies, wherein workers have an external loyalty to their profession and job hierarchies are less relevant. This intermediate group numbered 37 million U.S. workers in 1990.

Dunlop's classification is useful because it reminds us of the wide variety of work organizations in the economy and because it highlights the relevance of the ILM concept for a large segment of the economy. Depending on how you treat the intermediate group, 30% to 60% of U.S. production workers in 1990 worked in organizations that possessed some of the characteristics associated with ILMs. Similarly, Anna D'Addio and Michael Rosholm used cluster analysis on 1995 data from the European Community Household Panel to examine the structure of jobs in Europe.[14] They found that about a third of men and 40% to 50% of women had jobs that fit the ILM concept in several dimensions. And Hiroshi Ono's careful analysis indicates that in 2005 about 20% of all Japanese workers, but 46% of male college graduates in large firms and two-thirds of men employed by the government, had lifetime employment contracts.[15] These proportions are comparable to Dunlop's results for the United States.

The Evolution of ILMs

Many feel that the types of work organizations described in the preceding section first appeared in the United States, where manufacturing establishments grew to very large sizes early in the twentieth century. These large firms presented managerial difficulties that ultimately led to efforts to systematize the organization and direction of the enterprise. In the management of labor, this effort can be seen in the gradual emergence of formal personnel administration functions and offices in manufacturing firms beginning at the time of World War I. As informal management of labor was replaced by formal

---

[14] Anna Cristina D'Addio and Michael Rosholm, "Temporary Employment in Europe: Characteristics, Determinants and Outcomes," *Brussels Economic Review/Cahiers Economiques de Bruxelles* 48 (2005): 13–41.

[15] Hiroshi Ono, "Lifetime Employment in Japan: Concepts and Measurements," *Journal of the Japanese and International Economies,* 24 (2010): 1–27.

human resource management structures, the ILM began to replace the external market with a bureaucratic system of wage and employment determination.[16]

The U.S. Labor Market a Century Ago

If we look closely at U.S. labor markets around 1900, we see many features that resemble the competitive labor market model. Historical research has established that workers had a high level of mobility, which allowed them to move freely to take advantage of multiple opportunities. Wages generally seem to have been market determined. There is evidence of compensating differentials in pay for jobs that involved higher risks of injury or unemployment, and competition among employers seems to have been sufficient to eliminate labor market discrimination as measured by unequal pay for equal work. Not only did the market work to determine pay and employment along the lines suggested by the competitive model, but labor markets also seem to have worked rather smoothly in adjusting to supply or demand shocks.[17]

Within manufacturing firms, efficiency was ensured by the "drive system" of shop-floor management, which was most prominent in the machinery manufacturing firms of New England and the mid-Atlantic states.[18] Under this system, the department foreman had the ultimate authority on the shop floor: he hired, fired, and set the pay of workers; he organized work and assigned workers to tasks; and he attempted to maximize productivity through close supervision and his persuasive powers. The owners of the firm, or their agents, kept close tabs on the activities of the foremen, but in most ways the shop floor of a manufacturing firm around 1900 can be aptly described as the "Foreman's Empire."

The Emergence of ILMs in the United States

Why was this system, which worked pretty much along the lines of the competitive labor market model, replaced by the ILM in many large manufacturing firms? Several forces appear to have been at work leading to the bureaucratization of labor management in these firms.

- *Size and Complexity.* As manufacturing firms grew larger with economies of scale, as products became more complex in their design, and as the production process also increased in complexity, there was an increased interest in applying "science" to the management of industry and professionalization of workforce management.
- *Turnover Costs.* As we might expect in an economy where the law of one price prevailed in labor markets and where close supervision by an authoritarian foreman dominated the shop floor, there was an extremely high rate of worker turnover. With average annual turnover rates often exceeding 100%, this came to be perceived as a major problem. And the costs of turnover were significant. One study found

---

[16] Sanford M. Jacoby, "Managing the Workplace: From Markets to Manors, and Beyond," in *Labor Economics and Industrial Relations,* eds., Clark Kerr and Paul D. Staudohar (Cambridge: Harvard University Press, 1994).

[17] Price V. Fishback, "Operations of 'Unfettered' Labor Markets: Exit and Voice in American Labor Markets at the Turn of the Century," *Journal of Economic Literature* 36 (2) (1998): 722–765.

[18] Daniel Nelson, *Managers and Workers: Origins of the New Factory System in the United States, 1880–1920* (Madison: University of Wisconsin Press, 1975).

turnover rates in 1914 averaging 157% annually among 20 metalworking plants in the Midwest. The costs of hiring and training replacements for these firms averaged $88,000 a year, or more than $1 million in 1991 prices.[19] As they became fully aware of this turnover cost problem, employers began to look for ways of obtaining greater employment stability.

- *Union Activity.* The period from around 1880 to World War I was one of continual conflict over union organizing efforts, which frequently resulted in major, bloody strikes. One estimate shows almost 23,000 separate strikes, an average of three new strikes a day, occurred during the two decades from 1880 to 1900.[20] One response to both the turnover problem and the threat of union militancy was the "welfare capitalism" movement. Many employers felt that corporate programs for housing, education, health care, recreation, profit-sharing, pensions, and social work would pay off in a more contented, productive, stable, and loyal workforce that would be less attentive to the arguments of trade unionists or socialists. The implementation of welfare work and scientific management resulted in the creation of a bureaucracy that formed the basis for the centralization of human resources management within personnel departments.[21]

- *Government Wartime Policy.* During the two world wars, the U.S. government actively intervened in labor management relations to prevent strikes and other work actions from disrupting the production of goods necessary for the war effort. During World War I, the Committee on Welfare Work within the Council of National Defense pushed firms to adopt welfare programs to keep labor peace, and the government provided training for new personnel managers. During World War II, the War Labor Board played an instrumental role in consolidating the system of labor relations developed during the Great Depression, and institutionalizing labor relations as an activity carried out in connection with human resource management by a centralized personnel department.

- *New Deal Labor Policy.* The passage of the National Labor Relations Act in 1935 and the Fair Labor Standards Act in 1938 gave impetus to the professionalization of human resource management. The 1935 law gave most workers in the private sector the right to engage in collective bargaining, gave firms the duty to recognize that right, and created the National Labor Relations Board (NLRB) to ensure that the right to collective bargaining was an effective right. The 1938 law required overtime pay and minimum wages, and imposed other regulatory requirements on the management of the firm. This legislation reinforced the tendency toward a centralized personnel function in business organizations because specialists were needed to comply with the new legal requirements for labor relations and compensation practices.

As a result of these forces, U.S. businesses gradually moved from a decentralized, informal method of human resource management conducted by shop-floor supervisors to a centralized, formal, bureaucratic method run by personnel professionals. This process

---

[19] Paul H. Douglas, "The Problem of Labor Turnover," in *Trade Unionism and Labor Problems,* ed., John R. Commons (New York: Augustus M. Kelley, 1967).

[20] Stuart D. Brandes, *American Welfare Capitalism, 1880–1940* (Chicago: University of Chicago Press, 1976).

[21] Jacoby, "Managing the Workplace."

was gradual during the first half of the twentieth century, but by 1950 it had pervaded most large organizations and proceeded in a wave-like fashion, waxing and waning over time. The end result was that the characteristics of internal labor markets developed in almost all large businesses and in many medium and small businesses as well. ILMs had provided a solution to the "labor problems" facing the firm.

Lifetime Employment in Japan

The ILM concept is clearly present in the distinctive institution of **lifetime employment** in Japan, in which workers entering large companies after graduation also enter into an implicit agreement that commits the firm to protecting the worker's job security and commits the worker to staying with the firm until retirement. This feature of Japanese organizations was widely adopted beginning in the 1950s, when the rapid growth of the Japanese economy created shortages of skilled labor and firms focused on reducing employee turnover and providing incentives for individuals to invest in firm-specific skills.[22] While reflecting many of the same forces that drove the emergence of ILMs in the United States prior to World War II, the characteristics of lifetime employment in large Japanese firms also derive from the legacy of shared decision-making in agriculture and the extension of family relationships to the workplace.[23]

Japanese ILMs differ from their traditional American counterparts in providing more extensive protection against layoffs, larger investments in the development of human capital and employment relationships, and greater opportunities for worker participation in consultation and consensus-based decision making. Yet the basic nature of the lifetime employment system—substituting internal rules and procedures for market forces in determining wages and the allocation of labor within the firm—is broadly in line with the theory of ILMs developed previously.

Employment Protection

The adoption of ILMs in the United States and Japan was motivated mainly by the employer's need to reduce turnover and increase the payoff to the firm and its workers from investments in firm-specific human capital. Thus, these labor market institutions were developed by firms and their workers. In contrast, in many countries, particularly in Europe, long-term employment relationships and protection of insiders from external labor market developments are promoted by legislation and collective bargaining agreements that impose restrictions on the ability of firms to dismiss workers. Such restrictions are often referred to as **employment protection regulations**.

Employment protection regulations involve three main types of provisions. First, they set out conditions under which the dismissal of an individual worker would be considered to be for "just cause," administrative procedures to follow in such dismissals, and requirements for severance pay for "fair" and financial penalties for "unfair" terminations. The second type of provision imposes additional procedural requirements for mass layoffs

---

[22] Masanori Hashimoto, "The Industrial Relations System in Japan: An Interpretation and Policy Implications," *Managerial and Decision Economics,* 12 (1991): 147–157.

[23] T. Hanami, *Labor Relations in Japan Today* (Tokyo: Kodansha International, 1981).

or plant closings, where it is felt that such actions are likely to impose social costs on the community. Finally, restrictions on the use of temporary employment help buttress the effect of other provisions in creating greater job security for regular contract employees. In many countries the enforcement of such regulations is under the jurisdiction of labor courts or other government commissions.

Researchers at the OECD have attempted to quantify the relative strictness and enforcement of employment protection regulations across countries and to quantify the impact of these rules on various aspects of labor market performance.[24] Table 10.2 ranks the countries in the OECD study by the overall level of strictness with which employment protection regulations bind personnel decisions. Turkey and Portugal rank at the top of Table 10.2 with quantitative indexes of employment protection around 18 times larger than that for the United States at the bottom of the ranking. Most European countries have relatively high employment protection indexes while the United Kingdom and Canada are closest to the level estimated for the United States. Cross-country analyses by the OECD using these employment protection indexes suggest that regulations do indeed increase employment security for regular employees by increasing the cost of dismissals for employers, but this security often comes at the expense of reduced opportunities for women and youth.

TABLE 10.2   Overall Strictness of Employment Protection Regulations in 2003

Country	EP Index	Country	EP Index
Turkey	3.7	Italy	1.9
Portugal	3.5	Czech Republic	1.9
Mexico	3.1	Slovak Republic	1.9
Spain	3.1	Japan	1.8
France	3.0	Poland	1.7
Greece	2.8	Hungary	1.5
Poland	2.6	New Zealand	1.5
Norway	2.6	Denmark	1.4
Austria	2.2	Australia	1.2
Belgium	2.2	Ireland	1.1
Germany	2.2	Switzerland	1.1
Sweden	2.2	Canada	0.8
Netherlands	2.1	UK	0.7
Finland	2.0	US	0.2
Korea	2.0		

Source: "Chapter 2 Employment Protection Regulation and Labour Market Performance," *OECD Employment Outlook*. OECD, 2004.

---

[24] Chapter 2, "Employment Protection Regulation and Labour Market Performance," OECD Employment Outlook, 2004.

Are ILMs Becoming Less Important?

A number of changes in the world economy during the past two decades have led some to wonder whether ILMs have outlived their usefulness as an organizational solution to labor problems. This assertion is supported by three specific observations about economic changes. First is the argument that business firms face increased competition stemming from global economic integration and that this has reduced their ability to afford career compensation systems. Accompanying increased competition is technological change, which may have reduced the importance of firm-specific human capital and made workers with general skills more interchangeable among firms. These forces seem to be at work in the process of "downsizing," which might be viewed as a repudiation of the promised lifetime benefits associated with ILMs and the suggestion that firms are more willing to hire contingent workers than to commit to hiring permanent personnel. The third observation is that workers entering the labor force today must expect to change jobs, employers, and careers much more frequently than workers did in the past. Taken together, the image of leaner, more flexible businesses seems counter to the image of workers spending their careers moving up a hierarchical job ladder in an ILM.

One source of data relevant to the question of whether ILMs are becoming less important in the labor market is length of job tenure. The data in Table 10.1 suggested that in many countries the proportion of prime-age workers with very long tenure had decreased slightly over the last decade. However, when we look at the tenure experience for all workers, a different picture emerges. Over the period from 1996 to 2010, the median years of job tenure in the United States rose from 4 to 4.6 years for men and from 3.5 to 4.2 years for women.[25] And Table 10.3 shows that the average job tenure of male and female workers in the four largest European economies increased from 2000 to 2009. Finally, Dobbie and MacMillan find no evidence of decline in the importance of ILMs in Australia from 1993 to 2005, and Cazes and Tonin show that a weakening of employment protection regulations in many European countries had only a minimal impact on job tenure.[26] This quick look at job tenure data does not provide much evidence for a major change in the importance of long-term employment relationships over the past decade or so in large economies.

Another bit of evidence regarding ILM trends in the United States is data on the employment of contingent workers and the use of alternative employment relationships. Contingent workers are those in temporary jobs or those who believe that their tenure in their current job is limited regardless of their job performance or the overall strength of the economy. Using the broadest measure of contingency, Bureau of Labor Statistics surveys show that the percentage of workers in this category fell from 4.9% of the workforce in February 1995 to 4.1% in February 2005.[27]

---

[25] Bureau of Labor Statistics, "Employee Tenure in 2010," News release USDL-10-1278, September 14, 2010, available at: http://www.bls.gov/news.release/tenure.t01.htm.

[26] Michael Dobbie and Craig MacMillan, "Internal Labour Markets in Australia: Evidence from the Survey of Education and Training Experience," *Australian Journal of Labour Economics*, 13 (2010): 137–154; Sandrine Cazes and Mirco Tonin, "Employment Protection Legislation and Job Stability: A European Cross-Country Analysis," *International Labour Review*, 149 (2010): 261–285.

[27] Bureau of Labor Statistics, "Contingent and Alternative Employment Arrangements, February 2005" News Release USDL 05-1433, July 27, 2005; "New Data on Contingent and Alternative Employment Examined by BLS," News Release USDL 95-319, August 17, 1995.

TABLE 10.3 Average Job Tenure in Years for the Four Largest European Economies

	Men		Women	
Country	2000	2009	2000	2009
France	11.3	11.8	.10.7	11.6
Germany	11.2	12.1	9.2	10.5
Italy	12.6	13.3	9.4	10.3
UK	9.1	9.2	7.1	8.3

Source: http://stats.oecd.org/Index.aspx.

The same surveys asked about alternative employment arrangements. Between 1995 and 2005, the percentage of U.S. workers who were independent contractors increased from 6.7% to 7.4%; the fraction of on-call workers and day laborers rose slightly from 1.7% of the work force to 1.8%; the percentage of employees who were paid by temporary help agencies fell slightly from 1.0% to 0.9%; and the percentage of workers provided by contract firms rose a bit from 0.5% to 0.6%. While the proportion of independent contractors increased, this seems to be a matter of choice. Only 9% of these individuals in 2005 expressed a preference for a traditional employment relationship. In the United States, therefore, there is no evidence of a major shift in employment toward less secure and more market-related employment relationships.

Comparable data on contingent and alternative work patterns are not generally available for other countries. But the OECD does track the fraction of workers in permanent employment.[28] For men over age 25 in all OECD countries, the share in permanent employment was 91.9% in 2000 and 91.6% in 2009. The comparable figures for women were 90.2% in 2000 and 89.4% in 2009. For this large number of industrialized economies there is no sign that employment relationships have become less permanent over recent years.

In addition to looking at evidence on the stability of employment, we could examine data on the wages set by employers to determine whether wages have become more responsive to the external labor market in recent years. One study did just that, analyzing the wages paid to workers in a set of well-defined job titles by 228 large firms in Cincinnati, Cleveland, and Pittsburgh from 1955 to 1996.[29] The results of this study showed that the size and persistence of wage differentials between firms for workers in the same job and between jobs for workers in the same firm had not changed from 1985 to 1996, even for firms in industries facing increased competition due to deregulation or international trade. The wage structure within U.S. ILMs remained insensitive to external labor market forces during the period when downsizing and other changes were supposed to have reduced the importance of ILMs to employers.

---

[28] Data are available in the Labour section of the web page at: http://stats.oecd.org/Index.aspx.

[29] Erica L. Groshen and David I. Levine, "The Rise and Decline of U.S. Internal Labor Markets," *Research Paper 9819*, Federal Reserve Bank of New York, 1998.

PUTTING THEORY TO WORK

MANAGING YOUR INTERNAL LABOR MARKETS FOR LASTING COMPETITIVE ADVANTAGE

That's the subtitle of a book entitled *Play to Your Strengths*, authored by four human resource management consultants with wide international experience. Their thesis is that paying careful attention to many of the issues discussed in this chapter would permit a company to take a more strategic approach to managing its human capital resources to increase growth and profit performance. Maximizing the firm's value from human capital requires a systems approach to the quantitative analysis of issues like:

- What are the required workforce capabilities, behaviors, and attitudes needed to meet strategic performance objectives?
- In light of this, what is the firm's record in terms of which workers get hired, which stay, and which get promoted?
- Are there bottlenecks in the job hierarchy that limit opportunities for skill and career development?
- Are the right incentives, career ladders, and performance rewards in place to identify and develop talented employees?
- What are the empirical links between investment and management of human capital and business results? Can you measure the Return on Investment on human capital investment?

The potential for a firm to gain from effective management of the internal labor market can be seen in these comments about recruiting workers in the "millennial" age group from Dennis Nally, CEO of PricewaterhouseCoopers LLP:

"This millennial generation is not just looking for a job, they're not just looking for salary and financial benefits. They're looking for skill development, they're looking for mobility, they're looking for opportunities to acquire different skills and to move quickly from one part of an organization to another."

"The human capital agenda has to be driven by the CEO. It's so strategic today that you want to have great support coming from the HR organization, but if this isn't viewed as just as strategic as new products and services or research and development, it won't be successful."

Notes: Haig R. Nalbantian. Richard A. Guzzo, Dave Kiefer, and Jay Doherty, *Play to Your Strengths: Managing Your Internal Labor Markets for Lasting Competitive Advantage.* McGraw-Hill, 2004; and Javier Espinoza, "PWC's CEO Switches Tactics to Keep Millennials," *The Wall Street Journal,* July 11, 2011.

An interesting question is whether the "lost decade" in Japan following the late 1980s bursting of a real estate and stock market bubble led firms to move away from their commitment to lifetime employment. Takao Kato combines quantitative analysis of job retention rates with field research to conclude that lifetime employment appears to be an enduring practice of Japanese firms.[30]

---

[30] Takao Kato, "The End of Lifetime Employment in Japan? Evidence from National Surveys and Field Research," *Journal of the Japanese and International Economies,* 15 (2001): 489–514.

Hiroshi Ono looks at the percentage of Japanese workers in core employment, the percentage of employees staying with the same firm at different ages, and job tenure data to conclude that: "In order to be more flexible and responsive to changes in the global economy, companies are reducing their core, and expanding their periphery labor force. But companies, especially the large ones, are still honoring the implicit contract of lifetime employment and protect those who are in the core."[31]

A similar conclusion is reached by Shimizutani and Yokoyama in their study of tenure patterns among full-time workers in Japan.[32] They find that mean tenure increased by 1.5 years for men and 2 years for women between 1990 and 2003. However, the impact of poor macroeconomic performance can be seen in the variance among full-time workers: tenure lengthened for those who kept their jobs and for graduates who entered employment after the severe recession but fell for those in the 30–34 age range who were most adversely affected by the recession. Large Japanese firms attempted to keep their commitment to lifetime employment in the face of poor business prospects by transferring redundant workers to subsidiaries and reducing hiring. The labor market response to the lost decade seems to have been a tripling of the incidence of part-time employment, especially for women, and diminished job opportunities for youth rather than a dismantling of lifetime employment.

Despite the many changes in the world economy in the last two decades, ILMs continue to be an important labor market institution in both the United States and other industrialized countries.

High Performance Work Systems

There is one major way in which ILMs have evolved over the past two decades, particularly in the United States and United Kingdom. This has involved the widespread adoption of Japanese-style human resource practices that have replaced the traditional hierarchical job structure of many firms with a more flexible and decentralized labor-management structure. What have come to be known as **high performance work systems** incorporate one or more of the following practices: intensive worker screening in the recruitment process; problem-solving and self-managing work teams; on-the-job training, job design, and job rotation to enhance the range of skills and flexibility of workers; bonuses and other types of pay for performance and skill acquisition, and enhanced job security. One of the goals of these systems is to allow firms to flatten management structures by shifting decisions from mid-level managers and foremen to the production floor.

The diffusion of these work place innovations has involved a gradual increase in the number of firms adopting any of the practices listed above along with an increase in the number of practices employed by the typical firm. Implementation has been faster in new plants, nonunion establishments, organizations with broader networks, and those

---

[31] Hiroshi Ono, "Lifetime Employment in Japan: Concepts and Measurements," *Journal of the Japanese and International Economies,* 24 (2010): 1–27.

[32] Satoshi Shimizutani and Izumi Yokoyama, "Has Japan's Long-Term Employment Practice Survived? Developments Since the 1990s," *Industrial and Labor Relations Review,* 62 (2009): 313–324.

AROUND THE WORLD

Human Resource Management Innovations in Europe

Results for the 2008 Community Innovation Survey in Europe give us a glimpse of cross-country and regional differences in innovative activity by individual enterprises. The table below shows the percentage of enterprises in each country organized by region reporting that they had implemented new methods of organizing work responsibilities and decision making during the period from 2006 to 2008. This measure gets at some aspects of the high performance work systems discussed in this chapter since the survey identifies these new work methods as the "first use of a new system of employee responsibilities, team work, decentralization, integration or de-integration of departments, education/training systems, etc."

The data show that, on average, fewer firms in the emerging market countries of Central and Eastern Europe implemented new work methods in comparison with firms in Western Europe. Only the Czech Republic, and to a lesser extent, Croatia, Estonia, and Slovenia had rates of implementation similar to the average for Western Europe. Germany, Luxembourg, and Portugal lead all countries with a quarter or more of establishments reporting new methods of organizing work.

Percentage of Surveyed Enterprises Reporting New Methods of Organizing Work Responsibilities and Decision Making from 2006 to 2008

Austria	16.9	Bulgaria	7.1
Belgium	18.9	Croatia	15.4
Finland	15.4	Czech Rep.	19.2
France	16.9	Estonia	15.5
Germany	25.8	Hungary	7.5
Ireland	20.2	Latvia	5.0
Italy	17.4	Lithuania	8.1
Luxembourg	25.1	Poland	7.1
Netherlands	9.4	Romania	9.9
Norway	11.3	Slovakia	8.0
Portugal	25.0	Slovenia	15.8
Spain	13.7		
Sweden	15.8		
Average	17.8	Average	10.8

Notes: Survey questions for The Community Innovation Survey 2008 can be found at: http://innovacion.ricyt.org/files/CIS%202006%202008.pdf.

Data used to construct the table above are available at: http://epp.eurostat.ec.europa.eu/portal/page/portal/science_technology_innovation/database.

with more complex products and processes and has accompanied the adoption of new information technology.[33]

ILMs and Firm Efficiency

Implicit Contracts

The key features of an ILM can be described in terms of the provisions of an **implicit contract** between workers and their employer that is designed to maximize the rents achievable from the employment relationship. The main source of such rents that we have emphasized thus far is the avoidance of hiring and training costs associated with the turnover of the workforce. Other rents, which accrue largely to the employer, come from a number of sources. They include the gains from worker investment in acquiring specialized skills useful mainly at the current employer; gains from worker willingness to share information with and provide on-the-job training to new hires; gains from worker willingness to maintain targeted levels of effort and efficiency; and gains from the opportunity to observe performance over a lengthy period and use this information to select individuals to fill job openings at higher levels. In some circumstances, the firm may well share some of these benefits with its workers by offering higher remuneration than would otherwise be possible. But the main thing that attracts workers, who may well be risk averse, to engage in these implicit employment contracts is the utility derived from stable employment and income.

Why are such contracts implicit instead of being written down and signed by all the parties? There are several reasons for this.[34] First, it may be very difficult to define performance criteria for workers precisely because of the complexity of the production relationship and the need to consider various contingencies that might limit performance. This would greatly increase the time and energy devoted to the process of negotiating and writing an explicit contract. Second, it might be very difficult to monitor worker performance on the job because the worker engages in several tasks, works in teams on some tasks, or is involved in a complex product or process. In addition, the damages from the failure of a worker to live up to his end of the bargain might be difficult to specify in advance. In such cases, it might be impossible to write an explicit contract that would be enforceable through court action. This would remove one of the key advantages of going to all the trouble of writing a contract.

A third reason for implicit contracts is that at the time of contracting there are likely to be informational asymmetries: the worker knows more about his ability and motivation than the employer does, and the firm knows more about the state of the business than does the worker. This makes the negotiation process more difficult and creates the opportunity for one side to try to take advantage of the other in writing the contract. Knowledge of the existence of such a possibility might mean that some contracts that would yield rents to both parties wouldn't make it through the negotiations.

---

[33] Lisa M. Lynch, "The Adoption and Diffusion of Organizational Innovation: Evidence for the U.S. Economy," IZA Discussion Paper No. 2819, May 2007.

[34] Michael L. Wachter and Randall D. Wright, "The Economics of Internal Labor Markets," *Industrial Relations* (1990): 240–262.

Implicit labor contracts are designed to be self-enforcing in the sense that incentives are created to abide by the terms of the contract and to limit the perceived gains to cheating. For example, ILMs attempt to reduce turnover costs through incentives built into compensation and promotion policies. Meanwhile, workers rely on several mechanisms to deter opportunistic exploitation by employers. These include threats of quitting or unionization and the desire of the firm not to damage its own reputation. These mechanisms are viewed as being more effective than writing a contract that specifies damages for nonperformance. Implicit contracts tend to emphasize the decision process rather than the intended outcomes of the employment relationship. And implicit contracts, like explicit union collective bargaining agreements, define the powers of management to act and the rights of workers to react to management decisions.

Efficiency Aspects of ILMs

How does an ILM act to enhance the efficiency of the employment relationship? There are several features common to ILMs that serve the purpose of creating an incentive-based, self-enforcing implicit contract designed to maximize rents.[35]

First, the long-term relationship maximizes rents associated with the avoidance of turnover costs and the investment by workers in firm-specific skills. The long-term relationship makes it easier for the firm to evaluate workers for promotion and to employ efficiency wage incentives for worker effort. The long-term relationship itself is created by career compensation policies that provide rewards for longevity with the firm, including seniority effects on pay, promotion from within to higher paying jobs, and pension benefits that become vested with tenure and accrue at the end of the worker's life.

Second, the reliance on limited ports of entry into the firm and promotion from within is an important part of the compensation incentive to a long-term relationship. A worker is less likely to put forth maximum effort in his current job if the firm's policy is to fill all higher-level jobs with outside hires. Reliance on promotion from within allows the firm to base its promotion decisions on the relative ability of workers as revealed by their performance at lower-level jobs. Relative ability is easier to measure than absolute ability and automatically adjusts for common factors that affect the performance of all workers such as a business slowdown. Finally, promotion from within is a tangible way for the firm to demonstrate its commitment to the long-term relationship. By promising to fill jobs from within, the firm cannot be opportunistic and claim that no one is absolutely good enough to fill openings at higher job levels.

Third, by attaching pay to jobs and limiting the range of wage rates that can be paid to workers on a given job, the pay structure reduces the incentive for managers to be overly generous with pay increases to avoid the unpleasantness of taking a hard line on pay. It also reduces the incentive for workers to spend their effort trying to influence their supervisor's impression of their job performance or the performance of coworkers. Finally, the system of attaching pay to jobs may be the best way of rewarding workers in situations where individual performance is hard to measure.

---

[35] Paul Milgrom and John Roberts, *Economics, Organization and Management* (Englewood Cliffs, NJ: Prentice Hall, 1992).

Fourth, by sheltering worker pay from variation related to external labor market shocks, the ILM can engender a higher level of worker commitment and loyalty in response to the perception that the firm is following a more equitable employment policy. The ILM allows the firm to engage in an implicit psychological contract in which equity is defined in terms of performance according to accepted norms of behavior that have emerged over time in a particular workshop.[36]

Fifth, within an ILM, remuneration schemes may be designed in such a way as to align the interests of the worker to those of the firm.[37] Although pay may not be determined directly by external market factors, it is set in such a way as to ensure that workers behave in the firm's interests.

Following this line of reasoning, ILMs exist because they allow firms and workers to maximize the benefits each derives from the establishment of the employment relationship.

ILMs and Firm Performance

A large literature has emerged documenting efforts to estimate the impact of high performance work systems and other human resource management strategies on firm performance. Since it would be surprising to find firms spending time and money to implement new work management practices without a financial return, it should not be surprising that the general conclusion one quickly reaches from reading much of this literature is that these innovations do improve performance.

One set of results indicates that enhanced job security, training, communication, information-sharing, and joint problem-solving raises worker job satisfaction and commitment to the firm and lowers the likelihood that individuals quit their jobs.[38] One of our recent research papers tries to determine why small manufacturing firms with defense contracts or subcontracts in Eastern Pennsylvania had substantially lower quit rates than similar firms without defense contracts.[39] The answer is that managers of defense contractors are more likely to adopt new human resource practices, such as information sharing, worker self-management, and training, which lowers turnover. This heightened rate of human resource innovation by defense contracting firms parallels a higher rate of technical innovation also noted for these firms. The reason for this innovation advantage of defense contractors is not entirely clear.

Another set of results, from detailed case studies, case studies amplified by "insider econometrics", and cross firm and cross-industry studies show that human resource practices matter for unit productivity and firm profitability.[40] This can be seen clearly in

---

[36] David Lewin, "Explicit Individual Contracting in the Labor Market," in *Labor Economics and Industrial Relations,* eds., Clark Kerr and Paul D. Staudohar (Cambridge: Harvard University Press, 1994).

[37] Paul Osterman, "Supervision, Discretion and Work Organization," *American Economic Review* 84 (1994): 380–384.

[38] For example, Robert D. Mohr and Cindy Zoghi, "High-Involvement Work Design and Job Satisfaction." *Industrial and Labor Relations Review* 61 (2008): 275–296; Rosemary Batt, "Managing Customer Services: Human Resource Practices, Quit Rates and Sales Growth," *Academy of Management Journal,* 45 (2002): 587–597.

[39] Todd A. Watkins and Thomas Hyclak, "Why Are Quit Rates Lower Among Defense Contractors?" *Industrial Relations* 50 (2011): 573–590.

[40] Casey Ichniowsky and Kathryn Shaw, "Beyond Incentive Pay: Insiders' Estimates of the Value of Complementary Human Resource Management Practices," *Journal of Economic Perspectives* 17 (2003): 155–180.

the meta-analysis of 92 published research papers carried out by James Combs and his colleagues.[41] Meta-analysis is a method of statistically analyzing the results from a large number of individual studies in order to provide a more rigorous summary than a narrative review of the literature might permit. Combs et al. reach four main conclusions from their application of this method:

1. High performance work system practices are positively correlated with firm performance and have an important practical effect: a one standard deviation increase in the use of such practices would, on average, increase return on assets by 4.6 percentage points and lower quit rates by 4.4 percentage points.
2. The use of several practices in a system is more strongly correlated with performance than using just one high performance work practice. There seem to be economies of scope related to the employment of complementary practices.
3. These human resource management practices are equally important for measures of operational performance, such as productivity and worker retention and financial performance, in terms of accounting returns and sales growth.
4. The implementation of high performance practices is more closely correlated with outcomes in manufacturing firms in comparison with service firms.

This systematic review of empirical studies on data from many different countries suggests the strong conclusion that firms and employees enter into implicit contracts to establish ILM institutions, whether traditional or involving high performance work systems, because they provide gains to both parties.[42]

The Case of Academic Tenure

Perhaps the ultimate example of an internal labor market is the institution of tenure used at most institutions of higher learning and many secondary schools in the United States and other countries. After a lengthy probation period, a faculty member whose performance in research, teaching, and service activities meets with the approval of the senior members of the department and the administration of the institution may be awarded tenure. A tenured faculty member enjoys considerable job security for the rest of his or her working life and can only be fired for reasons of "moral turpitude" or "gross incompetence" or if the financial stability of the institution requires the elimination of an entire department or program.

The high degree of job security enjoyed by tenured faculty members has been the source of complaints about the tenure system. One issue that has been raised by many, including legislators evaluating the finances and managerial practices of state universities in the United States, is that tenure shelters faculty from accountability for poor performance. Another argument is that tenure makes the university inefficient in responding to

---

[41] James Combs, Yongmei Liu, Angela Hall, and David Ketchen, "How Much Do High-Performance Work Practices Matter? A Meta-Analysis of Their Effects on Organizational Performance," *Personnel Psychology* 59 (2009): 501–528.

[42] For a different viewpoint on the gains to workers see: John Godard, "What Is Best for Workers? The Implications of Workplace and Human Resource Management Practices Revisited," *Industrial Relations* 49 (2010): 466–88.

THE WAY WE WORK

Human Resource Management and Productivity

Can the type of human resource management (HRM) practices used by a firm enhance productivity? A recent study focusing on steel finishing lines indicates that the answer is "yes."* By focusing on one product line, this study was able to control for the technology and equipment features of the finishing process for steel coils. The measure of productivity used was the percentage of potential work time that a finishing line was up and running, or uptime.

Uptime was found to be positively related to profit sharing, line incentives, close screening of new hires, the use of formal teams, job security guarantees, job rotation systems, training, and information sharing. In addition, productivity was found to be even more responsive to clusters of HRM practices.

Four such clusters were identified. HRM4 is a traditional system with no innovative practices. HRM3 is a traditional system plus worker teams and enhanced communications. HRM2 adds extensive skills training and high levels of worker involvement in teams to the HRM3 package. The most innovative system, HRM1, incorporates incentive pay, worker screening, training in skills and in problem-solving, high worker involvement in teams, enhanced job duties and job rotation, regular information sharing, and an implicit job security pledge.

Controlling for other factors and relative to HRM4 finishing lines, uptime was 1.5% to 3% higher on HRM3 lines, 3% to 5% higher on HRM2 lines, and 7% to 10% higher on HRM1 lines. The authors estimate that shifting from HRM4 to HRM2 and maintaining this for 10 years would add more than $10 million to a finishing line's operating profits.

Note: *Casey Ichniowski, Kathryn Shaw, and Giovanna Prennushi, "The Effects of Human Resource Management Practices on Productivity: A Study of Steel Finishing Lines," *American Economic Review* 87 (1997): 291–313.

---

changing instructional demands. It is difficult to substitute computer engineering faculty for civil engineering faculty if most of the latter have tenure. In 1988, the Education Reform Act significantly "softened" the tenure system in the United Kingdom, making it easier to fire individual faculty members for financial reasons. More recently, some universities in the United States have taken steps to give university administrators more control over tenured professors.[43] And, in general, U.S. institutions of higher learning have tended to increase the use of part-time and nontenured instructors over time. In 1992, just 48% of all instructors had tenure or were in a tenure-track position[44] while more current estimates by the American Association of University Professors (AAUP) indicates that more than 50% of faculty are part-time instructors.[45]

---

[43] Robin Walsh and Sharon Walsh, "Tears in the Fabric of Tenure," *Chronicle of Higher Education*, 2003.

[44] Michael S. McPherson and Morton Owen Schapiro, "Tenure Issues in Higher Education," *Journal of Economic Perspectives* 13 (1999): 85–98.

[45] AAUP, "Background Facts on Contingent Faculty," available at: www.aaup.org.

The traditional argument in favor of tenure is based on academic freedom. In this view, tenure protects faculty members from retaliation for voicing unpopular views. For example, a labor economist might not present a complete examination of the costs and benefits of unions if he or she feared that a rabidly antiunion member of the board of trustees might seek to have the economist fired for speaking of the positive aspects of unions. In fact, the AAUP got its start in the wake of a 1901 decision by Stanford University to fire economics instructor Edward Ross at the insistence of Mrs. Leland Stanford, who objected to his liberal economic views.[46]

Going beyond academic freedom, the economics literature has recently turned to an emphasis on tenure as a labor market institution that may have a positive payoff to universities through the incentives it provides. For example, Lorne Carmichael's model of an academic department treats tenure as the means of providing incentives for incumbent faculty to participate in identifying the best candidates for new positions.[47] If incumbent faculty had to worry that more able new additions to the department might replace them one day, they would be less inclined to make hiring decisions that were in the best interests of the university. Incumbents are much better positioned to judge the talents of potential new hires than is the university administration, and long-term job security through tenure gives them the incentive to hire new faculty who might be more productive than the existing faculty in a department.

Michael McPherson and Morton Shapiro have also emphasized the notion that tenure has a positive payoff for the university by aligning the self-interest of individual faculty members with the long-run interests of the institution.[48] They see two valuable economic benefits from the tenure system beyond the incentive to hire and mentor more productive new faculty. First, job security allows tenured faculty the independence to perform credibly objective evaluations of students and other faculty. People outside the university who rely on the information provided by student grades or faculty reviews of papers or proposals can have greater confidence that these evaluations have not been colored by the faculty member's concern about job security. Second, tenure allows faculty to make long-run strategic decisions about educational policy and research even if these are in conflict with the short-run, career interests of administrators. The fact that tenured faculty often are viewed as obstacles to change by ambitious administrators looking to embellish their records for their next career move might well be a good thing for the long-run interests of the university.

Antony Dnes and Jonathan Seaton provide some evidence on the potential payoff to tenure as an internal labor market system.[49] They found that the research rating of UK universities was significantly higher in those institutions with "hard" tenure systems providing more complete job security than in institutions with "soft" tenure systems. The research productivity advantage of universities with more extensive tenure protection

---

[46] Joan Wallach Scott, "Critical State of Shared Governance," *Academe* (2002): 41–48.

[47] H. Lorne Carmichael, "Incentives in Academics: Why Is There Tenure?" *Journal of Political Economy* 96 (1988): 453–472.

[48] Michael S. McPherson and Morton Owen Shapiro, "Tenure Issues in Higher Education," *Journal of Economic Perspectives* 13 (1999): 85–98.

[49] Antony W. Dnes and Jonathan S. Seaton, "The Research Assessment Exercise and the Reform of Academic Tenure in the United Kingdom," *Contemporary Economic Policy* 19 (2001): 39–48.

was found to persist even after the 1988 act that legally softened tenure systems in all universities. They attribute this to tenure traditions that established a workplace culture associated with high research productivity, which proved relatively immune to legislative changes.

Empirical evidence also questions the notion that tenure leads faculty members to shirk their responsibilities. Robert Blackburn and Janet Lawrence suggest that teaching performance and research output does not decline systematically as faculty members are awarded tenure.[50] However, Daniel Hamermesh does find that the research output of academic economists is negatively correlated with their age[51] and, hence, that tenure might protect the jobs of less productive, older faculty members. Finally, Debra Barbezat and James Hughes find that tenure is positively correlated with faculty salary, controlling for individual experience, possession of an advanced degree, the number of articles and books published, individual rank and field, the type of university, and the person's history of job turnover.[52] This is at least suggestive of a productivity advantage of individual tenured faculty members.

Implications of ILMs for Labor Analysis

The existence of internal labor markets for a substantial fraction of the workforce has some important implications for the analysis of several important labor market situations. Several of these will be addressed in later chapters; however, we can outline here the main effects on our thinking resulting from the concept of the ILM.

Wage Determination

With wages set by the firm within ILMs to maximize the joint gains from establishing and maintaining the employment relationship, it is no longer possible to think of wages in general as being determined by the intersection of traditional labor supply and demand curves. External labor market forces do affect the wages of workers at the point of entry to the firm and may influence wage setting in general, but since wages are determined in a manner consistent with the long-run objectives of the firm, they are insulated to a great degree from current market vacillations. With this in mind, it is easier to see why wages would vary by firm, industry, or occupation even when we control for the education, experience, and compensating differentials on the job. In fact, variables indicating the firm, industry, and occupation of a worker often explain more of the variation in wages across workers than the human capital variables that are consistent with the competitive model of labor supply.

---

[50] Robert T. Blackburn and Janet H. Lawrence, *Faculty at Work: Motivation, Expectation, Satisfaction* (Baltimore: Johns Hopkins University Press, 1995).

[51] Daniel S. Hamermesh, "Aging and Productivity, Rationality and Matching: Evidence from Economists," *NBER Working Paper No. 4906*, 1994.

[52] Debra A. Barbezat and James W. Hughes, "The Effect of Job Mobility on Academic Salaries," *Contemporary Economic Policy* 19 (2001): 409–423.

Collective Bargaining

When you are used to thinking of wages as being determined by supply and demand, it is difficult to see how trade unions could have much influence on wages through collective bargaining. If unions raised the wage of some workers in a labor market where all the workers are close substitutes, it is hard to see how this wage increase wouldn't just price those workers out of their jobs. And yet, as you will see in Chapter 12, there is a lot of empirical evidence worldwide to indicate that union workers might get wages 10% to 20% higher than they could have commanded in the absence of union bargaining and that these union wage premiums have significant staying power without necessarily costing union members their jobs.

The ILM concept gives us another way to think about these union wage effects. The key fact leading to ILMs is that the employment relationship generates rents to the firm and its workers that are significant enough to warrant setting up an ILM as a form of implicit contract. How these rents are divided between the workers, their managers, and the owners of the enterprise is an open question. By engaging in collective bargaining with the threat of a strike or other work action, a trade union might be able to increase the share of the rent going to the workers it represents. The fact that this would lower the share going to managers and owners might be all we need to know to understand the vigor with which these groups resist union organizing efforts even in firms where there appear to be ample means to satisfy union demands.

Unemployment

The competitive labor supply and demand model of labor markets also makes it difficult to analyze the problem of unemployment. Any excess supply of workers, which is what unemployment indicates, should serve to depress wage levels and return the labor market to equilibrium. At equilibrium, the number of workers wishing to work at the going wage equals the number employed, so the only unemployment that might exist would be frictional or voluntary in the sense that some workers would be unwilling to accept work at the going wage and prefer, instead, to keep looking for better paying jobs. The solution is to assume that wages adjust to excess supply only in a very sluggish manner over time. In this view, wage rigidity leads to involuntary unemployment whenever labor supply exceeds labor demand.

The ILM model provides us with an explanation for wage rigidity. If the firm sets wages to provide incentives for worker investments, with the returns to be shared over the entire working life, the short-run appearance of excess labor supply might not have much of an effect on wages, except perhaps for the wages of new hires. Because the purpose of an ILM is to provide incentives for a long-term employment relationship, it is perhaps easier to see why unemployed workers would not be competitive for many jobs, even if they were willing to work for less than the people filling those jobs. With the concept of an ILM, the notion of wage rigidity appears less like jury-rigging the model to make it fit the facts and more like a central concept in the study of real-life labor markets.

Labor Market Segmentation

In labor economics, it often suffices to suppose that all workers are the same. This may be surprising, but it is true. For example, we have used the homogeneous labor assumption when investigating monopsonistic labor markets in which some workers are employed and others involuntarily unemployed. We have used the same assumption about homogeneous workers when studying search models of unemployment, attributing the differences that workers experience in the duration of unemployment periods to different fortunes in searching a labor market characterized by uncertainty. In later chapters we continue to use the homogeneous labor assumption when it is convenient to do so. It does, after all, simplify our analysis quite a lot (just as does the assumption of homogeneous outputs in perfectly competitive models of the product market), and it buys this simplification at relatively low cost in terms of explanatory power. However, it is important to be aware that the homogeneous labor assumption is really quite a strong one. One of the authors of this book may have become an airline pilot had it not been for his slight color blindness; from the air he could not distinguish between a runway and a river. It is a fact that not all people are equally able to do all jobs.

In the neoclassical model with which we have dealt in earlier chapters, this lack of equivalence is a matter of little interest. Indeed, the whole concept of a job sits rather uneasily within the neoclassical paradigm. In that model, workers are paid their marginal revenue product; a worker who is not very good at being a pilot (for example) can work as a pilot and be paid a low wage for doing so. This, we all know, is balderdash. In the world in which we live (as opposed to the neoclassical world), people work in jobs, they get paid a wage that is largely determined by the job they do, and they are only employed in a job if they are productive enough in that job to justify their wage. It is the job rather than the individual that should be the cornerstone of our analysis.[53] (This issue is discussed at greater length in Chapter 11.)

The standard analysis of ILMs is not neoclassical, and ILMs are jam-packed full of jobs. It is therefore instructive to explore what might happen when we confront the theory of ILMs with the observation that not all workers have the same characteristics.

Many workers will join an ILM at an entry port and will rapidly be promoted to a point further up the ladder of responsibility. These workers will then most likely remain with the firm for an extended period because they will be earning more in their promoted post with their current employer than they could possibly earn elsewhere. Should they change employers, they would have to start again at the bottom rung of the ladder. These workers are said to operate in a **primary labor market**.[54] Their jobs are secure, with the prospect of lengthy job tenure. There are well-established promotion ladders and pay progression, and remuneration is relatively high. A supportive infrastructure is present, characterized by good working practices. The high wage rates paid to primary sector workers encourage employers to invest in capital-intensive technologies, and this serves to make primary sector workers ever more productive—and ever more well paid. Such workers are on a virtuous spiral.

By way of contrast, some workers will join an ILM at an entry port but will fail to be promoted. These workers have no incentive to remain with the firm for an extended period. They can change employers without feeling that they have to "start over"; in a sense, they never really got started. Consequently, there tends to be a high rate of turnover among such workers: job security is not a feature of their work, and there is no

---

[53] This does not mean that the neoclassical approach is without value. Indeed we have already witnessed in earlier chapters just how useful it can be. But it is not the right tool for analyzing issues to do with jobs.

[54] Peter Doeringer and Michael Piore, *Internal Labor Markets and Manpower Analysis* (Lexington: Heath, 1971).

prospect of lengthy job tenure. Such workers are said to work in a **secondary labor market**. They have slim chances of promotion, and pay does not increase with experience. The jobs occupied by such workers are often referred to as "dead-end" jobs. Remuneration is low, and working conditions are often poor. And, since pay is low, there is no incentive for employers to invest in the capital that could make these workers more productive. In contrast to primary sector workers, workers in the secondary sector are on a vicious spiral of low pay, high labor intensity, low productivity, and sustained low remuneration.

This analysis paints a stark picture for workers allocated to secondary jobs. They occupy positions in the labor market that have undesirable characteristics, and decisions that affect them are taken by primary sector workers. Secondary workers cannot control their own destiny at work and so become alienated. Their lot is not a happy one.

It is rather important to establish whether **segmented labor markets** really do exist. An obvious way to check this is to consider the manner in which wages are determined in different jobs. Recall from Chapter 6 that the (log) wage is often modeled as a function of schooling, experience, and experience squared. Regression analysis can be used to estimate the coefficients of such a model. Now it makes sense to suppose that earnings are determined in this way in primary labor markets. In these labor markets, earnings do rise with experience. And it is reasonable to suppose that worker promotion prospects—and so also their pay—depend to some extent on the level of education that they have attained. But in secondary labor markets, it is not at all clear that wages depend on schooling and experience. Remember that these are "dead-end" jobs, with no pay progression or promotion structure. So it is likely that the human capital earnings function does not work so well when applied to data on secondary labor markets.

This issue has been investigated using U.S. data from the Panel Study of Income Dynamics.[55] The results confirm that a model in which there are two segments of the labor market significantly outperforms one in which there is only a single labor market.[56] Coefficients on the human capital variables are much higher in the primary sector than in the secondary sector. The rate of return to an additional year of schooling is estimated at about 7% in the primary sector, but it is close to (and insignificantly different from) zero in the secondary sector. A similar result obtains when we consider the effect on wages of experience. An extra year of experience adds about 1.5% to wages in the primary sector, but it adds nothing to wages in the secondary sector. Similar evidence of a dual structure to wage determination with differential wage returns to various dimensions of human capital in the two defined segments of the labor market has been found by the application of switching regression techniques to data on individual workers in Chile, Spain, and Argentina.[57]

---

[55] William T. Dickens and Kevin Lang, "A Test of Dual Labor Market Theory," *American Economic Review* 75 (1985): 792–805.

[56] The researchers used a neat technique known as switching regressions. This allows two regressions—one for each sector—to be estimated without a need for the analyst to specify in an ad hoc manner which individuals belong in which sector. The allocation of individuals to sectors is done by the statistical algorithm, based on what fits the data best.

[57] Michael Basch and Ricardo D. Paredes-Molina, "Are There Dual Labor Markets in Chile? Empirical Evidence," *Journal of Development Economics* 50 (1996): 297–312; Ana Huguet Roig, "Testing Spanish Labour Market Segmentation: An Unknown-regime Approach," *Applied Economics* 31 (1999): 292–305; Maria Laura Alzua, "Are Secondary Workers Informal Workers? Evidence for Argentina," *Desarollo y Sociedad* 63 (2009): 81–114.

It seems that there is a degree of dualism in the labor market. Whether this is important depends on two further questions: (a) what proportion of the working population is confined to secondary market jobs, and (b) can workers in the secondary market ever break through to become primary sector workers? Let's look at each of these questions in turn.

The technique used to identify the existence of a dual wage structure can also be used to estimate the percentage of a given sample of workers who are in the secondary sector. Dickens and Lang find that about 12.5% of a sample of 2812 U.S. male workers were in secondary sector jobs with higher percentages for those under age 25 (19.1%), those with less than 12 years of schooling (17.8%) and nonwhites (31.1%). John Baffoe-Bonnie[58] looks at a 1991 sample of 4,159 U.S. male workers over age 20 and finds that 2.5% to 3.5% of managerial, professional, and skilled and semi-skilled blue-collar workers were in secondary jobs, while as many as 25% to 35% of administrative support, services, and agricultural workers fell into that category. Roig's analysis of data on a 1991 sample of 2,265 Spanish nonagricultural wage earners finds that 11% of men and 33.6% of women held secondary sector jobs. Finally, Alzua's study of annual household surveys from 1975 to 1996 in the Greater Buenos Aires region of Argentina shows that the percentage of secondary jobs is related to macroeconomic performance. She finds that 35% of male private sector workers aged 15 to 65 held secondary sector jobs during 1975–1991, when the unemployment rate was relatively low, but that this figure more than doubled to 72% during 1992–2001, when unemployment rates fluctuated in the 10%–20% range. In all of these samples there are nontrivial numbers of workers found to be in the secondary sector, with the number rising depending on age, skill, education, gender, race, and the overall state of the labor market.

Can these workers break through to the primary sector? The fact that young workers are heavily represented in the secondary sector suggests that at least some of them can. The natural process of getting older helps because labor market experience increases the likelihood of gaining a primary sector job (it is reassuring to know that getting older does indeed have some compensation). Education and training can also help workers switch from the secondary to the primary sector. However, to the extent that ethnic minorities may be stuck in the secondary sector because of discrimination (as opposed to their human capital characteristics), the empirical evidence is that they might find it difficult to escape. This is both morally disturbing and frightening in terms of its implications for social cohesion. We discuss discrimination in much more detail in Chapter 13.

Summary

In the competitive model of the labor market, workers and jobs are perfect substitutes. In the real world, however, employers are willing to part with large sums of money to ensure that they hire the "right person for the job," and workers engage in extensive and expensive job search to find the "best opportunity out there." In the competitive model of

---

[58]John Baffoe-Bonnie, "Distributional Assumptions and a Test of the Dual Labor Market Hypothesis," *Empirical Economics* 28 (2003): 461–478. See footnote 19 for references to the other studies mentioned in this paragraph.

the labor market, high labor turnover is not a problem because acceptable substitute workers and jobs can always be found. In the real world, however, workers on average tend to stay with their employer for long periods of time, and this tendency has not been significantly eroded by changes in the competitive environment or workplace organization during the past decade.

The internal labor market model addresses these features of the real world that are not really a part of the competitive labor market model. Hiring costs and firm-specific investments create rents through avoidance of excessive turnover and maximization of the period of investment returns. Because it is difficult to write complete contracts to maximize these rents, firms turned to ILM mechanisms—career job ladders, wages sheltered from external labor market shocks, and rewards for long tenure—to provide incentives for long-term employment relationships. ILMs began to be implemented in large U.S. manufacturing firms during the first few decades of the twentieth century, and some estimates suggest that as many as two-thirds of the current U.S. workforce is employed in establishments with some ILM characteristics.

One upshot of broadening our approach to labor market analysis by including the ILM concept in our bag of tools is that we can more readily explain certain features of the labor market in addition to careful recruiting and long job tenure. Because wages are only partially affected by shocks to labor supply and demand, we can understand why many empirical studies find that wages are heavily influenced by "institutional factors," such as industry, occupation, unionization, and firm identity. It is also easier to understand why real wages might not readily adjust to eliminate the excess supply of labor during periods of high unemployment. And it becomes clear that access to an ILM might have an important role to play in determining wage differences across groups within the economy. As we continue to study these labor market situations, we will use both the competitive labor market model and the ILM model to develop a more complete analysis.

KEY TERMS

hiring costs

job tenure

job hierarchy

port of entry

lifetime employment

employment protection regulations

high performance work systems

implicit contract

primary labor market

secondary labor market

segmented labor markets

PROBLEMS

1. Have you held a job? If so, compare the key features of the best job you have held with the features of typical jobs in internal labor markets. Was this a job that required costly hiring and training by the employer?

2. Take a closer look at the syllabus for your course. In what sense can this be described as an implicit contract? How does it provide incentives for sustained effort and performance? How does it provide protection against risk?

3. Search the internet for an up-to-date list of good companies for which to work. The 2011 list compiled by CNN can be found at: http://money.cnn.com/magazines/fortune/bestcompanies/2011/full_list/

   Identify one firm from the list and prepare a brief summary of the practices and policies that make it a good place to work. To what extent are these similar to or different from the types of ILM policies and practices discussed in this chapter?

4. Try to find a list of companies that are identified as bad places to work. Compare and contrast your selection with the company you used to answer problem 3.

5. Hiring and training costs are one reason ILMs come into being. Consider the following businesses and determine the extent to which these costs matter for the typical firm. Rank them according to the likelihood of having an ILM.
   a. A farmer hiring workers to harvest tomatoes.
   b. A vineyard.
   c. A fast-food restaurant.
   d. A software development company.
   e. An emergency medical treatment ambulance service.
   f. A nursing home.

6. What is the difference between primary and secondary sectors in the labor market? What problems do economists encounter in testing for the existence of segmented labor markets? Why might the effect of schooling and experience on earnings be greater in the primary sector than in the secondary sector?

7. In most developed countries over the last 30 years employment has become polarized with job growth in both high skill occupations, like professional and managerial workers, and low-skill service occupations, like health care workers. At the same time, employment has decreased in middle-skill occupations, like office administration and production workers. How might these changes affect the prevalence of ILMs and the relative size of the primary and secondary sectors?

8. How does the traditional ILM compare with high performance work systems in terms of job hierarchy, wage policies, and employment security?

9. Why might large Japanese firms continue to protect workers already inside the firm and adapt to the economic slowdown by reducing hiring of new employees? How would this affect the ability of young workers to escape the secondary sector?

10. Explain why employment protection regulations that restrict the freedom of firms to fire workers would lead firms to reduce the rate at which they hire new employees? How would this affect the size of the secondary sector and the ability of young workers to move into primary sector jobs?

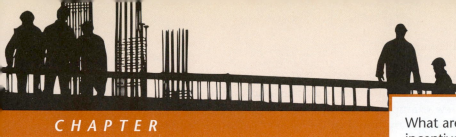

11

Personnel Economics

What are the advantages of incentive pay?

In what ways are organizations like tournaments?

How does the firm gain by tying wages and fringe benefits to worker seniority?

Chapter 10 illustrates how a firm's optimum response to hiring and training costs might be to create an internal labor market in which wage patterns could differ from those set in a perfectly competitive labor market. In this chapter we continue our analysis of the ways individual firms use compensation strategies to achieve profit maximizing outcomes. This subject, known as personnel economics, helps us understand why a variety of wage and employment relationships emerge in the real world where workers are not homogeneous and firms produce differentiated products with different technologies.

Personnel economics applies the tools of economic analysis to key questions facing human resource managers. We begin with a consideration of the means available to the firm for motivating workers to achieve their highest productivity levels. Then we examine how the compensation system of a firm might create incentives for the "right" workers to apply for openings. Personnel economics, like the analysis of internal labor markets, helps us understand why the "law of one price" does not often prevail in labor markets and why organization structure and management practices matter when considering wages and employment.

Motivating Worker Effort

In developing the basic model of production underlying the demand for labor in Chapter 2, we started from the notion that the output of the firm is related to the amount of labor employed by the firm. There we measured the amount of labor as the number of workers or worker hours hired by the firm. In reality there is a qualitative dimension to the output–labor relationship; how much product a firm makes from an hour's worth of labor depends in part on how much effort the worker puts into that hour of labor. This qualitative dimension is somewhat similar to the notion of efficiency wages—where higher wages lead to higher productivity because of better nutrition and health—which we examined in Chapter 3. Here are a few examples to clarify what we mean by **effort**.

Effort may be represented by how fast the worker performs the tasks required by the job. In a simple production setting, the quality of effort may actually be measurable. Assuming that all workers face similar conditions, we could define a high-effort fruit picker, for example, by the number of apples picked in an hour.

Effort might also be represented by the number of different tasks a worker completes in a given time period. Some people are high-energy gardeners who can mow, mulch, till, prune, and weed in the same Saturday afternoon in which others can barely get the lawn cut. It's not their ability or training that lets them accomplish more; rather, it's their willingness to work harder and take fewer breaks that accounts for the difference.

In some jobs effort can be more qualitative and is described by terms such as *care* or *attention to detail*. Homer Simpson is *not* a high-effort nuclear power plant operator.

Finally, in service jobs, effort might be found in the responsiveness of employees to customer needs and how courteously the worker treats a customer. If you have ever dealt with an airline agent in the wake of a canceled flight, you can attest to the importance of these aspects of effort.

Once we introduce effort into the production relationship, we have to recognize the existence of a classic **principal-agent problem** in the employment relationship—that is, a problem where a principal (for instance, an employer) wants to get an agent (say, a worker) to behave in a certain way despite the fact that agents have their own set of priorities that do not ordinarily coincide with those of the principal, and the fact that agents can usually conceal some aspects of their behavior. Employers would like all of their workers to be high-effort workers. But the amount of effort put into the job is to some extent under the control of the workers, and this is especially the case in jobs where effort is not easy to measure. Moreover, other things being equal, workers have the incentive to minimize the amount of effort expended. This principal-agent problem means that the owners of the firm (the principals) need to find some way to motivate the workers (the agents) to perform in a way that suits the interests of the owners rather than their own.[1]

Tackling this principal-agent problem is really what human resource management and personnel economics are all about. In common with many other applications of principal-agent analysis, personnel economics opens up the "black box" of the firm and encourages us to examine both the institutions that exist within an organization and the relationships between those institutions. So, for example, we are led to ask questions such as these: Why do jobs exist? Why do promotion hierarchies exist? Why do people in different positions within the firm get paid differently?

The answers to these questions may seem self-evident at first glance, but they are illustrative of just how insightful personnel economics can be. Why do jobs exist? Isn't the answer obvious? Well, actually, no. Neoclassical economics tells us that workers get paid a wage based on the value of their marginal product. In a neoclassical world, therefore, you could work as a rocket scientist even without any training in that field, but

---

[1] In the long-running daily comic strip *Blondie*, Mr. Dithers has chosen the method of pummeling Dagwood every time he catches Dagwood sleeping on the job. Given the number of times this has been the subject of this comic strip over the years, we might suggest that Mr. Dithers try another approach.

you probably wouldn't be paid a very high wage. Of course, we know that this is absurd. What we see in the world around us is that people can either get a job or they can't, and if they get a job, they get the wage associated with that job. Now the neoclassical model is certainly useful in many contexts, but it ignores what we know about the existence of jobs.

So, why do jobs exist? The answer must be that the bunching of tasks into an institution known as a "job" is efficient for the firm. It may be more efficient, for example, for a firm to set up a maintenance engineer's position than to buy engineering services from outside. It may be more efficient for a university to set up an institution known as a professor of economics rather than hire teachers separately for each economics lecture to be given. It may be more efficient for a newspaper to hire journalists rather than to rely on freelance workers. In each case, the rationale for setting up the job is that the institution of a job allows the firm to minimize transactions costs. And where jobs exist, it is possible to be hired to do a job, and it is possible to be fired from a job.

Within a firm, there may be many jobs, and the characteristics of these jobs may differ markedly. For instance, the way in which people are paid may differ from job to job. Senior managers may have a contract that requires them to work whatever hours are necessary (for given pay) to fulfill their contractual obligations; other workers may have the opportunity to earn overtime; sales staff may not be remunerated on an hourly basis at all but rather on the basis of their success in achieving sales. Some workers are paid more than others because they have achieved a level of seniority within the firm. In the remainder of this chapter, we focus primarily on the insights into the remuneration of employees that personnel economics provides.

Wages and the Supply of Effort

To begin with, let's look at how remuneration schemes can help firms regulate the level of worker effort. The principal-agent problem related to worker effort is illustrated formally in Figure 11.1. Here we depict the utility levels and trade-offs associated with different characteristics of a job. The worker is assumed to derive positive utility from the monetary and nonmonetary rewards from a job. Although nonmonetary rewards, such as prestige

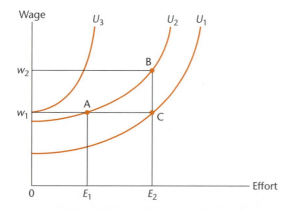

FIGURE 11.1 Wage, Effort, and Worker Utility

and personal fulfillment, are undoubtedly important, Figure 11.1 focuses attention on the wage as the source of positive utility.

The job also requires effort, which is assumed to generate disutility, or negative utility. Thus the indifference curves in Figure 11.1 are positively sloped. An increase in the amount of effort required on the job for a given wage level, for example, from E_1 to E_2, results in lower overall utility, and the worker is moved from indifference curve U_2 to U_1. For the worker to remain at the same level of overall satisfaction, an increase in required effort must be accompanied by a higher wage. Workers prefer jobs with higher wages and lower effort to jobs with lower wages and higher effort. Thus, in Figure 11.1, the worker prefers points A and B to C and is indifferent between points A and B.

This analysis suggests that workers will evaluate both the compensation level and the required effort in deciding whether or not to accept a job offer. The technology, product mix, size, location, and management style of different firms hiring a given type of labor are likely to vary across firms; therefore, it would not be surprising if the degree of effort associated with the job also varied across firms. Because workers would not knowingly accept a job that required greater effort without being compensated for it, some part of the variation in wages across firms for workers filling similar jobs may be accounted for by this factor. For example, janitors earning a higher wage in some firms could be receiving a compensating differential for the greater effort required of a janitor's job in those firms.

Two additional managerial issues arise in this situation. First, the worker's disutility from greater effort (the costs of effort) may present a constraint on the ability of the firm to maximize profits. Second, because workers prefer points like A in Figure 11.1 to points like C, they have an incentive to **shirk** on the job (if they can do so), reducing their effort below the level they agreed to when they took the job. Thus, managers have to expend scarce resources identifying applicants who can fulfill the effort requirements of the job and monitoring worker performance. Managers may have to dismiss workers and forgo the return on the investment in their hiring and training to make the penalties of shirking credible. One important contribution of personnel economics is explaining how the structure of compensation can be used to accomplish these same objectives and save managerial resources.

Effort and Output in a Fixed Wage System

Let's look at a simple model that illustrates the potential benefits of shifting from a fixed wage system to a system that ties compensation to worker effort. The problem facing the firm's manager is depicted in Figure 11.2. First, we graph a linear individual production function linking output, and hence total revenue (TR) at fixed output prices, to worker effort. This individual production function can be written as:

$$Q = \alpha E + v \tag{11-1}$$

where Q is the quantity of output per period produced by a given worker, E is the worker's effort, α is a parameter tying output to effort, and v captures the effect of factors beyond the worker's control on his or her output. Thus a machine breakdown, a power shortage, or an unexpected drop in market demand for the product might be measured by a negative value for v.

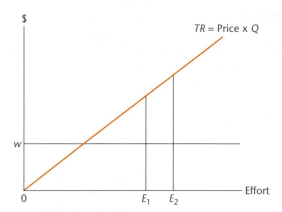

FIGURE 11.2 Returns from Effort

In Figure 11.2 we assume that α is constant, that there is a linear relationship between output and effort—the worker indeed can determine his or her own output. Think of the "beer man" at a sporting event. His output in sold bottles of beer is directly linked to the amount of time he spends selling versus watching the game, the enthusiasm with which he yells "Beer here!" and other aspects of his effort on the job. Contrast that with the situation facing an assembly-line worker whose output is determined mainly by the speed of the line and the effort of other workers at job stations ahead of the worker. The value of α in this case would be close to zero because the worker's own effort has little impact on his or her output.

Figure 11.2 also includes the fixed hourly wage paid by the firm (w). For a given wage level, the workers determine their supply of effort and the level of total revenue they earn for the firm. The firm requires a minimum level of effort (E_1). This level of effort would generate a surplus of revenue over the wage that was just sufficient to cover the fixed costs of production, including the normal profit. The firm essentially offers job applicants the combination of wage w and effort level E_1. Workers who agree to provide effort level E_1 for wage w presumably get greater utility from this choice than from their next best alternative.

Because the employment relationship involves an agreement on the amount of effort the employee will supply, two managerial problems are created for the firm. First, the manager must ensure that the worker indeed supplies a level of effort equal to E_1. Remember that Figure 11.1 showed that the worker has an incentive to reduce the amount of effort expended below E_1 at wage w because this would move the worker to a higher indifference curve. Thus a worker has an incentive to shirk and would do so as long as the utility gain is greater than or equal to the cost of shirking, which can be described as the product of the probability of getting caught and the wage lost if shirking led to dismissal. Monitoring worker effort is costly, and the worker could claim that fluctuations in v rather than E were responsible for output shortages, so the probability of getting caught shirking may be relatively small.

There is another difficulty with the monitoring approach to ensuring minimum effort. If w equals the prevailing wage in a competitive labor market, the threat of discharge may not carry much weight with the worker as he or she could always find another job paying

w. There are monetary and nonmonetary transition costs of changing jobs, however, and workers are likely to be motivated in part by pride in their work, so shirking may be somewhat self-limiting. If the probability of getting fired and the differential value of the current job relative to the market are both low, however, it may be difficult to get sustained effort at the required level.

The second managerial problem is to motivate workers to supply a greater level of effort than E_1. If managers can motivate workers to supply a level of effort of E_2, the difference between workers' contributions to total revenue and their wages will be greater. Perhaps managers could exert more of their own effort in recruiting and hiring in an attempt to identify workers who are able and willing to supply more effort than E_1 at the wage w. Or perhaps managers could attempt to motivate greater effort through exhortation or through employee-of-the-month campaigns or other nonmonetary appeals to workers' pride. When management controls the rate of usage of a complementary input, the firm could make people work harder by speeding up the assembly line, for example.

Performance Pay

An alternative method of influencing workers to supply required effort levels is by explicitly linking the wage received by the worker to effort. Performance pay systems induce workers to voluntarily increase their effort on the job to realize higher wages. The effects of a piece rate system, which encompasses what has been called an efficient contract linking compensation to output, are shown in Figure 11.3. Here the wage earned by the worker is a function of his effort level, as given by the following equation:

$$w = -B + \beta E \tag{11-2}$$

where B is a performance bond that the worker pays to get the job. If B is set equal to the producer surplus at the normal profit effort level (E_1 in Figure 11.3), the worker would have to supply at least this amount of effort to earn back the performance bond and make a wage equivalent to that in alternative jobs. In our example of the beer man at a sporting event, the performance bond might involve the vending firm selling cases of

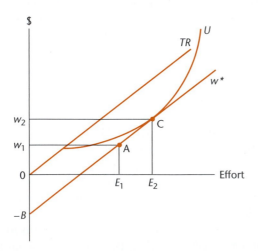

FIGURE 11.3 Incentive Pay versus Fixed Wage

beer to the beer man at a price that covered the cost of the beer plus the average fixed cost of running the concession. The beer man's net wage (w) would equal the money earned by selling beer through his efforts at the market price (βE) minus the upfront cost of buying the beer (B). This arrangement is common in taxi companies as well, wherein the firm rents the cab to a driver who keeps the fares.

This wage system would solve the managerial problems we identified in the previous section. Point A identifies the combination of effort level E_1 and wage level w_1 corresponding to the values in Figure 11.2. Only those whose indifference curves are tangent to the wage–effort line above point A will accept jobs at this firm. For example, a worker whose indifference curve is tangent at point C will supply effort level E_2 and earn as a result compensation level w_2. No workers whose indifference curves would put them on a point below A would accept a job with this firm because they could earn at least w_1 at other firms. The pay system encourages self-selection of workers in the hiring process, thus saving the firm from the need to pay close attention to the characteristics of applicants. More important, the firm would not incur the costs of monitoring worker performance because workers would move to a lower indifference curve by shirking.

The analysis in Figure 11.3 is sufficient to establish three key outcomes from the introduction of an incentive pay system in a firm that originally used a fixed wage system. First, effort and output per worker will rise. Second, the average level of earnings will rise as a reflection of increased effort. Third, the variance of effort and wages across workers within the firm would increase, reflecting the variation in preferences among workers. These three findings were all observed in the wake of the Safelite Glass Corporation's decision to shift from a fixed wage system to a **piece rate system** for glass installers.[2]

Performance bonds are not often seen in real-world piece rate systems. In part, this reflects the fact that workers may not be able to afford to pay the bond out of their resources or borrow funds to pay the bond. It's one thing to charge a vendor the cost of a case of beer plus a markup reflecting the average fixed costs of running the concession business. It is far more difficult for a worker to pay a bond covering the average fixed cost of an industrial plant or the overhead costs associated with research and development, marketing, and other administrative tasks.

In addition, if workers are risk averse, they would not be attracted to a pay system that made them the **residual claimant** to firm revenues. In this situation, the worker's income would be the amount left over after fixed costs, including a normal profit to the owners, were paid. We would expect workers to reject a performance pay system if the output of the firm is subject to large random shocks, that is, if it were not unusual for the term v in equation 11-1 to take on large positive or negative values. Workers would have to plan for the eventuality that their incomes could fall substantially due to factors beyond their control. Because the effects of a large negative v may be indistinguishable from low E, it is unlikely (owing to the presence of "moral hazard" effects) that workers would be able to buy insurance against adverse shocks.

Finally, a performance bond may not be in the interest of the employer. The value of B in Figure 11.3 is determined by the producer surplus that could be earned by the firm if the wage were set at w_1 and all employees worked at effort level E_1. But suppose all the workers hired by the firm chose to work at effort level E_2. If the workers are the residual

---

[2] Edward Lazear, "Performance Pay and Productivity," *American Economic Review* 90 (2000): 1346–1361.

PUTTING THEORY TO WORK

DO PAY INCENTIVES INCREASE EFFORT AND PRODUCTIVITY?

The central assumption in the analysis of incentive pay systems is that workers will respond with greater effort if by doing so they can positively affect their compensation. This assumption seems reasonable, but there is little direct empirical evidence to confirm it, perhaps because it is so difficult to measure individual effort at typical work sites. One study that does provide empirical support for this central assumption used data on the daily output of tree planters to measure the effort response to piece rates.*

Tree planters plant seedlings on harvested tracts of land for reforestation purposes. The job involves digging a hole, placing a seedling in the hole, and covering the roots. It is a physically demanding job but one that involves a simple production process and an easy-to-measure output. In British Columbia, which produces a quarter of the softwood lumber in North America, tree planting firms pay piece rates per unit of output to tree planters. The level of the piece rate varies according to the terrain and the difficulty of planting on a particular tract. But this feature presents problems in estimating the effect of incentives on output because piece rates are generally higher on tracts where it is harder to plant seedlings.

Holding planting conditions constant, the analysis of daily plantings by 88 workers over a five-month period showed that a 1% increase in the piece rate would increase productivity by slightly more than 2%. Therefore, raising the average piece rate of 25 cents per seedling by a penny would increase the average daily output by 67 trees. Once the characteristics of the plot are taken into account, tree planters' output depends solely on how hard they work. This study indicates that effort in this industry would respond significantly to a small increase in the amount of incentive pay.

Note: *Harry J. Paarsch and Bruce S. Shearer, "The Response of Worker Effort to Piece Rates: Evidence from the British Columbia Tree-Planting Industry," *Journal of Human Resources* 34 (1999): 643–667.

claimants, they would receive the entire amount of the extra producer surplus generated by the additional effort exerted. By setting a performance bond in advance, the firm surrenders the opportunity to earn any additional revenue stemming from its good fortune in attracting a particularly diligent workforce.

Effort is very difficult to measure, so real-world incentive pay schemes most often link compensation to output rather than to the effort of a worker. Salesmen are often paid a commission that is expressed as a fraction of the value of sales made. Machinists may be paid a piece rate that is expressed as a given amount of money for each unit produced or processed on their machine tools. Equation 11-1 suggests a close link between output and effort, but it also tells us that "other factors," captured by the term v, influence worker production regardless of the amount of effort expended by the individual.

The typical real-world piece rate or commission system looks more like Figure 11.4. Here there is a base wage, or draw against commission, equal to w_0. If the worker produces less than q_1 units of output, the worker's pay is equal to w_0. For output levels in excess of q_1 there is a positive link between output and the wage. In such a system, q_1 is set so that the positively sloped portion of the wage–performance relationship usually applies. Workers

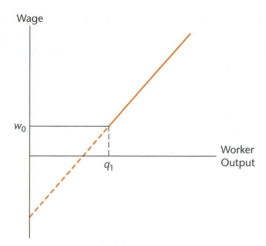

Wage

w_0

q_1

Worker
Output

FIGURE 11.4 Typical Piece Rate Relationship

who consistently earn w_0 during normal periods when other workers are on the positively sloped segment of the curve reveal themselves to be inferior, and the employer may discharge those workers. If economic circumstances force all workers onto the flat portion of the wage–performance relationship, however, the wage floor at w_0 protects their income. In addition, by comparing relative performance across workers, the firm's managers can be certain that the low output of individuals indeed reflects factors beyond their control.

Difficulties with Implementing Performance Pay

Piece rates and commissions can be found in many employment relationships, but the most common forms of pay are time-based. In addition to the difficulties with performance bonds previously noted, several other factors also are important in limiting the ability of a firm to link individual wages to individual output or effort.

- Individual output may not be easily measured in many jobs. Auto dealers can measure the sales of each salesperson and base their pay on commission, but what is the output of the service manager or an office assistant? If output or effort cannot be objectively measured so that workers can easily see the link between their pay and their effort, a performance pay system may not motivate greater work effort.
- It might take a long time to measure the performance of an individual. New lawyers, doctors, or research scientists might need several years to develop their stock of knowledge and customer base before a supervisor could evaluate whether they are high-output workers.
- Workers might not be able to influence their individual output by exerting greater effort on the job. This is certainly the case of much assembly-line work, where the output rate of a worker depends on the speed of the assembly line and the performance of others at preceding stations on the line. Similarly, a production process where labor and capital are complementary factors of production and where the available capital stock is fixed, thus limiting output, offers workers little opportunity to influence output by their effort.

- The output of an individual might be difficult to separate from the output of a work group or the firm. If you were the driver of a steamroller, how could your contribution to the number of miles of road paved be separated from that of the other drivers of trucks and equipment and the other laborers on the road repair crew? Because of free-rider incentives and the uncertain link between your performance and that of the work group as a whole, pay linked to output for the whole crew is likely to provide less incentive for you to work hard than individual pay for performance would.
- If workers perform several tasks, the incentive system has to be carefully constructed to ensure that performance of all tasks contributes to pay. Renting cabs to drivers and letting them keep the entire proceeds from fares might motivate them to drive until the marginal value of leisure equals the marginal return to continued work. But it might not motivate them to maintain the cab in good running condition. The drivers might regard that as the responsibility of the company that owns the vehicle, and may not perceive it to be their duty at all. It is possible to construct an incentive system for multiple tasks, but it is difficult to do so in a way that makes the link between pay and performance objective transparent to the worker.
- Traditional piece rate systems in industrial settings are often subject to attempts to manipulate the system, peer pressure on workers to meet group norms for production, and efforts by employers to initiate and by workers to resist so-called ratchet changes in the pay system in response to new equipment, technology, or product design.

One way of providing general incentive pay is to link compensation to the performance of the firm through ownership of shares of stock. Workers could be motivated to exert greater effort in order to insure profitable operations that increase the value of their share holdings. However, such incentives would be blunted if the actions of the individual had a minor effect on profits or if share prices were mainly driven by broad market forces. A recent study of the effect of stock ownership plans within a large multinational corporation reveals positive effects on employee behavior.[3] Membership in the share plan is correlated with lower quit and absence rates, greater work effort, and less interest in searching for another job. The strength of these relationships rises with the extent of individual participation in share ownership.

In cases where it is difficult to observe effort and where the employee engages in a number of different activities, making it hard to measure his output, the firm might attempt to use incentive pay by linking the wage to a subjective assessment of the worker's performance. Suppose the pay system is given by:

$$w = w_0 + b(P) \tag{11-3}$$

where P is an index of worker performance based upon the evaluation of supervisors and, perhaps, of coworkers and clients. In this case, the evaluation process needs to be carefully structured so that the activities that are measured and rewarded as indicators of good performance are also activities that add value to the firm. As the following box suggests, there are plenty of examples of incentive systems that reward one type of behavior while expecting another type of behavior to occur.

---

[3] Alex Bryson and Richard Freeman, "How Does Share Ownership Affect Employee Behavior? Evidence form a Multinational Corporation," Presented at the Mid-Year Fellows Workshop in Honor of Louis O. Kelso, Rutgers University School of Management and Labor Relations, February 25, 2011.

Suppose that there are two types of activities engaged in by the worker: a_1 and a_2 (these could be research and teaching activities of a university faculty member, research and writing activities of a journalist, or diagnostic and surgery work by a doctor). Then there are at least two ways in which this performance pay system might present the worker with misleading incentives:

- Suppose that by doing more of a_1 the worker enhances both his or her personal performance measure (P) and the firm's profitability, but doing more of a_2 contributes only to profitability. In this case the worker has little incentive to do a_2 even if the contribution of a_2 to the firm is very significant.
- Suppose doing more of a_1 positively affects P and profitability, but doing more of a_2 affects only P. In this case the worker has the incentive to do both a_1 and a_2 even though a_2 has no value to the firm.

These and other issues might lead a firm and its workers to prefer a time rate to a piece rate pay system, but other features of the work relationship, such as probationary periods, promotions, and periodic bonuses or merit pay increases, can be used to provide an incentive for greater work effort. In general, these features describe incentive pay systems that operate over the worker's tenure with the firm.

THE WAY WE WORK

You Get What You Pay For

Piece rates, merit pay increases, bonuses, and work-life compensation schemes attempt to increase worker effort and productivity. The construction of efficient incentive systems requires careful attention, especially when the worker has several different tasks to perform. A classic article by Steven Kerr* cited numerous examples "of reward systems that are fouled up in that behaviors which are rewarded are those which the rewarder is trying to *discourage*, while the behavior he desires is not being rewarded at all" (p. 769). Some examples are:

- Setting pay on the basis of quantifiable goals while hoping for efforts in team building, creativity, interpersonal relations, and so on
- Hoping that managers will pay attention to long-run costs and opportunities while rewarding them on the basis of short-run performance or achievement of stock price goals
- Hoping for budget discipline while allocating new budgets on the basis of past spending
- Hoping for innovation while rewarding conservatism and currying favor with supervisors
- Hoping for performance while rewarding attendance.

Kerr points to four reasons reward systems in organizations often fail to achieve their desired outcomes:

- A fascination with "objective" measures
- Overemphasis on highly visible behavior
- Hypocrisy about the desired behavior
- Emphasis on equity rather than efficiency

Note: *Steven Kerr, "On the Folly of Rewarding A, While Hoping for B," *Academy of Management Journal* 18 (1975): 769–783.

Work-Life Incentive Schemes

Work-life incentives work by making future wage levels contingent on satisfactory job performance. In a way, this is very similar to a piece rate system, albeit with a very long production period—years instead of an hour or day—and periodic adjustment of pay to performance. Under a work-life incentive scheme, the wage is less than the worker's value of the marginal product when the worker is young and greater than the value of the marginal product when the worker is older.

Basic Concepts

Because the objective of these pay systems is to enhance effort by deterring shirking by those on the job, a useful starting point is the Shapiro-Stiglitz model of the decision to shirk. A rational worker would choose to shirk if and only if the gain from doing so were greater than the cost, which consists of the potential lost income from getting caught and losing one's job. This can be written as:

$$G > \theta(w - w^*)N \tag{11-4}$$

where G is the utility gain from taking it easy on the job, θ is the probability of losing the job if one is caught shirking, w is the annual wage earnings on the current job, w^* is the alternative annual wage the worker could expect to earn, and N is the number of years the worker might expect to continue working with the firm.[4] The essence of this relationship is that the firm can deter shirking by increasing the probability of detection and punishment or by raising the value of the current job relative to the next best alternative. If monitoring costs or contracts make it difficult for the firm to raise θ, it may still be able to deter shirking by affecting lifetime wage differentials.

The essence of a work-life incentive scheme can be seen in Figure 11.5, which shows the profile of wages and the value of the marginal product over the tenure of an individual. *VMP* indicates the time profile of the value of the marginal product for a high-effort worker over the worker's span of employment with the firm. In a competitive market where the firm would set $w = VMP$ in each year, this relationship would also indicate the wage–tenure profile for the worker. *VMP* increases at a decreasing rate in line with both human capital theory, which posits eventually diminishing returns to experience, and considerable empirical evidence. For example, the results reported by Lori Kletzer indicate that a blue-collar worker whose entire career was with a single employer would have a wage profile that peaked after about 19 years of service with the firm.[5]

The line labeled w^* indicates the profile of the worker's opportunity cost for remaining in employment with the firm. When young, w^* would represent the best alternative wage outside the firm. However, as the individual approached retirement age, w^* might best be described as a combination of the utility from leisure and the nonlabor income from

---

[4] We assume a zero discount rate in this equation. Full details of this model are given by Carl Shapiro and Joseph Stiglitz, "Equilibrium Unemployment as a Worker Discipline Device," *American Economic Review* 74 (1984): 433–444.

[5] Lori Gladstein Kletzer, "Returns to Seniority after Permanent Job Loss," *American Economic Review* 79 (1989): 536–543.

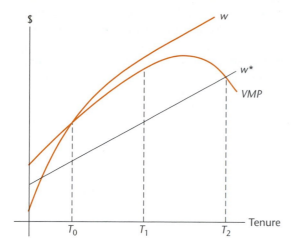

FIGURE 11.5 Work-Life Incentive Schemes

savings, private pension, and Social Security. It is clear that w^* increases with tenure with the firm, both because general labor market experience positively affects human capital and wages and because tenure with one firm has been found to enhance the wage a worker can command in the external labor market. In addition, the amount of nonlabor income available to the worker also rises with age. We draw w^* as following a linear relationship with tenure.

If workers are paid a wage equal to VMP at all times, the incentive to work hard begins to diminish after tenure equal to T_1 years in Figure 11.5. After that age, the difference $VMP - w^*$ diminishes steadily until at T_2 the two series intersect. It would be optimal for the worker to retire after T_2 years on the job. It is also likely to be the case that the probability of losing one's job if discovered to be shirking declines with tenure. In unionized settings, labor arbitrators clearly give deference to evidence of a long period of satisfactory performance when judging the propriety of disciplinary actions taken against a worker.[6] Finally, the number of years remaining until retirement decreases with a person's tenure with the firm. Thus, we could argue that all three components of the costs of shirking in equation 11-4 decrease with time on the job.

The wage profile represented by line w in Figure 11.5 offers the firm a way of maintaining the worker's incentive to work at a high-productivity level of effort. Assume that the wage path w has the same expected present value as that of VMP at the moment the worker is hired by the firm. Instead of setting the wage equal to VMP at each point of the person's career, the firm pays a wage less than VMP for the first T_0 years and a wage higher than VMP for the worker's remaining tenure, setting the present value of the wage over the worker's career equal to the present value of the worker's marginal product. The advantage of following a wage path like w is that the difference $w - w^*$ can be set to maintain a constant value as the worker's career progresses. Such a wage structure is

[6] Paul Prasow and Edward Peters, *Arbitration and Collective Bargaining: Conflict Resolution in Labor Relations* (New York: McGraw-Hill, 1983).

described as a work-life incentive scheme because it is designed to make the value of retaining the job for the employee higher, thereby creating an incentive for the worker to put forth satisfactory effort.

Two issues arise if the firm tries to follow a wage path like w. First, because the firm has an incentive to renege on the deal by firing a worker once w begins to exceed VMP, the firm must make a credible commitment to living up to the bargain to get workers to buy into the deal. A firm concerned with its reputation and the effect of reputation on its ability to attract good workers has an incentive to live up to its bargain. Several characteristics of internal labor markets—protection of senior workers, promotion from within, and limited ports of entry from the external labor market—could serve the purpose of establishing a formal commitment to the lifetime incentive system. Second, workers on the wage path w no longer have an incentive to retire voluntarily when their $VMP < w^*$. In the absence of compulsory retirement, the firm may have to provide financial inducements to get workers to retire "on time."

The Probation Period

One of the advantages of piece rate pay is that the compensation system provides an incentive for workers to self-select in their applications for employment with the firm. Those workers whose ability or motivation would not allow them to consistently perform along the rising portion of the wage relationship depicted in Figure 11.4 have little incentive to apply for the job. In the work-life incentive scheme, however, workers whose ability or motivation is inconsistent with high-productivity work still have an incentive to apply for a job because the expected present value of w exceeds the expected present value of w^* and because the firm may promise to protect senior workers to make its wage offer credible.

Thus many firms following this approach to incentive may employ **probationary periods** during which newly hired workers are observed closely to determine if their performance is satisfactory and are subject to dismissal if their performance doesn't measure up. It is also common for workers to receive a reduced wage during the probationary period and to get a significant raise upon completion of probation. Such periods serve as the means to screen out low-productivity workers and as the means of establishing the wage below VMP at the beginning of the worker's career. In fact, as we have drawn the curves in Figure 11.5, w may well be set initially below w^* to stimulate the kind of self-selection in applications that the piece rate system engenders.

To illustrate the effect of probationary period pay levels on the decision of a worker to apply for a job, let's consider a simple example. Suppose a worker could always get a job paying $30,000 a year. If he or she expects to work 30 years and if we assume the discount rate is zero, the expected present value of earnings in this job over his or her work life is $900,000. Suppose further that the Acme Manufacturing Company is accepting applications for a high-productivity job that would pay $35,000 a year after an initial one-year probationary period. The expected value of earnings for this worker would equal:

$$PV = \text{Probation Wage} + p(\$35\text{K} \times 29 \text{ years}) + (1 - p)(\$30\text{K} \times 29 \text{ years}) \qquad (11\text{-}5)$$

The critical values affecting a person's decision about applying for this job depend on the wage paid during the probationary period and on the probability (p) that the applicant will make it through the probationary period and retain the high-wage job. If the worker has low ability and motivation, the value of p would be quite low. Let's assume that $p = 0.10$ so that even a worker with low ability and motivation has some small chance of successfully completing the probationary period. In this case, the worker's estimated present value of applying for the high-wage position is:

$$PV = \text{Probation Wage} + \$884{,}500 \tag{11-6}$$

If the probation wage is equal to the wage paid in the low-productivity job, the expected present value of applying for the high-wage job is $914,500. Because this exceeds the present value for the low-wage position, a worker is likely to apply for the high-wage job even if he or she has a very low chance of meeting the requirements for keeping that job. However, a probation wage of $15,499 would make the expected present value of applying for the high-wage job less than the expected present value of the low-wage job for the low-productivity applicant. This should serve to deter low-ability workers from applying for the high-wage job. Such self-selection in applications means that workers with a reasonably high chance of succeeding in a job are induced to apply and those who would like to earn higher wages but are not really capable of doing the job well are deterred from applying. This is very advantageous to the firm because it may be able to avoid some of the costs associated with recruiting and screening job applicants and because it decreases the odds that the firm will lose its training expenses by having to fire someone during the probationary period.

The level of the probationary wage relative to the post-probationary wage needed to motivate self-selection depends on the effectiveness of the screening process. In our example, if the low-ability applicant has a fifty-fifty chance of making it through the probationary period, the worker will always apply for the high-wage job. It also depends on the wage differential between the high- and low-wage positions. If making it through the probationary period wins the person just a small wage increase then a small probationary wage differential should be sufficient to deter applications from low-ability workers.

Bonuses and Merit Pay

The positive slope of the w curve and the widening differential between w and w^* in Figure 11.5 provide an incentive to avoid the potential costs of shirking on the job. A more positive work-life incentive to induce greater effort is to tie the periodic increase in compensation to a performance review. This could be done with bonuses for exceeding objectives in excess of "normal" pay increases or with merit pay increases that provide larger raises for more productive employees. The difference between these alternatives is that bonuses are usually one-time payments whereas merit pay increases the worker's hourly rate or salary for the remainder of the worker's career. Because bonuses are one-time payments, they can be larger than merit pay increases and thereby provide more motivation for employees.

Recent surveys of U.S. businesses indicate rapid growth in bonus-based variable pay plans and a reorientation of such plans away from traditional **merit pay** programs.[7]

---

[7]Alvin M. Konrad and John Deckop, "Human Resource Management Trends in the U.S.A.: Challenges in the Midst of Prosperity," *International Journal of Manpower* 22 (2001): 269–278.

In 1990, 47% of firms surveyed had at least one type of bonus plan compared to 78% of surveyed businesses in 2000. Awarding bonuses, like merit pay decisions, is based on a periodic performance review by management. Increasingly, firms are relying on objective or quantitative performance measures tied to team, unit, or company goals rather than assessment of individual performance based on subjective evaluations by supervisors. These changes address some of the problems with the traditional system: supervisor ratings of worker performance often fail to distinguish outstanding and poor performers, and the link between performance and merit increase is blurred by relatively small wage increments received well after the work period being evaluated. Nonetheless, merit pay increases based on subjective supervisor evaluations still predominate in work-life incentive schemes.

A recent study examined the bonus system in effect at six large UK financial institutions as revealed in a survey conducted in 2003.[8] Indeed there was evidence of a shift from bonus formulas linking pay to objective measures such as new deposits or loans to bonuses based on subjective evaluations of the employee's contribution to good customer service and leadership in achieving operational goals. However, of the 487 managers surveyed, 72% received a formula bonus and just 24% earned a subjective bonus. The use of both types of bonuses was positively correlated with department or branch office net profit per employee.

The shift toward greater use of bonus systems for achievement of group or organizational objectives is interesting because there are several reasons to believe that the incentives for enhanced individual effort from such plans are quite small. First, it may be very difficult for an individual to see a direct link between his or her activities and the achievement of group goals. In addition, there are incentives for individuals to be free riders by reducing their own effort and hoping to benefit from the work of others. Finally, the profit gains must be spread over a number of workers, and it may be difficult for the firm to pay a bonus big enough to elicit increased effort. A key factor seems to be the size of the group and the importance of peer pressure to meet group norms. A recent study of Continental Airlines, for example, found that the promise of a $65 bonus for meeting a company-wide on-time goal was an effective motivating device.[9] The authors of that study speculate that the organization of the company into autonomous work groups enhanced the link between individual behavior and outcomes and limited the opportunity for free riding.

Tournaments and Promotions

Another way for the firm to use lifetime earnings as a motivating device for current behavior is to employ a hierarchy of job levels with opportunities for promotion from within the firm from lower to higher levels. Analysis of this type of incentive system has been labeled **tournament theory**. Tournament theory implies that the pay system of a firm will incorporate three key features:

- The firm offers promotions to better paying jobs as fixed "prizes" in a competition among workers at the next lowest job level.

---

[8] Tahir M. Nisar, "Evaluation of Subjectivity in Incentive Pay," *Journal of Financial Services Research* 31 (2007): 53–73.

[9] Marc Knez and Duncan Simester, "Firm-wide Incentives and Mutual Monitoring at Continental Airlines," *Journal of Labor Economics* 19 (2001): 743–772.

AROUND THE WORLD

The Reward Structure of UK Firms

The Chartered Institute of Personnel and Development (CIPD) conducts an annual survey of UK firms regarding their management of reward systems. The 2011 survey gives some insight into the prevalence of pay for performance plans, long-term compensation programs and management priorities among the 276 responding organizations. Here are a few key findings from that survey:

Rewards for Performance

- Bonuses and incentive pay plans were offered by two-thirds of the responding organizations (90.9% of private sector goods producers and 81.2% of private sector service providers).
- The most commonly used monetary rewards were merit pay raises (56.4% of all organizations) and individual bonuses (53.5%).
- Individual nonmonetary recognition was employed by 29% and group or team recognition awards by 15% of the respondents.
- Fewer than 20% of organizations offered some type of profit or gain sharing plan, 19.6% used sales commissions, and 0.9% had a piece rate pay plan.

Long-term incentives and pensions

- Long-term incentives were part of the pay plan in one-third of the responding organizations (63.6% of private sector goods producers and 41.2% of private sector service providers).
- These included save-as-you-earn programs (33.6% of firms), share incentive plans (31.6%), company share option programs (20%), and executive share options (about 18%).
- Contributory long-term pension plans were offered by 98.9% of responding organizations.

Top five compensation management priorities

- Align pay with business strategy: 58.5% of respondents
- Assure that the reward system is competitive: 41.1%
- Align pay with individual and/or business performance: 40.3%
- Ensure an internally fair-pay system: 35.2%
- Minimize costs: 32.6%

Note: "Reward Management: Annual Survey Report 2011," Chartered Institute of Personnel and Development (http://www.cipd.co.uk).

- The "winner" of this competition is the best worker among those in the competition; relative rather than absolute performance measures are used to make the promotion decision.
- A significant salary increase is needed to stimulate competition for the promotion; the size of the prize increases as the number of competitors rises.

PUTTING THEORY TO WORK

INCENTIVES FOR POOR PERFORMANCE IN SPORTS

Professional sports leagues in the United States are often structured to provide a positive incentive for teams to lose games at the end of the season. If the team has been eliminated from postseason playoffs, it can win by losing if it can gain an advantageous position in the annual draft of college or high school players. So the team management may have an incentive to relax its efforts to motivate team performance in a setting where, by doing so, it gets a top draft pick.

Taylor and Trogdon* examine this incentive to lose in the National Basketball Association, which has tinkered with its draft mechanism to reduce such incentives. They compare team behavior in 1983–84, when order of a team's draft pick was strictly inverse to its winning percentage, with the 1984–85 season, when all the teams not involved in the playoffs had an equal chance of winning the top draft pick in a lottery. They also look at behavior in 1989–90, when the NBA changed its system yet again to give teams with poorer records a slightly greater chance of winning the draft lottery than non–playoff teams with better records.

Controlling for home court and the winning percentages of the two teams entering the game, they measured the effect of being eliminated from the playoffs in each of the three seasons under study on the probability of winning a game. Their results show the following:

- In 1983–84, being eliminated from the playoffs lowered a team's chance of winning by 22%, and playing an eliminated opponent raised the chances of winning by about the same margin.
- In 1984–85, the playoff status of a team or its opponent had no effect on the probability of winning a game.
- In 1989–90, when losing again could enhance draft position, an eliminated team had a 19% lower probability of winning a game, and playing an eliminated opponent raised a team's probability of winning by 25%.

These results clearly suggest that NBA teams responded to incentives to lose once they were eliminated from playoff contention.

Note: *Beck A. Taylor and Justin G. Trogdon, "Losing to Win: Tournament Incentives in the National Basketball Association," *Journal of Labor Economics* 20 (2002): 23–41.

Figure 11.6 illustrates how tournament pay systems would be reflected in the wage profiles of winners and losers. Here are the wage profiles for three workers who were all hired at the same salary after successfully completing a probationary period. Tom never gets promoted, Dick is promoted once, and Harry is promoted three times. All three have salary increases from additional years of experience with the firm, but the discrete jumps in salary associated with promotions mean that the gap between the three workers widens over time. This view of tournament theory suggests the hypothesis that changes in job titles due to promotions would be a main determinant of wage differentials among similar workers within a firm using such an incentive pay system.

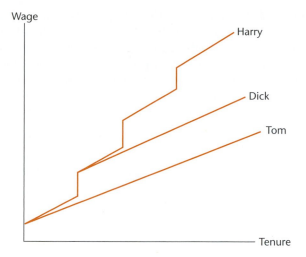

FIGURE 11.6 Promotions and the Wage Profile

The few studies available on intra-firm wage differentials have not been able to reject this hypothesis.[10]

Studies from the sports world support the notion that individual effort is positively related to the size of the winner's prize. Professional golfers register lower scores in tournaments with bigger prizes, and NASCAR drivers appear to drive faster in races with a higher payoff.[11] There is also empirical evidence to suggest that the structure of executive compensation in U.S. firms, in which the level of compensation rises at an increasing rate as one moves up the managerial hierarchy, can be explained as the outcome of the use of tournaments for allocating managers to different jobs. A study of individual managers at the top four managerial levels at more than 600 firms reached the following key conclusions:[12]

- About 80% of such jobs were filled by promotion from within the firm.
- The pay gap between levels rises as the job level increases, after controlling for personal characteristics.
- Pay increases were substantially greater for those promoted to the next highest level than for those staying at the same level.
- Job level and firm can explain almost two-thirds of the compensation differences across managers in the sample.
- An increase in the number of competitors for promotion to CEO is associated with higher CEO compensation and a bigger differential between CEO pay and pay at the next lowest level.

---

[10] George Baker, Michael Gibbs, and Bengt Holmstrom, "The Wage Policy of a Firm," *Quarterly Journal of Economics* 109 (1994): 921–955.

[11] Ron Ehrenberg and Michael Bognano, "The Incentive Effects of Tournaments Revisited: Evidence from the European PGA Tour," *Industrial and Labor Relations Review* 43 (1990): 74–89; Brian Becker and Mark Huselid, "The Incentive Effects of Tournament Compensation Systems," *Administrative Science Quarterly* 37 (1992): 336–350.

[12] Michael L. Bognano, "Corporate Tournaments," *Journal of Labor Research* 19 (2001): 290–315.

Conclusions consistent with the predictions of tournament theory also can be found in a study of absenteeism (as a measure of effort) derived from personnel records of 998 workers in a major UK financial firm.[13] The results show that absence rates fell (effort increased) as the size of the wage increase received when promoted to the next job level increased and that absences were reduced (effort increased) when the role of luck in winning a promotion was minimized.

Tournaments are similar to merit pay systems in that salary adjustments reflect individual performance as assessed by supervisors on a relative basis—comparing workers with each other rather than with an absolute standard for high performance. Tournaments have a couple of advantages for the firm. They provide the firm with the means of making a credible commitment to its promise of rewarding high-productivity workers by formally setting the prizes for such performance in advance. Merit pay or bonus systems are based on implicit contracts that invite the firm to renege on such a promise. Tournaments force managers to identify the top performer among a group of workers rather than opting for a less troublesome merit rating that fails to clearly distinguish between the best and worst performers. And tournaments clearly establish a positive relationship between higher pay and greater responsibility by linking big increases to changes in job titles.

Jed DeVaro has examined the importance of relative performance ratings using matched data on workers and establishments in Atlanta, Boston, Detroit and Los Angeles from 1992 to 1995.[14] He finds that the probability of promotion for recently hired workers was positively related to their own performance ratings and negatively correlated with the performance ratings of their peers. This suggests that indeed relative performance determined promotion chances in his sample. He also shows that effort, measured by the individual's performance rating, increased with the size of the promotion wage increase and fell as luck became more important in determining the tournament winner. So firms tended to increase the prize spread in situations where worker performance was heavily influenced by factors other than the individual's effort on the job. These results suggest that tournament theory provides significant insight into the behavior of firms in setting up promotion schemes and of workers in their response to promotion schemes.

The use of relative performance evaluations in merit pay and tournaments has the advantage of automatically removing from the evaluation system common factors (such as the state of the economy) that affect individual performance but are unrelated to worker effort. It also makes it more difficult for the firm to say that no one deserves a raise or promotion. Two problems with relative evaluations are that individuals have an incentive to devote effort to currying favor with their supervisors and that they have little incentive to work cooperatively with others. In fact, the prizes associated with winning a tournament may give workers the incentive to sabotage the efforts of others.

Because compensation gains are based on a relative ranking of competitors in promotion tournaments, the cardinal link between individual performance and pay seen in a piece rate system is broken in the tournament model. For example, the high pay of corporate CEOs can be regarded not so much as a reward for the high productivity or unusual

---

[13] Rick Audas, Tim Barmby and Jon Treble, "Luck, Effort, and Reward in an Organizational Hierarchy," *Journal of Labor Economics* 22 (2004): 379–395.

[14] Jed deVaro, "Internal Promotion Competitions in Firms," *RAND Journal of Economics* 37 (2006): 521–542.

effort of the person currently filling that position but rather as the incentive necessary to get managers further down the corporate ladder to strive to be promoted in the future.

A difficulty with the tournament model is that individuals who believe that they are less able than others competing for the same prize may give up and supply minimal effort because they see a low probability of winning. Some attention then has been paid to the effects of various prize structures on effort exerted in a tournament setting. However, since it is difficult to get real-world business firm data that would allow clear tests of the incentive impact of alternative promotion structures, much of the empirical evidence on tournament prize structures has been derived from experiments. Economists are paying increasing attention to the results obtained from the behavior of individuals in highly structured laboratory settings because only in such settings can we observe behavioral responses to clearly different institutional designs. So let's look at a couple of studies using experiments to test for tournament design effects.

Christine Harbring and Bernd Irlenbusch describe a tournament design experiment in which 216 students at the University of Bonn made effort choices in tournament settings in which the structure of prizes was altered systematically.[15] Over 20 rounds, each student selected an effort level knowing the monetary payoff matrix of choices, which reflected both a rising cost of effort and the potential effort decisions of other competitors. They find that chosen effort levels were higher in tournaments with a larger number of winners. For example, in tournaments with six competitors and two winners, the average effort was 63.3 and 38.6% of the students opted for zero effort. With six competitors and four winners the average effort level rose to 79.2 and the percentage of students with zero effort fell to 30.1%. More winners mean greater chances of winning for less able competitors, and so there is greater incentive for them to exert effort and compete.

Richard Freeman and Alexander Gelber report on an experiment designed to capture the effect of both prize structure and knowledge of one's relative ability on a person's effort.[16] Effort in this experiment was measured by output in the form of maze puzzles completed by 468 subjects at Harvard University in six-person groups in two rounds. In the first round, participants received a piece rate payment for each puzzle solved. In the second round, half of the subjects were given full information about the first round performance of each member of their group, the other half had no such information, and all groups faced one of three prize structures: an equal payout of $5 for each competitor, a single prize of $30 for the one with the most puzzles solved, and $30 divided into multiple prizes ranging from $15 to $1 depending on the number of puzzles completed.

Freeman and Gelber find that output was affected by the prize structure and information about relative ability. For those with no information about relative performance in round one, the tournaments with a single prize or multiple unequal prizes elicited the highest mean performance of 16.5 puzzles. Interestingly, mean performance was about the same (around 12 puzzles) for the piece rate performance in round one and the equal pay structure in round two. For those with information on round one performance of group members, mean output was 18.6 puzzles in the multiple prize tournaments versus

[15] Christine Harbring and Bernd Irlenbusch, "An Experimental Study on Tournament Design," *Labour Economics* 10 (2003): 443–464.

[16] Richard B. Freeman and Alexander M. Gelber, "Prize Structure and Information in Tournaments: Experimental Evidence," *American Economic Journal: Applied Economics* 2 (2010): 149–164.

16.2 in the single prize case, mainly due to higher output by those with the poorest round one performance. The mean number of puzzles solved was 15.5 in the equal pay case. In this experiment, tournaments appear to have had greater incentive effects than equal pay or piece rates, and multiple prize tournaments seemed able to elicit increased effort from workers who were not likely to produce the highest output level.

Fringe Benefits

Nonwage benefits such as health or life insurance, retirement pensions, and vacation time can also be used to enhance the work-life incentives for good performance. The value of these **fringe benefits** generally rises with tenure, thus increasing the future payoff to young workers for putting in sufficient effort to ensure longevity with the firm. The positive relationship between the value of health insurance coverage and tenure reflects the increased likelihood of encountering a serious medical problem as workers age.[17] Time off from work for rest and recreation might also be expected to have a higher value to older workers. And vesting and age requirements for pension plans mean that this portion of compensation is meaningful only for those workers with relatively long tenure with the firm.

Because these forms of compensation add to the value of the job for experienced workers, they provide the kind of lifetime effort incentive depicted in Figure 11.5. In addition, there are tax and regulatory advantages to both the firm and the employee for nonwage forms of compensation,[18] making these benefits less costly than direct wage payments and accounting for much of their use in pay systems.

Table 11.1 presents some comparative information on the relative importance of direct wage payments in the hourly compensation of production workers in manufacturing firms. This group of workers is a small minority of all employees, and the data for these workers may not be representative of the situation of all workers. Even so, these data reveal an interesting perspective on fringe benefit trends in different countries. The difference between 100% and the figures reported in Table 11.1 is the percentage of compensation accounted for by employer spending on legally required insurance programs and on contractual and private benefit plans. In Australia, Canada, the United States, and the United Kingdom, such benefits accounted for more than 30% of compensation in 2009, whereas in France, Germany, Japan, they accounted for more than 40% of compensation. There is a general downward trend in the relative importance of direct wage payments in manufacturing compensation over the last four decades.

One issue regarding fringe benefits and work-life incentive schemes that has received some attention is the question of disincentives for optimal retirement. If we return to Figure 11.5, the optimal retirement age for this worker is at tenure level T_2, where the marginal benefit of w^*, which at this point is the value of leisure rather than pay in an alternative job, is greater than the value of the marginal product of the worker. If pay followed VMP over the worker's tenure, the worker would voluntarily retire at tenure T_2.

---

[17] Employer-provided health insurance plans are a particularly important fringe benefit in the United States. This is not an important benefit in countries with comprehensive national health plans covering all citizens.

[18] Interesting examples of regulatory effects are the widespread use of company cars by white-collar workers in the United Kingdom during the 1970s and the initial adoption of employer provided health insurance in the United States during the late 1940s when in both situations wage and price controls limited the size of allowable salary increases.

TABLE 11.1   Hourly Pay for Time Worked as a Percentage of Hourly Compensation for Production Workers in Manufacturing

Country	1979	1989	1999	2009
Australia	75.20	75.47	72.97	69.60
Canada	77.97	76.17	73.39	69.23
France	58.68	53.67	54.74	56.33
Germany	60.51	57.89	59.01	57.82
Japan	58.75	58.10	58.26	58.92
Singapore	66.32	67.06	68.08	66.55
Sweden	62,72	59.28	60.04	59.79
UK	73.37	74.16	67.57	68.68
US	74.25	73.40	72.97	69.60

Source: US Dept. of Labor, Bureau of Labor Statistics. http://www.bls.gov/web/ichcc.supp.toc.htm#prod_worker

However, if the wage profile is w instead of VMP for work-life incentive reasons, the worker has an incentive to remain on the job for some time after reaching tenure of T_2 years.

In the absence of a mandatory retirement age, the firm could structure a pension plan to induce retirement at the optimal tenure. A defined benefit pension, which pays a specified retirement pension, usually defined as a fraction of the person's pay just before retirement, can be structured to provide an incentive for the worker to choose retirement at the optimal age. Because payments from a defined benefit pension last only until the worker's (or the worker's spouse's) death, the longer the worker stays on the job the less valuable is the total amount of pension income the worker can expect to earn. A defined contribution pension fund, which works like a mutual fund or savings account, doesn't have this retirement incentive. Workers can continue to accumulate pension wealth as long as they work, and this type of account can be passed on to the workers' heirs. Interestingly, many U.S. companies have switched their pension plans from defined benefit plans to defined contribution schemes in recent years. Apparently, the financial benefits from doing so outweigh the retirement incentives in these cases.

Behavioral Economics

The piece rate and work-life incentive models are equilibrium models of wage determination. In each case, the employer attempts to set wages, or their expected present value, equal to the value of the worker's marginal product, or its expected present value; and the employee determines the quantity of labor effort by weighing the wage versus the marginal utility of effort. In this sense, the analysis of labor market decisions is fully consistent with neoclassical microeconomic theory, and the wage set by the firm can be regarded as a market-clearing wage, even though firms faced with different monitoring costs and production technologies may develop quite different pay structures.

An alternative view with clear implications for managers interested in getting the most out of their workers is provided by **behavioral economics**. Behavioral economics draws on research largely drawn from experimental studies in psychology to develop an understanding of motives for behavior beyond the model of rational utility and profit maximizing behavior. In particular, the results of these experiments indicate that people care enough about fair outcomes to take on costs needed to avoid inequity; are motivated by strong feelings of reciprocity; are highly responsive to peer influence, emotions, and regard for personal respect in making economic decisions; and use simple heuristics rather than collecting and processing detailed information to work through problems.[19]

The effects on wage-setting behavior are revealed by numerous replications of the simple ultimatum game experiment, in which one participant proposes a division of a given amount between another participant and herself. The other participant can reject the offer, in which case both receive nothing. Rational analysis would suggest offering a token amount, thereby maximizing one's return, in the expectation that the other rational party would prefer to get a little rather than nothing at all. But in most such games the median offer is typical for an even division of the spoils of the game.[20] Employers motivated by the strong norms of fairness evident in these experiments could choose to pay a "fair" wage higher than the market clearing wage.

Other experimental research suggests that paying a higher wage would elicit a positive reciprocal response in terms of greater worker effort in what has come to be called the "gift exchange" model of the labor market.[21] Evidence for such a reciprocal response can be found in the results of gift exchange experiments, where a player acting as an employer offers a wage and another employer decides on the effort level he or she will provide, given the cost of effort, at various wage levels. One recent study reports on results of experiments designed to mimic an organization with several employees.[22] Instead of a purely rational response on the part of "workers" (offering a minimum level of effort regardless of the wage) participants in these experiments generally offered greater effort in return for a higher wage offer.

Instead of a laboratory experiment, Uri Gneezt and John List carried out a field experiment.[23] Students were actually recruited for two different one-day jobs in which their effort could be measured by their output. Half of the students hired for each job were told that their wage would be substantially higher than advertised when they reported for their day of work. In response, those workers who received the higher wage "gift" had significantly higher output at the beginning of the work day and for the first few hours of work. However, performance at the end of the day by those with the higher wage was similar to that recorded by the lower wage earners. Still, these findings suggest some validity to the gift exchange model in a more realistic experimental setting.

---

[19] Uschi Backes-Gellner, Donata Bessey, Kerstin Pull, and Simone Tuor, "What Behavioural Economics Teaches Personnel Economics," Working Paper No. 77, Institute for Strategy and Business Economics, University of Zurich, February 2008. Electronic copy at: http://ssrn.com/abstract=1092826.

[20] Colin Camerer and Richard H. Thaler, "Anomalies: Ultimatums, Dictators and Manners," *Journal of Economic Perspectives* 9 (1995): 209–219.

[21] George Akerlof and Janet L. Yellen, "Fair Wage-Effort Hypothesis and Unemployment," *Quarterly Journal of Economics* 105 (1990): 255–282.

[22] Sandra Maximiano, Randolph Sloof, and Joep Sonnemans, "Gift Exchange in a Multi-Worker Firm," *The Economic Journal* 117 (2007): 1025–1050.

[23] Uri Gneezy and John A. List, "Putting Behavioral Economics to Work: Testing for Gift Exchange in Labor Markets Using Field Experiments," *Econometrica* 74 (2006): 1365–1384.

Summary

The analysis of labor issues in modern industrial economies has always featured tension between market and institutional explanations for wage and employment outcomes. Market explanations emphasize the forces of supply and demand and their equilibrating interaction. Institutional explanations look to the labor market consequences of legal rights and restrictions, trade union actions, psychological and sociological factors, and human resource management policies of firms.[24] We have observed many of the institutions common to labor markets even in an economy with rational firms, unrestricted by laws or collective bargaining contracts.

Whether the firm follows a wage policy to provide incentives for maximum worker effort and self-selection by job applicants or to protect investments in establishing an employment relationship, it may be optimal for a firm to design a policy that insulates its wages somewhat from market forces and that provides different work-life incentives for its employees. Institutions such as job hierarchies, promotion from within, rewards to seniority, wage and employment security, and the array of activities associated with human resource departments could well be optimal responses to labor turnover costs, asymmetric information about skills and effort, and high costs of monitoring worker diligence.

One result of this is the notion that the firm may be a wage setter rather than a wage taker and that the law of one price is not likely to apply to a relatively homogeneous group of workers hired by different firms with different product market and production process characteristics. Another result is that the wage distribution across individuals is influenced by more than the human capital of workers and compensating differentials for job or area characteristics. Thus we should not be surprised by empirical wage studies in which firm, industry, and occupation have explanatory power. Finally, the fact that the firm may set its wage policy to achieve objectives other than the efficient allocation of labor might well mean that market forces will influence the wage structure only after a long period of adjustment.

KEY TERMS

effort
principal-agent problem
shirk
piece rate system
performance bonds
residual claimant
work-life incentives

probationary periods
merit pay
tournament theory
fringe benefits
behavioral economics
gift exchange

---

[24] See, for example, Bruce E. Kaufman, *The Origins and Evolution of the Field of Industrial Relations in the United States* (Ithaca, NY: ILR Press, 1993).

PROBLEMS

1. Think of this course as a job where your effort combined with this textbook and your instructor's guidance yields an output level equal to your enhanced knowledge of labor economics. Analyze how your effort affects this output. Assuming your parents or guardians are the principals and you are the agent in achieving learning, discuss how your interests can vary from theirs.

2. How does the structure of rewards (grades and credits) in this course provide an incentive for you to work harder? By comparison, if everyone knew they would receive the same grade in this course, what would happen to effort and learning? And if everyone knew that the student with the best grade would get an A and everyone else a C, what would happen to effort and learning?

3. In Figure 11.1, what factors would affect the slope of the indifference curve for an individual? Why wouldn't a worker always opt for zero effort at the fixed wage?

4. Evaluate equation 11-1 for two firms. At the Acme Company the value of α is 0.95 and v is either 0.10, 0, or -0.10 with equal probability for each outcome. At the Ajax Company the value of α is 0.50 and v is either 1.0, 0, or -1.0 with equal probability for each outcome. Which of these firms is less likely to employ a piece rate pay system? Why?

5. Why is the commission on sales usually a high fraction of compensation for traveling sales representatives who call on clients and a small fraction for sales clerks who wait on walk-in clients?

6. Carefully explain why the incentive to shirk might increase as a worker's tenure with the firm lengthens.

7. Does equation 11-4 help to explain why labor economists often find that wages are higher in larger firms, even after controlling for other wage determinants?

8. Using the information in equation 11-5, calculate the level of the probationary wage if the annual post-probationary wage at Acme Manufacturing Company was $31,000 a year and the other variables remained unchanged.

9. Assume you are a participant in an ultimatum game in which you could propose a division of $10 between you and an anonymous participant, who in turn could accept or reject your offer. If he or she rejects your offer you both get nothing. How much of the $10 would you offer to the other person?

10. Assume in your job you could choose a daily effort level ranging from 1 to 5. Assume that increasing your effort from one level has a marginal effort cost of $5. How much effort would you choose to offer if your employer paid you the going rate of $100 a day? How much would you choose if the employer instead offered $150 a day?

12

Unions and Collective Bargaining

Why do unions grow, and why do they decline?

Are there economic determinants of union growth?

What do unions seek to do? Can we model union goals and behavior?

What effects have unions had on the wages of both their members and nonunion workers and on employment, employee benefits, and the productivity of the firms with which they deal?

Wages and employment in labor markets are influenced by the market forces of supply and demand but also, to a large degree, by institutions operating in the marketplace. One very important institution is unionism. Unionism and collective bargaining are complex subjects, and there are many different approaches to studying them: from a legal perspective (What does the law allow unions to do?), a management perspective (How do unions affect operations in the workplace?), or a historical perspective (Why did unions come into being?). In this chapter we look at unionism from an economics perspective, leaving topics such as the law and the mechanics of collective bargaining to others.

A Profile of Unionism in the United States

In 2011 approximately 14.8 million wage and salary workers in the United States were union members. As a percentage of the labor force, this figure amounts to only 11.8%, a statistic economists refer to as the **union density**. In fact, union density has been declining rather steadily in the United States in the past several decades, as Table 12.1 shows. Some qualifications are in order, however. The table shows union members as a percentage of the total labor force, which includes the self-employed and employers, managers, and supervisors (who are generally not allowed to join unions). Removing these two groups would raise union density, although not the declining trend, by several percentage points.

These data also include (after 1960) members of certain employee associations that share some characteristics of unions but are not always involved in collective bargaining activity. Among these groups are the American Association of University Professors (AAUP), the

TABLE 12.1 Recent U.S. Union Membership Trends

Year	Union Membership* (in millions)	Percentage of Labor Force
1960	17.0	23.6%
1970	21.2	25.7
1980	22.4	20.9
1982	19.8	17.9
1984	19.8	16.0
1986	17.0	14.8
1988	17.0	14.0
1990	16.7	13.4
1992	16.4	12.9
1994	16.7	12.7
1996	16.3	12.2
1998	16.2	11.8
2000	16.3	11.4
2002	16.1	11.1
2004	15.4	10.4
2006	15.4	10.2
2008	16.1	10.4
2010	14.7	9.6
2011	14.8	9.6

Note: *These numbers include employee associations.
Source: U.S. Department of Labor, Bureau of Labor Statistics.

Fraternal Order of Police (FOP), and the American Nurses Association (ANA). At one time these groups were professional associations exclusively and were not part of the organized labor movement. Over time, however, they have become more actively involved in furthering the economic well-being of their members. Another such group, the National Education Association (NEA), is perhaps the best (and the biggest) example of such an organization, and despite its name and history, the NEA has transformed itself into a union of teachers.

Finally, these data do not include workers who are represented by a union—whose jobs are covered by a union contract—but who themselves are not union members. This group consisted of about 1.5 million workers in 2011.

Even though union density in the United States is low and has been falling, unions remain a very important force in the labor market. In fact, the degree of power and influence that unions exercise is disproportionate to their density figure in several respects. First of all, union membership is concentrated in key sectors of the economy, including autos, transportation, communications, and the public sector. These are industries with large employers who have some measure of monopoly power in the product market. These employers are likely to be making surpluses that the unions can try to capture in the form of wage increases for their members.

Second, unions sometimes bargain not just for their own members but also for any nonunion members they may represent. In other words, the collective bargaining *coverage rate* can exceed the union density rate. After winning a representation election, unions usually try to require that all workers in the bargaining unit join the union (an arrangement called a "union shop") or at least pay the equivalent of union dues (called an "agency shop"), but laws in 23 states and in many other countries make such requirements illegal. These are called **right-to-work laws**, although the term "right to work" is a misnomer. Such laws give no one the "right" to work.

Finally, nonunionized employers sometimes follow the lead of unions by paying their own workers union wage rates. Why would employers do this? One reason is to keep their workers sufficiently satisfied so that they will have no interest in unionizing, thereby possibly also warding off any union that might be thinking about organizing their workers. This tendency to match union pay scales is called the "threat effect," and we will discuss it later in the chapter.

Interestingly, despite the fact that unionism has been around a long time (as far back as the late 1700s in the United States and even earlier in many other countries), it has only been in the last three generations that unions have continuously represented a substantial number of workers in the United States. In fact, it wasn't until the 1930s that union growth really began to take off. Why did it take so long? A tempting answer might be that the Great Depression caused union growth in the United States to rise rapidly. After all, isn't it when times are bad that people need unionism the most? And times certainly were bad in the 1930s, with unemployment rates in some cities reaching levels as high as 25%. But the fact of the matter is that historically union membership has *declined* in times of recession and depression and has *risen* in times of prosperity. In other words, union density has tended to be positively correlated with the business cycle. In boom times jobs are plentiful, labor is in short supply, and employer resistance to unions and their demands is likely to be weak. In economically depressed times, on the other hand, when labor is abundant, employers are more likely to resist union demands and union attempts to organize.

Legislation and Labor Union Growth

If it wasn't the Great Depression itself, just what happened in the 1930s to stimulate union growth in the United States? One important factor was the passage of favorable labor legislation. Before the 1930s there was no comprehensive legislation at the federal level that guaranteed and protected the right of workers to organize themselves into unions and bargain collectively.

The Norris-LaGuardia Act of 1932 severely limited the use of court injunctions against striking workers. The act also outlawed so-called yellow dog contracts, agreements employees were forced to sign stating that they never would join a union under the penalty of being fired. By removing two very effective anti-union tactics, the Norris-LaGuardia Act helped pave the way for subsequent union growth.

The other important piece of legislation was the **National Labor Relations Act** of 1935, usually referred to as the Wagner Act. The Wagner Act contained several important provisions:

- It gave most workers in the private sector the right to elect their own bargaining representatives.
- It declared that employers were bound by law to recognize and bargain with the legally elected bargaining representatives of workers.
- It prohibited certain practices by employers that would interfere with workers' rights under the act, such as restraining, coercing, or discriminating against employees in their exercise of legitimate union activities, assisting or dominating a labor organization, or refusing to recognize or bargain with the legally certified bargaining representative.

TABLE 12.2   Union Membership in the United States Prior to 1960, Selected Years

Year	Union Membership (in millions)	Percentage of Labor Force
1930	3	6
1935	3	6
1940	9	16
1945	14	21
1950	14	22
1955	17	25

Source: U.S. Department of Labor, Bureau of Labor Statistics.

Furthermore, the act set up a federal agency—the National Labor Relations Board—to enforce the provisions of the act. Simply put, the National Labor Relations Act was the strongest piece of pro-union legislation ever enacted in the United States. It became public policy to foster and encourage the growth of labor unionism, and by 1935 union membership began to experience a growth surge unparalleled in the history of the United States (see Table 12.2).

It is important to note two additional pieces of federal labor legislation subsequent to the Wagner Act that attempted to restrict union power. The Labor-Management Relations Act of 1947 (usually called the Taft-Hartley Act) was passed in response to a rash of post–World War II strikes and a widespread feeling that restrictions on some union activities were in order. In addition to permitting states to pass right-to-work laws, the Taft-Hartley Act also banned a number of "unfair union practices," such as coercing workers who do not want to join unions to do so, refusing to bargain collectively with an employer, and forcing an employer to pay for work not performed (sometimes called "featherbedding"). We analyze featherbedding further along in this chapter. Still later, the Labor-Management Reporting and Disclosure Act of 1959 (the Landrum-Griffin Act) was passed, largely as a result of widely publicized congressional hearings on corruption and the abuse of power in several unions (e.g., the Teamsters). The Landrum-Griffin Act contained provisions to protect the rights of union members by providing for periodic free elections of union officers, free speech, and reporting of union finances.

But what can explain the decline of unionism over the most recent five decades? Although there has been no new significant federal labor legislation since the Landrum-Griffin Act, a number of other factors have been at work here:

- The fraction of the labor force that is female has increased greatly in recent decades as we reported in earlier chapters, and women have historically been less likely than men to become union members. However, the gap between male and female union membership rates has narrowed considerably in recent years.
- Many industries that have traditionally been highly unionized have declined (either relatively or absolutely) in recent decades. Among the industries affected are manufacturing, mining, and construction.
- Regional shifts in population and employment, probably the most important being the movement of firms and workers from the Northeast and Midwest to

the sunbelt states, have occurred. And union density in most of these states (especially the southeastern states) has long been substantially lower than in the Northeast and Midwest. Right-to-work laws that prohibit the union shop, the agency shop, and other forms of "union security" are largely concentrated in the southern states and, among other things, signify a much less favorable climate for unions to operate in.[1]

These three structural changes together may explain perhaps half of the decline in overall union density in the United States over the last several decades, according to many economists.

Some economists offer still other reasons for the decline, arguing that many U.S. employers have become increasingly hostile to unions in recent years and have adopted more aggressive tactics to keep them out of the workplace. Employers are limited by law in what they may do to counter union organizing attempts. For example, employers can legally present arguments to employees stating why they feel that their workers should vote against union representation. But employers may not legally promise to grant higher wage increases if workers vote against unionizing or threaten to cut back on wages if workers do vote to unionize. In addition, employers may not discriminate against workers involved in unionizing efforts. All of these are "unfair labor practices" under the Wagner Act. In the event of their occurrence, unions may file an unfair labor practice charge with the National Labor Relations Board (NLRB), which may issue a "cease and desist" order against the employer.

On the other hand, some say that the more hostile management behavior toward unionism may not so much reflect a change in managerial ideology as simply a desire to keep labor costs under control in an age of increased competition in the global marketplace. In recent years, many employers (especially large ones) have introduced a series of policies called high performance work systems (HPWS). These include extensive use of sophisticated hiring practices and training of the incumbent work force. HPWS also entails planning the career paths of employees to ensure that when a worker leaves the firm there will be someone with the skills to step into the missing person's shoes. Workers may be monitored on a regular basis to ensure that their motivation and application remain at satisfactory levels. And if a problem is identified with any worker, remedial action is taken. In the early stages at least, this might take the form of a chat with a line manager to establish the source of the problem. The worker and the manager then cooperate to find a means of working around the problem. HPWS has a "caring face," and the firm is seen to be making an investment in the attitude of its work force. Indeed, the whole ethos of HPWS is one of cooperation, with labor and management working together in the pursuit of a common set of goals.

The HPWS approach is interesting to economists for a number of reasons. First, it represents an attempt by firms to solve a principal-agent problem within the organization. Recall that principal-agent problems occur when management (the principal) has one set of goals (making profits, perhaps) and the agent (the worker) has another (say, exerting

---

[1] The list of right-to-work states includes Alabama, Arizona, Arkansas, Florida, Georgia, Idaho, Indiana, Iowa, Kansas, Louisiana, Mississippi, Nebraska, Nevada, North Carolina, North Dakota, Oklahoma, South Carolina, South Dakota, Tennessee, Texas, Utah, Virginia, and Wyoming.

little effort).[2] The second reason HPWS is interesting is because, despite its caring face, HPWS has an ethos that is in direct competition to the ethos of trade unions. It builds on the perception that workers are stakeholders in their firms and encourages workers to align their own personal goals with those of the company for which they work. It may well be that firms have adopted these HPWS strategies to undermine unions where they exist or to preempt them where they do not.

The adoption of HPWS policies by firms may therefore be further evidence of a hostile management attitude toward unionism. The end result is that workers end up being "cared for" by the firm rather than by the union. This may, coincidentally, be in the interests of both the firm and the worker, but HPWS is initiated by the firm and primarily serves the interests of the firm.

Still other explanations have been offered for the decline in union density in the U.S. Union organizing efforts, for example, have fallen off in recent years. In fact, the number of NLRB union representation elections held each year dropped from 2,645 in 2001 to 1,571 in 2010.[3] (Before 1980 the number of NLRB elections was more than 6,000 per year.)[4] And Farber and Western found that most of the decline in union membership over the period 1973–98 was due to declining employment in unionized firms compared to rising employment in nonunion workplaces.[5] All in all, as our discussion above indicates, there is disagreement among economists over just which factors have been primarily responsible for the long-term decline in the private sector union membership rate in the United States.

Unions in the Public Sector

So far, our discussion concerning union growth and decline and the factors responsible has pertained mostly to unions in the private sector of the economy. But since about 1960, unions have made great inroads in organizing workers employed by the local, state, or federal levels of government. In fact, had it not been for this new organizational beachhead, the decline in union density in the United States observed since about 1970 would have been considerably greater.

Let's look at some numbers. From about 1960 to the mid-1970s, the growth in public sector union membership in the United States was explosive, with membership rising from 900,000 to more than 6 million. In 1977 union density in the public sector (i.e., union membership as a percentage of public employment) was 32.7%. Since then the rate of growth has leveled off. In 2011, 37.0% of public sector workers at all three levels of government combined (federal, state, and local) were union members.[6]

---

[2] The task of the principal is to design an incentive system that will encourage the agent to act in such a way that the principal's goals are met. In the context of HPWS, this means that management will ensure that monitoring of workers is thorough and that workers are incentivized through well-defined promotion structures, bonus pay schemes, and representation in the company's decision making to behave in a manner that is in the firm's best interests.

[3] National Labor Relations Board, Representation Elections, http://www.nlrb.gov/graphs-data

[4] Jack Fiorito, "The State of Unions in the United States," *Journal of Labor Research*, 28 (1) (Winter 2007): 44–68.

[5] Henry Farber and Bruce Western, "Accounting for the Decline in Unions in the Private Sector, 1973–1998," *Journal of Labor Research*, 22 (3) (Summer 2001): 459–485.

[6] U.S. Department of Labor, Bureau of Labor Statistics, "Union Members Summary," January 27, 2012, USDL-12-0094.

THE WAY WE WORK

Name That Union!

When studying the organized labor movement in the United States, students are often bewildered by the large number of acronyms used to denote various labor unions. Here is a list of acronyms representing some well-known unions. See if you can guess which union belongs with each acronym. In their full titles you will also see that few unions today are homogeneous when it comes to the types of workers included in their ranks. Careful: we have thrown in a couple of "ringer" acronyms that have nothing to do with the U.S. labor movement.

1. IBT	9. RJT
2. AFSCME	10. SEIU
3. UAW	11. UMW
4. USWA	12. ALPO
5. IBID	13. IAFF
6. FOP	14. IBEW
7. NEA	15. CWA
8. AFT	16. LIU

Answers: 1. International Brotherhood of Teamsters, Chauffeurs, Warehousemen, and Helpers; 2. American Federation of State, County, and Municipal Employees; 3. United Automobile, Aerospace and Agricultural Implement Workers of America; 4. United Steelworkers of America; 5. Abbreviation for *ibidem* (the same place), sometimes used in footnotes; 6. Fraternal Order of Police; 7. National Education Association; 8. American Federation of Teachers; 9. The initials of one of the authors of this textbook; 10. Service Employees International Union; 11. United Mineworkers of America; 12. A dog food (but very close to ALPA, the Air Line Pilots Association); 13. International Association of Fire Fighters; 14. International Brotherhood of Electrical Workers; 15. Communications Workers of America; 16. Laborers International Union

Although unions of public employees in the United States are not a new phenomenon, their growth before 1960 was unremarkable due in large part to the fact that government employers generally resisted demands for collective bargaining. Such resistance was possible because public employees at any level (local, state, or federal) did not generally have legal rights to bargain collectively until after 1960. Government employees were specifically excluded from the National Labor Relations Act of 1935. Consequently, unions of state and local government employees have had to depend on state laws, executive orders, or other means to participate in collective bargaining.

In 1959 Wisconsin became the first state to grant collective bargaining rights to employees of local government. A surge of legislation in other states soon followed, and as a consequence about three dozen states now grant bargaining rights to at least some groups of public employees over wages, hours, and other working conditions. Some states (e.g., Hawaii) do not allow bargaining over health and retirement benefits. Several other states have passed laws requiring public employers to simply "meet and confer" with their employee unions. Meet and confer statutes typically require only that the public employer give their employee unions the opportunity to comment on proposed actions regarding terms and conditions of employment. In only two states (North Carolina and Virginia) is collective bargaining between public employers and labor organizations explicitly prohibited.[7] It is important to note, however, that strikes by public employee unions are for the most part banned. Only about 12 states either by statute or by court decision permit certain groups of public employees to strike (never public safety employees such as police and firefighters), and usually only under certain conditions.

One of the most striking recent developments in the field of public sector bargaining has been the movement to cut back on, or even eliminate, public employee bargaining rights. No state has received more attention on this front than Wisconsin—ironically the first state to grant state and local public employees bargaining rights back in 1959. In 2011, the Wisconsin legislature passed a law that eliminated collective bargaining rights for some workers (e.g., employees of the University of Wisconsin) and limited collective bargaining to wage increases no greater than changes in the Consumer Price Index. Other states, such as Ohio, Michigan, Indiana, and Oklahoma have also passed bills limiting collective bargaining for public sector employees.[8]

Unionism in Other Countries

How does the experience of unionism in the United States compare with that of other countries? Although it is impossible to provide more than a thumbnail sketch here, there are many interesting differences (as well as some similarities) among unions around the world.

The breadth of unionism is shown in Table 12.3 (column 3), and there is a tremendous range in union density rates across countries. With a union density rate of about 10%, the United States clearly ranks near the bottom compared to most other countries.[9] Although some other countries have experienced substantial density declines in recent decades (e.g., Japan, France, and the United Kingdom), in some other countries union density has either remained stable or increased (e.g., Denmark, Spain, and Norway).[10] This indicates that increasing globalization, one reason commonly offered to explain the density decline in the United States, may not be that important a factor after all.

Another interesting observation from the data in Table 12.3 is that collective bargaining coverage rates in many countries are sometimes much higher than union density

---

[7] Jon O. Shimabukuru, "Collective Bargaining and Employees in the Public Sector," Congressional Research Service, *CRS Report for Congress*, March 30, 2011, pp. 1–7.

[8] Joseph Slater, "The Assault on Public Sector Collective Bargaining: Real Harms and Imaginary Benefits," American Constitution Society, Issue Briefs, June 2011, 1–18.

[9] The density rates for the United States in Tables 12.1 and 12.2 show union membership as a percentage of the entire labor force whereas the data for the countries in Table 12.3 mostly show membership as a percentage of wage and salary earners. Dividing U.S. union memberships by the number of wage and salary workers would raise the U.S. density rate by about two percentage points.

[10] See David Blanchflower and Richard Freeman, "Unionism in the U.S. and Other Countries," *Industrial Relations* (1996): 31. Also, see David Blanchflower, "The Role and Influence of Trade Unions in the OECD," Bureau of International Labor Affairs, U.S. Department of Labor, available at http://www.dartmouth.edu/nblnchflr/papers/UnionsOECD.

TABLE 12.3   Union Density and Collective Bargaining Coverage Rates, Selected Countries

	Year	Union Density* (%)	Year	Collective Bargaining Coverage Rate (%)
Americas				
Argentina	2006	37.6%*	2006	60.0%*
Bolivia	2006	26.6	–	–
Brazil	2007	17.8	2006	60.0*
Canada	2007	26.6	2007	29.3*
Chile	2007	13.6	2007	6.5
Cuba	2008	70.6	2008	67.7
Mexico	2008	11.2	2007	6.9
United States	2007	10.7	2007	11.8
Uruguay	2006	13.3	–	–
Europe				
Austria	2008	23.6	–	–
Czech Republic	2006	17.3	–	–
Denmark	2008	71.5	2006	95.6
France	2005	7.9	–	–
Germany	2007	17.5	2006	35.1
Greece	2007	19.6	–	–
Hungary	2004	14.0	2007	35.4*
Ireland	2007	20.8	–	–
Italy	2007	24.0	–	–
Netherlands	2007	17.7	–	–
Norway	2006	65.5	–	–
Spain	2006	11.9	2006	68.6*
Sweden	2007	65.8	–	–
United Kingdom	2009	27.4	2009	32.7
Asia				
Australia	2008	17.1	2008	38.2*
India	2005	2.4	–	–
Japan	2007	15.5	–	–
Korea	2006	6.7	–	–
Malaysia	2007	7.6	2007	1.8
New Zealand	2008	17.2	2007	14.6
Philippines	2007	1.7	2008	1.1
Singapore	2007	33.3	2007	14.6
Taiwan, China	2006	35.9*	–	–
Thailand	2007	1.4	2007	1.4
Africa				
Egypt	2007	16.1	2008	2.1
Ghana	2007	70.0*	2006	70.0*
Kenya	2007	4.1	2007	0.4
South Africa	2008	24.9	2008	17.1

Note: *Density is defined here as union membership as a percentage of total employment except where noted (*) as a percentage of wage and salary earners.

Sources: International Labour Organization, Trade Union Density and Collective Bargaining Coverage, International Statistical Inquiry, Technical Brief, 2008–09. Data for the United Kingdom is from BIS, Department for Business Innovation & Skills, Trade Union Membership, 2009, Tables 1.1 and 4.2.

rates. Coverage rates can exceed density rates because union workers and nonunion workers frequently work side by side, and workers who refuse to join a union are not always compelled to as they may be via the "union shop" arrangements discussed earlier. In fact, in some countries compulsory union membership is illegal.

Another major difference between U.S. unions and those in many other countries is the degree of centralization in bargaining and wage setting. The system of collective bargaining is very fragmented and decentralized in the United States, with thousands of unions bargaining collectively with employers at the local level. In many other countries (e.g., Austria, Ireland, and the Scandinavian countries) wage determination and collective bargaining are much more centralized. Unions frequently negotiate national agreements with associations of employers, and often these negotiations take place in conjunction with the government and national economic policy. In France and Germany unions may negotiate industry-wide agreements (or even regional agreements) whose terms and conditions may cover nonunion workers as well.[11] In fact, this is one reason bargaining coverage rates are so much higher than union density rates in some countries.

Still another major difference between the United States and many other countries concerns goals and objectives. Although we have much more to say about this later, most U.S. unions practice "business unionism" and pursue "bread and butter" objectives. That is, it is the primary interest of unions to provide economic benefits to their own members such as higher wages and fringe benefits. In many other countries, however, unions have been more concerned with the interests of the working class as a whole, and they are often also closely associated with social reform issues such as reduced income inequality and reduced hours of work. In Great Britain, for example, the growth of the union movement was historically closely aligned to that of the Labour Party, though in recent years the two have become increasingly separate. U.S. unions have been largely independent political entities engaged in lobbying efforts to achieve policies favorable to their members, although they are traditionally more closely associated with the Democratic Party than with the Republican Party.

Finally, the countries of Central and Eastern Europe provide some interesting examples of how the structure and scope of unionism have, in some cases, changed abruptly. In the former command economies of this region (e.g., Poland, the former Czechoslovakia, and Hungary), trade unions had followed the old Soviet model, serving mainly as "transmission belts" for the goals of the state and the Communist Party. Unions were effectively partners with management, and their common major objective was to ensure attainment of the planned levels of production. These unions were not involved in collective bargaining over wages but instead took responsibility for worker welfare, recreation, access to housing, and vacation facilities. With the collapse of the socialist systems in these countries, unions became independent and have now become involved with collective bargaining, just as their counterparts in other countries are. However, they are encountering some employer opposition, and their membership totals have fallen sharply in some cases.[12]

---

[11] Richard Freeman, "American Exceptionalism in the Labor Market: Union–Nonunion Differentials in the United States and Other Countries," in *Labor Economics and Industrial Relations*, eds. Clark Kerr and Paul Staudohar (Cambridge, MA: Harvard University Press, 1994), pp. 274–275.

[12] Anna Pollert, "Trade Unions in Transition in Central and Eastern Europe," *European Journal of Industrial Relations* 5 (2) (1999).

Despite these major differences, some features are common to unionism across countries. Just as in the United States, in most countries men are more likely to belong to unions than are women (although the difference is narrowing and in some countries—such as the United Kingdom—women are more likely to be union members than are men).[13] Furthermore, union density rates are usually higher in the public sector than in the private sector, and clear interindustry patterns are consistent across countries.

Theories of Union Growth

Although legislation has been important in fostering union growth, especially in the U.S. economy, other factors are also at work in determining why unions grow or decline. In fact, questions relating to the determinants of union growth have intrigued economists and social scientists for many generations. For example, why do unions originate? What factors or conditions are most important in explaining their emergence and in influencing their growth? Why do unions take on the political characteristics that they do, conservative and embracing capitalism in some countries (such as in the United States) but socialistic in other countries? Many theories have been offered to answer these questions. Some stress economic reasons, such as widening product markets, which result in growing market competition and the consequent pressure to reduce costs that is brought to bear on employers and, in turn, on their employees. Other theories stress psychological reasons, such as workers being conscious of the scarcity of good jobs and joining together to protect these jobs. Still others stress the importance of institutional factors such as changing technology, the law, or even the emergence of great labor leaders. Although there is some truth in each of these explanations, we can explain why unions grow and decline, as John Pencavel has done, using the favorite tool of economists—supply and demand analysis.[14]

Figure 12.1 shows a demand schedule for union services where the quantity of union services demanded is a function of the "price" of such services. Here the price could be measured simply as the level of union dues and fees workers would have to pay to join a union, and the amount of "union services" on the horizontal axis could be measured (or proxied) by the number of workers who would join unions at various prices. It is also reasonable to argue that the demand schedule for union services would be negatively sloped. Using similar thinking, unions should be able and willing to supply more union services as the price they received for such services rises (or conversely as the cost of providing such services falls, including employer resistance to unions). In this "market," the demand for and supply of union services would determine the number of workers unionized as well as the going price of union services.

Now it is interesting to see how some of the factors associated with good times and bad times for unions fit neatly into this demand–supply framework. First, the legal protection given to unions in the 1930s with the passage of the Norris-LaGuardia and Wagner acts lowered the costs to unions of providing any given level of union services. With unions in the private sector no longer having to devote so much of their resources in

---

[13] Blanchflower, "The Role and Influence of Trade Unions in the OECD," p. 2.

[14] John Pencavel, "The Demand for Union Services: An Exercise," *Industrial and Labor Relations Review*, 24 (2) (1971).

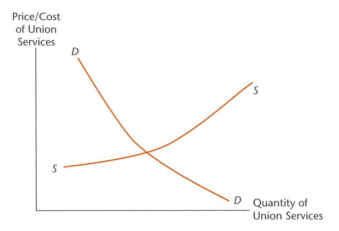

FIGURE 12.1 The Supply of and Demand for Union Services

their battles merely to be recognized by employers, the supply schedule of union services would shift to the right, resulting in an increase in union membership. The same rightward shift in the supply schedule took place in the 1960s as similar legal protection was accorded to unions in the public sector. In the public sector, employment was also growing at a faster rate than in the private sector, and the demand for union services was shifting to the right as well.

The decline in union membership that generally characterizes times of recession and depression can easily be explained as arising from greater employer resistance to unions—resistance in organizing as well as resistance to union bargaining demands. In any case, greater employer resistance means that any given level of union services is associated with higher costs, driving the supply schedule to the left. Additionally, in times when unemployment is high, the demand for union services falls because jobless workers are not always desirous of keeping their union membership.

Finally, can supply and demand forces explain the secular decline that we have seen in union density and absolute union membership totals in the last several decades? The changing gender, industrial, and regional mix of employment discussed earlier would result in a leftward shift of the demand schedule for unionism. Furthermore, the relative movement of population and employment to the sunbelt states, where, you will recall, right-to-work laws are more likely to be in place, has made it more difficult for unions to organize, and a leftward shift in supply is the result.

When we think of the various factors that have stimulated or deterred union growth over time, it is clear that all of them fit nicely into a demand–supply framework. However, we are still left with the challenge of trying to decide which of these factors have been most important in explaining union membership trends. In an early study, Orley Ashenfelter and John Pencavel tried to answer this question by formulating an econometric model to help "explain" annual percentage changes in union membership in the United States over the period 1900–60.[15] Recognizing that there is "a great deal more involved other than just

---

[15] Orley Ashenfelter and John Pencavel, "American Trade Union Growth: 1900–1960," *Quarterly Journal of Economics* 83 (3) (1969): 434–448.

economic factors," they hypothesized that changes in union membership could be explained by movements in the following variables:

- *The annual inflation rate.* Why? With wages usually lagging price changes, the benefits of unionism rise during periods of inflation.
- *The rate of change of employment in the unionized sector of the economy.* Employer resistance to unionism is likely to be weakest when labor is in short supply, which will be the case when employment is rising rapidly.
- *A psychological factor—worker discontent or the "stock of labor grievances."* To specify this factor, Ashenfelter and Pencavel use the amount of unemployment in the preceding trough of the business cycle, with a weight that "decays" over time. Their logic here is plausible: the severity of employment conditions (at their worst) in the past could influence workers' desires to unionize.
- *The proportion of total employment in the union sector that is already unionized.* This variable might be looked upon as reflecting diminishing returns to further organizing efforts. The greater union density is in the unionized sector, the less room for further gains.
- *A political factor: an index of legislative pro-union sentiment.* Remember the effect that the presence of favorable legislation seems to have had on labor's organizing efforts in the private sector after 1935 and in the public sector after 1960? This, along with the fact that the Democratic Party has long been considered the ally of organized labor, led Ashenfelter and Pencavel to try to capture legislative sentiment toward unions by the percentage of members of the U.S. House of Representatives who are Democrats.

Using annual data from 1900 to 1960 and least squares multiple regression, Ashenfelter and Pencavel found "remarkable support" for their hypotheses, with the variables discussed previously explaining about 75% of the variance in union membership growth in the United States. In particular, the rate of change of prices had a strong effect on union growth, with an increase of one percentage point in this rate of change associated with about a 0.65 percentage point increase in the rate of growth of union membership.[16] In short, the Ashenfelter-Pencavel results seem to indicate that (for the period studied, at least) we can explain the movements in union membership with a relatively small number of factors.

Later researchers have found, however, that the explanatory power of this model for years since 1960 is not as great.[17] Lee Stepina and Jack Fiorito, for example, suggest that "different models may be needed to explain union growth and decline at different times."[18] Henry Farber and Alan Krueger used a demand–supply framework to analyze the decline in union membership between 1977 and 1991 in the United States. They found that almost all of the decline is due to a fall in worker demand for union representation and not to a reduction in the supply of union jobs. Furthermore, they contend that

---

[16] Ashenfelter and Pencavel, "American Trade Union Growth," p. 441.

[17] Farouk Elsheikh and George S. Bain, "American Trade Union Growth: An Alternative Model," *Industrial Relations* 17 (1) (1978): 75–79.

[18] Lee Stepina and Jack Fiorito, "Toward a Comprehensive Theory of Union Growth and Decline," *Industrial Relations* 25 (3) (1986): 263.

very little of the decline in union density in the United States over this period seems to be attributable to structural shifts in the composition of the labor force (i.e., gender, education, age, occupation, and so forth).[19] This is in sharp contrast to the situation in some other countries, such as the United Kingdom, where there has been a marked shift in industrial structure away from heavily unionized manufacturing and toward services.

Although it is clear from this discussion that there is some disagreement among economists over just which factors can best explain union growth and decline, it is interesting to speculate what the next few years might hold for unions if those factors identified by Ashenfelter and Pencavel are still important. Using recent trends in the inflation rate, employment growth in the traditional unionized sectors of the economy, the unemployment rate during the last recession and the makeup of the U.S. Congress, would you predict that unions are likely to rebound with substantial new membership gains? Or are they in for more lean times in the years ahead?

Union Goals and Objectives

In the process of representing workers in the collective bargaining process, what is it that unions want? How does a typical union decide what wage to demand in negotiations? Many people simply respond that unions generally seek to raise the wages of their members and the workers that they represent, but this answer doesn't really tell us very much. Surely union wage demands are not without limit; in other words, unions don't "shoot for the moon" in contract negotiations. The reasons are simple. First, even if employers would agree to them, wages that are set too high might lead to layoffs and unemployment as employers move up their demand for labor schedules. Second, the presence of a large pool of unemployed workers willing to work for lower wages could threaten the wage levels negotiated by unions.

In this section we discuss various models of union goals and ask whether unions can be said to possess a common objective function. We have seen earlier that it is reasonable to assume that employers seek to maximize profits, but can unions also be assumed to maximize anything, perhaps wages? (We think you already know the answer to this question.) If not wages, is it reasonable to assume that unions try to maximize *anything* and, if so, what?

Theorizing about union goals and objectives is in some respects more complex than theorizing about employer goals and objectives. First of all, the union is both an economic and a political entity. Wage agreements reached by the union leadership often must be brought back to the workers, the rank and file, to vote upon and ratify. Therefore, the possibility of disagreements between the leadership and the rank and file emerges.[20] Contrast this situation with that of corporate management of a business firm, which generally has full authority to ratify collective bargaining agreements without consulting the stockholders.

---

[19] Henry Farber and Alan Krueger, "Union Membership in the United States: The Decline Continues," *NBER Working Paper No. 4216*, 1992.

[20] This situation is sometimes called a principal-agent problem in economics.

Second, the union itself is often made up of groups with diverse interests: older workers and younger workers, those with more seniority and those with less, men and women. Certainly support for a high union wage demand might be lower among workers with less seniority (and hence with a greater likelihood of being laid off) than among workers with more seniority. Furthermore, members of unions comprised of both private and public sector workers ("mixed unions," as they are sometimes called, such as the SEIU and the CWA) might have decidedly different views on the desirability of tax increases to finance increases in wages and benefits.

With these cautions in mind, let's now turn to some well-known models of union goals that have been proposed by labor economists.

Union Monopoly Models

Samuel Gompers, founder of the American Federation of Labor, was once asked by a reporter just what it was that labor unions wanted for their workers. Gompers's response was allegedly "More, more, and still more." This makes for an interesting anecdote, but it does not accurately describe the wage goals of most unions. Taken at its literal meaning, it would imply that a union seeks to maximize the wage rate. But this would mean moving up the demand curve for labor as far as it is possible to go before it intersects the vertical axis. This would hardly be reasonable because it would mean that just one worker would be left employed, although at a high wage.

One very popular class of union goal models considers unions to be monopolies. On the surface this view of unions has some appeal. Business monopolies sell products; union monopolies "sell" labor. In fact, Dave Beck, head of the Teamsters union during the 1950s until he was jailed on corruption charges, once described himself in the following way: "I am a businessman. I sell labor." Moreover, unions at one time were subject to prosecution under the Sherman Antitrust Act of 1890 as monopolies acting in restraint of trade. However, there are some difficulties with this view of unions as monopolies. In the first place, humans are not "products." Moreover, strictly speaking, unions don't sell labor; rather, they negotiate the terms of work.

Whether or not unions are reasonably viewed as a kind of monopoly, there remains the question of what they seek to do.[21] Business firms attempt to maximize profits. What, if anything, do unions attempt to maximize?

Rent Maximization

The union **rent-maximization model** is almost a mirror image of the business monopoly model of profit maximization. Reviewing quickly the monopoly model that you studied in basic economics, suppose we consider a monopoly firm facing a product demand schedule (*DD*) as in Figure 12.2. The firm is trying to decide what level of output to produce (*Q*) and what price (*p*) to charge for its product. Since *DD* is the *average* revenue schedule to the firm, there is also a schedule that represents the firm's *marginal*

---

[21] One economist who argues that unions do indeed act in accord with the monopoly model is Morgan Reynolds, "What Ever Happened to the Monopoly Theory of Labor Unions?" *Journal of Labor Research* 2 (1) (1981): 163–173.

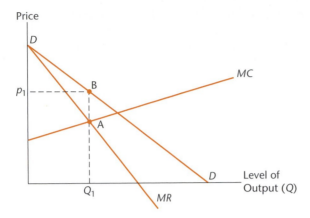

FIGURE 12.2 The Monopoly Firm Model

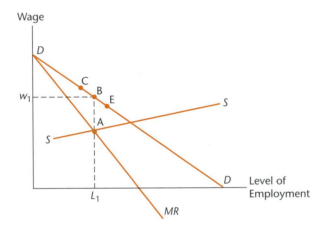

FIGURE 12.3 The Union Rent-Maximization Model

revenue (*MR*). If we then consider the firm's marginal cost schedule (*MC*), the firm's profit maximizing level of output (Q_1) would be where $MR = MC$ at a price (p_1) read off the demand curve.

Let's now turn to Figure 12.3 and consider a union to be a type of monopolistic "seller" of labor trying to decide what wage (*w*) to negotiate with an employer who is hiring union labor. The employer's demand curve for union labor could be depicted as *DD*, and the labor supply schedule as schedule *SS*. Although the demand for labor schedule would be a marginal revenue product schedule to the employer, to the union it represents the average revenue (or simply the wage) going to employed union workers. And just as the *MR* schedule in Figure 12.2 represents the marginal revenue to the firm, schedule *MR* in Figure 12.3 could be said to represent the change in revenue (more accurately, the change in the total wage payments, sometimes called the total wage bill) going to union workers. Finally, the labor supply schedule (*SS*) shows the wage necessary to call forth the services of the corresponding number of workers. Recalling our analysis of labor supply in Chapter 4, this is determined by the workers' subjective "costs" of giving up leisure. What is the point of all this? The point is simply that a labor supply schedule can be considered to be roughly analogous to an employer's marginal cost schedule. Both schedules represent the "cost" of supplying an additional unit of the product or of labor.

Now, to complete our analysis, if the union were to act in a fashion similar to a profit maximizing firm, the union in Figure 12.3 would desire to see L_1 of its members hired (at the point where the labor supply schedule SS intersects the MR schedule). And it would try to negotiate a wage equal to w_1 read off the demand schedule, which would ensure that workers would receive their marginal revenue product. But what is it that the union would be "maximizing"? Not profits, here, but rather what we could call the *rent* or surplus—the return over and above the supply prices or reservation wages of its members.

The close parallel between the profit maximizing monopolist firm model and the rent-maximizing monopolist union model should be clear; but the important question is how realistic is this model of union wage and employment goals? The model seems plausible, suggesting as it does that a union will attempt to get the greatest return it can for its members over and above their "costs" of supplying their labor. But one fundamental difficulty with the model is that it ignores the question of how to allocate union gains (and losses) among the membership. More specifically, suppose that in Figure 12.3 the union was considering negotiating a wage level just above the rent-maximizing level w_1 (say, at point C). If this wage could be reached, then those who retained their jobs at the higher wage would certainly consider themselves to be better off. But those who lost their jobs would rate themselves as worse off. With there being both gainers and losers, how can we realistically argue that the rent-maximizing wage is the "best" one for the union? Similar reasoning could be applied to a situation where the union was considering a lower wage (e.g., point E). Formerly unemployed union members who now found themselves with a job would say that they were better off, but certainly not those who were employed before at higher wages. In a nutshell, the difficulty here seems to be that the union is an entity comprising many individuals with a heterogeneity of preferences. And with any union wage goal potentially resulting in both gainers and losers, the model leaves unanswered the question of how (or why) one outcome is deemed superior to another.

Maximization of the Wage Bill

Another well-known model of union goals is the **wage-bill maximization model**. (Former U.S. Secretary of Labor and Harvard economist John Dunlop once referred to this model as probably the most plausible union goal model.)[22] As we mentioned earlier, the "total wage bill" is defined as the total amount of wage payments going to employed union members, or simply the multiplicative product of the wage and the number of workers.

To see what wage (and employment level) would maximize the total wage bill, refer to Figure 12.4. The MR schedule represents the change in the total wage bill associated with one more (or one less) employed union worker; therefore the wage that would maximize the total wage bill will be on the DD schedule above the point where $MR = 0$. In the figure, w_1 is that wage, and the area bounded by w_1BA0 represents the total wage bill.

---

[22] John T. Dunlop, *Wage Determination under Trade Unions* (London: Macmillan & Company, 1944).

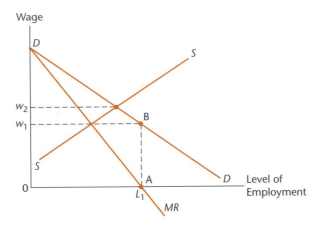

FIGURE 12.4 The Wage-Bill Maximization Model

Reasonable? Perhaps, but once again there are some difficulties. This model faces the same heterogeneity of preferences problem that the rent-maximization model encountered. Moreover, it also ignores the possible constraint imposed by the supply of labor. If, for example, the supply of labor schedule were SS, then wage level w_1 and its corresponding employment level L_1 are not even attainable. Furthermore, consider a situation where the current wage level (say, w_2) happens to be above the wage-bill maximizing wage w_1. To attain its goal of maximizing the wage bill, we would have to argue that the union would be asking for a *lower* wage during the next round of negotiations. That is not very likely.

The Median Voter Model

A major difficulty with the two models just discussed is that unions are composed of individual members with a diversity of interests. One model that specifically incorporates membership diversity is the **median voter model**. Although it was originally used to explain politicians' stances on issues of importance to voters (hence its name), the model can easily be modified to explain union goal setting.

For the sake of illustration, let's focus on seniority. In many firms, workers who have been hired most recently (those with the least seniority) are the first to be laid off in times of a fall in demand. Conversely, those with the most seniority are least likely to get the axe. It therefore follows that, *ceteris paribus*, more senior workers are more likely to favor high union wage demands whereas more junior workers would prefer lower union wage demands. Figure 12.5 shows the heterogeneity of wage demand preferences, with an employer's demand for labor schedule DD and the corresponding wage preferences of workers with high and low levels of seniority.

How would a union deal with the differing wage preferences of its members in formulating its wage demands? According to the median voter model, in a democratic system policies will be adopted that reflect the preference of the voter whose position is squarely in the middle. That is, if preferences were to be arrayed, that of the median

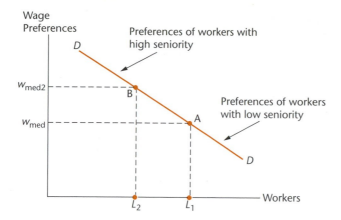

FIGURE 12.5 Wage Demand Preferences

individual would win the most support.[23] In Figure 12.5, the wage preference of the median-seniority union member is w_{med} at point A. According to the model, this is the wage the union will be most likely to demand in negotiations. Any wage that is either higher or lower than w_{med} would not receive the support of at least half of the union members.

This is a bit tricky to see, but Table 12.4 should help. The table shows the overall percentage of union members who would prefer wage levels at least as high as that given in the corresponding row. For example, all union members would prefer a wage of at least $16 per hour; so a union demand of less than $16 would capture no membership support whatsoever. Similarly, a wage demand below $18 would be supported by only 20% of the members. Wages of at least $24 would win the backing of 40% of the members. A wage of $22, the median preference, is the highest that would capture the support of a majority of union members.

Is it reasonable to argue that the median voter model is a plausible reflection of union wage-setting goals? Although it addresses the diversity of interests of union members rather well, the model runs into a serious difficulty. Remember that the distribution of wage preferences is largely due to the fear of layoffs that overly high wages threaten to bring about. In Figure 12.5 if the wage preference of the median union member (w_{med} at point A) is in fact realized, then only L_1 workers will be hired. But this means that in the next period the former median worker now becomes the worker with the *least* seniority, and there will be a new median worker with a higher wage preference (w_{med2} at point B). If the union succeeds in negotiating this higher wage, then $L_1 - L_2$ workers will be laid off, and the whole process begins anew in the next period. In short, what the median voter model of union wage preferences seems to imply is an ever-shrinking number of union workers! Although we analyzed the secular decline in union membership earlier in the chapter, the rate implied by the median voter model (50% per "period") does not seem consistent with our earlier observations. Of course the model doesn't bring into consideration

---

[23] Remember that the median is defined as the $(n + 1)/2$ value in an array where n refers to the number of items (here workers or "voters") in the array.

TABLE 12.4 Union Workers' Wage Preferences

Hourly Wage (w)	Percentage of Union Members Desiring a Wage of At Least w
$16	100%
18	80
20	60
22	50
24	40
26	20
28	10

employer resistance to higher wages, nor does it specifically define the period over which the reformulation of wage demands takes place.

The Utility-Maximization Model

This last union goal model has received considerable attention by labor economists. It has been referred to as the "monopoly model" or the "Cartter-Fellner model."[24] Its popularity is also due to the fact that it forms the basis for an interesting controversy over whether union monopoly outcomes are "efficient" or "Pareto optimal"; we will address this issue after we develop the model.

Instead of assuming that a typical union has a single objective, such as maximizing union rents, maximizing the wage bill, or satisfying the wishes of the median union member, the Cartter-Fellner model assumes that the union desires to maximize utility. This leaves open the possibility that unions can possess multiple objectives. Although any number of "arguments," as they are often called, might comprise a union's utility function, for simplicity let's assume that union utility is a function of the wage level (w) and the level of employment (L), or as equation 12-1 states:

$$U = f(w, L) \tag{12-1}$$

Figure 12.6 shows what the shape of the utility isoquant for any given level of utility might look like. Notice that the isoquant is curved and convex to the origin, but it is quite close to being L-shaped because wages and employment are not likely to be very close substitutes in the eyes of a union. To illustrate, suppose the union is currently at point A in Figure 12.6, with wage–employment combination w_1 and L_1, respectively. If the union were faced with the possibility of a cut in the wage level, it would no doubt feel that it would require a very large increase in the number of union members employed to

[24] The model was first developed most fully by Allan Cartter, *Theory of Wages and Employment* (Homewood, IL: Richard D. Irwin, 1959); and by William Fellner, "Prices and Wages under Bilateral Monopoly," *Quarterly Journal of Economics* 61 (1947): 503–532. For some more recent applications of the Cartter–Fellner model, see John Pencavel, "The Tradeoff Between Wages and Employment in Trade Union Objectives," *Quarterly Journal of Economics* 99 (1984): 215–231; and Ian McDonald and Robert Solow, "Wage Bargaining and Employment," *American Economic Review* 71 (1981): 896–908.

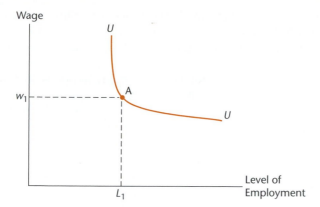

FIGURE 12.6 Union Preferences for Wages and Employment

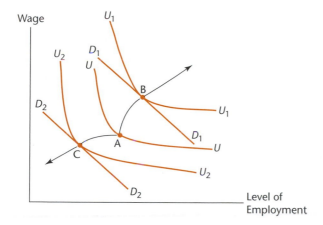

FIGURE 12.7 Wage–Employment Preference Path with Changes in Labor Demand

consider itself to be just as well off (in a utility sense) as before. Likewise, if the union were to face a cut in the number of its members who were employed, it would take a considerable increase in wages for it to feel that its overall level of utility was the same as previously. Another way of putting this is to say that the union's marginal rate of substitution of wages for employment is high.

What would the rest of the union's utility map look like? Turning to Figure 12.7, again note the differences from our prior utility maps. Assume that our union happens once more to be at point A on the employer's demand for labor schedule (which is not shown to keep Figure 12.7 uncluttered). Let's suppose that the employer's demand schedule for labor rises to D_1D_1. How would the union prefer to enjoy the "fruits" of this demand increase—with higher wages, a higher level of employment, or some combination of higher wages and employment? Most observers (and probably your intuition too) would say that the union would like both, but it would likely favor higher wage levels over higher employment levels. If this is the case, then the highest level of utility attainable by the union would be at point B on utility isoquant U_1, which in Figure 12.7 lies in a north-northeasterly direction above point A. Notice also that two utility isoquants U and U_1 appear "squeezed" to the left.

What if there were a decline in the demand for labor, as often happens in times of recession? Most observers would contend that unions try to resist wage cuts in times of slack demand, preferring to "bite the bullet" in the form of employment declines (layoffs) instead.[25] In Figure 12.7, this means that the highest level of utility now available to a union facing a demand decline (to D_2D_2) would be at point C on utility isoquant U_2. And the two utility isoquants U and U_2 appear to be "squeezed" from below.

In short, what the Cartter-Fellner utility maximization model implies is that unions possess a wage–employment preference path, depicted by the arrows through points A, B, and C in Figure 12.7. As we've noted, this wage preference path is asymmetrical, with union wage–employment preferences differing depending on whether the demand for labor is rising or falling.

Employer Wage–Employment Preferences

The Cartter-Fellner model has some other attractive features. In addition to recognizing that unions may have multiple goals (note that it would be possible to add still more arguments to the union utility function, such as fringe benefits or safety standards), the model can be extended to include employer wage and employment preferences as well. In this way we can see how union and employer preferences may differ and what the range of possible outcomes in a bargaining situation might be.

We have made frequent use of the marginal revenue product (MRP) concept, one of the most important tools of the labor economist. In Chapters 2 and 3, when we analyzed labor demand, we also introduced the concepts of average product and average revenue product (ARP). Simply put, the ARP is the total revenue product divided by the number of workers employed. Its relationship to the MRP can be seen in Figure 12.8. More important, though, with some minor adjustments, the ARP concept can be used to develop a wage–employment preference map for the employer.

The ARP schedule is a *gross* concept, telling us how much revenue the average worker produces for the firm. If we wanted to deduct the cost of capital (assume it to be a fixed cost), we could turn the ARP schedule into a *net* schedule simply by subtracting the cost of capital from the total revenue product and dividing by the number of workers (L). The resulting schedule is the average net revenue product (or ANRP) schedule, and as Figure 12.9 shows, ANRP (focus for the moment only on $ANRP_1$) lies below the original *ARP* schedule, although the distance between the two narrows as we move farther to the right. (Why is this?) If the cost of capital were greater, the ANRP schedule would be lower still, at $ANRP_2$.

---

[25] In collective bargaining, a union will almost always insist on maintaining the current wage, unless the employment decline is likely to be severe or unless without wage cuts the employer (or industry) is threatened with extinction. In fact, instances of union wage concessions are rare enough that they usually make the headlines when they do occur.

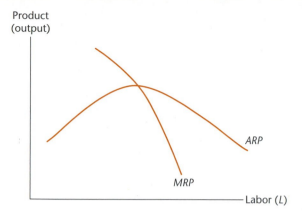

FIGURE 12.8 Relationship between Average and Marginal Revenue Products

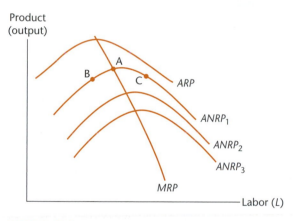

FIGURE 12.9 Employer Wage–Employment Preferences

But what does all of this have to do with employer wage–employment preferences? Suppose we were to treat *profit* as a fixed cost, just as we treated capital costs previously. Then there would be an ANRP schedule for each possible level of profit, with higher levels of profit associated with lower ANRP schedules as in Figure 12.9. Then we could think of any one ANRP schedule as depicting all possible combinations of wages and employment that would yield a certain level of profit to the employer, an *isoprofit curve*. On any one isoprofit curve (e.g., $ANRP_1$), an employer would be indifferent to any given combination of wages and employment (e.g., points A, B, or C). However, an employer would always prefer a lower isoprofit curve because it is associated with higher levels of profit. And the collection of all isoprofit curves could be viewed as an employer preference map, much like the union's preference map that we have just analyzed.

Things become interesting (and a little more complex) when we superimpose the employer's preference map on the union's preference map, as we have done in Figure 12.10. Suppose that the existing wage–employment combination is at point A on demand schedule D_1D_1. We could assume that this represents the result of a collective bargaining

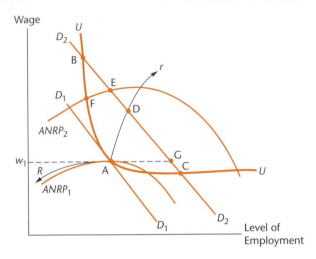

FIGURE 12.10 Union–Employer Bargaining Possibilities with Rising Labor Demand

contract agreed to by both labor and management during past negotiations. If possible, the union would like to see the wage rise above w_1. In fact, the union would like to see wages and employment rise along the wage–employment preference path Ar, but this would result in a lower level of profit for the employer (a higher ANRP schedule), and of course the employer would resist. Similarly, the employer would prefer a lower wage level, moving down demand schedule D_1D_1 to a lower (but higher profit) ANRP schedule. But such a position would result in the union being on a lower utility isoquant, and of course the union would resist. So point A appears to be, at least for the time being, a point of stability. It appears that neither party could nudge the other away from point A without making the other party worse off.

But suppose now that since the last contract negotiation period the employer's demand for labor has risen, and D_2D_2 is the new demand schedule. It is now time for negotiation of the new contract. What can be said about the wage and employment preferences of the union and of management? The union, of course, would again simply prefer to move up its wage–employment preference path Ar. The "best" (i.e., highest utility) wage–employment combination the union could hope to achieve would be point D on the employer's new demand for labor schedule. But any wage–employment combination between points B and C would leave the union at least as well off as before. Now, what about the employer? Because the demand for labor has risen, the old ANRP schedule will now be associated with a higher level of profit. In other words, because of the rise in labor demand, continuing to pay the existing wage would make the employer better off.[26] This being the case, a new higher ANRP schedule will represent the same level of profit as

---

[26] Because the labor demand schedule is the MRP schedule, which is the multiplicative product of the marginal product and the price of the product (or marginal revenue if the product market is imperfectly competitive), the demand for labor will rise if either labor productivity or product price rises.

before. Another way of putting this is to say that the former $ANRP_1$ schedule has shifted upward to $ANRP_2$.

What does all this tell us about the possible wage and employment outcomes during the new round of negotiations? The union would prefer to see agreement reached at point D on its wage preference path, but any w-L combination on the demand for labor schedule D_2D_2 between B and C would leave the union at least as well off as before. For the employer, any point on the demand schedule below point E would make the employer better off because it would be associated with higher levels of profit than before. Given the preferences of the union and the employer, there is a *range of possible agreement* bounded by points B and D over which range both parties would prefer to move down the demand schedule! However, below point D the interests of the two clash. The employer, of course, would wish to reach the lowest (highest profit) ANRP schedule possible, and the union hopes to attain the highest level of utility that it can. Here is the region where the interests of the two parties diverge—the *range of disagreement* in bargaining. Generally this range is defined by the line between D and C. But if we assume that the employer would not seek to lower the wage from its former level (after all, the demand for labor has risen), then this range of disagreement can be depicted rather more precisely as the distance DG.

Given this range of disagreement, where might an eventual collective bargaining agreement occur? Realistically, we would expect the actual outcome to be determined by the relative bargaining power of the two parties. Although we will more precisely explain what we mean by bargaining power shortly, intuitively we would expect the agreement to be closer to point D if the union's bargaining power exceeds that of the employer and closer to G if the reverse were the case.

Efficient Contracts

The model that we have just analyzed is attractive in several respects. First, it incorporates both wages and employment in union objectives. Second, it recognizes that in bargaining situations there may not be a deterministic solution but instead a range of possible outcomes. However, as with each of the other models we have examined, the model implicitly assumes that unions and management bargain over the wage but that the level of employment is ultimately determined by the employer. In other words, once the wage level is decided upon, the employer simply "reads" the level of employment off the demand for labor (MRP) schedule. Is this a realistic assumption? Can unions sometimes succeed in getting employers to hire more workers than they would otherwise wish to hire? In other words, do "off the demand curve" outcomes sometimes occur?

This question is closely related to what has been called the **efficient contracts** controversy, and to explain it we must return for a moment to Figure 12.10. Suppose the current wage–employment combination is at point A on demand schedule D_1D_1 and that there has been no change in either the employer's or the union's preference functions. Now let's focus on (and magnify) the area around point A (see Figure 12.11). What if the union were to demand an increase in the level of employment, and try to "push" the employer off the demand curve, perhaps to point H? Notice that the union would find point H to be preferable to point A (it is above utility isoquant *UU*). But here is the surprising observation: the employer would also find point H preferable to point A because

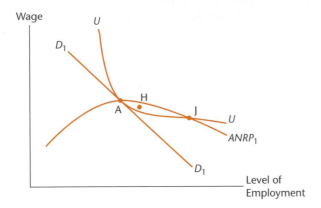

FIGURE 12.11 Bargaining Outcomes "Off the Demand Curve"

point H is below the former isoprofit curve $ANRP_1$ and hence will yield a higher level of profit. In fact, any wage–employment combination within the lens-shaped area bounded by A and J will result in at least one of the two parties being better off than at point A, with neither one being worse off.[27] If this is the case, then we can state that point A is not an "efficient" contract in the Pareto sense.[28]

Are there any possible wage–employment outcomes that could be called "efficient"? Any such outcome would have to make the union better off only if the employer were made worse off. And it would have to make the firm better off only by making the union worse off. Such a situation in turn implies that a union's utility isoquant would have to be tangent with the employer's isoprofit (ANRP) curve. Figure 12.12 illustrates one such efficient contract outcome at point K, but in fact any point along the band KM would indicate points of co-tangency between union utility isoquants and employer's isoprofit curves. Therefore, band KM is the range of possible efficient contracts that might be negotiated.

Two important questions should be addressed at this point. First, why is the subject of off-the-demand-curve outcomes (and efficient contracts) an important one? The answer is that in negotiating higher wages unions may not always have to fear that such wages will bring with them lower employment levels and job losses for union members. To the extent that off-the-demand-curve outcomes might make both unions and employers better off, it seems to imply that for unions there may be such a thing as a free lunch after all! You just need to negotiate for it.

The second question is to what extent do unions actually try to bargain not just over wages but over employment levels as well? There are examples, although they are not all that numerous. Teachers' union contracts sometimes contain language capping class size,

---

[27] There may not be any such area if the slope of the employer's ANRP schedule to the right of A is greater than the slope of the union's utility isoquant (the union's marginal rate of substitution of wages for employment).

[28] Remember that a Pareto efficient outcome occurs when no other possible outcome can make one party better off without making another party worse off. Another way of putting it is that a Pareto efficient outcome is an allocatively efficient outcome.

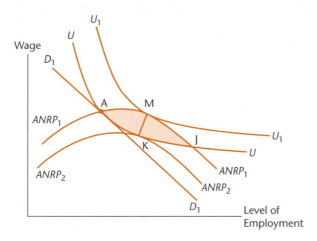

FIGURE 12.12 Range of Possible "Efficient" Contracts

thereby obligating schools to hire more teachers than they would otherwise choose to hire. Some police collective bargaining contracts require on-duty patrol cars to be staffed by two uniformed officers rather than just one. And airline contracts usually stipulate a minimum number of crew members for flights. Whether these practices can be called "efficient" is another matter, however, and to date there is only limited econometric evidence supporting the theory of efficient contracts in union–employer bargaining. If unions bargain only over wages, then we would expect that only variables that concern worker characteristics and the characteristics of their employers would affect the wage–employment settlement. For instance, wages would be determined by the human capital stock of the worker, and—if workers are able to capture rents earned by their employers—by the profitability of the firm. Once wages are determined, the employer characteristics would determine employment. Other factors, such as the rate of unemployment or the level of welfare benefits paid to unemployed workers, should not affect the settlement at all. But if the union bargains over outside employment levels, these "outside" factors should matter in determining the settlement. This is because the union is likely to be more reluctant to opt for a high-wage, low-employment settlement when conditions are not favorable. That is, when unemployment is high and when welfare payments are low, unions are unlikely to want to press for high wages at the cost of pushing some of their members out of work and into a hostile environment. So the key question is: Do outside variables affect the negotiated settlement in unionized industries? One interesting study of this issue concerns the highly unionized coal industry in the United Kingdom.[29] The conclusion drawn by the authors is that outside variables do affect employment. So there is evidence to suggest that the efficient bargains model is more realistic than models in which the union bargains only over the wage.

In some instances unions have insisted on certain work practices that have the effect of causing the number of workers to be higher than the employer desires or that limit the

---

[29] See C. Bean and P. J. Turnbull, "Employment in the British Coal Industry: A Test of the Labor Demand Model," *Economic Journal* 98 (1988): 1092–1104. Since the time of this study, the coal industry in Britain has shrunk dramatically and unions in that industry are no longer powerful.

amount of work or output. These practices are often pejoratively labeled **featherbedding**[30] (or overmanning in the United Kingdom). Examples include the following:

- Limitations on the number of bricks that bricklayers may lay in a day
- Limitations on the number of "squares" of roofing material that can be placed in a day
- Requirements that prepackaged meats sent to supermarkets be unwrapped and then wrapped once more
- Restrictions on the sizes of the brushes or rollers that painters may use
- Minimum orchestra sizes for Broadway plays, even though a musical might be scored for a smaller number of musicians.[31]

Many featherbedding practices appear to be outrageous. For example, for many years after coal-burning steam locomotives disappeared from railroads (in the 1950s), train crews still included firemen, whose original function was to stoke the furnaces with coal. U.S. longshoring operations on the west coast once prohibited lifting loads of more than 2,100 pounds. Printers union contracts sometimes required that type set for material that would run for several days in a newspaper (e.g., an advertisement) be broken down and reset each day that the material would run.[32] Clearly, advances in technology have resulted in the elimination of many practices such as these. But the question remains: Why and how do such practices arise in the first place?

Two explanations have been offered. In almost all instances where such practices have arisen, unions have sought to justify them (sometimes convincingly, sometimes not) on the grounds of quality, consumer protection, or worker safety.[33] For example, the requirement for rewrapping prepackaged meats means that bad meat will stand a better chance of being detected. Limitations on the sizes of painting materials have been defended both on the grounds of quality of painted surfaces and for safety considerations. (Painters often must work high above the ground.) And railroad unions once justified the presence of railroad firemen by arguing that they provided an extra measure of safety in case there was an obstruction on the tracks (perhaps a cow?) or if the locomotive engineer should become incapacitated.

It's safe to say, however, that the major reason underlying most featherbedding practices is the fear of job loss. Simply put, it is the fear of unions and their members that by negotiating higher wages or by working too quickly or producing too much there will be

---

[30] The word *featherbedding* originally meant to make one's position comfortable by favorable economic or financial treatment. (What could be more comfortable than a bed of feathers?) But the word is used today to refer almost exclusively to rules requiring more workers than necessary or rules limiting output.

[31] For a detailed discussion of various union featherbedding practices, see Albert Rees, *The Economics of Trade Unions*, Chapter 7 (Chicago: University of Chicago Press, 1977).

[32] One of the most hilarious examples of featherbedding occurred in the radio broadcasting industry before the dawn of television. The same radio show broadcasting live band music (have you ever heard of Lawrence Welk?) would sometimes be aired over both AM and FM channels. The American Federation of Musicians (AFM) once negotiated a contract requiring that in such cases *two* bands be hired, although only one would actually be playing music. The justification that the AFM used is that this would keep more musicians employed.

[33] See "Exploring Restrictive Building Practices," *Monthly Labor Review* (1969): 31–39; and Steven Allen, "Union Work Rules and Efficiency in the Building Trades," *Journal of Labor Economics* 4 (1986): 212–242.

less work and fewer jobs available. But can such practices actually work? Remember that all such practices result in higher costs associated with producing goods and services and consequently higher prices. And with higher prices, consumers will choose to buy fewer of the goods and services in question. Instead of hiring higher-priced painters, some consumers will choose not to have their houses painted or perhaps do it themselves. Higher-priced musicals on Broadway will lead some people to seek other forms of entertainment. And if brick walls and houses become too expensive, some will simply have them built out of wood. In other words, over time restrictive featherbedding practices are usually doomed to failure.

Before we leave the efficient bargains model of union–firm negotiation altogether, we ought to consider a special case.[34] If unions care only about the wage, then the union's utility isoquant will be flat. In this case the points of tangency that define the contract curve will be where the isoprofit curves of the firm peak. Because the peaks of the isoprofit curves lie along the labor demand curve, in this special case the efficient bargain contract curve will coincide with the demand for labor curve. In other words, the idea that efficient bargaining can lead to employment levels above those that the firm would choose if left to its own devices does not hold if all the union cares about is wages. This is an important observation because it nicely clarifies for us the fact that it is union pressure on employment that generates the off-the-demand-curve result. But are union utility isoquants really flat? Recall the evidence we gave earlier about the British coal mining industry. That evidence suggests that unions do care about employment as well as about wages.

Union Bargaining Power and Strikes

Bargaining Power

One implication of the Cartter-Fellner model is that in any union–management bargaining situation there is usually a *range of indeterminacy* within which the eventual wage–employment outcome will fall. In Figure 12.10 this range is depicted as the distance DG. Furthermore, the actual wage–employment outcome will be determined by the relative **bargaining power** of the two parties. In Chapter 3 when we first explained the Marshall-Hicks determinants of the elasticity of the demand for labor, we also said that they could be used to evaluate the potential bargaining power of unions. But just what is bargaining power? What does it mean to say that a union might possess a high or a low degree of bargaining power relative to an employer? Can we measure bargaining power, and if so, how?

Neil Chamberlain and James Kuhn provided one simple but very insightful and widely recognized definition of bargaining power:[35] the ability of one party (e.g., the union) to secure the agreement of another party (e.g., the employer or management) on the first party's terms. The union's ability or power to secure an agreement on its own terms will in turn depend on the costs to the employer of disagreeing relative to the costs

---

[34] This was first observed by A. Oswald, "Efficient Contracts Are on the Labor Demand Curve," *Labour Economics* 1 (1993): 85–114.

[35] Neil Chamberlain and James Kuhn, *Collective Bargaining*, 2nd ed. (New York: McGraw-Hill, 1965).

of agreeing. But let's put this into formula terms to see it more clearly. Using Chamberlain and Kuhn's reasoning, the union's bargaining power can be expressed as a ratio:

$$\text{Union Bargaining Power} = \frac{\text{Cost to Mgt. of Disagreeing with Union's Terms}}{\text{Cost to Mgt. of Agreeing to Union's Terms}} \qquad (12\text{-}2)$$

Similarly, for management:

$$\text{Management Bargaining Power} = \frac{\text{Cost to Union of Disagreeing with Mgt.'s Terms}}{\text{Cost to Union of Agreeing to Mgt.'s Terms}} \qquad (12\text{-}3)$$

But what are these "costs" of agreeing and disagreeing? To both management and the union, the costs of disagreeing with the other's terms could include, for example, those that would be incurred in the event of a strike, and the costs of agreeing could be considered as the "opportunity cost" of giving in to a certain demand when a better offer might have been made later. In any case, it is clear that in a bargaining situation no agreement will be forthcoming if both parties find it costlier to agree than to disagree. In other words, no agreement will be reached unless the bargaining power ratio for at least one party is greater than 1.

But what about the sources of bargaining power? What specific tactics do unions and employers use in collective bargaining to increase their own bargaining power while attempting to reduce the bargaining power of the other side? As we've mentioned, in the case of a union it's primarily the strike or threat of a strike, but other union tactics include boycotts[36] (such as the "Please Don't Patronize" request shown in the box), picketing, and occasionally even seeking political support for their cause. In the case of management, the tactics include the lockout (more rarely used than strikes, though), continuation of production with managerial personnel, and even replacement of striking workers. This last tactic, contrary to what many believe, is perfectly legal in the United States although not in many other countries.

But this is only half of the story. Each of these tactics is intended to impose costs on the other party, but most also impose costs on the party implementing them. In the case of a union, a strike may shut down a plant but it also means lost wages for workers. Similarly, a lockout affects both parties as well. As a consequence, we often see actions taken by each side to render itself immune or less vulnerable to such tactics. Some unions, for example, provide strike benefits for their members. Such benefits lower the costs of disagreement to the union (thus lowering management's bargaining power) while the strike itself increases the costs of disagreement to management (thus raising the union's bargaining power). Similarly, firms in some industries have set up strike insurance funds for a similar purpose.

The timing of offensive tactics designed to increase the costs of disagreement (and hence raise one's bargaining power) can also be important. For example, the "best" time for farm workers to strike or threaten a strike might well be at harvest time, and the "best" time for baseball umpires to strike might be during the World Series. If your college professors

---

[36] A boycott is an organized refusal to deal with another party. For example, you might boycott the university bookstore because you don't like its policy on buying back used textbooks. Interestingly, the word owes its origin to Captain Charles Boycott, an English land agent in Ireland, who in the late nineteenth century was ostracized for his refusal to reduce rents on land.

THE WAY WE WORK

Boycott!

PLEASE DO NOT PATRONIZE
<u>PRICE RITE</u>

The Wakefern Corporation and Price Rite are attempting to operate this store nonunion in an effort that we believe could potentially lead to a total phase out of their already unionized Shop Rite supermarket division in the Lehigh Valley. The Shop Rite jobs, and jobs like those at Super Fresh and Laneco, provide livable wages and quality benefits. If they are successful here, there is little doubt that they will open many other locations, which may result in the loss of hundreds of good jobs at both Shop Rite and Super Fresh, in the Lehigh Valley. These good union jobs have provided excellent wages, health and welfare benefits, pensions, etc. to the Lehigh Valley for many years.

We cannot let yet another company erode our community!

In the last 10 years, we have seen the demise of Pathmark, Acme, and most recently Laneco in the Lehigh Valley. These were all good union jobs that were lost, not because these companies were not profitable, but because these companies were successful at doing what we believe the Wakefern Corporation and Price Rite is attempting to do now.

How much longer can the Lehigh Valley sit back and watch good jobs be replaced by mediocre ones? We have to take a stand! Let's send a strong message to Price Rite and Wakefern that the Lehigh Valley will not patronize the store until they do the right thing!

On behalf of the hundreds of men, women, and their families that work at Shop Rite, Super Fresh, and Laneco in the Lehigh Valley, we thank you and would greatly appreciate your support!

Source: Reprinted by permission of Local 1776, United Food & Commercial Workers AFL-CIO, CLC.

happen to be threatening to strike (we hope not), during what time of year would such a walkout carry with it the highest costs?

Strikes, as well as lockouts and other tactics associated with bargaining impasses, are costly, and a logical question arises: Do such tactics generally pay off? The answer will surprise you, and let's focus here on strikes. Strikes impose costs on *both* parties but can clearly "pay off" for *at most* one party (and perhaps for neither); it is impossible for *both* unions and employers to be better off after a strike than before. If this is the case, why do strikes ever occur? If it is impossible for both parties to gain from a strike, it would always seem possible for one party (perhaps the one that would lose the most from a strike) to compensate the other party so that each side would be at least as well off without the strike occurring. Visualize a large pie that would become smaller if there were a strike. Clearly both sides cannot have bigger shares (pieces) of a smaller pie. Even though one side's share (the winner's) *may* be bigger after a strike, the side whose share would be smaller (the loser) would always be better off paying the eventual winner *beforehand* the amount that the winner would gain by the strike. This being the case, we repeat the question: Why do strikes ever occur?

Models of Strike Activity

J. R. Hicks (the same economist whose name we associate with the Marshall-Hicks determinants of demand elasticity) has offered a simple model of strike activity that can shed some light on the question.[37] Suppose that a bargaining impasse exists, as depicted in Figure 12.13, with the union initially demanding a wage of A and the employer initially willing to grant a wage of B. If a strike occurs, however, the employer knows that he will budge on his initial offer. Furthermore, the longer the strike is expected to last, the more the employer will be likely to give in to a higher wage demand. (Why would this be so?) Suppose that we depict the relationship between the highest wage an employer would pay to avoid a strike of a certain length and the expected strike length, calling it the employer's *concession curve*. Clearly it would be positively sloped as shown in Figure 12.13.

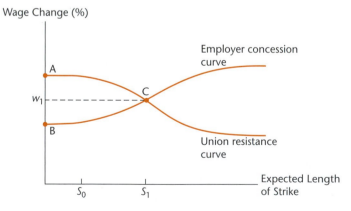

FIGURE 12.13 Hicks's Model of Strike Activity

---

[37] See John R. Hicks, *The Theory of Wages*, Chapter VII (New York: St. Martin's Press, 1968).

Similarly, the expected length of a strike would also determine what wage striking union members would be willing to accept. If a strike were expected to last a long time, the wage the union would be willing to accept to avoid the strike would be lower. (Again, why should this be so?) The relationship between this wage and the expected strike length is the union's *resistance curve*, as in Figure 12.13.

As the figure shows, given the employer's concession curve and the union's resistance curve, a strike would be expected to occur in this situation, and it would be of duration S_1. A strike of any duration shorter than S_1 (e.g., S_0) would still find the union's wage demand exceeding the wage that the employer would be willing to pay. As time passes, however, and the costs associated with the strike mount for both union and employer, the wage the union would be willing to settle for falls while the wage the employer would be willing to offer rises. Equivalently, in terms of our bargaining power ratios (equations 12-2 and 12-3), the costs to each side of disagreeing continue to rise while the costs of agreement fall as each side modifies its initial demand or offer. Eventually an agreement is reached at wage w_1 after a strike of length S_1.

The Hicks model of strikes together with the Chamberlain and Kuhn concept of bargaining power illustrate the forces that lead to eventual agreement in a bargaining impasse. We've previously established that it is impossible for both parties to be better off with a strike than without a strike, so why wouldn't the two parties choose to settle at w_1 to begin with and avoid all the costs associated with a strike? There are several reasons this is unlikely to happen. In the first place, in any bargaining situation the union will not ordinarily have precise information about the employer's concession curve, nor will the employer know the shape of the union's resistance curve. In other words, some strikes may be the result of imperfect information and the "faulty negotiation" that arises as a consequence. As Hicks himself put it, "Adequate knowledge will always make a settlement possible."[38] This, by the way, is the reason *mediation* (where a neutral third party is called on to bring the parties closer together and assist them in reaching an agreement) and *fact-finding* (where a neutral third party issues a report summarizing the issues in dispute and may even propose a settlement) are often used to facilitate the negotiation process. Furthermore, to a union a strike is a weapon, and like most weapons it will become rusty if not used from time to time. In other words, another reason strikes occur is that they serve as a signal to employers that union strike threats are credible and that union demands are therefore to be taken seriously.

Another theory of strike activity (and to many economists one of the most convincing) is the strike model of Ashenfelter and Johnson.[39] Building on the Hicks notion that faulty information is at the root of most strikes, Ashenfelter and Johnson argue that three parties, not just two, play important roles in labor–management negotiations: management, the union rank and file, and the union leadership. We've analyzed the goals of the union, but Ashenfelter and Johnson maintain that the union leadership also has a personal goal of its own: survival in office.

But don't the interests of the union and the union leadership coincide? In other words, if the union leadership desires to stay in office, won't it make sure that it doggedly

---

[38] John R. Hicks, *The Theory of Wages*, p. 147.

[39] Orley Ashenfelter and George Johnson, "Bargaining Theory, Trade Unions, and Strike Activity," *American Economic Review* 59 (1) (1969): 35–49.

pursues the objectives of the union rank and file, whether these objectives be the maximization of union rents, the total wage bill, or simply union "utility" as we discussed earlier? For the most part, the answer to this question is "yes," but there are occasional instances where the interests of the two parties may diverge. Consider this scenario: the wage increase expected by the rank and file is unrealistic and is much greater than what management will agree to or perhaps even be able to pay. Assume also that the union leadership is well aware of this situation but wonders how to convince the rank and file that their wage expectations are too high. In such a situation there may be only three courses of action:

1. Try to encourage the rank and file to tone down its demands
2. Sign a collective agreement the rank and file may be extremely unhappy with and perhaps turn down
3. Call for a strike.

The first two actions could well be political suicide for the union leadership. The rank and file might believe that their leaders have "sold them out" and in the next union election vote them out of office. (Remember, the Landrum-Griffin Act of 1959 expanded union democracy and in the process made it easier for the rank and file to bring about changes in leadership.) A strike, however, would make it seem to the rank and file that their leaders are aggressively pursuing their demands (thus solidifying their political status in the eyes of the membership). But as the strike wears on and the costs of continued disagreement rise, rank and file expectations as to what would constitute an acceptable wage increase fall. The union moves down its resistance curve until eventually an agreement is reached.

Viewed this way, strikes become a method of adjusting union demands that might be excessive because of faulty information. But it is important to notice here that the faulty information is *asymmetric*—that is, it is not characteristic of all parties in the negotiations.[40] Furthermore, the channel through which information about the acceptability of wage demands is conveyed is not the union leadership, because that would not be in the leadership's political best interests, but rather through the strike action itself. Some evidence on how faulty negotiation can lead to strikes is provided by the research of Melvin Reder and George Newmann, who have demonstrated that in situations where negotiators are relatively inexperienced strikes are more common.[41]

The Effects of Unions

Now that we've addressed union goals, bargaining power, and work stoppages, the logical next question is that of the impact of unions on wages and on other important economic variables as well. Through the process of collective bargaining, unions attempt to raise the wages of the workers whom they represent to levels higher than the employer would have presumably chosen to pay—but by how much? Is the average impact of unions on wages large or small? How can we measure it?

---

[40] O. Ashenfelter and J. Currie, "Negotiator Behavior and the Occurrence of Disputes," *American Economic Review, Papers and Proceedings* 80 (1990): 416–420, analyze the nature of negotiation failures in greater detail.

[41] M. W. Reder and G. R. Newmann, "Conflict and Contract: The Case of Strikes," *Journal of Political Economy* 88 (1980): 867–886.

Understanding the effects of unions is critical for several reasons:

- It has been public policy for nearly 80 years to provide workers in the private sector of the U.S. economy with certain collective bargaining rights, ever since the Wagner Act of 1935. But has this policy been a sound one? A fair one? Is the relative bargaining power of unions versus employers reasonable, or should existing labor legislation be modified to change this balance? The answers to all of these questions certainly depend at least in part on what the effects of unions on wages have been.

- Although the Wagner Act did not extend bargaining rights to workers and unions in the public sector, many states have passed laws giving unions of teachers, firefighters, police, and other state and local public employees the right to bargain collectively. These laws vary considerably, with a few states even giving certain groups of public employees the right to strike. How sound is such policy? Has the bargaining power of public sector unions tended to be excessive, or has it been no greater (perhaps even less) than that of unions in the private sector? Should public sector bargaining laws be modified, and if so in what way? Certainly the magnitude of the impact of public sector unions on wages will help us answer these questions.

- Most recently, employers of all nations find themselves competing in the global marketplace and facing increased pressures to hold down the costs of the goods and services they produce. Because unions can affect wages and costs of production, to what extent may unions be responsible (maybe even "blamed") for the declining fortunes of some firms and industries? Once again, the question of the magnitude of union wage effects looms as important.

In this section, we first analyze the difficulties in accurately measuring the effects of unions on wages; then we turn to some of the models that have been utilized. The big question—How much have unions raised wages?—comes next, and in the process we compare the effects of private sector unions with those in the public sector. Finally, we measure the effects of unions on some important nonwage variables, including fringe benefits, employment, and productivity.

Measuring Union Wage Effects: The Problems

Let's conduct a little experiment. If you have a friend or relative who is a member of a union, ask what effect he or she thinks the union has had on wages. You're not likely to get a precise numerical answer, but chances are the response will be something like "reasonably large" or "fairly sizeable." In fact, most people believe that unions have had a substantial effect on wages. For example, a Gallup poll once asked a sample of the American public this question: "Do you agree that the wage gains that workers have made in this country are *chiefly* due to unions?" About 66% of those sampled did agree with the statement, and only 17% disagreed. The other 17% didn't know. Incredibly (to us, anyway), a Roper public opinion poll in the late 1970s found that 47% of the American public thought that without unions "U.S. living standards would be like those in underdeveloped lands."[42] Impressions like these are no doubt reinforced by newspaper headlines that give major coverage to large settlements or by articles such as one that appeared in an issue of *Teamster* magazine

---

[42] *Wall Street Journal*, October 1977.

reporting what truck drivers working in Philadelphia were earning in the year 1920 (about 25 cents per hour). But does anyone really believe that had it not been for their union Philadelphia truck drivers would *still* be earning only 25 cents per hour?

Let's look at some of the difficulties that arise when we try to answer the seemingly simple question, "How much have unions raised wages?" First, we would have to respond, "Raised wages relative to what?" If the reply is "relative to what wages *would have been* without unions," we are in trouble (though not hopelessly so as you will soon see). Without a crystal ball, we can never know for certain what wages would have been in the absence of unions—what economists have sometimes referred to as the *absolute union wage effect* or the **wage gain**. Of course we may be able to answer the "relative to what" question by comparing union wages to the wages of nonunion workers—or what economists call the *relative* union wage effect or the **wage gap**; but as we explain next, the relative wage effect of unions is not necessarily the same as their absolute wage effect.[43]

Why is this so? Let's define w_u to be the union wage for a certain group of workers and w_0 to be the wage that these workers would have been paid had they not been unionized. Of course, we do not ordinarily know w_0; it is "unobservable." Then the union wage gain, expressed as a proportion, can be defined as:

$$\text{Wage Gain} = (w_u - w_0)/w_0 \tag{12-4}$$

Again, because w_0 is unobservable, suppose we compare the union wage to that of a similar group of workers who are not unionized. Ideally, the nonunion group should be as similar as possible to the union group to which it is being compared. If we define the wage of the nonunion group as w_n, then the union wage gap (in proportion terms) can be defined as:

$$\text{Wage Gap} = (w_u - w_n)/w_n \tag{12-5}$$

But would the magnitude of the union wage gap be a good estimate of the union wage gain? Or to put it another way, do relative union–nonunion wage differentials accurately reflect the "true" effect that unions have on wages? If w_n could ordinarily be expected to be equal to w_0, the answer would be "yes."

However, there are a number of reasons the nonunion wage might be different from the wage that would have prevailed in the absence of the union. (This is a mouthful: perhaps we could call the latter the "would-have-been wage.") The **threat effect** is one such reason. Sometimes even when their work forces are not unionized, employers will choose to pay higher wages to ward off the possibility or "threat" of unionization. If this is so, then the wage gap will be smaller than the wage gain and will not give a reliable picture of the true union effect on wages.[44] In fact, nonunion employers will sometimes pay the union wage, in which case the relative union wage effect is zero.

---

[43] The terms *absolute wage effect* and *relative wage effect* were first introduced by H. Gregg Lewis in his classic study *Unionism and Relative Wages in the United States* (Chicago: University of Chicago Press, 1963). The "wage gain" and "wage gap" concepts were introduced in his later book, *Union Relative Wage Effects: A Survey* (Chicago: University of Chicago Press, 1986).

[44] In such cases, we would say that the relative wage effect (the wage gap) is a downward-biased estimate of the absolute union wage effect (the wage gain).

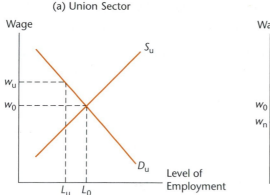

(a) Union Sector

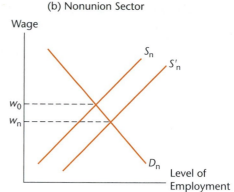

(b) Nonunion Sector

FIGURE 12.14 Spillover Effects in the Labor Market

Another reason the nonunion wage w_n might not equal w_0 is due to **spillover effects**. To see this, suppose that we categorize the labor market into two sectors, the unionized sector and the nonunionized sector. In the unionized sector unions have managed to raise the wage level to w_u, as shown in Figure 12.14a. Because the demand for labor in the union sector is not perfectly inelastic, the higher wage level will cause the level of employment in this sector (L_u) to be lower than it would have otherwise been (L_0). Put another way, the positive effect of unions on wages has caused *disemployment* in the union sector, the magnitude of this disemployment being $L_0 - L_u$. But what happens to those workers who would have had jobs in the union sector had it not been for the union-caused higher wage level? Unless they drop out of the labor force, they will seek employment in the nonunion sector of the economy, with a resultant increase in labor supply in that sector. But this increase in labor supply (from S_n to S'_n in Figure 12.14b) will tend to drive down the level of wages in this sector to w_n. What has happened, in short, is that the spillover of workers from the unionized to the nonunionized sector of the economy has caused the nonunion wage (w_n) to be lower than it would have been otherwise. In this case, the union wage gap will be larger than the union wage gain.

Threat effects and spillover effects are two reasons it is difficult to determine the impact unions have had on wages. But there is a further difficulty as well and that is the need to "net out" the union effect by controlling for other factors. To illustrate this problem, let's compare data from the U.S. Department of Labor for 2011 on average (median) weekly earnings for unionized and nonunionized workers in a few selected broad industries. Table 12.5 shows that the average earnings of union workers exceed those of nonunion workers for five of the eight industries, and in some cases by a substantial margin. But it is not necessarily correct to conclude that unions are responsible for these differences because in these broad industry groups factors other than unionism may explain the difference. For construction the difference between union and nonunion earnings is nearly 52%. For various reasons, union density in construction is higher in the North than in the South. But earnings in general also tend to be higher in the North than in the South because of cost-of-living differences, so at least part of the union differential in the construction industry reflects these cost-of-living differences. Similarly, although the union earnings difference in the mining industry is −3.6%, we should not conclude that unionism in mining has actually *lowered* wages. The mining industry is diverse, consisting of

TABLE 12.5 Difference Between Median Weekly Earnings of Union Members and Nonunion Full-Time Workers, 2011, Selected Industries

	Earnings of Union Members	Earnings of Nonunion Workers	Percentage Difference
Construction	$1,059	$698	51.7%
Public sector	981	810	21.1
Transportation and public utilities	987	762	29.5
Wholesale and retail trade	622	612	1.6
Manufacturing	836	780	7.2
Professional and business services	872	880	−0.1
Finance and insurance	819	908	−9.8
Mining	1,030	1,069	−3.6

Source: U.S. Bureau of Labor Statistics, *Union Members – 2011*, January 27, 2012.

coal mining, metal mining, petroleum and natural gas extraction, and quarrying; and both union density rates and pay scales differ across these industry subsectors.

Generating precise estimates of the effects of unions on wages is fraught with problems. In the next section we analyze some of the methods economists have used and summarize what they have found.

Measuring Union Wage Effects: The Methods

More than 200 studies of union effects have been undertaken over the last several decades: studies of different unions, different time periods, different occupations and industries, different countries, and so on.[45] Some of the early studies were quite simple, even crude, with little or no effort made to control for other factors (e.g., cost-of-living differences in the areas studied) that could explain union–nonunion differentials. But most recent studies have utilized multiple regression analysis to try to control as best they can for these other factors.

For example, suppose we specify a simple earnings function (much like earnings functions that we have seen earlier) of the following form:

$$\ln w = b_0 + b_1 U + \sum b_i X_i + e \tag{12-6}$$

where $\ln w$ is the natural logarithm of wages, U is a variable indicating union status (1 = union member, 0 = nonunion), X is a set of human capital and other variables (e.g., experience and education) specifying worker quality, the bs are the estimated coefficients of the equation, and e is a residual term reflecting both random error and perhaps omitted variables. Now suppose we would like to estimate the effects of unionism on the earnings of retail clerks in an area for which we have information about a large sample of both union and nonunion clerks, as Table 12.6 partially depicts.

---

[45] For summaries and critiques of many of these studies see H. Gregg Lewis, *Unionism and Relative Wages in the United States* (Chicago: University of Chicago Press, 1963); and his later *Union Relative Wage Effects: A Survey* (Chicago: University of Chicago Press, 1986).

TABLE 12.6   Estimating Union Wage Effects for Retail Clerks: An Exercise*

Workers	Hourly Wage (w)	Union Status (U)	Experience (in years) (X)	Education (in years) (E)
John Rutt	$8.80	1 (unionized)	4	10
Hugo Smedley	9.35	0 (nonunion)	2	12
Sharon Sloan	7.60	1	1	12
Judy O'Rourke	8.40	1	1.5	12
Jen Stevens	10.00	0	6	16
Steve Thome	10.25	1	7	16
...	...	...	...	...
...	...	...	...	...
...	...	...	...	...
Alice B. Gown	8.75	0	3	13

Note: *Data are hypothetical.

When we use multiple regression analysis to estimate the coefficients of equation 12-6, we generate the following equation:

$$\ln w = 6.5 + 0.12U + 0.07X + 0.02E \tag{12-7}$$

To keep the discussion simple, we won't test to see whether the coefficients are statistically significant; but the coefficient of the union status variable (0.12) indicates that unionized clerks enjoy about a 12% wage advantage over their nonunion counterparts once experience (X) and educational differences (E) are taken into account.[46]

This earnings function model may be applied to situations where we have information about the earnings and union status of individual workers, or microdata. Sometimes, however, we do not have such information but must work with aggregate data instead, and a somewhat different model can be the result.

As the exercise shows, modeling and trying to estimate union effects can be arduous. It is also rare for a labor economist to have data that include *all* the important factors that might influence the level of wages. Therefore, **omitted variable bias** can affect our results. For example, it might be the case that union workers are also more productive workers than nonunion workers, a possibility that we will address later in this chapter. To the extent that the values of such omitted variables may be positively correlated with the union status or unionization variable, our union effect estimates might be biased upward as we wind up attributing to unionism wage effects that are due, at least in part, to other factors.[47]

Another problem frequently encountered in union effect models is the fact that the propensity to unionize might itself be a function of the wage level. In other words,

---

[46] The actual percentage difference is $e^{.12}-1$, or 12.7%.

[47] One way of dealing with the problem of omitted variables is to use panel data such as longitudinal (time series) data on individual workers. For a technical explanation of how the use of such data can circumvent the problem of omitted variable bias see Lewis, *Union Relative Wage Effects*, pp. 60–61.

unionization might be endogenous. There are several reasons this might be so. In seeking new members, some unions may channel their recruiting efforts toward certain areas or occupations where wages are already high. In urban areas, for example, with greater concentrations of workers, the payoffs to union recruiting efforts may be greater than they are in sparsely populated areas. Furthermore, highly paid workers are better able to afford higher union dues. We do not mean to imply that pecuniary motives are foremost in union organizing drives, but recruiting members can be viewed as a type of investment and, *ceteris paribus*, investments with a higher expected return are more likely to be undertaken.

The Effects of Unions on Wages

Now that we've looked at some of the major difficulties associated with estimating union wage effects as well as one of the models used, what does the evidence tell us? With more than 200 studies analyzing the United States alone in the last several decades, we can make the following generalizations. First, *different unions vary in the extent to which they have been successful in raising the wages of their members*. This certainly should not be surprising. We have already seen how the Marshall-Hicks factors affect union bargaining power, and it is obvious that the Marshall-Hicks conditions are not equally favorable or "ripe" for all unions. But how much variation is there? Some unions, such as those of commercial airline pilots and skilled building craftspeople, have generated wage gaps for their members as high as 25% to 30%. Other unions, such as those of clothing and textile workers, have had very little effect on the wages of their members. On average, though, few unions have succeeded in producing wage gaps greater than 30%, at least not for very long periods of time.

A second important generalization is that *the wage effects of unions—the pay gaps that they generate—vary with economic conditions*. In "normal" times (when inflation is moderate and unemployment is neither extremely low nor extremely high), U.S. unions have on average tended to generate pay gaps of about 10% to 20%. However, during periods of rapid and unexpected inflation, the average union pay gap has tended to decline. Conversely, during times of depression (such as that of the 1930s), the union–nonunion pay gap has risen sharply. This result may strike you as surprising, even counterintuitive, because earlier in this chapter we found that unions tend to see their memberships rise during times of economic prosperity and fall during recessions (*ceteris paribus*, again). Why should the wage effects of unions be more pronounced when, organizationally speaking, they seem to be weakest?

The key to this apparent dilemma lies in the rigidity that unions build into the wage determination process when they negotiate contracts. Many union contracts are negotiated for two or even three years. In times of rapid unexpected inflation, a union might therefore be locked into a contract with scheduled pay increases that do not reflect the rise in the price level. In the nonunion sector, on the other hand, wages may rise more rapidly. The result is that the difference between w_u and w_n can shrink or even become negative.[48] But, you might be wondering, don't unions routinely negotiate cost-of-living adjustments (sometimes called COLAs, escalators, or indexation) into their contracts? Some do in fact

---

[48] Albert Rees found evidence that unionism in the post–World War II steel industry may actually have resulted in a *negative* pay gap for a brief period. The rapid unexpected surge in prices came after the steelworkers had already negotiated a five-year contract with steel manufacturers (Rees, *The Economics of Trade Unions*, p. 79).

try to negotiate COLAs, but they are not as common as they once were. Even so, most COLA provisions are not fully indexed to the rate of inflation, usually providing for a certain cents-per-hour adjustment for a given rise in the Consumer Price Index. As a result, they compensate workers for only a fraction of the rise in the price level. Many COLAs are capped with maximum adjustments as well.

What explains the tendency for the union wage gap to rise during times of severe downturns in the economy? Two factors are at work here. First, the same rigidity that can prevent union wages from rising quickly during times of unexpected inflation works to keep union wages from falling during times of deep recession or depression. Second, unions generally fiercely resist wage cuts except during extremely depressed conditions (remember the shape of the union preference curve in Figure 12.10). These two factors tend to widen the gap between w_u and w_n during such times.

Table 12.7 depicts estimates of the average economy-wide adjusted union wage gap from various studies for various periods of time. Notice that the wage gap was at its

TABLE 12.7 The Average (Adjusted) Union–Nonunion Wage Gap, 1920–2002

Time Period	$\dfrac{w_u - w_n}{w_n}$ %
1920–24	16%
1925–29	23
1930–34	38
1935–39	20
1940–44	6
1945–49	2
1950–54	11
1955–59	15
1960–64	22
1965–69	17
1970–74	17
1975–79	26
1980–84	25
1985–89	15
1990–94	14
1995–99	17
2000–02	16

Sources: H. G. Lewis, *Unionism and Relative Wages in the United States* (Chicago: University of Chicago Press, 1963); George Johnson, "Changes over Time in the Union–Nonunion Wage Differential in the United States," in *The Economics of Trade Unions: New Directions*, ed. Jean-Jacques Rosa (Boston: Kluwer-Nijhoff, 1983); David Blanchflower and Alex Bryson, "Changes over Time in Union Relative Wage Effects in the U.K. and the U.S. Revisited," *NBER Working Paper No. 9395* (National Bureau of Economic Research, 2002); David Blanchflower and Alex Bryson, "What Effects Do Unions Have on Wages Now and Would Freeman and Medoff Be Surprised?" *Journal of Labor Research* 25 (3) (Summer 2004).

highest level, a whopping 38%, during the early years of the Great Depression of the 1930s and at its lowest level during the inflationary period of the immediate post–World War II years. On the whole, though, over the nearly 80-year period that Table 12.7 covers, the union wage gap in the United States has averaged a little over 15%.

Many people would be surprised by this finding. As our public opinion poll evidence revealed, the prevailing opinion is that unions have had a much larger effect on wages than 15%. Why is this? Milton Friedman has suggested several reasons.[49] First, unions negotiate infrequently, sometimes only once every two or even three years. The *total* wage increase over such a long period may seem deceptively large. Unions also make headlines, especially those that strike and those that have negotiated large settlements. Settlements that are newsworthy are by their nature not likely to be "typical."

Our discussion so far has been restricted to the wage effects of U.S. unions, but over the last few decades a number of studies have estimated union wage gaps for other countries. *A priori*, we would probably not expect union wage effects to be about the same in all countries. As you saw earlier in this chapter, union density, union coverage, and the degree of centralization in wage setting vary considerably across countries. And, as Richard Freeman has observed, unions have in fact raised wages by widely different amounts.[50] David Blanchflower reports that the union wage gap in Canada is in the range of 10% to 15%, in Great Britain about 10%, in Australia between 7% and 17% (and probably closer to the lower end of the range), in Germany under 6%, and in South Korea about 5%. Viewed comparatively, then, the union wage gap in the United States appears to be relatively high.[51] In fact, the relatively high union wage premium in the United States may have been partly responsible for the decline in union density we have observed over the past several decades insofar as it has induced employer opposition to unions.[52]

So far in our assessment of the effects of unions, we have made no distinction between unions in the public sector and unions in the private sector. Have wage gaps for unions in the public sector been of the same order of magnitude as wage gaps for private sector unions? The question is not a trivial one. If there is a much more pronounced gap for unions of government workers, a case might be made for changing public policy in this area. Those who have taken strong stances against allowing public sector unions to strike have expressed precisely this concern. And the proposals to scale back public employee bargaining rights in Wisconsin (successful), Ohio (unsuccessful), and other states reflect the importance of the issue.

---

[49] Milton Friedman, "Some Comments on the Significance of Labor Unions for Public Policy," in *The Impact of the Union*, ed., David M. Wright (New York: Harcourt Brace, 1951).

[50] Richard Freeman, "American Exceptionalism in the Labor Market: Union–Nonunion Differentials in the United States and Other Countries," in *Labor Economics and Industrial Relations*, eds., Clark Kerr and Paul Staudoher (Cambridge, MA: Harvard University Press, 1994), pp. 273–274.

[51] David Blanchflower, "Changes over Time in Union Relative Wage Effects in Great Britain and the United States," *NBER Working Paper No. 6100*, 1997. Also, David Blanchflower and Alex Bryson, "Changes over Time in Union Relative Wage Effects in the U.K. and the U.S. Revisited." *NBER Working Paper No. 9395*, National Bureau of Economic Research, 2002.

[52] David Blanchflower and Richard Freeman, "Unionism in the United States and Other Advanced OECD Countries," *Industrial Relations* 31 (1992): 56–79.

Before we examine the evidence, though, let's first speculate as to what we might *expect* to find. On the one hand, the elasticity of demand for some (though not all) types of workers in the public sector is quite low (e.g., police and firefighters). Recalling the Marshall-Hicks determinants of demand elasticity, the services that many public employees provide are essential and without close substitutes. Furthermore, in the public sector there is usually no danger of the government being shut down, much less being "driven out of business," by excessively high wage increases. On the other hand, unions of public employees in the United States do not possess the full spectrum of bargaining rights enjoyed by workers in the private sector. In particular, public employees are usually denied the right to strike (although illegal strikes, especially by teachers unions do occasionally occur.) The point, though, is that *a priori* we cannot predict whether public sector union effects should be greater or smaller than private sector union effects.

What does the empirical evidence show? Numerous studies have attempted to measure the effects of unionism on the wages of (mostly local) government employees. On average most studies have found that the impact of public sector unions has not been extraordinarily large. Typically the estimated union-nonunion wage gap is under 10% and is often considerably less. The gap seems to be somewhat larger for police and firefighters than for other groups such as teachers, perhaps reflecting their greater bargaining power. All in all, the average union wage gap in the public sector appears to be smaller than that in the private sector, although Blanchflower and Bryson have argued that the gap has been rising in the past several decades.[53]

The Effects of Unions on Other Economic Variables

Nearly all union impact studies undertaken in the United States have focused exclusively on the wage effects of unions, the reason largely being the paucity of data. But unions in both the public and the private sectors have been successful in raising the level of nonwage benefits as well.[54] By nonwage benefits (also called "fringe benefits") we are referring to compensation in the form of vacation and holiday pay, life and health insurance, sick leave, and retirement benefits. In fact, there is evidence that union effects on fringe benefits may be proportionately greater than union effects on wages. John Budd finds that workers in union jobs receive fringe benefits that are between 15% and 40% higher than workers in similar nonunion jobs.[55] Such a finding is probably not too surprising if you think about it. As we've seen, in competitive labor markets in the absence of unions, firms tend to hire up to the point where the wage equals the marginal revenue product. A typical firm will thus tend to give greater weight to the marginal worker and the marginal worker's preferences when it comes to the mix of wages and fringe benefits in the total compensation package. But in a unionized situation, a union will tend to give greater weight to the preferences of the median worker (or so our median voter model predicts) who is more likely to be older and more experienced and hence more interested

---

[53] David Blanchflower and Bryson, 2004, p. 391.

[54] See Richard Freeman, "The Effect of Unionism on Fringe Benefits," *Industrial and Labor Relations Review* 33 (1980): 489–510.

[55] John Budd "The Effect of Unions on Employee Benefits: Updated Employer Expenditure Results," *Journal of Labor Research* 26 (4) (Fall 2005): 669–676.

in nonwage benefits such as pensions, insurance, and so forth. Interestingly, Blanchflower and Freeman claim that unions in other countries seem to have had effects on nonwage outcomes that are similar in magnitude to those of U.S. unions.[56]

There is also some evidence that union effects on fringe benefits in the public sector may likewise be greater than union wage effects. For one thing, it is sometimes easy to hide the long-run costs of generous fringe benefit settlements made at the public sector bargaining table. This is particularly true for pensions, which can be underfunded for years before the consequences become apparent. By the time the "bill" comes due, the government officials responsible have long since departed. Some empirical evidence supports this suspicion, but it is limited. One study of firefighters, for example, found that unionism's effect on fringe benefits was several times larger than its effects on wages.[57] And another study of police, fire, sanitation, and other municipal departments (excluding education) found that the average effect of bargaining on wages (only 3.6%) was dwarfed by the effect of bargaining on pensions and paid time off from work.[58]

In comparing the effects of unions in the private sector with those in the public sector, one extremely important question arises: Are public sector workers overpaid? The question has recently taken on even more importance with, as we have already mentioned, attempts by some states in the United States to cut back on collective bargaining rights of public employees. Such attempts have usually been couched in terms of the claim that the recent fiscal difficulties that many states and municipalities have experienced are due in large part to overly generous pay and benefit levels that government workers enjoy—pay and benefit levels that allegedly are the result of powerful public employee unions.

But what is the evidence? Are public workers overpaid? Should public sector bargaining rights be curtailed? According to Lewin, Kochan, and Keefe, state and local government employees in the United States earn wages that are on average between 5.8% and 8.5% *lower* than those of comparable private sector workers (comparable with respect to human capital and personal characteristics, such as education, and experience.) On the other hand, public employers on average do provide relatively better health insurance and pension benefits than private sector employers. But when wages and benefits are considered together, average compensation in the public sector is actually found to be about 5% *lower* than in the private sector.[59]

Finally, let's address the question of the effects of unions on output and productivity. This is a difficult question to answer, for the magnitude of the net effect will depend on several factors:

- Output losses due to restrictive work rules, such as featherbedding
- Output losses due to strikes

[56] David Blanchflower and Richard Freeman, "Unionism in the United States and Other Advanced OECD Countries," *Industrial Relations* 31 (1992): 67.

[57] Casey Ichniowski, "Economic Effects of the Firefighters Union," *Industrial and Labor Relations Review* 33 (1980): 405–425.

[58] Jeffrey Zax, "Wages, Compensation, and Municipal Unions," *Industrial Relations* 27 (1988): 314.

[59] David Lewin, Thomas Kochan, and Jeffrey Keefe, "Toward a New Generation of Empirical Evidence and Policy Research on Public Sector Unionism and Collective Bargaining," *Working Paper*, April 12, 2012, pp. 1–39.

- Output losses due to union effects on employment and the resulting misallocation of resources
- Possible *positive* effects of unions on productivity.

Let's briefly consider how large each of these effects tends to be. In the case of feather-bedding, we've noted some examples earlier in this chapter (and could have mentioned quite a few more). But many of these practices have disappeared with advances in technology and consequent changes in production processes. John Addison and others have argued that featherbedding has been prevalent in a relatively small number of industries that are monopolistic rather than competitive, and some of the historical examples (railroads, longshoring, and construction) certainly support this assertion.[60] However, a few attempts have been made to empirically estimate the output loss to the economy that featherbedding generates. One early study by Albert Rees cited a statistic that obsolete work rules in one industry alone (railroads) were costing $500 million per year (about 0.1% of gross national product [GNP]), but the number was put forth by management and is probably exaggerated.[61]

The Business Roundtable once analyzed a sample of collective bargaining agreements in the construction industry. It found that about 20% of the contracts contained minimum crew size provisions (restrictions that were especially prevalent among ironworker, boiler-maker, and operating engineer agreements). The Business Roundtable estimated that such restrictions resulted in an annual excess cost of $42 million.[62]

Steven Allen has estimated the effect of union work rules in the building trades by comparing demand elasticities for different types of labor among union and nonunion contractors. Allen's hypothesis is that union featherbedding restrictions would be expected to result in lower labor demand elasticities in the union sectors. Focusing on construction of commercial office buildings and school buildings, Allen found that both the own-wage elasticities of demand and the elasticities of substitution among different skill categories of labor were (as expected) lower in union construction than in nonunion construction. However, he also found that the costs of such work rules, although sizeable, were "not as alarmingly large as journalistic accounts and nonacademic studies suggest."[63] Furthermore—and we will return to this shortly—Allen finds that worker productivity in the union sector is sufficiently higher than in the nonunion sector to offset the adverse cost effects of such work rules.

What about output losses due to union strike activity? Table 12.8 presents information on the number and incidence of strikes in the United States since 1960, and it tells a surprising story. First of all, the number of strikes is relatively small and has been declining sharply in recent years. Second, the percentage of working time lost due to strikes is also extremely small. In fact, if one were to add up all the man-days lost to strikes since

---

[60] John T. Addison, "Trade Unions and Restrictive Practices," in *The Economics of Trade Unions: New Directions*, ed., Jean-Jacques Rosa (Boston: Kluwer-Nijhoff, 1984). Also see Albert Rees, "The Effects of Unions on Resource Allocation," *Journal of Law and Economics* (1963): 69–78.

[61] Albert Rees, "The Effects of Unions on Resource Allocation," p. 75.

[62] Business Roundtable, "Constraints Imposed by Collective Bargaining Agreements, Construction Industry Cost Effectiveness Project Report C-4" (New York: Business Roundtable, 1982).

[63] Steven Allen, "Union Work Rules and Efficiency in the Building Trades," *Journal of Labor Economics* 4 (1986): 212–242.

TABLE 12.8 Strikes* in the United States, 1960–2011

Year	Number of Strikes	Workers Involved (1,000s)	Percent of Estimated Working Time	Year	Number of Strikes	Workers Involved (1,000s)	Percent of Estimated Working Time
1960	222	896	0.09%	1990	44	185	0.02%
1965	268	999	0.10	1991	40	392	0.02
1970	381	2,468	0.29	1992	35	364	0.01
1971	298	2,516	0.19	1993	35	182	0.01
1972	250	975	0.09	1994	45	322	0.02
1973	317	1,400	0.08	1995	31	192	0.02
1974	424	1,796	0.16	1996	37	273	0.02
1975	235	965	0.09	1997	29	339	0.01
1976	231	1,519	0.12	1998	34	387	0.02
1977	298	1,212	0.10	1999	17	73	0.01
1978	219	1,006	0.11	2000	39	394	0.06
1979	235	1,021	0.09	2001	29	99	<.005
1980	187	795	0.09	2002	19	46	<.005
1981	145	729	0.07	2003	14	129	.01
1982	96	656	0.04	2004	17	171	.01
1983	81	909	0.08	2005	22	100	.01
1984	62	376	0.04	2006	20	70	.01
1985	54	324	0.03	2007	21	189	<.005
1986	69	533	0.05	2008	15	72	.01
1987	46	174	0.02	2009	5	13	<.005
1988	40	118	0.02	2010	11	45	<.005
1989	51	452	0.07	2011	19	113	<.005

Note: *Excludes strikes involving fewer than 1,000 workers and lasting less than one day.

Source: U.S. Bureau of Labor Statistics, Work Stoppages Summary, USDL 12-0215, February 8, 2012.

1960, they would sum to far less than all the man-days lost by unemployment in a single typical year. Clearly, the output losses from union strike activity are not large despite the headlines that strikes sometimes generate. The fact that strikes are rare is consistent with the view we expressed earlier: strikes occur as a result of mistakes made in bargaining.

The third way unions can affect output is less direct and less obvious. Union effects on employment and the resulting misalloction of resources can affect output. When unions raise wages to levels higher than would otherwise have existed in a competitive labor market, employment levels will be lower (disemployment occurs) as long as the demand for labor is not perfectly inelastic. What this means, of course, is that there are fewer jobs in the unionized sector of the economy (*ceteris paribus*) than there would be otherwise. But what happens to those workers who would otherwise have worked in the union sector? Although some may drop out of the labor force, most will seek jobs in the nonunion sector. The result is an "output loss" to the economy. Figure 12.15 tells the story.

Let's assume for simplicity that the economy comprises two sectors, a union sector and a nonunion sector, and that initially the wage levels in each sector are the same (w_0). Let's assume next that in the union sector the wage level is bargained up to w_u. The demand

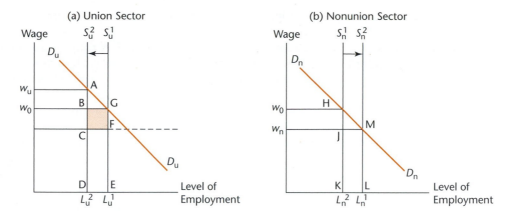

FIGURE 12.15 Output Loss to the Economy Due to Union Employment

for labor is not perfectly inelastic, so employers in this sector will reduce the level of employment from $L_u{}^1$ to $L_u{}^2$. Those workers who no longer have jobs in the union sector ($L_u^1 - L_u^2$) will then seek jobs in the nonunion sector, the result being an increase in the supply of labor in that sector and a drop in the wage level to w_n. With fewer workers employed in the union sector, output will fall there by an amount designated by the trapezoid ADEG[64] in Figure 12.15a; but with more workers employed in the nonunion sector (although at a lower wage w_n), output there will rise by the amount HKLM in Figure 12.15b. The important point is that the output changes in the two sectors will not offset one another. Rather, the fall in the union sector's output will exceed the output gain in the nonunion sector, resulting in a net loss in output for the economy as a whole. If we assume for simplicity that the employment gain in the nonunion sector is exactly equal to the employment loss in the union sector, then the net loss in total output will be represented by shaded area BCFG.

Before we estimate the size of this output loss—sometimes called the welfare or deadweight loss due to unionism—let's explain more concretely what this loss represents with a simple example. Suppose you are a painter; you have been trained to perform this work, and this is the type of work you are best at. However, because of fewer employment opportunities in the unionized sector, you are not able to obtain a job as a painter but instead wind up in another line of work where your marginal product and pay (alas) are lower. The difference in marginal products between the job you would have had and the job you wind up taking is an output loss that, when aggregated for all individuals like you, is represented by the BCFG area depicted in Figure 12.15a.

In the figure we have implicitly assumed that the supply of labor in both sectors is vertical, or perfectly inelastic. But if we assume instead that the labor supply schedules are positively sloped, the output loss will be greater still. Some people who are unable to

---

[64]Remember that total output (Q) associated with a particular level of employment (L) can be depicted as the area under the marginal product function up to L. An equivalent way of explaining the output loss is that there is too little labor (and too much capital) in the union sector and too much labor (and too little capital) in the nonunion sector.

find work in the union sector will drop out of the labor force rather than work at a lower wage w_n.

How large is the output or welfare loss we are talking about? A rough estimate of its magnitude would require knowledge of labor demand elasticities in each sector, the average union–nonunion wage gap, and the size of the unionized labor force. Albert Rees first estimated the size of this loss to be approximately $600 million for the U.S. economy in 1957, a number that in absolute terms seems large (we certainly wouldn't mind winning a lottery prize of this amount). As a percentage of GNP, however, the output loss was extremely small, a paltry 0.14%.[65] How large would this output loss be today? We have left this for you as a simple exercise in problem 9 at the end of this chapter.

So far, all of the union effects on output that we've analyzed have been negative effects: output losses due to restrictive work rules, strikes, and lower employment in the union sector. But unions sometimes have positive effects on productivity as well, a fact that has not been widely appreciated by many economists or by the public at large. This other view of unions is not new, but in recent years it has been given new life largely due to the work of Richard Freeman and James Medoff.[66] More specifically, Freeman and Medoff argue that the traditional view or "face" of unions as labor market monopolies is too narrow. It overlooks the fact that unions are also institutions that channel information between workers and management, thereby serving as a **collective voice**.[67]

Let's use an analogy to see how the voice mechanism works. Suppose you are unhappy with the way things are going in a particular class (*not* labor economics, of course) because of your grade, the difficulty of the material, the pace of the course, and so forth. You have two options. One is to simply drop the class or "walk," the exit option. The other option is to talk with the instructor about the way things are going in hopes of coming to a resolution or understanding. The exit option can be costly: you may have to take the course all over again or take another course to substitute for it. The "voice" option may resolve the matter to your satisfaction and allow you to complete the course. In a similar fashion, by serving as the collective voice of workers, unions can help resolve grievances and conflicts at work, thereby improving worker morale and reducing quits. Both poor morale and quits can be costly to the firm. Poor morale can result in lower levels of output or inferior quality of goods and services produced; quits can result in additional search, hiring, and training costs, not to mention wasting firm-specific human capital already invested in workers. Table 12.9 contrasts the strikingly different productivity implications of unionism according to these two faces of unionism.

What evidence is there to support the collective voice view? There is quite a bit of evidence that quit rates do indeed tend to be lower in union firms. Of course, higher union wages as well as the collective voice mechanism that unions provide are no doubt responsible for these lower quit rates. A fair number of studies have compared productivity in union and nonunion establishments and industries, and here the evidence is mixed. Freeman and Medoff cite evidence showing that in many sectors (construction, paper mills, cement, to name a few) unionized establishments are more productive than

---

[65] Albert Rees, "The Effects of Unions on Resource Allocation," p. 70.

[66] Richard Freeman and James Medoff, *What Do Unions Do?* (New York: Basic Books, 1984).

[67] The "voice" concept was first advanced by Albert O. Hirschman, *Exit, Voice, and Loyalty* (Cambridge, MA: Harvard University Press, 1971).

TABLE 12.9   Union Effects on Productivity: The Monopoly Face Versus the Collective Voice Face

Monopoly Face	*Collective Voice Face*
▪ Unions raise wages above competitive levels, leading to too little labor relative to capital in unionized firms. ▪ Union work rules decrease productivity.	▪ Unions have some positive effects on productivity—reducing quit rates, inducing management to alter methods of production and to adopt more efficient policies, and improving morale and cooperation among workers. ▪ Unions collect information about the preferences of all workers, leading the firm to choose a better mix of employee compensation and a better set of personnel policies.

Source: From Richard B. Freeman and James L. Medoff (1979), The two faces of unionism, The Public Interest, 57, 69–93. Reprinted by permission of National Affairs, Inc.

nonunion establishments, but there are also many cases (education, libraries) where no differential has been found.

There is an obvious question lurking here, and you've probably already guessed what it is. If unions often have favorable effects on productivity, could it be that at least on average their (positive) effect on productivity outweighs their (negative) effect on costs and thereby actually increases the profitability of firms? The simple answer to this question is "no." If it were not the case, we might then expect profit maximizing employers to actually welcome union attempts to organize their firms. But the fact is that unions generally reduce the profitability of firms. Evidence from studies of stock prices confirms this; generally, the price of a company's stock falls when a union wins a certification election.

Summary

In this chapter we have given unions a rather thorough "physical examination." We've looked at how widespread unionism is, where it is most heavily concentrated, what unions strive for, the tactics they use, and, finally, the effects of unions on the economy. Unionism is a far more complex institution in nearly all respects than many people (including some economists) are willing to admit. Furthermore, such generalizations as "unions are good [or bad]" or "unions once had an important role to play but not in today's global economy" are simplistic. And as far as policies toward unions are concerned, perhaps Freeman and Medoff put it best when they state: "Because … unions do much social good, … the 'union-free' economy desired by some business groups would be a disaster for the country. [At the same time] we also think that 100 percent unionization would also be economically undesirable."[68]

---

[68] Richard Freeman and James Medoff, *What Do Unions Do?* p. 250.

KEY TERMS

union density

right-to-work laws

National Labor Relations Act

rent-maximization model

wage-bill maximization model

median voter model

utility-maximization model

efficient contracts

featherbedding

bargaining power

wage gain

wage gap

threat effects

spillover effects

omitted variable bias

collective voice

PROBLEMS

1. Given the changing character of the economy, assess the prospects for union membership growth over the next 10 years.

2. If you were in a position to try to raise union density in the private sector of the economy, what strategies would you pursue?

3. Do you think workers in the southern states are less likely to become union members than workers in the North? If so, why do you think this is true?

4. Suppose all union contracts included cost-of-living adjustments. How might this affect the union–nonunion wage gap over time?

5. Suppose that Congress is debating a proposal for tax reductions for employers who purchase capital equipment. Some prominent union leaders have been asked to comment on the proposal from the standpoint of how it will affect the well-being of their members. Would you expect the union leaders to favor or not favor the tax reduction?

6. Sometimes nonunion companies in a particular city or industry pay higher wages and fringe benefits than do their unionized competitors. Would you conclude that unions in these areas are ineffective in gaining higher wages and benefits?

7. The city of Jonesburg has an ordinance requiring that all electrical installations and repairs must be made by union electricians. Analyze the effects of this ordinance on workers, consumers, and the general well-being of people living in Jonesburg.

8. The first unions in the United States (in the nineteenth century) were formed among skilled craft workers such as shoemakers and carpenters rather than among unskilled laborers. Why was this the case?

9. The estimates of the output loss (or welfare loss) attributed to unionism in the United States undertaken by Albert Rees are now 50 years old. How large would you estimate the welfare loss to be today, both in absolute ($) terms and as a percentage of GNP? You may use the following information for your calculations:
   - η_d (elasticity of labor demand) = −1 (in both the union and nonunion sectors)
   - Union density rate = 0.10 (10%)

- η_s (elasticity of labor supply) = 0 (both sectors)
- Average annual worker pay (union and nonunion combined) = \$30,000.

10. If you wanted to lower the output loss (welfare loss) caused by unions, what changes in the law regarding unions would you suggest? How likely would U.S. society (unions, politicians, and workers in general) be to support or embrace your suggestions?

APPENDIX

Occupational Licensing*

Another important labor market institution—but one that is growing in importance in the United States (and in many other countries as well)—is occupational licensing. Although union membership as a percentage of the labor force has been declining since 1970 (see Table 12.1), the percentage of workers affected by occupational licensing has nearly tripled from about 10% in 1970 to about 29% as of 2005.[69] Today, not just doctors and lawyers need a license to practice, but also barbers, massage therapists, egg graders, tattoo artists, interior designers, auctioneers, locksmiths, and workers in hundreds of other fields (depending on the state or locality).

An occupational license is, in the simplest of terms, a government-issued "permit" allowing one to work in a particular occupation. If an occupation is licensed, a prospective practitioner of the occupation is usually required to have attained a specified level of education or training in the field, passed an examination, paid a fee to be given the license, and met certain additional requirements (e.g., be of good moral character and not have a criminal record). It is important to differentiate occupational licensing from other less-restrictive forms of job regulation such as certification (which is effectively "title protection"). Unlike licensing, certification does not restrict the right of a person to practice in a field, but allows only individuals who have met certain requirements to use the job title. For example, certification laws prohibit individuals who have not met a minimum set of requirements from using the title "certified public accountant" (or CPA) in every state in the United States, but individuals are still allowed to perform the tasks of an accountant so long as they do not use the protected CPA title. Licensing laws are much more restrictive. Doctors, for example, are not permitted to *practice* in any state in the United States without obtaining a license.

How do occupations become licensed? As Milton Friedman noted:

In the arguments that seek to persuade legislatures to enact such licensure provisions, the justification is always said to be the necessity of protecting the public interest. However, the pressure on

---

*This appendix was written by Edward Timmons of St. Francis University.

[69] These figures are taken from Morris Kleiner, *Licensing Occupations: Ensuring Quality or Restricting Competition* (Kalamazoo, MI: W.E. Upjohn Institute for Employment Research, 2006); and Morris Kleiner and Alan Krueger, "The Prevalence and Effects of Occupational Licensing," *British Journal of Industrial Relations* 48 (2010).

the legislature to license an occupation rarely comes from the members of the public who have been mulcted [a good word to look up in the dictionary!] or in other ways abused by members of the occupation. On the contrary, the pressure invariably comes from members of the occupation itself.[70]

What Friedman is arguing, of course, is that it is the self-interest of the practitioners, rather than the interests of the public, that usually constitutes the real motivation for licensing. Furthermore, any lobbying group that has a strong pecuniary interest in licensing legislation can devote a great deal of time and resources to their lobbying efforts. Consumers, on the other hand, typically spend a very small percentage of their income on services that may become licensed and find it not worthwhile to spend time lobbying against, or even learning about, licensing legislation. As a result, licensing interest groups have a much better chance of initiating and maintaining licensing laws than consumers have of eliminating them.

What effect do occupational licensing laws have on labor markets? Economists contend that, by restricting labor supply, licensing will increase the earnings of practitioners in the occupation.[71] Entry requirements into the occupation impose higher costs upon potential practitioners and thus discourage entry into the occupation. In the labor market for barbers, for example (who must be licensed in every state except Alabama), we would expect to see a labor supply curve that is lower (further to the left) with occupational licensing than without licensing.

Economists have attempted to estimate the economic effects of licensing on earnings. Table 12.A.1 provides a snapshot of what some of these studies have found. Estimates of the effects of occupational licensing on wages range from little or no effect to as much as a 30% wage premium. Recent nationwide estimates of the occupational licensing premium find that the average premium is probably between 10% and 15%—very similar in magnitude, by the way, to estimates of the overall union–nonunion wage gap (see Table 12.7).

Although economists agree that licensing will increase the earnings of practitioners, there is some disagreement as to how occupational licensing affects consumers. Consumers of medical services, for example, have different access to information about the credentials and skills of a doctor than the doctor herself. Depending upon the degree of asymmetric information between consumer and practitioner, it is possible that occupational licensing may increase the quality of services delivered to consumers.[72] It is therefore possible that occupational licensing may increase demand for practitioners in a labor market and perhaps this can also explain the higher earnings of practitioners resulting from occupational licensing.

Measuring the quality of the services delivered to consumers is difficult, however. The few existing studies that have attempted to measure the effects of occupational licensing

---

[70] Milton Friedman, *Capitalism and Freedom*, p. 140.

[71] In the *Wealth of Nations* Adam Smith discussed how more restrictive entry requirements into a craft will have the effect of increasing earnings. The Nobel Laureate Milton Friedman has also discussed how licensing limits entry into an occupation in *Income from Independent Professional Practice* (New York: National Bureau of Economic Research, 1945); and *Capitalism and Freedom* (Chicago: University of Chicago Press, 1962).

[72] See George Akerlof, "The Market for Lemons: Quality Uncertainty and the Market Mechanism," *Quarterly Journal of Economics* 89 (1970); and Hayne Leland, "Quacks, Lemons and Licensing: A Theory of Minimum Quality Standards," *Journal of Political Economy* 87 (1979).

TABLE 12.A.1   Selected Studies of the Economic Effects of Licensing

Author(s)	Profession(s)	Findings
Benham and Benham (1975)	Optometrists	Stricter licensing increases price of services by 25% to 40%
Shephard (1978)	Dentists	More restrictive licensing increases price of services by 8.5% to 18%
Muzondo and Pazderka (1980)	12 Licensed occupations	Stricter licensing increases the wages of professionals in Canada by 10% to 30%
Feldman and Begun (1985)	Optometrists	Stricter regulation increases the price of an examination by $4.11 on average
Kleiner and Kudrle (2000)	Dentists	Dentists in states with strict regulation have hourly wages that are 12% higher than dentists in the least-regulated states
Kleiner (2000, 2006)	Several occupations	Licensing increases the wages of dentists and lawyers. In general, licensing increases earnings by 10% to 12%
Adams, Ekelund, and Jackson (2002, 2003)	Cosmetologists and Midwives	Licensing increases the price of cosmetology and midwifery services
Timmons and Thornton (2008, 2010)	Radiologic technologists and Barbers	Licensing and specific licensing requirements increased the wages of radiologic technologists (as much as 7%) and barbers (as much as 22%)

Notes: A. Frank Adams III, Robert Ekelund, and John Jackson, "Occupational Licensing in a 'Competitive' Labor Market: The Case of Cosmetology," *Journal of Labor Research* 23 (2002): 261–278; A. Frank Adams III, Robert Ekelund, and John Jackson, "Occupational Licensing of a Credence Good: The Regulation of Midwifery," *Southern Economic Journal* 69 (2003): 659–675; Lee Benham and Alexandra Benham, "Regulating Through the Professions: A Perspective on Information Control," *Journal of Law and Economics* 18 (1975): 421–447; Roger Feldman and James W. Begun, "The Welfare Cost of Quality Changes due to Professional Regulation," *The Journal of Industrial Economics* 34 (1985): 17–32; Morris Kleiner, "Occupational Licensing," *Journal of Economic Perspectives* 14 (2000): 189–202; Morris Kleiner and Robert Kudrle, "Does Regulation Affect Economic Outcomes? The Case of Dentistry," *Journal of Law and Economics* 18 (2000): 547–576; Morris Kleiner, *Licensing Occupations: Ensuring Quality or Restricting Competition* (Michigan: W.E. Upjohn Institute, 2006); Timothy Muzondo and Bohumir Pazderka, "Occupational Licensing and Professional Incomes in Canada," *Canadian Journal of Economics* 13 (1980): 659–667; Lawrence Shephard, "Licensing Restrictions and the Cost of Dental Care," *Journal of Law and Economics* 21 (1978): 187–201; Edward Timmons and Robert Thornton, "The Effects of Licensing on the Earnings of Radiologic Technologists," *Journal of Labor Research* 29 (2008): 333–346; and Edward Timmons and Robert Thornton, "The Licensing of Barbers in the U.S.," *British Journal of Industrial Relations* 48(4) (2010): 740–757.

on quality generally find that licensing has had little effect.[73] As we already noted, though, practitioners are generally far more likely to lobby for occupational licensing than consumers. This observation would be consistent with larger benefits from occupational licensing accruing to practitioners than those received by consumers.

---

[73] See Morris Kleiner, *Licensing Occupations: Ensuring Quality or Restricting Competition* (Kalamazoo, MI: W.E. Upjohn Institute for Employment Research, 2006).

13

Labor Market Discrimination

Is there evidence that racial and gender discrimination affects labor market outcomes?

How important is discrimination as a determinant of wages and employment opportunities?

Are affirmative action and comparable worth effective anti-discrimination policies?

So far we have assumed that employers would have no reason to prefer one group of workers over another group as long as workers' marginal products are expected to be the same. Such an assumption, however, is not always tenable in real world labor markets. Many characteristics, including skin color, gender, age, ethnic group, and sexual preference, may be considered by employers in hiring, pay, and promotion decisions.

We begin by defining what is meant by labor market discrimination and then look at the many ways such discrimination can manifest itself. Next we explore some "fast facts" on labor market discrimination, concentrating particularly on gender and racial discrimination. Then we analyze the major theories of labor market discrimination that seek to explain both why such discrimination arises and the best policies for eliminating it. We look at gender and racial "earnings gaps" to determine what portion of these gaps reasonably can be attributed to labor market discrimination. Finally, we discuss the various policies that have been enacted in the United States and in other countries to combat labor market discrimination, and we analyze how effective these policies have been.

The Many Faces of Labor Market Discrimination

Discrimination is a long-standing problem that knows no national borders. In Northern Ireland, for example, some Catholics have been subject to religious discrimination. In many countries, discrimination has been directed against ethnic minorities: the Native American population and the Aboriginal people in Australasia are two examples that affect Anglophone countries today. In South Africa, apartheid policies have had a severe impact on blacks. In Kosovo, the plight of ethnic Albanians is well known, and the list goes on and on.

Discrimination also goes back a long way in history. The Old Testament Book of Leviticus (27: 3-4) states that "thy estimation shall be of the male from 20 years old even unto 60 years old … 50 shekels of silver, after the shekel of the sanctuary. And if it be a female, then thy estimation shall be 30 shekels." This refers not to the labor market remuneration of the sexes but rather to the legal value of an individual based on compensation claims. Nonetheless, it suggests that the market valuation of a female in biblical times amounted to around 60%, a little more than half that of a male. It is also noteworthy that the ratio of women's wages to men's wages remained at this 60% level well into the late twentieth century and that in many economies it remains roughly the same even to this day. For example, in the couple of decades leading up to the early 2000s, the mean hourly wages of women in the United States was just 68% that of men; in the United Kingdom the corresponding figure was just 65%.[1] Evidence on ethnic wage differentials suggests that these, too, are considerable in magnitude.

Of course, not all discrimination occurs in the context of labor markets. For example, in the United States blacks were for a long time denied access to equal education and housing opportunities (residential segregation), and societal pressures frowned on married women with children working outside the home. Although this kind of discrimination is fading in the United States, it is still quite strong in some other countries. Even so, the focal point of this chapter is restricted to labor market discrimination.

Labor market discrimination can manifest itself in many ways:

- At the hiring stage, employers may prefer not to hire persons of a particular group (let's call it a "minority group"[2]), or they may insist on higher qualifications for members of this group.
- Employers may not promote members of a certain group to better-paying positions.
- Employers may pay lower wages to persons in a particular group, even though their qualifications are the same and the work they perform is equal to that of other workers.
- Consumers may exercise labor market discrimination in their refusal, for example, to purchase the services of particular persons simply because of their gender, ethnic background, or race.
- And fellow workers may practice labor market discrimination by their unwillingness to work alongside other workers simply because they happen to be members of a certain group.

The word *discriminate* has several different meanings. If a person is said to have "discriminating tastes," it is generally understood that the person shows good judgment in food, clothes, choice of friends, and so forth. But if a person is said to "discriminate" against another person, that action is rightly considered to be unfair and reprehensible. For the purposes of our discussion, we define **labor market discrimination** in the following way: employment, wage, and promotion practices that result in workers who are equal with respect to their productivity being treated differently because of their race,

---

[1] See Martina Zweimüller, Rudolf Winter-Ebmer, and Doris Weichselbaumer, "Market Orientation and Gender Wage Gaps: An International Study," *Kyklos* 61 (2008): 615–635.

[2] The term *minority group* is widely used in the discussion of discrimination, but it is a misnomer when applied to women as a class.

gender, age, ethnic group, or other characteristics unrelated to their job performance. The qualification "equal with respect to their productivity" is an important one. Not all pay or employment differences between groups can necessarily be attributed to labor market discrimination. Some such differences may reflect productivity differences.

Gender and Racial Differences in Labor Markets

Gender Differences

The single fact that can best describe the secular labor market experience of employed women in the United States is that they have been concentrated in a limited number of occupations. Table 13.1 shows the extent of this employment concentration for two years, 1983 and 2010, in several dozen selected occupations. Although women comprised 47% of all those employed in 2010, tremendous variation in the gender composition of the various occupations still exists. Some occupations are largely female (e.g., nurses, dieticians, and therapists) whereas others are largely male (e.g., airline pilots and the engineering occupations). In addition, substantial changes in the male–female composition have occurred in only a few occupations since 1983, with lawyers and pharmacists being in this group; but in many other categories **occupational segregation** still exists.

Why the concentration? As recently as several decades ago, many jobs were stereotyped as "men's work" or "women's work," and job notices in the classified ad sections of newspapers typically advertised for either men or women to fill certain types of jobs. In fact, the classified ad sections in many newspapers were often broken down into separate sections for men's and women's jobs. Men's listings typically included such jobs as restaurant cook, automobile salesman, driver, and welder, whereas women's listings included openings for secretaries, maids, bookkeepers, and waitresses.[3] Such advertising is now illegal unless there are justifiable reasons for such restrictions, and these are rare. However, many occupations remain, for all practical purposes, male occupations and others remain female occupations, both in numbers and in people's minds. To verify that this is so, cover the numerical data in Table 13.1 and read down the list of occupations. When you see an occupation that strikes you as a "male" or "female" occupation, check the percentage figures in the right-hand columns to see if your impression is supported by the evidence. Is such concentration due to job discrimination, or are there other reasons for it? We address this question later in the chapter.

One widely used measure of the actual degree of gender concentration across occupations is known as the **Duncan index of dissimilarity (DID)**,[4] which is defined as follows:

$$DID = \sum |m_i - f_i|/2 \tag{13-1}$$

where m_i is the proportion of all males in the labor force who are in occupation i and f_i is the proportion of all females in the labor force who are in occupation i. This is a

---

[3] William Darity and Patrick Mason, "Evidence on Discrimination in Employment: Codes of Color, Codes of Gender," *Journal of Economic Perspectives* 12 (1998): 64.

[4] The Duncan index of dissimilarity is also sometimes called the index of segregation.

TABLE 13.1 Employed Civilians for Selected Occupations, Sex, Race, and Hispanic Origin, 1983–2010

Occupation	1983				2010			
	Total Employed (in 1,000s)	Percent of Total			Total Employed (in 1,000s)	Percent of Total		
		Female	Black	Hispanic		Female	Black	Hispanic
Total	100,834	43.7%	9.3%	5.3%	139,064	47.2%	10.8%	14.3%
Architects	103	12.7	1.6	1.5	184	24.4	2.1	7.8
Aerospace engineers	80	6.9	1.5	2.1	126	10.8	6.7	3.8
Civil engineers	211	4.0	1.9	3.2	318	9.7	4.9	6.9
Electrical and electronic engineers	450	6.1	3.4	3.1	307	7.2	5.3	7.0
Industrial engineers	210	11.0	3.3	2.4	159	20.0	5.0	7.8
Mechanical engineers	259	2.8	3.2	1.1	293	6.7	3.2	3.7
Mathematical and computer scientists	463	29.6	5.4	2.6	3,531	25.8	6.7	5.5
Chemists, except biochemists	98	23.3	4.3	1.2	103	33.5	9.9	4.3
Biological and life scientists	55	40.8	2.4	1.8	113	45.8	8.0	6.2
Physicians	519	15.8	3.2	4.5	872	32.3	5.8	6.8
Dentists	126	6.7	2.4	1.0	175	25.5	0.3	5.7
Registered nurses	1,372	95.8	6.7	1.8	2,843	91.1	12.0	4.9
Pharmacists	158	26.7	3.8	2.6	255	53.0	5.2	4.3
Dietitians	71	90.8	21.0	3.7	105	92.3	14.9	5.2
Respiratory therapists	69	69.4	6.5	3.7	187	68.5	5.8	5.4
Physical therapists	55	77.0	9.7	1.5	132	96.3	2.9	6.1
Speech therapists	51	90.5	1.5	—	99	68.7	5.0	9.2
Elementary school teachers	1,350	83.3	11.1	3.1	2,813	81.8	9.3	7.3
Secondary school teachers	1,209	51.8	7.2	2.3	1,221	57.0	8.0	6.7
Special education teachers	81	82.2	10.2	2.3	387	85.1	6.8	6.2
Librarians	193	87.3	7.9	1.8	216	82.8	9.2	5.2

TABLE 13.1 Employed Civilians for Selected Occupations, Sex, Race, and Hispanic Origin, 1983–2010 (continued)

Occupation	1983 Total Employed (in 1,000s)	1983 Percent of Total Female	Black	Hispanic	2010 Total Employed (in 1,000s)	2010 Percent of Total Female	Black	Hispanic
Psychologists	135	57.1	8.6	1.1	179	66.7	3.9	7.3
Social workers	407	64.3	18.2	6.3	771	80.8	22.8	11.3
Clergy	293	5.6	4.9	1.4	429	17.5	12.6	6.3
Lawyers	612	15.3	2.6	0.9	1,040	31.5	4.3	3.4
Authors	62	46.7	2.1	0.9	199	63.5	3.8	1.5
Designers	393	52.7	3.1	2.7	793	53.7	3.3	9.0
Musicians and composers	155	28.0	7.9	4.4	182	31.9	13.9	8.7
Painters, sculptors, craft-artists	186	47.4	2.1	2.3	195	47.1	2.7	6.6
Photographers	113	20.7	4.0	3.4	161	39.4	6.5	8.1
Clinical laboratory technologists and technicians	255	76.2	10.5	2.9	342	76.8	15.1	7.4
Dental hygienists	66	98.6	1.6	—	141	95.1	4.3	3.0
Licensed practical nurses	443	97.0	17.7	3.1	573	91.7	24.4	6.2
Airplane pilots and navigators	69	2.1	—	1.6	110	5.2	1.0	6.3
Child care workers	408	96.9	7.9	3.6	1,247	94.7	16.0	19.1
Food preparation and service occupations	4,860	63.3	10.5	6.8	7,660	55.1	11.3	22.2
Waiters and waitresses	1,357	87.8	4.1	3.6	2,067	71.1	7.1	16.6
Maids and housemen	531	81.2	32.3	10.1	1,407	89.0	16.3	40.8
Janitors and cleaners	2,031	26.6	22.6	8.9	2,186	33.2	17.1	30.9
Textile sewing machine operators	806	94.0	15.5	14.5	170	78.5	13.3	40.2

Source: U.S. Census Bureau, *Statistical Abstract of the United States*, various issues.

TABLE 13.2 Duncan Index of Dissimilarity by Gender in Three Scenarios

	Case 1		Case 2		Case 3	
	A	G	A	G	A	G
Male	0.60	0.40	0	1.00	0.20	0.80
Female	0.60	0.40	1.00	0	0.40	0.60

simple but easily confused measure. To see how it works, let's assume that we have an economy with only two types of occupations, which we'll call A (for awful) and G (for great). Table 13.2 presents three different scenarios, each depicting different concentrations of males and females in these two different occupations. In Case 1, 60% (0.60) of all males in the labor force are in occupation A, as are 60% of all females, leaving 40% of males and 40% of females in occupation G. With no difference in the distribution of males and females across the two occupations, the value of the Duncan index is equal to 0. In Case 2, the exact opposite situation occurs—maximum occupational segregation. All of the males in the labor force (100%) but none of the females are in occupation A, and vice versa for occupation G. Here the Duncan index would take on its maximum value: 1.00 (or 100%). In Case 3, there is some occupational concentration present, with 20% of males and 40% of females in occupation A, and 80% of males and 60% of females in occupation G. Here the Duncan index would take on a value of 0.20. Interestingly, the magnitude of the index tells us more than just how strong the degree of occupational segregation happens to be, with the index rising as concentration becomes higher and falling as concentration decreases. It also indicates the percentage of males (or females) that would have to change occupations for there to be no occupational segregation (in other words, for the index to be 0). For example, in Case 3 either 20% of males or 20% of females (or some combination of the two totaling to 20%)[5] would have to change jobs for there to be the same proportion of males and females in both occupations.

Values of the Duncan index of dissimilarity for a number of countries are reported in Table 13.3. Occupational segregation appears to be particularly high in the Czech Republic, Hungary, and Sweden. Paul Swanson has noted a high degree of segregation in the Eastern European countries in general.[6] Sweden has a very high female participation rate, with many women in part-time employment. By way of contrast, occupational segregation is much lower in Australia and the United States. Nevertheless, the figures in the table do not suggest that there is any room for complacency, because even in the latter countries more than one-third of all women would need to change jobs to achieve parity across the sexes.

Further work on U.S. data suggests that women, especially married women, do not succeed in gaining access to the most challenging and remunerative jobs, which may be

---

[5] More precisely, the change would be in *percentage points* rather than percent. This is a common mistake made in interpreting the Duncan index of dissimilarity.

[6] Paul Swanson, "Occupational Sex Segregation and Economic Development," *Journal of Business and Economic Research* 3 (2005): 43–51.

TABLE 13.3   Gender Occupational Segregation Indices

Country	Index
Australia	0.381
Austria	0.537
Czech Republic	0.609
Germany	0.422
Hungary	0.567
Ireland	0.558
Italy	0.463
Netherlands	0.522
New Zealand	0.492
Norway	0.434
Sweden	0.577
Switzerland	0.531
United Kingdom	0.530
United States	0.357

Sources: Australia, Germany, Norway, and the USA—Francine Blau and Lawrence Kahn, "Wage Structure and Gender Earnings Differentials: An International Comparison," *Economica* 63 (1996): S29–S62; remaining countries—Paul Swanson, "Occupational Sex Segregation and Economic Development," *Journal of Business and Economic Research* 3 (2005): 43–51.

due to occupational segregation. The occupational choices of men are much more responsive to wage differentials between occupations than is the case for women, especially married women. This suggests that, for whatever reason, women are more restricted than men in the occupations they can choose.[7] A considerable amount of evidence also suggests that women often move to less demanding and remunerative jobs in order to enjoy more flexibility in their hours of work once they take on family commitments—and that they subsequently find it hard to return to more challenging jobs that match their skills.[8]

Further evidence, this time from the United Kingdom, shows that fewer women enter business, and more enter public administration, than would be expected if the occupational choices of women were based on the coefficients estimated for the male occupational choice model. For men, exactly the opposite is true.[9] These results imply either that women are denied opportunities in business or that the nonmonetary returns to different types of work vary in a systematic way across genders. If the former explanation holds true to any extent, this should be regarded as a source of concern because it implies inefficiency and unfair treatment.

---

[7] Geraint Johnes, "It's Different for Girls: Participation and Occupational Segregation in the U.S.," *The Manchester School* 68 (2000): 552–567.

[8] Geraint Johnes, *Career Interruptions and Labour Market Outcomes* (Manchester: Equal Opportunities Commission, 2006). Available at http://bit.ly/r0vSgD.

[9] Peter J. Dolton, Gerald H. Makepeace, and Willy van der Klaauw, "Occupational Choice and Earnings Determination: The Role of Sample Selection and Other Non-pecuniary Factors," *Oxford Economic Papers* 41 (1989): 573–594.

To complete our statistical profile, let us see how female income compares to that of the average male. Table 13.4 presents information on median annual incomes in the United States for various groups (male, female, black, white, Hispanic) over the period 1998–2010. It is important to note that the data in the table represent average *incomes* (which include mostly earnings from work but also other types of income as well) and are only for individuals employed full time. As can be seen from the middle third of the table, median income for females averages just under three-quarters of median income for males.[10] Similar differences between male and female earnings can generally be observed in the cross-countries data.

Be careful not to conclude at this point that *all* of the income gap (about 25 percentage points) represents the effects of **gender discrimination** against females in the labor force. As you will see very soon, there are many reasons average female earnings might lie below average male earnings: among them, fewer years of work experience on average and disproportionate concentration in certain types of occupations (which may also pay lower wages). In fact, one of the most important research questions tackled by labor economists has been just how much of the gender earnings gap can be attributed to discrimination. Later in this chapter we discuss what they have found.

The female–male earnings gap in the United States has not declined steadily over time. In fact, for about 30 years (from roughly the end of World War II to the late 1970s) the ratio of female-to-male pay in the United States seemed "stuck" at about 59%. This led to the popularity of the "59 cent" button back in the 1960s and 1970s, a button whose message was that women's pay had for too long averaged only about 59 cents for every dollar earned by men. But then the gender pay gap began to decline rapidly—at a rate of about 1% per year from the late 1970s to 1990. The decline was due to a number of factors, among them increases in female work experience as well as increases in both the level of and returns to schooling for women.[11] Since about 1990, however, the rate of convergence in gender pay has slowed considerably and now seems to have plateaued, for reasons that are not completely clear.[12]

It is conceivable that the differences between men and women (or between ethnic groups or religious groups or whatever) are due not to discrimination but to choice. Perhaps women prefer to be in occupations that happen to be relatively low paying. Is there any way to verify whether this is so? Fortunately, yes. A number of recent studies have attempted to tackle head-on the issue of tastes and job satisfaction and how these might vary between women and men. Panel data have been used to develop models of male and female earnings that take full account of differences across individuals in tastes.[13] Recall from Chapter 1 that panel data allow us to control for unobserved

---

[10] Some year-to-year variation in the income levels (and hence the income ratios) is due to "sampling error": that is, the fact that the data come from sample information rather than from the entire population. Therefore, we cannot put too much importance on small year-to-year movements.

[11] June O'Neill, and Solomon Polachek, "Why the Gender Gap in Wages Narrowed in the 1980s," *Journal of Labor Economics*, Part 1 11 (1) (January 1993): 205–228.

[12] Francine D. Blau and Lawrence M. Kahn, "The U.S. Gender Pay Gap in the 1990s: Slowing Convergence," *Industrial and Labor Relations Review* 60 (1) (October 2006): 45–66.

[13] A nice example of how this can be done is provided by Sol W. Polachek and Moon-Kak Kim, "Panel Estimates of the Gender Earnings Gap," *Journal of Econometrics* 61 (1994): 23–42.

TABLE 13.4   Some Income Facts. Median Annual Income and Ratios, Full-Time Workers in the United States, 1998–2010

Income

	1998	1999	2000	2010
Males				
All	36,252	37,450	38,891	50,063
White	37,196	39,212	40,253	50,852
Black	27,472	30,154	30,489	37,805
Hispanic	22,505	22,717	24,175	31,671
Females				
All	26,855	27,366	29,123	38,531
White	27,304	28,000	29,659	38,729
Black	23,864	25,141	25,750	33,918
Hispanic	19,817	20,021	21,196	28,944

Ratios

	1998	1999	2000	2010
All Females / All Males	0.741	0.731	0.749	0.770
Black Females / White Females	0.874	0.900	0.868	0.876
Hispanic Females / White Females	0.726	0.715	0.715	0.747
Black Males / White Males	0.739	0.769	0.757	0.743
Hispanic Males / White Males	0.605	0.579	0.601	0.623

International Gender Earnings Ratios

Australia	0.733	USA	0.654
Austria	0.727	Hungary	0.649
Italy	0.723	Switzerland	0.646
Germany	0.702	United Kingdom	0.614

Sources: U.S. Bureau of the Census, Current Population Survey, Annual Social and Economic Supplements. Francine Blau and Lawrence Kahn, "Wage Structure and Gender Earnings Differentials: An International Comparison," *Economica* 63 (1996): S29–S62. The Blau-Kahn data are adjusted for hours.

characteristics of individuals (such as tastes) that can be assumed to remain unchanged over time. Hence, if women are paid less than men because they prefer jobs that (for one reason or another) are less remunerative, this will be captured by a fixed effect associated with each individual. Sol Polachek and Moon-Kak Kim find that about one-half of the gap between male and female wages is explained by this "unobserved heterogeneity." However, even after allowing for systematic gender differences in tastes, a substantial unexplained wage differential remains between men and women. So the male–female differential, at least, is not a red herring.

THE WAY WE WORK

Women's Pay and Family Responsibilities

Which came first, the chicken or the egg? This is a familiar, yet unanswerable, question. Economists refer to it as the *endogeneity problem*. The chicken-and-egg problem is particularly serious when we want to identify or measure the extent of labor market discrimination. Consider the following:

Q. Why is it that women (rather than men) stay home to raise children?

A. Because women's market work is paid less than men's market work.

Q. Why is women's market work paid less than men's?

A. Because women have on average fewer marketable skills than men.

Q. Well, why do women have fewer marketable skills than men?

A. Because they stay home to raise children.

Source: Adapted from Michael Gold, *A Dialogue on Comparable Worth* (Ithaca, NY: ILR Press, 1984).

Racial and Ethnic Differences

Just as was the case for women, a high degree of occupational concentration also characterizes the employment of blacks and Hispanics in the U.S. labor market. Table 13.1 (line 1) shows that in 2010 blacks comprised about 11% of the U.S. labor force and Hispanics 14%. However, by scanning down the two right-hand columns you will see that blacks and Hispanics are greatly underrepresented in many occupations. On the other hand, the two groups are disproportionately represented in many service jobs that require lower skills such as food preparation and cleaning and maintenance (maids and janitors). (Notice the last several job categories in Table 13.1.) However, two differences from the data for women stand out: (1) there are no particular occupations held almost exclusively by blacks and Hispanics, and (2) the degree of occupational concentration is much less for blacks and Hispanics than for women. The Duncan index confirms this observation, at least for blacks, with studies finding values of the index of dissimilarity by race to be much lower than values found by gender.

Just as was the case for "women's jobs" in the 1960s and earlier, it was also very common for newspapers to publish classified ads for job openings expressing racial preferences. Some striking examples of such racial preferences expressed openly in newspaper ads are shown in Table 13.5. After the Civil Rights Act of 1964, ads like these largely disappeared. However, it then became common to see ads expressing a preference for "European" workers, a thinly veiled way of stating that the employer wanted to hire only whites. Ads of this type too have now disappeared, but it would be a mistake to conclude that racial discrimination in employment no longer exists. Such discrimination simply takes on more subtle forms.[14]

[14] If the ads in Table 13.5 shock you, take a look at the personal ads in today's newspapers. There are still signs of discrimination.

TABLE 13.5 Examples of Racial Preference in Newspaper Job Listings, 1960

Chicago Tribune January 3, 1960	Los Angeles Times January 2, 1960	New York Times January 3, 1960	Washington Post January 3, 1960
LABORATORY TECHNICIAN. Experienced, Modern southside medical center. White. Salary open. Call Vincennes 6-3401	COMPANION. White. Lite hswk, for single lady. Must drive. Local refers. CR 1-7704	COOK, housekeeper, Negro preferred, experience essential, prominent family, permanent position, high salary, MA 7-5369	NURSE (practical) white, for small nursing home, Silver Spring area. Car nec. Good salary. EV 4-6161
WAITRESS. White. Good tips. 7611-15 Stoney Island RE 4-8837	GIRL, white, 25-40. Lite household duties. Rm, board, sal. Apply eves. After 5, 10572 S. Vermont Ave.	COOK - hswkr, fine position, to salary + bonus. Start Jan. Must be capable, white; ref. HU 2-7222	BOYS-WHITE Age 14 to 18. To assist Route manager full or part-time. Must be neat in appearance. Apply 1346 Conn. Ave. NW, room 1006, between 9 to 11 a.m. or 3:30 to 4:30 p.m.
MAN. Empl. White, for small mfg. Hse. North. 4-rm. furn. apt. and sa. Write MXB303.Tribune	HOUSEKEEPER – European or Oriental – 2 adults, pri. quarters, under 45. Ref. GR, 2-4891	COOK-HOUSEKEEPER European own room and bath. Family of four. Long Island Home. $70 weekly. 7-3212 TIMES	DRIVERS (TRUCK) Colored, for trash routes; over 25 years of age; paid vacation, year-around work; must have excellent driving record. Apply SHAYNE BROS. 1601 W ST., NE
WHITE married men who can furnish and opr. late aircond. Cadillac Limo. - Good opportunity. ID 2-4864	HSKPR, white, 22-45, 2 school boys, must live in. Refs. BR, 2-7041	COUPLE, $400-500, white for business couple with 2 adult children. Private home Forest Hills. Man to work in business. BO 3-2649	PAINTER - White, for apts. in S.E. area exp. apply. Rm. 7, 140 Eye St., NW
SINGLE, white man – work in first class tables. Room, board + $60 per month, CR2-0299		HOUSEKEEPER-cook, European; must be honest, clean, reliable; own room & bath; other help; recent references; good salary; 70's East Side. Re 4-25581	MEN-COLORED $125 WEEK. I will teach three men the selling profession. Earnings will start from the first day on the job. If you are ambitious you can earn as high as $250 a week after 30 days training. Apply 705 Park Rd., NW, 9:30-12 noon only. See Mr. Jackson
TOW TRUCK DRIVERS. White, also work around station. See Carl, 530 N. La Salle St.		HOUSEKEEPER, white, sleep out, 5 1/2 days. 10 thru dinner, experienced, must love children; recent references; East Side TH 9-6001	AMBITIOUS MEN (WHITE) National concern requires services of 3 neat-appearing young men, 18-35, to work in the library dept. for executive person. For appt call MR. Albright, ME, 8-1484, 9 am-2 pm
DOORMAN-WHITE age 30 to 45 married. Neat in appearance and at least 5'11" or taller in height. Address MEK			STUDENTS Boys, white, 14 yrs. and over, jobs immediately available. Apply 3:30-4:30 p.m., rm. 724 9th St., NW. See Mr. Faulkner

Source: William Darity and Patrick Mason, "Evidence on Discrimination in Employment: Codes of Color, Codes of Gender," *Journal of Economic Perspectives* 12 (1998): 66-67. Reprinted by permission of the American Economic Association, and William Darity, Ph.D.

Income gaps by race are fairly similar in magnitude to those we have observed by gender (see Table 13.4). In particular, black males employed full time have average annual incomes that are about 75% that of white males. The income gap is slightly larger for Hispanic males when compared to white males. Interestingly, the income gap is smallest for black females compared to white females, with black females in recent years earning about 85% to 90% of what white females earn. Surprisingly, not much progress has been made in closing these racial income gaps over the last several decades. Although wages for black men rose at a faster rate than wages of white men during the 1960s and 1970s in the United States, there has been virtually no further closing of the gap since then. Although the ratio of black women's wages to white women's wages came very close to unity in the 1970s, this gap has actually widened since that time.[15]

Theories of Labor Market Discrimination

The existence and persistence of occupational segregation and gender and racial wage differentials lead to some interesting and important questions. Among them are these:

1. *Why does discrimination exist?* Before you are tempted to dismiss this as an inane question, consider this. Assume that women have the same abilities, skills, education, and other characteristics as do men. In other words, they are equally productive. But suppose wage discrimination exists, and women are paid less and therefore cost less to hire than men. Shouldn't profit maximizing employers actually prefer to hire women instead of men? And won't such a preference for equally productive but less expensive women continue with demand rising until the pay gap disappears and, with it, pay discrimination? Why doesn't this happen? Our reasoning here would be the same even in the absence of wage discrimination against females. If employers simply had a preference for hiring men over equally productive women (what we would call *employment discrimination*), the demand for male labor would rise, creating a wage premium for males. And, of course, this reasoning could also be applied to any other groups subject to labor market discrimination: ethnic minorities, the young, the elderly, religious groups, etc.

2. *Who gains and who loses from discrimination?* The answer to this may seem obvious. Clearly, the group that is discriminated against loses from labor market discrimination, but it is not necessarily the case that the perpetrators of discriminatory actions gain, at least in a pecuniary sense. Remember that employers who discriminate may be hiring more expensive labor than they need to.

3. *What kinds of policies are best suited to eliminate labor market discrimination?* Since the middle of the twentieth century, many countries have instituted a variety of policies designed to eliminate wage and employment discrimination: for example, equal pay and employment legislation, affirmative action, and "pay equity" (comparable worth) laws. But which ones are best designed to eradicate discrimination?

---

[15]Joseph Altonji and Rebecca Blank, "Race and Gender in the Labor Market," in *Handbook of Labor Economics*, eds., Orley Ashenfelter and David Card (Amsterdam: Elsevier Press, 1999), 3C, p. 3149.

To answer these questions and to help us understand why, how, and with what effects employers discriminate, we turn to the theory of discrimination. Economists have formulated several such theories, and we examine them in the following sections.

Personal Prejudice Theory

Economic theories of discrimination owe their origins principally to Gary Becker.[16] In his pathbreaking work on **personal prejudice theory**, Becker suggested that we can assign a monetary dimension to labor market discrimination. According to Becker, an individual with a propensity to discriminate against members of a certain group can be said to have a "taste for discrimination" (or, simply, a prejudice). That is, the individual acts *as if* he or she were willing to pay some amount not to be associated with members of this group. Note that this does not in any way help us *explain* discrimination—but it does help us understand the ramifications of it.

To explain Becker's model more fully, let's look at how an employer who possesses a "taste for discrimination" in the hiring of female workers would act. This employer could hire a female worker or a male worker at wage w. However, the employer acts as if the female wage were higher by some proportion d, where d is a measure of the employer's taste for discrimination against women (we could also call it the discrimination coefficient). In other words, the employer acts *as if* the female's wage were $w(1 + d)$. If d is small, so also is the employer's taste for discrimination, and vice versa if d is large. What's the point? For this employer to be indifferent to hiring either a female or a male, the actual wage offered to a female would have to be lower than that of a male by an amount sufficient to offset the employer's taste for discrimination.

Becker recognizes that not all labor market discrimination is due to employer preferences. Employees, who may not like working alongside of or being supervised by members of another group, may also exercise discrimination. Suppose that some white employees resent working with black workers. Although these white employees are paid a wage of w, they act as if the wage they receive is lower by some amount $1 - d$, where d again represents their taste for discrimination. The upshot is that they will choose not to work with black workers unless they are paid a wage that is high enough to offset their taste for discrimination.

Consumers also may practice labor market discrimination in their purchases of goods and services. For example, if a consumer could employ the services of a Hispanic attorney for a certain price p but has a taste for discrimination against Hispanics, that consumer acts as if the attorney's price is higher by some amount: that is, as if his price is $p(1 + d)$. For the consumer to be indifferent between hiring the services of a Hispanic and a non-Hispanic attorney, the price of the Hispanic attorney would have to be lower by an amount sufficient to offset the consumer's discrimination coefficient. Another example of such consumer discrimination is a situation where consumers might prefer not to shop in stores that hire a large number of minority salespersons.

In sum, according to Becker, three major sources of personal prejudice discrimination are working in labor markets: employers, employees, and consumers. These sources of discrimination have important implications for the Becker way of viewing labor market discrimination. First, although we have been discussing discrimination against

---

[16] Gary Becker, *The Economics of Discrimination* (Chicago: University of Chicago Press, 1957).

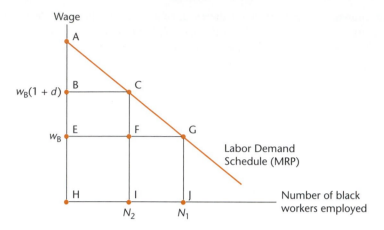

FIGURE 13.1 A Firm with a Taste for Discrimination against Employment of Blacks

blacks, women, and Hispanics, the Becker notion of discrimination could be applied to discrimination on the basis of any characteristic: religion, age, sexual preference, accent, hair color, and so on.

Second, the Becker notion of discrimination implies that employers who indulge in their discriminatory tastes are not profit maximizers. To understand this clearly, look at Figure 13.1, which depicts the demand for labor schedule (marginal revenue product [MRP]) of an employer with a taste for discrimination against blacks. Assume that the wage at which this employer could hire a black worker is w_B. If this employer had no propensity to discriminate against black workers, the employer would hire up to the point where w_B was equal to MRP at point G, employing N_1 black workers. Assume that the employer has a discrimination coefficient of d and acts as if the wage of black workers were higher—that is, equal to $w_B(1+d)$. The employer would now choose to hire where $w_B(1+d)$ equals MRP at point C, employing only N_2 black workers. (Of course, if either d or the elasticity of the demand schedule were high enough, this employer might hire no black workers at all.) In this case, the employer would be underemploying black workers because at point C their MRP is higher than the wage they are being paid. And instead of receiving a level of profit represented by triangle AEG (total revenue product minus total labor cost), the discriminating employer would receive a level of profit of only AEFC. The consequent loss of profit that would be suffered by the employer is represented by the area CFG. In short, employers who practice their discriminatory tastes must "pay" for them by sacrificing profits and are in fact utility maximizers (with discrimination as a term in their utility function) rather than profit maximizers.

A third interesting implication of the Becker model concerns the magnitude of the market pay gap that is due to discrimination. Assume, as is reasonable, that the labor market comprises many employers whose tastes for discrimination vary. Some employers possess ds that are high, some possess ds that are low, and some have no propensity to discriminate at all, and their ds are zero.[17] Suppose also that we could construct a market

---

[17] It is possible that some would have ds that are negative.

demand for labor schedule that would rank employers by the magnitude of their ds, as portrayed in Figure 13.2 where a market demand schedule for female labor is depicted. The vertical axis depicts the ratio of female wages to male wages (w_f/w_m) and the horizontal axis the number of female workers hired. If the supply of female labor in this market were low (as depicted by supply schedule S_1), then female workers could find employment with nondiscriminating employers, and no gender wage gap would emerge. In other words, w_f/w_m would equal 1. However, if the supply of female labor were greater (e.g., at S_2 or S_3), then some females would have to find employment with employers who possess nonzero ds and a market pay gap (or market discrimination coefficient) would result. The larger the supply of female labor, the larger would be the gender pay gap, *ceteris paribus*.

Fourth, Figure 13.2 can also be used to make a quick observation about laws designed to combat discrimination. Suppose lawmakers passed an equal pay law outlawing pay discrimination against women, claiming that this law would eliminate gender pay differences caused by discrimination. Clearly, those lawmakers would be wrong; such an equal pay law alone would, if effective, simply prevent the female–male wage ratio from falling below a value of 1.0, and those employers with nonzero ds would simply refuse to hire female workers. In other words, employers would now indulge in their tastes for discrimination by engaging in *employment* discrimination rather than wage discrimination.

Finally, as we've already noted, employers who indulge their tastes for discrimination are not profit maximizers. Therefore, discriminating employers who refuse to hire blacks and women will be at a cost disadvantage relative to those that do hire them. Employers who discriminate would either have to sell their goods and services at higher prices to cover their higher costs or experience lower levels of profit. In either case, it would seem that in competitive markets such employers would eventually be driven out of business. Some would argue that forces of competition themselves would eliminate discrimination in the long run and that anti-discrimination statutes are not necessary. Of course, such a prediction would not be valid if there are monopoly elements in product markets or if consumer discrimination (Becker's third type of discrimination) exists. So the fact that discriminating firms are not profit maximizers suggests that discrimination must be a symptom of market imperfection—it is a type of market failure.

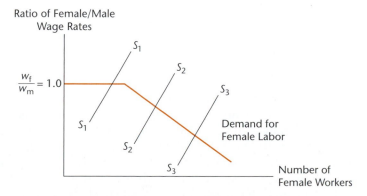

FIGURE 13.2 Labor Supply and the Gender Pay Gap

Statistical Discrimination

Becker's model of discrimination is not the only one that has attracted a good deal of attention among economists. Theories of **statistical discrimination** (there are a number of variants) also provide very plausible explanations of why, how, and with what effects labor market discrimination occurs. Unlike the Becker model, which does not provide a *reason* for employers, employees, and consumers to discriminate—it's merely a "taste" or prejudice, which could be either rational or irrational—theories of statistical discrimination argue that discrimination results from imperfect information.

Consider an employer who is considering hiring a new worker for a job. We know that employers usually don't have complete information about applicants (see Chapter 8). Therefore, they can't judge for certain how well particular individuals will work out if hired: how quickly they will learn, how motivated they will be, how conscientious, and so on. So employers try to use *signals* to help them in their hiring decisions including whether the individual has a college degree, his or her grade point average, and letters of recommendation, for example. These are all examples of signals based on individual performance. Other signals, however, might be based on the average characteristics of the group to which an individual belongs, or what would better be called "stereotypes." And here lies the potential problem. To the extent that the individual might not be representative of the group to which he or she belongs, the possibility of statistical discrimination or "unfair stereotyping" arises.

To illustrate this point, let's use a couple of examples. Suppose an individual graduated from Sloth University, a (fictional) university with a justifiably bad reputation. This university has almost no academic standards, its graduates are generally poorly equipped to enter the workforce, and its most popular major is Pizza Studies (with a concentration in pepperoni). But suppose the job applicant is actually a person of considerable talents who just happened to attend a poor university. Some employers may simply look at where the applicant graduated and refuse to consider him or her further. These employers are evaluating an *individual* based on average characteristics of a *group*, and we can say that this individual has been subjected to statistical discrimination.

Using another example, suppose two people (one man and one woman) apply for a job involving a considerable amount of specific training. Because employers bear some of the costs of specific training, the employer in question wishes to hire a person who is likely to remain with the firm for a long time. Now we know that women on average tend to remain in the labor force (and with a particular employer) for fewer years than men. If the employer chooses to hire the man rather than the woman simply on the basis that there is a higher probability that she may quit, a situation of statistical discrimination has occurred.

Figure 13.3 depicts in a simplified way how statistical discrimination can manifest itself and how it can result in outcomes that are "unfair." Clearly individuals differ with respect to the characteristic called "ability" both within each group and across the two groups. Although the average ability of persons in Group A (μ_A) is lower than the average ability of persons in Group B (μ_B), many individuals in Group A have abilities that exceed those of many individuals in Group B. For example, the individual in Group A called Chuck actually has an ability level that is higher than the mean of individuals in Group B. Yet, if an employer decided that Chuck's membership in Group A was sufficient reason for denying him a job, Chuck would have experienced statistical discrimination and would be justifiably upset.

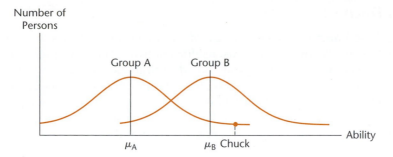

FIGURE 13.3 Statistical Discrimination

It is not necessary for the average qualifications of two groups to differ for a situation of statistical discrimination to occur. For example, employer perceptions about group averages may be in error: that is, the stereotyping itself may be false. Or the tests that employers use to gather information about individuals may be less reliable for one group than for another group. Furthermore, an employer that is risk averse may discriminate against a group whose distribution of abilities is unusually wide, even though average ability in that group is in line with that of other groups. The important point is that firms can engage in statistical discrimination against members of a particular group even when the means of the qualifications in question are the same for both groups.[18]

This type of discrimination—using group characteristics rather than individual characteristics to evaluate people—is sometimes controversial. In fact, some defend the practice by arguing that it can lead employers to make correct hiring decisions on average. Others defend it by pointing out that the evaluation of individuals on the basis of group characteristics is done all the time in situations not involving employment. Young drivers, for example, pay higher automobile insurance premiums than older drivers because on average young drivers have more accidents than older drivers. You might be 20 years old with a perfect driving record, but your premiums are probably still much higher than those paid by your parents. On the other hand, your life insurance premium rates are much lower.[19]

The United States and many other countries have enacted laws banning gender, race, and certain other characteristics from being used in pay and employment situations. Therefore, even though employers using group characteristics to evaluate individuals may indeed be making "correct" decisions on average, such practices have been deemed illegal. Another major problem with statistical discrimination (as we've already implied) is that the information about the group may be incorrect or outdated, yet the unfair stereotyping continues to take place.

---

[18] Dennis J. Aigner and Glenn G. Cain, "Statistical Theories of Discrimination in Labor Markets," *Industrial and Labor Relations Review* 30 (1977): 175–187.

[19] Young male drivers sometimes pay higher automobile insurance premiums than young female drivers because young males tend to have more accidents. Yet this type of gender-based statistical discrimination is legal in most states in the United States but not in the European Union.

Other Models of Discrimination

In the Becker model discrimination arises because of employer (or employee or consumer) preferences, but it effectively treats the reasons for discrimination as pure prejudice. Models of statistical discrimination also posit that discrimination arises from employer preferences, but here the preferences arise because of informational deficiencies, with information about individuals being either lacking or incorrect. Still another set of models, referred to as noncompetitive models, are based on the idea that discrimination can arise because markets are not competitive; that is, employers can and do collude because they possess monopoly or monopsony power.

One of the most important of these models, known as the **crowding model**, is often used to explain the sizeable female–male pay gap. Certain occupations (a relatively small number) have a very high degree of concentration of women; they are literally "crowded" with women. Figure 13.4 depicts what will happen in such a situation. If women are disproportionately concentrated in a small number of occupations, then the large supply of female workers (relative to demand) will keep female wage levels low. Precisely the opposite situation will characterize the labor market for "men's jobs," and as a consequence male wage levels will be high.

Why don't women simply move from the lower-paying female jobs into the higher-paying male jobs? Proponents of the crowding hypothesis contend that employer prejudice has kept, or at least hindered, women from moving into these jobs. In fact, using the Becker model, we could think of employers as possessing a taste for discrimination against hiring females for some jobs (men's jobs) but not for other jobs. An equivalent way of expressing this is to think of men and women as "noncompeting groups" in the labor force. Effectively, this means that women are not able to move freely into and out of occupations; hence, the gender wage differential remains.[20]

The crowding model has not been free of criticism, however. The critical question is *why* certain occupations are marked by relatively high or low concentrations of female labor. Employer discrimination is one explanation, but other possible explanations include societal role prejudice (see the Way We Work feature on societal prejudice) and the preference of

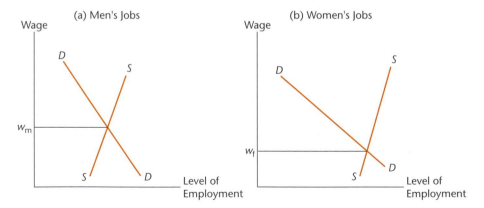

FIGURE 13.4 The Effects of Occupational Crowding

---

[20] In fact, approximately 40% of all women employed work in only 10 occupations.

THE WAY WE WORK

Societal Prejudice at Work?

Kindergarten Awards Categories

Boys' Awards	Girls' Awards
Very Best Thinker	All-Around Sweetheart
Most Eager Learner	Sweetest Personality
Most Imaginative	Cutest Personality
Most Enthusiastic	Best Sharer
Most Scientific	Best Artist
Best Friend	Biggest Heart
Mr. Personality	Best Manners
Hardest Worker	Best Helper
Best Sense of Humor	Most Creative

At a ceremony marking his daughter's graduation from kindergarten, T. Gary Mitchell noticed something about the awards conferred on every student in the class.

The boys got pats on the back for analytical skills and intellectual ability; girls were acknowledged primarily for their pleasing personalities. "I thought to myself, 'This is [what year]?'" Mr. Mitchell says.

Mr. Mitchell, an attorney with Epstein Becker & Green in Newark, NJ, says he was particularly surprised because he and his wife like the school and consider their New Jersey community, a suburb of New York City, to be quite progressive.

Mr. Mitchell and his wife wrote a letter to the school about the awards, which, he says, will probably result in changes in next year's graduation ceremony. And his fight against gender-stereotyping continues. Mr. Mitchell is about to buy new readers that include female characters for everyone in his daughter's first-grade class.

Source: Adapted from Kathleen Deveny, "Chart of Kindergarten Awards," *Wall Street Journal*, December 5, 1994. Copyright © 1994 by Dow Jones & Company Inc. Reprinted by permission of Dow Jones & Company Inc. via Copyright Clearance Center.

some women for certain occupations (such as teaching) because of various advantages that they afford, such as the chance to have their summers free to care for their children who are also no longer in school. We return to each of these points a little later in the chapter.

Still another explanation of discrimination-caused gender and racial wage differences builds on both the monopsony model (see Chapter 9) and the job search model (see Chapter 8). In the monopsony model, we noted that the elasticity of labor supply can affect the wage paid by the monopsony employer.[21] Specifically (and *ceteris paribus*), the

---

[21] A nice model of monopsony and discrimination is provided by Robin Naylor, "Pay Discrimination and Imperfect Competition in the Labor Market," *Journal of Economics* 60 (1994): 177–188.

lower the elasticity of labor supply (η_s), the lower the wage that the monopsony employer can pay and the greater the difference between the monopsony wage level and the wage that would be paid in a competitive labor market. A low η_s can be the result of workers being relatively immobile, ignorant of alternative job opportunities, or having high employment search costs.

How does this relate to discrimination in the context of gender and racial wage differences? Minorities may be unable to search as extensively for jobs as majority workers due to an unwillingness or inability to migrate or to limited opportunities to commute. Women and ethnic minorities thus, in effect, face higher search costs in their efforts to secure employment, making their supply of labor schedules less elastic and resulting in their becoming more subject to monopsony wage exploitation. Figure 13.5 (a variant of which appears in Chapter 9) shows the effect that low η_s can have on the difference between the wage level in a competitive labor market (w_c) and the wage levels of women (w_f) and men (w_m). In each case, employers seek to hire the number of workers under the point where the marginal labor cost (MLC) equals the MRP. But with women facing higher search costs resulting in their having a lower η_s, the gap between w_f and w_c in Figure 13.5a is much higher than the corresponding gap between w_m and w_c in Figure 13.5b. If this analysis seems unconvincing, simply ask yourself this question: If you decided to limit your own job search to one or two employers or to employers within a couple of blocks from your home, would you expect the wage offers you received to be as high as those of your classmates who participated in a much more extensive search?

There isn't a lot of evidence on the effects of labor market monopsony on discrimination. One interesting study from Austria, conducted by Rudolf Winter-Ebmer,[22] does provide support for this theory. Winter-Ebmer used regression methods to estimate a wage equation in which the explanatory variables include information about workers' human capital stock (schooling and experience) and measures of concentration of the product and labor markets in which workers are employed. The product market concentration index is the ratio of value added accounted for by the largest four firms in the industry to total industry value added. The labor market concentration index is defined as the ratio of employment in the largest four firms in the region to total regional employment. The findings of the study are that this last variable has a significantly negative influence on wages only in the case of married women. This is consistent with the predictions of the theory in that it shows how the wages of married women can be depressed by firms operating in a labor market monopsony.

A final model of discrimination applies specifically to the case of gender discrimination. This model was developed by Edward Lazear and Sherwin Rosen,[23] and it hinges on two simple assumptions. First, assume that women and men both have the same ability distribution in connection with labor market activities but that women have higher ability in connection with nonmarket activities. Hence, women are assumed to be

---

[22] Rudolf Winter-Ebmer, "Sex Discrimination and Competition in Product and Labor Markets," *Applied Economics* 27 (1995): 849–857.

[23] Edward P. Lazear and Sherwin Rosen, "Male-Female Wage Differentials in Job Ladders," *Journal of Labor Economics* 8 (1990): S106–S123.

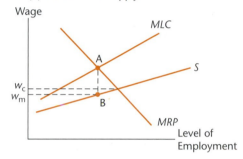

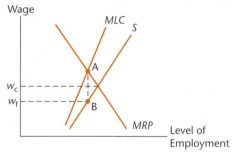

(a) Inelastic Labor Supply of Women

Wage

MLC S

A

w_c

w_f B

MRP

Level of
Employment

(b) Elastic Labor Supply of Men

Wage

MLC

A

w_c

w_m B

S

MRP

Level of
Employment

FIGURE 13.5 Supply Elasticity and Gender Wage Differences under Monopsony

especially strong in the field of household production. In consequence, in comparison with men, women tend to have a higher rate of separation from their employers; that is, they quit more. This is borne out empirically—though, as shown in Figure 13.6, which is based on U.S. data, the gap between the sexes has been narrowing over time.

The second assumption is that firms must pay for any training undertaken by workers as a consequence of promotion. Typically a promotion involves changing the worker's job description, and so some period of training or induction is needed once the worker begins his or her duties in a new post.

Three implications can be drawn from this pair of assumptions. First, because firms are reluctant to promote workers who have a relatively high propensity to quit and risk the sunk cost of training the newly promoted employee, women must generally have greater ability than men to be promoted. Second, across the whole distribution of abilities women are less well paid than men because they are not so readily promoted, and women do not, therefore, gain access easily to the better paid jobs. Within each grade, however, the mean productivity of women is likely to exceed that of men because they have, on average, greater ability. As long as productivity is reflected in earnings, this implies that *within each grade* women should earn a higher wage than men. The third implication is that promotion rates at the top end of the ability distribution are likely to differ less between the sexes than they do at low levels of ability. There are two reasons for this: it is easier for firms to assess workers' propensity to quit on an individual-by-individual

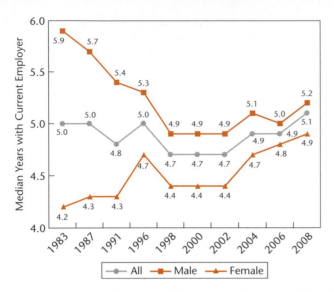

FIGURE 13.6 Median Years of Tenure for Wage and Salary Workers Age 25 or Older, by Gender, 1983–2008

Source: Employee Benefit Research Institute compilations from Bureau of Labor Statistics, http://economix.blogs.nytimes.com/2010/01/15/how-long-have-you-been-at-your-job-if-you-have-one/#

basis when workers are near the top of the promotion ladder, and workers near the top have already demonstrated a commitment to the employer.

The Lazear and Rosen model is interesting, but how well does it stand up to empirical scrutiny? To test the model, personnel records from a firm must be used. For reasons of confidentiality these are not easy to come by, but one study has succeeded in using data from a major international firm in the financial sector to test the implications.[24] In some respects, the results support the predictions of the model quite strongly. In particular it is established that women are indeed less likely than men to be promoted. However, it is also found that, within each grade, women earn slightly less than men. This is, of course, at variance with one of the predictions of the model. So, overall, the Lazear and Rosen model seems to explain some aspects of gender differentials quite well, but it clearly needs some refinement.

Measuring the Effect of Discrimination on Pay Gaps

We have described several major economic theories that seek to explain why labor market discrimination occurs and how it can manifest itself. Now let's turn our attention to *how much* of the various pay gaps may be due to labor market discrimination. Some of you might be wondering why we don't attribute *all* of the gender (or racial) pay gap to discrimination. The answer is simple. Men and women, blacks and whites, Hispanics and

---

[24] Rick P. Audas, Tim Barmby, and John G. Treble, "Gender and Promotion in an Internal Labor Market," 1997. Available online at: http://www.bangor.ac.uk/~abs003/promo.pdf

non-Hispanics may differ on average with respect to the types of occupations at which they work, the years of education they have, their work experience, and many other factors.[25] This is the old *ceteris paribus* difficulty again. To measure the *net* pay gap attributable to discrimination, we need to control for these other factors or at least for those that we suspect could influence earnings. But how can this be done?

Case Studies

Let's focus on the gender pay gap first. One way of ascertaining the magnitude of the net pay gap is to utilize the "case study" approach. We could analyze pay at a firm or firms that hire both men and women who work at the same jobs and then observe what kinds of pay differences exist *within* these firms. At first blush, this approach seems to be ideal as it largely solves the *ceteris paribus* difficulty. We would automatically be holding constant such factors as firm profitability, location, industry, job types, and so on. However, if we only analyze firms that hire both men and women to perform the same types of work, we are likely to find little or no difference in pay. These firms, to use Becker's terminology, probably have little or no taste for discrimination to begin with.[26] Moreover, any gender pay differentials that did appear within a particular firm would easily stand out and invite litigation. If we broaden our approach and compare gender pay differences *across* many firms, however, we are again faced with the problem of how to control for nondiscrimination-related reasons for whatever pay differences are observed.

In fact, this is one reason economists have rarely used the case study approach in their efforts to measure that portion of the gender or racial pay gap attributable to discrimination. (However, a type of case study approach sometimes referred to as the "audit study" has seen limited use in economic research to determine whether members of different groups are treated differently in the hiring process. We will discuss this approach shortly.) Generally, economists have relied heavily on the earnings function approach described in Chapter 6.

The Earnings Function Approach

An earnings function is an equation that relates the earnings of an individual or a group of individuals to various factors (including human capital factors such as schooling, experience, and occupation and other personal characteristics) that would be expected to "explain" earnings. For example, we could specify the following equation:

$$\ln w = \beta_0 + \beta_1 S + \beta_2 E + \beta_3 O \tag{13-2}$$

where w stands for earnings (in logarithmic form, ln), S for years of schooling, E for years of experience, and O for occupation.[27] This is a highly simplified example of an earnings

---

[25] Of course these differences might themselves be due to discrimination as well.

[26] We must be careful, however, not to imply that pay discrimination no longer exists at all at the level of the firm. One particularly interesting example of substantial gender pay differences that some have alleged are due to discrimination is at colleges and universities. Because female professors are disproportionately concentrated in lower-paying academic disciplines (the arts, humanities, and social sciences), the average pay of female faculty members is generally lower than the average pay of male faculty members.

[27] To designate occupation, a series of dichotomous or "dummy" variables would ordinarily be used.

function, but it will suffice for our explanation. Suppose now that we have a large number of men and women (or blacks and whites, if we want to examine racial differences) who differ with respect to their earnings. Moreover, suppose that we would like to see to what extent these earnings differences reflect differences in the levels of human capital and various other variables and to what extent they reflect possible discrimination in the labor market. We could examine this question by adding another explanatory variable to our earnings function, a gender dummy variable (G) that takes on a value of 1 if the person is a female and a value of 0 if the person is a male (or vice versa). Our earnings function then becomes:

$$\ln w = \beta_0 + \beta_1 S + \beta_2 E + \beta_3 O + \beta_4 G \tag{13-3}$$

We could then use multiple regression analysis to estimate the coefficients (the β values) of our earnings function; and the sign and statistical significance of the coefficient of β_4 will tell us whether females in our sample are receiving lower earnings than males after the influence of the human capital and other variables are taken into account. And, since the dependent variable is in natural log form, the magnitude of the coefficient gives us a measure of the extent of the pay gap, other things being equal, in percentage terms (about $100\beta_4$.)

Although this approach has been used in many studies of gender and racial discrimination, it suffers from one important shortcoming. It assumes that the effects of discrimination will be observed *only* in the coefficient of the dummy variable. But as we've already seen, discrimination can manifest itself in many ways. For example, females might not experience the same returns to schooling or the same returns to experience as males. Therefore, the coefficients (βs) of earnings functions estimated for females might be different from the coefficients of earnings functions estimated for males. The simple method just described implicitly assumes that there are no differences in these coefficients and would fail to pick up these other kinds of discrimination.

An extension of the earnings function approach, commonly known as the **Oaxaca decomposition method**, can deal with this difficulty, however.[28] To understand what this approach entails, let's again look at our two groups, one composed of males and the other of females, but this time we will specify and estimate a separate earnings function for each group (without the gender dummy variable). The male earnings equation could then be written as:

$$\ln w_{\mathrm{m}} = \beta_{0\mathrm{m}} + \sum \beta_{\mathrm{m}} X_{\mathrm{m}} \tag{13-4}$$

where for simplicity the set of human capital and other variables and their coefficients have been expressed as $\Sigma \beta_{\mathrm{m}} X_{\mathrm{m}}$. Similarly, the female earnings equation could be written as:

$$\ln w_{\mathrm{f}} = \beta_{0\mathrm{f}} + \sum \beta_{\mathrm{f}} X_{\mathrm{f}} \tag{13-5}$$

[28] Ronald L. Oaxaca, "Male-Female Wage Differentials in Urban Labor Markets," *International Economic Review* 9 (1973): 693–709.

Suppose now that we use regression analysis to estimate the coefficients of each of the earnings functions using our male data set to estimate the coefficients of the male earnings function and the female data set to estimate the female earnings function coefficients. Thus we would calculate numerical values for the β terms in each of our equations.

Suppose next that we estimate the average log earnings $(\overline{\ln w_m})$ for males with average levels of the human capital and other variables $(\overline{X}_m)$ in equation 13-4, and likewise the average log earnings for females $(\overline{\ln w_f})$ with average levels of the (same) variables $(\overline{X}_f)$ in equation 13-5. These equations could then be written as:

$$\overline{\ln w_m} = \beta_{0m} + \sum \beta_m \overline{X}_m \tag{13-6}$$

and

$$\overline{\ln w_f} = \beta_{0f} + \sum \beta_f \overline{X}_f \tag{13-7}$$

If we then subtract equation 13-7 from equation 13-6, we have an expression that defines the *difference* between average male and average female earnings as:

$$\overline{\ln w_m} - \overline{\ln w_f} = (\beta_{0m} - \beta_{0f}) + \left(\sum \beta_m \overline{X}_m - \sum \beta_f \overline{X}_f\right) \tag{13-8}$$

In other words, the average female–male salary gap depends on two factors: (1) the different amounts of human capital and other characteristics that each group possesses, and (2) the different regression coefficients (the β coefficients) associated with these amounts of human capital and other characteristics. The second factor signifies how employers reward characteristics and shows the presence of labor market discrimination against females.

You may be wondering how much of the gender earnings gap can be attributed to each of these two factors. The answer can be found by some algebraic sleight of hand and rearranging of terms. Let's add the following term (which is equal to zero) to the right-hand side of equation 13-8:

$$-\sum \beta_m \overline{X}_f + \sum \overline{X}_f \beta_m \tag{13-9}$$

Then, by rearranging terms, equation 13-8 can be rewritten as:

$$\overline{\ln w_m} - \overline{\ln w_f} = (\beta_{0m} - \beta_{0f}) + \sum \beta_m (\overline{X}_m - \overline{X}_f) + \sum \overline{X}_f (\beta_m - \beta_f) \tag{13-10}$$

Equation 13-10 shows that we can "decompose" the average female–male earnings gap $(\overline{\ln w_m} - \overline{\ln w_f})$ into two components:

1. The difference in the average levels of human capital $(\overline{X}_m - \overline{X}_f)$;
2. The differences in the way in which the average levels of human capital are evaluated (rewarded) in the male and female earnings functions: in other words, the difference between β_m and β_f.

In a nutshell, our earnings decomposition should tell us how much of the difference between average female and male earnings appears to be due to differences in such human capital factors as education and experience $(\overline{X}_m - \overline{X}_f)$ and how much is due to employers rewarding men and women differently for their human capital $(\beta_m - \beta_f)$. The latter is what we might refer to as unjustified discrimination. (The earnings decomposition described above is not the only one possible. See footnote 29.)[29]

Another way to understand this analysis is to look at things graphically. The two positively sloped lines in Figure 13.7 represent two earnings functions, one for males and one for females. The functions depict what we would expect earnings to be for different levels of human capital (X). The male earnings function has the greater slope, and we can see that increases in human capital levels seem to "pay off," in terms of earnings, more for males than for females. In other words, there is a clear sign that labor market discrimination exists. But males also have higher levels of human capital (e.g., more years of work experience) than females. In other words, $\overline{X}_m$ is greater than $\overline{X}_f$ How do we estimate the amount of the actual female–male earnings difference ($\overline{w}_m - \hat{w}_f$) that is due to different treatment by employers or due to human capital differences? One solution is to insert the level of human capital that females have $\overline{X}_f$ into the male earnings function. This would give us an estimate of what females would earn (point B or earnings level $\hat{w}_f$) if they were treated no differently from men. The remainder of the actual gender earnings difference (AB or $\overline{w}_m - \hat{w}_f$) would represent the portion of the earnings difference that is not due to discrimination but instead to human capital differences.

The earnings function decomposition method also possesses some shortcomings of its own, shortcomings that could result in either an overestimate or an underestimate of the market discrimination coefficient. First, the earnings function decomposition method assumes that the effects of discrimination will be observed through differences in the coefficients (the β values) of the earnings functions *but not* in the levels of human capital or other independent variables (such as occupation). In other words, the X variables are

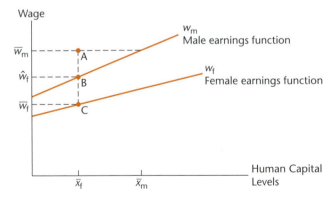

FIGURE 13.7 The Decomposition Method of Measuring Discrimination Wage Gaps

[29] Note that, instead of adding equation 13-9 to the right-hand side of equation 13-8, we could have added $-\Sigma\beta_f\overline{X}_m + \Sigma\beta_f\overline{X}_m$. This would yield an alternative decomposition to equation 13-10; namely, $\overline{\ln w_m} - \overline{\ln w_f} = (\beta_{0m} - \beta_{0f}) + \Sigma\beta_f(\overline{X}_m - \overline{X}_f) + \Sigma\overline{X}_m(\beta_m - \beta_f)$. This gives estimates of the characteristics effect and the discrimination effect that are different from those obtained in equation 13-10. In fact an infinity of different decompositions can be made based on various weighted averages of the β_m and β_f coefficient vectors. Typically, however, the differences between results obtained in empirical studies using different decompositions are fairly minor. An excellent discussion of these decompositions is provided by Ronald Oaxaca and Michael Ransom, "On Discrimination and the Decomposition of Wage Differentials," *Journal of Econometrics* 61 (1994): 5–21.

TABLE 13.6   Some Variables Used to Explain Wage Differences
in Studies Measuring Discrimination

Education	Marital Status
Experience	Union Status
Training	Health
Occupation	Region
Quality of Education	Family Background
College Major	Age
Industry	Seniority
Turnover	Distance to Work
Full Time/Part Time	

assumed to be exogenous. If, however, discrimination results in members of a minority group not having the same access to education as white males do, or access to the same types of jobs, or the same levels of experience, then our model will *underestimate* the true effect of discrimination. A second shortcoming of our model is that it implies that earnings differences that cannot be explained by human capital differences are, by default, attributed to discrimination. However, this earnings function may have omitted other variables (other human capital or personal characteristics) that have nothing to do with discrimination (see Table 13.6). If this is the case, then our model might be overestimating the market discrimination coefficient. And third, if minority groups *choose* to work in jobs that are poorly remunerated, where the returns to their characteristics are unusually low, then it is not clear that we can attribute their low earnings to discrimination.[30]

Discrimination and the Distribution of Earnings

In equation 13-10 the decomposition between the characteristics effect and the discrimination effect is carried out at the mean values of all the variables (that's what the bar above the variables means). In many instances, that's fine because working with the means gives us a good idea of the sources of the wage differential between the two groups of workers. But on some occasions it might be limiting simply to examine the discrimination experience of some mythical average person. To illustrate, consider the following scenarios: in Case 1 all members of a minority group suffer discrimination so that their wage is 10% below that of otherwise identical members of the majority; in Case 2 discrimination is suffered by only one in five of the minority group, but those who do suffer discrimination receive only half of the wage paid to members of the majority group. Although the *average* experience is identical in both cases, the distribution of experience across workers, and hence also the appropriate policy response, differs considerably. If, for example, discrimination against minorities is especially severe at the bottom and top ends of the labor market, it follows that policies that exacerbate inequalities also exacerbate discrimination. It would help, therefore, if there were a way of analyzing the distribution of discrimination experience.

---

[30] It's well to recall, at this point, our discussion earlier in this chapter. Even after allowing for differences in tastes across individuals, we saw that the gap between male and female pay remains substantial.

THE WAY WE WORK

Religious Discrimination and the Irish Troubles

The history of troubles in Ireland is a long one, going back at least to the twelfth century with the Norman invasion of Ireland in 1169. During the seventeenth century, much land was confiscated from the Irish and allocated to English and Scots immigrants following the defeat of the Irish at the Battle of Kinsale in 1601. The immigrants were predominantly Protestants, who settled mainly in the North, whereas the indigenous Irish were Catholics. This clear-cut split along religious as well as regional and political lines has allowed the divisions to be perpetuated across centuries.

In 1922 a treaty was agreed to that effectively gave 26 counties independence, and these counties make up what is now known as the Republic of Ireland. But 6 counties in Northern Ireland have remained part of the United Kingdom. This partitioning has brought its own problems, and from 1968 until 1997 (with some short interruptions) Northern Ireland suffered a period of intense turbulence and violence.

A major factor underpinning the troubles of the twentieth century was the perception that Catholics were discriminated against in the labor market. The average age of Catholics in Northern Ireland was lower than that of Protestants, as was the average level of educational attainment. Both these factors contributed to the adverse position of Catholics in the labor market. Even allowing for these differences in characteristics, however, Catholics seem to have been disadvantaged. One study* suggests that the unemployment probability faced by a typical Catholic in Belfast (controlling for age, education, and other characteristics) during the mid-1980s was 39.3% compared to 23.9% for a typical Protestant.

More recent work[†] has suggested that one possible reason for this is that Protestants are much more likely than Catholics to migrate out of Northern Ireland to other regions of the United Kingdom. One reason the unemployment rate is so much lower for Protestants, therefore, is that unemployed Protestants leave to find work elsewhere.

For a similar reason, small countries such as Switzerland and the Netherlands, which have an internationally mobile workforce, experience perpetually low rates of unemployment.

Notes: *David J. Smith and Gerald Chambers, *Inequality in Northern Ireland* (Oxford: Clarendon Press, 1991); [†]Graham Gudgin and Richard Breen, *Evaluation of the Ratio of Unemployment Rates as an Indicator of Fair Employment* (Belfast: Central Community Relations Unit, 1996).

Fortunately, a method has been developed by Chinhui Juhn and others that offers a way around this problem.[31] The method is quite complicated, and we won't go into detail about it here. The gist of the method, though, is that there are *three* major sources of the wage gap: characteristics, the distribution of wages, and discrimination.

---

[31]Chinhui Juhn, Kevin M. Murphy, and Brooks Pierce, "Wage Inequality and the Rise in Returns to Skill," *Journal of Political Economy* 101 (1993): 410–442.

We are now in a position to revisit an argument introduced earlier in the chapter: namely, that the wage differential between majority and minority workers, particular between men and women, is intimately connected to the spread of the overall wage distribution. (This argument can be used to explain the limited extent of gender wage differentials in Australia.) A decrease in inequality can, as a by-product, result in a decline of the wage differential between worker groups.

Armed with the techniques of the Oaxaca decomposition method (and its refinement by Juhn et al.), we can now proceed to study what the real world data tell us about gender and ethnic discrimination in a variety of countries.

What Does the Research Show?

Earnings Gaps

Economists first became interested in measuring the effects of discrimination several decades ago. Since that time hundreds of studies have attempted to measure just how much of the pay gap between men and women (or between ethnic groups) is due to discrimination and how much seems to be attributable to other factors. These studies differ with respect to the groups studied, the time periods investigated, the explanatory variables used, and so on. Many of the more recent studies also investigate how much of the gap is due to changes in the income distribution. Here we report on the results of a few of these studies.

The original study by Ronald Oaxaca is quite old, but it's interesting to see what things were like in the United States in the 1960s and to evaluate how the world has changed since then. The wage differential estimated by Oaxaca between white men and white women amounted to 0.4307 (i.e., white men were paid around 43% more than white women). Using equation 13-10, he finds that 53% of this wage differential was due to unjustified discrimination, the remainder being due to differences in characteristics.[32] The corresponding figure for black workers, where the wage differential between genders was 0.3989, was somewhat lower at 50%.[33] Numerous other studies have confirmed that about one-half of the gap between male and female earnings can be explained by gender differences in human capital and other characteristics.

Two further studies of gender differentials by Francine Blau and Lawrence Kahn examine changes over time and allow international comparisons to be drawn. In analyzing the decline over time in the gender wage differential,[34] Blau and Kahn have found quite a dramatic reduction in the gap between female and male earnings between 1979 and 1988 in the United States. The reasons underpinning this change are shown in Table 13.7. The total change in the log wage differential between men and women between these two years was −0.1522 (i.e., the differential narrowed by about 15%).

---

[32] Using female regression weights, as in footnote 29, the proportion of the wage differential accounted for by unjustified discrimination is somewhat higher at 64%.

[33] Or 61% using the female regression weights.

[34] Francine Blau and Lawrence Kahn, "Swimming Upstream: Trends in the Gender Income Differential in the 1980s," *Journal of Labor Economics* 15 (1997): 1–42.

TABLE 13.7   Decomposition of Changes in the
Gender Pay Gap, 1979–88

Total change in the wage differential	−0.1522
Change due to	
Observed characteristics	−0.0755
Observed prices	0.0419
Distributional effects	−0.1456
Unobserved effects	0.0269

Source: Francine Blau and Lawrence Kahn, "Swimming Upstream:
Trends in the Gender Income Differential in the 1980s," *Journal of
Labor Economics* 15 (1997): 1–42.

Assuming a simple earnings function, some −0.0755 of this change in the differential can
be attributed to changes in characteristics. So about half of the changing differential may
be "justified" by reference to differences across the genders in characteristics.

Another large chunk of the eroding differential may be explained by the "distributional effects" term. This term shows how much the wage differential between men and
women would have changed if the level of male inequality (after controlling for changes
in characteristics) had been unchanged across the two years but the corresponding measure of female inequality had been allowed to change. We can interpret this effect as
being a mix of characteristics effects that are not measured by the variables in the wage
equation (so-called unobserved characteristics) and discrimination. Both of these effects
would explain why women's positions in the distribution relative to men could change
over time. The results reported in the table suggest that some −0.1456 of the total change
in the wage differential is due to this effect. It is clear, therefore, that the distributional
impact over this period was favorable to women.

Clearly, the sum of this distribution effect and the characteristics effect amounts to
more than the total of −0.1522 that we seek to explain. The reason for this is that the
impact on the change in wage differential of changes in the regression coefficients (the
change due to unjustified discrimination) works in the opposite direction.[35] Relative to
men, the returns to human capital characteristics faced by women have become increasingly unfavorable over time. Although women's position in the labor market has
improved, it has improved less than would be justified by their improving human capital
stock and by their changing position in the distribution. Women are striving hard to better
their marketability, but the market has become increasingly hostile to them. For this reason, the experience of women in the labor market has been described as "swimming
upstream."

Further evidence on the impact of the wage distribution on gender wage gaps is
provided by a number of studies that use quantile regression methods[36] to estimate the

---

[35] A small amount of the change in the wage differential is also accounted for by "unobserved effects."

[36] With quantile regression, the dependent (y) variable is expressed in quantiles (e.g., percentiles, quartiles, or
deciles). And the coefficients of a quantile regression can be interpreted as showing the effect of changes in the
independent variables on quantile values of the dependent variable.

TABLE 13.8   Percentage Wage Gap [and the Percentage of That Gap due to Characteristics] between Men and Women, Various Countries, at Various Points of the Earnings Distribution

	10th centile	25th centile	50th centile	75th centile	90th centile
Austria	21.2 [74]	20.7 [72]	21.5 [78]	23.3 [85]	26.9 [101]
Belgium	9.0 [75]	12.0 [88]	14.4 [120]	17.4 [124]	21.8 [110]
Great Britain	20.1 [75]	22.4 [74]	24.6 [80]	27.2 [83]	30.2 [97]
Denmark	4.5 [44]	8.1 [71]	11.0 [122]	16.3 [98]	20.9 [87]
Finland	13.4 [111]	16.5 [122]	20.7 [142]	25.0 [126]	28.4 [117]
France	19.7 [110]	17.4 [112]	18.9 [111]	23.6 [117]	29.4 [129]
Germany	13.9 [47]	14.2 [56]	14.6 [63]	15.9 [64]	20.0 [71]
Ireland	18.5 [70]	21.5 [81]	24.0 [91]	25.6 [96]	26.9 [86]
Italy	15.6 [108]	13.8 [124]	14.6 [112]	16.9 [116]	20.5 [106]
Netherlands	2.9 [16]	6.8 [38]	10.7 [61]	17.2 [79]	24.9 [90]
Spain	21.4 [85]	21.1 [102]	20.7 [101]	20.2 [83]	20.5 [99]

Source: Wiji Arulampapam, Alison Booth, and Mark Bryan, "Is There a Glass Ceiling over Europe? Exploring the Gender Pay Gap across the Wage Distribution," *Industrial and Labor Relations Review* 60 (2007): 163–186.

coefficients of the earnings equation separately at different points in the distribution of earnings. As an example of this work, consider the results reported in Table 13.8.[37] These concern gender wage gaps in various European countries. The figures show the percentage wage gap between men and women working in the private sector at each of several points of the distribution, and the numbers in square brackets indicate the percentage of this wage gap that is due to gender differences in characteristics. It is easily seen that, in some countries, the wage gap varies little across the earnings distribution—examples are Austria and Spain. In other countries, however, the wage gap is far greater at the top end of the earnings distribution than at the bottom end. In the Netherlands, for example, the wage gap is 3% at the 10th centile (also called percentile), but rises to 25% at the 90th centile. While much of the gap at the top end is due to differences in characteristics, these data nonetheless suggest that, in certain countries, the extent to which women are disadvantaged is particularly high at the top end of the earnings distribution. This has often been referred to as a "glass ceiling" effect—where an invisible barrier prevents women from access to the highest-paying jobs.

The United States has a high gender earnings differential in comparison with a lot of other countries. In Table 13.9 the first column shows the differential between logged wages of men and women in each of 10 countries, including the United States. In the second column, the difference between the value of the differential reported for each country in the first column and the value reported for the United States is calculated. Of the countries examined here, only Hungary, Switzerland, and the United Kingdom have higher gender earnings differentials than does the United States.

---

[37] Wiji Arulampapam, Alison Booth, and Mark Bryan, "Is There a Glass Ceiling over Europe? Exploring the Gender Pay Gap across the Wage Distribution," *Industrial and Labor Relations Review* 60 (2007): 163–186.

TABLE 13.9 Decomposing International Differences in the Gender Wage Differential

Country	Log Wage Differential between Men and Women	Difference between Country and USA in Log Wage Differential	Explained by Differences in Observed Characteristics	Explained by Differences in the Income Distribution	Explained by Differences in the Gender-Specific Return to Characteristics
Australia	0.31	−0.12	0.06	−0.06	−0.07
Austria	0.32	−0.11	0.06	0.28	−0.15
Germany	0.35	−0.07	0.03	0.24	−0.10
Hungary	0.43	0.01	−0.06	0.63	−0.03
Italy	0.32	−0.10	0.03	−0.02	−0.01
Norway	0.35	−0.09	−0.08	0.58	−0.09
Sweden	0.26	−0.17	−0.03	−0.01	−0.03
Switzerland	0.44	0.01	0.10	0.07	−0.01
United Kingdom	0.49	0.06	0.01	0.42	−0.04
United States	0.43	—	—	—	—

Source: Francine Blau and Lawrence Kahn, "Wage Structure and Gender Earnings Differentials: An International Comparison," *Economica* 63 (1996): S29–S62.

What causes these international differences? Column 3 reports differences between the United States and other countries in the amount of the differential that is due to international differences in human capital characteristics. The figures in column 3 are mostly greater than zero, which means that the gap between women's and men's human capital characteristics is greater in most countries than it is in the United States. American women are relatively well endowed with human capital and other characteristics, so human capital differences across countries cannot explain why women fare so much better (relative to men) in many other countries. Column 4 reports the extent to which the income distribution is responsible for these differences and is a little more helpful. In some countries, notably Australia and Sweden, the distribution effect is important in explaining the fact that women's performance relative to men's is superior to that observed in the United States. And column 5 reports the extent to which unjustified discrimination accounts for the international differences observed here.[38] It shows that in *every* country studied the extent of the wage differential between men and women that is due to what we have called unjustified discrimination is less than it is in the United States.

In Table 13.9 notice that the values in columns 3 and 5 are quite small in relation to the values in column 1. This means that the balance between the characteristics effect and unjustified discrimination is fairly similar across all of the countries in this table.

We have devoted most of this section to explaining how much of the gender earnings gap seems attributable to discrimination; now let's direct this same question to the racial earnings gap. First, "premarket" human capital differences are much more pronounced

---

[38] You might have noticed that the sum of columns 3, 4, and 5 does not equal column 2 because there is also an unobserved effects component of the difference in international experience.

when focusing on race than when focusing on gender. In particular, in the United States, black workers are much more likely than white workers, *on average* (we have to stress that), to have come from families with lower incomes, to have lived in poor neighborhoods, and to have attended inferior schools. As a result, black workers both have fewer years of schooling than white workers and are more likely to have experienced poorer quality schooling.[39]

The hourly earnings of black men in the United States are considerably lower than the hourly earnings of white men. Black men also on average work fewer hours per week and fewer weeks per year than white men. Furthermore, black men are more likely to be unemployed at any moment in time. In fact, over the past several decades, the unemployment rate of black males has been about twice that of white males. All of these factors help explain the sizeable income differences by race such as those shown in Table 13.4. But how much of the black–white earnings gap can be attributed to discrimination, and how much to human capital and other factors? A large number of studies have been undertaken in recent decades to analyze this question (not as many as for women, however). Although the results vary somewhat, we can draw a few generalizations from some representative studies.

The results of decomposition exercises, which aim to ascertain the source of racial earnings differentials, vary considerably across countries. Much recent work has suggested that none of the wage gap between white and minority workers in the United States is due to discrimination; it can *all* be explained by differences in characteristics.[40] Interestingly, the decomposition of the earnings differential is somewhat different for blacks than for women. Education differences explain very little of the gender gap, but such differences are a major determinant of the racial earnings gap. For example, in 2010 more than 30% of whites aged 25 years or older had completed four or more years of college compared to just under 20% of blacks. In 1990 the difference was about the same (22% versus 11%).[41] It is difficult to interpret such figures. Certainly they imply that blacks accumulate less human capital on average than do whites, but there could be many reasons for this. One possibility is that there is discrimination in the market for education.

Not only are there differences between blacks and whites in the number of years of formal education but also in their levels of educational achievement. Years of education are, at best, an imperfect measure of educational achievement. (Remember our Sloth University example earlier.) A number of researchers have assessed the importance of differences in achievement using test scores from the Armed Forces Qualifications Test (AFQT), which is a better measure of actual skill levels than the number of years of formal education. For example, using data for the years 1977 through 1987 for a sample of 3,000 full-time male workers, June O'Neill estimates that the actual black–white wage ratio of 0.829 would have risen to 0.877 if blacks had the same years of education, region, and

---

[39] This isn't true everywhere. In the United Kingdom, for example, ethnic minority workers of Indian origin have a higher average level of schooling than do whites. See David H. Blackaby, Derek G. Leslie, Philip D. Murphy, and Nigel C. O'Leary, "The Ethnic Wage Gap and Employment Differentials in the 1990s: Evidence for Britain," *Economics Letters* 58 (1998): 97–103.

[40] See, for example, Derek A. Neal and William R. Johnson, "The Role of Premarket Factors in Black-White Wage Differences," *Journal of Political Economy* 104 (1996): 869–895.

[41] U.S. Department of Commerce, Census Bureau, *Statistical Abstract of the United States* (2012), p. 151 (Table 229).

potential work experience as whites. And if the blacks in her sample had the same AFQT scores as whites, the estimated wage ratio would have been 0.955, with about three-quarters of the gap being explained. When differences in actual experience and occupational and industry characteristics are accounted for, virtually all of the black–white earnings gap is "explained."[42] As O'Neill concludes, "Differences in school quality or family and social background that lead to differences in the acquisition of human capital … now have even a greater impact on economic outcomes than they did in the past."[43]

Just as in the case of women, differences in labor market experience also account for a large proportion of the earnings gap between blacks and whites. Unlike in the case of women, however, it is difficult to make an argument that "choice" can explain racial differences in the accumulation of experience. In addition to experience levels, there is some evidence that blacks may also have lower returns from experience than whites. This could in turn be due to the fact that blacks tend to receive less on-the-job training.

Differences in the characteristics of the various ethnic groups provide the main source of the wage differential in the United States, but in the United Kingdom differences in characteristics explain very little of the gap in earnings across racial groups.[44] On average, there is an 11% wage differential between whites and minorities in the United Kingdom, although the gap varies across ethnic groups (from 7% for Indians, to 13% for blacks, to more than 30% for Pakistanis). Almost none of these substantial gaps can be explained by anything other than discrimination.

A number of factors serve to explain the racial earnings gap and the fact that the gap has not narrowed in the last several decades. To these factors we can also add the decline in unionism (black workers are more likely to be unionized than white workers), the shift in jobs from central cities to the suburbs (the spatial mismatch hypothesis), the effects of globalization and skill-biased technical change, and changes in the real value of the minimum wage. Perhaps the conclusion reached by John Bound and Richard Freeman about the recent decline in the relative earnings of young black males best describes what we know about ethnic earnings gaps in general: "There is too much diversity in the black economic experience for a *single-factor* story … to stand up under scrutiny."[45]

Evidence from Audit Studies

For various reasons economists have not often used the case study approach to measure that portion of the gender or racial pay gap attributable to discrimination. However, the audit study (a type of case study) has recently been used in economic research to determine whether members of different groups are treated differently in the hiring process. Audit studies have been used for some time to ascertain the existence of housing discrimination and to enforce fair housing laws. The procedure consists of auditors being sent out to rent apartments or to purchase homes to see whether the probability of renting or

---

[42] June O'Neill, "The Role of Human Capital in Earnings Differences between Black and White Men," *Journal of Economic Perspectives* 4 (1990): 40–41.

[43] O'Neill, "The Role of Human Capital," p. 42.

[44] Blackaby et al., "The Ethnic Wage Gap and Employment Differential in the 1990s."

[45] John Bound and Richard B. Freeman, "What Went Wrong? The Erosion of Relative Earnings and Employment among Young Black Men in the 1980s," *Quarterly Journal of Economics* 107 (1992): 230.

buying is adversely affected by race. In a similar fashion, the audit study has been used in labor economics to see whether a person's race or gender affects the probability of being hired. Only a limited number of audit studies have been conducted, and we discuss two that are particularly interesting.

In a study of sex discrimination in hiring in the restaurant industry, David Neumark sent two male and two female college students to apply for jobs as waiters and waitresses at a number of restaurants in Philadelphia.[46] Why would there be a suspicion of discriminatory hiring in this industry? Previous research suggested that male waiters seem to be favored in higher-priced, "classier" restaurants where wages and tips are higher.[47] Neumark's results for job offers and interviews provide significant evidence of sex discrimination against women hired for jobs in higher-priced restaurants. Specifically, in higher-priced restaurants a job application from a woman had a probability of receiving an interview that was lower by about 0.35 and a probability of receiving an offer that was lower by about 0.40 than a job application from a man. The nature or source of the discrimination was not absolutely clear (a limitation of audit studies in general), but a likely candidate is Becker-type "taste" discrimination on the part of employers or customers. Alternatively, statistical discrimination could be the culprit if employers undertake investment in their workers and believe that women are more likely to quit than men.[48]

A second labor market audit study that has attracted considerable attention is that of Claudia Goldin and Cecilia Rouse, who studied the selection of musicians for symphony orchestras.[49] Until fairly recently, the members of the most renowned symphony orchestras in the United States were handpicked by music directors, and the proportion of female musicians was extremely small; none contained more than 12% until about 1980. There had been a long-standing bias against female musicians on the part of many renowned conductors. Some claimed that women had "smaller techniques" than men and were "more temperamental and more likely to demand special attention or treatment." For example, Zubin Mehta of the Los Angeles Symphony is said to have once stated, "I just don't think women should be in an orchestra."[50] Moreover, many European orchestras had explicit policies against hiring female musicians.

---

[46] David Neumark, Roy J. Bank, and Kyle D. Van Nort, "Sex Discrimination in Restaurant Hiring: An Audit Study," *Quarterly Journal of Economics* 111 (1996): 915–941.

[47] See, for example, Louise Kapp Howe, *Pink Collar Workers* (New York: G. P. Putnam's Sons, 1977); Barbara Bergmann, *The Economic Emergence of Women* (New York: Basic Books, 1986).

[48] Ethical concerns have been raised recently about some audit studies. For example, an audit study may consist of sending fake resumes to employees to see whether employers are less likely to interview candidates with names more likely to be associated with gender, race, or other characteristics. In such cases, employers are effectively recruited without their knowledge and consent to participate in studies that may be costly (time-wise) or potentially embarrassing to them. See Daniel Hamermesh, "Are Fake Resumes Ethical for Academic Research," http://www.freakonomics.com/2012/01/15/are-fake-resumes-ethical-for-academic-research/; and Devah Pager, "The Use of Field Experiments for Studies of Employment Discrimination: Contributions, Critiques, and Directions for the Future," *The Annals of the American Academy of Political and Social Science* 609 (2007):104–133.

[49] Claudia Goldin and Cecilia Rouse, "Orchestrating Impartiality: The Impact of 'Blind' Auditions on Female Musicians," *American Economic Review* 90 (2000): 715–741.

[50] Cited by Goldin and Rouse, from George Seltzer, *Music Matters: The Performer and the American Federation of Musicians* (Metuchin, NJ: Scarecrow Press, 1989), p. 215.

A change in the audition procedures took place in the 1970s and 1980s, and screens were used to hide an auditioning musician from the judges to ensure impartiality in the selection process. Using information from eight major symphony orchestras, Goldin and Rouse found that the use of screens increased by 50% the probability of women advancing from preliminary rounds. Furthermore, they claimed that the switch to blind auditions explained as much as 25% of the increase in the female composition of major symphony orchestras from 1970 to 1996.[51]

Discrimination in Sports[52]

The professional sports industry in the United States lends itself to studies of racial discrimination as there is extensive publically available data on race, pay, and productivity. However, there is mixed evidence on the extent and type of discrimination across several sports.

The long-standing racial barrier in baseball was not broken until Jackie Robinson was signed by the Brooklyn Dodgers in the late 1940s. Although early studies of baseball provided little evidence of salary discrimination against black players,[53] there was clear evidence of employment discrimination. It is also notable that teams that integrated more quickly in the 1940s and 1950s achieved greater success on the field.[54] In addition, there is anecdotal evidence of coworker discrimination in the era of integration, as attested to by the refusal of some white ballplayers to play with, or against, Jackie Robinson. In the 1960s there was evidence of customer discrimination, with black players found to significantly reduce team revenue.[55] Recent research has confirmed the apparent absence of salary discrimination in general although it may still exist in the lower half of the salary distribution for black players.[56]

Other professional sports in the United States have also shown evidence of discrimination. Earnings equation regressions for basketball players in the National Basketball Association (NBA) in the 1980s revealed that black players earned 11% to 25% less than white players when performance and market-related statistics were controlled

---

[51] Goldin and Rouse, "Orchestrating Impartiality," p. 738.

[52] This section was written by Simon Medcalfe of Augusta State University.

[53] For a review of the discrimination literature in U.S. professional sports though the 1980s, see Lawrence M. Kahn, "Discrimination in Professional Sports: A Survey of the Literature," *Industrial and Labor Relations Review* 44 (1991): 395–418.

[54] This was first analyzed by Brian L. Goff, Robert E. McCormick, and Robert D. Tollison, "Racial Integration as an Innovation: Empirical Evidence from Sports Leagues," *American Economic Review* 92 (2002): 16–26. However, their empirical approach has been criticized by F. Andrew Hanssen and James W. Meehan Jr., in "Who Integrated Major League Baseball Faster: Winning Teams or Losing Teams?" *Journal of Sports Economics* 10 (2009): 141–154.

[55] Estimates from the 1970s suggest that if the percentage of black players on a team increased by one percentage point, team revenue would fall by $58,523. See Gerald W. Scully, "Pay and Performance in Major League Baseball," *American Economic Review* 64 (1974): 915–930.

[56] The premiums for white and Hispanic players are as high as 25% of salary for the bottom quintile of players. See Paul Holmes, "New Evidence of Salary Discrimination in Major League Baseball," *Labour Economics* 18 (2011): 320–331.

for.[57] This gap had generally disappeared by the mid-1990s, but the differential effects of the racial composition of teams on attendance and revenue persisted into the 1990s.[58] Customer preferences have also been found that reflect the racial mix of the population in cities with National Football League (NFL) teams, with the salaries of white and nonwhite players varying positively with the percentage of the surrounding population.[59]

In baseball, blacks faced discrimination in promotion from the minor to the major leagues.[60] In the 1960s and 1970s, black minor league baseball players were 9.3% less likely to be promoted to the majors than whites and 8.1% less likely in the 1990s. Hispanics seem to have suffered similar discrimination in the 1960s and 1970s, but apparently this phenomenon had disappeared by the 1990s. Significantly, promotion discrimination seems to have subsided in expansion years, just as the Becker model would predict. Allegations of discrimination by playing position have also been raised, with black baseball players underrepresented at the pitcher, catcher, and infield positions.[61] In the late 1980s nonwhite football players were underrepresented at quarterback, kicker, punter, and offensive line.[62] As late as 2006, black quarterbacks in the top half of the salary distribution in the NFL appeared to be penalized for their race.[63]

In Europe, recent research on discrimination in association football (sometimes called "soccer" but more commonly simply "football") has found that English soccer clubs with a below-average proportion of black players tended to win fewer games per season from 1978 to 1993.[64] However, black players transferring between English soccer clubs do not command lower transfer fees than white players.[65] The evidence on customer

[57] Lawrence M. Kahn and Peter D. Sherer, "Racial Differences in Professional Basketball Players' Compensation," *Journal of Labor Economics* 6 (1988): 40–61; James V. Koch and C. Warren Vander Hill, "Is There Discrimination in the 'Black Man's Game'?" *Social Science Quarterly* 69 (1988): 83–94; Michael Wallace, "Labor Market Structure and Salary Determination among Professional Basketball Players," *Work and Occupations* 15 (1988): 294–312.

[58] See Richard C. K. Burdekin, Richard T. Hossfeld, and Janet Kiholm Smith, "Are NBA Fans Becoming Indifferent to Race? Evidence from the 1990s," *Journal of Sports Economics* 6 (2005): 144–159.

[59] For example, a one standard deviation increase in the percentage of the nonwhite population in a metropolitan area was found to raise nonwhite player salaries, all else being equal, by 2.6% to 4.4% and a corresponding decrease was found to raise white salaries by 1.2% to 3.1%. See Lawrence M. Kahn, "The Effects of Race on Professional Football Players' Compensation," *Industrial and Labor Relations Review* 45 (1992): 295–310.

[60] Fred A. Bellemore, "Racial and Ethnic Employment Discrimination: Promotion in Major League Baseball," *Journal of Sports Economics* 2 (2001): 356–368.

[61] Kevin J. Christiano, "Salary and Race in Professional Baseball: Discrimination Ten Years Later," *Sociology of Sport Journal* 5 (1988): 136–149.

[62] Kahn, "The Effects of Race on Professional Football Players' Compensation."

[63] For example, a black quarterback throwing 3,000 yards per season who is in the top decile of the salary distribution would have a salary that is only 61% of a similarly productive white quarterback. See David J. Berri and Rob Simmons, "Race and the Evaluation of Signal Callers in the National Football League," *Journal of Sports Economics* 10 (2009): 23–43.

[64] Stefan Szymanski, "A Market Test for Discrimination in the English Professional Soccer Leagues," *Journal of Political Economy* 108 (2000): 590–603.

[65] See Barry Reilly and Robert Witt "English League Transfer Prices: Is There Racial Discrimination?" *Applied Economics Letters* 2 (1995): 220–222; Simon Medcalfe, "English League Transfer Prices: Is There a Racial Dimension? A Re-examination with New Data," *Applied Economics Letters* 15 (2008): 865–867.

discrimination is more straightforward: the proportion of black players on a team does not seem to affect either attendance or revenues in England.[66]

Economists have started to look into the possibility of discrimination by national origin, finding evidence that South American players received preferential treatment in the English Premier League (soccer) and that international players in the NBA received lower salaries than their U.S.-born counterparts.[67] From 1985 until 1991 additional foreign-born players decreased ticket demand in Major League Baseball (MLB). However, from 1992 until 2005 the net effect on ticket demand was positive.[68] Finally, evidence of salary discrimination against French Canadians in the National Hockey League (NHL) has been found, but apparently only against those who play on defense.[69]

Recent research has also found that referees (in the NBA) and umpires (in MLB) discriminate against players whose race or ethnicity is different from their own. Strikes are called less often in baseball when a pitcher and umpire are of different race or ethnicity. More personal fouls are awarded against NBA players when they are officiated by an opposite-race refereeing crew than if the crew were of their own race. However, there is no evidence that referees in the English Premier League discriminated when penalizing soccer players.[70]

Coaches are in a unique position in sports with regard to discrimination: they may discriminate against players on their team and be discriminated against by the team's owner(s). There is evidence that coaches in the NBA gave greater playing time to players of their own race during the 1996–2004 seasons.[71] The evidence on hiring and retention of coaches varies by sport: race does not seem to affect hiring or retention decisions in the NBA nor the promotion of assistant coaches to head coach in the NFL. However, in major league baseball minorities are actually more likely to be retained for the next season.[72]

---

[66] Stefan Szymanski, "A Market Test for Discrimination in the English Professional Soccer Leagues," *Journal of Political Economy* 108 (2000): 590–603.

[67] Roberto Pedace, "Earnings, Performance, and Nationality Discrimination in a Highly Competitive Labor Market: An Analysis of the English Professional Soccer League," *Journal of Sports Economics* 9 (2008): 115–140; Chih-Hai Yang and Hsuan-Yu Lin "Is There Salary Discrimination by Nationality in the NBA? Foreign Talent or Foreign Market," *Journal of Sports Economics* 13 (2012): 3–19.

[68] Scott Tainsky and Jason A. Winfree, "Discrimination and Demand: The Effect of International Players on Attendance in Major League Baseball," *Social Science Quarterly* 91 (2010): 117–128.

[69] Marc Lavoie, Gilles Grenier, and Serge Coulombe, "Discrimination and Performance Differentials in the National Hockey League," *Canadian Public Policy* 13 (1987): 407–422.

[70] Christopher A. Parsons, Johan Sulaeman, Michael C. Yates, and Daniel S. Hamermesh, "Strike Three: Discrimination, Incentives, and Evaluation," *American Economic Review* 101 (2011): 1410–1435; Joseph Price and Justin J. Wolfers, "Racial Discrimination among NBA Referees," *Quarterly Journal of Economics* 125 (2010): 1859–1887; Barry Reilly and Robert Witt, "Disciplinary Sanctions in English Premiership Football: Is There a Racial Dimension?" *Labour Economics* 18 (2011): 360–370.

[71] Jesse L. Schroffel and Christopher S. P. Magee, "Own-Race Bias among NBA Coaches," *Journal of Sports Economics* 13 (2012): 130–151.

[72] Lawrence M. Kahn, "Race, Performance, Pay, and Retention among National Basketball Association Head Coaches," *Journal of Sports Economics* 7 (2006): 119–149; Brian Volz, "Minority Status and Managerial Survival in Major League Baseball," *Journal of Sports Economics* 10 (2009): 522–542; Benjamin L. Solow, John L. Solow, and Todd B. Walker, "Moving on Up: The Rooney Rule and Minority Hiring in the NFL," *Labour Economics* 18 (2011): 332–337.

Men and women rarely compete against each other, so studies of gender discrimination in sports are rare. When they do compete, the evidence on gender discrimination is mixed: female horse jockeys secure fewer mounts than male jockeys, while National Collegiate Athletic Association female basketball coaches are compensated the same as male coaches.[73]

Anti-Discrimination Policies

The existence and persistence of labor market discrimination have prompted enactment of **anti-discrimination legislation**. The most important statutes and policies in the United States include:

- Equal Pay Act (1963)
- Civil Rights Act (1964)
- Age Discrimination in Employment Act (1967)
- Americans with Disabilities Act (1990)
- Affirmative Action
- Comparable Worth

We discuss each of them briefly and appraise their effectiveness and then look at some of the policies other countries have implemented.

The Equal Pay Act

The oldest federal anti-discrimination statute in the United States is the **Equal Pay Act** of 1963. Put simply, this act mandates that men and women should receive the same pay if the work that they are doing is substantially the same, requiring similar skills and under similar working conditions. The act includes those occupations covered by the federal Fair Labor Standards Act (the minimum wage law); therefore, its coverage, although broad, is not universal. The Equal Pay Act also eliminated some prior protective labor laws that limited the hours of work that women were able to perform and restricted night work or working during pregnancy. These laws were enacted by many states with the best of intentions during an age when workplace abuses were more common, but they had the effect of legally sanctioning differential treatment of women in the workplace.[74]

Although its focus was on equal pay, the act said nothing about requiring equal treatment in hiring and promotions. As the Becker theory of discrimination shows, an equal pay law in the absence of equal employment requirements can function as a minimum

---

[73] Margaret A. Ray and Paul W. Grimes, "Jockeying for Position: Winnings and Gender Discrimination on the Thoroughbred Racetrack," *Social Science Quarterly* 74 (1993): 46–61; Stacey L. Brook and Sarah Foster, "Does Gender Affect Compensation among NCAA Basketball Coaches?" *International Journal of Sport Finance* 5 (2010): 96–106.

[74] Protective labor statutes for women were not unique to the United States, of course, but some of them remained on the books until fairly recently. For example, the Republic of Ireland did not remove its ban on women working at night until 1986.

wage law, resulting in employers with a "taste for discrimination" perhaps simply refusing to hire women at all.

The Civil Rights Act

The **Civil Rights Act** of 1964 is a landmark piece of U.S. legislation. Title VII made it an unlawful practice for an employer to discriminate against any employee on the basis of race, color, religion, sex, or national origin. Similar prohibitions apply to employment agencies and unions as well. The Equal Employment Opportunity Commission (EEOC) is responsible for enforcing the act and attempts to persuade parties to comply with the act's requirements, although it may bring suits on its own when it believes that violations have occurred. Employees, of course, may also sue employers directly.

The rights guaranteed to employees under the Civil Rights Act were qualified in several ways. For instance, discriminatory treatment is allowable for prison guards in a single-sex jail who may have to undertake strip searches of inmates. Another exemption from the act allows Roman Catholic high schools to hire only Catholic teachers of religious studies.

Discrimination on the Basis of Age and Disability

The Age Discrimination in Employment Act (ADEA) of 1967 protects individuals who are 40 years of age or older from employment discrimination based on age. The ADEA covers both employees and job applicants and applies to all employers with 20 or more employees, including the federal, state, and local governments. Under the ADEA, it is unlawful for an employer to discriminate against a person because of age with respect to any terms or conditions of employment, including hiring, firing, promotion, layoff, and compensation. Furthermore, it is unlawful for an employer to retaliate against a person for filing an age discrimination complaint or for participating in an investigation or litigation under the ADEA.

The Americans with Disabilities Act (ADA) was passed in 1990 and came into effect in 1992. The act gives civil rights protections to individuals with disabilities much like those provided to individuals on the basis of race, color, sex, national origin, age, and religion. Title I of the act prohibits private employers, state and local governments, employment agencies, and labor unions from discriminating against *qualified* individuals with disabilities in hiring, firing, promotion, compensation, and other terms and conditions of employment. A qualified employee or applicant with a disability is an individual who, with "reasonable accommodation," can perform the essential functions of the job in question. Reasonable accommodation may include making existing facilities used by employees accessible to persons with disabilities, for example, by providing ramps for people in wheelchairs. Under the act an employer is required to make an accommodation for the disability of a qualified applicant or employee only if it would not impose an "undue hardship" on the operation of the employer's business. Undue hardship is defined as one that would result in significant difficulty or expense in light of such factors as an employer's size and financial resources.[75]

---

[75] The U.S. Equal Employment Opportunity Commission, *Facts about the Americans with Disabilities Act, 2008.*

Affirmative Action

Probably the most controversial (and often misunderstood) anti-discrimination program in the United States is **affirmative action**. The federal affirmative action program has its roots in World War II, when President Franklin D. Roosevelt issued an executive order barring discrimination against blacks in the federal government and by defense contractors. Several decades later in 1961, President John F. Kennedy created a Committee on Equal Employment Opportunity and issued Executive Order 10925, which first used the term "affirmative action" to refer to measures designed to reduce discrimination in employment. In 1965, President Lyndon Johnson issued Executive Order 11246, which required those doing business with the federal government (federal contractors) to undertake affirmative action so as to bring about equality of employment opportunity without regard to race, religion, or national origin. Gender, disability, and status as a Vietnam War veteran were later added as additional protected categories.[76]

What does affirmative action entail? The Office of Federal Contract Compliance Programs (OFCCP) requires every federal contractor with at least 50 employees and government contracts of at least $50,000 to develop and implement a written affirmative action program. Such a program is to include the following:

- A self-analysis by the contractor to see whether any barriers to equal employment opportunity exist within the firm.
- A self-analysis of the contractor's workforce to see whether minorities and women are "underutilized." Underutilization is defined as employing fewer minorities and women in a particular job group than would reasonably be expected given their availability in an area within which the contractor can reasonably recruit workers.
- Establishment of numerical goals and timetables to eliminate any underutilization of minorities and women. To attain these goals, good faith efforts (affirmative action steps) are to be taken, such as expanded efforts in recruitment and training to increase the firm's utilization and qualified pool of minorities and women.

These numerical goals were not supposed to be interpreted as quotas, nor were they intended to lead to "set-asides" (places reserved only for minorities or women). In fact, federal regulations specifically prohibit quotas and preferential hiring, which would themselves be forms of discrimination.[77]

Affirmative action has generated much controversy and criticism. Opponents of affirmative action sometimes claim that affirmative action does mean setting de facto quotas, placing unqualified people in jobs, or preferences for members of a protected class over those who are not in a protected class. However, neither quotas nor preferential hiring are required—or even allowed—by affirmative action. Exceptions can occur, however, if courts find that past discrimination has taken place and issue orders for remedial action. In some of these cases, courts have set quotas, and companies have been ordered to follow hiring procedures to reach these quotas. Companies are not required to hire people who are unqualified for the job even in these cases.

---

[76] Affirmative Action Review Report to the President (1995).

[77] U.S. Department of Labor, Employment Standards Administration, "Facts on Executive Order 11246—Affirmative Action," 2002.

Critics have also argued that affirmative action means that the "best qualified" person may not be hired. Supporters sometimes take issue with what it means to be judged "best qualified," contending that test scores and educational qualifications are not necessarily the best predictors of a worker's future success. According to this argument, affirmative action does not mean that unqualified people will be hired, but that people who may not have the highest test scores or grades but who are still perfectly capable of doing the job may be hired. Most employers consider not just test scores but also factors such as personal appearance, personality, and family and school connections, thereby demonstrating that "qualified" can be defined in many ways. (If they didn't, why would you bother to dress up for a job interview?)

Comparable Worth

Beginning in the mid-1980s, the issue of **comparable worth**—also known as "pay equity"—emerged as a significant gender pay issue in the context of labor market discrimination in the United States.[78] The motivation behind comparable worth is that, despite several decades of anti-discrimination legislation, women on average still earn only about 70% of what men earn. As we have seen, the problem does not arise primarily from wage discrimination. Instead, much of the wage disparity reflects the fact that female workers tend to be heavily concentrated in a small number of occupational categories that pay relatively low wages. The Equal Pay Act of 1963 prohibits employers from paying women less than men for the *same* jobs. The comparable worth notion proposes that equal pay be required for jobs that, although dissimilar, can be shown to be of *comparable worth* or *value* as judged by job evaluation methods. Job evaluation is a method that assigns point values to jobs on the basis of such factors as skill, effort, responsibility, and working conditions. Jobs with higher point values would be considered to have higher worth or value than jobs with lower point values and, according to the comparable worth notion, should therefore command higher pay.

Comparable worth and pay equity policies have met with some criticism. One major criticism is that such policies determine pay by job evaluation rather than by market forces of supply and demand. But what's the problem with this? According to basic economic analysis, attempts to set wages or prices that differ from those determined in a competitive market will generally produce difficulties. To use just one example, in the academic labor market in the United States supply and demand conditions determine that the salaries for beginning professors of history are lower than those of beginning economists. (Our historian friends are not happy that this is the case.) But suppose (as is likely) that a job evaluation study finds the "worth" of the jobs that economists and historians perform to be the same. Pay equity principles would then dictate that the salaries of the two groups be equal. If the pay of history professors were raised, then a surplus of professors of history would be the result. If pay equity is achieved by lowering the pay of economists, however, a shortage of economists will take place. In either case, by ignoring the market a misallocation of resources has occurred.

---

[78] Some parts of this section have been taken from Robert J. Thornton, "Unions in the Local Government Sector," in *Management Policies in Local Government Finance*, eds. J. Richard Aronson and Eli Schwartz (Washington: International City/County Management Association, 2004).

Steven Rhoads presents several examples to show how comparable worth policies can distort resource allocation in labor markets. For example, he notes that in Minnesota (a state that mandates that local governments implement comparable worth policies) some libraries had 40 to 60 applications for every opening, yet they were still required to raise salaries 20% to 60% because the work of librarians had been "undervalued." At the same time, he notes that public sector nurses could not be offered wages high enough to attract them to government jobs.[79]

Ignoring the market and allowing pay levels to be set by other means can lead to further undesirable side effects. For example, in raising the pay of women above levels desired by the employer or by the market, comparable worth policies may lower women's employment levels. Mark Killingsworth cites the following evidence:

- In San Jose, California, where pay equity adjustments for female municipal workers were implemented throughout the 1980s, a reduction of nearly 7% occurred in female–male relative employment.
- In Minnesota where local governments are required to set pay according to comparable worth principles, a decline of about 7% occurred in the total employment of women relative to that of men.[80]

Another criticism of comparable worth schemes is that job evaluation is a very subjective process. This subjectivity can mean differences among experts in the job factors selected, in the assignment of weights to the factors, and in the number of points assigned to factor categories. But the problems with job evaluation go deeper than its subjectivity. Simply put, job evaluation is a procedure for placing a value *on the job itself*—on the tasks, the responsibilities, the effort and skills required to perform the job satisfactorily, as well as on the working conditions associated with the job. Job evaluation is not a procedure for placing a value on how well the *individual* actually performs the job.

Although comparable worth has had only limited success in the United States, in many other countries the notion has become widely accepted. In the countries comprising the European Union, for example, claims for equal pay for work of equal value are common and are covered by equal pay legislation. In fact, Article 119 of the 1957 Treaty of Rome (which set up the European Common Market, predecessor to the European Union) required that each member state should "ensure and subsequently maintain the application of the principle that men and women should receive equal pay for equal work." At a very early date, equal work was interpreted broadly to mean not only identical work but also work of equal value. It should be noted, however, that the manner in which member states have adopted comparable worth policies—and the enthusiasm for the principle of comparable worth—has varied. In the United Kingdom, for example, a decentralized policy is operated. Firms may conduct job evaluations, but they are not required to do so. If a job evaluation has been conducted, then the wages paid to men and women must reflect the outcome of the evaluation. If no evaluation has taken place, any dispute concerning

---

[79] Steven Rhoads, *Incomparable Worth* (New York: Press Syndicate of the University of Cambridge, 1994), p. 5.

[80] Mark Killingsworth, "Benefits and Costs of Comparable Worth," in *Pay Equity: Means and Ends*, ed. Michael G. Abbott (Kingston, Ontario: John Deutsch Institute for the Study of Economic Policy, Queen's University, 1990). In other areas of the United States where comparable worth has been tried (Iowa, Michigan, and Washington), these efforts too met with, at best, very limited success.

unequal pay across genders must be handled by an industrial tribunal (a small panel of experts chosen by government). The tribunal then conducts an evaluation. In constructing a job evaluation, neither the firm nor the tribunal has legal guidance concerning the factors that should be considered. This affords both firms and tribunals considerable discretion and has led to a lack of transparency. Meanwhile, the tribunals, which were set up to be quick and easy decision-making bodies, typically take about a year to report. This long drawn out process is costly both to firms and to complainants and is not terribly effective; it may at best be regarded as a lukewarm variant of comparable worth.

In Australia, the principle of pay equity has had a checkered history. The principle of equal pay for equal work has been accepted by the Commonwealth Conciliation and Arbitration Commission since 1969, and in 1972 this was extended to the principle of equal pay for work of equal value. The equal pay principle was reaffirmed in 1985, but at that time the notion of comparable worth was rejected. By the late 1990s, comparable worth principles had once again come to the fore, with passage of the 1996 Commonwealth Workplace Relations Act. These moves have generally been praised for helping to close the gender pay differential in Australia, but it is also recognized that they come at a cost in terms of employment, especially the employment of women,[81] and they remain controversial.

In January 1988 the world's most comprehensive comparable worth law was put into effect in Ontario, Canada. Ontario's Pay Equity Act is significant in several respects. Its scope, first of all, includes not just Ontario's public sector but also all firms with at least 10 employees in the private sector. In addition, the Ontario law is proactive rather than complaints-based. In other words, instead of leaving to female employees the burden of initiating a complaint or suit and then proving that they are underpaid, the Ontario law places the responsibility on employers to base pay levels on comparable worth principles in the first place.

Interestingly, despite the comprehensive and aggressive nature of the Ontario comparable worth law, its effect on the gender earnings gap in Ontario appears to have been modest. There was a rise of several percentage points in the female–male earnings ratio after the passage of the act in 1988. However, studies suggest that even this modest rise in the ratio may not necessarily have been due mainly to pay equity legislation.[82]

International evidence also points to an important policy that while not explicitly being an anti-discrimination measure may have a profound impact on discrimination. In our section on Theories of Labor Market Discrimination, we pointed out that competition ought to eliminate discrimination. The extent of competition or economic freedom varies across countries, and so it is possible to evaluate the extent to which such freedom impacts on gender (and other) wage gaps. In Figure 13.8, the (logged) wage gap evaluated from International Social Survey Program data for each of 31 countries is plotted against a measure (calculated by the Fraser Institute in Vancouver) of economic freedom. It is clear

---

[81] John Madden, "The Economic Consequences of Pay Equity for Female Intensive Occupations: A Multiregional CGE Analysis," mimeo, University of Tasmania, 2000.

[82] Judith A. McDonald and Robert J. Thornton, "Private-Sector Experience with Pay Equity in Ontario," *Canadian Public Policy* 24 (1998): 185–208; Michael Baker and Nicole Fortin, "Comparable Worth Comes to the Private Sector: The Case of Ontario," Conference "Équité Salariale." CIRANO, Montreal, October 15–16, 1999.

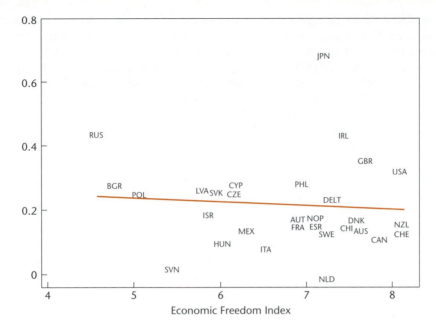

FIGURE 13.8 Gender Wage Gaps and Economic Freedom

Source: Martina Zweimuller, Rudolf Winter-Ebner, and Doris Weischelbaumer, "Market Orientation and Gender Wage Gaps: An International Study," *Kyklos* 61 (2007): 615–635.

that as economic freedom improves, there is a tendency for the wage gap to decline.[83] Encouraging competition seems to be, therefore, a further way of tackling the problem of discrimination.

The Effects of Anti-Discrimination Policies

Many different types of public policies have been formulated to combat labor market discrimination. How effective have these policies been in reducing or eliminating racial and gender wage gaps?

Turning to race, first of all, we noted earlier in this chapter that wages for black men rose at a faster rate in the United States than wages of white men during the 1960s and 1970s. However, since that time there has been virtually no further closing of the gap. Moreover, the ratio of black women's wages to white women's wages came very close to 1 in the 1970s, but the gap has widened since then. In the case of gender differences, the female–male pay ratio, long constant at about 0.60, began to rise at the end of the decade of the 1970s and is about 0.75 today.

---

[83] Martina Zweimuller, Rudolf Winter-Ebner, and Doris Weischelbaumer, "Market Orientation and Gender Wage Gaps: An International Study," *Kyklos* 61 (2007): 615–635.

Can we attribute these changes to anti-discrimination policies? Evidence suggests that lawsuits (actual and threatened) under Title VII of the Civil Rights Act during the 1960s and 1970s improved the employment and occupational experiences of blacks.[84] And in his analysis of more than 68,000 establishments over the period 1974–80, Jonathan Leonard found that both black and female employment increased more rapidly at establishments subject to affirmative action. Leonard also claims that the increase in the demand for black male labor induced by affirmative action accounted for a significant portion of the decline in the racial earnings gap.[85] In short, both blacks and women were helped by anti-discrimination policies in the 1960s and 1970s.

After 1980, however, the story is somewhat different. Enforcement of anti-discrimination statutes became more lax as funding was reduced and legal standards for proving discrimination were tightened. It is difficult to prove whether this had a pronounced effect on earnings gaps, however. Although the decline in the racial earnings gap came to a halt during this period, these were also the years when the gender earnings gap experienced its most rapid decline.

In probably the most comprehensive assessment of the record of affirmative action to date, Holzer and Neumark provide the following inferences regarding its magnitude as well as some of its other effects:

- Although affirmative action programs have redistributed employment and government business from white males to minorities and women, the extent of the redistribution is probably not large.
- There is virtually no evidence of weaker qualifications or job performance among females who have benefited from affirmative action relative to males.
- There is some evidence of weaker labor market *credentials* of minority beneficiaries of affirmative action compared to their white counterparts. But evidence of weaker *performance* in the labor market on the part of these groups is much less frequently observed.
- There is some evidence of positive externalities from affirmative action. For example, minority doctors are more likely to treat minority and low-income patients than are white physicians.[86]

Overall, Holzer and Neumark conclude that the most current evidence best supports the view that "*affirmative action offers significant redistribution toward women and minorities with relatively small efficiency consequences*" [italics added].[87]

In concluding our assessment of the effects of anti-discrimination policies, let's look briefly at evidence from other countries. Apart from the United States, most other studies have been undertaken for the Australian, Canadian, or United Kingdom labor markets and have examined the effects of equal pay legislation; a summary of the results appears in Table 13.10. Not unexpectedly, the evidence is rather mixed. Two studies of British

---

[84] Altonji and Blank, "Race and Gender in the Labor Market," p. 3246.

[85] Jonathan Leonard, "The Impact of Affirmative Action on Employment," *Journal of Labor Economics* 2 (1984): 439–463.

[86] Harry Holzer and David Neumark, "Assessing Affirmative Action," *Journal of Economic Literature* 38 (2000): 558–559.

[87] Holzer and Neumark, "Assessing Affirmative Action," p. 559.

TABLE 13.10 Representative Studies of the Effects of Anti-Discrimination Legislation on Female Wages

Study	Country	Impact
Baker and Fortin (2004)	Canada (Ontario)	No effect on aggregate wages in female jobs or on gender wage gap.
Drolet and Mumford (2009)	Canada	Aggressive pay-equity policies have not worked to narrow the gender pay gap
Cassidy, Strobl, and Thornton (2002)	Ireland	Only a very small part (c. 4%) of the rise in the female–male pay ratio is attributable to Irish equality legislation.
Gunderson (1975)	Canada (Ontario)	No significant impact.
Gunderson (1976)	Canada (Ontario)	Statistically significant reduction in gender gap in only two occupational groups.
Gunderson (1985)	Canada (Ontario)	No significant effect on gender gap.
McDonald and Thornton (1998)	Canada (Ontario)	Very modest. Average pay adjustment for females was less than 1.5% of payroll.
Chiplin and Sloane (1988)	United Kingdom	Statistically significant increase of 8 percentage points in relative female earnings, although some of this may have been due to other wage policies.
Zabalza and Tzannatos (1985)	United Kingdom	Statistically significant increase of 19.4% in relative female earnings.
Gregory and Duncan (1981)	Australia	Increased relative female earnings by 30%, although no statistical test of this was done.

Sources: Michael Baker and Nicole M. Fortin, "Comparable Worth in a Decentralized Labour Market: The Case of Ontario," *The Canadian Journal of Economics/Revue canadienne d'Economique* 37(4) (2004): 850–878; Brian Chiplin and Peter Sloane, "The Effect of Britain's Anti-Discriminatory Legislation on Relative Pay and Employment: A Comment," *Economic Journal* 98 (1988): 833–838; Mark Cassidy, Eric Strobl, and Robert Thornton, "Gender Pay Differentials and Equality Legislation in the Republic of Ireland," *Canadian Public Policy* 28 (2002): S149–S169; Marie Drolet and Karen Mumford, "The Gender Pay Gap for Private Sector Employees in Canada and Britain," *IZA Discussion Paper Series No. 3957*, 2009. Accessed online March 27, 2009; Robert G. Gregory and Ronald C. Duncan, "Segmented Labor Market Theories and the Australian Experience of Equal Pay for Women," *Journal of Post Keynesian Economics* 3 (1981): 403–428; Morley Gunderson, "Male-Female Wage Differentials and the Impact of Equal Pay Legislation," *Review of Economics and Statistics* 57 (1975): 462–470; Morley Gunderson, "Time Pattern of Male-Female Wage Differentials," *Relations Industrielles* 31 (1976): 57–71; Morley Gunderson, "Spline Function Estimates of the Impact of Equal Pay Legislation: The Ontario Experiment," *Relations Industrielles* 40 (1985): 775–791; Judith McDonald and Robert Thornton, "Private Sector Experience with Pay Equity in Ontario," *Canadian Public Policy* 24 (1998): 185–208; Antonio Zabalza and Zafiris Tzannatos, "The Effect of Britain's Anti-Discrimination Legislation on Relative Pay and Employment," *Economic Journal* 95 (1985): 679–699.

legislation have investigated the effects of the Equal Pay Act of 1970 and the Sex Discrimination Act of 1975; the results of the studies suggest that the relative wages of females have risen by somewhere between 8% and 20% in response to the new laws. Equal pay legislation in Australia seems to have been more successful, increasing the average earnings of full-time female employees by 30% relative to the average earnings of full-time male employees. In Ontario, Canada, equal pay legislation seems to have had little or no effect. Finally, Irish legislation of the 1970s may have increased female relative wages by just under 4%. In all of these studies, the equal pay laws alluded to were comparable worth laws requiring equal pay for work of equal value.

Summary

The labor market is a particularly interesting "place" because casual observation suggests that it may have a tendency to fail. This observation has been confirmed by the existence of discrimination against women and minority workers. In addition to being morally offensive, discrimination is, as we have seen, also inefficient. Its existence may, therefore, be viewed as something of a puzzle, though perhaps not more of a puzzle than the existence of other market failures.

Discrimination in the labor market can take on a number of different forms. The most obvious, and the two we have focused on, are discrimination by gender or ethnicity, but discrimination on the basis of age, religion, disability, health, and other personal attributes is often observed as well.

Gender differences in access to different occupations are considerable. The earnings gap between men and women still amounts to about 25% in most Western countries although not all of this is due to discrimination. Part of it results from men and women having different human capital characteristics. There is also occupational concentration and wage discrimination along racial lines. A number of theories of discrimination have been developed by economists, including Gary Becker's model of personal prejudice, the statistical discrimination model, the occupational crowding model, monopsony models, and the Lazear and Rosen model of gender differentials within an internal labor market.

The extent to which discrimination explains the wage differential between minority and majority groups is commonly analyzed using the Oaxaca decomposition method; this allows that part of the differential that is due to differences in human capital to be separated out from the part that is due to unjustified discrimination. Studies show that one-third to two-thirds of the wage differential between men and women is due to discrimination; the proportion of the differential between ethnic majority and ethnic minority workers that is due to discrimination varies considerably from country to country. Professional sports provides a good laboratory for testing for the presence and extent of discrimination because data on individual performance are kept, and a great deal of discrimination has been witnessed in this arena. Legislation to combat discrimination has had mixed success; equal pay and civil rights legislation has helped to reduce differentials, but the success of comparable worth policies has been less clear.

The prevalence of discrimination has potentially serious social consequences. Racial discrimination has been the root cause of violent disturbances in a number of countries, and discrimination on the basis of religion has caused serious disruptions, contributing to the Irish troubles and some of the problems in the Middle East. This, in addition to the moral and efficiency reasons mentioned earlier, makes it essential that discrimination should be better understood so that policies can be formulated to reduce or eliminate it.

KEY TERMS

labor market discrimination
occupational segregation
Duncan index of dissimilarity (DID)
gender discrimination

ethnic discrimination
personal prejudice theory
statistical discrimination
crowding model

monopsony model

Oaxaca decomposition method

anti-discrimination legislation

Equal Pay Act

Civil Rights Act

affirmative action

comparable worth

PROBLEMS

1. Think of jobs that you and others in your class have had. Is there a gender difference in the types of work that people do? What might explain this? Is there a gender difference in pay levels? What might explain this? Are there racial differences in the types of jobs and levels of pay?

2. The size of the wage differential between majority and minority groups that is due to differences in coefficients between the earnings functions for the two groups is often called "unjustified discrimination." But can you think of any other explanation for this?

3. Discrimination occurs in many areas of life, not just in the labor market. How would you evaluate the extent of discrimination in the market for education? What implications does this have for subsequent wage and employment differentials in the labor market?

4. Why is the gender earnings differential in Australia so much smaller than in many other countries?

5. What happens to the relative magnitude of the "characteristics effect" and the "unjustified discrimination" effect when more explanatory variables are added to the earnings functions for the majority and minority groups? Of the following, which variables should be included and which should be excluded from the list of explanatory variables: experience, experience squared, schooling, schooling squared, occupation, industry, union membership, tenure with firm, tenure with firm squared, region of residence? Why?

6. What problems are associated with comparable worth legislation? Does the benefit of reducing discrimination offset these problems?

7. Consider an economy in which the distribution of workers across occupations is as follows:

Occupation	Males (%)	Females (%)
Managers	18%	12%
Professional occupations	17	14
Technicians	14	2
Sales workers	4	20
Administrators	5	23
Other services	3	13
Craft workers	14	9
Operatives and laborers	21	5
Agricultural workers	4	2

Calculate the Duncan index of dissimilarity. What would you conclude from this about the distribution of men and women across "good" and "bad" jobs?

8. Consider an economy in which the earnings function for males is given by:

$$\ln w = 0.5 + 0.10S + 0.08X - 0.003X^2$$

while that for females is given by

$$\ln w = 0.2 + 0.13S + 0.05X - 0.003X^2$$

where S represents years of schooling and X represents years of experience. What do the above equations imply about the rate of return to education for men and women? (*Hint:* Think back to Chapter 6.)

9. Use the information from question 8 and the following additional information: The average value of S for men is 13.7, and for women it is 13.5; the average value of X for men is 23, and for women it is 13. Using the Oaxaca decomposition method, find the log wage differential at the means of the variables. Identify how much of this differential is due to differences in characteristics and how much to "unjustified discrimination."

10. Suppose that there are just two types of hair: blond and brown. Suppose further that people with blond hair are discriminated against in Alabastria and Bluxonnia. In Alabastria, all blonds earn a wage that is 20% below that of brown-haired workers with otherwise identical characteristics. In Bluxonnia, half of the workers with blond hair earn exactly the same as brown-haired workers with identical characteristics, but the other half earn only 60% of the blond wage. In which country do you think discrimination is the more severe problem? On what does your judgment depend?

Why did the unemployment rate rise so rapidly in the "Great Recession" of 2008 and 2009?

Why did unemployment stay high even as economies around the globe recovered in 2010 and 2011?

Why is the unemployment rate much higher in some economies than in others even during periods of economic growth?

If the labor market worked perfectly, it would always clear. Everybody who wanted to work for the wages currently on offer could find a job, and nobody would be forced to work for a wage he or she found to be unacceptable. In such a world, only those who chose not to work at the prevailing wage would be unemployed. In this scenario, unemployment would be wholly voluntary, and economists would not regard it as a problem. Indeed, **voluntary unemployment** would be a good thing because economic welfare is maximized when individuals choose freely.

An examination of the voluntary nature of some unemployment is provided by job search theory. As we saw in Chapter 8, unemployed workers who choose to prolong their search after receiving a wage offer less than their reservation wage are behaving efficiently. They are investing a sum equal to the cost of prolonged search in the hope and expectation of receiving enhanced future wages. The process of job search, and the existence of search unemployment, ensures that productive matches are made between workers and firms.

There is plenty to suggest, however, that the labor market does not work well enough to ensure that all unemployment is search unemployment. Numerous studies suggest that, on average, the unemployed are less happy than the employed. Indeed, over and above the pecuniary cost of being unemployed and hence forgoing an income, the psychic cost of a year's unemployment to a typical individual has been estimated at $60,000.[1] It would be curious indeed if something that made people so unhappy were voluntary.

Further evidence comes from the severity of the business cycle. At times the overall rate of unemployment in an economy fluctuates extremely sharply. Few observers find it plausible to suppose that people's preferences change this rapidly, and many economists

---

[1] David G. Blanchflower, and Andrew J. Oswald, "Well-Being Over Time in Britain and the USA," *Journal of Public Economics* 88 (2002): 1359–1386.

view the sharp up and down swings of unemployment as evidence that not all unemployment results from choices about work versus leisure or from the necessities of efficient job search. The implication of this is that for some workers unemployment is involuntary. These workers are unable to find jobs even though they are willing to work for the going wage or even less than the going wage.

In this chapter, we explore several aspects of the complex phenomenon that is unemployment in a modern industrialized country. We begin by reviewing the way we measure unemployment and by examining the key statistical properties of the time series evidence on the unemployment rate. The unemployment rate can be separated into a component that stays fairly constant over time and a more volatile component that rises and falls with the business cycle. The stable component best matches the concept of search unemployment, and search theory proves useful in explaining why this level of unemployment varies from place to place and sometimes changes over time.

The volatile, cyclical component of the unemployment rate is harder to characterize in terms of search theory. An important factor explaining this volatility is the inability of the short-run labor market to easily adapt to demand changes by adjusting the real wage rate to keep the market in equilibrium. This requires that we pay careful attention to explanations for short-run wage rigidity based on models of contracts, efficiency wages, and insider–outsider behavior. Finally, unemployment has serious social and political consequences, and it has always been viewed as an important public policy matter. We conclude this chapter with a summary of the policy recommendations suggested by modern analyses of search and cyclical unemployment.

Measures of Unemployment

The two most widely used measures of the extent of unemployment in a given labor market are the unemployment rate and the duration of unemployment. The unemployment rate measures the incidence of unemployment at any point in time and provides an indicator of the average individual's risk of experiencing a spell of unemployment. Duration measures the severity of unemployment. A spell of unemployment may be fairly easy to deal with if the individual finds a new job within a couple of weeks, while a spell of unemployment lasting several months is likely to have a more severe impact on the economic and psychological well-being of the individual.

The Unemployment Rate

In all countries, government agencies devote considerable resources to the collection of statistical data that enable them to calculate the **unemployment rate**. But what does the unemployment rate measure, and how is it calculated?

The starting point is an estimate of the civilian working-age population. This usually excludes military personnel and those institutionalized in hospitals and prisons of various types because these persons are not available for work in the private labor market. The working-age population also excludes young children, with the minimum age used to define "working age" varying by country. In the United States, those younger than age 16 are excluded from the working-age population.

The civilian working-age population is then divided into three groups: those who are employed, those who are not employed and who are actively looking for work, and those who are not employed but who are not able or willing to work. The last group, which includes retirees, students, the ill or disabled, and those working in the home, is defined as being "out of the labor force." Only those without a job who are actively looking for one and willing to accept one are counted as "unemployed."

Because it is very costly to count everyone in a census, the most common way of estimating the number employed, unemployed, and out of the labor force is by using the results of statistically designed surveys of samples of individuals and households. The results of these surveys are used to estimate the proportion of the working-age population in each of the three labor market categories. Some countries, such as France, Germany, and the United Kingdom, use administrative data drawn from unemployment insurance registries, trade union rolls, and firm surveys to supplement labor force surveys in the estimation of the unemployment rate. In the United States, the Current Population Survey is conducted monthly to obtain information from around 60,000 households that is used to estimate the unemployment rate.

To summarize, if P is the working-age population, E is the number of jobholders, U is the number of unemployed job seekers, and N is the number of people not in the labor force, then $P = E + U + N$ and the unemployment rate is:

$$\% \text{ Unemployed} = \{U/(U + E)\} \times 100 \tag{14-1}$$

The important point to make is that N does not enter the calculation of the unemployment rate at all.

Figure 14.1 and Figure 14.2 graph the unemployment rates experienced by the major economies of the world during the past two decades. In Figure 14.1 we compare the

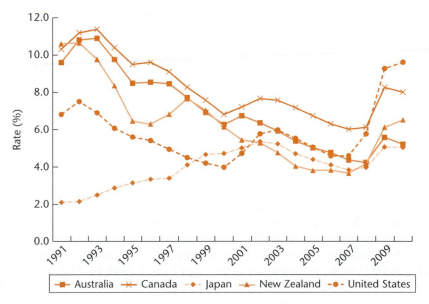

FIGURE 14.1 Unemployment Rates in Five Pacific Rim Countries, 1991–2010

Source: http://stats.oecd.org/index.aspx?queryid=21760

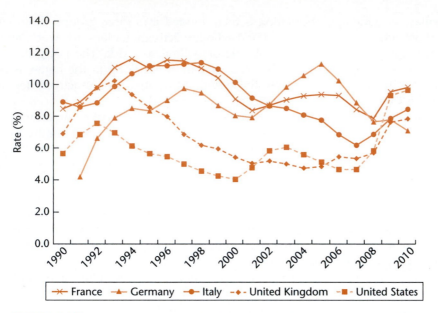

FIGURE 14.2 Unemployment Rates in Europe and the United States, 1990–2010

Source: http://stats.oecd.org/index.aspx?queryid=21760

unemployment rates for five Pacific Rim economies, and Figure 14.2 contrasts the unemployment experience of the United States with that of Europe. The rates in these figures have been calculated by the Organization for Economic Cooperation and Development (OECD) in a way that minimizes the effect of nation-specific differences in definitions and procedures.

Both charts use the U.S. situation as a point of comparison. In the United States, the unemployment rate followed a distinct cyclical pattern that clearly identifies three recessions. The rate rose during and after the recession of the early 1990s, reaching a peak of 7.5% in 1992. The strong economic recovery of the mid- to late 1990s pushed the unemployment rate to 4% in 2000. However, the reappearance of recession in 2001 led the U.S. unemployment rate to rise to 4.8% in that year and to a peak of 6.0% in 2003. Again recovery took over, and the unemployment rate fell to 4.6% in 2007 before rising sharply to 9.6% in 2010 following the "Great Recession" of 2008 and 2009.

The unemployment rates for Australia, Canada, and New Zealand in Figure 14.1 follow a time series pattern that is remarkably similar. The unemployment rates in these three countries were much higher than in the United States at the beginning of the period, with rates peaking around 10% in 1993. After that unemployment rates in these three countries trended downward, albeit with interruptions in this movement in the late 1990s and early 2000s, until they were essentially equivalent to U.S. rates in 2007. All three countries experienced a sharp rise in unemployment during the recessionary period from 2007 to 2010.

In stark contrast to the data for the other countries in Figure 14.1, the Japanese unemployment rate showed a steady rise throughout the 1990–2001 period. This period has

AROUND THE WORLD

Emerging Markets in the Great Recession

Unemployment rate data for emerging market countries are available from the International Monetary Fund (IMF) database. While it is not clear that these estimates are derived in the same manner as the U.S. figures and one might raise questions about measurement error and overall accuracy, they provide a glimpse of the effect of the global spread of the Great Recession from 2008 to 2009.

The table below shows unemployment rates for a sample of nine emerging market economies. In every country, save Indonesia, the unemployment rate rose from 2008 to 2009; on average, rates increased by 0.87 percentage points. But these countries were less affected by the global downturn than most of the major developed economies. For example, the unemployment rate increased by 3.5 points in the United States and 2.0 points in the United Kingdom from 2008 to 2009.

Country	2008	2009	2010
Brazil	7.9%	8.1%	6.7%
China	4.2	4.3	4.1
Colombia	11.3	12.0	11.8
Egypt	8.8	9.5	9.0
Indonesia	8.4	7.9	7.1
Korea	3.2	3.7	3.7
Russia	6.4	8.4	7.5
South Africa	22.9	23.9	24.9
Turkey	10.9	14.0	11.9

Source: http://www.imf.org/external/pubs/ft/weo/2011/02/weodata/weoselgr.aspx

become known as Japan's "lost decade" as economic growth stagnated following the collapse of real estate and stock market bubbles in 1990. During the period from 2001 to 2010, the unemployment rate followed a pattern that is indistinguishable from that traced by the U.S., Australian, or New Zealand data although the Great Recession seems to have had a smaller impact on Japan's unemployment rate. In general, we might conclude that the unemployment experiences of these five major Pacific Rim countries were quite similar during the decade up to 2010.

Figure 14.2 reveals a different story when we compare the United States with Europe. The U.K. unemployment rate followed roughly the same trajectory as the U.S. rate. On the continent, however, unemployment rates continued to rise until late in the decade of the 1990s and were well above the U.S. and U.K. figures in much of the period up to about 2005. There is an interesting feature to the German time series: that country managed to lower its unemployment rate sharply from 2005 to 2007 and to avoid almost completely the recessionary rise in unemployment starting in 2008. The data in Figures 14.1 and 14.2 suggest that unemployment rates vary considerably across countries both at a given moment of time and over longer time periods. This cross-country variation allows us to test for the effects of various policies and different economic developments on unemployment.

Measurement Issues

The calculation of unemployment rates appears to be a relatively straightforward process. However, a number of measurement issues have been debated over the years, and these debates have led at times to the development of alternative unemployment indicators. These measurement issues fall into three categories:

1. *When to count someone as employed.* The U.S. Department of Labor says a person is employed if he or she did at least one hour of work for pay during the survey week. What about those working part time when they would prefer a full-time job? Or those working outside of the occupations they have trained for?
2. *Issues concerning the unemployed.* If a person is actively searching for work, does it matter if he or she refuses a job because the pay offered is too low? What if the person was unemployed because he or she had just started to look for work after finishing school or a stint in the army? Is this the same as someone who was laid off or fired from a job and became unemployed as a result?
3. *Issues surrounding those classified as out of the labor force.* How should so-called **discouraged workers** be counted? These people have stopped actively searching for jobs because they don't think they can find work, yet they would be willing to accept a job offer if one came along. Should they be included among the unemployed?

Table 14.1 presents data on alternative estimates of the U.S. unemployment rate that take into account some of these considerations. In these estimates the unemployed category is progressively expanded to include discouraged workers, marginally attached workers, and workers with part-time jobs who want full-time positions. The marginally attached group includes those without a job who said in the survey that they would like a job and that they had looked sometime in the past. By expanding the definition of those we count as "unemployed" versus "out of the labor force," we increase the

TABLE 14.1   Alternative Estimates of the U.S. Unemployment Rate

	2006	2007	2008	2009	2010
Official Rate	4.6	4.6	5.8	9.3	9.6
Plus Discouraged Workers	4.9	4.9	6.1	9.7	10.3
Plus Marginally Attached	5.5	5.5	6.8	10.5	11.1
Plus Part Time for Economic Reasons	8.2	8.3	10.5	16.2	16.7

Source: U.S. Department of Labor, Bureau of Labor Statistics. Available online at: http://www.bls.gov/cps/cpsatabs.htm

estimated unemployment rate, although the estimated rate increases only marginally for the first two alternative definitions. It is only when we count part-time workers who want full-time jobs as unemployed (and many would regard that as a big stretch) that we get a large differential between the official and the alternative unemployment rates.

Labor Market Flows

The data we have discussed are presented as annual average unemployment rate estimates. That is, at any moment during 2010, 9.6% of the U.S. labor force was unemployed, on average. However, the same 9.6% of the labor force was not unemployed for the entire year, nor did only 9.6% of the workforce experience a period of unemployment during the whole of 2010. In fact, the U.S. Department of Labor estimates that during 2010 152.3 million people worked or looked for work and that 25.2 million (or 15.9%) of them experienced at least one spell of unemployment.[2] Because of continuous flows between employment, unemployment, and out of the labor force, the number unemployed at a given time within a year is usually less than the number who find themselves out of work at any time during the year.

Although the unemployment rate may appear to describe a static condition, the composition of the unemployed is always changing. Some of the unemployed in one month will leave unemployment to take a job, and others will leave unemployment by dropping out of the labor force. Some of those currently employed will lose their jobs because of a layoff or plant closing, and others will quit their jobs without having obtained another position. As students or housewives or others decide to look for work, there are flows over time from the out of the labor market state to employment or unemployment.

The Duration of Unemployment

Important information about the state of the labor market can be found in data on unemployment spells and unemployment duration. Spells are the number of times during a given time frame that a person becomes unemployed. Duration is the length of time a person remains unemployed during an unemployment spell. In 2010 in the United States, 25.2 million workers had a single spell of unemployment, 1.9 million had two spells of unemployment, and 2.1 million had three or more spells of unemployment. The median duration of an unemployment spell for U.S. workers in 2010 was 19.9 weeks, with about 12% of the unemployed experiencing a month or less of unemployment and 32.3% having unemployment spells longer than six months.[3]

The **duration of unemployment** is an important measure of the severity of unemployment in a labor market. An important feature of the Great Recession in the United States has been a sharp increase in the duration of unemployment. From 1994 to 2008, about

---

[2]"Work Experience of the Population in 2010," *U.S. Department of Labor News*, 2010. Also available online at: http://www.bls.gov/news.release/pdf/work.pdf.

[3]See footnote 4.

TABLE 14.2   Percentage Unemployed One Year or Longer

Country	2007	2008	2009	2010
Australia	15.4%	14.9%	14.7%	18.5%
Canada	7.4%	7.1%	7.8%	12.0%
France	40.2%	37.5%	35.2%	40.1%
Germany	56.6%	52.6%	45.5%	47.4%
Italy	47.3%	45.7%	44.4%	48.5%
Japan	32.0%	33.3%	28.5%	37.6%
New Zealand	6.1%	4.4%	6.3%	9.0%
Spain	27.6%	23.8%	30.2%	45.1%
Sweden	13.0%	12.5%	12.8%	16.6%
United Kingdom	23.7%	24.1%	24.5%	32.6%
United States	10.0%	10.6%	16.3%	29.0%

Source: http://stats.oecd.org/Index.aspx?DataSetCode=DUR_I

half of those out of work found jobs within five weeks, but in 2010 only about a third of the unemployed were so lucky.[4]

In addition, research has demonstrated that unemployed workers have a lower chance of finding a new job the longer they remain unemployed. It has been suggested that a long period of unemployment reduces an individual's human capital as skills deteriorate from lack of use. In addition, a long spell of unemployment may work as a negative signal of an individual's productivity to potential employers. Human resource managers may wonder what is "wrong" with a person who has been unemployed for a long period of time. The problem of joblessness is more severe for those with long unemployment spells than for individuals out of work for brief periods of time.

Table 14.2 presents information on the duration of unemployment for different countries during the Great Recession, measuring the incidence of long-term unemployment in terms of the percentage of unemployed persons who were out of work for one year or more. As the United States slid into recession in 2008, the duration of unemployment began rising and continued to do so after the recovery began in mid-2009. In just three years, the incidence of long-term unemployment in the United States about tripled. In the other countries, the recession didn't begin until 2009, and the impact on duration can be seen in rises from 2009 to 2010. In most of Europe and Japan there was a tendency for high rates of long-term unemployment even before the Great Recession began, while Canada and New Zealand stand out for single digit duration percentages until the effects of the global downturn were felt fully in 2010.

This brief review of recent data from a number of countries around the globe is sufficient to identify four key characteristics of the time-series and cross-section pattern of unemployment rates that have been the focus of much research. These are:

1. The unemployment rate has a pronounced cyclical component. This is perhaps best illustrated by the U.S. unemployment rate, as depicted in Figure 14.1, where sharp

---

[4] US Bureau of Labor Statistics, "How Long Before the Unemployed Find Jobs or Quit Looking?" *Issues in Labor Statistics*, Summary 11-1, May 2011.

spikes in the unemployment rate occurred with each of the three recessions since 1990. But in almost every country we've looked at the unemployment rate rose in response to the global recession of 2008–2009.

2. The cyclical response of the unemployment rate varies considerably from country to country. From 2008 to 2010 the rate rose by 2 points in France and 1.6 points in Italy but actually fell in Germany.

3. The unemployment rate also has a strong noncyclical component—rates are never zero—that varies considerably across countries. In 2007, before the start of the Great Recession, the unemployment rate in France was 8.4%, and 40.2% of the unemployed had been out of work for a year or longer. Across the English Channel, 5.3% of U.K. workers were unemployed, and only 23.7% of them had been looking for work for as long as a year.

4. Trends in the unemployment rates in some countries suggest that the noncyclical component is changing over time. Figure 14.1 suggests that the rates in Australia, Canada, and New Zealand all trended lower over the two decades in the chart, while the Japanese rate moved steadily higher during the decade of the 1990s. And Figure 14.2 suggests that rates in Europe rose in the early 1990s and generally stayed high thereafter, although in recent years German and Italian unemployment rates have moved down a bit. The search for causes of the variability across countries and over time within countries in the noncyclical component of unemployment has occupied much research interest.

The Natural Rate of Unemployment

The noncyclical component of unemployment is embodied in the concept of the **natural rate of unemployment**, which plays an important role in macroeconomic policy analysis. Milton Friedman[5] defined the natural rate as "the level which would be ground out by the Walrasian system of general equilibrium equations, provided that there is imbedded in them the actual structural characteristics of the labor and commodity markets, including market imperfections, stochastic variability in demands and supplies, the cost of gathering information about job vacancies and labor availabilities, the costs of mobility, and so on." This very influential definition suggests that the natural unemployment rate is determined by market equilibrium conditions, given the structural and institutional influences on a particular labor market.

Estimating the Natural Rate

The natural rate of unemployment is a theoretical concept, and there are no direct measures of its value. Attempts to estimate the value of the natural rate from data on the observed unemployment rate have taken a number of different paths, many of which have led to the coinage of alternative names for this theoretical concept. This proliferation of nomenclature causes confusion, and makes it necessary to consider alternative estimates and characterizations of the natural rate of unemployment. Analysts have attempted to match numbers to the concept of the natural rate of unemployment using four different techniques: the

---

[5] Milton Friedman, "The Role of Monetary Policy," *American Economic Review* 58 (1968): 1–17.

long-run equilibrium unemployment rate, the natural rate with full employment, a measure of noncyclical unemployment using moving averages, and the non-accelerating inflation rate of unemployment (NAIRU). Let's examine each of these in turn.

One easy way to estimate the natural rate is to assume that it is equivalent to the mean value of the actual unemployment rate over some period of time. In a statistical sense, the mean is the expected value of the unemployment rate, so we could conceivably think of this as an estimate of the long-run **equilibrium unemployment rate**. Looking at the U.S. data in Figure 14.1, the mean is 5.8% over the years from 1990 to 2001. Since the U.S. data can be seen as rising and falling around this mean with no evidence of a significant trend, 5.8% might be a good estimate of the equilibrium rate for this country. However, the same exercise for Canada would not work. The mean unemployment rate there is 7.9% over the 1990–2001 decade, but the yearly values are all higher than this in the 1990s and, except for the last two years, all lower in the 2000s. It doesn't look like the mean unemployment rate in Canada over this time span describes an equilibrium level.

Another approach is to use our judgment about the macroeconomic environment to select a value for the natural rate. To emphasize the fact that the actual unemployment rate would equal the natural rate when there is **full employment**, we might use the actual unemployment rates at business cycle peaks as an estimate of the natural rate. On this basis, the U.S. natural rate was 4% in 2000 and 4.6% in 2007, and the Canadian natural rate was perhaps 6.8% in 2001 and 6% in 2007 (see Figure 14.1). The problem with this method is the difficulty of determining whether the figure for a particular period is indeed consistent with the equilibrium concept of the natural rate or whether the unemployment rate at a particular cyclical turning point was actually above or below the "true" natural rate due to special circumstances. There is also the problem of interpolating the value of the natural rate between cyclical peaks.

A third method of estimating the natural rate uses statistical methods to separate the time series of unemployment rate data into cyclical and trend components. In this method, the natural rate is defined as a measure of **noncyclical unemployment**. One simple way of doing this is by using a **moving average** of the unemployment rate while a more complex approach often used to extract a trend from time series data is the Hodrick-Prescott filter.[6] These are both "mechanical" methods of identifying underlying trends in a data series with arbitrary aspects that are not based on a theory of the natural rate.

The most widely used approach, and one that often incorporates a purely statistical decomposition of trend and cycle, is the estimation of the **nonaccelerating inflation rate of unemployment (NAIRU)**.[7] This method uses the Phillips curve relationship (which we introduced back in Chapter 7) to estimate the value of the unemployment rate that is predicted to result in a constant rate of inflation from one period to the next. A very simple Phillips curve can be written as:

$$\pi_t - \pi_{t-1} = \alpha - \beta U_{t-1} + \varepsilon_t \qquad (14\text{-}2)$$

---

[6] Andrew C. Harvey and Albert Jaeger, "Detrending, Stylized Facts and the Business Cycle," *Journal of Applied Econometrics* 8 (1993): 231–247.

[7] Professor Friedman's analysis of the natural rate placed particular emphasis on the unemployment rate consistent with wage and price stability.

TABLE 14.3   NAIRU Estimates

	1990	2000	2010
Australia	6.5%	6.3%	5.2%
Japan	2.2	4.1	4.1
New Zealand	7.0	6.3	4.2
Canada	9.0	7.7	6.6
United States	6.3	5.3	5.3
France	9.3	9.0	8.7
Germany	5.3	7.7	7.6
Italy	9.1	8.9	7.2
United Kingdom	8.6	6.1	5.8

Source: Data for 1990 are from: *OECD Economic Outlook* Issue 68, December 2000.
Information for the later years is at: http://stats.oecd.org/Index.aspx?QueryId=29819.

where π is the rate of price inflation, the expected rate of inflation is assumed to equal the value of π from the preceding period, U is the unemployment rate, and ε is a random error term with an expected value of zero. In this case, the estimated value of the NAIRU, the level of U that keeps inflation from increasing, is $\frac{\alpha}{\beta}$. For example, Douglas Staiger, James Stock, and Mark Watson[8] estimate equation 14-2 using U.S. annual data from 1962 to 1995. They find that $\alpha = 2.73$ and $\beta = 0.44$, so the NAIRU = 2.73/0.44 or 6.2%.

Most researchers go beyond the simple Phillips curve to incorporate longer lags on the inflation and unemployment rates to account for persistence, to control for episodes of supply shocks or wage and price controls, and to test for changes over time in the NAIRU using statistical smoothing functions.[9]

Table 14.3 presents estimates of the NAIRU at different points over the last two decades for the large economies we have been tracking so far in this chapter. As suggested by Figure 14.1, the NAIRU estimates for Australia, Canada, and New Zealand have all dropped substantially over time; the U.S. data shows a lower rate for the 2000s versus the 1990s; while in Japan the NAIRU almost doubled between 1990 and 2000 and remained steady after that. A general lowering of the NAIRU is also seen in the estimates for the United Kingdom and, to a lesser extent, in France and Italy. Germany started with a very low NAIRU in 1990, but after the reunification of East and West Germany, the NAIRU moved sharply higher during the 1990s and stayed there during the most recent decade. The highest NAIRUs in the table are those for the continental European economies.

Determinants of the Natural Rate

What factors determine the level of the natural rate of unemployment? Professor Friedman's definition seems to point to three sets of determinants. First, labor market frictions

[8] Douglas Staiger, James H. Stock, and Mark W. Watson, "The NAIRU, Unemployment and Monetary Policy," *Journal of Economics Perspectives* 11 (1997): 33–49.

[9] See Staiger, Stock, and Watson, "The NAIRU, Unemployment and Monetary Policy"; and Robert J. Gordon, "The Time-Varying NAIRU and Its Implications for Economic Policy," *Journal of Economic Perspectives* 11 (1997): 11–32.

determine the volume of unemployment associated with the normal turnover of jobs and workers occurring even when labor markets are in equilibrium. Second, structural changes in the demand for labor, perhaps related to technological change or changing international trade patterns, could add to the volume of job seekers let go by declining industries while making it more difficult for these workers to find jobs in growing sectors of the economy. Third, institutional factors might prevent labor markets from reaching equilibrium by pushing wages above market-clearing levels.

Recall from Chapter 8 that the critical variable affecting the individual's decision to continue searching for a job is his or her reservation wage. The higher the reservation wage, the more likely it is that a job seeker will turn down a job and continue to search for a better offer. In the aggregate, higher reservation wages are associated with longer durations of job search unemployment, which would make the natural unemployment rate higher.

One of the factors raising the reservation wage is the availability of nonlabor income, which reduces the cost of continuing to search. This has led many to focus on the impact of unemployment compensation and other income transfers on the natural rate. The hypothesis is that a more generous income transfer program for those out of work will increase the natural rate of unemployment by reducing the costs of continued job search and, thereby, lengthening the duration of unemployment periods.

Another factor raising the reservation wage is the individual's expected income from continuing to search for a better job. This may be an important factor in the long duration of structural unemployment, when workers must revise their estimation of the wages they can expect to earn because structural change has made some of their skills obsolete. In the aggregate this has been characterized as a **wage aspiration effect,**[10] with the hypothesis that, in situations where workers expect higher real wages than the market can provide, there will be longer than "normal" job search and, as a result, a higher natural rate.

A third factor affecting job search unemployment is the "offer-arrival rate." In our examination of search theory, we adopted the conventional assumption of a known distribution of job offers that arrive at a constant rate, once a week, for example. In the real world, the offer arrival rate is much less certain due to the difficulties of matching workers with jobs. In the context of high unemployment in Europe, this idea has led to the hypothesis that government programs that make it difficult to fire workers also reduce the hiring rate by increasing the employer's cost of making a bad match when filling a vacant job.[11]

The notion of matching job seekers with open positions points to another set of factors. If the matching process is made more efficient, for example, by enhancing the quantity and quality of information on jobs and seekers, then frictional unemployment will be lower as people move more quickly into jobs. Similarly, if the process of retraining and relocating individuals is more efficient, then structural unemployment will be lower. This leads to the hypothesis that government programs focused on enhanced information, training, and mobility may lead to a lower natural rate of unemployment.

Another hypothesis is that institutional forces that limit the ability of wages to adjust to equilibrium will increase the natural rate of unemployment by keeping labor markets in a state of excess labor supply at the "going wage." Such institutional forces include the

---

[10] Joseph Stiglitz, "Reflections on the Natural Rate Hypothesis," *Journal of Economic Perspectives* 11 (1997): 3–10.

[11] *The OECD Jobs Study: Facts, Analysis, Strategies* (Paris: OECD, 1994).

importance of minimum wages, the power of trade unions or workers to influence the wage level, the extent to which firms use wages to motivate worker effort, and the extent to which employers are sheltered from competitive pressure in their product markets.

Another force pushing wages above the equilibrium level are payroll taxes, which are used to finance unemployment insurance, worker's compensation or health care plans, and government-provided retirement programs (such as Social Security in the United States). These taxes create a "wedge" between the cost to the employer of using a unit of labor and the wage received by the worker. The higher cost of labor associated with higher tax rates could be expected to reduce the quantity demanded of labor.

A final factor to consider is the presence of **hysteresis** in unemployment.[12] Hysteresis occurs when the level of the natural rate is positively correlated with previous period actual unemployment rates so that business cycle movements in the unemployment rate in one period may move the natural rate up or down over time. An environment of rising cyclical unemployment over some period of time would lead to an increase in the duration of unemployment because job vacancies will be less than the number of job seekers. Those who are unemployed for a long time have a reduced chance of exiting unemployment for a job because their skills deteriorate or employers view their unemployment record as a signal of low productivity. Essentially, the macroeconomic environment will have created some structurally unemployed workers who need to revise their reservation wages, undergo retraining, and perhaps relocate to another region to move into employment.

The hysteresis hypothesis is that a period of rising cyclical unemployment will eventually lead to an increase in the natural unemployment rate, whereas a period of falling cyclical unemployment will eventually lower the natural rate. The sharp increases in the fraction of the unemployed who were out of work for a year or longer in 2010 seen in Table 14.2 have raised concerns that the long-run hysteresis effects of the Great Recession will offset the tendency in the last decade toward a lower natural unemployment rate in many countries.

Table 14.4 reports regression coefficients from a recent study of the determinants of the annual unemployment rate in 20 large countries from 1985 to 2003, controlling for the effect of the business cycle, general country specific effects and time specific effects on the unemployment rate. These estimates provide some support for the hypothesis that cross-country differences in the natural rate of unemployment are correlated with differences in public policy.

The results suggest that the noncyclical component of unemployment is higher in countries with more generous unemployment benefits, a higher tax wedge between labor cost to employers and compensation received by workers, and more extensive government regulation of product markets giving monopoly power to firms. The results also indicate that a high degree of "corporatism"—close interaction between the government, firms, and unions in wage setting—lowers the natural rate of unemployment as does a higher rate of spending on active labor market policies focused on retraining the unemployed and matching them with job vacancies. In this particular sample, the extent of employment protection legislation and the degree of unionization are not statistically

---

[12] Olivier Blanchard and Lawrence Summers, "Hysteresis and the European Unemployment Problem," in *NBER Macroeconomics Annual*, ed., Stanley Fischer (Cambridge: MIT Press, 1986), p. 1.

TABLE 14.4   Determinants of the Natural Rate of Unemployment in
20 countries from 1985–2003

Variable	Regression Coefficient
Unemployment insurance replacement rate	0.012*
Active labor market policies	−0.028*
Union density	−0.029
Degree of corporatism	−1.91*
Labor tax wedge	0.023*
Employment protection legislation	−0.177
Product market regulation	0.35*

Note: *statistically significant at the .05 level. $R^2 = .98$
Source: Andrea Bassanini and Romain Duval, "The Determinants of Unemployment Across OECD
Countries: Reassessing the Role of Policy and Institutions," *OECD Economic Studies No. 42,* 2006/1, pp. 7–86.

significant determinants of unemployment. The variables listed in Table 14.4, along with measures of the output gap and country and time fixed effects can explain 98% of the variation in the mean unemployment rate across the 20 countries over time.

Changes in the Natural Rate

According to the estimates reported in Table 14.3, most countries experienced significant changes in the NAIRU at some point in the 20 years covered. What could cause these changes in the natural rate as measured by the NAIRU? In contrast to our discussion of the determinants of the *level* of the natural rate, we are less certain of the answers to this question.

One explanation for changes in the natural rate concerns the response in the labor market to a major change in the frictional, structural, or institutional factors that set the level of the natural rate. For example, Robert Gordon's estimates of the U.S. NAIRU show a higher rate in the 1960s than in the 1990s.[13] He attributes the difference to a shift from strong unions and a high minimum wage, leading to a rising labor share of national income in the 1960s, to weak unions and a low minimum wage, contributing to a decrease in labor's share of national income in the 1990s.

This type of "regime change" explanation has also been offered for the significant decrease seen in the NAIRU estimates for Ireland and the Netherlands in the 1990s.[14] Starting in the late 1980s, Ireland took policy steps to achieve wage moderation in union–management negotiations; to reduce the tax wedge between labor cost and wages received; to reduce the unemployment insurance replacement rate; to make the receipt of benefits contingent on job search; and to increase spending on training, mobility, and labor market efficiency. Similarly, the Netherlands enacted a series of reforms to significantly lower

---

[13] Robert J. Gordon, "The Time-Varying NAIRU and Its Implications for Economic Policy," *Journal of Economic Perspectives* 11 (1997): 11–32.

[14] Cedric Tille and Kei-Mu Yi, "Curbing Unemployment in Europe: Are There Lessons from Ireland and the Netherlands?" Federal Reserve Bank of New York, *Current Issues in Economics and Finance* 7 (2001): 1–8.

negotiated wage increases, to tighten unemployment benefits, and to remove important barriers to part-time work that had limited labor force participation of women.

More general empirical analysis has attempted to estimate the relationship between policy changes and changes in the NAIRU. The decrease in the NAIRU in Australia, Canada, and the United Kingdom, which we observed in Table 14.3, has been linked mainly to substantial reductions in the generosity of unemployment insurance and the deregulation of important product markets.[15]

Fluctuations Around the Natural Rate

Even allowing for a natural unemployment rate that changes over time, it is clear that the actual unemployment rate varies quite a bit more than the natural rate from year to year. In examining efforts to explain fluctuations that take the unemployment rate above or below the natural rate, we need to pay attention to the distinction between the concepts of voluntary and involuntary unemployment.

Involuntary unemployment occurs if, for some reason, the going wage fails to adjust downward to its equilibrium level[16] when there is excess supply in the labor market. When this occurs, some workers will be unable to find jobs even though they are willing to work for less than the going wage. Such workers are said to be involuntarily employed. One explanation for the deviation of actual from natural unemployment rates looks at shocks to aggregate demand or supply in product markets feeding into labor markets with rigid wages. Wage rigidity in the face of falling labor demand then results in involuntary unemployment.

However, the notion of involuntary unemployment poses something of a challenge for economists because its very existence relies on the failure of a market to equilibrate. This failure calls for an explanation, and arriving at satisfactory explanations for the existence of involuntary unemployment has proved rather difficult. We look at several attempts to do so a bit further along in this section. We begin, however, with a model in which all unemployment, even that associated with the business cycle, is voluntary, that is, when individuals choose to be without a job to search for better offers.

The Real Business Cycle Model

One of the most famous stylized facts about a modern economy is the tendency for economic activity to fluctuate according to a periodic cycle. The existence of the business cycle has generally been attributed to a constant bombardment of **random shocks**, the

---

[15] Christian Gianella et al., "What Drives the NAIRU? Evidence from a Panel of OECD Countries," *OECD Economics Department Working Papers*, No. 649, 2008.

[16] In a search theoretic context, the whole notion of a going wage is blurred because the wage follows a distribution, and there is no unique equilibrium wage. It does not make sense, therefore, to talk of involuntary unemployment in the context of search models. This does not mean that search models are useless; in economics as in carpentry, the trick is to choose the right tool for the task at hand. Search models are not good at analyzing involuntary unemployment, but they are great for helping us to understand patterns in the duration of unemployment or in the process whereby matches are made between workers and firms. They also serve to remind us that the distinction between voluntary and involuntary unemployment is not always an easy one to make.

effects of which undergo some kind of **smoothing process**. Until fairly recently, this smoothing process had been little analyzed by economists. One insight into the process by which random shocks become smooth cycles involves the notion of **intertemporal substitution**—that is, the idea that economic agents have a choice not only about *how much* to consume, work, or invest but also about *when* to do it. If, rather than working steadily, it is better for a worker to work very hard in one period and not at all in another, then that is what he or she will do. This insight has led to the development of a family of theories known as **real business cycle models**.[17]

To keep things simple, suppose that all individuals are self-employed and that each person produces output, which is used exclusively by the individual either for current consumption or for investment. To fix ideas we might suppose that each individual owns and runs an orchard. The fruit, which is the output of this orchard, can either be sold and eaten (i.e., consumed) or used to plant trees for the future (i.e., invested).

One of the hazards of running an orchard is that the producer is subject to the vagaries of the weather. If the weather is good, output is likely to be high, so the self-employed individual enjoys high productivity and will be able to consume and invest at high levels. If the weather is unkind, output will be relatively low, and the opportunities for the individual to consume and invest will not be so great. So far as the individual is concerned, weather activity may be regarded as random. In effect, the producer is subject to a series of random productivity shocks. In real business cycle models, these shocks are the source of cyclical fluctuations. In our example, the shocks come from the weather, but in the more general context, productivity shocks may come from any source. For example, in manufacturing industries, these shocks may come from the erratic timing of the invention and development of new processes.

When conditions are adverse, productivity is low, and the returns to work effort are also low. Conversely, when conditions are favorable, the returns to effort are high. Although consumption is relatively smooth over the life cycle, this does not necessitate an equally smooth income stream, which is when the notion of intertemporal substitution becomes important. An individual may prefer to work doubly hard at times when the shock is favorable and the returns from work are highest and perhaps not at all during periods when there is an adverse productivity shock. By increasing savings during high productivity periods, the individual can keep consumption at normal levels during slack periods. This may represent rational optimization behavior on the part of the individual, yet it suggests that sometimes the individual will be unemployed. Of course, because this is through the individual's own choice, the unemployment is voluntary in nature.

How do random productivity shocks lead to the relatively smooth business cycle we see over time? Recall that adverse shocks may lead to a choice by the individual to exert less work effort. This means that, both because of the productivity shock itself and because of the reduction in effort, less is produced. Therefore, less output will be available to be used both for consumption and for investment. Clearly, if investment in one period is reduced, productive capacity in subsequent periods will also be reduced. So an adverse shock in one period, through its impact on investment, has an effect on production that spills over into subsequent periods. Consequently, a particularly severe adverse shock

---

[17] Finn E. Kydland and Edward C. Prescott, "Time to Build and Aggregate Fluctuations," *Econometrica* 50 (1982): 1345–1370.

can lead to a sequence of periods in which output, employment, consumption, and investment are below par, even if that severe shock is followed by more moderate adverse shocks or even by favorable shocks.

Exactly the same argument can be made in reverse. A favorable shock can likewise have long-lasting effects because the immediate response to a favorable shock is to increase work effort. This, in turn, raises the opportunity for investment, which stimulates future output. Through the effects of shocks on output, work methods, investment, and future output, the impact of the random sequence of shocks is smoothed over time to produce the type of business cycle we observe in the world.

Three features of this model are noteworthy:

1. The model relies on a sequence of random, probabilistic shocks to drive the cycle. Such shocks are often referred to as "stochastic."
2. The model is necessarily dynamic. The smooth cycle arises from the impact of events in one period on real variables in subsequent periods.
3. The model is in general equilibrium. At every stage, the economic agents in the model are making optimizing decisions and the markets clear.

Bearing these three features in mind, it is perhaps unsurprising that real business cycle models have recently come to be known also as "stochastic dynamic general equilibrium" models.

Having discussed the theory of real business cycles, it is appropriate now to ask the following question: How well does it match the empirical evidence? The model suggests that changes in productivity and real wages over time bring about changes in labor supply that are sufficient to explain the unemployment swings we observe in the world. A recession is therefore explained by falling real wages, which bring about a decline in employment. This requires two things: that real wages indeed fall during a recession and that the elasticity of labor supply with respect to the real wage is fairly high. In fact, neither of these conditions seems to be met in practice. As Katharine Abraham and John Haltiwanger report, there is no clear evidence to suggest that real wages are systematically pro-cyclical (or, indeed, countercyclical).[18] Moreover, empirical studies suggest a relatively inelastic aggregate labor supply curve, with the best estimates being somewhere between zero and one-half.[19] At best, then, the real business cycle model can explain only a fraction of the observed variations in the unemployment rate over time.

In addition, evidence against one of the fundamental assumptions of real business cycle models comes from a study of New York taxi drivers. These drivers rent their cabs and keep the revenue earned from a day's work, so they are in a perfect position to exercise intertemporal labor substitution by working more when a shock (the weather, perhaps) increases the demand for cab rides and working less when a shock decreases demand. However, a study by Colin Camerer and colleagues[20] found that the labor

[18] Katharine G. Abraham and John C. Haltiwanger, "Real Wages and the Business Cycle," *Journal of Economic Literature* 33 (1995): 1215–1264.

[19] John Ham, "Testing Whether Unemployment Represents Life-Cycle Labor Supply Behavior," *Review of Economic Studies* 50 (1986): 559–578.

[20] Colin Camerer, Linda Babcock, George Loewenstein, and Richard Thaler, "Labor Supply of New York City Cabdrivers: One Day at a Time," *Quarterly Journal of Economics* 112 (1997): 759–789.

supply of drivers was best explained as the result of setting a daily target income level and quitting work once the target was achieved. There was no evidence that labor supply among these workers responded positively to transitory changes in income opportunities caused by random productivity shocks.

Wage Rigidity Models

The most salient characteristic of the real business cycle model is the assumption that markets clear at all times. An alternative view of the labor market assumes that real wages are unresponsive to excess supply or demand for labor in the short run. As a result, a negative output shock, whether from real or monetary forces, would shift the demand for labor to the left and put the market in a state of disequilibrium, in which the unemployment rate would be higher than the natural rate. If the real wage were indeed unresponsive to this labor market disequilibrium, some workers would experience involuntary unemployment.

In this view of the labor market, unemployment fluctuates over time due to the interaction of three forces: aggregate demand or supply shocks that move the labor market out of equilibrium, **real wage rigidity** that prevents wage adjustments from restoring the market to equilibrium in the short to medium term, and hysteresis effects that result in a high correlation between the unemployment rate in the current period and that prevailing in preceding periods. The importance of wage rigidity in this scheme has led to a number of theoretical attempts to explain why real wage levels do not restore the labor market to equilibrium in the short run.

Implicit Contracts

In the first model we consider, workers strike "deals" (contracts) with their employers concerning the wage at which they will be employed. When workers make these deals, they understand that a possible consequence could be unemployment, and they bear this in mind when agreeing to the terms of work. From a before-the-event perspective, therefore (i.e., *ex ante*), any unemployment that arises is voluntary and efficient. In effect, workers and firms set up a contract with one another. This contract need not necessarily be formal or written; it may take the form of an **implicit contract**.[21]

To capture the flavor of implicit contract models, let's examine a particularly simple variant[22] in which a single firm makes a decision whether to employ a single worker. If the worker is employed, he or she produces a single unit of output. Suppose next that the price at which this output can be sold on the product market is unknown by both the worker and the firm at the time the contract is set, but that both know that the price can take one of only two values, $1 or $0, and the probability that each of these prices obtains is exactly one-half. Finally, assume that only the firm can observe the realized product

---

[21]Costas Azariadis, "Implicit Contracts and Underemployment Equilibria," *Journal of Political Economy* 83 (1974): 1183–1202.

[22]Alan Manning and Jonathan Thomas, "A Simple Test of the Shirking Model," mimeo, Centre for Economic Performance, London School of Economics, 1997. Available online at: http://cep.lse.ac.uk/papers/discussion/download/dp0374.pdf

market price. The firm may relay information about the product market price to the worker, but the worker has no way of knowing whether the firm is telling the truth. The model is therefore one of asymmetric information.

The task faced by the worker is to design a contract with the employer that maximizes the worker's expected remuneration subject to the constraint that the expected profit of the firm is not negative. The worker could ensure that he or she always remains employed by setting a wage equal to zero. But working for nothing is no fun. The worker could try for a wage equal to $1, but the firm would never agree to hire the individual at that wage because the expected revenue of the firm at the time the contract is set would be 50 cents (0.50 × $1 + 0.50 × $0).

By designing a contract in which the wage is always 50 cents, the worker ensures that he or she will be hired and paid that wage if the product market price turns out to be $1. With this contract in place, suppose the product market price turns out to be zero. In this instance, the firm would make a loss if it engaged in any production at all, and to prevent this from happening, the firm would lay off the worker. When designing this contract, therefore, the worker is aware that, with probability one-half, he or she may earn 50 cents, and, also with probability one-half, the worker may become unemployed and earn nothing. A worker's expected wage from this contract therefore is 25 cents. In this model, this is the best wage the worker can expect to earn. So this particular contract is optimal.

Remember that the unemployment generated by this model is, in an *ex ante* sense, voluntary. Once the worker has become unemployed, however, full information about the true product market price is revealed,[23] and the worker will inevitably feel that he or she would be willing to work for less than the 50 cents that was agreed to in the contract. With the benefit of hindsight, then (*ex post*), the worker's unemployment is involuntary. This distinction between *ex ante* voluntary unemployment and *ex post* involuntary unemployment is a consequence of the **asymmetric information** in the model.

Any assessment of the value of implicit contract theories must rely on two issues. First, is it plausible that product market prices are unobserved by workers? Second, is it likely that contracts (whether explicit or implicit) are of sufficient duration to be a plausible explanation of rigid wages and involuntary unemployment? Explicit wage contracts typically last a year or longer, but it is possible that implicit contracts, which are by definition unobservable, last longer.

Efficiency Wages

Models of efficiency wages were first constructed in the 1950s and have their origins in the literature on development economics. The earliest such model, now known as the nutrition model, was based on the premise that, in developing countries where the work force receives subsistence level wages, a firm could pay above equilibrium wages to its workers so that they can eat better, become stronger, and increase their productivity. A by-product of these higher wages is involuntary unemployment. Although interesting, models of this kind are of limited applicability in the context of developed Western economies.

---

[23] The fact that the worker has been made redundant confirms that the product market price must be zero.

Nevertheless, the underlying idea that a firm can gain from paying wages above the equilibrium level has been an enduring one. Further variants of the efficiency wage model have been developed, and these are much more persuasive in the context of modern economies.

Shirking

A fundamental assumption of the shirking model (see Chapter 11) is that firms cannot observe the effort put in by their workers without incurring significant supervision costs. Consequently, it may be cheaper to provide workers with an incentive to work hard, in the form of higher wages, than to introduce a perfect monitoring system. When the wage rate is being used to motivate worker effort, the firm might not be willing to lower the wage even when there is excess supply in the labor market. Consider an efficiency wage model with the following features:

1. Individual effort rises as the wage becomes more attractive relative to income from outside opportunities. The worker risks losing a well-paying job by shirking, so an increase in the efficiency wage premium raises the costs of shirking relative to the benefits, thereby inducing greater effort.
2. We assume that the firm is efficient in the sense that it chooses a value of the wage that minimizes its labor cost per unit of effort. The resulting wage rises as outside opportunities improve because a premium is needed to induce greater effort. The firm will also choose to offer a higher wage with a larger payoff to the firm from increased worker effort.
3. The outside opportunities can be described as the weighted sum of an individual's income in and out of work. Hence,

$$x = (1 - u)w + (u)bw \qquad (14\text{-}3)$$

where b denotes the benefit replacement ratio (i.e., the ratio of income while unemployed to income while working), and u is the unemployment rate (expressed as a proportion). In calculating the value of outside labor market opportunities, then, the worker supposes that there is a probability of u that he will be unemployed and receive an income of bw, and a probability of $1 - u$ that he will be employed and earn an income of w.

Under these conditions it can be shown that, if all firms are identical and follow a similar pay policy,

$$u = \theta/(1 - b) \qquad (14\text{-}4)$$

where θ is the gain to the firm from increased worker effort. Hence, the unemployment rate will increase as the replacement ratio (b) increases. This is an intuitively plausible result that is consistent with our discussion of the determinants of the natural unemployment rate. However, unemployment also rises as the productivity enhancing effect of the wage increases because the higher is θ, the greater is the incentive for firms to pay wages above the market clearing level.

Even very small values of θ could generate quite high unemployment rates. For instance, if the replacement ratio was 50% and θ equaled 0.05, the unemployment rate would be 10%. Hence, one does not need to believe that the shirking effect is very substantial for it to have a significant effect on unemployment. Unemployment is a by-product of the high wage, but it is nonetheless essential to the workings of the model. It is the prospective penalty of unemployment that deters workers from shirking.

The key assumption of the shirking model is that the wage is not the only cost of labor. To be specific, the additional cost of labor is the cost of monitoring the effort exerted by workers in the firm's employ. However, this need not be the only cost of labor other than the wage. The second main class of efficiency wage models, which like the shirking model exploit the property that some nonwage labor costs exist, is the family of turnover models.

Turnover

The essence of turnover models of efficiency wages is that firms may pay their workers a wage that exceeds the equilibrium wage to reduce their propensity to quit. In doing so, firms incur higher wage costs, but by reducing the quit propensity, they reduce their non-wage costs. In particular, because there is less labor turnover, firms experience lower costs of hiring and training new workers. In effect, firms balance the extra cost of higher wages against the benefit of lower turnover costs. Once again, the higher wages effectively create an externality because the consequence of paying wages above the equilibrium level is that involuntary unemployment will be generated.

If all firms paid the same wage, there would be no reason for workers ever to quit their current employer. However, firms typically set their own wage levels with less than complete information about the wages paid by other firms. In effect, each firm enters a "game" with its competitors in which its task is to ensure that the firm maximizes its expected profits by adjusting its wage offer, fully recognizing the interdependence of its own wage and those offered by other firms (which impact on quits). Despite the uncertain environment that characterizes models of this kind, it is often possible to establish a pattern of behavior in which each and every firm is maximizing its expected profit given the decisions made by every other firm. This is known as a Nash equilibrium.[24] Game theory models of this type have been analyzed extensively in economics.[25] Now suppose that the game being played between firms has a Nash equilibrium where each firm sets a wage above the market-clearing wage. The outcome will be involuntary unemployment because, at this relatively high wage, the demand for labor will not be sufficient to meet supply.

An interesting feature of the turnover model is that it provides an explanation for the common observation that different firms pay different wages for similar work. Some firms

---

[24] Nash equilibria are not always efficient. A classic example is that of the prisoners' dilemma. Suppose the police interrogate two suspected criminals separately. Each is told that, if both partners confess, they will each receive 3 years' imprisonment. If neither confesses, then both will go free. If one confesses but the other does not, the latter will receive a 10-year sentence, but the former will go free as a state's witness. Under these circumstances, each prisoner is sure to confess; each prisoner is indifferent between confessing and not confessing if his partner does not confess, but there is a severe penalty to not confessing if the partner confesses. So, with each prisoner acting independently, each optimizes his outcome by confessing. They are therefore each imprisoned for three years. But if the prisoners could have colluded, neither would have confessed and both would have been freed.

[25] See James W. Friedman, *Oligopoly and the Theory of Games* (Amsterdam: North Holland, 1977); and Hal R. Varian, *Intermediate Microeconomics: A Modern Approach*, 5th ed. (New York: Norton, 1999).

opt to pay relatively low wages and endure a high turnover rate, whereas others offer high wages in return for low costs of labor turnover. The model also provides an explanation for why workers who have received much training, and hence are more costly for the firm to lose, tend to be paid more than other workers. (This is complementary to the human capital explanation in Chapter 6.)

Critics have identified three potential problems with the turnover model. First, there is no guarantee that, at the margin, the saving in turnover cost will justify raising the wage above the market-clearing level. In addition, the costs of turnover are, for each worker, one-shot costs (i.e., they do not recur each year), so it is entirely plausible that the impact of a wage increase on savings in turnover costs may be quite small.

Second, if workers could pay for their own training, turnover costs would collapse to (close to) zero, and the whole efficiency wage mechanism would be absent. In Chapter 6, you learned that firms will not normally pay for the acquisition of general human capital in any event and that they will typically seek to pass some of the cost of specific human capital investment on to the worker.

Third, the equilibrium obtained in the turnover model is inefficient. It is, in effect, a prisoners' dilemma. To demonstrate this, note that a coordinated move to bring the wages of all firms down to the market-clearing level would remove the source of unemployment and would result in a new equilibrium from which no firm has an incentive to deviate. This is because quits (and so also turnover costs) are absent whenever all firms pay the same wage. Because all firms would gain by coordination, it might seem rather surprising that they do not coordinate their wage policies.

Adverse Selection, Sorting, and Gift Exchange

A third category of efficiency wage models results from the costs of adverse selection in hiring. If a firm is unable to assess fully the productivity of a prospective worker through interviews and references, it may choose to use the wage as a kind of **sorting** mechanism. By offering a wage above the equilibrium level, the firm can ensure that it will attract a superior pool of job applicants. By comparing the attributes of applicants in such a pool, the firm would be able to increase the probability of identifying and hiring the most productive workers.[26]

A final variant of the model of efficiency wages is the **gift exchange** model developed by George Akerlof.[27] In this theory, the relationship between a firm and its employees is based on goodwill. This is both evidenced and fostered by the firm awarding an above equilibrium wage to its workers, who, in exchange, offer the firm enhanced productivity.

This model is grounded in sociology rather than economics. Nevertheless, there may be an economic interpretation of the patterns of behavior observed by Akerlof. Wages are sustained above the market-clearing level because unemployed workers fail to bid down the wage. But if wages are determined in the setting of an infinitely repeated game between workers and firms, it may not be in the interests of unemployed workers to bid

---

[26] Andrew Weiss, "Job Queues and Layoffs in Labor Markets with Flexible Wages," *Journal of Political Economy* 88 (1980): 526–538.

[27] George A. Akerlof, "Labor Contracts as Partial Gift Exchange," in *Efficiency Wage Models of the Labor Market*, eds., George A. Akerlof and Janet Yellen (Cambridge: Cambridge University Press, 1982).

the wage down.[28] In this context, if any one unemployed worker were to bid the wage down, it would remain low—at the reservation wage level—forever. In such a dynamic model, therefore, social norms may initiate a wage settlement above the equilibrium. It is then in the self-interest of unemployed workers to ensure the perpetuation of the above equilibrium wage; otherwise they will be poorly remunerated when they eventually find work.

The various theories of efficiency wages have not been without critics.[29] The turnover and shirking variants in particular have attracted the criticism that they rely on a "missing price." That is, in efficiency wage theories of unemployment, firms use the wage not just to regulate the supply of labor but to control something else as well. In general, if there are x objectives, there should be no fewer than x controls. To control the speed and direction of a car, you need a steering wheel and an accelerator. Likewise, to control both the supply of workers to a firm and the effort those workers expend, two "controls," in this case two prices, are needed, the wage and something else. To control both the supply of workers to a firm and their rate of turnover, again two prices are needed. Unemployment occurs in the efficiency wage models because there is only one price. The wage is trying to perform two tasks, ends up doing neither particularly well, and unemployment is the by-product. Critics of efficiency wage theories argue that, in the real world, the missing price is not missing at all.

In the shirking model, for example, if the firm needs to regulate the effort exerted by its work force, it does not need to use the wage to do so. A variety of other options exists, such as productivity bonuses, share ownership schemes, piece rates, and the promise of promotion. Alternatively, unemployed workers could offer to post bonds with firms in return for an offer of a job at the efficiency wage similar to the type of deposit often posted by tenants renting a house; the worker would then have an incentive not to shirk because he or she would regard the bond as a sunk cost. Any of these mechanisms could be used to motivate the workforce, leaving the wage to perform the task of equating demand and supply in the labor market.

Likewise, in the turnover model, reserve clause contracts or salary supplements, which vary with tenure, could be used to regulate the quit rate. To the extent that any of these are used in practice, the harmful effect of the efficiency wage on unemployment will not be observed. And, if these mechanisms are not used, we can only suppose that the impact of shirking or turnover is not sufficiently deleterious to warrant their introduction. This critique is quite potent. In effect, it says that there is no reason for the missing price (on which the efficiency wage theories of unemployment rely) to be missing. So, despite the existence of a moderate degree of empirical support, economists have continued to search for models of involuntary unemployment that do not rely on efficiency wages.

Insider–Outsider Theories

The failure of the wage to clear the labor market when there is an excess supply of labor has also been attributed to union negotiations resulting in an above-equilibrium wage for

---

[28] Robert Solow, *The Labor Market as a Social Institution* (Cambridge: Blackwell, 1989).

[29] See H. Lorne Carmichael, "Efficiency Wage Models of Unemployment: One View," *Economic Inquiry* 28 (1990): 269–295; Kevin Lang and Shulamit Kahn, "Efficiency Wage Models of Unemployment: A Second View," *Economic Inquiry* 28 (1990): 296–306.

union members. This has been an enduring notion, and it is supported by much empirical evidence of a union markup on wages averaging about 10%. However, such an explanation remains rather unsatisfactory inasmuch as it fails to explain why unemployed workers cannot bargain down the wage.

A new breed of model known as insider–outsider theory attempts to address this issue.[30] According to this, model workers are divided into two groups, insiders and outsiders. **Insiders** are incumbents who hold jobs. **Outsiders** are prospective employees who may currently be employed in another firm or who may be unemployed. The theory, in a nutshell, is that outsiders are unable to price their way into work because it is in the self-interest of insiders to prevent them from doing so. Insiders are able to do this because they possess a degree of monopoly power in their dealings with the firm.

This insider monopoly power may take a number of forms. First, if outsiders are hired, the firm must incur some training and hiring costs. Any such costs for insiders were expended a long time ago and are regarded by the firm as sunk. Therefore, at any given wage it is more expensive to employ outsiders than it is to employ insiders. Consequently, insiders are in a position to bargain their wage up above the level of the wage that would be paid to outsiders. So, to gain employment, outsiders must offer their services at a wage that undercuts the going wage of insiders by a considerable degree.

This mechanism may, on its own, be sufficient to deter some outsiders from seeking employment with a firm, but there are some additional mechanisms that insiders might use to strengthen their position. For example, insiders might refuse to cooperate in training newly recruited outsiders. If this occurs, the costs to the firm of training new recruits must rise. This makes outsiders even less attractive to the firm, which will respond by lowering the wage at which it would be prepared to employ outsiders. Again, to price their way into employment, outsiders would need to drop their reservation wage still further below the going wage.

Other action on the part of insiders might make this extremely unlikely even if some of the jobless had extremely low reservation wages. Insiders may decide to harass newly recruited outsiders. That is, they may behave in a manner that makes life at the firm unpleasant for new recruits. If outsiders anticipate such behavior, they may be unwilling to work for the firm unless they are compensated for a poor working environment by a higher wage. Noncooperation by insiders effects a reduction in the wage at which firms are willing to hire outsiders, but harassment by insiders raises the reservation wage at which outsiders are willing to work. As a result, the wages diverge. Some unemployed workers might be willing to work at wages below the firm's wage, but others will not, and the latter will remain unemployed even though their reservation wage lies below the wage being paid to the insiders.

Both noncooperation and harassment by insiders is designed to reinforce their monopoly position within the firm. By making the recruitment of outsiders less likely, these actions render the insiders less dispensable. They can, therefore, push more vigorously for an increase in their own remuneration. In effect, the continued unemployment of outsiders is a consequence of the rent-seeking behavior of insiders.

---

[30] Assar Lindbeck and Dennis J. Snower, *The Insider–Outsider Theory of Employment and Unemployment* (Cambridge: MIT Press, 1988).

PUTTING THEORY TO WORK

EXCESS SUPPLY AND SALARY OFFERS FOR PHD ECONOMISTS

The analysis of unemployment rests heavily on the observation that wages do not respond to excess supply in labor markets in a way that would quickly restore equilibrium between labor demand and labor supply. Here are some data from the U.S. academic market for new PhDs in economics to illustrate this point.

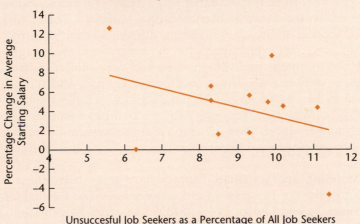

Excess Supply and Wage Growth for New PhD Economists, 1999–2000 to 2010–2011

Source: Data for the chart are from annual issues of the *Survey of the Labor Market for New PhDs in Economics* published by the Center for Business and Economic Research at the University of Arkansas. Available online at: http://cber.uark.edu/369.asp.

In every year, a substantial fraction of new PhD Economists (ranging from 5.6% to 11.4% of all job seekers) were unable to find an academic or nonacademic position. The graph indicates that increases in the percentage of unsuccessful job seekers are correlated with lower rates of growth in the average starting salary over this time period, revealing a fairly typical Phillips curve relationship. However, the only decrease in the level of average nominal wage offered by the surveyed departments came during the 2010–2011 academic year, reflecting perhaps the cumulative effects of the Great Recession on college budgets and state support for public institutions.

Deans and department chairs would probably justify this situation by the argument that salary offers have to increase for their university to be competitive for the subset of seekers who promise the best fit for their needs. This is one of the efficiency wage theory explanations for wage rigidity. If salary increases for new faculty members are part of the rationale for increases for existing faculty members, then insider bargaining might also help explain rising wages in the face of an excess supply of new PhD economists.

Evidence on Wage Rigidity

Do the theories we have examined provide good explanations for the existence of wage rigidity and unemployment in the labor market? Empirical evidence from both econometric studies and surveys of business managers suggests that the lack of a short-run wage response to excess labor supply indeed reflects various aspects of the implicit contract, efficiency wage, and insider–outsider models.

Econometric Studies

Important evidence on efficiency wages comes from the careful study of industry wage differentials by Alan Krueger and Lawrence Summers.[31] Along with many other analysts, they find that there is substantial wage dispersion across industries even after controlling for the typical array of human capital variables. Their work is able to rule out unmeasured worker ability, compensating differentials for job attributes, and the threat of union organizing as explanations for the observation that wages are higher in some industries than in others. In addition, they find very similar industry wage differentials for workers in different size firms, in different regions, and with different job tenures. Finally, their evidence that employee turnover is lower in industries with high industry-specific wage differentials suggests that such differentials are noncompetitive rents rather than compensation. They conclude that the empirical evidence on industry differentials is best explained by differences in management's use of efficiency wages in different industries.

Alan Manning and Jonathan Thomas have taken advantage of a rather unusual data set to test for the presence of efficiency wages due to shirking.[32] The British Survey of Incomes In and Out of Work (SIIOW) contains information about workers' reservation wages while unemployed and about the wages workers receive once they gain employment. If efficiency wage effects are observed in line with those predicted by the shirking model, Manning and Thomas argue that the distribution of actual wages observed once workers gain employment should lie above the reservation wage plus "something" (which is the extent of the efficiency wage effect). Their empirical analysis amounts to a test for the existence of this "something."[33] The results obtained using a sample of men and women provide modest support for the shirking hypothesis.[34]

Empirical evidence on insider–outsider models focuses on the extent to which insiders appear to engage in rent-seeking behavior. David Blanchflower and colleagues estimate wage functions using standard regression techniques, including measures of the financial

---

[31] Alan B. Krueger and Lawrence H. Summers, "Efficiency Wages and the Inter-Industry Wage Structure," *Econometrica* 56 (1988): 259–293.

[32] Alan Manning and Jonathan Thomas, "A Simple Test of the Shirking Model," mimeo, Centre for Economic Performance, London School of Economics, 1997. Available online at: http://cep.lse.ac.uk/papers/discussion/download/dp0374.pdf.

[33] In essence, it is a type of regression analysis in which a rather complicated functional form, designed so that the "something" may or may not be there, is imposed. The parameters of the model are estimated by maximum likelihood methods.

[34] The estimate on the "something" parameter is marginally significant at the conventional 5% level.

TABLE 14.5 Determinants of Wage Flexibility, 48 U.S. States

Variable	Coefficient
Constant	−7.23*
Importance of efficiency wages	−24.28*
Importance of small firms	12.88*
Importance of union membership	−4.26*
Right-to-work law state	0.53*
Importance of the minimum wage	−7.80*
Importance of layoffs in unemployment	3.58*
Importance of long-term unemployed	−6.32*

Note: *statistically significant at the .05 level.

Source: Thomas Hyclak and Geraint Johnes, *Wage Flexibility and Unemployment Dynamics in Regional Labor Markets* (Kalamazoo, MI: W. E. Upjohn Institute, 1992).

performance of the firm and the market structure of the industry in which the firm operates as wage determinants.[35] Strong financial performance and a high degree of industrial concentration are both found to influence the wage in a positive direction with a high level of statistical significance. Their results suggest that workers within a firm do engage in rent-seeking behavior.

The degree of wage flexibility in a labor market can be estimated by the coefficient on the unemployment rate in a Phillips-type wage adjustment equation.[36] The closer the absolute value of this coefficient is to zero, the greater the degree of wage rigidity in the particular labor market. Estimates using this method have shown that wage rigidity varies significantly across countries and that it is positively correlated with the level and change in the unemployment rate.[37] One of our own research studies used estimates of wage rigidity for states in the United States derived from Phillips curve regressions as the dependent variable in a regression analysis of the interstate determinants of wage rigidity. Some results from this study are reported in Table 14.5.

These results are supportive of the theories we have discussed. Wages were found to be less flexible in states with an industry mix more heavily weighted toward those reliant on efficiency wages and in states where the minimum wage was a more important factor in the regional wage structure. Wage flexibility was higher in states with a larger share of small businesses, which might be thought to rely more on managerial supervision than wages to deter shirking. Wage flexibility also was higher in states with lower union density and right-to-work laws that limit union organizing strength. And wage flexibility was enhanced by a higher incidence of layoff unemployment and a smaller risk of long-term unemployment. A higher incidence of layoff unemployment

---

[35] David G. Blanchflower, Andrew J. Oswald, and M. D. Garrett, "Insider Power in Wage Determination," *Economica* 57 (1990): 143–170.

[36] David T. Coe, "Nominal Wages, the NAIRU and Wage Flexibility," *OECD Economic Studies* 5 (1985): 87–126.

[37] Dennis Grubb, Richard Jackman, and Richard Layard, "Wage Rigidity and Unemployment in OECD Countries," *European Economic Review* 21 (1983): 11–39.

could be seen as more threatening to insiders whereas the long-term unemployed are most often regarded as distinct outsiders with little impact on insider bargaining power.

Survey Evidence

In recent years, economists have attempted to judge the validity of various wage rigidity theories by surveying business managers about the factors that limit their willingness to consider wage reductions in response to a business cycle downturn. Table 14.6 summarizes the results reported from five such surveys of firms in the United States, the United Kingdom, and Sweden. In all five surveys, managers reported reluctance to cut wages in periods of high unemployment; the preferred method of scaling back labor costs in the face of falling output was temporary or permanent layoffs.

The reasons for this reluctance to cut wages seem to be quite consistent with the conclusions of efficiency wage theory. In four of the five surveys, the key reason cited for wage stickiness was the belief that a reduction in wages would hurt employee morale and, in turn, result in lower effort and productivity. Managers in these firms seemed to feel that worker morale and effort respond more to changes in wages than to the level of the wage and that wage reductions would have a much bigger impact than wage increases. The efficiency wage formulation is also supported by beliefs that worker perceptions of fairness are important for performance and that wage cuts would be seen as unfair.

There is also evidence in a couple of the surveys for the turnover variant of the efficiency wage model. Managers in many firms suggest that they would risk losing their most productive workers if wages were reduced, whereas layoffs could be targeted at the

TABLE 14.6   Survey Responses on Wage Stickiness

Study	Firms Surveyed	Key Reasons for Avoiding Wage Cuts
Kaufman (1984)[1]	26 small British firms	Morale and work effort would suffer
Blinder and Choi (1990)[2]	19 large firms in New Jersey and Eastern Pennsylvania	Labor turnover would rise and wage cuts would be seen as unfair
Bewley (1995)[3]	258 firms in Connecticut	Morale and motivation would decrease
Agell and Lundborg (1995)[4]	179 large manufacturing firms in Sweden	Would be seen as unfair because worker motivation depends on relative wages
Campbell and Kamlani (1997)[5]	184 U.S. firms	Quits by best workers would increase and morale and effort would suffer due to implicit agreement to keep wages stable over the business cycle

Notes: [1]Roger T. Kaufman, "On Wage Stickiness in Britain's Competitive Sector," *British Journal of Industrial Relations* 22 (1984): 728–741; [2]Alan S. Blinder and Don H. Choi, "A Shred of Evidence on Theories of Wage Stickiness," *Quarterly Journal of Economics* 105 (1990): 89–96; [3]Truman F. Bewley, "Depressed Labor Markets as Explained by Participants," *American Economic Review* 85 (1985): 250–254; [4]Jonas Agell and Per Lundborg, "Theories of Pay and Unemployment: Survey Evidence from Swedish Manufacturing Firms," *Scandinavian Journal of Economics* 48 (1995): 295–307; [5]Carl M. Campbell II and Kunal S. Kamlani, "The Reasons for Wage Rigidity: Evidence from a Survey of Firms," *Quarterly Journal of Economics* 112 (1997): 759–789.

least productive employees. In addition, in at least one study, managers agreed with the concept that an implicit contract existed that compelled them to stabilize wages over the business cycle. The study of Swedish firms indicated that relative wages were very important to worker morale, suggesting that firms would be reluctant to be the first in the market to cut wages even if wage reductions were their optimal response to an economic downturn.

Two recent papers have collected data on firm wage setting behavior from international surveys and administrative sources to estimate the determinants of downward rigidity in nominal and real wages. Data from the International Wage Flexibility Project cover 31 different data sets for twelve countries over various time spans yielding information on over 31 million wage changes.[38] Analysis of these data sets revealed substantial variation in rigidity across countries with the percent of workers affected by downward nominal rigidity ranging from 4% of Irish workers to 58% of Portuguese employees, with an overall average of 28%. Downward real wage rigidity was found to affect 26% of workers, on average, across the countries in the project. Public policy providing a high degree of employment protection was positively correlated with nominal rigidity while real rigidity was highly correlated with union density in cross-country comparisons.

Similar conclusions were drawn from an analysis of firm level data for 15 European countries drawn from surveys coordinated by the International Wage Flexibility Project.[39] There was considerable variation in measures of nominal and real wage rigidity across these countries with institutional factors, such as collective bargaining, employment protection legislation, and share of permanent contract workers correlated with less flexible nominal and real wage levels.

This brief review of studies of wage rigidity leads to two conclusions. First, wages are relatively unresponsive to excess labor supply in most labor markets although the degree of wage rigidity varies across markets. And second, the hypotheses about the causes of wage stickiness drawn from the implicit contract, efficiency wage, and insider–outsider theories are generally supported by econometric and survey research. The existence of wage rigidity suggests that fluctuations in the aggregate demand for labor will largely be reflected in quantity changes rather than in wage changes. Decreases in demand lead to decreases in employment and a short-run unemployment rate that is higher than the natural rate. On the other hand, increases in aggregate labor demand are associated with rising employment opportunities and an unemployment rate temporarily below the natural rate.

Recent empirical studies of business cycle dynamics in the United States lend additional support for the demand-shock-plus-wage-rigidity explanation of variations in the unemployment rate about the natural rate.[40] Simulations of the effect of technology shocks

---

[38] William T. Dickens, Lorenz Goette, Erica L. Groshen, Steinar Holden, Julian Messins, Mark E. Schweitzer, Jarkko Turunen, and Melanie E. Ward, "How Wages Change: Micro Evidence from the International Wage Flexibility Project," Federal Reserve Bank of New York, Staff Report no. 275, February 2007.

[39] Jan Babecky, Philip Du Caju, Theodora Kosma, Martina Lawless, Julian Messina, and Tairi Room, "Downward Nominal and Real Wage Rigidity: Survey Evidence from European Firms," *The Scandinavian Journal of Economics* 112 (2010): 884–910.

[40] Jordi Gali, "Technology, Employment, and the Business Cycle: Do Technology Shocks Explain Aggregate Fluctuations," *American Economic Review* 89 (1999): 249–271; Neville Francis and Valerie Ramey, "Is the Technology-Driven Real Business Cycle Hypothesis Dead? Shocks and Aggregate Fluctuations Revisited," *Journal of Monetary Economics* 52 (2005): 1379–1399.

on the economy tend to find that these additions to productivity are correlated with reduced hours of labor used in production. This conclusion is the opposite of that suggested by real business cycle analysis. However, demand shock simulations are consistent with the observed data on cyclical movements in output, labor hours, and output per labor hour.

The Wage Curve

We first discussed the **wage curve** in Chapter 7, but it is worth paying a bit more attention to this empirical relationship here. We can use the wage curve to examine the macro concept of the responsiveness of real wages to unemployment in the context of the familiar human capital model of the determinants of individual earnings.

Although we might expect a high wage to result as a compensating differential for high unemployment, David Blackaby and Neil Manning[41] observed that people living in regions with high unemployment rates tend to have relatively low wages, other factors being held constant. Far from being paid more to live with a high risk of unemployment, workers in high unemployment areas seem to be paid less! David Blanchflower and Andrew Oswald[42] refer to this inverse relationship between the unemployment rate and the real wage rate as the wage curve. Wage curves have been estimated for numerous countries, including the United States, the United Kingdom, Canada, South Korea, Australia, Germany, Austria, Italy, the Netherlands, Ireland, Switzerland, Norway;[43] Luxembourg, Spain, Portugal, Greece, Denmark, Belgium, Hungary, Israel, New Zealand, the Philippines, Poland, Russia, Slovenia;[44] Cote d'Ivoire;[45] and India.[46]

The preferred specification of the wage curve has been logarithmic, using data on individual workers and their characteristics and regional unemployment rates. The typical wage curve equation is:

$$\ln w_{ij} = \alpha + \beta(\ln u_j) + \gamma(X_{ij}) + \varepsilon_{ij} \tag{14-5}$$

where the dependent variable is the log of the real wage per hour or week received by worker i living in region j. On the right-hand side are the log of the unemployment rate (u) in region j and controls for other determinants (X) of the real wage of person i in region j. Finally, ε_{ij} is a random error term. The coefficient β measures the responsiveness of individual real wages to unemployment in the aggregate labor market, controlling for the other determinants of wage levels.

---

[41] David H. Blackaby and D. Neil Manning, "Regional Earnings Revisited," *The Manchester School* 55 (1987): 158–183.

[42] David G. Blanchflower and Andrew J. Oswald, *The Wage Curve* (Cambridge: MIT Press, 1994).

[43] Blanchflower and Oswald, *The Wage Curve*.

[44] David G. Blanchflower and Andrew J. Oswald, "Unemployment, Well-Being and Wage Curves in Eastern Europe," mimeo, Dartmouth College, 1998.

[45] John Hoddinott, "Wages and Unemployment in an Urban African Labor Market," *Economic Journal* 106 (1996): 1610–1626.

[46] Sonia Bhalotra, "The Spatial Unemployment-Wage Relation Revisited: An Investigation of Interstate Urban Unemployment Differentials in India," University of Bristol DP 96/409, 1996.

Nijkamp and Poot have attempted to identify the average estimate of the coefficient β from the large international literature on the wage curve through the use of **meta-analysis**.[47] Meta-analysis combines the results of a number of individual studies of a given relationship to attempt to identify a common measure of effect size, taking into consideration differences in sample sizes and sample characteristics across the studies and using statistical techniques to address potential biases. Their application of meta-analysis to 17 studies of the wage curve published between 1990 and 2001 results in an unbiased estimate of β of -0.07.

Let's pause for a moment to consider just what this coefficient means. Because the estimated regression is logarithmic in both earnings and unemployment, the coefficient can be interpreted as the unemployment elasticity of the wage. With a value of -0.07, a 10% increase in regional unemployment will typically bring about a 0.7% reduction in the real wage. Hence, if unemployment were to rise from 10% to 11% (a rise of 1 percentage *point* but a percentage increase of 10%), the wage would fall by about 0.7%. But if unemployment were to rise by one percentage point from 5% to 6% (a 20% increase), the wage would typically fall by about 1.4%. The relationship between the wage and unemployment is therefore negative and nonlinear, with a bigger wage response to a given change in the unemployment rate at lower levels of unemployment.

This has two implications for the analysis of unemployment. First, there is considerable evidence in these studies for an inelastic response of the real wage to the unemployment rate, controlling for other wage determinants. This is consistent with the evidence from macro analyses of wage rigidity using the **Phillips curve** approach and average wage data for aggregate labor markets. Second, the wage curve suggests that the real wage becomes less responsive to a change in the unemployment rate as we move from low-unemployment to high-unemployment labor markets. This is consistent with the conclusion of the insider–outsider theory that the existence of large numbers of long-term unemployed has little effect on insider wage bargaining power.

A Model of the Aggregate Labor Market

To pull together the various strands of analysis we have been considering in this chapter, let's examine the model of the aggregate labor market developed by Richard Layard, Stephen Nickell, and Richard Jackman (LNJ).[48] The **LNJ model** goes beyond a simplified aggregate labor supply and demand market framework to incorporate wage- and price-setting behavior consistent with implicit contracts, efficiency wages, and insider–outsider bargaining power. The equilibrium in the LNJ model does not necessarily involve market clearing and allows for involuntary unemployment. This approach has received considerable attention as a method of analyzing the macroeconomic relationship between wages and unemployment.[49]

---

[47] Peter Nijkamp and Jacques Poot, "The Last Word on the Wage Curve?" *Journal of Economic Surveys* 19 (2005): 421–450.

[48] Richard Layard, Stephen Nickell, and Richard Jackman, *Unemployment* (Oxford: Oxford University Press, 1991).

[49] See the treatment of this model in Olivier Blanchard, *Macroeconomics*, 3rd ed. (Upper Saddle River, NJ: Prentice Hall, 2003).

Suppose wages are set by the following simple relationship:

$$w/p^e = a^e(\alpha_0 - \alpha_1 u) \tag{14-6}$$

where w denotes the nominal wage rate, p^e is the aggregate price index expected to prevail during a given time period, a^e is the expected level of output per worker (anticipated average productivity), and u is the unemployment rate. Here nominal wages are set as a markup over the expected price level, which declines as the rate of unemployment rises. As in the wage curve or Phillips curve models, the real wage falls as unemployment rises with the coefficient α_1 as a measure of real wage flexibility. The inverse relationship between the wage markup and the unemployment rate reflects the impact of rising unemployment on wage setting in perfectly competitive segments of the labor market and diminishing bargaining power in periods of weak economic activity. It also reflects a lower efficiency wage premium in labor markets where high unemployment itself raises the costs of low effort.

The term α_0 of this wage-setting relationship captures the net effect on wage setting of variables that influence the reservation wage and the bargaining power of workers. An increase in the generosity of the unemployment benefit system or an increase in union strength would be reflected in a larger value of α_0.

An increase in anticipated worker productivity would also act to increase the real wage level desired by workers; in the long run, workers would attempt to increase nominal wages in proportion to changes in the price level and productivity for a given unemployment rate.

Business firms are seen as operating in imperfectly competitive product markets with constant marginal and average costs over the relevant range of output. In this case, the marginal cost of producing one more unit of output is the wage divided by the average productivity of workers, or unit labor costs. The prices set by firms can be treated as a markup over marginal cost in the following manner:

$$p = \beta(w/a) \tag{14-7}$$

The size of the price markup over unit labor costs (β) will be determined in part by the extent of competition among sellers in the product market, with lower markups in more competitive settings. If there were an increase in the price of some other variable input (e.g., energy), we could treat that as also increasing the markup of p over w. Finally, the tax wedge between the wage received by workers and the labor cost (wage plus payroll taxes) paid by employers would also be reflected in β. This price markup relationship can be rewritten as:

$$w/p = a/\beta \tag{14-8}$$

Figure 14.3 depicts the wage- and price-setting relationships in the LNJ model. Equilibrium in the labor market would occur when the expected levels of prices and productivity equaled the actual values of these variables and when the real wage acceptable to workers was equal to the real wage business firms desired to pay, given productivity and the markup rate. The unemployment rate prevailing at the intersection of the relevant wage-setting (WS) and price-setting (PS) curves then would be the equilibrium unemployment rate. We might refer to this long-run equilibrium rate as the natural rate although we need to keep in mind that market clearing is not assumed by the LNJ concept of equilibrium.

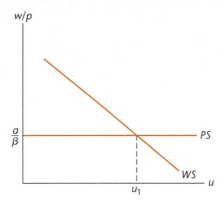

FIGURE 14.3 Long-Run Equilibrium in the LNJ Model

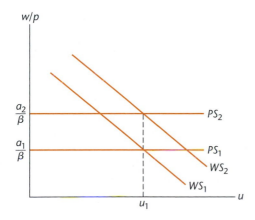

FIGURE 14.4 Effects of an Increase in Actual and Expected Productivity

We can use this graphical version of the LNJ model in Figure 14.4 to examine how the equilibrium unemployment rate would change in response to changes in the underlying determinants of wage and price setting. For example, higher productivity that was fully anticipated would shift the WS and PS curves up by equal amounts, from WS_1 to WS_2 and from PS_1 to PS_2. Higher productivity will result in a higher equilibrium real wage but will not affect the equilibrium unemployment rate. This prediction of the model is consistent with the empirical evidence on the long-run impact of productivity growth on aggregate labor markets.

Increases in worker bargaining power due to trade union growth, high minimum wage levels, protective legislation making it difficult for firms to fire workers, or generous unemployment compensation and welfare benefits would shift the WS curve from WS_1 to WS_2 in Figure 14.5. This would cause the equilibrium unemployment rate to rise from u_1 to u_2. The effort by workers to secure higher real wages is inconsistent with the profit maximizing real wage employers are willing to pay. Firms would react to the wage

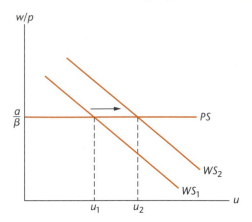

FIGURE 14.5 Effect of an Increase in Bargaining Power

AROUND THE WORLD

Unemployment in Eastern Germany

Ever since the reunification of Germany, unemployment in the former communist states has been significantly higher than in the rest of the country. For example, in April 2003, the unemployment rate in eastern Germany was 19.1%, whereas in western Germany it was 8.6%. High unemployment in eastern Germany reflects substantial job erosion. At the end of 2002, employment in western Germany plus Berlin was at about the same level as at the beginning of 1994, but the number of jobs in the five states of eastern Germany at the end of 2002 was just 82% of the number recorded in 1994.

The explanation for this situation can be found in the labor market aftereffects of the politics of reunification. A strong effort to equalize negotiated wage rates in the two regions has resulted in wage levels in the eastern states that are 65%–75% of western levels even though productivity in the eastern region is less than 60% of western levels. As a result, unit labor costs are dramatically higher in the eastern region. The federal government also engages in substantial transfer programs that on average tend to put disposable income of eastern Germans on par with western levels. It is estimated that every third euro spent in the east on final goods comes from transfer payments or loans from western Germany.*

In terms of the LNJ model, the lower productivity would cause the price-setting curve in the east to lie well below the western price-setting curve. The national bargaining objective of equalized wages and the existence of generous welfare payments would greatly increase the insider bargaining power of those employed in eastern firms. As a result, the wage-setting curve in eastern Germany might even lie above the wage-setting curve for the west. We could easily draw regional price- and wage-setting curves under these conditions that are consistent with the evidence of lower real wages and higher unemployment in eastern Germany.

Note: *Hans-Werner Sinn, "The Laggard of Europe," CES ifo Forum 4 (2003): Special Issue No. 1.

pressure by reducing employment and increasing equilibrium unemployment. In the new equilibrium, the higher unemployment rate offsets worker bargaining power in determining prevailing real wage levels.

A greater real wage response to the unemployment rate would lead to a lower equilibrium unemployment rate. This is shown in Figure 14.6 where we assume that α_0 and α_1 in equation 14-6 both initially equal 1. An increase in wage responsiveness increases the absolute value of α_1, rotating the WS curve from WS_1 to WS_2 and lowering the equilibrium unemployment rate from u_1 to u_2. A large body of evidence points to greater wage flexibility in the United States as a key factor leading to lower unemployment rates there than in Europe.

Finally, Figure 14.7 looks at the effect of increases in the price markup set by firms on the equilibrium unemployment rate. Two factors are of particular relevance. Both higher payroll taxes to finance unemployment and Social Security benefits would increase labor costs relative to the wage paid and lead to a higher markup β. Reduced product market competition, perhaps as a result of limits on imports or controls on entry into certain industries, would also allow firms to raise p relative to w/a. An increase in β shifts the

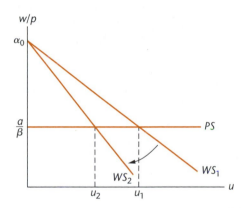

FIGURE 14.6 Effect of an Increase in Wage Flexibility

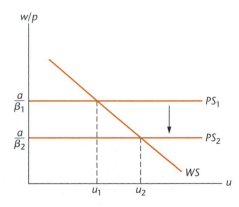

FIGURE 14.7 Effect of an Increase in Price Markup

price-setting curve down from PS_1 to PS_2, leading to a rise in the equilibrium unemployment rate from u_1 to u_2.

We can also use the graphic LNJ model to examine fluctuations in the unemployment rate around its long-run equilibrium level. We can only do so, however, in a rudimentary way because it is very difficult to consider the dynamic evolution of the wage and unemployment rate over time and because we would need to supplement this model of the labor market with a model of the determinants of aggregate demand or supply shocks in a fuller treatment. However, we can still get a sense of what happens over the business cycle.

Let's look at the case of a recession when the unemployment rate rises above the natural rate. In doing so, it will help to rewrite the wage- and price-setting relationships (equations 14-6 and 14-8) so that the dependent variable is the nominal wage rather than the real wage. This is easily done as:

$$\text{Wage Setting}: \ w = p^e a^e (\alpha_0 + \alpha_1 u)$$
$$\text{Price Setting}: \ w = pa/\beta \tag{14-9}$$

Following modern macroeconomic theory, we can identify a short-run equilibrium that temporarily diverges from the long-run equilibrium as long as expectations differ from the realized values of key variables. Figure 14.8 illustrates how a short-run equilibrium could result in an unemployment rate that is higher than the eventual long-run equilibrium rate. Suppose we start with the wage- and price-setting relationships labeled WS_1 and PS_1 in Figure 14.4. These curves yield an equilibrium unemployment rate of u_1, which is a long-run equilibrium rate since $p^e = p_1$ and $a^e = a_1$.

Now suppose there is a cyclical contraction in aggregate demand caused by a decrease in planned investment spending. This cyclical decrease in aggregate demand would cause the price and output levels to decrease. During a business cycle contraction, output per worker tends to drop along with total output as firms delay cutting employment. As p and a fall, the price-setting curve will shift down. If p^e and a^e do not change, the resulting short-run equilibrium would lead to a higher unemployment rate at u_2 and

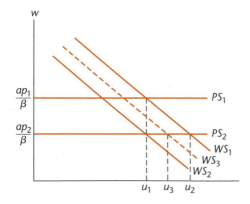

FIGURE 14.8 Effects of a Decrease in Aggregate Demand on Unemployment in the Short Run

a lower nominal wage at w_2.[50] This type of analysis lies behind the typical treatment of a recession using the aggregate demand–aggregate supply model in courses in intermediate macroeconomics.

Two things could move the labor market depicted in Figure 14.8 back to long-run equilibrium. First, there might be a recovery of aggregate demand, either because investment spending recovered or because of expansionary monetary or fiscal policy. In this case, the price-setting curve would return to PS_1, and the unemployment rate would fall back to u_1. This might be thought of as the typical case because most business cycles since World War II have been relatively short in duration. But what happens if aggregate demand remains at a depressed level for a very long time? Then the adjustment to long-run equilibrium would involve a downward adjustment in p^e and a^e, which would shift down the wage-setting curve to WS_2, yielding an equilibrium unemployment rate at u_1. The dynamics of such an adjustment and the speed at which it might occur require a much more sophisticated model than the one we have portrayed.

If the second adjustment process were required to respond to a long-lasting change in the level of aggregate demand, we might see the short-run high-unemployment rate translated into an increase in the long-run equilibrium unemployment rate. If the unemployment rate remains in the neighborhood of u_2 for a considerable period, the duration of unemployment will lengthen, and the number of people out of work for a very long time will increase. If the long-term unemployed become less competitive for job openings the longer they remain unemployed, the bargaining power of insiders may increase as long as the unemployment rate remains high. This would tend to offset the downward shift of the wage-setting curve, which would be to WS_3 instead of WS_2, meaning that the new long-run equilibrium unemployment rate might end up at u_3 instead of u_1. This is one way that hysteresis can affect the natural rate of unemployment.

The LNJ model offers an approach to the study of unemployment that is quite different from its predecessors. It has clear policy implications for lowering the natural rate of unemployment: weaken union bargaining power, reduce benefits and taxes, and make the product market more competitive. These conclusions have clearly driven policy in a large number of countries over the last 15 years.

Unemployment in the Great Recession

The economic history of the early years of this century will fascinate analysts for a long time to come. The recession of 2008 and its aftermath cast a shadow over economies around the world lasting well beyond the actual recession itself.

Unlike many recessions, the origins of the 2008 downturn are to be found in the financial sector. Over a number of years, banks had sought new ways of extending their business. In doing so, they developed new products which allowed them to make loans to groups of people that they had not previously been able to access. In particular, mortgage style loans were made available to low income households in order to help them buy their

---

[50] Given the fact of ongoing inflation in most economies, it would be perhaps better to say that *the rate of increase* of prices and wages, rather than the *level* of p and w, fell as a result of this cyclical downturn (or that p and w ended up lower than they otherwise would have been).

own homes. These loans carried an element of risk for the banks, but there were two reasons why the banks felt comfortable with this new risk.

First, so long as house prices continued to rise, the loans were secured on a safe asset—if the borrower failed to keep up with repayments, the bank could reclaim the house. Secondly, many banks financed the loans by packaging up a number of loans, some riskier than others, into derivatives which could then be sold to other financial institutions and because of the portfolio effect of bundling, labeled as safe assets. But problems arose when house prices started to fall and banks were left with unpaid debts; the loans which banks made were suddenly transformed into "toxic assets."

These problems multiplied when it became clear that many of the derivatives held by banks were made up, in part, of such toxic assets and that the extent to which these derivatives themselves represented safe assets was unclear. Banks no longer had confidence in the products that they had previously been freely trading; one bank would no longer lend to another (it would no longer buy the other's assets); and, unable to sell their assets to other financial institutions, banks could not generate the funds needed to continue to invest in industry, real estate, and so on. The day-to-day activities of the banking system—borrowing and lending—thus slowed down considerably in this so-called credit crunch.

As soon as the public loses confidence in a bank, the consequences can be alarming. Customers who hold their assets in the bank seek to withdraw those assets and a "bank run" can ensue. Since any bank only holds a proportion of its customers' deposits as cash—it loans out the rest so that it can earn interest—the bank can quickly run out of liquid assets with which to pay back its depositors. ATMs can run out of cash. Firms can find it impossible to take money out of banks in order to pay wages to their workforce. In a nightmare scenario, lack of confidence in the banking sector can lead the whole economy to grind to a halt. Fortunately this was avoided in 2008—but not without some banks failing and others, which were deemed to be too important to fail, being bailed out by national governments.

The credit crunch had an obvious consequence for the real economy. Businesses found it harder to invest in new capital because they could not get loans from the banks with which to finance these investments. This reduced the demand for investment goods. Meanwhile, consumers found it harder to borrow in order to finance their own purchases. At one end of the spectrum people could not obtain mortgage loans to buy homes, and this had additional effects in that they would not then spend on alterations, decoration, furnishings, and so on. At the other end of the spectrum, people found that the limits that they could borrow on their credit cards were being squeezed. Both demand and the capacity of the economy to produce fell. The consequent recession was severe in many countries.

The aftermath of this recession has also been severe. Public finances were adversely affected. This occurred partly because governments received less in tax revenues as incomes, spending, and employment fell and because they spent more as the number of welfare recipients rose. In addition, governments in many countries brought forward large-scale investment projects that would help mitigate the effects of the recession on employment. Many governments also needed to finance bailouts of the banks. The impact on the government's budget deficit was, in the case of many countries, substantial. The governments of most countries were able to cope with this; they run deficits in some years, surpluses in other years, and are able to borrow from the public and from financial institutions to cover the gap.

In the case of some countries, however, the budget deficit has risen so dramatically that confidence in the country's ability *ever* to pay back its debt has been eroded. When this happens, it becomes impossible for the government to borrow more money to finance its budget deficit—people will not lend money if they do not believe that they will get it back. To reduce the deficit, a country in this position will need to close the gap between government spending and revenue by introducing austerity measures. Moreover, in one form or another, the country is likely to default on its debt obligations (though, to sweeten the pill, the default may go under another name, such as a "restructure" or a "haircut"). Defaulting in this way means that the government of the country does not pay back everything it owes to its creditors.

These creditors may include governments and banks in other countries. So, just as one bank failing can lead to other banks coming under pressure, one country's default can lead to adversity in other countries. The financial problems faced by the governments of Iceland, Portugal, Ireland, Italy, and, especially, Greece have been well publicized, but these difficulties have serious implications also for the level of economic activity that can be sustained elsewhere. In 2008, private borrowing led to the credit crunch, and in 2011, public borrowing led to a similar readjustment, severely damaging the prospects for growth. This period has thus been characterized by a "double-whammy."

A characteristic of financial crises is that the recessions to which they give rise are typically longer and more severe than other recessions.[51] On average, such recessions last for about 2 years, and the loss of output approaches 10%. Indeed, the recent recession has been especially severe, and, hence, it has been dubbed the Great Recession. It is, in many respects, useful to think of it as two recessions rolled into one—the first being associated with private debt and the second with public debt. Inevitably it has had a very marked impact on labor markets, but as we shall see this impact has been very different in different countries.

In Figure 14.9, the time series for unemployment in four countries is graphed over the period 1982 through 2011. These series illustrate the very different experience of the various countries over the course of the recent recession. In the United States, after many years in which the unemployment rate was around 5% or 6%, the rate rose to just under 10% in the wake of the 2008 recession and has remained high. In the United Kingdom, the years following the 1991 recession saw a gradual fall in the unemployment rate, but this rose after 2008, albeit not to the same extent as in the United States. It appears likely that job losses in the United Kingdom led partly to a rise in unemployment; partly to a rise in the numbers of economically inactive people who we may deem to be discouraged workers; and partly to outmigration of workers who had, over the previous few years, migrated in substantial numbers into the United Kingdom from Eastern Europe.

In Spain, the impact of recession on unemployment has been much more pronounced; it is easily seen from the graph that unemployment in Spain is highly sensitive to the business cycle. In view of the dependence of the Spanish economy on exports of tourism services (which are highly income elastic), this is perhaps not altogether surprising. In many respects, the most curious series in the graph is the one for Germany, where the unemployment rate *fell* throughout the 2008–2011 period. Michael Burda and Jennifer Hunt have argued that this is due partly to a reticence on the part of employers to hire workers

---

[51] Carmen Reinhart and Kenneth Rogoff. "The Aftermath of Financial Crises," *American Economic Review* 99 (2009): 466–472.

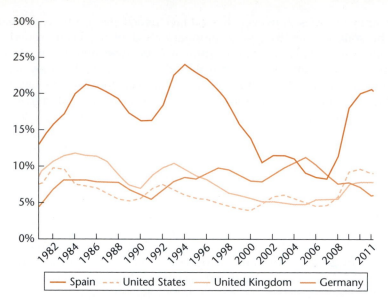

FIGURE 14.9 Unemployment Rate, Various Countries, 1982–2011

Source: International Monetary Fund.

during the upturn of the early 2000s; it is partly due to low rates of wage growth in Germany; and it is partly due to some distinctive policies that moderate labor costs, including the introduction of working time accounts which allow employers to avoid paying overtime rates if workers work more in some periods but less in others.[52]

Differences across countries in the responsiveness of unemployment rates to changes in real GDP have attracted considerable attention. Severe recessions, as defined by periods in which output falls drastically, tend to be accompanied by pronounced rises in unemployment which may also be boosted by financial crises and housing price busts. Arthur Okun conducted some highly influential research on this many years ago, and his results suggested that Gross Domestic Product needs to rise by around 2.5% per year in order to keep unemployment constant—if GDP falls, or even if it rises only slowly, then the unemployment rate will tend to rise.[53] This figure of 2.5% seemed to serve as a good rule of thumb over many years, and the notion that 2.5% growth is needed in order to keep unemployment from rising came to be known as **Okun's law.**

However, the behavior of unemployment and real GDP changes in many countries during the 2008–2009 downturn has led many to wonder if "Okun's broken." For example, the increase in U.S. unemployment seems "too high" relative to the change in real output when these variables are compared to outcomes in other countries. As a result, researchers at the IMF have reexamined the performance of Okun's law during the Great

---

[52] Michael Burda and Jennifer Hunt. "What Explains the German Labor Market Miracle in the Great Recession," *NBER working paper 17187*, 2011, available at http://ftp.iza.org/dp5800.pdf.

[53] Arthur Okun. "Potential GNP: Its Measurement and Significance," *Cowles Foundation Paper 190*, 1962, available at http://cowles.econ.yale.edu/P/cp/p01b/p0190.pdf.

Recession.[54] For the United States, United Kingdom, and Spain, it turns out that the peak-to-trough rise in unemployment during the Great Recession is largely consistent with the predictions from Okun's Law once an additional unemployment increase explained by measures of financial stress and the housing price bust are included in the analysis. Okun's law alone would predict an increase of a percentage point or so in the German unemployment rate, but this predicted effect from declining real output was offset by the use of short-time work programs that kept workers on company payrolls and by unexplained factors.

In fact, the IMF study found that unexplained factors worked to reduce the unemployment rate relative to the level predicted by the combined effects of output declines and financial and housing crises for several European countries and Canada during the Great Recession. This may be due to the effects of the Great Recession on wages. Real wages fell by 0.4% in Germany, and by 0.5% in the United Kingdom during 2009. In 2008, they fell by a massive 1.1% in the United States.[55] And when real wages fall, the Okun relationship breaks down. The cut in demand for business output is accommodated by a cut in firms' (labor) costs. Rather than coping with the decline in demand by cutting production and employment, firms can lower prices. Hence the need to shed labor is reduced as a direct consequence of the downward flexibility of real wages. Unemployment has risen somewhat in most economies during the recession, but by much less than would have been the case had real wages not fallen, and the extent of this fall in real wages during the years following 2008 has been unusual and remarkable.

The atypical behaviour of real wages in recent years makes it difficult for economists to predict how unemployment rates will change in the near future. If real wages continue to be flexible, then the labor market may prove to be unusually robust to adverse changes in demand. If, on the other hand, worker militancy increases,[56] further downward pressure on real wages will face resistance. In this scenario, Okun's law would be mended and a further downturn or a period of sluggish growth would once more lead to an increase in unemployment. Even with moderation in real wages, the sluggish pace of economic growth during the recovery from the Great Recession helps explain why unemployment rates remained stubbornly high in the United States and many other countries for a long period of time following the mid–2009 trough in the U.S. business cycle.

Summary

Unemployment is a critical problem facing many countries today. Joblessness is highly correlated with individual medical and psychological difficulties. Youth unemployment, in particular, is associated with criminal activity, and an extensive period of joblessness for youths just out of school may significantly diminish their lifetime income possibilities.

---

[54] "Unemployment Dynamics During Recessions and Recoveries: Okun's Law and Beyond," Chapter 3, *World Economic Outlook: Rebalancing Growth*, International Monetary Fund, April 2010.

[55] Interestingly, real wages in Spain continued to rise during this period, and unemployment rose dramatically in that country. These data come from the International Labor Office publication, Global Wage Report 2010/11, available at http://bit.ly/qr295v.

[56] The Occupy Wall Street movement of late 2011 may be an early indication of this in the United States.

Those out of work for an extended period suffer a diminution of their skills and confidence and may carry a negative stigma with them when they seek a new job. The social and political consequences of high unemployment give greater urgency to the efforts of economists to understand the causes and the cures of unemployment. Several key conclusions can be drawn from our survey of these efforts in this chapter.

First, an important part of the measured unemployment rate is a relatively constant, noncyclical component generally known as the natural rate of unemployment. The natural rate will be higher in economies where the costs of remaining an out-of-work job seeker are low, where the hiring rate from the pool of jobless people is low, where significant retraining or relocation is required to match seekers with openings, and where institutional or managerial influences keep the going wage above the market-clearing level.

The unemployment rate moves around the natural rate in a manner that is highly correlated with other indicators of the business cycle. Some economists treat cyclical unemployment as an equilibrium phenomenon, but the typical view is that aggregate demand and supply shocks coupled with real wage rigidity lead to short-run labor market disequilibria in which the actual unemployment rate is above or below the natural rate. Wage rigidity stems from managerial decisions to use the wage level as an effort-enhancing or turnover-reducing incentive and from insider bargaining power. Empirical evidence from wage curve or Phillips curve studies shows that wages do respond in the right direction to excess supply of labor but that this response is too small to eliminate excess supply in the short run.

Cyclical and noncyclical unemployment may be interrelated by the process known as hysteresis. A period of high cyclical unemployment may contribute to a subsequent increase in the natural rate if it leads to an increase in unemployment duration. The long-term unemployed find increasing difficulty in moving out of unemployment, and wage levels seem to be much less responsive to long-term than to short-term unemployment. The extent of the connection between cyclical and noncyclical unemployment is difficult to measure because we cannot observe the natural rate and usually infer the level of the natural rate from a moving average of actual rates of unemployment.

The analysis of the causes of cyclical and noncyclical unemployment outlined in this chapter generally supports the argument for policy reforms designed to make labor markets more flexibly responsive to changing economic circumstances. Steps to increase the responsiveness of wages to unemployment, to enhance the ability of the market to match job seekers with vacant positions, to remove disincentives to hire the unemployed, and to create a macroeconomic environment conducive to job growth should lower the natural rate of unemployment in an economy. The experience of Ireland and the Netherlands gives added validity to this policy prescription. The fear of some, however, is that this unemployment prescription has undesirable side effects, such as reducing the influence of institutions of labor-management-government cooperation and increasing inequality in earnings and income.

KEY TERMS

voluntary unemployment
unemployment rate
discouraged workers

duration of unemployment
natural rate of unemployment
structural unemployment

equilibrium unemployment rate

full employment

noncyclical unemployment

moving average

nonaccelerating inflation rate of unemployment (NAIRU)

wage aspiration effect

hysteresis

random shocks

smoothing process

intertemporal substitution

real business cycle models

real wage rigidity

implicit contract

asymmetric information

sorting

gift exchange

insiders

outsiders

wage curve

meta-analysis

Phillips curve

LNJ model

Okun's law

PROBLEMS

1. Distinguish between voluntary and involuntary unemployment. Why is wage flexibility important for this distinction?

2. When surveyed about her labor force activity, Jane replies that she is not employed but has been actively looking for a job. Explain how it is possible that her unemployment might be voluntary.

3. Suppose an economy had 100 jobs available each month, the labor force consisted of 100 people, and the real wage kept labor demand equal to labor supply. Explain why the unemployment rate would probably not equal zero in this case.

4. Using the data in Table 14.1, choose the version of the unemployment rate that you think best measures the risk of joblessness in the United States, and explain your reasoning.

5. Suppose that each month 10% of the unemployed manage to find a new job. If 1,000 people are unemployed on January 1, what would the average length of a completed period of unemployment be for these people? What would the average duration be if 1,200 people were unemployed in January? What if the hiring rate were 5%?

6. Look again at the case study on "Excess Supply and Salary Offers for PhD Economists." The chart there shows an estimated linear relationship between the percentage change in starting salaries and the percent of PhD job seekers who could not find a position. This linear relationship has an intercept of 13.4 and a slope coefficient of -1.01. Use these values to estimate the NAIRU for this labor market. Does this estimate seem high?

7. The NAIRU estimates in Table 14.3 suggest that the natural unemployment rate may be lower in smaller countries. Is there an inverse relationship between the NAIRU and land area or population density? Does the theory of search unemployment suggest why such an inverse relationship might exist?

8. From 1981 to 1982 the level of employment in the United States fell by 0.86% and the real wage dropped by 0.13%. If this represented a shift in labor demand along a fixed

labor supply curve, what would be the elasticity of labor supply? Is your estimate consistent with typical estimates of the wage elasticity of labor supply? How does the existence of wage rigidity help reconcile your elasticity estimate with the typical estimate?

9. Psychologists have long noted a negative effect of unemployment on a person's self-esteem and psychological well-being. How does this square with the hypothesis that unemployment resulting from a productivity shock can be described as intertemporal labor substitution? Explain.

10. The case study on "Unemployment in Eastern Germany" suggests that the LNJ model can be used to explain why real wages were lower and unemployment rates higher in eastern Germany in the decade following the reunification of Germany. Try to do this.

11. Use the LNJ model to analyze the effect of the following on the unemployment rate:
    a. A decrease in union bargaining power
    b. A more generous unemployment compensation benefit
    c. Increased efficiency in matching job seekers to job vacancies
    d. Legislation requiring firms to pay a year's severance pay to workers they fire

12. Why do policy recommendations for labor reforms also call for more price competition in product markets among business firms as a way of lowering unemployment in labor markets? Use a graph like that in Figure 14.3 to analyze how such a policy would affect unemployment.

13. Select a country and find the data to describe the way its unemployment rate changed in the decade prior to the Great Recession, during the Great Recession, and in the years after the Great Recession. Can you distinguish between changes in the natural rate of unemployment and cyclical movements of the unemployment rate?

14. Search online for a definition and explanation of "jobless recoveries." Is there evidence of a jobless recovery in the data you used to answer question 13?

15

Wage Inequality, Income Inequality, and Poverty

What is the evidence on wage inequality trends in various countries?

What are the causes of rising wage inequality in the United States?

How is wage inequality related to income inequality and poverty?

The study of labor economics focuses on developing systematic explanations for the commonplace observation that different workers have very different experiences in the labor market. Some are more prone than others to unemployment, and different workers often earn widely differing levels of compensation for their work. We have developed a number of explanations for wage differences among workers, starting with the observation that wages are highest for workers possessing scarce skills and ending with an analysis of the ways institutions such as trade unions, corporate human resource policies, and race and gender discrimination affect the earnings potential of similar workers. In all of these explanations, we have narrowed our view to explain why the wages of a particular group of workers are higher or lower than the wages earned by some other reference group of workers.

In this chapter we take a somewhat broader view of wage differentials among workers. Like the analysis of unemployment in Chapter 14, the questions addressed here are relevant to an economy-wide evaluation of labor market performance. This chapter examines in turn the measurement and explanation of differences in wage inequality, income inequality, and poverty across countries and over time within countries. The explanation of wage differentials among workers is one of the central issues of labor economics, and we address the ways labor market changes and changes in labor market institutions have resulted in growing wage inequality in developed economies. We then turn our attention to the way in which wage inequality translates into inequality in the distribution of income among families and individuals. We examine the measurement and explanation of poverty, concentrating on poverty in the United States because this country has experienced the deepest cuts in the inflation-adjusted pay of low-wage workers and the biggest increases in family income inequality and poverty in the past 20 years. This chapter ends with a discussion of policy options available to a government interested in achieving a reversal of recent inequality trends by reducing wage disparity.

Wage Inequality and Labor Market Performance

The analysis of **wage inequality** is an important element in the evaluation of the performance of an economy for several reasons. The first is that people place a positive value on increasing social equality. A society is generally willing to sacrifice some portion of its annual standard of living in return for greater equality in income among its citizens. Of course, societies will differ in their willingness to make such trade-offs. In the United States, where a high value is placed on economic efficiency and the free market policies that bring that about, people are generally willing to tolerate much greater wage inequality than that of most European countries.

A second reason for our interest in economy-wide measures of wage equality is that questions about the distribution of income are, in some sense, the Achilles' heel of the free market economy. The vast disparities between the standards of living of the average worker and the owners of businesses generated by the industrial revolution in Great Britain, as described in the novels of Dickens and others, lay at the root of the development of socialist and communist alternatives to the market system. The existence of disparities in labor market outcomes has served as one of the strongest arguments for government regulation of wages and the labor market. This can be seen even in the countries undergoing the transition from failed centrally planned economies under communism to market-oriented economies under democratic governments. Most of these countries have experienced recurrent waves of nostalgia for the "good old days" largely occasioned by the greater wage inequality generated by newly unfettered labor markets.

Wage and income inequality became a major news item in the wake of the Great Recession. Anger over high executive pay and bonuses boiled over when financial institutions saved by government "bail outs" maintained prerecession pay policies. The Occupy Wall Street Movement, coining the slogan "We Are the 99%," took up residence in New York's Zuccotti Park and stimulated protests against inequality around the globe in the autumn of 2011. In the United Kingdom, 2012 brought a "shareholder spring" when an increasing number of individual and institutional owners of corporate shares voted against proposed executive pay packages. And an underlying theme to the ongoing sovereign debt crises facing Greece, Ireland, Portugal, and Spain in 2012 was the disparate effects of government tax increases and austerity programs required as the condition for financial support from the European Union, the European Central Bank, and the International Monetary Fund.

Social and political concerns about wage inequality are found in the relationship between the distribution of wages and poverty. The extent of poverty in a country can be defined by the fraction of workers whose potential earnings in the labor market are too low to afford them a decent standard of living. Increased wage inequality can occur because rising wages for the best-paid workers outstrip the wage increases being received by average or low-paid workers. In this case, everyone is better off, but the top-paid workers are "way better off," and we might expect to see fewer people in poverty.[1] While the increased disparity between

---

[1] We should recognize, however, that definitions of poverty change over time. To stay out of a state people would generally deem to be poverty, a poor household may need to have rising income over time because our definition of necessities changes through the years. For instance, 50 years ago few people in the developed world would have deemed a TV, a refrigerator, or a car to be a necessity.

rich and poor may cause some concern, the fact that the poor are, at least in absolute terms, getting less poor may mean that issues of inequality are not, in these circumstances, likely to be at the top of the political agenda. In contrast, a situation where wage inequality rose because the wages of the poorest-paid and average workers decreased while the wages of the best-paid workers increased would be expected to lead to greater poverty and increased public attention.

During the last three decades the U.S. labor market has generated changes in the wage distribution that match both scenarios over different time periods. From the late 1970s to the early 1990s the evolution of the wage structure followed the second scenario, with wages at the top of the distribution rising relative to the median and wages at the bottom falling relative to the median. Since the early 1990s the U.S. situation has followed the first scenario. The wages at the top of the distribution have continued to rise relative to the median while the wages at the bottom of the distribution relative to the median have exhibited little trend. The onset of the Great Recession in 2008–2009 and the slow recovery from that downturn portend sharp rises in inequality and poverty.

This rise in wage inequality in the United States has been accompanied by increased disparities in family income and in the incidence of poverty. Rising wage inequality has also been experienced in many other countries, reversing a tendency toward more equal wage distributions in developed economies around the world since World War II. Labor economists have been asking why this change occurred and what should and can be done to address the problems of income inequality and poverty associated with this trend.

Another important recent development is the major reevaluation of public policy subsumed under the heading of "welfare reform." One traditional response to the existence of poverty in Europe and North America was the institution of government programs designed to transfer income from taxpayers to the poor, thereby providing them with the means of attaining a more socially acceptable standard of living. These "welfare programs" have come under severe attack for blunting the incentives to work and, thereby, perpetuating poverty. In the United States and the United Kingdom, welfare reform legislation has been enacted to make income transfers temporary sources of aid to the poor while forcing transfer recipients to reenter the workforce. Other countries have also experimented with legislation designed to reduce the generosity of welfare benefits and increase the transition from welfare to work. Because of the heated debate surrounding such legislation, we also examine the economics underlying the welfare reform movement.

Measuring Inequality

The distribution of wages across workers in an economy at a given point in time generally looks like the hypothetical drawing in Figure 15.1. The distribution is often skewed to the right: the majority of workers earn wages that are close to the average wage level while a very small fraction of the workforce earns very large incomes from work. For example, if we were to chart the distribution of wages for all professional baseball players, we would find that the largest fraction, those in the minor leagues or on independent teams, earns quite modest salaries. A smaller fraction, rookies and utility players in the major leagues, earns higher salaries, and a very small fraction of all professional players earns the very high salaries paid to starting players and stars.

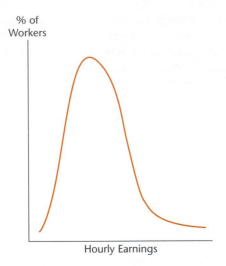

FIGURE 15.1 A Typical Earnings Distribution Graph

Because the typical distribution of wages measured in dollars is so skewed, analysts often express wage levels in their logarithmic values when drawing the wage distribution. This has the advantage of changing a skewed distribution into a symmetrical, bell-shaped normal distribution, which has more desirable statistical properties. Figure 15.2 was taken from a study[2] showing the distribution of the logarithm of real hourly wages among all wage earners aged 17 to 64 in the United States and Canada in 1981 and 1988.[3] In both countries and in both years, the largest fraction of workers earned an inflation-adjusted wage of around $10 an hour, a very small fraction of workers earned as much as $25 an hour, and an equally small fraction earned as little as $2 an hour.

Figure 15.2 shows why we could use a numerical index of the degree of wage inequality. It is clear that both in Canada and the United States the wage distribution changed between 1981 and 1988. It is not clear, however, whether that change was in the direction of more or less equality. Similarly, if we look closely at the graphs, we can see differences in the distribution of wages between Canada and the United States in both 1981 and 1988. The U.S. distribution appears to be more spread out than the Canadian distribution. We might interpret that as suggesting greater wage inequality in the United States, but we would be hard-pressed to say how much more unequal the U.S. distribution was. Over the years, economists and statisticians have devised several numerical measures of the degree of inequality in a particular income distribution. With such a numerical measure (e.g., the difference in the logarithm of real wages earned by workers at the 10th and 90th percentiles) we could say that inequality increased in the United States by 12% between 1981 and 1988 and that there was 8% less wage inequality in Canada in 1988.

---

[2] John DiNardo and Thomas Lemieux, "Diverging Male Wage Inequality in the United States and Canada: Do Institutions Explain the Difference?" *Industrial and Labor Relations Review* 50 (1997): 629–651.

[3] While data from the 1980s may be "ancient history" to the typical reader of this text, it is worthwhile paying some attention to this period since this is when increasing wage inequality became a prominent feature of labor market developments in the U.S. and many other countries.

(a) United States

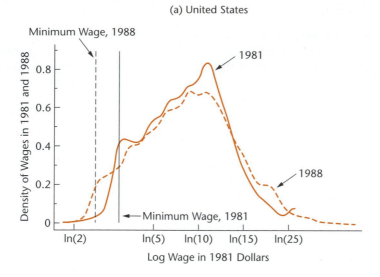

(b) Canada

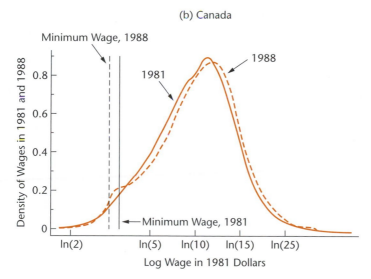

FIGURE 15.2 Wage Distributions in Canada and in the United States, 1981 and 1988

Source: John DiNardo and Thomas Lemieux, "Diverging Male Wage Inequality in the United States and Canada: Do Institutions Explain the Difference?" *Industrial and Labor Relations Review* 50 (1997): 629–651.

Rather than studying all of the proposed indexes of inequality, we concentrate on three that have been used extensively in the recent literature on changes in wage inequality: the percentile wage differential, the Gini coefficient, and the variance of the logarithm of earnings. We will explain how these measures of inequality are calculated and how to interpret the information they provide about wage inequality.

Percentile Wage Differentials

One relatively easy way of numerically depicting the degree of inequality in a given wage distribution is by a comparison of the differences in wage levels at various percentiles of the distribution. This gives us a measure of dispersion similar to the range in statistics. To illustrate the calculation of the various wage inequality indexes, we use data on the distribution of hourly wages paid to janitors working for firms in Los Angeles County in 2000 and 2010. These data are derived from employer surveys carried out by the U.S. Bureau of Labor Statistics and give us a view of the level and change in wage inequality for a very homogeneous group of workers. Despite the fact that these workers have a common skill level and work in the same metropolitan area, their wages are widely dispersed. As we work through the calculation of different measures of wage dispersion for these workers, recall what you have learned that can help explain why the "law of one price" doesn't apply to these workers.

Table 15.1 reports the inflation-adjusted hourly wage level at the 10th, 25th, 50th, 75th, and 90th percentiles of the distribution of janitors ranked from the lowest wage earner to the highest wage earner. Read the figures in Table 15.1 as follows: In 2000, 10% of the janitorial workers in Los Angeles earned a real wage of $8.09 per hour or less, and 90% earned a real wage of $20.32 or less. Most college students are familiar with such percentile rankings from their college entrance exam reports, which usually give both a test score and a percentile ranking indicating the percentage of students taking the test who scored less than your test score. The janitors in Los Angeles feel the same way about their wages as most college-bound students feel about SAT scores: they would like their level to be above the 99th percentile.

The **percentile wage differential** measures inequality by the spread or distance between high and low wages, with high wages defined as those at a high percentile of the distribution and low wages similarly defined as those at a low percentile. If the data are in dollars, as in Table 15.1, the percentile wage differential can be calculated as the

TABLE 15.1 Real Hourly Wage Level (in 2010 Prices) at Various Percentiles of the Wage Distribution and Percentile Wage Ratios for Los Angeles Janitors, 2000 and 2010

Percentile	2000	2010
10	$8.09	$8.51
25	9.02	9.08
50	10.71	10.71
75	15.12	14.06
90	20.32	19.84
w90/w50*	1.80	1.85
w50/w10	1.32	1.26
w90/w10	2.51	2.33

*This equals the wage at the 90th percentile divided by the median wage.

Source: Authors' calculations from the U.S. Department of Labor, Bureau of Labor Statistics, Occupational and Wage Estimates available at: http://www.bls.gov/oes/oes_dl.htm.

ratio of high wages divided by low wages. If the wage data have been converted to logarithms, the percentile wage differential is calculated by subtracting the logarithm of the lower wage from that of the higher wage. Table 15.1 reports three ratios of high to low wages that provide us with useful information about how dispersed the distribution of wages among L.A. janitors was in 2000 and in 2010. These ratios are identified by a symbol. For example, w90/w50 is the wage at the 90th percentile divided by the wage at the 50th percentile. You can figure out the others.

What do these ratios tell us? First, they indicate that there was a fairly high dispersion in janitor's wages in Los Angeles in these two years. The wages earned by those at the 90th percentile of the distribution were about two and a half times larger than the wages earned by janitors at the 10th percentile. Second, the spread between high and median wages in this local labor market increased over time; the w90/w50 ratio rose from 1.80 to 1.85 from 2000 to 2010. Third, at the same time the wage disparity between the median earner and the janitor earning the 10th percentile wage rate decreased with the w50/w10 ratio falling from 1.32 to 1.26 from 2000 to 2010. Finally, overall inequality, as measured by w90/w10, the spread between high and low wages, fell by 7.2%, from 2.51 in 2000 to 2.33 in 2010.

If the data are available, the percentile wage differential is an easy to calculate and easy to interpret measure of the distance between high- and low-wage earners in a given distribution. As a result, this measure has been used quite frequently in empirical studies of wage inequality. It does have one drawback as a comprehensive index of inequality. The percentile wage differential concentrates attention on just a few bits of information from the wage distribution and ignores what might be happening to wages at other percentiles than the ones under study. The Gini coefficient is an inequality index that attempts to encompass information about the entire distribution in a single number.

The Gini Coefficient

The starting point for an explanation of the **Gini coefficient** is the **Lorenz curve** depicted in Figure 15.3. Along the horizontal axis of this diagram we plot the cumulative percentage of workers, starting at zero and ending at 100%, with workers ranked by their wage level. The number 10 on the horizontal axis would indicate the 10% of workers with the lowest wage levels. The vertical axis measures the cumulative share of total wages earned

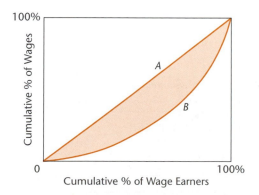

FIGURE 15.3 The Lorenz Curve

by workers, again starting at zero and running to 100%. The 45-degree diagonal line, marked A, is called the *line of perfect equality* because along this line the cumulative percentage of workers ranked by income equals the cumulative percentage of income earned. Thus the poorest 10% of workers receive 10% of income and the poorest 50% receive 50% of income along line A. Line B is the Lorenz Curve, which plots the actual share of earnings going to each fraction of the workforce. If wages are not equal for all workers, the Lorenz curve lies below the line of perfect equality, and the poorest 10% of workers receive less than 10% of earnings.

The Gini coefficient is defined as the shaded area between lines A and B divided by the area under line A and, hence, is a number that lies between zero and 1 in value. In a market with a greater degree of wage inequality, the Lorenz curve will lie farther away from the line of perfect equality, and the Gini coefficient will have a larger value. Because it takes into account the full array of data available on the share of earnings going to workers at different percentiles of the distribution, the Gini coefficient is a more comprehensive measure of wage inequality than the percentile wage differential. It is also more difficult to calculate in that it requires far more comprehensive data about the income distribution.

Table 15.2 presents data on the cumulative distribution of real wages among L.A. janitors in 2000 and 2010, which we can use to calculate the Gini coefficients for these distributions. In this table, the workers are divided into quartiles ranked by the average wage level in each fourth of the workforce. The second and third columns in Table 15.2 show the percentage of workers in each quartile (which by definition is 25% in each case) and the cumulative percentage of workers. The first column for each year shows the percentage share of the total hourly wages paid by employers to all janitors that went to those in each quartile. So the 25% of Los Angeles janitors with the lowest wages earned 17.4% of all wages paid by employers to janitors in 2000 and 18.3% in 2010. The second column for each year cumulates the fraction of wages earned across quartiles as we go from the lowest paid 25% of janitors in the first row to 100% of janitors in the last row.

The Gini coefficient can be calculated as:

$$\text{Gini} = 1 - \sum_i f_i(z_i + z_{i-1}) \tag{15-1}$$

where f_i is the fraction of workers in each income class (0.25 for each income class), z_i is the cumulative fraction of income up to income class i, and z_{i-1} is the cumulative fraction

TABLE 15.2   Quartile Distribution of Workers and Wages for Janitors in the Los Angeles Area, 2000 and 2010

Wage Quartile	% of Workers	Cumulative %	2000 % of Wages	2000 Cumulative %	2010 % of Wages	2010 Cumulative %
1	25	25	17.4	17.4	18.3	18.3
2	25	50	20.1	37.5	20.6	38.9
3	25	75	26.3	63.8	25.8	64.7
4	25	100	36.2	100	35.3	100

Source: See footnote to Table 15.1.

of income up to the income class preceding income class i. Using the data for 2000 in Table 15.2 and this formula, we get:

$$\text{Gini} = 1 - \big(0.25[0.174] + 0.25[0.375 + 0.174] + 0.25[0.638 + 0.375]$$
$$+ 0.25[1.0 + 0.638]\big) = 0.156 \tag{15-2}$$

The Gini coefficient for 2010, calculated in a similar manner, equals 0.140. Thus, by using this numerical inequality index we can conclude that wage inequality for janitors in Los Angeles was about 9% lower in 2010 than in 2000, a rate of decrease in inequality that is slightly larger than that shown by the w90/w10 ratio. By the way, a Gini coefficient of 0.156 or 0.14 indicates a very low level of inequality; Gini coefficients for all workers in the United States would be around 0.35 in value. The low level of wage inequality among Los Angeles janitors is partly because these workers are very similar in terms of skill.

Another reason for the fairly low estimated Gini coefficient for these data is the fact that we calculated the coefficient with the entire distribution of janitors compressed into just four groups. We assumed a linear relationship between the share of income and the share of workers within each of the four wage quartiles. This was done to make the calculations easier; but to estimate the Gini coefficient more accurately, we should divide the workforce into a greater number of wage groups. Because of the data requirements and computational difficulty in estimating Gini coefficients for a large number of wage groups, many analysts turn instead to the variance of earnings as a comprehensive wage inequality index. The variance is especially useful if the analyst is working with microdata covering individual workers rather than with data on worker groups.

The Variance of the Logarithm of Earnings

Another way of measuring wage inequality is to use a statistical measure of dispersion about the mean level of earnings. The standard deviation or the coefficient of variation has been used for this purpose, but most recent studies using a statistical measure of dispersion have relied on the **variance of the logarithm of earnings**. A small value for the variance of earnings indicates that most of the observations in the earnings distribution are closely clustered around the average wage, indicating that there is relatively little wage dispersion. Wage inequality, then, is directly related to the variance of the logarithm of wages.

If we have information on the fraction of workers receiving various wages, we can calculate the weighted average wage using the following formula:

$$\overline{\ln(w_i)} = \sum_i f_i(\ln(w_i)) \tag{15-3}$$

where $\ln(w_i)$ is the logarithm of the real hourly wage of level i and f_i is the fraction of workers earning that wage. Then the variance is:

$$\text{Var}(\ln w_i) = \sum f_i \Big(\ln(w_i) - \overline{\ln(w_i)}\Big)^2 \tag{15-4}$$

The data we have been using thus far in this section on Los Angeles janitors doesn't lend itself to a meaningful estimate of the variance of the log real wage since we have information on just a few points in the 2000 and 2010 wage distributions for these workers.

We can use the percentile wage differentials, the Gini coefficient, and the variance of the log of real earnings to estimate the degree of inequality in the distribution of hourly wages; weekly, monthly, or annual earnings; or annual income across individuals or families. Be sure that you can replicate the calculations for the Los Angeles janitorial labor market used as illustrations in this section, and hone your skills in measuring inequality using these three indices by completing the problems at the end of this chapter. The math is simple, and a spreadsheet program almost makes the calculation of these measures of inequality fun!

Trends in Wage Inequality

Now that we have an understanding of the key measures of inequality, we can turn to an examination of changes in the distribution of wages over time. Rising inequality in the U.S. wage distribution and the search for explanations for this development has attracted the attention of many labor economists. But as we will see, the U.S. experience has differed considerably from that seen in many other highly developed economies.

International Comparisons

Data from the Organization for Economic Cooperation and Development (OECD) are sufficient to describe how inequality has changed in the United States and elsewhere. The evolution of wage inequality during the past 30 years in four countries is depicted in Figures 15.4 to 15.7. These graphs show percentile wage differentials, comparing wages at the 90th, 50th, and 10th percentiles, for male and female full-time workers in the United States, the United Kingdom, and Japan over the years from 1979 to 2009 and in France from 1979 to 2007.

Changes in the relative wage of the highest-paid full-time male workers, as measured by the w90/w50 ratio, are described in Figure 15.4. From 1979 to 1989 this measure of the spread between wages of the highest paid workers and wages earned by workers at the middle of the distribution rose by 13.2% in the United States, 14.6% in the United Kingdom, and 10.5% in Japan. The increase in France was less pronounced at 4.4% and in this country the w90/w50 ratio essentially stabilized at around 2.08 from 1999 to 2007. In contrast the w90/w10 ratio continued to rise for the other three countries in the last two decades depicted in Figure 15.4.

Figure 15.5 presents information on changes in the relative position of the lowest-paid full-time male workers, as measured by the w50/w10 ratio. There is a sharper contrast here between developments in the United States and the United Kingdom, on one hand, and trends in France and Japan, on the other. The distance between the wages of the median worker and the wages earned by the lowest wage earners grew by a bit more than 9% in the United States and the United Kingdom from 1979 to 1989 and then by around 1.5% in both countries from 1989 to 2009. In Japan, the w50/w10 ratio rose by 3.8% from 1979 to 1989 but then reversed itself by falling 1.8% from 1989 to 2009. In France the w50/w10 ratio fell steadily over the entire period, indicating that wages at the 10th percentile of the distribution gained relative to the median at a modest pace in this

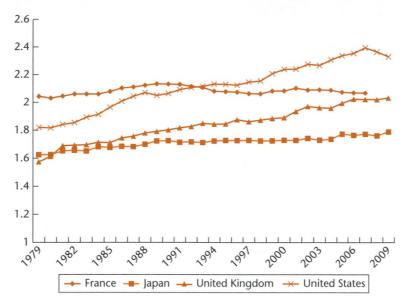

FIGURE 15.4 Wages at the 90th Percentile Relative to the Median Wage, Male Full-Time Workers

Source: http://stats.oecd.org/Index.aspx?DataSetCode=DEC_I.

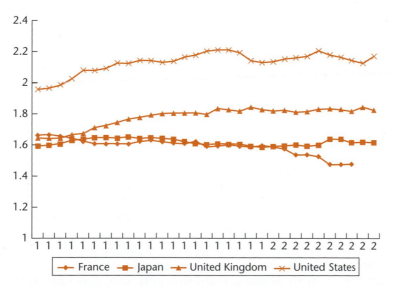

FIGURE 15.5 Median Wages Relative to Wages at the 10th Percentile, Male Full-Time Workers

Source: http://stats.oecd.org/Index.aspx?DataSetCode=DEC_I.

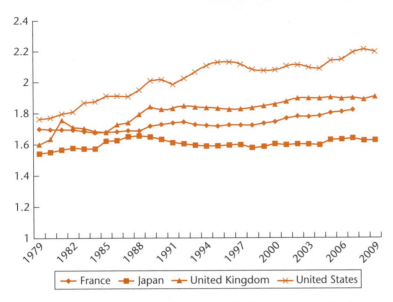

FIGURE 15.6 Wages at the 90th Percentile Relative to the Median Wage, Female Full-Time Workers

Source: http://stats.oecd.org/Index.aspx?DataSetCode=DEC_I.

country. The data for full-time male workers in these four countries indicate that wage spreads rose most rapidly during the decade of the 1980s and that developments since then differ when we compare the top and bottom of the distribution in each country.

Figure 15.6 shows the trend in the w90/w50 ratio for full-time female employees. As was the case for men, the w90/w50 ratio rose steadily in the United States, increasing by 14.2% from 1979 to 1989 and by 9.4% from 1989 to 2009. During the 1980s this ratio in the United Kingdom increased at about the same pace as in the United States but the post-1989 increase was much slower at 3.3%. In Japan, this inequality indicator rose by 7.1% during the 1980s and then fell slightly over the following 20 years. Finally, France saw very little rise in the w90/w50 ratio for women during the 1980s but then saw an increase of 6.4% from 1999 to 2007.

Finally, Figure 15.7 illustrates changes in the w50/w10 ratio for women. Again, the spread between the wages of the median female employee and the wages earned by the lowest-paid workers rose substantially in the United States and the United Kingdom, increasing by 20.4% and 12.6%, respectively, from 1979 to 2009, with the bulk of the change occurring in the 1980s. The w50/w10 ratio hardly budged for Japanese women during the 1980s but then rose by 5.6% from 1989 to 2009. In France this index rose by 3.8% from 1979 to 1989 and then fell sharply from 1989 to 2007.

The general conclusion from all of this is that wage inequality generally rose in these four countries during the 1980s but the pattern of change after that was more complex. In the United Kingdom and in the United States there was an increase in inequality over the entire 30-year period that was fairly large and encompassed a rise in the wages of the top-paid workers relative to the median and a fall in the wages of the poorest-paid workers relative to the median. In Japan the rise in inequality was less pronounced and mainly

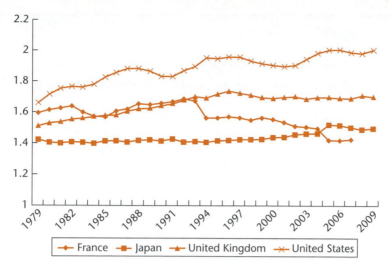

FIGURE 15.7 Median Wages Relative to Wages at the 10th Percentile, Female Full-Time Workers

Source: http://stats.oecd.org/Index.aspx?DataSetCode=DEC_I.

reflected an increase in the relative earnings of high-wage workers. In France wage inequality increased during the 1980s and then reversed its trend movement for men and for the lowest paid women while the w90/w50 ratio for women rose slowly over the entire period.

This conclusion from a look at recent trends in four countries is similar to the findings from a more comprehensive examination of new data on changes in the earnings distribution across 20 OECD countries from 1965 to 2005.[4] This study found no evidence for a general rise in wage inequality, particularly for those at the low end of the wage distribution. However, in many countries the w90/w50 ratio rose substantially. This was especially true for the United Kingdom, the United States, Australia, New Zealand, Germany, and Italy.

What's Different About the United States?

The United States stands out in international comparisons of wage inequality. First, by the end of the 1980s, the United States had a substantially less equal distribution of earnings than did other industrialized countries. This is seen quite clearly in the Luxembourg Income Study database, which allows for fair comparisons between countries by carefully adjusting national currencies for differences in purchasing power related both to price levels and exchange rates. Table 15.3 shows information from one study using these data for seven countries.

---

[4] Anthony B. Atkinson, "The Distribution of Earnings in OECD Countries," *International Labour Review* 146 (2007): 41–60.

AROUND THE WORLD

Changes in Inequality during Chile's "Economic Miracle"

Chile has often been cited as a model for developing countries of the favorable patterns of growth and development they might achieve by adopting market-oriented policies favoring free trade and private enterprise. The return to democratic government after the military dictatorship of General Pinochet brought commitment to maintaining the growth policies he formulated but, in addition, concern over the distributional consequences of the free market economy.

A World Bank study* of household surveys carried out in 1987, 1990, 1992, and 1994 gives us a detailed examination of the evolution of inequality and poverty in Chile during the final years of Pinochet's regime and the first few years under democratic government. The data suggest that inequality and poverty fell significantly from 1987 to 1994. Some highlights are:

- From 1987 to 1994 the average real earnings of workers in the poorest 10% of families rose by 58%, and the average real earnings of workers in the richest 10% of families increased by 53%.
- The Gini coefficient for household income, defined to include all earnings, cash transfers, imputed rents on owner-occupied housing, and gifts, fell from 0.547 in 1987 to 0.530 in 1994. Despite this decrease, income inequality in Chile was still much higher than was typical in the mid-1990s in South America.
- The percentage of people in households with household income less than 120,400 pesos a year, twice the cost of a standard food basket, fell from 40.7% in 1987 to 23.1% in 1994.

While economic growth and development have continued to reduce poverty and inequality in Chile since 1994, student protests and political demands increasingly focused on these issues during 2011 and 2012. Concerns about inequality in education leading to inequality in wages and incomes have led politicians to consider reforms to the market-oriented policies followed by Chile's governments for the past 20 years.**

Notes: *"Chile: Poverty and Income Distribution in a High-Growth Economy," *World Bank Report*, No. 16372-CH, November 25, 1997.
**"Progress and its Discontents," *The Economist*, April 14, 2012.

In Table 15.3 real wages at the 10th, 50th, and 90th percentiles in each country are expressed as a fraction of the real wage at the 50th percentile in the United States, allowing for a direct comparison of inequality among these economies. Even though the median real earnings level in all countries is lower than that in the United States, the earnings of workers at the 10th percentile in each country is higher relative to the U.S. median than it is for American workers. The clear implication is that workers at the 10th percentile in the United States receive much lower relative wages than do workers at the 10th percentile in the other countries. At the same time, U.S. workers at the 90th percentile earn relative wages that are substantially higher than similar workers in other countries. Among these

TABLE 15.3   International Comparisons of Wage Inequality

Country	10th percentile earnings/U.S. median	50th percentile earnings/U.S. median	90th percentile earnings/U.S. median
Netherlands, 1987	0.51	0.72	1.24
Germany, 1984	0.51	0.79	1.28
Australia, 1989–90	0.51	0.90	1.44
United Kingdom, 1986	0.42	0.69	1.30
Sweden, 1992	0.41	0.84	1.40
Canada, 1987	0.35	0.92	1.61
United States, 1991	0.34	1.00	1.93

Source: Peter Gottschalk and Timothy M. Smeeding, "Cross-National Comparisons of Earnings and Income Inequality," *Journal of Economic Literature* 35 (1997): 633–687.

seven countries, only Canada has a level of overall earnings inequality that is in the U.S. ballpark; the European countries all have much smaller wage spreads between their highest and lowest earners.

While the comparisons in Table 15.3 are dated as of the late 1980s or early 1990s depending on the country involved, our discussion of inequality trends thus far in this chapter gives us no reason to expect that the conclusions drawn from that data have changed materially in the last decade or two. Indeed, a second distinguishing characteristic about U.S. performance, amply illustrated in Figures 15.4 through 15.7, is that this country experienced a rapid increase in wage inequality during the decade of the 1980s and that increases in the w90/w50 and w50/w10 ratios continued, albeit at a more moderate pace for the latter ratio, from 1989 to 2009. Only the United Kingdom experienced a rise in wage inequality of a magnitude and pattern similar to that in the United States. So the data on wage ratios across countries presented in Table 15.3 show that there were substantially higher wage disparities in the United States than in the other countries in the table at about the midpoint of a period of steadily rising wage disparities in the United States. As we examine various factors that economists believe are driving changes in wage inequality, carefully consider how each in turn can help account for the differences between the United States and other countries.

Other Aspects of Rising Wage Inequality

Our discussion of trends thus far has focused on percentile wage differentials as the index of inequality. Like our example of the labor market for janitors in Los Angeles, studies using the Gini coefficient and the variance of the logarithm of real wages also show evidence of rising wage disparity during the past 20 years in the United States and in other countries. Among the major world economies, only Germany and Italy experienced no perceptible increase in wage inequality during the 1980s. Researchers have identified several reasons for this major change in labor market performance around the world: wage structure changes, increased skill differentials, rising within-group inequality, and industrial and demographic changes.

Wage Structure Changes

Because most of the data used to analyze wage inequality comes from surveys of workers, it is possible that the measured increase in inequality reflects changes in the number of hours worked, the incidence of multiple job-holding, or other labor supply characteristics. However, it appears that the increase in inequality is due mainly to changes in the distribution of hourly wages and represents a change in the wage structure. Thus the changes in wage inequality we have observed can be traced to changes in the price paid by employers for an hour of various types of labor in the labor market.

Increased Skill Differentials

There is very strong evidence of rising wage differentials for skilled workers relative to unskilled workers.[5] This can be seen most dramatically in the rise in the wage difference between U.S. workers with a college degree and those with only a high school diploma. Figure 15.8 demonstrates this good news for the typical reader of this text. The wage advantage for young men with a college degree rose by about 41% between 1980 and 2009, and the wage premium for young college-educated female workers rose by 33%. Along with rising relative wages, the employment of college-educated workers has also increased as a fraction of the overall workforce. This suggests that there has been an increase in the demand for these workers in the United States relative to supply.

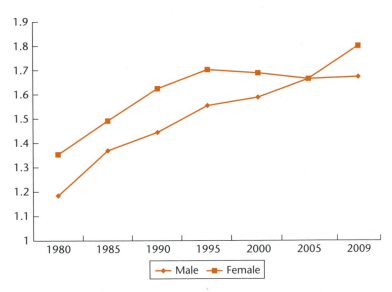

FIGURE 15.8 U.S. Median Annual Earnings of College Graduates Relative to Earnings of High School Graduates, Ages 25–34

Source: National Center for Education Statistics at: http://nces.ed.gov/programs/coe/tables/table-er2-1.asp.

---

[5] Moshe Buchinsky, "Changes in the U.S. Wage Structure 1963–1987: Application of Quantile Regression," *Econometrica* 62 (1994): 405–458; Richard J. Murnane, John B. Willett, and Frank Levy, "The Growing Importance of Cognitive Skills in Wage Determination," *Review of Economics and Statistics* 77 (1995): 251–266.

This supply-demand explanation for rising educational premiums is seen in data for other countries as well. Since 1980 demand growth has exceeded the increase in the supply of college-educated workers in Australia, Canada, Japan, Sweden, the United Kingdom, and the United States. As a result, the college wage premium rose in every case but for Japan, where it was unchanged. In the Netherlands, however, the increase in supply of college-educated workers outstripped demand growth during the 1980s with a resulting decrease in the college wage premium.

Recent studies of the United States and the United Kingdom indicate that over the last three decades young people have generally increased their skill levels but that the distribution of skills among them has become more uneven.[6] In particular, the least skilled individuals appear to have fallen behind those in the middle and upper reaches of the distribution in terms of their rate of skill augmentation since the early 1980s. This suggests that there will be a further increase in wage inequality due to increased inequality in worker skills over the coming decade or so.

Rising Within-Group Inequality

Inequality has risen among workers with the same level of education and experience and among workers in the same occupation and locality. The rise in between-group inequality started in most countries around 1980, but the increase in within-group inequality started in the late 1960s or early 1970s. Some have suggested that this reflects a rising demand for skilled workers because the measures of skill we generally can observe, such as education or experience, do not encompass the full range of skills that are of value to employers.[7] Under this interpretation, increases in wage inequality among college graduates would be due to increased demand for the most able among them. Still this rise in within-group inequality represents something of a mystery to most labor economists who have studied the wage inequality issue.

Industrial and Demographic Changes

The earliest studies of rising inequality, which appeared in the mid-1980s, placed great emphasis on industrial change as the cause of what was referred to as "The Great U-turn." The argument was that deindustrialization resulted in a shift in the job composition away from middle-income jobs and toward low-wage jobs. It is somewhat surprising, then, that changes in the industrial mix have been found to have little impact on the rise in wage disparity in the United States.[8] It also appears to be the case that the changing racial and gender composition of the workforce has not been an important determinant

---

[6] Joseph G. Altonji, Prachant Bharadwaj, and Fabian Lange, "Changes in the Characteristics of American Youth: Implications for Adult Outcomes," *NBER Working Paper 13883*, 2008; Geraint Johnes, "Changes in the Characteristics and Skills of British Youth," *Economics Bulletin* 29 (2009): 368–374.

[7] Chinhui Juhn, Kevin M. Murphy, and Brooks Pierce, "Wage Inequality and the Rise in Returns to Skill," *Journal of Political Economy* 101 (1993): 410–442.

[8] Kevin M. Murphy and Finis Welch, "The Structure of Wages," *The Quarterly Journal of Economics* 106 (1992): 285–326.

of increased pay inequality.[9] Wages have become less equally distributed within all industries and demographic groups in a way that accounts for the relative unimportance of shifts among these categories of workers in understanding the wage inequality trend.

Causes of Increased Wage Inequality

The rise in wage inequality has attracted considerable attention from labor economists in recent years, and a large number of empirical studies have emerged both in the United States and in the rest of the world. Economists have focused on the reasons for the substantial rise in the relative wages and employment of skilled workers. The data suggest that wage inequality has risen because the average wage of skilled workers has gone up in comparison with the average wage of unskilled workers, where skill is measured by education level, amount of experience, or occupation. In addition, among workers of a given measurable skill level (e.g., college graduates), the wages of the best workers have risen relative to the wages of average workers. Even the most sophisticated studies of these types of relative wage changes use a very simple supply and demand model as the theoretical basis for interpreting empirical results.

A Relative Supply and Demand Model

The type of supply and demand model useful for thinking about relative wage changes is shown in Figure 15.9. On the vertical axis the wage of skilled workers is divided by the wage of unskilled workers, and this ratio is identified as r_w, which could be the average

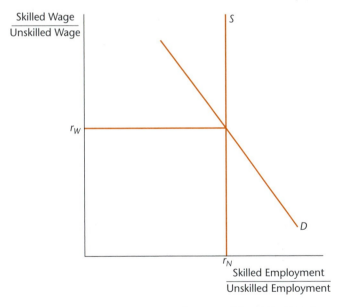

FIGURE 15.9 Relative Supply and Demand for Skilled Workers

[9] Mark E. Schweitzer, "Workforce Composition and Earnings Inequality, Federal Reserve Bank of Cleveland," *Economic Review* 33 (1997): 13–24.

wage of college-educated workers divided by the average wage of high school graduates. Alternatively, r_w might be calculated as the wage of college graduates at the 90th percentile of the college wage distribution divided by the wage of college graduates at the 10th percentile. The horizontal axis represents the number of skilled workers employed in a given time period divided by the number of unskilled workers hired in that period.

The demand curve in this model is downward sloping with respect to r_w. If skilled workers became cheaper for employers to hire in comparison with unskilled workers, the model predicts that employers would substitute skilled for unskilled workers on the job. The key idea here is that skilled workers are more productive than unskilled workers in all jobs and that the productivity advantage of skilled workers increases as jobs become more complex. Of course some jobs are so complex that only skilled workers will be hired to do them. There are also likely to be some jobs for which skilled workers are deemed to be "overqualified"; these jobs will be open only to the unskilled. Because jobs vary in complexity and employers face a problem of matching job openings with applicants with various and imperfectly observed qualifications, the relative demand curve may be quite inelastic in the short run. The uncertainty involved in this matching problem is likely to make employers reluctant to attempt to substitute less skilled for more skilled workers even in the face of higher relative wages for skilled employees.

The supply curve is also likely to be completely inelastic in the short run because it takes time, energy, and money to acquire skills. In the long run, however, people will have time to respond to the financial returns to skills; therefore, we might expect the long-run relative supply curve to be quite flat. Indeed, if there were absolutely no impediments to acquiring the skills needed to enter the labor market, we might draw the long-run relative supply curve as a horizontal line at the value for r_w that was just high enough to make the marginal worker indifferent between the skilled and unskilled job.

The intersection of demand and supply serves to determine an equilibrium value for r_w and for the relative skill composition of the workforce. Changes in the equilibrium value of r_w are traced to the net effect of shifts in the relative demand and supply curves. In the case of the rise in the relative wage of college-educated workers in the United States and elsewhere, we can observe an increase in r_w accompanying an increase in the fraction of the workforce with a college degree and infer that there must have been a large enough increase in relative demand to outstrip the effect of the increase in relative supply on wages.

The relative demand and supply model leads to the following equation used by George Johnson to explain relative wage growth:[10]

$$\%\Delta r_w = (\%\Delta D - \%\Delta S)/\sigma \tag{15-5}$$

Here the percentage change in the relative wage rate ($\%\Delta r_w$) is determined by the elasticity of substitution (σ), the percentage change in the position of the relative demand curve ($\%\Delta D$), and the percentage change in the position of the relative supply curve ($\%\Delta S$).[11] Assuming that the value of σ is 1.5, Johnson then calculates the percentage shift in

---

[10] George E. Johnson, "Changes in Earnings Inequality: The Role of Demand Shifts," *Journal of Economic Perspectives* 11 (1997): 41–54.

[11] It is convenient to divide the U.S. workforce into college-educated and high-school-educated segments by allocating those with "some college" to both groups.

TABLE 15.4   Shifts in Labor Demand and Labor Supply for Skilled and Unskilled Workers, and Their Effects on the Relative Wage

Period	$\%\Delta r_w$	$\%\Delta D$	$\%\Delta S$
1963 to 1970	0.8	3.6	2.3
1970 to 1979	−0.7	3.7	4.8
1979 to 1989	1.3	4.7	2.7
1989 to 1993	1.1	5.0	3.3

Source: George E. Johnson, "Changes in Earnings Inequality: The Role of Demand Shifts," *Journal of Economic Perspectives* 11 (1997): 41–54.

demand that would generate the observed percentage change in r_w given the known rate of growth in the relative supply of college workers. His results are shown in Table 15.4.

These calculations lead to the conclusion that both the relative demand curve and the relative supply curve for college-educated workers have been steadily shifting to the right in the United States since the 1960s. The decade of the 1970s was characterized by a larger rightward shift in supply than demand as baby boomers went to college and graduated; this caused r_w to fall by 0.7% during that decade. In the 1980s, however, demand growth accelerated and supply growth slowed, causing a sharp increase in relative wage growth. This situation continued into the early years of the 1990s.

Work by Autor et al. (2008) extends this analysis to 2005, reaching very similar conclusions.[12] They estimate a value of $\sigma = 1.57$, quite close to the value used by Johnson, and find that the trend toward increased relative demand for more highly educated workers offset the continued rise in the college-educated fraction of the workforce to push relative wages higher. They do note a slowdown in the growth rate of relative demand for college-educated workers after 1992.

This analysis suggests that we can look for an explanation for rising wage inequality driven by increases in the wage advantage going to the most skilled workers to factors causing the relative demand for skilled workers to shift to the right faster than the relative supply of skilled workers.

Causes of Shifts in Demand for Skilled Workers

Two main causes of the rising demand for skilled labor have been emphasized in the literature: international trade and technological change. International trade has caused a decrease in the demand for low-skill workers that has, in effect, shifted the relative demand curve for skilled workers to the right. And technological change, perhaps related to the widespread use of computers, has led to an increase in the complexity of jobs and the substitution of more skilled for low-skilled workers in filling those jobs.

---

[12] David H. Autor, Lawrence F. Katz, and Melissa S. Kearney, "Trends in U.S. Wage Inequality: Revising the Revisionists," *Review of Economics and Statistics* 90 (2008): 300–323.

International Trade

During the 1980s the volume of trade between developed countries and less developed countries expanded rapidly as general tariffs and other restraints on trade were relaxed. In addition, less developed countries abandoned import substitution policies and opened their economies to trade in the hope that exports would become the engine of development. Finally, multinational companies took advantage of new opportunities to outsource production to regions of the world with lower costs. The net effect of these trade-related developments is hypothesized to be a decrease in the demand for low-skill workers in the developed world as consumers substitute the products of low-skill workers in less developed countries for the products of low-skill domestic workers. This hypothesized effect of trade on workers in developed countries has remained an important factor in public policy debates and political elections.

A number of empirical studies tested the hypothesis that trade, in particular trade with less developed countries, was an important determinant of the rise in wage inequality during the 1980s. In most of these studies, however, the identified trade effect was quite small.[13] Breau and Rigby found that trade with emerging economies was correlated with lower relative wages for less-educated Canadian workers and that this effect was more pronounced in labor-intensive industrial and geographic labor markets.[14] In an interesting study, Guy Michaels examined the effect on rural U.S. labor markets of increased internal and international trade resulting from the completion of the interstate highway system in the early 1970s.[15] He found that increased trade raised the relative demand for skilled workers in localities with a more highly skilled workforce and lowered the relative demand for skilled workers in areas with a low-skilled workforce. While this result supports one key hypothesis for the effects of trade in the relative demand and supply model, Michaels also finds that these effects are too small to explain much of the observed change in the relative wage of skilled workers.

In large developed economies, the sectors affected by trade are quite small relative to the sectors that do not face much import competition, but wage inequality has risen among workers in all industries and occupations, regardless of their sensitivity to imports. And the relative demand for college-educated workers has been rising faster than the relative supply in most countries throughout the post–World War II era and only accelerated slightly during the 1980s when trade expanded the most.

Technological Change

Many economists believe technological change is the primary determinant of shifts in the relative demand for highly skilled workers, even though the difficulty of measuring technology makes it hard to document such an effect. During the 1980s a number of developments lent plausibility to the technology explanation. First, the sharp decrease in the cost

---

[13] George J. Borjas, Richard B. Freeman, and Lawrence F. Katz, "How Much Do Immigration and Trade Affect Labor Market Outcomes?" *Brookings Papers on Economic Activity* (1997): 1–67.

[14] Sebastien Breau and David L. Rigby, "International Trade and Wage Inequality in Canada," *Journal of Economic Geography* 10 (2010): 55–86.

[15] Guy Michaels, "The Effect of Trade on the Demand for Skill: Evidence from the Interstate Highway System," *Review of Economics and Statistics* 90 (2008): 683–701.

of computing power led to widespread adoption of computers in the production process for all goods and services. This raised the demand for computer programmers, systems analysts, and engineers. Information technology has also increased the complexity of many jobs, which can now be done only by workers with sufficient computer skills. Another type of technological change has been the reorganization of the workplace. One such change, often in response to downsizing, is to shift some of the responsibilities for quality control and scheduling from supervisors to production workers, thereby increasing the complexity of those jobs.

Changes in the relative wage and employment of skilled workers in manufacturing industries are closely correlated with such technical change measures as capital investment, research and development spending, and computer intensity.[16] Workers who use computers at work have been found to earn substantially higher wages than those who don't use computers, and the adoption of computer technology can explain a large part of the interindustry differences in changes in the employment of skilled workers.[17]

The debate about the relative importance of globalization and technology change in driving the relative demand for skilled workers is still alive. Yet Stephen Machin and John Van Reenen's empirical analysis of skill upgrading in seven countries indicates that this phenomenon is very closely correlated with measures of technical change.[18] And recent work suggests that the foreign trade effect on relative wages may well be due to trade-induced technical change.[19] A study of changes in the skill composition of work in transition economies reveals that upgrades to the production process and new quality control methods were significant determinants of the decrease in the employment shares of unskilled workers in Hungary, Romania, and Russia.[20]

However, recent work by Card and DiNardo raises questions about the importance of skill-biased technological change as a determinant of skill-related wage differentials.[21] Their argument focuses on timing—while technological changes associated with information technology has proceeded apace, much of the rise in the relative wage of college educated workers occurred in the early 1980s—and on a very strong correlation between relative wages and the inflation-adjusted minimum wage. Atkinson countered this argument by pointing out that relative supply shifts could obscure the effect of technological change on relative wages and that evidence for a large number of developed countries showed relative

[16] Eli Berman, John Bound, and Zvi Griliches, "Changes in the Demand for Skilled Labor Within U.S. Manufacturing: Evidence from the Annual Survey of Manufacturers," *Quarterly Journal of Economics* 109 (1994): 367–397.

[17] Alan B. Krueger, "How Computers Have Changed the Wage Structure: Evidence from Microdata, 1984–1989," *Quarterly Journal of Economics* 108 (1993): 33–60; David H. Autor, Lawrence F. Katz, and Alan B. Krueger, "Computing Inequality: Have Computers Changed the Labor Market?" *Quarterly Journal of Economics* 113 (1998): 1169–1213; Peter Dolton and Gerry Makepeace, "Computer Use and Earnings in Britain," *Economic Journal* 114 (2004): C117–C129.

[18] Stephen Machin and John Van Reenen, "Technology and Changes in Skill Structure: Evidence from Seven OECD Countries," *Quarterly Journal of Economics* 12 (1998): 1215–1244.

[19] Roberto A. DeSantis, "Wage Inequality Between and Within Groups: Trade-Induced or Skill-Bias Technical Change? Alternative AGE Models for the U.K.," *Economic Modeling* 19 (2002): 725–746.

[20] Simon Commander and Janos Kollo, "The Changing Demand for Skills: Evidence from the Transition," *Economics of Transition* 16 (2008): 199–221.

[21] David Card and John E. DiNardo, "Skill-Biased Technological Changes and Rising Wage Inequality: Some Problems and Puzzles," *Journal of Labor Economics* 20 (2002): 733–783.

wage increases at the upper end of the distribution dominated those at the lower end of the distribution where, presumably, minimum wages would have the biggest effect.[22]

Autor et al. offer a slightly more complex explanation of the effect of technological change, suggesting that information technology in particular raises the demand for the most highly educated workers engaged in abstract tasks, reduces demand for those with slightly less education whose jobs involve more routine tasks, and has a small effect on the demand for the least-skilled workers.[23] This approach shifts the role of technological change to explaining mainly the observed increases in the w90/w50 ratio, which have continued to the present, rather than the w50/w10 ratio, which increased the most during the 1980s.

Changes in Labor Market Institutions

Labor market institutions, such as trade unions, government regulations, and internal labor markets, often have an important effect on wage setting and the level of employment. So we need to supplement our supply and demand shifts discussion of the causes of the rise in wage inequality with an analysis of the effects of changes in institutions. The labor market effects of technological change, international trade, college education, and immigration are likely to be similar in many countries, so differences in labor market institutions may be critical to explaining the differences we have seen in the level and change in pay inequality across developed countries. Particular attention has been focused on minimum wage policy and the role of collective bargaining as the main institutional factors determining wage inequality.

Changes in Minimum Wages

By effectively putting a floor on the market wage level, a minimum wage pushes up the lower boundary of the wage distribution, increasing the wages received by workers at the lower percentiles of the distribution. This effect of the minimum wage on the distribution of wages can be seen in Figure 15.2, which graphs the wage distributions in Canada and the United States for 1981 and 1988 and indicates the level of the real minimum wage. In both Canada and the United States, the minimum wage fell from 1981 to 1988 as legislated changes in the nominal minimum wage failed to keep up with inflation. The effect of the decline in the real minimum wage in both countries was to make the lower tail of the distribution "thicker." That is, the percentage of workers receiving the lowest real wage levels increased.

This effect of the minimum wage on pay disparity helps explain the differences in inequality between the United States, which led the developed world in increased pay inequality during the 1980s, and Canada, which had a much smaller rise in inequality. The decline in the real minimum wage between 1981 and 1988 was 23% in the United States and 12% in Canada, and we can see in the graphs that the thickening of the lower tail of the wage distribution was much more pronounced in the United States. The differences between these two countries in the real minimum wage can account for as much as 20% of the difference in the level of inequality and 34% of the difference in the growth of inequality between Canada and the United States during the 1980s.

---

[22] Anthony B. Atkinson, "The Distribution of Earnings in OECD Countries," *International Labour Review* 146 (2007): 41–60.

[23] David H. Autor, Lawrence F. Katz, and Melissa S. Kearney, "Trends in U.S. Wage Inequality: Revising the Revisionists," *Review of Economics and Statistics* 90 (2008): 300–323.

Other studies have also found that the minimum wage is an important determinant of wage inequality. In France, for example, the real minimum wage increased throughout the 1980s. Unlike the situation in the United States or the United Kingdom, the wage gap in France between the median male worker and the worker at the 10th percentile became progressively smaller during the period from 1979 to 1995. There is also evidence that minimum wage policies helped prop up the wage of 10th percentile workers in Belgium, Finland, and Germany. In the United States the minimum wage was found to be particularly important in explaining the sharp rise in wage disparity among female workers.

Unlike the evidence on international trade or technology, there is considerable agreement with the notion that a policy of allowing a substantial erosion of the real value of the minimum wage, which was the policy followed in the United States during the 1980s, will result in an increase in the w50/w10 ratio and an increase in overall wage inequality. Of course, as we saw in Chapter 9, minimum wage policy decisions have to consider potential employment effects as well as wage distribution effects.

Changes in Collective Bargaining

Empirical research has determined that one effect of trade union activity through collective bargaining is a reduction in wage disparity. As we saw in Chapter 12, the positive effect of union coverage on wages is significantly more pronounced for lower skilled workers, and union wage policies may spill over to nonunion firms. In the United States, the United Kingdom, and several other countries, union membership and contract coverage declined sharply during the 1980s, partly as a result of economic change and partly as a result of government policy. It is not surprising, then, that many analysts point to the decline in unionization as an explanation for rising wage inequality and that differences in collective bargaining trends help explain differences in wage inequality across countries.[24]

In countries like Germany, where labor agreements are centrally negotiated and automatically extended to all employers in a region or industry, the rise in inequality has been minimal. In contrast, in the United States and the United Kingdom, the erosion of trade union influence has been substantial in the last two decades, and they top the standings of countries ranked by increases in wage inequality. Although some observers question whether union effects on the wage distribution are independent or merely reflections of underlying market developments, the evidence seems to consistently show a close correlation between low/declining unionization rates and high/rising wage inequality.

Another aspect of the decline in collective bargaining in the United States, along with organizational changes to reduce the middle ranks of the managerial hierarchy, is a rise in the fraction of workers receiving at least part of their pay as bonuses linked to their individual or unit productivity. According to one study, this fraction increased from 38% in the late 1970s to 45% in the early 1990s in the United States, and this rise in the use of performance-related pay could account for about a fifth of the increase in the variance of male wages in that period.[25] Enhanced wage rewards for individual performance eliminate

---

[24] Richard B. Freeman, "Labor Market Institutions and Earnings Inequality," *New England Economic Review* (1996): 157–168.

[25] Thomas LeMieux, W. Bentley MacLeod, and Daniel Parent, "Performance Pay and Wage Inequality," *The Quarterly Journal of Economics* 124 (2009): 1–49.

the wage equalizing influence of equal pay raises and rigid wage structures commonly seen in union contracts and organizations with well-defined job hierarchies.

The Effect of Unemployment Rates

One factor that has not had much attention in the analysis of wage disparity is the role of unemployment, even though the unemployment experience in the United States and Europe was unusually severe during the period of rising inequality. In the United States, unemployment rates rose to post–World War II highs during the early 1980s, the unemployment rates of blue-collar workers relative to white-collar employees remained high for most of the 1980s, and the recovery from the 1990–1991 recession was unusually prolonged. In Europe, unemployment rates increased steadily during the 1980s to post–World War II highs in many countries and stubbornly resisted efforts to lower them during the first half of the 1990s.

Some have argued that the trend in wage disparity has been so dominant that cyclical factors don't appear to have played much of a role. However, one of our own research projects found a significant correlation between wage inequality and the level of unemployment in U.S. labor markets, controlling for other factors associated with inequality. In addition, the impact of local unemployment rates was equivalent to the effect of decreases in the real minimum wage and union contract coverage in terms of its relative importance as an inequality determinant.[26] Also, news reports indicate that the sharp drop in unemployment rates during the late 1990s resulted in the first significant increases in real wages for low-wage earners in decades.[27] Further study to determine how much of the increased wage inequality reflects long-lasting structural changes in the labor market and how much is due to more temporary and reversible changes in unemployment is needed.

This brief review of a large and growing literature is sufficient to outline an explanation for rising wage inequality that is consistent with the logic of the relative supply and demand model of the labor market for skilled workers and with much of the empirical evidence presented by labor economists. Wages have been rising most rapidly at the high-wage end of the distribution during the last three decades largely because technological change has caused employers to seek out the most able workers to fill increasingly complex jobs. Wages are rising more slowly or falling at the low-wage end of the distribution because technological change and import competition coupled, perhaps, with an influx of immigrants have made the least skilled workers less competitive in the labor market. The wages of the least skilled are also adversely affected by the declining importance of the minimum wage and collective bargaining and by periods of high unemployment. As we turn our attention to **income inequality** and poverty, be sure you can use a simple supply and demand graph (see Figure 15.9) to explain how the factors discussed here could lead to increased wage inequality by increasing the wage spread between the most-skilled and least-skilled workers.

---

[26] Thomas Hyclak, *Rising Wage Inequality: The 1980s Experience in Urban Labor Markets* (Kalamazoo: W. E. Upjohn Institute, 2000).

[27] Louis Uchitelle, "Raises Arrive at Bottom Rung of Labor Force," *New York Times,* May 23, 1997.

From Wage Inequality to Income Inequality

Turning our attention to income inequality requires a shift in emphasis from the previous discussion of wage inequality. Wages are paid to individuals, so we usually measure inequality across those individuals; and our examination of the wage distribution analyzes the structure of wages paid to the holders of different jobs. When we look at the distribution of income or the rates of poverty, we examine the economic well-being of individuals or families. Although the degree of pay disparity across jobs is an important determinant of the degree of disparity in living standards across families, this shift in emphasis toward well-being raises several important measurement issues.

Earnings Mobility

The measurement of wage inequality typically is done on a year-by-year basis using cross-sectional data for each year as the basis for measurement. This is sufficient if we are analyzing changes in the structure of wages across jobs from year to year. In thinking about the distribution of well-being across individual workers or their families, however, this year-by-year approach to measuring inequality may be misleading if there is sufficient earnings mobility. **Earnings mobility** refers to the movement of individual workers up and down the wage distribution as they change jobs during their working careers. If there were substantial earnings mobility and we were able to measure the degree of inequality of lifetime earnings for a sample of workers, we might get a radically different picture of the level and trend in inequality than we would from a series of year-by-year measures of the degree of annual income inequality for the same sample of workers.

A few studies have used longitudinal databases (panel data), which collect data from the same sample of workers for several years in a row, to estimate the relationship between annual earnings inequality, earnings mobility, and inequality measured over longer time horizons of several years. A survey of this research[28] found the following:

1. Annual earnings inequality indexes overstate lifetime earnings inequality because many low-wage workers do not remain low-wage workers for their entire career.
2. Longitudinal databases present problems in measuring lifetime inequality because subjects drop out of the sample in a nonrandom way, and the inevitable reporting errors on wages and other data are amplified over time.
3. Earnings mobility is highest among young workers at the beginning of their careers and is more prominent the longer the time period covered by the data.
4. Two-thirds of the measured annual earnings inequality represents persistent, long-run (lifetime?) differences in relative earnings among workers. This finding is remarkably consistent across countries.

Studies have found no significant change in earnings mobility during the period of rising wage inequality; therefore, increases in annual earnings inequality must have been accompanied by similar changes in hard-to-measure lifetime earnings inequality. In one such study, the United States and United Kingdom, with very high rates of wage

---

[28] Anthony B. Atkinson, François Bourguignon, and Christian Morrison, *Empirical Studies of Earnings Mobility* (Philadelphia, PA: Harwood Academic Publishers, 1992).

AROUND THE WORLD

Comparing Intergenerational Income Mobility

The statistics usually used to examine earnings and income distributions help us see the degree of inequality in a given place at a given time and allow us to compare inequality in different places and/or times. But we need studies of earnings and income mobility to see if people who are in one part of the distribution today tend to stay there or if they tend to move up or down the distribution over time. A high level of wage inequality might be more socially acceptable if it were accompanied by a high rate of upward mobility.

An important question is how much mobility there is from one generation to the next. With longitudinal data, intergenerational mobility can be measured by estimating the elasticity of the child's earnings with respect to his or her parents' earnings (often measured by father's earnings). Values close to zero would suggest high mobility, since the child's earnings would be independent of the parent's in this case; and values close to one would suggest low mobility, with the child's earnings (and position in the earnings distribution) the same as the parent's.

A number of studies have attempted to estimate this elasticity for many different countries. The results generally show values of around 0.4 to 0.5 for the United States and Great Britain, 0.2 to 0.3 for Germany, and 0.1 to 0.2 for Sweden and Finland. Studies that explicitly compare intergenerational earnings elasticities for the United States and other countries generally find higher values for the former, although the U.S and U.K. estimates are usually quite similar. Not only is there greater earnings inequality in the United States than in Europe, but these results suggest there is also a greater chance that the children of low-wage American workers will also have low earnings when they are adults.

Note: Gary Solon, "Cross-Country Differences in Intergenerational Earning Mobility," *Journal of Economic Perspectives* 16 (2002): 59–66.

inequality, had earnings mobility measures comparable to those in Germany or Italy, with low and stable inequality indexes.[29] This implies that international comparisons of annual earnings inequality are relevant also for lifetime earnings inequality, at least for large, highly developed economies.

Measuring Inequality in Living Standards

Another serious difficulty in examining the disparity in income across individuals, households, or families as a measurement of well-being is finding a monetary equivalent of living standards. The ideal measure, known as the **Haig-Simons concept**, is the real value of

---

[29] "Earnings Inequality, Low-Paid Employment and Earnings Mobility," *OECD Employment Outlook* (July 1996): 59–108.

goods and services consumed, including the consumption of leisure time and public goods, plus or minus changes in net worth (the value of assets owned minus debt owed by the living unit). However, the difficulty in accurately measuring consumption means that most practical approaches focus instead on disposable income, which is income after taxes and transfer payments available for consumers to spend or save. Even here there are two important measurement concerns:

1. Disposable income before taxes and transfers includes income receipts from nonlabor sources (rents, interest payments, dividends, and profits) in addition to wage and salary income. To correspond closely with the Haig-Simons measure, disposable income should also include capital gains, imputed rents from home ownership, the value of goods and services produced in the home, and the value of leisure time. This is seldom done in practice.
2. Disposable income after taxes and transfers is usually calculated by subtracting income and payroll taxes from earned income and adding income transfers. In-kind transfers, if included in the transfer adjustment, are valued at the cost of provision rather than the value to the household, and adjustments for indirect taxes paid and the value of public goods consumed are not usually made.

The income data usually available from government sources to measure income inequality are therefore an approximation of the ideal data necessary to measure the standard of living of a person, a family, or a household. Inequality in available data on disposable income can be measured with the Gini coefficient, percentile income ratios, or the variance of the logarithm of income, just as with wage inequality.

The Recipient Unit

Another measurement question concerns the recipient of income. Should we measure income inequality across individuals, households, or families? A household is defined as a group of individuals residing together, and a family is a group of individuals related by birth or marriage who are living together. To cover the entire population, individuals residing alone can be classified as single-person households or families. Typically we focus on the relative well-being of families because we are often more concerned about the number of children living below the poverty line than we are about the poverty status of individual workers or nonworking adult family heads.

When studying income inequality across households or families, we must decide whether to adjust the data to reflect possible economies of scale or scope in consumption. These adjustments would acknowledge that larger families may be able to consume a greater quantity of goods and services or a greater variety of goods and services for the same income as that for a smaller family. Assumptions about the equivalence scales used to adjust for the presence of such economies can make a big difference in estimates of the level of income inequality, but they don't appear to affect trends in inequality.

Trends in Income Inequality

Wages and salaries account for 70 to 75% of household income from all sources. Therefore, it would not be surprising to find that indexes of income inequality for developed economies followed trends during recent years similar to the trends we observed for wage inequality measures. This is indeed the case. Figure 15.10 shows Gini coefficients of U.S. household income from 1979 to 2003. These data from the U.S. Department of Commerce are designed to measure inequality using income definitions that come close to the ideal measure of household living standards. The line designated *Before Taxes* shows the Gini coefficient of income from all sources, including capital gains and the value of health insurance benefits provided by employers. The *After Taxes* line shows the Gini coefficient for this income total after subtracting taxes and adding transfer payments. The latter include the value of the earned income tax credit; means tested and non–means tested cash transfers; the value of Medicare, Medicaid, and school lunch programs; and the value of means tested in-kind transfers such as food stamps and subsidized housing. The adjusted line therefore shows the degree of inequality among U.S. households using the most comprehensive measure of household disposable income available in published sources.

Both Gini coefficients in Figure 15.10 indicate that the degree of inequality in the distribution of income across U.S. households increased over the years from 1979 to 2003. The Gini coefficient for comprehensive before-tax and transfer household income rose by 12%, and the Gini coefficient for comprehensive after-tax and transfer household income rose by 15% from 1979 to 2001 before dropping slightly from 2001 to 2003. The time series pattern is the same for both measures: the Gini coefficients rose from 1979 to 1993 and followed a fairly flat trajectory after that. In addition, the tax and transfer system in the United States acted to redistribute purchasing power in a way that substantially lowered the level of measured household income inequality. The after-taxes Gini coefficient is about 20% lower than the before-taxes coefficient throughout this time period.

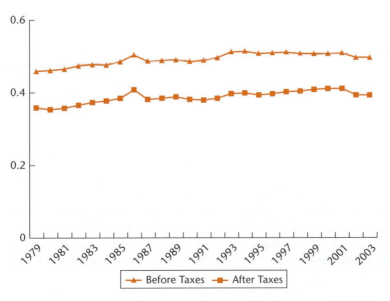

FIGURE 15.10 Gini Coefficients for U.S. Household Income, 1979–2003

Source: U.S. Bureau of the Census at: http://www.census.gov/hhes/www/income/data/historical/measures/rdi5.html.

The international evidence on recent income inequality[30] trends in a larger group of developed economies leads to these conclusions:

1. Inequality is highest in the United States and the United Kingdom and lowest in the Nordic countries and Northern Europe. Low-income residents of the United States, those at the 10th percentile of the income distribution, have lower real income than similarly situated individuals in other countries.
2. Post-tax and transfer income is much more equally distributed than income received from labor and nonlabor earnings, and in many countries the tax and transfer system works to offset increases in wage inequality almost completely.
3. Income inequality has risen in most but not in all countries. The fastest increases were registered in the United Kingdom, the United States, and Sweden; income inequality changed only slightly in Canada, Israel, Finland, France, Portugal, Spain, Ireland, West Germany, and Italy. In no country was there evidence of a significant *decrease* in income inequality since 1980.
4. In many countries social welfare expenditures for working age individuals have been reduced significantly, and reductions in the marginal income tax rates for the highest income earners made the tax system less progressive. But these tax and transfer system changes had only minor effects on the evolution of inequality.
5. Substantial increases in the labor force participation rates, hours of work, and real wage levels of married women interacted with a moderate increase in the correlation between the earnings of husbands and wives to increase measured inequality among households and families.

Poverty

The evidence presented thus far clearly demonstrates that labor market developments in the last two decades have worked decidedly to the disadvantage of workers in low-wage labor markets in the United States. Wage inequality in this country increased rapidly to the highest levels in the developed world largely because the real wages of the lowest-paid workers fell dramatically from the mid-1970s to the mid-1990s, registering increases only in the very tight labor markets at the end of the 1990s. In other countries, the real wage of high-paid workers grew at a faster pace than the real wage of low-wage workers, but the latter group did see their real wages rise over time. When we compare the relative wages of workers or the relative income of individuals across countries, those at the 10th percentile of the U.S. distributions are substantially worse off than those at the 10th percentile of the wage and income distributions in other countries.

At the same time, the political debate in the United States has been largely focused on welfare reform, which has generally meant finding ways to lower government spending in support of the poor. The welfare reform measure signed into law in 1996 by President Clinton would accomplish this by putting lifetime limits on the availability of welfare

---

[30] As summarized in Gottschalk and Smeeding, "Cross National Comparisons of Earnings and Income Inequality." Gini coefficients for a large number of countries, including many less developed economies, can be found at: http://data.worldbank.org/indicator/SI.POV.GINI/countries/1W?display=default?

THE WAY WE WORK

Income Inequality and Marketing Strategy

By 2011 the distribution of incomes across households in the United States and many other countries had been twisted by the confluence of three decades of increasing wage and income inequality, little growth in the purchasing power of median household incomes for a decade or more, and the effect of high unemployment and falling house values during the global financial crisis.

One of the business consequences of these changes was a corresponding twist in the potential for retail sales in different segments of the consumer market place. The continued rise in relative earnings and incomes at the top of the distribution meant that upscale markets for high-price, high-quality consumer goods remained strong even in a weak economy. Price-conscious families at the bottom of the income distribution formed the basis of a fairly strong market in the low-price, low-quality segment served increasingly by "dollar" or "pound" stores. And this strong low-price retail scene was reinforced by changes in the middle of the distribution which induced more families to "trade down" in their purchases.

The extent and depth of increased income inequality in the United States is dramatically illustrated by the changing product strategy of Procter & Gamble (P&G). After a century or more of mass producing and marketing a wide range of consumer goods to middle income buyers, P&G is now looking at data on Gini coefficients and developing products and marketing programs for both upscale and downscale markets. As you might imagine, this shift of business strategy to address the "new normal" in American retail sales has presented significant challenges to the managers of this iconic consumer products firm.

Note: Ellen Byron, "As Middle Class Shrinks, P&G Aims High and Low," *The Wall Street Journal*, September 12, 2011.

benefits and by moving people from welfare to work. Welfare reform is also a major topic of political interest in the United Kingdom, where the 2012 Welfare Reform Bill has considerably simplified the benefits system. The aim of this reform was to provide support to the neediest while ensuring that no one is prevented from working as a result of being caught in a "poverty trap"—where wage income is more than offset by the loss of benefits.

Given these developments, it seems worthwhile to pay a bit more attention to the topic of **poverty** in the United States. As usual, we start with the measurement of poverty. In this case, poverty measures are written into legislation defining the qualifications for and benefits of a number of government programs, so the debate about the correct way of measuring poverty has more than academic significance.

The Measurement of Poverty

The United States has an "official" poverty measure, which was developed in the 1960s. This official measure of poverty has four main features:

1. This measure is based on U.S. Department of Agriculture research establishing the expenditure required for a "low-cost food plan" for households differing by size, number of children, and gender of the household head. After substantial revisions to the index in 1981, households are no longer differentiated by the head's gender.

2. The low-cost food plan spending level was multiplied by three for households with three or more persons (higher multipliers are used for smaller units) to reflect research on the average fraction of income spent on food by low-income households. The product of this multiplication is the poverty threshold.
3. The poverty threshold has been adjusted upward each year to keep value relative to the consumer price index constant. In 2011 the poverty threshold was $22,811 for a four-person family with two children under 18 years of age.
4. All individuals in household units with total income lower than the poverty threshold are counted as poor, and the difference between household income and the poverty threshold is defined as the income deficit, or poverty gap. Income is defined as money income, including cash transfers, received by the household before payments for taxes and doesn't include the value of in-kind transfer payments.

Each of the four aspects of the official poverty measure has come under scrutiny by those concerned with developing more accurate measures of U.S. poverty. Questions have been raised about the correct measurement of the "equivalence scales" linking the income needs of households with different household characteristics, the use of the consumer price index, and the definition of income used to identify those below the poverty threshold. In response to these critiques, the Census Bureau now uses an improved consumer price index (known as CPI-U-X1) to adjust poverty thresholds, and it reports poverty data for a number of different definitions of household income.

A final important issue in the measurement of poverty is whether the poverty threshold should be adjusted for changes over time in the average standard of living as well as for changes in prices. Adopting such a change would shift the poverty index from an *absolute* poverty index to a *relative* poverty index. A relative index recognizes the fact that people with low incomes in rich societies could be considered in poverty even though the purchasing power of their incomes greatly exceeded that received by average consumers in poor societies. The official U.S. poverty measure, however, remains an absolute poverty index. With such an index it is possible for the number of people falling below the poverty threshold to shrink even though wage and income inequality are increasing.

Poverty Trends in the United States

Developments in the incidence of U.S. poverty from 1980 to 2010 under two definitions of household income are depicted in Figure 15.11. The *Official* line shows the percentage in poverty using the money income of persons and families to gauge those below the poverty threshold. The line labeled *Adjusted* uses an expanded income definition, subtracting taxes, and adding income from capital gains, transfer payments, and earned income tax credits to define those living below the poverty line. The adjusted poverty figures are available only up to 2002. Even after adjusting for the redistributive effects of the tax and transfer system on income, nearly 10% of the American population was still below the poverty threshold in 2002.

Unlike previous figures describing trends in wage and income inequality, Figure 15.11 is dominated by cyclical movements rather than trends, showing a sharp rise in the incidence of poverty during the recessions of the early 1980s, 1990–91, 2001, and 2008–09. Poverty decreases markedly during the intervening periods of economic growth. During the Great Recession the official poverty rate rose from 12.5% in 2007 to 15.1% in 2010, the highest rate since 1993. Clearly situations with high unemployment, reduced working hours, and lower pay push many below the poverty threshold for personal and family income.

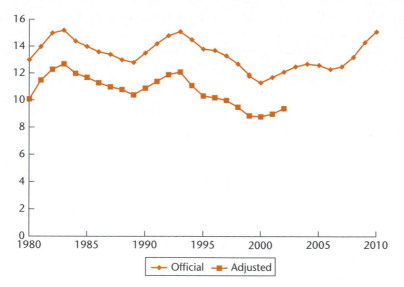

FIGURE 15.11 Percentage of U.S. Population in Poverty from 1980 to 2010

Source: Official data are at: http://www.census.gov/hhes/www/poverty/data/historical/people.html and the adjusted data are at: http://www.census.gov/hhes/www/poverty/data/historical/rdp05.html.

A look at information on poverty using a longitudinal database covering 2004–2006, a period of full-employment in the United States, gives us a good idea of the structure and dynamics of American poverty.[31] On average, during this period, 10% of the population was in poverty at any given point in time, but about 20% had a spell of two or more months with income below the poverty line, and 2.8% were in poverty for the entire three-year period. The median length of a poverty spell for all people was 4.5 months. This suggests a substantial amount of movement in and out of poverty during this period of low unemployment.

The incidence of poverty, measured by the percent experiencing a spell of 2 or more months with income below the threshold, was highest for Blacks and Hispanics, for those under 18 years of age, and for those in families with a female householder and no husband present. Of the 39 million people in female householder families during 2004 to 2006, 51.8% had a spell of poverty lasting at least 2 months, and 9.7% were in poverty for all 36 months. These racial, age, and gender characteristics of the American poor have been a constant feature of the structure of poverty for a long time.

Poverty in Other Countries

From a global perspective, there is good news about poverty developments in the last three decades. The number of poor people is estimated to have declined by 375 million,

---

[31] Robin J. Anderson, U.S. Census Bureau, Current Population Reports, P70-123, *Dynamics of Economic Well-Being: Poverty, 2004–2006*, U.S. Government Printing Office, Washington, DC, 2011.

and the percentage living on less than a dollar a day has dropped by 50%.[32] This drop in global poverty has been fueled by strong economic growth in developing countries leading to rapid job creation, a shift of people into urban, nonagricultural employment, and rising wages and incomes. Many of the gains in poverty reduction have been centered in the populous low-income countries of China, India, and Brazil and have followed a commitment to open economies and free trade—policies long advocated by economists. It is important to recognize that those who are poor in high income countries generally enjoy significantly better standards of living than the poor residing in low income and emerging middle income economies.

Table 15.5 shows indicators of poverty for a sample of European economies in 2005. Here poverty is measured by the fraction of people living in households with disposable income, adjusted for the size of the household, below 60% of the median income in the country. This is a relative measure of poverty; and hence the results cannot be compared with the United States, which measures poverty relative to an absolute income threshold. The indication is that poverty affects a substantial fraction of the European population with rates in Table 15.5 generally higher than 10% and often above 20%.

Among the largest European economies, poverty is highest in Spain, the United Kingdom, and Italy where the rates fall just short of 20%. But poverty is still 11%–13% in Germany, France, Norway, and Sweden. This general picture of poverty also prevails among the economies still making the transition from central planning to a market system, although the Czech Republic is the only country listed with a poverty rate less than 10%. Poverty seems to be particularly high in the Baltic countries of Lithuania and Latvia.

The determinants of poverty are similar across developed economies. Those whose human capital, race, and region of residence make them particularly vulnerable to job loss during periods of recession and rapid job turnover during periods of low unemployment

TABLE 15.5   Poverty Rates in Europe in 2005

Countries in Western Europe	Poverty rate (%)	Countries in Central Europe	Poverty rate (%)
Germany	12.7	Czech Republic	9.8
Spain	19.9	Hungary	15.9
France	12.9	Lithuania	20.0
Italy	19.6	Latvia	23.2
Norway	11.1	Poland	19.1
Sweden	12.2	Slovenia	11.7
UK	19.3	Slovakia	11.7

Poverty is measured as the percentage of people in households with household-size-adjusted disposable income below 60% of the national median.

Source: Orsolya Lelkes and Eszter Zólyomi, "Poverty Across Europe: The Latest Evidence Using the EU-SILC Survey," European Centre for Social Welfare Policy and Research, Policy Brief, 2008.

---

[32] David Dollar, "Globalization, Poverty, and Inequality since 1980," *World Bank Policy Research Working Paper 3333*, 2004.

generally have a high incidence of poverty. Children, particularly those living with their mothers as the sole head of household, are also at a high risk for living in poverty.

The Feminization of Poverty and the Family Pay Gap

Wage inequality, income inequality, and poverty have increased by comparable proportions in the United States over the past two decades. Because wages and salaries are the largest source of family income, we could rely on our analysis of changes in the labor markets for skilled and unskilled workers for an explanation for all three trends. An additional factor to consider as a cause of increased family income inequality and poverty is the **feminization of poverty**.

AROUND THE WORLD

The Dynamics of Poverty

Most of the data we have on poverty consists of snapshots of the situation facing a given population at various moments in time. It is rare to have data that allow us to follow the same group of people over a period of time. Three OECD economists were able to put together such a longitudinal database to describe the poverty experience over a six-year period in the early 1990s for households in Canada, Germany, the United Kingdom, and the United States.[*] Here are some of their findings:

- A small percentage of people (about 2% in Canada and Germany and 6% in the United Kingdom and the United States) spent all six years in poverty.
- A fairly large fraction (20% in Canada, 27% in Germany and the United States, and 38% in the United Kingdom) experienced at least one period in poverty during the six years.
- Out of those in poverty in a given year, 45% in the United Kingdom and the United States and more than 50% in Canada and Germany were able to escape poverty during the following year.
- The average duration of a completed period of poverty was two years in the United Kingdom and the United States and slightly less than two years in Canada and Germany.
- Unfortunately, there was a fairly high reentry rate for those who managed to escape poverty. In the United Kingdom and United States one-third saw their income slip below the poverty line again within a year, and reentry into poverty was 25% in Germany and 17% in Canada.

These data paint a picture of considerable turnover among the poor: relatively few households were in poverty for the entire study period, and many moved into and out of poverty over time. Canada and Germany seem to have been somewhat more successful than the United Kingdom and the United States in getting poor households above the poverty line and in keeping them from reentering poverty at a later date.

Note: *Pablo Antolin, Thai-Thanh Dang, and Howard Oxley, "Poverty Dynamics in Four OECD Countries,"* OECD Economics Department, *Working Paper No. 212,* 1999.

In 2010, those in female-headed families with no husband present accounted for 34% of all poor persons and 48% of all poor persons residing in family units. Both of these percentages were twice as great as those found in data for 1959 when poverty among the elderly accounted for the lion's share of the poor. This development partly reflects the effect on family structure of higher divorce rates and the greater frequency of births outside marriage. Between 1965 and 2010, the number of persons in all female-headed families increased by 283.5%, while the number in all families increased by 159.7%.[33]

Another factor to consider in the feminization of poverty is the evidence for a **family pay gap** in the relative wages of female workers. Wage differences generally widened during the 1980s, but the wages of women workers rose in comparison with the wages of their male counterparts. However, divorced, separated, and never-married women with children did not share in this improvement in the male–female wage gap. A comparison of real hourly wage growth from 1978 to 1994 for men and women in the prime working ages of 24 to 45[34] shows that the real wage for all men in this age range fell by 8%, from $16.25 per hour in 1978 to $15.95 in 1994. Real wages between those years grew by 9.4% for women without children and by 12.1% for married mothers, substantially narrowing the gap between these two groups of women workers and all male workers. However, real hourly wages for previously married mothers dropped by 2.1%, and those for never-married mothers fell by 9.6% between 1978 and 1994. Econometric tests indicate the presence of a family wage gap that has increased over time even when controlling for human capital characteristics and unobserved heterogeneity among workers. By the middle of the 1990s, the pay gap between single and previously married mothers and women without children was larger than the pay gap between women and men.

This deterioration in the relative wage of non-married women with children is an important contributing factor to the rapid rise in poverty among female-headed families. Research has not clearly documented the cause of this relative wage deterioration, but it appears that the continuity of a woman's attachment to the labor force and to a given employer is a highly significant determinant of her labor market success. The pay gap between mothers and women without children is high in the United States and low in Canada, perhaps because liberal maternity leave and child care policies in Canada promote greater labor force and employer continuity for women with children.

Periods of separation from the workforce caused by childbirth and child care have lasting negative effects on a woman's wages over her working life. The growing importance of skills in the U.S. labor force might be expected to increase the pay penalty associated with child-related separation from the labor market.

Welfare Reform

The substantial increase in the relative importance of female-headed families among the poor during the 1970s and 1980s drew attention to the possible adverse side effects of the U.S. welfare system on the work effort and family structure of welfare recipients.

---

[33] See Table 2. Poverty Status by Family Relationship, Race, and Hispanic Origin at: http://www.census.gov/hhes/www/poverty/data/historical/people.html.

[34] Jane Waldfogel, "Understanding the 'Family Gap' in Pay for Women with Children," *Journal of Economic Perspectives* 12 (1998): 137–156.

The argument that the welfare system itself was responsible for the feminization of poverty, because of the work disincentives we discussed in Chapter 4, formed the basis for the **welfare reform** efforts culminating in passage of the Personal Responsibility and Work Opportunity Reconciliation Act in 1996.

This act replaced welfare payments with Temporary Assistance to Needy Families (TANF). To address the problems of welfare disincentives, TANF benefits are time limited, and recipients are required to actively prepare and search for work. The timing of the welfare reform legislation was propitious; the strong economy and low unemployment rates during 1997, 1998, and 1999 led to a sharp drop in welfare rolls.

Research shows that welfare reform plus the Earned Income Tax Credit, which works much like a negative income tax, helped contribute to a drop in the poverty rate among families with a female householder.[35] These families actually experienced an increase in the number of poverty spells, but each spell was shorter and family income rose more quickly after the start of each spell as the female head found a new job or higher paying work. The economic lives of these families may have become more turbulent, but the net effect on their incidence of poverty has been positive.

Spatial Isolation and Urban Poverty

The fact that the poor are highly concentrated in central city neighborhoods of large metropolitan areas in the United States is readily apparent to most people living in or visiting these communities. Poverty rates in the United States were 1.5 times higher for central city residents than for suburban or nonurban residents in the mid- to late-1990s, and research suggested that the residential concentration of the poor in the one hundred largest metropolitan areas increased substantially from the census of 1970 to the census of 2000. A final factor to consider in our analysis of U.S. poverty is the extent to which the spatial development of metropolitan labor markets has contributed to the evolution of poverty.

John Kain[36] was one of the first to concentrate attention on the spatial mismatch hypothesis, which pointed to the interaction of housing segregation and the suburbanization of employment in creating reduced access to jobs that limited employment opportunities for minority residents of metropolitan areas. More recently, the role of **spatial isolation** in creating a culture of urban poverty has been a central thesis of William Julius Wilson.[37] He argues that the suburbanization of middle-class Blacks has left impoverished central city areas without the means of developing a vibrant local economy. He further hypothesizes that the decline of manufacturing and the shift of many remaining manufacturing firms from the city to the suburbs has resulted in relatively few jobs, paying low wages and offering little career opportunity, in inner-city neighborhoods. This has negative externalities on children, leading to behavioral patterns that are not conducive to labor market success and may play an important role in the perpetuation of poverty among inner-city residents.

---

[35] David Card and Rebecca Blank, "The Changing Incidence and Severity of Poverty Spells among Female-Headed Families," *American Economic Review: Papers and Proceedings* 98 (2008): 387–391.

[36] John F. Kain, "Housing Segregation, Negro Employment, and Metropolitan Decentralization," *Quarterly Journal of Economics* 82 (1968): 175–197.

[37] William Julius Wilson, *When Work Disappears: The World of the New Urban Poor* (New York: Alfred A. Knopf, 1996).

Attempts to test these hypotheses about central city isolation and lack of access to suburban jobs with data on the wage and employment characteristics of workers have yielded mixed results. Labor economists face two problems: it is difficult to separate residential location from employment location decisions, and it is difficult to separate the effects of racial discrimination in employment from the effects of residential location on employment. Nonetheless, the preponderance of the empirical evidence lends support to the conclusion that the spatial decentralization of jobs plus the spatial concentration of the disadvantaged within metropolitan labor markets contributes to wage inequality and poverty, especially for young Black workers.

Developments in the last decade may force a rethinking of the conventional wisdom on the spatial aspects of poverty. A new look at this issue found that between 2000 and 2008 the suburbs of the largest U.S. metropolitan areas were the home of the largest and fastest growing number of poor people in the country.[38] This reflected the relative economic decline of Midwestern cities and suburbs, gentrification of inner city neighborhoods of large Northeastern metropolitan areas, and the local effects of the housing collapse leading to the financial crisis and recession of 2008–2009 in the South and West. More research is needed to firmly establish the existence and causes of high levels of suburban poverty.

Poverty represents a special aspect of the study of wage and income inequality. With the official U.S. definition, the poor are defined as those living in family or household units whose incomes are below an absolute minimum income standard. Over the years poverty has come to be concentrated among children and their mothers living in households without a father present, so the search for causes must go beyond the labor market to examine why divorce rates and the frequency of births to unwed parents who live apart have increased over time. In addition, it is necessary to consider carefully the possibility that the receipt of public assistance has corrosive effects on the behavior of recipients that makes the system itself an important determinant of poverty.

Three labor market issues are relevant for the study of U.S. poverty. First, there is evidence of a significant wage penalty for being an unmarried woman with children. Second, there is the question of whether welfare-to-work programs will continue to be successful in an economy that increasingly favors the most-skilled workers. Finally, there is the role of spatial isolation from the location of most jobs and the impact of inner-city residence on the quality and quantity of human capital and on behavioral patterns that are detrimental to labor market success. These labor market issues must be considered in the formulation of policies designed to reduce the incidence of poverty in the United States.

Policy Options

Our analysis of the evolution of inequality and poverty in the United States and other developed economies suggests several policy options for reducing wage inequality and poverty. The first step in implementing any such policy option is the political acceptance of a concrete goal to reduce wage and income inequality. Labor economists have outlined

---

[38] Elizabeth Kneebone and Emily Garr, "The Suburbanization of Poverty: Trends in Metropolitan America, 2000 to 2008," *Brookings* (2010): 1–23.

the causes of recent trends toward greater inequality, but discussion of a concrete policy goal has been lacking in three respects:

1. We have done little to define the social welfare consequences of different degrees of inequality beyond subjective assessment that existing wage and income disparities are "too great." Of course, some degree of inequality is necessary to provide incentives for people to work.
2. We have not been able to quantify adequately the trade-offs between equity and efficiency embodied in various policy options.[39] This is amply illustrated by the debate over the employment consequences of increases in the minimum wage, which we examined in some detail in Chapter 9.
3. We have not paid enough attention to the possibility that increases in inequality might be reversed eventually by the operation of the labor market even in the absence of policy, perhaps through a long-run increase in the relative supply of skilled workers.

Nevertheless, policy options to lower inequality have been presented in the literature, and the rest of this section reviews a few of them.

Keeping Unemployment Low

A macroeconomic policy designed to keep the economy on a sustained path of growth with low unemployment is one way to boost the demand for low-wage workers and increase their real wage levels in the short run. A long-run benefit would be to enhance the upward lifetime earnings mobility of young workers by allowing them to begin their careers with better jobs providing opportunities for training and meaningful experience. Of course, the drawback of a low unemployment policy is the risk of higher inflation and some analysts have argued that the anti-inflation bias of central banks is an important cause of increased wage inequality.[40]

Increasing the Relative Supply of Skilled Workers

Education and training programs designed to lower the cost of acquiring relevant labor market skills are a staple item in the labor economist's antipoverty tool kit. Germany's ability to avoid an increase in wage inequality during the 1980s has been traced to the German educational system.[41] This system is seen as working to reduce significantly the extent of educational disparities among German workers and to enhance the ability of the labor market to meet a rising demand for skilled workers with training programs that effectively increase the elasticity of the relative supply curve for skilled workers. In the United States over the decades since Lyndon Johnson's "War on Poverty," a number of educational and training programs have been geared toward raising the ability of the disadvantaged to compete in the labor market. The general assessment of these programs is

---

[39] Some interesting recent work suggesting that most people regard equity to be very important in comparison with efficiency comes from Alberto Alesina, Rafael Di Tella, and Robert MacCulloch, "Inequality and Happiness: Are Europeans and Americans Different?: *NBER Working Paper 8198*, 2001.

[40] James K. Galbraith, *Created Unequal: The Crisis in American Pay* (New York: Free Press, 1998).

[41] Stephen Nickell and Brian Bell, "Changes in the Distribution of Wages and Unemployment in OECD Countries," *American Economic Review* 86 (1996): 302–308.

positive, but their high costs and lack of political support has meant that their impact has been marginal.

Shifting Demand Toward Low-Skill Workers

A policy option suggested by the relative supply and demand model used in this chapter is to shift demand away from skilled workers and toward lower-skilled applicants. This could be done by providing tax incentives or wage subsidies to private sector employers hiring more disadvantaged applicants. Or public sector employers could increase their employment of low-skill workers through expanded programs of public works. It appears that wage subsidies and tax incentives do work to improve the short-term employment and wage opportunities of the disadvantaged. The long-term effects are uncertain, however, and funding limits and limited participation by employers have meant that experiments have involved very small numbers of workers. Moreover, subsidies are necessarily distortionary and will have an adverse effect on economic efficiency.

Increasing Labor Market Access

Our analysis of poverty suggested two ways in which policies might reduce wage inequality by improving access to the labor market. By following the lead of other countries in providing expanded maternity leave rights and greater support for child care, the United States could lower the family pay gap by making it easier for mothers to maintain labor market continuity. Second, our analysis of urban poverty suggested that spatial isolation might be an appropriate policy target. However, studies of initiatives such as Enterprise Zones, which use tax breaks to attract employers to inner-city locations, show that these are very costly ways of increasing employment opportunities for inner-city residents. Policies to improve public transportation or access to suburban housing may be more fruitful.

Maintaining the Real Minimum Wage

There is agreement among many labor economists that increases in the minimum wage result in an improvement in the relative wages received by the poorest wage earners. In terms of the number of workers affected, an increase in the minimum wage may be the most effective policy option for lowering the wage disadvantage of low-skilled workers. The minimum wage plus the earned income tax credit work to reduce income inequality and the incidence of poverty among families with a full-time worker at their head. Of course, when we discuss the benefits of the minimum wage in terms of raising the earnings of low-wage workers, we must address the possible adverse employment consequences of an increase in the minimum wage.

Summary

This chapter has examined the measurement and determinants of wage inequality, income inequality, and poverty. Various indices are available to measure, with a single number, the extent to which wages or incomes are unequally distributed among workers, individual income recipients, families, or households. We examined the methods of calculating three commonly employed indices: the percentile wage differential, the Gini coefficient, and the variance of the logarithm of wages.

Wage disparity among workers has grown considerably over the past two decades, but especially during the 1980s, in a large number of developed countries. Wage disparity has grown the fastest in the United States and the United Kingdom. The United States currently has the greatest wage inequality among developed countries and is one of the few countries to experience steadily falling relative wages for the lowest paid workers. The rise in wage inequality is due largely to rising relative wages and relative employment for skilled workers in comparison with unskilled workers. The relative demand for skilled workers has increased over time because of technological change and import competition. In the United States the relative supply of skilled workers may have been adversely affected by immigration and college enrollment rates during the 1980s. In addition to demand and supply shifts, rising wage inequality has also been due to declining real minimum wages and collective bargaining coverage rates. Institutional changes are important in explaining international differences in the level and trend in wage inequality.

Income inequality across families or households has increased along with wage inequality in most countries. The tax and transfer system works to lower the level of income inequality and, in a few countries, has been able to offset the rise in wage inequality completely. The percentage of the U.S. population in poverty has risen over time. Two additional factors of importance in explaining the rise in U.S. family income inequality and poverty are the increase in the number of female-headed households and the large drop in the relative wages of divorced, separated, and never-married mothers.

Policies to maintain low unemployment rates, increase the relative supply of skilled workers, shift labor demand toward the less skilled, improve access to the market for mothers and inner-city residents, and increase the minimum wage could potentially reduce inequality and poverty. The full implementation of such policies awaits a greater political commitment to increased pay equality. The policy discussion would be enhanced by better information about the efficiency trade-offs of equity-enhancing policies and the social benefits associated with a more equal distribution of wages.

KEY TERMS

wage inequality

percentile wage differentials

Gini coefficient

Lorenz curve

variance of the logarithm of earnings

income inequality

earnings mobility

Haig-Simons concept

poverty

feminization of poverty

family pay gap

welfare reform

spatial isolation

PROBLEMS

1. Select a metropolitan area with data from the National Compensation Survey at the BLS website: http://www.bls.gov/ncs/ocs/compub.htm.

    a. Find the most recent report and one from about ten years ago. Calculate the w90/w50, w50/w10, w90/w10 percentile wage differentials for all workers in both years.

    b. Describe the changes in wage inequality in this local labor market.

    c. Is there evidence in these data for an increase in the demand for skilled occupations relative to unskilled occupations?

2. Use the data on the wage distribution and the incidence of low wage work available for OECD countries at: http://stats.oecd.org/Index.aspx?DatasetCode=DEC_I%20. Pick a country that has not been highlighted in this chapter, and compare trends in the percentile wage ratios in that country with the United States. Which country has greater wage inequality according to this measure? How do the trends compare?

3. Check out the information on earnings by educational level in Britain at: http://www.guardian.co.uk/news/datablog/2011/aug/24/earnings-by-qualification-degree-level. What has happened to the wages earned by the most educated relative to those earned by the least educated over time? Use the relative demand and supply model to explain these developments.

4. Review George Johnson's estimates of relative demand growth for college-educated workers.

    a. What is the estimated value for $\%\Delta D$ if $\sigma = 2$? Explain σ. Is a value of $\sigma = 2$ plausible?

    b. Suppose from 1995 to 2005, $\%\Delta S = 4.0$ and $\%\Delta D = 5.0$. What would be the predicted $\%\Delta r_w$?

5. Draw the relative demand and supply curves. Analyze the short- and long-run effects of the following on r_w.

    a. Technological change reduces the time, effort, and money required to get a college degree via the Internet.

    b. Technological change makes it easy for firms to replace accountants and financial analysts with smart computers.

    c. The government commits itself to keeping the minimum wage at a fixed real level.

    d. The number of unskilled immigrants rises dramatically.

6. Carefully explain why measured inequality for one year is likely to be higher than inequality measured with the lifetime earnings of workers. How is this related to earnings mobility?

7. Use what you've learned about human capital theory, gender discrimination, and employer selection to explain the evidence for a family pay gap.

8. Do inner-city residents seem to behave in a manner consistent with search theory when they concentrate their job search to firms located in the central city? Why might suburban employers discriminate against central city residents?

9. What are the possible causes of the rapid rise in suburban poverty from 2000 to 2008? How would the onset of recession in 2008 affect your thinking about the purely spatial aspects of poverty?

10. Develop a list of policies that could be used to increase the relative supply of skilled workers. For each policy list the political arguments likely to be raised in opposition to its implementation. Are you optimistic about the adoption of any of these policies?

11. Welfare reform requires benefit recipients to leave welfare for work. Given the trends in U.S. pay inequality and the family pay gap, can this reform succeed and lift the poor above the poverty line?

Index